AFRICA YEARBOOK

AFRICA YEARBOOK

Volume 8

Politics, Economy and Society South of the Sahara in 2011

EDITED BY

ANDREAS MEHLER

HENNING MELBER

KLAAS VAN WALRAVEN

SUB-EDITOR

ROLF HOFMEIER

BRILL

LEIDEN • BOSTON
2012

Buyers of this book get free access to the Africa Yearbook Volume 8 E-Book. Please visit and register at booksandjournals.brillonline.com and activate your content subscription under My Account by using token code **AYB82012Fr13ac0EB7c**

ISSN 1871-2525
ISBN 978-90-04-23398-0 (paperback)
ISBN 978-90-04-24178-7 (e-book)

This book is printed on acid-free paper.

Contents

Preface

In May 2003, the Africa-Europe Group of Interdisciplinary Studies (AEGIS) encouraged some of its member institutions to publish an Africa Yearbook with a wider international appeal. The African Studies Centre in Leiden (ASC), the Institute of African Affairs in Hamburg (IAA) and the Nordic Africa Institute in Uppsala (NAI) – all very active AEGIS centres sharing similar profiles – accepted this challenge and their joint efforts first bore fruit in the initial volume of the series in 2004. In 2007, the Dag Hammarskjöld Foundation in Uppsala (DHF) joined this international project, while the NAI ended its involvement with the fifth volume published in 2009. For this current volume Rolf Hofmeier once again joined us as sub-editor for the Eastern Africa section.

The country-specific articles cover domestic politics, foreign affairs and socioeconomic developments in the states of sub-Saharan Africa during the calendar year under review. This year, the newly independent sovereign state of South Sudan is included the first time. While we recognise the impossibility of finding fully objective indicators for the relative importance of each of the states covered by the Yearbook, the length of the country-specific articles aims to reflect the approximate weight of each country. The four sub-regions are also introduced by means of an overview article. Further overviews summarise general continental developments, European-African relations and the United Nations and Africa.

The Yearbook is based on scholarly work, but is oriented towards a wider target readership, including students, politicians, diplomats, administrators, journalists, teachers, practitioners in the sphere of development cooperation and business people. Without forcing the individual contributions too much into a straitjacket, the volume is primarily concerned with providing factual (though not necessarily neutral) information. Each issue, in focusing almost exclusively on developments during the particular calendar year, provides a completely fresh annual overview of events and thereby adds to the cumulative record of ongoing developments.

We wish to express our gratitude to all the contributors for their collaboration in this endeavour; to the partner institutions in AEGIS for encouraging us to embark on this ambitious project; to Carol Rowe for her meticulous language editing; to Bas van der Mije for his unfailing coordinating assistance; and to Brill Publishers for their continued commitment. Last but not least, we note with appreciation and gratitude the ongoing support of our three institutions and their remaining loyal to turning the original idea into reality.

The Editors
(Hamburg, Leiden and Uppsala, June 2012)

List of Abbreviations

ABN	Autorité du Bassin du Niger (Niamey)
ACP	African, Caribbean, and Pacific Group of Countries (Lomé/Cotonou Agreement)
ADF	African Development Fund (Abidjan)
AfDB	African Development Bank (Tunis)
AFD	Agence Française de Développement (Paris)
AGOA	African Growth and Opportunity Act
AI	Amnesty International
APRM	African Peer Review Mechanism
AU	African Union (Addis Ababa)
BCEAO	Banque Centrale des Etats de l'Afrique de l'Ouest (Dakar)
BEAC	Banque des Etats de l'Afrique Centrale (Yaoundé)
CAR	Central African Republic
CBLT	Commission du Bassin du Lac Tchad (N'Djaména)
CEEAC	Communauté Economique des Etats de l'Afrique Centrale (Libreville) = ECCAS
CEMAC	Communauté Economique et Monétaire de l'Afrique Centrale
CEN-SAD	Community of Sahel-Saharan States (Tripoli)
CEPGL	Communauté Economique des Pays des Grands Lacs (Gisenyi/Rwanda)
CFAfr	Franc de la Communauté Financière Africaine (BCEAO; BEAC)
COMESA	Common Market for Eastern and Southern Africa (Lusaka)
CPLP	Comunidade dos Países de Língua Portuguesa
DAC	Development Assistance Committee (Paris)
DDR	Disarmament, Demobilisation and Reintegration
DFID	Department for International Development (London)
DRC	Democratic Republic of the Congo
EAC	East African Community
ECA	Economic Commission for Africa (United Nations; Addis Ababa)
ECCAS	Economic Community of Central African States (Libreville)
ECF	Extended Credit Facility (IMF)
ECOWAS	Economic Community of West African States (Abuja)
ECOMOG	ECOWAS Ceasefire Monitoring Group

EDF	European Development Fund (Brussels)
EIB	European Investment Bank (Luxemburg)
EPA	Economic Partnership Agreement
ESAF	Enhanced Structural Adjustment Facility (IMF)
EU	European Union (Brussels)
FAO	Food and Agricultural Organisation (Rome)
FDI	Foreign Direct Investment
FTA	Free Trade Area
GDP	Gross Domestic Product
HDI	Human Development Index (UNDP)
HIPC	Heavily Indebted Poor Countries
HRW	Human Rights Watch
ICC	International Criminal Court
ICG	International Crisis Group
IDA	International Development Association (Washington)
IDP	Internally Displaced Person
IFAD	International Fund for Agricultural Development (Rome)
IFC	International Finance Corporation (Washington)
IGAD	Intergovernmental Authority on Development (Djibouti)
ILO	International Labour Organisation (Geneva)
IMF	International Monetary Fund (Washington)
IOC	Indian Ocean Commission (Quatre Bornes)
IOR-ARC	Indian Ocean Rim Association for Regional Cooperation (Port Louis)
MDGs	Millennium Development Goals
MDRI	Multilateral Debt Relief Initiative
MRU	Mano River Union (Freetown)
NEPAD	New Partnership for Africa's Development
NGO	Non-Governmental Organisation
OAU	Organization of African Unity
ODA	Official Development Assistance
OECD	Organisation for Economic Cooperation and Development (Paris)
OIC	Organisation of Islamic Cooperation (Jeddah)
OIF	Organisation Internationale de la Francophonie
OPEC	Organisation of Petroleum Exporting Countries (Vienna)
PALOP	Países Africanos de Lingua Oficial Portugesa
PPP	Purchasing Power Parity
PRGF	Poverty Reduction and Growth Facility
PRSC	Poverty Reduction Support Credit
PRSP	Poverty Reduction Strategy Paper

PTA	Preferential Trade for Eastern and Southern African States (now COMESA)
SACU	Southern African Customs Union (Pretoria)
SADC	Southern African Development Community (Gaborone)
SAF	Structural Adjustment Facility (IMF)
SDR	Special Drawing Right (IMF)
TI	Transparency International
UAE	United Arab Emirates
UEMOA	Union Économique et Monétaire Ouest-Africaine (Ouagadougou)
UMA	Union du Maghreb Arabe
UN	United Nations (New York)
UNCTAD	United Nations Conference on Trade and Development (Geneva)
UNDP	United Nations Development Programme (New York)
UNEP	United Nations Environment Programme (Nairobi)
UNESCO	United Nations Educational, Scientific and Cultural Organisation (Paris)
UNHCR	United Nations High Commissioner for Refugees (Geneva)
UNICEF	United Nations Children's Fund (New York)
UNSC	United Nations Security Council
USAID	United States Agency for International Development (Washington)
WFP	World Food Programme (Rome)
WHO	World Health Organisation (Geneva)
WTO	World Trade Organisation (Geneva)

Factual Overview (as of 31 December 2011)

West Africa

Country	*Area (in sq km)*	*Population (in m)*[1]	*Currency*	*HDI (2011)*	*Head of State*	*Prime Minister*
Benin	112,622	9.1	CFA Franc	0.427	Boni Yayi	Pascal Irénée Koupaki
Burkina Faso	274,122	17.0	CFA Franc	0.331	Blaise Compaoré	Luc-Adolphe Tiao
Cape Verde	4,033	0.52	Cape Verdean Escudo	0.568	Jorge Carlos Fonseca	José Maria Pereira Neves
Côte d'Ivoire	322,462	22.6	CFA Franc	0.400	Alassane Ouattara	Guillaume Kigbafori Soro
Gambia	11,295	1.84	Dalasi	0.420	Yahya Jammeh	
Ghana	238,500	25.0	Cedi	0.541	John Atta Mills	
Guinea	245,857	10.6	Guinean Franc	0.344	Alpha Condé	Mohamed Said Fofana
Guinea-Bissau	36,125	1.61	CFA Franc	0.353	Malam Bacai Sanhá	Carlos Gomes
Liberia	111,370	4.1	Liberian Dollar	0.329	Ellen Johnson-Sirleaf	
Mali	1,240,000	15.4	CFA Franc	0.359	Amadou Toumani Touré	Kaidama Cissé
Mauritania	1,030,700	3.5	Ouguiya	0.453	Mohamed Ould Abdel Aziz	Moulaye Ould Mohamed Laghdaf
Niger	1,267,000	16.1	CFA Franc	0.295	Mahamadou Issoufou	Brigi Rafini
Nigeria	923,768	162.3	Naira	0.459	Goodluck Jonathan	
Senegal	197,162	12.8	CFA Franc	0.459	Abdoulaye Wade	Souleymane Ndéné Ndiaye
Sierra Leone	71,740	5.4	Leone	0.336	Ernest Bai Koroma	
Togo	56,785	5.8	CFA Franc	0.435	Faure Gnassingbé	Gilbert Fossoun Houngbo

Central Africa

Country	*Area (in sq km)*	*Population (in m)*	*Currency*	*HDI*	*Head of State*	*Prime Minister*
Cameroon	475,442	20.1	CFA Franc	0.482	Paul Biya	Philemon Yang
Central African Republic	622,984	5.0	CFA Franc	0.343	François Bozizé	Faustin Archange Touadéra
Chad	1,284,000	11.5	CFA Franc	0.328	Idriss Déby	Emmanuel Nadingar
Congo	342,000	4.1	CFA Franc	0.533	Denis Sassou-Nguesso	
DR Congo	2,344,855	67.8	Congolese Franc	0.286	Joseph Kabila	Adolphe Muzito
Equatorial Guinea	28,051	0.7	CFA Franc	0.537	Teodoro Obiang Nguema Mbasogo	Ignacio Milam Tang
Gabon	267,667	1.5	CFA Franc	0.674	Ali Bongo	Paul Biyoghe Mba
São Tomé and Príncipe	1,001	0.2	Dobra	0.509	Manuel Pinto da Costa	Patrice Trovoada

Eastern Africa

Country	*Area (in sq km)*	*Population (in m)*	*Currency*	*HDI*	*Head of State*	*Prime Minister*
Burundi	26,338	10.2	Burundi Franc	0.316	Pierre Nkurunziza	
Comoros	1,862	0.8	Comorian Franc	0.433	Ikililou Dhoinine	
Djibouti	23,200	0.9	Djibouti Franc	0.430	Ismail Omar Guelleh	Dileita Mohamed Dileita
Eritrea	124,320	5.9	Nakfa	0.349	Isaias Afewerki	
Ethiopia	1,121,900	87.1	Birr	0.363	Girma Wolde-Giorgis	Meles Zenawi
Kenya	569,259	41.6	Kenya Shilling	0.509	Mwai Kibaki	Raila Odinga
Rwanda	26,338	10.9	Rwanda Franc	0.429	Paul Kagame	Pierre-Damien Habumuremyi
Seychelles	455	0.1	Seychelles Rupee	0.773.	James Michel	
Somalia	637,600	9.9	Somali Shilling	n.a.	Sheikh Sharif Sheikh Ahmed	Abdiweli Mohamed Ali
(Somaliland)	137,600	3.5	Somaliland Shilling	n.a.	Ahmed Mohamed Mahamoud 'Silanyo'	
Sudan	1,886,060	35.7	Sudanese Pound	0.408	Omar Hassan Ahmad al-Bashir	
South Sudan	619,745	8.9	South Sudanese Pound	n.a.	Salva Kiir Mayardit	
Tanzania	945,087	46.2	Tanzania Shilling	0.466	Jakaya Kikwete	Mizengo Pinda
Uganda	197,000	34.5	Uganda Shilling	0.446	Yoweri Kaguta Museveni	Amama Mbabazi

Southern Africa

Country	*Area (in sq km)*	*Population (in m)*	*Currency*	*HDI*	*Head of State*	*Prime Minister*
Angola	1,246,700	19.6	Kwanza	0.486	José Eduardo dos Santos	
Botswana	581,730	2.0	Pula	0.633	Ian Khama	
Lesotho	30,344	2.2	Loti	0.450	King Letsie III	Pakalitha Mosisili
Madagascar	592,000	21.3	Ariary	0.480	Andry Rajoelina (contested)	Jean Omer Beriziky
Malawi	118,484	15.9	Kwacha	0.400	Bingu Wa Mutharika	
Mauritius	2,040	1.3	Mauritius Rupee	0.728	Sir Anerood Jugnauth	Navinchandra Ramgoolan
Mozambique	799,380	23.1	Métical	0.322	Armando Guebuza	Aires Bonifácio Ali
Namibia	824,269	2.3	Namibian Dollar	0.625	Hifikepunye Lucas Pohamba	Nahas Angula
South Africa	1,219,090	50.5	Rand	0.619	Jacob Zuma	
Swaziland	17,364	1.2	Lilangeni	0.522	King Mswati III	Sibusiso Dlamini
Zambia	752,614	13.5	Kwacha	0.430	Michael Chilufya Sata	
Zimbabwe	390,580	12.1	Zimbabwe Dollar	0.376	Robert Gabriel Mugabe	Morgan Tsvangirai

(Population figures are for mid-2011 according to Stiftung Weltbevölkerung, www.weltbevoelkerung.de)

I. Sub-Saharan Africa

The impact of the global financial crisis did not prevent the resource rich countries on the continent from achieving positive economic growth rates, although forecasts were adjusted downwards. Economic performance remained generally above the levels seen in other parts of the world. Africa's natural wealth continued to attract many external players, not least several more emerging economies, which openly joined the competition for access to these resources. While there were many demands for crisis management on the political front and politically related violent turmoil, the AU did not exercise its responsibilities vigorously but was preoccupied with efforts to appear united despite internal differences of opinion. The independence of South Sudan added another member to the continental body, but also brought some additional problems that required a solution. Democratic political transitions in several countries, most notably a change in government in Zambia, contrasted with undemocratic seizures or retention of power in several other countries. The continent had several political violence hot spots, mainly in West and Central Africa and the almost notorious state of civil war in parts of the Horn of Africa persisted. The East and Southern African states continued to benefit from greater stability, though the fragile situation in Zimbabwe, Swaziland, Madagascar, and to some extent also Malawi, continued to give cause for concern. Initiatives within NEPAD and the APRM did not result in any spectacular progress towards creating a positive image or enhancing efforts to promote good governance. Piracy, abductions and acts of terrorism remained a challenge, mainly in West Africa and the Horn of Africa. The human cost of disease and natural disasters was less than in the previous year, though the drought in the Horn of Africa ranked among the world's worst catastrophes during the year in terms of loss of life.

Africa in the Global Economy

Optimism reigned with regard to sub-Saharan economies, but in the course of the year expectations subsided somewhat as gloom set in about Western economic performance and several commodity prices experienced a downturn. The IMF, with its own way of making the calculations, as usual came up with the highest forecasts: a 6% **growth rate** and 5.5% in real terms. While this average masked considerable differences between high- and low-performing countries, it was expected by the first quarter that continental growth might be more sluggish as a result of high food prices and the effects of the Libyan revolution, which led to higher fuel costs. Perhaps more important was the indirect effect of reduced growth in the debt-ridden economies of the West, leading to a reduction in Asian exports, a fall in demand for African raw materials and a consequent cutback in Asia's investments. Also, with OECD countries still receiving more than half of all sub-Saharan exports (figures for 2010), Africa was still very dependent on the West's economic performance and Asian demand could not yet completely make up for this. A fall of 1% in Western growth was said to lead to an identical drop in Africa's GDP rate. In the second half of the year, the World Bank thus predicted an average growth of 4.8%, but the IMF still thought 5.2% feasible for the sub-Saharan zone, pointing to the overall resilience of low-income countries, including non-oil producers. Nevertheless, at year's end, warnings were being given of the effects of a downturn in the West.

Although Africa's oil-producing countries did better in this equation than non-oil producers, a fall in demand for oil and **minerals** put prices under pressure. Initially, oil was still booming, pushed on by the temporary collapse in Libyan production, as was the crisis-indicator, gold, and mining investment in a range of minerals continued unabated. By September, however, heavy falls were reported in the prices of nickel, copper, zinc and bauxite – sometimes even forcing the suspension of mining operations, as in Zambia, for example. With natural resource extraction over the preceding decade accounting for one-third of African real GDP, and more than 80% of continental export earnings dependent on primary commodities, Africa remained vulnerable to volatility in price developments.

On 21–26 September, the **World Bank** and **IMF** held their annual meetings in Washington. The so-called emergent economies, Brazil, Russia, India, China and South Africa (BRICS), expressed concern over the pace of reform in quota and voting rights, which continued to grant the West over-representation, and said they would refuse to increase their contribution to the institutions' resources until this issue was resolved. Africa again called for an extra seat on the IMF's ruling body. The World Bank presented a new African strategy, which shifted the focus from general economic stability to more specific targets, such as competitiveness, vulnerability and governance. In this connection, the IMF introduced a fourth African Regional Technical Assistance Centre (AFRITAC), to be established in Mauritius, aimed, among other things, at capacity building in poverty-reducing strategies.

In September, the annual change in **consumer prices** was calculated to be 8.4% (against 7.5% in 2010). Much of this was pushed by fuel and food prices – global food prices were 26% higher than in 2010 and the FAO cereal price index reached a new record (though below its 2008 peak). A poor harvest in the Sahel was expected to push up cereal prices further, while the cost of rice, a middle-class staple food, rose by 5% in one month alone. Although global food prices fell after March, they had more than doubled overall since 1990, according to FAO, and Oxfam claimed that the world's poorest now spent around 80% of their income on food. Besides the Sahel, East Africa also faced serious food shortages as a result of persistent drought, which affected at least 8 m people. Of 29 countries worldwide requiring food aid, 21 were in Africa. These difficulties also pointed to the constraints facing **agricultural production**, such as farmers' subsidies in the North, underinvestment, and pests and poor post-harvest technology leading to grain losses. In Eastern and Southern Africa, such losses totalled more than 13% of grain production and cost the whole of sub-Saharan Africa as much as $ 4 bn annually, i.e. roughly the same amount as the price of cereal imports. New initiatives included an improvement scheme for processing and post-harvest storage of rice launched by the Africa Rice Centre and funded by Canada (one-third of global rice imports are African). The G20 group of countries decided to exempt food aid from export restrictions and high taxation – thus eliminating a hurdle in the humanitarian work of WFP.

While South Africa, as the economic gateway to the continent, had been invited in December 2010 to join the BRIC countries, **Brazil** maintained its higher economic profile, despite the more limited enthusiasm for Africa evinced by its new president, Dilma Roussef. The country now boasted 35 embassies on the continent, rivalling **Turkey**, which had opened a spate of legations over the previous decade and continued to boost its trade, notably in the construction business. In 2010, bilateral trade totalled $ 16 bn (as against $ 5 bn in 2003). Overall, Africa's trade with emerging economies now made up 39% of continental activity (as compared with 23% in 2001), but this must be principally attributed to its partners in the Far East.

China's trade was expected to set new records, as bilateral trade expanded by 30% over the previous year. As confirmation of its new status, the Chinese currency, the Yuan, grew in importance in the currency reserves of some of Africa's principal economies. By contrast, **India** was reported to be concerned that its trade would not grow as fast as expected. Thus, on 24 May, the Indian prime minister, making a six-country tour of the continent, announced a comprehensive plan for Africa involving $ 5 bn in loans and better access to Indian markets. Extra training and education programmes would be established in conjunction with the AU, and 10,000 scholarships made available for an India-Africa virtual university. (India had been helping the AU with internet infrastructure projects, hoping to compete with the Chinese in the field of telecommunications.) Despite the impatience of some, bilateral trade stood at $ 46 bn in 2010, as compared with $ 3 bn a decade earlier. **Japan** announced that it would maintain the level of its foreign assistance after earlier plans for cutbacks. Numerous African countries made donations after Japan was struck by an earthquake and tsunami on 11 March. More than 30 African countries participated in a follow-up ministerial meeting in Dakar (1–2 May) of the Tokyo International Conference on African Development, held at summit level in 2008.

As in the previous two years, FDI declined, although **investment** in the extractive sector increased. The focus on natural resources confirmed Africa's traditional role: UN organisations reported that Africa still accounted for just 1% of global manufacturing and that it was losing share in labour-intensive manufacturing, the entry-level in industrial development. In the overall economic equation, **development aid** therefore continued to be a necessity. Developed countries reaffirmed a commitment to ODA, although popular sentiment in Western countries – including, significantly, the Netherlands – was turning increasingly against it. The **AfDB**, however, continued to be an active player in the field and launched, among other initiatives, a Migration and Development Fund jointly with France and the UN to deepen knowledge about remittances (which were expected to be hit as a result of the crisis in the West and the turbulence in Libya). The AfDB approved more than 130 projects totalling $ 6 bn, which was partly due to greater demand from some of the new governments in North Africa. With the political crisis in Côte d'Ivoire seemingly past its high point, it was expected that the bank would move its headquarters back to Abidjan from Tunisia if conditions allowed.

At the **G 20**'s Cannes summit on 3–4 November a commitment was made to an action plan on food security, while several countries supported the French proposal, opposed by Britain and the US, for a tax on international financial transactions, known as the 'Robin Hood' tax, aimed to benefit the world's poorest. A report by Bill Gates on new ways of financing development helped to keep aid issues in the limelight. By contrast, the **G8** summit in the French resort of Deauville on 26–27 May was more preoccupied with developments in North Africa. Sub-Saharan Africa was represented at a session that included several African leaders, including the new head of state of Côte d'Ivoire.

The AU endorsed several projects put forward by NEPAD's **infrastructure** committee, which published plans for a single standardised SIM card to reduce the cost of mobile phone services and pursued implementation of the Pan-African e-network project, funded by India to connect all public administrations on the continent. International consortiums continued with the laying of new submarine cables linking Africa to Europe and improvements to internet connectivity. UNDP launched a pilot project to give up to 3 m of Africa's poor access to their own mobile phone number – the continent is leading a new trend in mobile money transfer systems useful in microfinance. An estimated 30% of the continent's population (more than 350 m people) now had mobile phones and network coverage had increased from 10% to 60% in over a decade. Power was another priority. Plans were made for regional hydropower **energy** pools and, on 21 April, the Paris-Nairobi initiative was launched, seeking to attract investor interest in renewable energy. Africa currently had a 30% rate of access to electricity, with average costs far too high ($ 0.18 per kWh against $ 0.04 per kWh in Asia).

The IMF assessed per capita GDP to be 2.9%. However, some experts argued that, in order to really escape **poverty**, Africa's economies would have to grow to double digit figures through high investment in agriculture. **Migration** produced largely sorry tales, notably those of thousands of African workers in Libya, who were accused of connivance with the Kadhafi regime and forced to flee – across the Sahara to other neighbouring countries, or in flimsy boats to Europe. Many perished, whilst those who made it across the desert or into Europe added to a **refugee crisis**.

African Union

Amidst the turbulence of violent regime change north and south of the Sahara, the AU found itself sidelined. The organisation proved incapable of breaking the impasse in **Côte d'Ivoire**, where President-elect Alassane Ouattara was beleaguered in his hotel by the forces of his predecessor Laurent Gbagbo, who was unwilling to step down. On 29 January, heated exchanges took place at the Peace and Security Council (PSC) in Addis Ababa, as Nigeria argued in favour of maintaining AU recognition of Ouattara as president and reserving as a formal possibility the use of armed force to remove his predecessor. South Africa and Angola were less enthusiastic, and the latter seemed willing to offer Gbagbo outright support. The PSC therefore appointed a high-level panel headed by the president of Mauritania to come up with a binding proposal to resolve the crisis. The PSC also called for an end to the siege of Ouattara's hotel headquarters, but appeared to favour a way out that might lead to a power-sharing deal with Gbagbo. However, the latter refused to accept the panel's findings in March, promising an honourable withdrawal, and the PSC could do little more than deplore Gbagbo's stubbornness and the fact that the military deadlock had led to a wave of refugees and thousands of casualties. The following month, as a result of the financial pressures on the Gbagbo camp and the military push by Ouattara's forces (assisted by the French), the conflict was ended in Ouattara's favour, revealing the continental body to be a powerless bystander.

The fall-out from Pan-African impotence in the **Libyan crisis** was worse, as it involved military intervention by NATO powers on Africa's northern shores. At the first of the two annual summits in Addis Ababa on 30–31 January, Equatorial Guinea's dictatorial president was elected as the Assembly's new chairman. He expressed confidence in the continent's ability to resolve the rebellion in Libya and even to ensure respect for human rights and stability there. However, the organisation did little more than oppose foreign intervention in the conflict, with a call for the rhetorical 'African solution'. At the second summit in Malabo, Equatorial Guinea, on 30 June–1 July, a 'roadmap' and UN peacekeeping force were discussed but "intense" talks could not conceal the divisions between countries that called for action against Kadhafi (including Nigeria, Rwanda, Ethiopia and Senegal) and those, such as Zimbabwe and, to some extent, South Africa, that tended to stand by the maverick Libyan leader. The Assembly could only find consensus on opposition to the extradition of Kadhafi to the ICC in The Hague. Libya's leader, who had been a lavish funder of both the Union and numerous heads of state, was not criticised for his brutal governance, which had given rise to the rebellion. This divided posture left the way open for Western intervention, which helped depose the Libyan dictator. In the process, however, the Libyan rebels plundered heavy weapons depots, which led to a dangerous proliferation of arms that boded ill for sub-regional security, particularly in West Africa. On 20 September, the AU recognised Libya's new National Transitional Council, which a month later was invited to take up the Libyan seat. The organisation went out of its way to call for the protection of harassed sub-Saharan nationals.

In this context, the continuing deadlock faced by troops of the AU Mission in **Somalia** (AMISOM) attracted much less attention. Apart from maintaining its deadlocked peacekeepers in the capital, Mogadishu, the organisation promised that it would help neighbouring Kenya in strengthening border security. It also optimistically decided, by way of the defence ministers of member states, to deploy a Regional Intervention Force in the fight against the elusive rebels of the Ugandan Lord's Resistance Army (LRA), now active in the Central African-South Sudan-DRC border zone. It was to be based on voluntary contributions and made up of troops from the member states concerned. **South Sudan** formally became the AU's 54th member state on 15 August, having become independent on 9 July.

The loss of face suffered over the 'Arab Spring' at least led to a new verbal resolve to call for ratification by member states of the AU's conventions on democratic governance. The organisation also decided on Douala, Cameroon, as the venue for the logistical base of its future intervention force. It also signed an accord with the EAC on implementing its peace and security strategy in the East African sub-region. However, the dramatic regime changes in North Africa, notably in Egypt and Libya, were likely to complicate the organisation's existing **financial difficulties**. Around 80% of AU programmes were already funded by foreign donors (particularly the EU) and, since Nigeria and South Africa refused to pick up the bill left by the Libyans (who in the past also took care of the arrears of some of the poorer member states), Commission President Jean Ping could do little more than hope for member states collectively to make up the shortfall. Ping himself was damaged politically as a result of the Commission's ineffectual posturing in the Ivorian and Libyan crises, with internal and outside observers apportioning some of the blame – not completely without reason – to the uncharismatic Commission chief. Although the fall of Kadhafi also had potential benefits insofar as his unrealistic institutional proposals had for years hijacked the AU's **internal functioning**, some of the perennial institutional soul-searching continued. The Malabo summit, however, characteristically deferred discussions of a progress report on the transformation of the Commission into an 'AU Authority' until the first summit of 2012.

Governance

On 29 June, the AU heads of state and government marked the tenth anniversary of **NEPAD** in Malabo, Equatorial Guinea. Originally established as an umbrella organisation with far-reaching ambitions for enhancing good governance in the broadest sense, NEPAD had turned into a kind of economic arm of the AU, which mainly concentrated on the promotion of economic programmes based on sub-regional or transnational infrastructural projects and cooperation, not least through the Comprehensive Africa Agriculture Development Programme, signed by 26 countries, and the Programme for Infrastructure Development in Africa. Established with its own secretariat in Midrand (between

Johannesburg and Pretoria), where the Pan-African Parliament is also headquartered, NEPAD had, over the years, turned into a kind of mega-NGO. It was revealing that in his speech at Malabo the AU chairperson Jean Ping called for a "revitalisation of NEPAD and strengthening of its role though the full integration into AU". This was the intended and expected effect of transferring the secretariat to the AU headquarters in Addis Ababa after the establishment of the NEPAD Planning and Coordinating Agency in February 2010, signalling NEPAD's formal incorporation into the AU. On 11 October, the 66th General Assembly Plenary of the UN, in its 32nd and 33rd sessions, hailed NEPAD as the "embodiment of African rebirth and renaissance", while the anniversary was at the same time viewed as an opportunity for "sober reflection on unfinished tasks".

The **APRM** remained the most prominent political instrument established and applied by NEPAD to promote good governance through mutual appraisal of best practice and the identification of shortcomings. The 14th Summit of the APRM Forum was held in Addis Ababa on 29 January, and the 15th Summit on 29 June in Malabo, when the host country, Equatorial Guinea, joined. By the end of the year, a total of 31 states had signed the memorandum of understanding for accession to the APRM, and 14 peer reviews had been completed. The APR Panel held a retreat in October with the AU Commission and promoted the idea of the APRM having its legal status elevated to autonomous specialised agency of the AU. This would allow South Africa to host the secretariat and grant full diplomatic immunity and privileges to its staff.

A **country review** mission to Zambia was conducted from 7 to 25 February and another to Sierra Leone from 21 May to 6 June. A second country review for Kenya, as a follow-up to the first in 2004/5, took place from 16 to 31 July in the form of a partial review, which focused on the achievements of the country's political and democratic governance. This made Kenya the first country to go through a second stage of the APRM process. The results led to disagreement between the Kenyan government and the APR secretariat on the process and the content of the report. At the core of the disagreements were the issues of IDPs, resettlement policies and the ethnic distribution in government personnel and in youth unemployment, although there seemed to be no controversy over other issues, including impunity, corruption and gender.

Elections

With one single exception, national elections were conducted in a foreseeable way and most of them produced predictable winners. While governments at the authoritarian end of the political spectrum either had discouraged their opponents well in advance or made sure of their own victory by manipulation, the more democratic political systems conducted free elections – nothing spectacular for the island republics of **São Tomé and Príncipe** and **Cape Verde**.

Liberia, still under the control of a large UN mission, held somewhat acceptable presidential elections that may not have met all the requirements to be considered exemplary, but led to the re-election of Ellen Johnson-Sirleaf. Only a few days before the election, she was awarded the Nobel Peace Prize, leaving a strong aftertaste given the scarcely appropriate way in which this influenced domestic politics. Elections in West Africa's 'model democracy', **Benin**, gave a second term to the incumbent, Thomas Boni Yayi, but had to cope with both technical irregularities and the outright contestation of the result by the second-placed candidate and veteran politician Adrien Houngbédji.

Nigeria, famous for widespread electoral violence, held elections for all important positions within the country (president, Senate, National Assembly and governors). Although those were deemed fairer and more peaceful than all previous exercises, they still fell short of international standards. President Goodluck Jonathan, who had succeeded Umaru Yar'Adua upon his death in 2010, started his first term as elected head of state. Noteworthy was the election of long-time opposition leader Mahamadou Issoufou as the new president of **Niger** after the interlude of military rule that followed the coup against Mamadou Tandja in 2010.

Zambia's exemplary democratic elections, which led to a change of government and the access to power of the somewhat populist opposition candidate Michael Sata, contrasted with many deeply flawed elections (e.g. in **Djibouti, the CAR and the DRC**). Those – together with the post-electoral crisis in Côte d'Ivoire, which triggered a short, but bloody civil war – showed that democracy was still not the only game in town on the continent. In places such as **Cameroon, Chad, Gambia and Uganda**, elections were simply not the most promising approach to changing a sitting government, The re-election – never exempt from a dose of manipulation – of long-serving presidents there proceeded as usual, with low and even declining public interest. To avoid all risk, some heads of state proved inventive. In the **DRC**, President Kabila changed the electoral rules and was consequently able to win in a single-round election based on a simple majority, but the elections were again overshadowed by widespread acts of violence. Similar manoeuvres would permit **Angola**'s President Dos Santos to stay on eternally; he secured a change in the Constitution that would provide for the complete avoidance of direct popular elections.

Coups and Unconstitutional Rule

The AU and sub-regional bodies had limited opportunities to show their commitment to countering unconstitutional rule on the continent. **Madagascar**'s Andy Rajoelina continued to govern the island republic after his coup in 2009, without international recognition and with limited domestic legitimacy. He was not threatened by military intervention, even though he unilaterally postponed presidential and legislative elections, and made few concessions. This contrasted somewhat with the fate of his Ivorian counterpart. In close connection to resolutions on Libya by the UNSC (where both the African heavyweights,

Nigeria and South Africa, were non-permanent members) and subsequent international intervention there, the crisis in **Côte d'Ivoire** was 'solved' by the decisive support of UN peacekeepers and French troops for the former rebel army backing Alassane Ouattara, and ended with the arrest of former president Laurent Gbagbo.

Army and police mutinies were recorded in two countries. When protesting soldiers took to the streets in **Guinea-Bissau** in December, it could be interpreted as another coup attempt. The revolt was contained after the arrest of the top naval commander. In **Burkina Faso**, President Compaoré was even forced to leave the capital after soldiers went on the rampage, incensed by the conviction of fellow soldiers for human rights violations. Rioting soldiers, and later policemen, in several parts of the country demanded better financial conditions and the revolt was only quelled with the appointment of a new government and a restructuring of the security forces. In a "re-civilised military regime", in which the security forces wielded massive political influence, these events were highly dangerous. The smooth election in **Niger** ended the short military interlude after the previous year's coup, to the great relief of policy-makers in the entire sub-region. A coup plot against newly elected President Issoufou was detected early and led to the arrest of a handful of high-ranking officers. In the **DRC**, an armed attack on President Kabila's residence in Kinshasa was foiled, but nevertheless took nine lives.

Peace and War

The topography of violent conflict changed only gradually, with new concerns focusing on West Africa (the Sahel region plus Côte d'Ivoire). The most serious conflicts were still to be observed in the Horn (Sudan, South Sudan and Somalia) and the Great Lakes (mainly the Kivu provinces of the DRC, plus Burundi).

The independence of **South Sudan** in July was arguably the year's major landmark event in Sub-Saharan Africa. After decades of a secessionist war and a prolonged peace process, a new state was finally born as a consequence of the much-awaited referendum on 9 January and with official independence celebrations on 9 July. But it soon became clear that the peace was a fragile one. On-going animosities between North and South, coupled with internal divisions within the two now separated states, meant that widespread violence could not be averted. Despite a relative decline in violence, peace was a distant goal in **Sudan**'s Darfur province after a new peace agreement was signed with just one rebel faction. In Southern Blue Nile and Southern Kordofan and the still disputed Abyei area, rebellions continued to pose challenges to the government in Khartoum. But the new government in Juba, the capital of the South, also immediately faced resistance from groups in outlying areas, suggesting that both governments discretely supported the other's armed opposition across the common border. In fact, the two governments' irritations with each other, unsurprisingly mainly about the control of oil production sites and the sharing of oil revenue, started without delay after South Sudan's independence.

Some of the civilian casualties in South Sudan's conflicts were the consequences of 'traditional' cattle raids between opposing groups. This pattern was equally observable in all neigbouring states, including the relatively stable **Kenya**, but, with the use of modern weaponry, the confrontations were tending to become ever more violent. The military intervention by Kenya in **Somalia** was a new element in the complex and decisively transnational conflict zone, which had its epicentre in south-central Somalia. The UN system, the AU and sub-regional organisations desperately searched for some basis on which to build a new viable state, but the internal rifts in Somalian society, which had partly religious overtones, could not be healed. Eritrea, by supporting radical Islamist groups in Somalia, and Ethiopia – and now Kenya – by sending troops, arguably added fuel to the fire, and repercussions were felt in the entire sub-region. Careless official talk brought the strong Somali minority in Kenya under general suspicion and small-scale terrorist attacks were reported in several Kenyan localities, even in Nairobi.

Chad was at relative peace, with most rebel movements now either engaged in a peace process or simply irrelevant. Civilians in large parts of the neighbouring **CAR**, however, continued to be plagued by confrontations between rebel movements or between these groups and the army. The dreaded LRA, although of Ugandan origin, continued to terrorise people in the CAR, but also in South Sudan and the north-east DRC, looting, raping and kidnapping. Increased cooperation between the relevant governments and a first deployment of a special US commando unit were meant to end this nightmare, but not all observers believed that the US involvement would be good news for the sub-region.

International relations in the **Great Lakes region** remained relatively good, despite some continued tensions. The Kivu provinces in the DRC faced a reconfiguration of armed factions, both as a result of the formation of new alliances within non-state armed movements and as a consequence of the difficult integration of former rebels into the official armed forces. Local mass killings continued to take place. The repercussions of the 2010 electoral crisis in Burundi were still felt and the main armed rebel movement tried to reorganise on DRC territory.

Repercussions of the Libyan crisis south of the Sahara, including the massive reflux of migrants, doubts on the sustainability of Libyan investment and an increase in the circulation of small weapons, had destabilising effects on Mali and Niger, for example, but they could mostly be contained for the time being.

The military victory of rebel forces, critically supported by international intervention, ended the extremely violent post-electoral episode in **Côte d'Ivoire** after the then president Laurent Gbagbo refused to accept electoral defeat in late 2010. ECOWAS pondered military intervention to install the internationally recognised winner, Alassane Ouattara, as president, but had to accept that its military options were extremely limited. When Gbagbo rejected the comparatively milder proposals of an AU high-level panel, ECOWAS requested the UNSC to authorise the implementation of its own decisions, i.e. to remove Gbagbo by force. This set the scene for the decisive UNSC resolution 1975. One day later, the re-formed rebel army ('Forces Nouvelles') advanced towards Abidjan, making good progress. The army, the majority of whom were till then still loyal to Gbagbo, quickly lost heart, and the final battle in Abidjan proved difficult and costly in human lives. Only when French infantry and helicopters participating in the UN Operation in Côte d'Ivoire were directly involved in taking the presidential palace did resistance collapse, though care was taken to ensure that Gbagbo was arrested by forces supporting Ouattara and not by foreign peacekeepers. All sides committed serious human rights violations in this, the end-game in a protracted power-struggle, with civilian casualties put at about 3,000. Public opinion in Africa was divided over the legitimacy of international involvement. The new regime in Abidjan, heavily dependent on former rebel commanders, did little to allay concerns about its lack of reconciliatory spirit.

The **ICC** in The Hague played an important role in the domestic politics of an increasing number of African countries. After the DRC, the CAR, Sudan and Uganda, it was now the turn of Kenya. The political fate of two major political leaders (William Ruto and Uhuru Kenyatta) appeared intrinsically connected to the outcome of on-going investigations by the ICC into their role in the post-electoral violence of early 2008. When the Ivorian authorities transferred Gbagbo to The Hague shortly before parliamentary elections took place, it could only be interpreted as a step against national reconciliation. All forms of 'international' and 'transitional' justice were, of course, signs of the failure of the formal judicial system, but they were themselves not free of suspicions of political manipulation. An African woman, Fatou Bom Bensouda of Gambia, was elected general prosecutor of the ICC at year's end, succeeding the high-profile Luis Moreno Ocampo (from Argentina).

Liberia's President Ellen Johnson-Sirleaf and her compatriot and women's rights campaigner Leymah Gbomee received the 2011 **Nobel Peace Prize** (along with Yemenite Tawakkol Karman). The disclosure of the jury's decision occurred less than a week before presidential elections in Liberia, producing a bad aftertaste given the way it influenced domestic political affairs.

Terrorism and Piracy

Terrorist activities (or activities labelled as such) strongly shaped foreign views on the African continent, particularly in the EU and USA. This was mainly related to headlines made by Nigeria's Boko Haram plus the perceived progress of al-Qaida in the Islamic Maghreb (AQIM) in all the states bordering the Sahara. A number of kidnappings again took place, including the abduction of six Europeans from hotels in Mali in November. The **EU** drafted its so-called Strategy for Development and Security in the Sahel, which was intended to be a holistic response to new threats and highlighted in particular the illicit trafficking of drugs as a source of funding for terrorists. The presence of AQIM in the north of Mali, focusing on Western targets, was presented as a major discouragement to investment in the region. Another concern was the associated restrictions on development cooperation and on the delivery of humanitarian assistance and aid. However, what was somewhat new was the fact that concerns focused on problems for the sub-region itself were rather less pronounced than concerns about consequent structural risks for Europe (such as drugs finding their way to Europe and the potential for terrorist attacks being prepared in an increasingly less controlled and ever expanding space in the Sahara). The short-term security interests of individual EU member states (first and foremost France) were easily discernible in the early stages of the strategy's discussion, but more and more other factors came into play. At least analytically, the strategy paper acknowledged that lack of employment opportunities and education would make young people more vulnerable to recruitment by Al-Qaida and other organisations. Weak justice and law enforcement systems, corruption and unresolved internal conflicts were equally seen as important background conditions for terrorism and other kinds of radicalised activity. More or less explicitly, the EU criticised its partner governments in states bordering the Sahara for unilateral and poorly coordinated action against terrorism. The proposed measures to counter the threat were mostly not new, but promised better coordination between member-states and the EU's instruments.

The **US Africa Command** (AFRICOM) made no big headlines this year in Sub-Saharan Africa – most activities were focused on the military intervention in Libya. Formally, the sending of US Special Forces to Central Africa to fight the LRA was attributed to AFRICOM. The Command strengthened its ties with Rwanda with a view to Kigali supporting the build-up of a South Sudanese army. In May, AFRICOM chief General Carter F. Ham announced that the USA would help Kigali set up a military academy and training school. Ham visited Juba, South Sudan, on 24 August.

The International Maritime Bureau (IMB), in its **global piracy report**, revealed that pirate attacks against vessels off East and West Africa accounted for the majority of attacks, while piracy significantly declined in South-East Asia. The IMB reported a total of 439 attacks, of which 237 took place off the Somali coast and 38 in the Gulf of Guinea. The number of attacks off the Somali coast rose slightly as compared with the previous year, while successful hijackings off East Africa decreased from 49 to 28 (still considered to be high). A major international gathering in Dubai on 18–19 April was intended to craft new policies and raise more money to fight the piracy threat off Somalia. The considerable international efforts were deemed partially effective insofar as the number of successful attacks might have been much higher without the numerous pre-emptive strikes. However, it was also clear that the pirates were adapting their strategy. For the first time, Somali pirates attacked an anchored vessel within the territorial waters of Oman, far from the Somali coast. In West Africa, Nigeria and Benin were mostly affected. The IMB was concerned about underreporting of attacks in Nigeria, where ten where officially reported, while the IMB itself had counted at least 34 additional incidents. On 30 August, the UNSC voiced concern over increasing maritime piracy, armed robbery and reports of hostage-taking in the Gulf of Guinea, followed by a resolution on 31 October calling on ECOWAS, CEEAC and the Gulf of Guinea Commission to engage into coordinated action against piracy there.

Continuously under UN mandate, the Combined Task Force 151 **(CTF-151)**, consisting of international warships patrolling the Gulf of Aden, the Arabian Sea and the Somali Basin, countered piracy and secured freedom of navigation rather satisfactorily. The command changed every three months (Pakistan, Singapore, New Zealand and Pakistan again). The separate Combined Task Force 150 **(CTF-150)**, which focused on counter-terrorism and associated illegal activities, carried out several operations to deter, detect and disrupt the smuggling of illegal cargo (particularly targeting narcotics). CTF-150 strengthened ties with the Kenyan and Tanzanian navy. The command changed every six months (from France to the United Kingdom). The European Naval Force Operation **'Atalanta'** escorted vessels sent by WFP, AMISOM and other agencies bringing humanitarian aid to Somalia. With the hunger crisis in the Horn, not least Somalia, more shipments had to be accompanied. Atalanta vessels also continued to operate to deter piracy off the Somali coast and to ensure free navigation for peaceful vessels. The mission was extended following Kenya's invasion of southern Somalia (to fight against al-Shabaab), formally because the Kenyan army had joined AMISOM.

Epidemics and Disasters

Malaria remained a major health threat. Close to 90% of deaths due to malaria worldwide occurred in sub-Saharan Africa, which, according to WHO Director-General Margaret Chan, was "the heartland of malaria". Most deaths were registered among children living in Africa. Nevertheless, according to the World Malaria Report 2011, mortality rates had fallen by more than 25% globally since 2000, and by 33% in the WHO African Region. On the occasion of World Malaria Day (25 April), the WHO regional director for Africa declared in Luanda that by the end of 2010, a total of 11 countries (Botswana, Cape Verde, Eritrea, Madagascar, Namibia, Rwanda, São Tomé and Príncipe, South Africa, Swaziland, Zambia and Tanzania) had registered a higher than 50% reduction in malaria cases and deaths.

The latest statistics on the global **HIV/AIDS** epidemic were published by UNAIDS, WHO and UNICEF in November, with figures for the end of 2010. Sub-Saharan Africa remained by far the worst affected region, with an estimated 22.9 m infected people out of an estimated total of 34 m worldwide. The number of newly affected people was estimated at 1.9 m out of a world total of 2.7 m new patients, with an adult prevalence rate of 5% compared with 0.8% worldwide and 1.2 m deaths out of a global total of 1.8 m. The overall growth of the epidemic had stabilised in recent years, however. The annual number of new HIV infections had steadily declined and, due to the significant increase in people receiving antiretroviral therapy, so had the number of AIDS-related deaths.

The **drought in East Africa** was considered to be the world's second worst natural disaster during the year. The biggest famine in decades affected people in parts of Kenya, Somalia, Ethiopia, Eritrea and Djibouti, with Somalia hit by far the hardest. According to a UN report in September, half of the country was in need of emergency aid. The war situation, with al-Shabaab operating locally as an offshoot of al-Qaida, exacerbated the dimensions of the problem and testified to the relative meaning of the term 'natural'. Hostile to Western intervention, al-Shabaab, which was in control of large parts of the territory, forced 16 relief agencies to abandon their humanitarian deliveries in November. It was estimated that as many as 30,000 children died as a result of the catastrophe, not least due to lack of international humanitarian aid and secure supply channels. The deadly combination of war and drought affected an estimated 13 m people in the Horn of Africa. While the food crisis in Somalia was no longer at emergency levels by the end of the year, needs remained huge. According to an estimate by the International Committee of the Red Cross, the country would take at least another two years to recover. Beyond the sub-region, the continued upward trend of **food prices** on international markets resulted in new tensions in local markets and increased the risks to food security for poor households that were already severely affected. Over 200 m Africans were said to be undernourished and suffering from vitamin and mineral deficiencies.

Floods resulting from high rainfall at the beginning of the year once again affected parts of Southern Africa, where the rainy season's rising waters caused close to 500 deaths – the highest death toll in recent years. In terms of fatalities, (southern) Angola was the most acutely affected country, followed by (northern) Namibia and the Eastern Cape in South Africa, where around 100 people died as a result of floods in January. There were a similar number of flood victims around the Nigerian city of Ibadan during the rainy season in August and floods also wreaked havoc in Accra at the end of October. The worst floods in 50 years hit Dar es Salaam at the end of December, killing over 20 people. Cyclone Bingiza caused flooding in Madagascar on 14 February.

As of 29 April, UNHCR estimates suggested that over 170,000 refugees had left **Côte d'Ivoire** as a result of the political violence there to seek shelter in neighbouring countries, primarily in Liberia, and there were also estimated to be over 800,000 Ivorian IDPs. The massive numbers of uprooted people negatively affected an already fragile food and nutrition situation. Food and water supplies and the availability of shelter became even more precarious.

Andreas Mehler, Henning Melber & Klaas van Walraven

II. United Nations and Sub-Saharan Africa

The AU-UN collaboration was affected by the global financial crisis, and both organisations struggled to mobilise the requisite funds for joint activities such as their peacebuilding and humanitarian operations in Sudan and Somalia. The AU and African issues were receiving serious international attention, according to experts and the media. The AU had won a voice at meetings of the G20 and played a part in getting the World Bank, the IMF and the WTO to take Africa's concerns more seriously. However, for the organisation to grow stronger, more of its member states would need to invest in the Union as well as follow its norms and rules. The AU's budget crisis deepened, since Egypt and Libya contributed less. The AU was criticised for its silence on the 'Arab Spring' developments and for its lack of progress in pushing rich countries to compensate for climate change damage. UN Secretary-General Ban Ki-moon presented the UN General Assembly's (UNGA) priorities for the year: inclusive and sustainable development ranked highest, followed by climate change, women's empowerment, a safe and secure world, human rights, improving the response to major humanitarian crises, and disarmament and nuclear non-proliferation. Africa-UN relations focused mainly on security. Major joint efforts included responses to conflict in Côte d'Ivoire, and peacekeeping operations in Sudan. Both examples bear witness to the AU-UN peace and security partnership; the postures and policies of the UN were shaped and implemented in close collaboration with actors such as the AU, ECOWAS and IGAD. The evolution of this partnership was not always smooth. There were quite heated debates between the UNSC and the AU Peace and Security Council (AUPSC) regarding the military intervention in Libya, the peace process in Sudan and the boosting of African troops fighting in Somalia.

Africa in the UN

Africa's presence and voice within the UN system manifested itself through events such as the election crisis in Côte d'Ivoire, the 'Arab Spring' and especially Kadhafi's death in Libya, the pronouncements and decisions of the ICC in relation to African leaders, the African intervention in Somalia, and the Southern Sudan independence referendum. Ban Ki-moon and his counterpart, AU Commission chief Jean Ping, were frequent interlocutors. Ban Ki-moon attended the AU Summits and also co-chaired high-level meetings on Côte d'Ivoire, Sudan and Somalia.

The UNSC condemned attempts to usurp the will of the people in **Côte d'Ivoire**, and urged all the Ivorian parties and stakeholders to respect the outcome of the election in view of the recognition by ECOWAS and the AU of Alassane Ouattara as the newly elected president. It also condemned the human rights and humanitarian law violations committed against civilians. An AU-led diplomatic initiative was seen as the best way to prevent renewed civil war in the country. A divided ECOWAS, with Nigeria taking a particularly hard line, preferred a tough stance on the crisis, even urging the UN to sanction the use of 'legitimate force' to remove Laurent Gbagbo to prevent a return to civil war. Thabo Mbeki, head of the AU initiative, preferred talks and stirred up controversy in the sub-region by proposing a transitional power-sharing mechanism. The UNSC supplied 2,000 additional troops for the nearly 9,000-strong UN Operation in Côte d'Ivoire (UNOCI), extended the temporary loan of UN Mission in Liberia troops and material to UNOCI, and imposed targeted sanctions on key individuals. UNOCI struggled to support some provision of security for the government and key politicians. UN Under-Secretary-General (USG) for Peacekeeping Operations Alain Le Roy decried restrictions imposed by Gbagbo on the freedom of movement of UNOCI in the capital and in the west. Access restrictions and political controversies severely hampered UNOCI's implementation of its protection of civilians mandate.

The AU's relationship with the **ICC** remained decidedly sour. The AU's Jean Ping, who had been a fierce critic of the ICC, accused its prosecutor, Luis Moreno-Ocampo, of adopting double standards by turning a blind eye to war crimes in places such as Myanmar, Iraq and Gaza. The AU stance was one of non-cooperation with the ICC by not arresting and surrendering al-Bashir and Khadafi. The AU renewed its call for the UNSC to suspend ICC proceedings against al-Bashir and asked for the lifting of sanctions against Khartoum and the comprehensive relief of Sudan's external debt, especially in view of Khartoum's acceptance of the outcome of the self-determination referendum for the South. Rome Statute signatories Malawi and Djibouti received visits from al-Bashir and did not arrest him. However, some top African officials were becoming less patient with Sudan. According to a Wikileaks report, Ping acknowledged in closed talks with the US, the UK and France that Khartoum had not done enough to address the issue of justice in Darfur and must engage with the ICC. Mbeki admittted in November that the AU High Level Implementation Panel on Sudan (AUHIP) he headed had been unsuccessful in implementing the justice component as mandated by the AU. The AU supported Kenya's appeal to defer the charges brought by the ICC against six high-ranking government officials, dubbed 'the Ocampo Six', in relation to the post-election violence in 2008. Botswana supported the arrest warrant against Khadafi and called on fellow African states to support the ICC.

With two high level appointments in March, the UN strengthened its **diplomatic presence** and recognised the continent's increasing importance in global affairs. The post of head of the UN Office in Nairobi was upgraded to USG, which gave greater authority within the hierarchy. Sahle-Work Zewde, a veteran Ethiopian diplomat, was appointed to the position. Nairobi became a more important regional hub for the UN's diverse operations in East and Central Africa. Ban Ki-moon also appointed Abou Moussa of Chad as his Special Representative and head of the UN Regional Office for Central Africa (UNOCA) based in Libreville, Gabon, which opened in March. UNOCA – one of only three regional centres in the UN system, along with the UN Office for West Africa and the UN Office for Preventive Diplomacy in Central Asia – had a mandate to promote peace and stability in the region.

The AU and the UN began elaborating a comprehensive capacity building programme for the AU, under the UN-AU **Ten Year Capacity Building Programme**. A retreat on this topic was held on 7–9 September in Debre Zeit, Ethiopia. An AU strategic plan was the starting point for the formulation of the programme, which aimed to particularly strengthen the NEPAD Planning and Coordinating Agency and the Regional Economic Communities. The plan had six programme areas: peace and security, shared values, integration, development, cooperation, and institutional capacity building. AU Commission Deputy Chairperson Erastus Mwencha and ECA Executive Secretary Abdoulie Janneh regarded the plan as a way of better linking objectives with concrete results.

Peace and Security

The **AUPSC-UNSC meeting** on 21 May in Addis Ababa was dominated by discussions on Libya, Côte d'Ivoire, Sudan and Somalia. The meeting documented the tensions in the relationship. African leaders and AU officials, Jean Ping and Ramtane Lamamra, vented their disappointment that the UN and international partners did not sufficiently support AU conflict resolution initiatives. The AU requested political, financial and material support from the UN, in particular for UNSC authorised peace operations. The AUPSC also at times sought more parity in the relationship with the UNSC. The UNSC for its part consistently reaffirmed its primary responsibility for the maintenance of international peace and security. The huge complexities of joint management of the UN-AU Mission in Darfur (UNAMID) also led to concerns that this support model was not a suitable precedent. The Council was reluctant, despite repeated African calls, to transform the AU operation in Somalia into a UN mission. According to AU Peace and Security Commissioner Ramtane Lamamra, some African countries felt the UNSC was selective; AU proposals for Somalia were not sanctioned, while the Arab League's request to impose a no-fly zone on Libya was immediately enacted. The meeting nonetheless committed to the full implementation of UN resolutions 1970 and 1973 on the protection of civilians in Libya and called for a political solution to the crisis that "responds to the legitimate demands of the Libyan people". It committed to helping Côte d'Ivoire rebuild its institutions and return to peace following Ouattara's inauguration as president on 21 May. It also called for a speedy resolution of the dispute surrounding the status of Abyei, Sudan.

The new **UN Office to the AU** (UNOAU) officially opened in Addis Ababa on 22 February, with the head of office, Zachary Muburi-Muita, having the status of an Assistant Secretary-General. This signalled an upgrade in strategic importance and closer institutionalisation of the AU-UN peace and security partnership. UNOAU's objective was to help operationalise the African peace and security architecture, provide technical advice to the AU in the management of complex operations and provide coordinated and consistent UN advice on both long-term capacity building and short-term operational support. The UNOAU is important for the implementation of the remainder of the Ten-Year Capacity Building Programme. Implementation had so far suffered from numerous challenges, including a lack of strategic vision for the programme. The UN Secretariat worked during the year on an overdue report to define a strategic vision for UN-AU cooperation in peace and security, submitted to the UNSC on 29 December.

Africa's largest country was split in two after the independence of South Sudan on 9 July. The UN's multidimensional role in **Sudan** was tightly coordinated with AU policies. The UN monitored the independence vote, provided aid to returning Southerners, and prepared options for a worst-case scenario of renewed warfare. The top UN brass applauded the fact that leaders in Sudan and South Sudan held the vote as scheduled in an atmosphere of "peace and cooperation". The UN reminded the parties to agree on key post-referendum issues, including wealth-sharing, the management of assets and debts, citizenship and border security arrangements. The nearly 10,000-strong UN Mission in Sudan (UNMIS) ended on 9 July. The UNSC created the UN Mission in the Republic of South Sudan (UNMISS), but the new mission had no mandate to operate in Sudan. There was soon criticism that the UNSC and UN troop contributing countries had downplayed the violent dynamics in Sudan after the independence vote. Violent conflict erupted in Abyei, Blue Nile and Southern Kordofan. Abyei did not hold its referendum on whether to join the North or the South. The Sudan People's Liberation Movement North and the Sudanese Armed Forces fought in the border states of South Kordofan and Blue Nile. After criticism over its 'failure to protect', the UNSC called for investigation into Khartoum's use of violence in Southern Kordofan on 15 August. A preliminary report, produced jointly by the Office of the High Commissioner for Human Rights (OHCHR) and UNMIS, described a wide range of alleged violations of international law. These could, if substantiated, amount to crimes against humanity or war crimes. The OHCHR recommended better access for human rights monitors to conduct investigations and for humanitarian actors trying to bring relief to the affected populations. Since 16 March, the UN Secretary-General's Special Advisers on the Prevention of Genocide and the Responsibility to Protect (R2P), Francis Deng and Edward Luck, had expressed grave concern over deaths and displacement in Abyei. Due to al-Bashir's criticism of UNMIS and the UN, and the lack of good options, at the end of June, the UNSC, under Chapter VII of the UN Charter, swiftly authorised the deployment of up to 4,200 Ethiopian peacekeepers to Abyei as the UN Interim Security Force (UNISFA). The Ethiopians acted unilaterally even though the AU welcomed the initiative. They enforced the demilitarisation of Abyei as per a 29 June agreement between the parties, to protect civilians and maintain security throughout the Abyei region, and to facilitate the delivery of humanitarian aid and free movement of humanitarian personnel. UNISFA enabled more AUHIP-led talks on the future status of Abyei. The UN said both countries had failed to withdraw their troops by 30 September as agreed.

The AU and the AUHIP advocated a three-track strategy to resolve the **Darfur** conflict: talks in Doha, Qatar, between the belligerents aimed at achieving a ceasefire; involving the people of Darfur in an inclusive Darfur Political Process (DPP); and early recovery and development in Darfur. The AU and the African Group in New York pushed for the earliest possible commencement of the DPP. This displayed the differences of approach between the AU and the UNSC. The AU criticised AU-UN Joint Chief Mediator Djibril Bassolé for not having liaised sufficiently with the AUHIP, since he had followed the UNSC line (pushed strongest by Western powers and Darfur armed groups) that, due to continued violence, the necessary conditions for dialogue between Darfurians had not yet been met. The AUHIP, on the other hand, believed soft diplomacy would encourage Sudan to create an enabling environment for the DPP, including suspending the state of emergency in Darfur. A Doha Document for Peace in Darfur (DDPD) was signed by the government and the Liberation and Justice Movement in July. At the end of July, the UNSC extended the UNAMID mandate for another 12 months, underlining that UNAMID should prioritise the protection of civilians; safe, timely and unhindered humanitarian access; and complementary efforts to promote the peace as well as the Doha talks. South Africa, Nigeria and Gabon expressed their disappointment that the UNSC had not launched the DPP, while Sudan argued that the UNSC was interfering in Sudan's internal affairs and said that any "mandate change" would lead Sudan to cancel the mission (referring to the resolution's call for coordination between UNAMID, UNISFA and UNMISS). It was up to the 'Tripartite Mechanism', involving senior representatives from the AU, UN and Sudan to solve these sovereignty and access issues. UNAMID noted that inter-ethnic violence had declined during the second half of the year and that the overall number of deaths in Darfur had fallen from 2,321 in 2010 to 724 so far in 2011. Ibrahim Gambari, head of UNAMID, said the mission had pursued its "new approach" to protection – more patrols and a "quick reaction force". This followed severe criticisms from the US ambassador to the UN in the UNSC in January. UNAMID's 'Operation Spring Basket' had expanded humanitarian access to previously inaccessible parts of Jebel Marra and elsewhere. At year's end, the 'joint commission' central to the implementation of the DDPD held its inaugural meeting, chaired by Gambari. He on many occasions deplored attacks on UNAMID peacekeepers, and repeatedly called on holdout movements to engage in the peace process.

On 17 March, South Africa, Gabon, and Nigeria supported UNSC resolution 1973, which authorised military intervention in **Libya**. However, this unity soon crumbled when African leaders felt Western powers had acted well beyond the spirit of the authorisation with NATO airstrikes over residential areas and Tripoli. In May, Mbeki complained that the UNSC had "marginalised" the AU's roadmap for Libya and that Western powers had used the cover of civilian protection when the no-fly zone was really about regime change. The AU's Libya Panel believed that an AU-negotiated ceasefire was the best option to bring about the reforms needed to end Kadhafi's rule.

On 12 July, the UNGA held an informal thematic debate on the role of **regional actors and R2P**. A UN Secretary-General report had stressed that effective global-regional collaboration was essential to realise the promise embodied in the R2P. The UN R2P strategy had three pillars: the primary responsibility of the state to protect; international assistance and capacity building; and a timely and decisive response. Many African states stressed the need for the principle to be strongly focused on preventative action, targeting the root causes of insecurity and focusing on non-military measures. They said Libya exemplified the way that certain states abused the R2P doctrine. Non-military means to protect civilians had not been exhausted prior to the use of military options. Côte d'Ivoire and Libya demonstrated that "timely and decisive response was most likely when intergovernmental bodies favoured similar courses of action". Therefore a multilateral alternative was important to Africa: the UN, with its regional and subregional partners, should enact the collective will. The International Conference on the Great Lakes Region expressed regional support for the R2P and gratitude for the support and training it had received in areas such as the prevention and punishment of genocide. Deng praised the AU's sound regional approaches to R2P.

At a UNSC open debate in November on **protection of civilians in armed conflict**, Ban Ki-moon and UN Human Rights Commissioner Navanethem Pillay stressed the need for accountability and enhanced compliance with international human rights and humanitarian law. They asked the UNSC to respond to violations with appropriate action, such as the threat of targeted sanctions or referrals to the ICC. Nigeria said that the effectiveness of the UN and UNSC was measured against its ability to protect civilians. South Africa said that civilians could not be harmed in the name of protecting civilians, adding that the UNSC's authorisation of protection for Libyan civilians had been a cover for regime change. Pillay encouraged the UNSC to secure follow-up to their resolutions in view of access restrictions to Abyei, Southern Kordofan and Blue Nile State.

Ban Ki-moon, citing the risk of increased international terrorism, called in January for the support packages for the AU's intervention in **Somalia** to be upgraded to match the standards of the support provided to UN peace operations. The UNSC did not support an increase in the force level estimated to be needed for the African Union Mission in Somalia (AMISOM), keeping it at the pledged level of 12,000 troops. The AU endorsed a call for the increase of AMISOM strength to 20,000 troops, with requisite air and maritime capabilities. It also requested the UNSC to deploy a UN peacekeeping force, by transforming AMISOM into an UN operation, with a fixed timeline. The UNSC, however, still considered the situation was not ripe for this. The UN Political Office for Somalia (UNPOS) and UN Support Office for AMISOM remained in Nairobi from where visits were carried out to Mogadishu. A joint regional strategy was adopted by UNPOS, AMISOM and IGAD on 23 February. UN Special Envoy for Somalia Augustine Mahiga, Boubacar G. Diarra, the AU envoy for Somalia and head of AMISOM, and Kipruto arap Kirwa, the IGAD peace facilitator, sought in this way to enhance cooperation and information sharing between the three institutions, the international community and other partners in order to improve their work of helping the Transitional Federal Government to manage the transitional period. In April, the EAC backed the AU request to boost AMISOM and called upon member states to deal jointly with the Somali terrorism threat and piracy. AMISOM's forces on the ground amounted to approximately 9,800 soldiers. On 12 July, Diarra recognised that AMISOM was bound by international law and that the protection of civilians was an implicit duty. The AU's guidelines for the protection of civilians in peace operations were being mainstreamed into AMISOM's work. The AMISOM mandate was expanded from peacekeeping to peace enforcement and, in August, it was lauded for its military success: it had secured control of Mogadishu and forced al-Shabaab to withdraw. From October onwards, Kenya's military was fighting al-Shabaab in the south of Somalia.

Ethiopia made a case for a tougher approach on **Eritrea** in the sub-region, which gained continental support. IGAD discussed Eritrea's support for al-Shabaab and other armed groups inside Somalia and the security threat this posed to the region. Ethiopia said it was pushing for regime change in Eritrea by supporting the Eritrean people and groups that wanted to dismantle the regime. The UN's Somalia/Eritrea Sanctions Committee recommended tougher sanctions against Eritrea, which the UNSC adopted in December despite some concerns that this would adversely impact on ordinary Eritreans. The decision was heavily influenced by pressure from African members of the UNSC, who accused Eritrea of harbouring armed groups, sponsoring terrorist attacks including a plot against the AU summit in January, and supporting al-Shabaab with finance and weapons.

In July, a joint UN assessment mission confirmed that the 'Forces Armées de la République Démocratique du Congo' (FARDC) in the **DRC** had committed mass rape and acts of pillage in several villages in the east of the country. The OHCHR initiated more in-depth investigations. Moreover, an OHCHR-MONUSCO (UN Organization Stabilization Mission in the Democratic Republic of the Congo) report said that the rape of hundreds of people in 2010 by rebel groups could be considered crimes against humanity and war crimes. MONUSCO provided technical and logistical support for the Congolese Independent National Electoral Commission for the conduct of the presidential and legislative elections held on 28 November.

On 1 April, leaders at a SADC security organ summit in Zambia criticised **Zimbabwe**'s delay in implementing the Global Political Agreement. It was even-handedly worded yet signalled a break with past appeasement of Zimbabwean President Robert Mugabe. South

African President Jacob Zuma, as the SADC mediator, was joined by Zambian President Rupiah Banda and Mozambique's President Armando Guebuza, forming a SADC Troika.

The UN and concerned countries gave attention to the piracy threat in the **Gulf of Guinea**. In October, the UNSC encouraged the intention of states in the region to develop a regional strategy to combat maritime piracy. An assessment mission was sent, led by the Africa II Division in the UN Department of Political Affairs, and the UN Office on Drugs and Crime (UNODC) in Nigeria. The initiative also involved UNOCA, the UN Office for West Africa (UNOWA), ECOWAS, ECCAS and the Gulf of Guinea Commission. After a coup attempt in **Guinea** in July, the UN Envoy to West Africa reaffirmed the UN's determination to support military reforms in Guinea. On 28 March, UNODC lauded Kenya's role in counter-piracy, police reform and combating illicit drug trafficking. UNODC's work in **Kenya** formed part of the wider Eastern Africa regional approach, designed to take into account overlapping geographic and thematic issues, such as capacity building for international cooperation on law enforcement, strengthening of border control, anti-corruption and prison reform.

Ban Ki-moon raised serious concerns in April over the continued recruitment of children by armed groups in the **CAR**, and called for measures to address the ongoing "protection crisis". The CAR appealed to the UNGA in September for aid to help consolidate peace and prevent fighting following the withdrawal of the UN Mission in the Central African Republic and Chad in December 2010, at the request of the Chadian government. Special Representative of the UN Secretary-General (SRSG) Margaret Vogt and the UN Integrated Peacebuilding Office in the CAR assisted in consolidating peace and national reconciliation and promoting and protecting human rights. Together with ECOWAS and other regional partners, UNOWA and Said Djinnit, the SRSG for West Africa, supported the conclusion of the transition processes in **Guinea and Niger**. UNOWA engaged in preventive diplomacy actions, including in Burkina Faso and in Côte d'Ivoire.

Governance and Human Rights

Two-thirds of developing countries were on track or close to meeting the MDG targets for curbing extreme poverty and hunger, according to the World Bank and the IMF Global Monitoring Report released in April. The report projected that by 2015 only 4.8% of China's population would be in extreme poverty compared with 36% in Sub-Saharan Africa. Seventeen African countries were still 'off-track'. The **UN MDG Report** released in July ranked Rwanda among the countries that had made rapid progress in ensuring the achievement of goals. Rwanda had made most progress in universal primary education and reduction of maternal deaths. The Sub-Sahara region led in steadily reducing new HIV infections, in addition to treating the disease. Other countries specially mentioned alongside Rwanda for the achievement of universal primary education included Burundi, Togo, Tanzania, Burkina Faso, Ethiopia, Guinea, Mali, Mozambique, Niger and São Tomé and Príncipe. The report also said that, between 2000 and 2009, Sub-Saharan Africa had seen the greatest fall in deaths from malaria. Rwanda still had the highest level of female participation in parliament with 56.3%. In July, a UN Women report credited Rwanda for the high representation of women in politics and participation in the development of their country.

The January **AU Summit** took place as 'Arab Spring' protests began in Tunisia and Egypt. African statesmen gathered under the theme of 'shared values'. But their silence on the popular uprisings revealed that democracy, governance, human rights and rule of law norms remained contested values. Incoming AU chairman, Equatorial Guinea's President Teodoro Obiang, voiced his view that universal values should be "adapted to the African value system", spurring others to request the AU to present a workable alternative. **Anti-imperialism** had strong rhetorical purchase: several African leaders complained that "western-controlled institutions" such as the ICC triggered African conflicts rather than preventing or ending them, imposing short-sighted or misguided prescriptions. Ping interrupted a journalist who asked Obiang about his governance record. He said that no one said anything when other organisations chose leaders with questionable backgrounds: "You are not being fair," he quipped, "and you have to treat us and place us on the same footing as other organisations. It's as if you're applying double standards."

AU leaders debated the establishment of a **continental criminal court** to prosecute Africans accused of crimes against humanity at home. For some, this would help bring the ICC trials to an end. Judging by the poor progress on the possible trial of former Chadian president Hissene Habré, which was the first case to be brought by the AU against a former head of state, African leaders were not ready to go after their colleagues who committed war crimes and crimes against humanity. Côte d'Ivoire requested an ICC investigation into the post-election violence there. On 23 November, an arrest warrant was issued by the ICC against Laurent Gbagbo. He faced charges of four counts of crimes against humanity allegedly committed in Côte d'Ivoire between 16 December 2010 and 12 April 2011. In February, the UNSC referred the situation in Libya to the ICC. In March, the ICC confirmed war crimes charges against two rebel leaders, Abdallah Banda and Saleh Jerbo, accused in the September 2007 'Haskanita attack' that resulted in the death in Darfur of 12 peacekeepers with the African Mission in Sudan (shortly afterwards reconstituted as UNAMID).

At the UNGA, Liberia urged the international community to place more focus on preventive mediation. South Sudan, the UN's 193rd member state, appealed for international assistance and the solving of contentious issues with north Sudan. In June, the UNGA adopted a consensus resolution on reinforcing mediation in the peaceful settlement of disputes. Nigeria intensified its quest for a permanent seat on the UNSC. Ban Ki-Moon said during a May visit to Nigeria that its chances of achieving this were good. Nigeria contributed to the UNSC's mandate as the world's 4th contributor to UN peace operations and was an active member of ECOWAS. At the UNGA in September, Benin proposed 2015 as the target date for giving Africa permanent representation on an enlarged UNSC. The UNGA held a meeting on **UNSC reform** on 8–9 November. Key issues were the urgent need to expand the UNSC by ensuring effective negotiations on UNSC reform, guaranteeing greater input from non-members, and improving transparency. Speaking on behalf of the African Group, Sierra Leone urged UN members to be flexible in the quest for a global governance system that was more representative and democratic, "to generate the necessary political will to advance progress on this very crucial issue". UN member states recognised the need for "flexibility and compromise" if the nearly decade-long effort towards reform was to bear fruit.

The **Human Rights Council** (HRC) suspended Libya on 1 March for its government's violent attacks on protesters. The final tally of the vote on the resolution calling for its suspension far exceeded the two-thirds majority required. The UNGA later voted to suspend Libya from the HRC in one of the UN's most unanimous votes. Sudan sought to terminate the mandate of the UN's human rights monitor for Sudan at the 15th session of the HRC, refusing to have a rights expert monitoring its affairs. The expert, Chande Othman, had criticised Khartoum's crackdown on political opposition leaders, journalists and students, and called for a probe into militia attacks on civilians in Sudan's western region of Darfur. He had also urged the National Intelligence and Security Services to release 11 human rights activists and journalists arrested between 30 October and 3 November 2010. On 7 January, the UN's Special Rapporteur on the **rights of indigenous peoples** welcomed a new law adopted in the Republic of Congo, saying it was "the first of its kind on the African continent, and it provides an important example of a good practice in the region for the recognition and protection of the rights of indigenous peoples". On 3 March, a UN report commissioned by the OHCHR highlighted the deprivations endured by thousands of victims of **sexual violence in the DRC**, including poverty, denial of justice and lack of access to medical and psychological care, and recommended the establishment of a reparations fund. The management of the fund might include representatives of the government, the UN, donors, civil society, and survivors themselves. Anthony Lake, the head of UNICEF, said the report was a valuable contribution to efforts to end sexual violence in the DRC. In some parts of Africa, it was deeply unpopular that an HRC resolution in June expressed grave concern about discrimination based on sexual orientation and gender identity. In March, it was reported that 26 states had signed the **Convention for the Protection and Assistance of Internally Displaced Persons in Africa**, but only five had ratified it. The treaty was adopted by the AU in 2009 and would come into force once 15 states had taken the steps necessary to become party to it. The 'Kampala Convention' builds on international humanitarian law and international human rights law, as well as the Guiding Principles on Internal Displacement. In September, human rights organisations urged UNESCO to reject a bid to honour President Teodoro Obiang of Equatorial

Guinea with a life sciences prize in his name. At the end of October, South Africa as a non-permanent member of the UNSC, threw its weight behind Palestine's bid to become a full member of the UN. Palestinian President Mahmoud Abbas made the historic application to a standing ovation in the UNGA in September.

Humanitarian Assistance

During mid-year, the AU engaged in a new way in the **Horn of Africa crisis**. Though not designed to raise funds to fight disasters, the organisation held a first-of-its-kind fund-raising conference that raised more than $ 350 m for famine aid. Only four African leaders attended the AU summit in Ethiopia, but the AU said it was not a question of who showed up, but rather how much money was raised. The Tanzanian UN Deputy Secretary-General Asha Rose Migiro attended the conference. Notable pledges came from Algeria, Egypt, Angola, South Africa and South Sudan. However, the bulk of the money – $ 300 m – came from the AfDB, to be used for long-term projects in the region. Some $ 1.2 bn of the $ 2.5 bn the UN said was needed had been raised worldwide. In July, Somalia was termed by the head of UNHCR the "world's worst humanitarian crisis". Tens of thousands of Somalis starved to death and more than 3.2 m others – almost half the population – were in need of life-saving assistance. The famine affected some 13.3 m people in Somalia and in Djibouti, Ethiopia and Kenya. In addition, fighting displaced 200,000 people within Somalia, bringing the number of IDPs up to 1.5 m. UNICEF provided food aid and set up feeding centres to treat acutely malnourished children. The number of people overall receiving food aid nearly doubled from July to August. In July, 770,000 Somalis received food aid and that figure stood at 1.4 m as of 19 September. UNICEF warned at the beginning of July that 2 m children were malnourished as a result of the drought, and half a million could soon die or suffer long-lasting mental or physical damage. The agency appealed for nearly $ 3 m to assist millions of children and women in Kenya, Somalia, Ethiopia and Djibouti. In mid-July, UN agencies resumed aid delivery to drought victims in al-Qaida-inspired al-Shabaab-controlled areas of Somalia, following a lifting of the ban on foreign aid operations. On 6 July, al-Shabaab appealed for help, saying they would allow aid through to their fiefdoms. UNICEF airlifted food and medicines for malnourished children to Baidoa. WFP, which had pulled out of southern Somalia in early 2010, considered resuming operations in the area.

In mid-August, the opening of an extension camp for **Somali refugees** in Kenya became controversial. Kenya said the flow of Somali refugees – at around 1,500 per day – was unsustainable and wanted the international community to address the humanitarian crisis within Somalia itself. The refugee population at Dadaab, the world's largest refugee camp, hit nearly half a million people by end-year. Kenya was becoming increasingly concerned by the refugee crisis and the terror threat posed by al-Qaida-affiliated insurgents.

The Horn of Africa crisis acted as a wake-up call for many working in humanitarian aid. The Office for the Coordination of Humanitarian Affairs (OCHA) and the Office for Disaster Risk Reduction supported a 'Never Again' campaign and a **Charter to End Extreme Hunger**. On 27 September, experts deplored the fact that warning signs were evident but ignored, long before drought and famine began killing tens of thousands of people in the Horn of Africa. The campaign wanted to make the international emergency response system more flexible in responding to early warnings, and sought more regular support for risk reduction at national and community level. The Charter had five essential elements: fixing the flaws of the international emergency system; supporting local food production; ensuring services and protection for the poorest; availability of affordable food; and reducing armed violence and conflict. Kenyan Prime Minister Raila Odinga was the world's first leader to sign it.

In March, UN agencies began complex **humanitarian operations in Libya**. UNHCR raised the alarm at violence and discrimination in Libya against Sub-Saharan Africans in both the rebel-held east and the government-controlled west. It said the number of people who had fled the violence since the start of mass protests in February exceeded 212,000, including 112,000 in Tunisia, more than half of them Tunisian and Egyptian migrants; 98,000 in Egypt, over two-thirds of them Egyptians; and 2,000 in Niger, mainly Niger nationals. WFP arrived in Benghazi in March with the first delivery of UN food aid to enter the country. WFP mobilised food as part of a $ 39.2 m emergency operation to feed more than 1 m people in Libya, Egypt and Tunisia over a three-month period. In July, WFP started using ferries to transport aid supplies and aid workers by sea from the Libyan city of Benghazi to Misrata. This unusual step was deemed necessary for security and humanitarian reasons. WFP also reported that it had distributed more than 6,000 tonnes of food aid to at least 543,000 people across Libya from January to April.

According to UNHCR, at least 113,000 people had been displaced from the contested territory of Abyei in **Sudan**. UN estimates suggested that at least 73,000 people were displaced throughout the central and eastern parts of South Kordofan. OCHA said access restrictions and funding significantly constrained the delivery of relief supplies to the displaced. Air strikes in Sudan's Blue Nile State sent increasing numbers of refugees fleeing into Ethiopia. UNHCR reported that an estimated 25,000 Sudanese had found refuge in western Ethiopia since the influx started on 3 September. UNHCR, UNICEF, WFP and others launched a formal appeal for funds to help refugees fleeing into western Ethiopia from Blue Nile State. The joint appeal raised some $ 18.3 m and was intended to help up to 35,000 refugees. The Sudan humanitarian appeal was greatly underfunded, with only 24% of the required $ 1.7 bn received. Agencies such as UNICEF and FAO renewed their involvement in the now independent **South Sudan**. Between January and mid-May, violent clashes displaced over 117,000 people and killed almost 1,400 in South Sudan alone. In July, UNICEF called for increased resources to help the country's 4 m children.

FAO said it had drawn up a $ 50 m plan to help build capacity in South Sudan's agriculture sector, prevent conflict over water resources and develop the livestock sector.

On 23 March, OCHA allocated $ 10.4 m to seven agencies to assist people affected by the post-election violence in **Côte d'Ivoire**. The unrest displaced up to a million people inside the country and an estimated 150,000 Ivorian refugees sought safety in Liberia. WFP reported that it had airlifted 5 metric tonnes of high-energy biscuits into Liberia for distribution in the border area, enough to feed 7,000 refugees for three days. WFP with UNHCR set up an emergency relief operation to assist 18,000 IDPs in Côte d'Ivoire and 15,000 refugees in Liberia for 45 days. FAO rushed in food aid and supplies for around 12,000 farming households in both Côte d'Ivoire and Liberia.

Environment

The 17th Conference of the Parties (COP 17) to the **UN Framework Convention on Climate Change** (UNFCCC) took place from 28 November to (officially) 9 December in Durban. Countries agreed to work towards and adopt a new global pact that would bring all major emitters into its fold. The legally binding 'Durban Platform for Enhanced Action' was adopted on 11 December (36 hours beyond the scheduled end of the talks). This EU proposal required that countries begin in 2012 to negotiate a new global regime for climate change. The new legal framework was to be in place by 2015, and would be implemented from 2020. There was agreement that countries would ramp up funding for the 'Green Climate Fund' and towards the $ 100 bn a year of long-term climate finance they had already agreed to provide by 2020. South Africa was keen to see the event as a success; Zuma called it "a moment of glory for South Africa and Africa". The AU was satisfied that Africa had spoken with one voice and that it had been heard. Speaking on behalf of the AU, Ethiopian Prime Minister Meles Zenawi complained that only 7% of the short-term climate funding promised to the developing world by 2013 had been delivered. Less than a quarter of the $ 30 bn promised by 2013 for the developing world was 'new' money, while the rest was reassigned from standing commitments, such as existing aid budgets. African campaigners and environmentalists said the agreement betrayed Africans already affected by the adverse impacts of climate change. There was suspicion that diplomatic pressure had been put on large developing countries (Brazil, South Africa, India and China) to accept a deal that would commit them to legally binding CO2 cuts. They had toned down the demand that it was the countries that had created the problem with their historical emissions that should shoulder most of the burden for sorting it out.

A United Nations Environment Programme (UNEP) report in February said Kenya, among other developing countries, would achieve higher growth by moving into what was known as a **Green Economy**, referring to sustainable development that takes care of the environment while growing the economy. The report, 'Toward a Green Economy', demonstrated that investing in green projects would result in rapid growth and poverty eradication. The report called on countries to invest 2% of global GDP into ten key sectors to kick-start a low carbon, resource efficient economy.

Africa presented a good opportunity for carbon offset projects, UN experts said at the **Africa Carbon Forum** in Marrakech, Morocco. UNFCCC told the Forum that the growing interest in Clean Development Mechanism (CDM) projects contributed to firmly positioning Africa's opportunities for the carbon market landscape beyond 2012. UNEP said there were approximately 190 CDM projects at various stages of development in Africa, up from 170 projects at the end of 2010 and 53 in 2007.

Christian Aid warned in a report launched in October ('Healthy Harvests: The Benefits of Sustainable Agriculture in Africa and Asia') that lessons learned from Asia's **Green Revolution** about the damage intensive farming could cause were being ignored in the race for food security in Africa. Africa needed sustainable farming techniques, not quick-fix solution modern seed varieties (MVs) that produced better yields if treated with synthetic fertiliser and pesticides. In Asia, the use of MVs had accelerated soil degradation, destroyed crop diversity and encouraged farmers to go into debt. The report recommended: diversification; nutrient recycling; maximum use of renewable, locally available resources; low external-input organic soil: and crop management techniques such as integrated pest management and zero or low till farming.

Linnéa Gelot

III. African-European Relations

European awareness that Africa was changing fast and that many dimensions of the Africa-Europe relationship would also have to change deepened in 2011. The dawning realisation that the tired stereotype of 'rich' Europe and 'poor' Africa was becoming less appropriate began to be reflected in the tone of policy statements and the placing of new emphasis on business relationships in European and African capitals. The influential British publication 'The Economist' even led its 3 December edition with a piece entitled "The hopeful continent: Africa rising". Nevertheless, for many Europeans, relations with the rest of the world were overshadowed by the ongoing sovereign debt crisis and existential questions about the EU's future that the crisis forced them to face. Such navel-gazing was not conducive to long-term European policymaking in a momentous year marked by the 'Arab Spring', which toppled several North African governments and sent shock-waves through the rest of Africa. Major events in Sub-Saharan Africa from a European perspective included the post-election violence in Côte d'Ivoire, the devastating famine in the Horn of Africa, the independence of South Sudan, and ongoing instability in Somalia and the Sahel. From an African perspective, if introspectiveness prevented Europeans from responding adequately to fast-moving events and taking steps to deepen relationships with African countries and institutions, there were other options for partnerships – most notably China.

The **post-Lisbon Treaty reforms** to the EU's external policy bureaucracies continued. On 1 January, the merger of former Commission Directorate Generals (DGs) for Development and EuropeAid took place, and a new organisational structure, DG EuropeAid Development and Cooperation (known as DG DEVCO), was formed. Although the former country desks for African, Caribbean and Pacific countries had previously been absorbed by the European External Action Service (EEAS), DEVCO was launched with an Africa directorate to manage relations between the European Commission, the AU and the African group in Brussels. The merger meant that DEVCO would be both a policy and an implementation organisation, but it raised coordination challenges between DEVCO and the EEAS regarding which organisation would perform which tasks. Given that many non-Europeans see the EU as a single actor and consider the finer points of the EU Treaties as less important than what is actually delivered, these complex institutional reforms were not well understood by many people outside Europe, including in Africa.

The **'Arab Spring'** took European policymakers by surprise, and gave them cause to reflect on their strategies for Sub-Saharan Africa as well as long-standing policies in the EU's neighbourhood. The Arab Spring did not fit with the models of change that European aid programmes were designed around. Rather than being driven by donor civil services and ministries in aid recipient countries, change in Tunisia and Egypt was brought about by ordinary people. Popular uprisings toppled long-standing leaders despite their countries' strong recent performances against human development indicators. For European development agencies, events in North Africa signified that seemingly immovable autocratic regimes were vulnerable to collapse, and that economic growth did not equate to development if political institutions did not mature at the same time. Moreover, the Arab Spring also signified that the Millennium Development Goals (MDGs) may have outlived their usefulness. Youth unemployment and lack of a political voice were cited as the major grievances behind the uprisings north of the Sahara, but neither was targeted by the MDGs.

The European Council meeting held on 11 March announced that the EU would work with the UN, the Arab League, the AU and other international partners to respond to the regional upheaval. Despite these belated efforts to bring multiple partners on-side, European responses to the **Libya crisis** in particular aroused mixed feelings in Sub-Saharan Africa. While few Africans shed tears at the demise of Muammar Kadhafi, there was discomfort at the way in which his dictatorship ended. As one newspaper report put it, exasperation at Kadhafi's meddling in Africa was often offset by admiration for his defiance of the West. Germany's abstention from UNSC Resolution 1973, which legitimised NATO air strikes in support of a no-fly zone, was not perceived by many Africans as a principled division in Europe, as was the case before the 2003 Iraq invasion. Indeed, with the USA taking a back seat, 'Europe' was seen to be intervening militarily in support of a rebel movement waging a civil war against a sitting African head of state – and thereby disregarding the AU's own 'roadmap' to end the Libyan crisis, even if this document was widely considered unrealistic. Following Kadhafi's death at the hands of a lynch mob in Sirte, AU Commission Deputy Chairperson Erastus Onkundi Mwencha said, "The AU has never believed in force to settle disputes." While such a statement may have reflected the disquiet of less democratic AU member state leaders, the feeling that former colonial masters were seizing the chance to rid themselves of the troublesome leader of an oil-rich state was widespread.

European policymakers and media followed the **post-election crisis in Côte d'Ivoire** closely and were ready to intervene to support the winner of the November 2010 poll, Alassane Ouattara. On 14 January, the EU Council extended asset freezes and visa bans originally imposed in December 2010. EU leaders condemned the violence and killings as ex-president Laurent Gbagbo clung to power, and backed African-led efforts in the first months of the year to ensure respect for the election results. The EU election observation mission to Côte d'Ivoire released its final report on 1 February. It praised the Ivorian people, noting that the ballots took place in a well-ordered and peaceful atmosphere with high voter turnout. The report identified irregularities but noted that they did not affect the result. The report was highly critical of Gbagbo for stimulating an atmosphere of tension and of the Ivorian Constitutional Court for unlawfully annulling the result.

Following Gbagbo's arrest on 11 April, after days of heavy fighting during which French and UN helicopters fired rockets at the presidential residence, EU High Representative for Foreign and Security Policy Catherine Ashton deplored the high price the Ivorian people had had to pay. She praised the actions of the UN and French forces, and announced that the EU would help bring peace back to the country. The EU Council welcomed President Ouattara's commitment to national reconciliation and promised support for the proposed Truth and Reconciliation Commission. It also urged the international commission of inquiry into human rights violations, established by the UN on 25 March, to investigate allegations swiftly and thoroughly, and to hold those found responsible for crimes accountable. As was the case with regard to Libya, military intervention by European countries in Côte d'Ivoire was sometimes equated with a return to colonial rule by African intellectuals and media.

The devastating **famine in the Horn of Africa** brought images of starving Africans back to European television screens, evoking memories of the 1980s and prompting politicians and NGOs to respond. Many Europeans were deeply disturbed by the realisation that such a tragedy could happen in 2011 and joined Africans in asking how, given that the disaster was widely forecast, the situation could have been allowed to deteriorate to such an extent.

Aid agencies responded to criticism that they were slow off the mark with a major collective endeavour. The Commission allocated € 184 m in humanitarian aid to drought-affected populations in the Horn of Africa in several tranches during the year. EU funds provided food aid, targeting malnourished children, as well as healthcare and clean water, sanitation facilities and supplies. The Commission's Humanitarian Aid and Civil Protection directorate (ECHO) coordinated these activities from its regional support office in Kenya, from where ECHO experts liaised with aid organisations and monitored relief projects.

Following the deterioration in the humanitarian situation in Somalia, Kenya, Ethiopia, Eritrea and Djibouti in July, German Foreign Minister Guido Westerwelle and Development Minister Dirk Niebel issued a statement expressing their deep concern about the famine and announcing a € 5 m increase in emergency aid, bringing the total German contribution to around € 30 m. The Ministers also appealed to the German people to show their willingness to help through private donations to German aid NGOs. The French government was also spurred into action and doubled its contribution to € 10 m. On 16 July, the UK government pledged £ 52.25 m, on top of £ 38 m pledged earlier that month and £ 57 m raised by the Disasters Emergency Committee.

The **independence of the Republic of South Sudan** on 9 July was greeted with enthusiasm in Europe, tempered with awareness of the magnitude of the challenges that lay ahead. Europe had six months to prepare for South Sudan's independence after the resounding result of the 9 January referendum. EU Development Commissioner Andris Piebalgs told the AU Summit in late January that he considered the division of Sudan to be Africa's greatest challenge, despite the turmoil in North Africa. He visited Khartoum and Juba in May, stressing to both governments that the Commission was ready to do all it could to support the world's newest country. On a similar note, during his June visit to Sudan, German Foreign Minister Westerwelle said that South Sudan's independence "must not be allowed to fail on the home stretch". As it turned out, the major conflict between the North and South that many Europeans expected following the referendum did not materialise, despite violent incidents in the disputed border areas. The initial response of the Sudanese government in Khartoum was well received by Europeans and there were whisperings that Sudanese President Omar al-Bashir would receive a reprieve from the indictment of the ICC. Such talk petered out when border conflicts escalated in November.

All 27 EU member states officially endorsed the independence of South Sudan, a significant step, given their differences about the recognition of Kosovo. High Representative Ashton attended the independence celebrations in Juba. The EU and the ACP group of states decided to use a "flexible procedure" to enable South Sudan to become a party to the **Cotonou Agreement**, which Khartoum had not ratified due to a clause referring to the ICC. The Commission was subsequently able to increase development assistance to South Sudan by around € 200 m for 2011–2013. In consultation with the South Sudan government and in coordination with international partners including the UN, the EU announced that it would lead on the joint programming of development assistance in the areas of justice/rule of law, education, health, water management, urban development and the rural economy. A draft joint programming document centred on South Sudan's national development plan was drawn up to serve as a reference for EU member state development programmes in the country. The EU also committed to deepen cooperation with South Sudan on trade and to ensure duty-free and quota-free access to EU markets under the 'Everything But Arms' regulation as soon as conditions were met. Commissioner Piebalgs visited Juba again in November and EU representatives took part in the Washington international conference on South Sudan in December. An Establishment Agreement between the EU and the new Republic was signed in Brussels on 9 December, allowing for recognition of the South Sudanese Embassy to the EU and the new EU Delegation in Juba.

EU-AU Relations

Commissioner Piebalgs announced ahead of his trip to the January AU Summit that the EU intended to support Africa's evolution towards more integration, democracy and good governance. This theme was stressed repeatedly throughout the year. The 4th consultative meeting between the AU Peace and Security Council (AUPSC) and the EU Political and Security Committee in Addis Ababa on 11 May expressed the joint intention of the two continental organisations to work together on Libya, Côte d'Ivoire, Sudan and Somalia. The EU Council General Secretariat published a large brochure in May that mapped out the implementation of the Joint Africa-Europe Strategy's (JAES) 2011–2013 Action Plan, with heavy emphasis on governance issues. The AU Commission's Mission to the EU hosted a conference in Brussels on 24 May on "The African Charter on Democracy, Elections and Governance and the Africa-EU political dialogue". Questions centred on the extent to which the Charter would be implemented by AU member states. A week later, several AU and EU Commissioners met with chief executives from the African Regional Economic Communities (RECs) in Brussels to discuss cooperation on short-term challenges and long-term structural change. The meeting concluded with the usual promises to enhance cooperation further and invited EU and AU member states, RECs, parliaments, the private sector, civil society and media to join in and deliver results that would be visible to ordinary people on both continents.

The AU Mission in Brussels organised another conference on the implementation of the JAES on 22 September. Discussions mainly focused on the financing of the Joint Africa-EU Action plan; the role of the EEAS and of DEVCO in Africa relations, and alternative sources of finance for the AU. There was an exchange on the EU Commission's proposal for a new **pan-African financial instrument**. The 'Pan African Programme' emerged from the Tripoli Declaration at the Third Africa-EU Summit in November 2010, which announced the intention to expand cooperation into new areas and promote the common interests of Africa and the EU on the international stage. The financial proposal was officially submitted to EU member states and the European Parliament on 7 December as part of the Commission's post-2014 EU budget.

The 8th **AU-EU Human Rights Dialogue** was held in Dakar on 11 June. Participants reaffirmed joint commitment to the promotion of human rights on both continents and the importance of AU-EU collaboration on the protection of human rights defenders, human rights in democratic transitions, and women, peace and security. They took note of positive developments in both Africa and Europe, such as the adoption of the Human Rights Strategy for Africa, AU member states' commitment to accelerate the ratification of international and continental human rights agreements, the AU Assembly's decision to establish the African Governance Platform, the binding nature of the EU Charter of Fundamental Rights through the adoption of the Lisbon Treaty, and progress made on the EU's accession to the Convention for the Protection of Human Rights and Fundamental Freedoms. The meeting noted achievements in the Africa-EU Partnership on democratic governance and human rights, particularly the holding, on 9 June, of the first working group meeting on governance of natural resources, including in conflict and post-conflict situations.

On 3 May, Europe's ACP partners finally backed the EU's bid to be granted enhanced **observer status** in the UN General Assembly, giving it the right to speak in debates, to submit proposals and amendments, the right of reply, to raise points of order and to circulate documents. These rights were also made open to other international organisations that requested them. In order to win the vote, the EU had to agree to changes to the resolution so that the same arrangements could be adopted for other regional organisations allowed to speak on behalf of their member states. Potential candidates for similar status included the AU, the Caribbean Community, the Arab League and the South American Union.

EU Relations with ECOWAS

The EU stepped up its support to ECOWAS' own efforts to create a borderless region in West Africa with the March launch of an EU-funded cross-border project that would seek to set up a regional customs union and a common market. Liberia's Vice President Joseph Nyuma Boakai launched the six-month project in Monrovia. The project aimed to train state law enforcement officers, including port and city police, immigration, customs and commerce inspectors, anti-drug agents and forest rangers. This was part of a strategy aimed at boosting inter-African trade, estimated to constitute only around 10% of overall African trade in 2011. On 4 February, the EU Delegation to Nigeria and ECOWAS jointly hosted a ceremony in Abuja to mark the signature of contracts worth € 37 m for the construction of three joint border posts in West Africa.

EU-South Africa Relations

The fourth **South Africa-EU Summit**, held at Kruger National Park on 15 September, was a chance to discuss a broad range of issues including global governance, climate change, trade, development, the JAES, the South Africa-EU strategic partnership and peace and security in Africa. The EU was represented by European Council President Herman Van Rompuy, Commission President José Manuel Barroso, Development Commissioner Piebalgs and Trade Commissioner Karel de Gucht. South Africa was represented by President Jacob Zuma, accompanied by Foreign Minister Maite Nkoana-Mashabane, Planning Minister Trevor Manuel, Finance Minister Pravin Gordhan, Science Minister Naledi Pandor, Trade Minister Rob Davies and Environment Minister Edna Molewa. Delegates discussed South Africa's preparations for the UN climate conference (COP 17) to be held in Durban in November and December and the 'Rio+20' conference on global sustainable development scheduled for 2012. Discussions about coordination on development cooperation in the framework of the EU-South Africa strategic partnership were timely, given South Africa's intention to become active as a donor itself.

Bilateral Relations

President Nicholas Sarkozy addressed the AU Summit on 30 January, the first time since 1963 that a French head of state had done so. He noted that **France** was also president of the G8 and G20, and he promised to involve Africa as closely as possible in this double presidency. He said that he had been convinced for a long time that Africa had not had its rightful place in international governance, and he urged the UN Secretary-General to reform the UNSC by expanding its membership. He did not say whether France would be willing to give up its veto as part of these reforms. Sarkozy also spoke of the opportunities recent growth in Africa provided for Europe, and stressed the two continents' common values and joint destiny.

South African President Jacob Zuma accepted Sarkozy's invitation to make a state visit to France on 2–3 March. During their meeting at the Elysée Palace, the two presidents discussed global issues as well as bilateral relations. They resolved to strengthen their countries' strategic partnership through regular consultations and high level exchanges. As South Africa was a major player on the African continent and a G20 member, the priorities of the French G20 Presidency and South Africa's hosting of the COP17 climate change convention were also discussed in detail.

Although French attention was concentrated mainly on the crisis in Côte d'Ivoire and its aftermath, France was also active in East Africa, French Minister for Cooperation Henri de Raincourt visited Uganda, Kenya and Tanzania in early December. The purpose of the trip was to reaffirm bilateral ties and de Raincourt visited several project sites co-financed by France through the AFD , including the Bujagali dam in Uganda and the Kenya-Ethiopia Interconnection power-line project. The French minister met with Ugandan President Yoweri Museveni, with whom regional cooperation between the Great Lakes countries and security in Somalia were discussed. In Kenya, he met with Prime Minister Raila Odinga, and talked about the crisis in the Horn of Africa and the fight against maritime piracy. In Tanzania, the minister met with President Jakaya Mrisho Kikwete and discussed the opportunities and challenges of integration in the East Africa sub-region.

Germany announced a new Africa policy on 15 June. The 'Africa concept' was divided into six categories: peace and security, economics, human rights, environment, energy and development. Foreign Minister Westerwelle presented the plan to African diplomats in a ceremony in Berlin. "What we are experiencing in Africa is possibly *the* most fascinating sign of our world in flux," he said. "Our aim is to use the potential of our cooperation for the good of the people in Africa, but also, and let's not forget this, also for our own good, also in our own interests." The concept envisaged increased trade ties with Africa and promised closer cooperation between the various German ministries whose work concerned Africa. The German government's openness about economic interests in

Africa troubled some critics, who considered that the concept prioritised markets for German exports, rather than overcoming poverty in Africa. It was also noted that, at around 30 pages, the policy document was short on detail, particularly regarding its timeline for implementation.

German Chancellor Angela Merkel visited Kenya, Angola and Nigeria in July. Her aim was to show support for inclusive and sustainable development in Africa as well as to promote German engagement in the energy sector. Merkel visited several projects supported by Germany, including a livestock research facility in Kenya, Africa's largest photo-voltaic solar energy system, and media organisations in Angola. While she was in Nigeria, ECOWAS Commission President James Victor Gbeho asked Merkel for a bigger German contribution to the $ 108 m electricity programme for Conakry.

United Kingdom Prime Minister David Cameron hailed the potential of aid, trade and democracy to lift millions of Africans out of poverty during his visit to Nigeria in July. He spoke at the Pan African University in Lagos, arguing that the continent had a real chance to end aid dependence. Cameron paid tribute to fast-growing economies and democratic transformation in Africa, which he said was happening in a way no one had thought possible 20 years ago. He urged African students to "seize these opportunities, grab them, shape them". Cameron reiterated that trade, not aid, was the key to Africa's future prosperity and could be better enhanced through economic restructuring, inward investment, improved infrastructure and good governance. He quoted research that argued that an African Free Trade Area could increase continental GDP by as much as $ 62 bn a year, $ 20 bn more than the world gave Sub-Saharan Africa in aid.

Cameron's speech echoed Development Secretary Andrew Mitchell's address to a London audience a week earlier, entitled "Africa is open for business". Mitchell announced that Britain would increase its support for businesses in Africa in a bid to boost economic growth and break aid dependence. Three new business projects (the Africa Enterprise Challenge Fund, the Food Retail Industry Challenge Fund and the Business Innovation Facility) were launched, which aimed to create thousands of jobs in food production, deliver low-cost energy to African businesses and help supermarkets bring ethically traded African food products to UK consumers.

In May, the UK foreign office announced that Minister for Africa Henry Bellingham spent ten days in Africa promoting British interests. His visit started in Côte d'Ivoire, where he attended the inauguration of President Ouattara. He then travelled to Ghana where he met parliamentarians and discussed Ghana's success in good governance. In Kenya, he discussed shared interests, including counter terrorism, piracy and regional security. Bellingham spent four days in Tanzania, where he promoted British trade and investment in meetings with members of the Tanzanian government. He also gave a speech to a British business group on the UK government's prosperity agenda.

The Netherlands' government announced a new development cooperation policy in June, focussing on 15 countries and four themes in which the country supposedly had proven success: security and the rule of law, water management, food security, and sexual and reproductive health care. Emphasis on human rights goals was to be maintained. Minister for European Affairs and International Cooperation Ben Knapen told the Dutch parliament that development spending in the areas of sexual and reproductive health and HIV/AIDS would be aimed at prevention and human rights. This would enable the Netherlands to heighten its profile as an advocate of human rights for all. The DRC was removed from the list of countries with which the Netherlands had a bilateral development relationship. However, Knapen was quick to note that this did not mean that the Netherlands had abandoned the DRC, and he said that it would continue to support the country through UN programmes and international trust funds.

Knapen told African ambassadors to the Netherlands in September that the image portrayed by some news reports of the Horn of Africa famine that Africa was a continent that could not provide for itself was false, and disregarded the impressive economic growth Africa had experienced in recent years. He said that the continent's élan and potential were such that it was time to think further than aid. Knapen said that he wanted to see development cooperation used as a catalyst for sustainable economic growth, ultimately enabling Africa to be self-reliant, and for the relationship to evolve into a mutually profitable economic partnership. The Netherlands announced that it would invest in long-term improvements in the business climate in African countries, and Dutch businesses would be encouraged to use their knowledge and experience in Africa to help bring about lasting improvements in living standards.

The principal focus of **Italy**'s policy towards Africa was in stemming migration across the Mediterranean following the downfall of North African governments with which Italy had closely cooperated. Italy made several efforts to solicit Europe's help in confronting illegal immigration, not only in terms of economic aid but also in terms of a plan for the distribution of refugees among EU member states. In late March, Foreign Minister Franco Frattini drew a distinction between "real refugees" from Eritrea and Somalia, and Tunisians who were not fleeing war and should instead be proud to go home and help their country's democratic transition.

The Italian government was also active in supporting famine alleviation efforts in the Horn of Africa. Frattini stressed the need for measures in Somalia that addressed push-factors for piracy on land and trials for pirates caught at sea. Two additional contributions were made to drought-stricken Somalia: € 1 m to FAO for a project in Puntland, and € 600,000 for the UN Office for Project Services for regional hospitals. Political, environmental and social turmoil in Africa were the main focus of Frattini's speech at the Italian Cooperation Steering Committee meeting in October. € 530,000 was earmarked for the training of Libyan port authority and coast guard staff and Italy made a voluntary contribution to the ILO for the social reintegration of former female inmates of Ethiopian prisons.

Unsurprisingly, **Spain**'s main focus was also on upheaval in North Africa. The country nevertheless took steps to deepen its relationship with South Africa. The 7th Session of the South Africa-Spain Annual Consultations was held in Pretoria on 1–2 February. Spain briefed South Africa on its Africa Plan and commitment to the AU and NEPAD. The parties reviewed the latest political developments and issues of conflict resolution, peace building and post-conflict reconstruction programmes on the African continent, such as Sudan/Darfur, Zimbabwe, and developments in the Maghreb, Madagascar and Côte d'Ivoire. Both countries agreed to explore together further opportunities for triangular co-operation in Sub-Saharan Africa.

Portugal's economic woes meant that Prime Minister Pedro Passos Coelho's visit to oil-rich Angola in November was closely watched by other European countries. The IMF agreed to give Portugal a $ 107 bn bailout on condition that it introduced a wide range of economic reforms, including privatisation. Some commentators argued that this created pressure for a reversal of former roles, with cash-strapped Portugal considering selling shares in state-owned companies to its former colony. Coelho denied suggestions of opportunism on account of his country's debts. Speaking at a press conference, he said Portugal was facing a difficult phase, but that Angola was a strategic partner and relations had nothing to do with Portugal's problems. Anti-corruption campaigners warned that Portugal should be careful not to become a laundromat for Angolan cash.

Poland held the rotating EU Presidency for the second half of the year, and in this capacity hosted the 6th **European Development Days**, which did not focus on Sub-Saharan Africa to the same extent as in previous years. Instead, the forum, held on 15–16 December, concentrated on democracy and development in the context of the Arab Spring and the Commission's new development policy proposals released in October. High-level panels discussed several issues of relevance to sub-Saharan Africans, including the Horn of Africa famine and strategies for modernising European development policy "beyond aid" The event provided Poland with an opportunity to stress its own experience of transition as an example for African countries north and south of the Sahara to emulate.

In Poland itself, Zambian born Killion Munyama became the second African to be elected to parliament after Nigerian-born John Godson. The economist and politician, who arrived in Communist Poland on a government scholarship in the early 1980s, lamented that few Africans know much about what Poland was capable of. He promised to facilitate interaction between Poland and Africa and encourage strong bilateral relations with African countries.

Development Cooperation

2011 may turn out to be the year in which European development cooperation started to react to several existential questions about its future. The Euro crisis increased pressure on European development budgets. In briefings to journalists, EU officials spoke of increasing public pressure to show that Europe's aid programmes, totalling € 54 bn, are worthwhile at a time of economic crisis. Research published by the Institute of Development

Studies (Sussex, UK) showed that three quarters of the world's poor now lived in middle-income countries. More importantly for EU development policy, the shifting priorities of EU member state leaders described above began to be reflected in changes in the way the Commission set its own agenda.

Following almost a year of public consultation, internal negotiation and numerous drafts, the Commission published its latest mission statement on development policy. On 13 October, Commissioner Piebalgs presented the grandly titled **'Agenda for Change'** together with a second paper setting out a new policy for EU budget support. The documents promised to re-prioritise Commission aid through more targeted funding allocations, both on sectors where aid could make a difference in reducing poverty and by targeting countries in the greatest need of external support. The Agenda announced the Commission's intention to focus aid on good governance, including human rights and democracy; gender equality, civil society and corruption; social protection, health and education; support for a favourable business environment and deeper regional integration; and sustainable agriculture and clean energy for inclusive and sustainable growth. The Agenda announced that, in order to generate more resources, the EU would explore innovative ways of financing development, such as the blending of grants and loans. More controversially, the Commission said that it would encourage EU member states to jointly prepare country strategies (so called "joint programming") and better divide labour among themselves to increase aid effectiveness. The Agenda also proposed to reassess aid to countries that seemed wealthy enough to fund their own development. This was welcomed by many, even though initial proposals to base aid allocation decisions on average per capita income failed to recognise that aggregates say little about a country's capacity to address poverty, even if, like Ghana and Zambia, they were classed as 'middle-income' by some measures.

The Commission's budget support proposals were welcomed by many African partner governments, even if some expressed scepticism at the declared intention to make funds more conditional on results. The Commission announced that "Good governance and Development contracts" would govern general budget support where the partner country could demonstrate commitment to "fundamental values" such as human rights, democracy and the rule of law. The Commission also announced that budget support would be used in fragile countries on a case by case basis to ensure vital state functions and support transition through "state building contracts".

European NGOs Bond and CONCORD expressed concerns that the most important change in the new agenda was that aid to the world's poorest was being cut, diverting funds towards energy and private sector investments which were in the interest of the EU only. Critics noted that the Agenda was an "aid concept", light on detail about how Europe intended to address "beyond aid" global public goods challenges, such as climate change, communicable diseases and food insecurity. However the proposals were cautiously welcomed by African officials as an indication of the EU's continued commitment to development and its intention to improve performance on accountability and the timeliness of aid delivery.

Security and Development

The European Council adopted two strategic frameworks on which intra-European agreement had proved difficult due to disagreements over the balance between security and state capacity-building measures. The two strategies had also been difficult to discuss with African partners because of their overt emphasis on European security concerns.

The EEAS released the EU's **Strategy for Security and Development in the Sahel** in September, some three years after it was first requested by the 2008 French EU presidency. The Strategy had four key themes: first, that security and development in the Sahel could not be separated; second, that progress was only possible through closer regional cooperation, which the EU pledged to support; third, that all states in the region would benefit from capacity building in areas of core government activity; and fourth, that the EU had an important role to play both in encouraging economic development and in helping achieve a more secure environment in which the interests of EU citizens and companies were also protected. High Representative Ashton said that the strategy would help Europe coordinate its engagement in the Sahel, making more effective use of various instruments to foster security, stability, development and good governance in the sub-region. Nevertheless, some EU member states were sceptical about certain aspects of the strategy and remained unconvinced that it could be implemented, despite formally welcoming its release.

The strategy responded to long-standing European concerns about security in the Sahel, where organised crime networks had been able to take advantage of weak state control over desert areas and kidnap Europeans for ransom. In this environment, it had become highly risky for development actors to continue operations, while French energy company AREVA had to institute expensive security measures to protect its operations in Niger. The final draft of the strategy was negotiated following the kidnapping and murder of two young Frenchmen in Niger's capital, Niamey, in a gun battle, which also killed several Nigerien security officers. Another five French citizens captured in Niger in September 2010 were held in northern Mali by al-Qaida in the Islamic Maghreb. One was released, but four remained hostage at year's end. Late in the year, the same group claimed responsibility for the killing of a German man and the abduction of three other Europeans in the centre of the ancient tourist city of Timbuktu. Another Jihadi group abducted two French geologists from their hotel in the Malian town of Hombori in late November.

On 14 November, the European Council adopted the EU's **Strategic Framework for the Horn of Africa**. The strategy aimed to establish a comprehensive framework for a range of policy proposals to address security and development challenges. It also openly stated Europe's interests in the region, largely stemming from its geo-strategic importance.

The strategy focussed on five priority areas for EU action: building robust and accountable political structures; contributing to conflict resolution and prevention; mitigating security threats emanating from the region; promoting economic growth and supporting regional economic cooperation. Specific goals included tackling piracy and supporting stabilisation in Somalia and peaceful transition in Sudan. Greek diplomat Alexander Rondos was appointed as the new EU Special Representative for the Horn of Africa on 8 December, a step taken to give the EU greater visibility and influence with other international partners. EU member states generally agreed that the Horn of Africa strategy presented a long-term perspective for European policy in the region and the next step would be to coordinate on its implementation.

In June, EU foreign ministers decided to make use of the Lisbon Treaty to widen and deepen Europe's conflict prevention policy. They put their money where their mouth was in late August, when the Commission replenished the **African Peace Facility** (APF) with € 300 m for the period 2011–2013, to support continental and regional conflict prevention and resolution and peace building efforts. € 40 m of this envelope was earmarked for supporting the implementation of the African Peace and Security Architecture (APSA), bringing total EU support for APSA to € 84.5 m since 2004. The AU announced that the funds would contribute to several areas of work, including enhancing synergies between the AUPSC and the RECs; increasing the capacity of the Continental Early Warning System; improving the functioning of the Panel of the Wise and mediation structures; supporting the operational capability of the African Standby Force; enhancing analytical and strategic capacity; and improving project and financial management capacity.

In early April, the European Commission published a detailed report on activities funded by the APF. The report praised the APF's support for the Early Response Mechanism's mediation operations, including the AU High Level Implementation Panel on Sudan. The report noted that the bulk of funding went to support the operations of the AU Mission in Somalia (AMISOM). On 28 March, Commissioner Piebalgs confirmed the Commission's support for the AMISOM mission by announcing an additional € 65.9 m to provide the peacekeepers with more medical care, transport and allowances. The Commissioner noted that EU support helped AMISOM provide protection for the transitional federal government, facilitate humanitarian operations and support disarmament and stabilisation efforts. In December, the Commission provided a further € 50 m to AMISOM, bringing the total EU contribution to € 258 m since 2007.

No new **EU peace-building missions** were launched, but several continued throughout the year. European Naval Force Somalia-Operation Atalanta **(EU NAVFOR-Atalanta)**, the mission to patrol the pirate-infested shipping lanes off the East African coast, had its mandate extended until the end of 2012. The mission reported some success: EEAS Africa Managing Director Nicholas Westcott said in a speech in October that, in the previous three months, Atalanta had been directly responsible for foiling three attempted pirate attacks on merchant ships and had deterred many more. According to the BBC, there were

25 successful hijacks in 2011 compared with 47 in 2010. The business was, however, highly lucrative: pirates earned some $ 146 m in 2011, an average of $ 4.87 m per ransom payment.

To complement and support counter-piracy operations, the EU agreed to transfer suspected pirates captured by operation Atalanta to face trial in Kenya, the Seychelles and, after 16 July, Mauritius. The EU offered support through its Instrument for Stability for prosecution, and for court, police and prison services in the three partner countries. An apparent change in tactics by pirates during the year to cooperate with al-Shabaab in seizing Western hostages from the Kenyan coast led to calls to attack pirates in their bases. Unsurprisingly, this was not universally popular. German opposition politicians from the Green and Social Democratic parties warned against the unpredictable consequences of expanding the EU's "military adventure" into Somalia's coastal towns.

The **EU Training Mission (EUTM) to Somalia** celebrated its first anniversary on 11 April. The mission's progress was followed closely and the Bihanga training facility in Uganda received visits from Members of the European Parliament, member state ministers and senior European military staff. Trainees were also reminded of Europe's own wars. Representatives from EUTM Somalia attended the Armistice Day ceremony at the Commonwealth War Graves Cemetery in Jinja, Uganda, in November. During the first week of November, 869 Somali men and women went back to Mogadishu after ten months of training, and the return flights carried 619 new trainees to Uganda.

Trade and Development

The Commission started a major review of its trade and development agenda with a view to adjusting to recent global changes. In April, the Commission launched a public consultation for a Trade and Development policy paper, due to be published in early 2012. On 19 July, Commissioner Piebalgs represented the Commission at the WTO's Third Global Review of Aid for Trade (AfT) in Geneva. The meeting was a key opportunity for donors and developing countries to discuss achievements since the launch of the AfT Initiative at the 2005 WTO Ministerial Conference in Hong Kong. The focus of the Third Global Review was on results, impact and how best to maximise the future potential of AfT.

EPA negotiations resumed after delays in late 2010 and continued on their tortuous path during the year. Optimism expressed early in the year that mutually beneficial agreements would be reached was not borne out by events. At the 4th EAC-EU EPA Negotiations Session held on 15 September in Zanzibar, parties agreed on a joint work programme for comprehensive negotiations until December 2011. However, at year's end a range of issues still needed to be resolved, including provisions dealing with export subsidies and taxes, special agricultural safeguards, rules of origin and EPA-related adjustment support.

There were stumbling-blocks on both sides. For instance, EAC Secretariat Director General of Customs and Trade Peter Kiguta said that negotiators were not well informed about the interests of the African countries they were representing. In December, on the fringes of the WTO ministerial meeting in Geneva, EU Trade Commissioner De Gucht informed journalists that a comprehensive EPA with Uganda, Kenya, Tanzania, Rwanda and Burundi would now be in sight. However, Ugandan trade negotiators were reported to be unaware of any deadline for concluding negotiations with the EU. At the ACP trade ministers' meeting in Brussels, in early December, Kenya's delegation described a Commission proposal of 30 September to amend market access as "not in good faith".

After almost a decade of negotiations, the EU finally set a deadline for the EPA talks. In late September, the Commission announced that countries that had concluded an EPA but not taken the necessary steps to ratify and implement it by 1 January 2014 would no longer benefit from EPA market access. Although some countries would still qualify for tariff-free access without signing an EPA, under the EU's 'Everything But Arms' initiative, countries such as Côte d'Ivoire, Ghana, Nigeria and Kenya – not classified as 'least-developed countries' – would have to pay duty of between 8.5% and 15.7% on their exports to Europe.

Mark Furness

IV. West Africa

The sub-region saw a dramatic end to the civil war in Côte d'Ivoire, where rebel forces, buttressed by UN and French firepower, dragged former president Laurent Gbagbo, still unwilling to step down after his defeat at the polls the previous year, out of his bunker at gunpoint. This paved the way for the accession to the presidency of electoral winner Alassane Ouattara and a return to some sort of civilian rule after a decade-long civil war. The other major event was the fall of Muammar Kadhafi in Libya, also assisted by European powers but mishandled, as arms depots were plundered and weapons fell into the hands of an assortment of non-state forces. As mercenaries in the pay of the Libyan leader returned home, there was an inevitable impact on sub-regional security, especially in the Sahelian zone, where new al-Qaida-inspired kidnappings of Western citizens took place. Burkina Faso was rocked by a mutiny and Guinea-Bissau characteristically saw an alleged coup attempt. Neighbouring Guinea, however, followed in the post-war footsteps of Liberia and enjoyed markedly more calm than in previous years, and, while Mali felt the menace of the Tuareg separatist agenda, Niger benefited from the conclusion of an exemplary transition from military to civilian rule. Nigeria, by contrast, faced sectarian violence on an unprecedented scale, while tensions in the context or ahead of elections rocked the body politic in Benin and Senegal. Economic trajectories varied, as some countries boasted considerable growth while others were confronted with a range of problems.

Coups and Electoral Politics

No successful coups took place, although in some countries an unruly military jeopardised security or put the normal political process at risk. In **Guinea-Bissau** mutinous soldiers went onto the streets in December and reportedly tried to arrest the army chief of staff. Gunfire and rocket blasts were heard and barricades erected in the capital, but relative quiet returned with the arrest of the naval chief of staff. **Burkina Faso** suffered worse when army rank and file went on the rampage after soldiers were convicted for maltreating a civilian. The sentenced men were released but this did not prevent looting in the capital and the spread of violence to provincial garrisons. Even the elite presidential guard joined in the rioting, forcing President Compaoré to flee Ouagadougou. It was several months before he was able to reassert control by appointing a new cabinet, shaking up the security forces and letting special army sections suppress the rebel soldiers. Although the armed forces in **Niger** returned to barracks after the completion of the transition to civilian rule, a few leading officers were arrested in the summer on charges of plotting a coup that was to include the assassination of the new civilian president. Most significant, however, were the country's elections (presidential, local and parliamentary) in January-March, which led to a peaceful shake-up of the party landscape and the rise to the presidency of long-time opposition leader Mahamadou Issoufou.

Such orderly elections were less exceptional in the case of **Cape Verde**, where, after legislative polls in February, the ruling party's candidate lost to an opposition contender in August. **Liberia**, too, was up for a scheduled round of electoral contests, preceded by a referendum in which the government failed to win endorsement of some constitutional revisions. However, incumbent President Sirleaf, having just been co-recipient of the Nobel Peace Prize, managed to defeat her rivals in presidential elections in October-November, though not without some violent incidents and an opposition boycott of the run-off. Accompanying parliamentary polls, in which just a third of sitting MPs were re-elected, completed an electoral process considered by the UNSC as free and fair. Similarly, **Nigeria** held a spate of electoral contests (legislative, presidential, gubernatorial and state) in April, which led to the confirmation as president of incumbent Goodluck Jonathan. While they were considered the most credible elections to date, despite numerous shortcomings and a postponement that cut short a parliamentary poll already under way, around 100 people died in a series of violent incidents. The aftermath was much worse, as northerners reacted in anger to the victory of Jonathan, a southerner and a Christian, vandalising and burning polling booths, which led to a steady stream of refugees and the death of up to 1,000 people. Even set against Nigeria's record of violence, this was without parallel since the end of the civil war in 1970.

Gambia was spared such incidents, but international observers nevertheless criticised the conduct of its general elections, citing voter intimidation and an uneven playing field that allowed incumbent President Jammeh to sweep up all constituencies. Known for his repressive policies and poor human rights record, Jammeh routed the opposition, though he still enjoyed little support among the Gambian diaspora. The dramatic violent scenes that engulfed **Côte d'Ivoire** in the first quarter were followed by an investiture ceremony on 21 May, in which Alassane Ouattara was sworn in as president, confirming the oath of office he had taken under UN protection the previous December. With violence dying down, the return to a more peaceful politics included legislative elections in December. While they were won by Ouattara's party, their boycott by Gbagbo's party and the low turnout showed that national reconciliation was still a long way off, and this was underlined by an incident involving a rocket attack west of Abidjan. **Guinea** and **Mauritania** should both have held legislative elections, but they were postponed beyond year's end. In Guinea, this was because the electoral role was considered hopelessly flawed (although the opposition refused to participate if the chairman of the electoral commission was not replaced too). In Mauritania, the opposition and the prime minister agreed to postpone the polls, without fixing a new date, because of dissatisfaction with existing electoral standards.

Benin demonstrated that the actual conduct of elections could spoil the political climate. Presidential and parliamentary polls were delayed but were finally held in March and April, respectively, though with government and opposition disagreeing on virtually every aspect of them, including the register, the electoral process, the counting of the votes and the announcement of the results. Incumbent President Boni Yayi faced a broad-based opposition that was, however, weakened by considerable splintering and opportunistic floor-crossing; he won 53% of the votes in the first round, thus avoiding a run-off. Although these results were confirmed by the constitutional court and international observers deemed the polls free and transparent in spite of irregularities, Yayi's principal challenger, Adrien Houngbedji, contested the results – even going so far as to declare himself president instead. The opposition boycott of Yayi's inauguration, which was attended by fellow heads of state, symbolised the deep rift that the elections had caused. Street protests, however, were met with tear gas, and the opportunism of many an opposition figure allowed Yayi to consolidate his position and re-establish some political calm. Similarly, pre-electoral manoeuvring ahead of presidential polls in 2012 led to considerable tension in **Senegal**. The principal bone of contention dividing government and opposition – the question of whether or not incumbent President Wade was entitled to renew his candidature – led to a lot of frustration, not only among opposition parties, which were unable to unite on a common candidate and saw several politicians declare themselves for the 2012 contest, but also in society at large. In the context of the country's economic difficulties, tensions rose and new movements were established aiming at political change, but the president and his opposition challengers did not back down.

Human Rights and the Rule of Law

Various issues pertaining to the rule of law impinged on political debate in the countries of the sub-region. In Mali, the saga around a new **family code** continued unabated. A version that had been watered down to the detriment of women's and girls' rights successfully passed a second reading in parliament, but the president then appeared to be hesitant to promulgate a law that contained clauses that would enforce by statute women's obedience to men, a minimum marital age of 15 or 16 years and gender inequality in inheritance. Islamic associations staged demonstrations to press the government to implement the law. Guinea-Bissau passed a law banning **female genital mutilation**, which was practised in the country's Muslim areas. The issue of **gay rights** attracted hostile attention in both Ghana and Nigeria. In Ghana, parliament refused to legalise homosexuality, retaining the country's criminal code as it stood, while Nigeria's senate proposed a strict ban on same-sex marriage. The phenomenon of **slavery** continued to be an issue in Mauritania, where it is a criminal offence. In January, a woman was sentenced to imprisonment for keeping children in bonded labour. However, later in the year police broke up a demonstration by anti-slavery NGOs and four activists were given suspended prison sentences.

Instances of **death in detention**, allegedly as a result of police torture, occurred in Burkina Faso and Gambia. In Burkina, the victim was a high school student and his case led to mass protests by students, which deteriorated into riots, with several youths and one police officer reported killed. In Gambia, the security men who had allegedly tortured to death a man accused of theft were themselves sentenced to death. By contrast, in Nigeria governors commuted several death sentences and the courts discharged suspects for lack of evidence. They included those who had been convicted of murdering a regime critic in 1995, who had spent more than 15 years in gaol. If the Nigerian **judiciary** still functioned because of its independence, in Guinea-Bissau the judicial authorities were hesitant to get their fingers burned in the investigation of the 2009 assassinations of President Vieira and several top-rank military men. (The head of the judicial police resigned over death threats in drug trafficking cases.) A UN official suggested referral of the 2009 murders to the **ICC**, to which the new Ivorian government transferred Laurent Gbagbo in November. (A national commission of inquiry had already begun investigations into the massive human rights violations that occurred in the wake of the post-electoral crisis.) The Special Court for Sierra Leone, in session at the ICC's premises, concluded the case against Charles Taylor, with judgement expected in the spring of 2012. The Senegalese government, however, continued to drag its feet with regard to the prosecution for human rights violations of Hissène Habré, the former Chadian dictator exiled in Senegal. They rejected a Belgian extradition request, which led to an AU decision to establish an ad hoc international court.

In several countries, the media were taken to task for slander or libel. In Benin, several newspapers were forced to close down and, in the context of the presidential elections, a broadcast by 'Radio France Internationale' was interfered with. Benin dropped several places on the **press freedom** index of 'Reporters sans Frontières'. In Togo, several private radio stations were forced to close down, while in Ghana the media were rocked by the sackings of key officials. By contrast, in Guinea-Bissau the authorities reversed a decision to close a weekly newspaper for besmirching the country's image and in Mauritania press freedom improved as media laws were liberalised and several new radio and television stations started broadcasting.

Anti-graft measures, both in and outside the context of political manipulation, were taken in several countries. In Benin, where numerous areas of economic activity suffer from **corruption**, the authorities notably targeted the customs sector (the port of Cotonou is of sub-regional importance), leading to strikes by customs officers and civil servants in the finance ministry. Guinea's low standing with regard to corruption improved somewhat as the new government continued its overhaul of mining contracts. Similarly, the new civilian administration in Niger seemed determined to continue the clean-up operation started by the previous junta. A report was published on financial irregularities over the period 1996–2009. In Mali, the health minister was arrested on suspicion of involvement in a $ 4 m corruption scandal. While the anti-corruption commission in Sierra Leone presented its 2010 report and a cheque for nearly $ 600,000 in recovered cash (though corruption levels remained high), the activities of its Nigerian counterpart produced few concrete results, as several cases were thrown out of court or suspects were released on bail. The chairperson of Nigeria's Economic and Financial Crime Commission was sacked. Pre-electoral manoeuvring in Senegal worsened the country's standing, as government spending increased substantially and reforms in the field of tenders, auditing and financial crimes led to deep concern among donors.

Conflict, Instability and Violence

The two events that had the profoundest effect on sub-regional stability, in both a positive and a negative sense, were the conclusion of **Côte d'Ivoire**'s post-electoral crisis and the fall of the Kadhafi regime in Libya, coupled to the rising tide of al-Qaida-inspired kidnappings and a growth in Tuareg separatist ambitions in the Sahelian zone. However, before Laurent Ggagbo was dislodged from his presidential bunker, intense fighting took place between former northern rebel forces backing the internationally recognised new President Ouattara and the pro-Gbagbo army, which was dominated by southerners. Militias and death squads were also active in this clash of wills, exacting a high toll in civilian lives, as much of the fighting took place in the commercial capital, Abidjan. As pro-Ouattara forces began an offensive from bases in the country's western region and swiftly swept through southern Côte d'Ivoire towards Abidjan, a humanitarian crisis threatened when city dwellers were trapped amidst the fighting and faced water and food shortages. In the background, French and UN forces assisted in the capture of Gbagbo and his wife, which was the prelude to de-escalation, though not before Ouattara's army had engaged thousands of pro-Gbagbo militiamen in several days of heavy fighting. It was reported that some 3,000 people died during the crisis, which had begun the previous December. Many fell victim to ethnically targeted killings, reportedly also carried out by pro-Ouattara forces active in the western region. Liberian security forces went on the alert as numerous Liberian mercenaries had been recruited by Gbagbo's camp and upon the latter's defeat were feared to be returning home with their arms.

In the **south-western forest zone**, Guinea was markedly calmer than in previous years and the newly elected government of civilian President Condé normalised its relations with the international community. However, distrust and ethnic polarisation continued to mark the country's politics and clashes took place on a number of occasions between demonstrators and security forces. In Liberia, where the UN still maintained peacekeepers, some violence erupted in the course of land disputes and communal tensions. Violent incidents also occurred in Sierra Leone between supporters of the country's opposing parties in the south and east of the country, leading to a ban on political rallies. This was a minor matter, however, compared with the continuing volatility in Guinea-Bissau, with its mutinous military and the destabilising effects of its role as sub-regional hub in the international cocaine trade. The chronic violence involving separatist forces in Senegal's Casamance region continued unabated. Numerous incidents took place, leading to the death of several government soldiers, mopping-up operations and civilian casualties of separatist guerrilla actions. Violence increased towards year's end.

Ghana and **Togo** experienced continuing calm (the latter in a relative upswing of stability since 2009). However, as in previous years, populous **Nigeria** saw some of the worst violence. This did not have the serious consequences for the sub-region that resulted from the crisis in Côte d'Ivoire, though there was speculation that the Islamist activists of Boko Haram – among others active in the country's north-east – might link up with al-Qaida in the Islamic Maghreb (AQIM). Clashes between Boko Haram and the Nigerian security forces continued, leading to a wave of retaliatory and well-orchestrated attacks by militants (bomb attacks, suicide bombings, raids on police stations, prisons, drinking spots and Christian churches, in addition to an attack on the UN headquarters in the capital, Abuja). Hundreds of people died and a state of emergency was declared on New Year's Eve in 15 local government areas across four of the federation's states, not just in the north but also in the Middle Belt where neighbouring Christian and Muslim communities have regularly clashed. Such communal conflicts also took place during the year, especially close to the capital of Plateau state, Jos, leading to dozens of casualties. This was in addition to election violence, whose thousand or so victims fell mainly in the north of the country, sectarian youth violence in Bauchi state, which led to the displacement of 4,000 inhabitants, incidents in the Niger Delta, and the violence associated with the country's kidnapping industry and armed robberies.

The **Sahelian zone** was also rocked by kidnappings. In Niger, two Frenchmen were snatched from a restaurant close to the presidential palace at the beginning of the year – an incident that had a profound impact on the life of Westerners in the capital. French forces based in Ouagadougou responded by tracking down the kidnappers and engaging them in a shoot-out just across the border in Mali, leading to the deaths of the hostages, the kidnappers and some of the pursuing Nigérien gendarmes. One of the militants involved was later reported to have had contact with Boko Haram in Nigeria's north-eastern city Maiduguri, and if this AQIM challenge was clearly calculated to provoke the authorities, the swift French response at least managed to draw a precarious line. In neighbouring Mali, however, such kidnappings continued unabated, effectively bringing the country's tourist industry to a standstill. A joint Mauritanian-Malian operation in the north of the country was botched and the Malian army could only establish temporary control. Some of the Mali kidnappings took place south of the Niger River and led to worries in neighbouring Burkina Faso. Meanwhile, returning Tuareg fighters who had been in the pay of Kadhafi and were well armed were returning home in droves. Although a few hundred were persuaded to join the national army, it was speculated that there might be as many as 2,000–4,000 returnees, giving rise to serious concerns over the country's short-term stability. Mauritania shored up its military spending.

Socioeconomic Developments

Growth prospects were good for Cape Verde, which benefited from increased tourist revenues as a result of the turmoil in North Africa, and for Burkina Faso, which benefited from an end to the Ivorian crisis. New oil-producers Ghana and Niger saw or hoped for higher growth rates, but resource-rich Nigeria battled with the continuing north-south divide, and non-oil producing Liberia, which enjoyed robust growth, continued to face high unemployment. The negative effects of the global economic crisis still affected Benin, while Côte d'Ivoire could only begin its long climb back to prosperity.

GDP rates thus varied across the sub-region, the variations being influenced by, among other things, the existence or absence of an important mining sector and poor agricultural performance as a result of drought and crop failure. Thus, growth was sluggish in Mali (2.3%), where the collapse of the tourist industry added to the effects of a failed cereal harvest; in Senegal (2.2%), also mainly due to insufficient rainfall; and in Niger, where initially optimistic forecasts were toned down to 3.8% for similar reasons. A low 3.1% for Benin reflected, among other things, logistical problems in the port of Cotonou. Higher

GDP rates were found in countries that had important mining activity, such as Burkina (just below 5%), Liberia (7.3%), Guinea (4%), Mauritania (5.2%) and oil-producing Ghana (a record 14.4%). Predictably, the worst performer in the sub-region was Côte d'Ivoire, with a negative rate of –4.7%, although it was expected that recovery would be speeded up by a good cocoa crop and the swift resumption of foreign aid.

The **drought** in the Sahelian zone was one of the most negative factors, complicating food security in Mali, Niger, Gambia and Senegal, especially for the coming year. Gambia saw a 70% reduction in the total harvest of rice, groundnuts and millet, and in Senegal too food and export crop production fell dramatically, with a negative growth rate for the primary sector overall of –12.6%. The autumn harvests in Niger were catastrophic, totalling 11% less than the average for the preceding five years. **Food security** was severely impaired there, as in Mali, where the government and humanitarian agencies also planned action.

Niger's new government announced a massive new **agriculture** programme aimed at improving livestock and cereal production, including by irrigation, but harvest failure made realisation of targeted production impossible. At a time when global cotton prices were high, cotton production in Benin rose significantly (partly as a result of new planting and a reduction in the costs of fertiliser), as it did in Burkina, Africa's largest cotton producer. As in Côte d'Ivoire, the cocoa yield in Ghana increased substantially, but farmers still benefited from a government-announced increase in the producer price. In Sierra Leone, an opposition party criticised land deals that leased out a reported 10% of available arable land to foreign companies. The **fishing** sector in Guinea-Bissau and Mauritania faced continuing problems as a result of over-fishing and illegal fishing activity. The EU recommended a reduction in the Mauritanian quota (a fisheries agreement with the EU was to expire in 2012), while Guinea-Bissau signed a new one-year accord. The World Bank provided a grant to Sierra Leone for the development of its pelagic stocks.

As a result of the failed harvests in the Sahel, food prices there were already rising significantly towards year's end. Average consumer price **inflation** in Mauritania was estimated at 6.5%. Inflation also rose in other countries, reflecting global food price increases. In Liberia, for example, inflation reached 8.1% and in Ghana 8.6%. In Guinea inflation was much worse, at 16%–20% (although this was down from 20.8% in 2010).

In several countries, **infrastructural projects** continued. In Benin, a one-stop window was intended to improve the efficiency of the port of Cotonou, although landlocked Niger, highly dependent on the harbour facilities, criticised its performance. A new inter-island ferry service in Cape Verde improved communication and hotels and airports were upgraded to boost tourism. Across the sub-region, energy was an important priority in infrastructural projects. In Ghana, plans were revealed for the extension of the power supply (access was already a high 60% but was planned to increase to 90%). More modestly, the World Bank and the AfDB approved plans for the improvement of the power and water supply in Bissau, the capital of Guinea-Bissau, including the purchase of new generators. A water project in Sierra Leone was to improve the supply to several provincial towns. In Senegal, which suffers severe shortages of electricity, plans were revealed for the amelioration of oil supplies and generating capacity, with financial support from donors. In Guinea, plans for a trans-country railway to transport iron ore remained on the drawing board, but the mining companies involved remained lukewarm, preferring to ship the ore via an existing railway in Liberia instead. The plan, pushed by Guinea for more than 40 years, included the construction of a new deep-water port. In Mali, construction began on a hydro-electric dam, while road and airport infrastructure also received a boost (as in Senegal). Mobile telecommunications development continued apace in Nigeria, a major market.

Mining benefited from high prices. Gold production rose considerably in Burkina, though at one mine local people (said by the mine company to be artisanal miners) protested against the environmental consequences of the use of cyanide. In Ghana, production rose by 3%. The lucrative mining sector in Guinea (including iron ore and bauxite) was in the midst of an overhaul of contracts, a process in which numerous foreign companies manoeuvred to improve their prospects. In Liberia, an ArcelorMittal concessions area made its first iron ore shipment in 20 years and blocks for off-shore oil exploration were also sold. New uranium finds were announced in Mauritania, while in Niger, where oil production also began, the Chinese started up a uranium mine, the first that was not in the hands of French-run Areva. New bauxite deposits were announced in Sierra Leone, as well as finds of rutile, zircon, ilmenite and some rare earth minerals. Iron ore mining received a boost there with the completion of a new railway and deep-water port. The government continued renegotiating contracts with mining companies to increase the country's share in the revenues.

Trafficking in drugs, but also in cigarettes, people and arms, remained an important activity in the sub-region. Cocaine continued to be important in Guinea-Bissau; smuggling networks helped to increase the conflict potential in Mali's northern region and Liberia, too, was reported to be vulnerable in this field. By contrast, Gambia's President Jammeh used his compliance with the West's anti-drugs crusade to ward off criticism of his human rights record. Mauritania improved its co-operation with Spain in combating drugs and human trafficking. In Britain, Nigerians were sentenced for trafficking children into domestic servitude or prostitution elsewhere in Europe. Sierra Leone confiscated a ship coming from Ecuador with a significant quantity of drugs on board, thus confirming the importance of the south-western forest zone as a link in the cocaine trade between South America and Europe. Togo, too, saw seizures of cocaine (here from Brazil), and of cannabis coming from Nigeria.

Floods hit part of the Ghanaian capital, Accra, causing a dozen deaths, and there was a small outbreak of **polio** in Nigeria, as well as the continuous spread there of HIV/AIDS. There were social **protests and strikes** in some countries, including Benin, Burkina, Guinea-Bissau, Niger and Senegal.

Sub-regional Organisations: Cooperation and Conflict

Security issues, ranging from the threats posed by AQIM and Boko Haram to piracy in West Africa's coastal waters, dominated some sub-regional agendas. On 7–8 November, ministers from Niger, Mali, Mauritania and Algeria met with US officials in Washington to discuss their multilateral approach to Sahelian security. The African countries had earlier agreed on a regional counter-terrorism partnership at a Sahel security summit in Algiers, but now the fallout of the Libyan crisis also caused concern. As in previous years, however, political sensitivities still complicated cooperation. Burkina Faso, Chad and Nigeria, for example, were not present at the Washington meeting. By contrast, in November, Niger formally asked for international support to combat **terrorism**. Earlier, on 10–12 October, ECOWAS member states met with officials from Morocco, Algeria and Mauritania to discuss **money laundering** in relation to terrorism financing. Experts from Switzerland and the BCEAO attended the summit. The representative of the Anti-Money Laundering Intergovernmental Working Group in West Africa, which monitors suspect money flows, pointed to the porosity of the sub-region's borders as one of the problems in this field. The financial aspect of (sub-)regional terrorism was also discussed at a counterterrorism forum in Algiers on 17–18 November. **Piracy** was another matter of concern, as observers reported in the course of the year a considerable upsurge of attacks on ships in Nigerian, and now especially Beninese, waters. The ECOWAS Council of Ministers, meeting in Abuja in August, ordered the ECOWAS Commission to convene a meeting of the chiefs of defence staff when Benin sounded the alarm bell. (Its port of Cotonou, the lifeline for its own and landlocked Niger's economy, was said to be severely affected.) Benin and Nigeria therefore launched joint sea patrols in September. Pirates (mostly based in Nigeria's Niger Delta) were attempting to profit from Benin's more limited capability to maintain off-shore security. Ghana and the new government in Côte d'Ivoire expressed strong concern about the possible spread of piracy towards their own waters. The United States, whose US Africa Command **(AFRICOM)** also monitors these issues, participated in a naval exercise in the sub-region in March.

The ECOWAS Committee of **Chiefs of Defence** met in Abuja on 3–5 October to discuss both piracy and terrorism issues. The membership of its sub-committee on maritime security was doubled to include Benin, Côte d'Ivoire, Senegal, Togo and Sierra Leone, alongside its existing members (Nigeria, Guinea-Bissau, Ghana, Gambia and Cape Verde). The chiefs of defence also agreed to continue joint security patrols along the Liberian-Ivorian border (where Liberian mercenaries formerly in the pay of Laurent Gbagbo's camp were causing concern). The ECOWAS Small Arms Programme, based in the Malian capital, Bamako, was extended for five years and the ECOWAS Standby Force would get more command posts and field training. An exercise in Ghana in November was part of the collective training.

In March, **ECOWAS** lifted the sanctions it had earlier imposed on Niger and Guinea, as these countries now had normally elected civilian governments. Meanwhile, the Ivorian crisis was reaching a climax and the sub-regional body could do little to resolve a problem that was finally ended on the battlefield. On 19 August, a small summit meeting in Abuja discussed Côte d'Ivoire's security challenges and the president of the ECOWAS Commission, Victor Gbeho, visited Abidjan later to discuss the possibilities of sub-regional help in the aftermath of the conflict. In the field of conflict mediation or political developments more generally, the sub-regional body also continued to monitor events in other countries. It considered the continuously volatile situation in Guinea-Bissau, the Gambian, Liberian and Nigérien presidential elections, problems in Guinea (the attack by rebel soldiers on the presidential residence) and the political situation in Benin. One of the organisation's institutional problems was the arrears in member states' contributions, which are derived from levies on imports from outside the sub-region and should be collected by member states and paid into an ECOWAS account. Kadré Désiré Ouedraogo, a former Burkinabè prime minister, became ECOWAS Commission president, taking over from the Ghanaian Victor Gbeho, after a prolonged battle that divided member states. The Nigerian Bashir Ifo managed to become president of the ECOWAS Bank for Investment and Development, an appointment that was not consensual, but since Nigeria contributes the lion's share of the bank's funds, this could not be prevented by other countries.

Economic and technical issues in the region included, among other things: plans for joint responses to disasters afflicting the sub-region; plans to develop a railway connecting Benin, Niger, Burkina Faso and Côte d'Ivoire (finance was still an open matter); World Bank-funded programmes to boost internet connectivity by installing fibre optic broadband (the so-called West Africa Regional Communications Infrastructure Programme); dialogue frameworks for national chambers of mines to promote mining activities; and the perennial issue of improving the free movement of people. In August, it was decided to launch two Border Information Centres (BICs) on the Ghana-Togo border to improve sub-regional trade. Among the intended benefits of the BICs, an ECOWAS-UEMOA initiative supported by USAID, were the cutting of transport costs and customs paper work. The ECOWAS-UEMOA Committee for the Management of the ECOWAS Common External Tariff (CET) agreed a 'roadmap' for finalising a draft CET as a step towards a future sub-regional customs union. (This was also said to be critical for concluding the negotiations with the EU on an EPA.) Former British colonies took a symbolic step further towards establishment of a monetary zone with a joint training course for employees of the central banks of the countries concerned. Sub-regional monetary cooperation, aimed at launching an ECOWAS-wide single currency in the future, also came slightly closer, as could be observed at a seminar in Bamako in the spring. ECOWAS and India signed a memorandum of understanding to boost cooperation on a host of issues, including food and agro-industries and infrastructure. Togo hosted an ECOWAS Trade Fair, replacing Côte d'Ivoire.

On 30 May, **UEMOA** heads of state in the Togolese capital Lomé elected a new governor of the BCEAO. The Ivorian Tiémoko Koné took over from his fellow countryman Philippe-Henri Dacoury-Tabley, a Laurent Gbagbo confidant who was sacked by the UEMOA summit conference on 22 January over his refusal to implement a BCEAO decision giving control of Ivorian assets in the central bank to Alassane Ouattara. UEMOA would also provide $ 300 m in reconstruction aid to the country. On 12 September, UEMOA finance ministers met in Dakar, Senegal, and sounded a more optimistic note regarding Côte d'Ivoire's macroeconomic prospects, which earlier in the year had threatened to destabilise the sub-region's economies. In contrast to the swift replacement of the central bank's governor, for much of the year UEMOA countries fought each other over the succession to the chairmanship of the UEMOA Commission. On 16 November, it became known that Hadjibou Soumaré, a Senegalese technocrat and confidant of President Wade, had won the battle for the presidency, prevailing over Niger and Guinea-Bissau on the issue, which had both also coveted the appointment of a national to the post.

Klaas van Walraven

Benin

The main issue of the year was the presidential and legislative elections planned for February and April. Despite protests over the functioning of the computerised electoral register, the electoral process and the results of the polls, incumbent President Thomas Boni Yayi succeeded in remaining at the helm of the state. The overall pre- and post-electoral process was marked by high levels of social and political tension. Although he faced fierce opposition from a broad-based coalition, the president was able to gain a dominant position in the Assembly. This new political deal caused new splits among opposition political parties and transfers towards the political majority. The adverse effects of the global economic crisis continued to put pressure on the country's economic growth, despite important investment in infrastructure (particularly roads and the Port of Cotonou), economic measures and initiatives to promote the private sector, and efforts to implement reforms, boost diversification and reinvigorate the cotton sector. Industrial action hit numerous sectors, including education and health.

Domestic Politics

On 4 January, Abdoulaye Bio Tchané, one of the main opponents of President Boni Yayi, officially declared his candidacy for the presidential election to be held on 27 February.

In the context of the approaching presidential and legislative elections, disputes about the computerised electoral register ('Liste Electorale Permanente Informatisée') were fierce. Control of the 'Commission Electorale Nationale Autonome' (CENA), which organised the polls, was at the heart of these political battles. The opposition first adopted a strategy of blocking the electoral process by preventing parliament from voting for the members of the CENA. On 13 January, a new alliance of political parties led to a **realignment of MPs** into five parliamentary groups in the National Assembly. By joining the 'Mouvance Présidentielle', MP Joachim Dahissiho from the opposition group G13 allowed the parties supporting the president to take a fourth seat among the nine CENA representatives to be designated by parliament. Politicians of several other parties – 'Force Cauris pour un Bénin Emergent' (FCBE), 'Sursaut Patriotique', 'Unité Nationale', and 'Alliance pour une Dynamique Démocratique' ('ADD-Paix et Progrès') – moved into various new alliances ('ADD-Nation et Développement' [15 members], 'Parti pour le Renouveau Démocratique', 'Parti pour la Rénovation Sociale' [17 members] and G13 [17 members]). After the president and the constitutional court designated two additional members, the CENA was established on 26 January. Boni Yayi officially declared himself a candidate on 29 January. On 1 February, MPs voted for a list of members to represent them on the electoral commission at the level of 'Départements'.

Following complaints that over 1 m people were not registered on the new electoral roll, the CENA twice postponed the presidential elections. On 21 February, protests about this took place in Cotonou. Initially scheduled for 27 February, the **presidential elections** were then planned for 6 March but finally took place on 13 March, even though opposition candidates called for a further postponement because the electoral list was not available. Boni Yayi ran for re-election against 13 other candidates, including Adrien Houngbédji, representative of opposition parties from the south and former head of the National Assembly, and Abdoulaye Bio-Tchané, president of the West African Development Bank and originating from the north. On 18 March, the CENA announced provisional results. According to the commission, Boni Yayi won 53% of the vote in the first round – thus allowing him to avoid a run-off – against 35% and 6% for Houngbédji and Bio-Tchané, respectively.

On 19 March, Houngbedji, the main challenger, **contested these results**, claiming he had secured 47% of the votes. However, on Monday 21 March, the constitutional court confirmed CENA's provisional results and declared Boni Yayi re-elected. On 22 March, Houngbedji said that the presidential vote had been rigged and declared himself president. Created that same day, the 'Front Républicain des Candidats pour la Sauvegarde des Acquis Démocratiques' (FRC-SAD) denounced the entire electoral process, including the counting of the votes. FRC-SAD, which gathered eight of the presidential candidates (Abdoulaye Bio Tchané, Christian Enock Lagnidé, Janvier Yahouédéou, Cyr M'Po Kouagou, Victor Topanou, Kessilé Tchala, Issa Salifou and Jean-Yves Sinzogan), declared that it rejected the results announced by the constitutional court, alleging widespread fraud and voting irregularities. Although the polls were judged as "mainly free and transparent" by international observers such as those from ECOWAS and the AU, other sources (such as the 'Centre Afrika Obota') spoke of flaws and irregularities. The opposition's appeals to the constitutional court were all rejected, however, on the grounds that the reported irregularities were not significant enough to have altered the final outcome.

The opposition organised **protests** in Cotonou on 24 March, accusing the government of electoral fraud and calling for the president to resign. Banned by the ministry of the interior, the protests were repressed by the police, who fired tear gas and arrested some politicians. On 29 March, the local transmission of 'Radio France Internationale' was disrupted when a popular phone-in programme called 'Appels sur l'actualité', hosted by Juan Gomez, was about to discuss the disputed elections. 'Reporters sans Frontières' said it was hard not to think that the disruption had been engineered by the authorities. On 31 March, the 'Bureau Exécutif de l'Union des Professionnels des Médias du Bénin' expressed regret about the lack of action from the independent mass media regulatory body, the 'Haute Autorité de l'Audiovisuel et de la Communication' (HAAC). Although a number of countries (including Nigeria, China, France and the EU) congratulated Boni Yayi on his re-election, Houngbédji held a meeting in the capital, Porto-Novo, on 1 April, reasserting that he had been elected president of the republic. He invited his supporters to protest peacefully against the declared results. On 6 March, Boni Yayi's **inauguration** (boycotted by most opposition leaders) took place in Porto Novo, attended by heads of state from neighbouring countries (Congo, Sierra Leone, Gabon, Togo, Senegal and Liberia).

Initially scheduled for 17 April but postponed by the constitutional court, **legislative elections** were held on 30 April after the CENA announced that voters could use an identity card to vote because voter cards were not available. Nineteen parties and coalitions of parties entered the contest. Although several polling stations opened late because ballot papers failed to arrive on time, voting took place without major incident. Of the 83 seats in the National Assembly, the FCBE won 41 and other pro-presidential parties eight, thus securing a majority in parliament. The opposition won 34 seats (30 going to Houngbédji's 'Union pour la Nation' coalition). Two-thirds of the Assembly's MPs (56 out of 83) were re-elected. There were 3.6 m registered voters, but turnout was reportedly much lower than in the presidential polls. On 16 May, the new legislature held its first session. On 21 May, MPs re-elected Mathurin Nago (FCBE) as speaker and elected members of the Office of the Assembly (a key body, which selects members of various institutions including the supreme court, the constitutional court and the high court of justice). The opposition failed in its negotiations with the presidential camp for representation on this body, gaining only one post. On 23 May, the 'Renaissance du Bénin' (RB), led by Rosine Soglo, joined the presidential majority, bringing it to 58 seats. Opposition MP Antoine Dayori ('Union Pour la Relève-Force Espoir') had already declared that he would join the presidential camp. On 27 May, five pro-presidential parliamentary groups were constituted: 'Union-Solidarité-Progrès', 'Refondation-Paix et Développement', 'Refondation et Emergence', 'Nation et Développement', and 'Refondation et Progrès'. On 30 May, the opposition parliamentary group 'Union Fait la Nation' (comprising the 'Parti du Renouveau Démocratique', 'Parti pour la Rénovation Sociale', 'Mouvement Africain pour la Démocratie et le Progrès' and 'Force Clé') followed. Led by MP Antoine Kolawolé Idji, it included 21 MPs after the RB joined the presidential camp.

On 29 May, Boni Yayi formed his **cabinet**, appointing 26 ministers. Pascal Irénée Koupaki became prime minister and MP Nassirou Bako-Arifari, head of the controversial electoral register and part of the opposition group G13, was made minister of foreign affairs. RB members, now affiliated to the presidential majority, also gained posts. The election of Bako-Arifari and Issa Salifou in the 1st electoral district (Karimama, Kandi, Malanville), was challenged after allegations of fraud, but both were confirmed as MPs by the constitutional court on 9 August. The election of other MPs, including Chantal Yayi (FCBE), the first lady, was also contested by an appeal to the constitutional court but this was later withdrawn.

On 7 October, MP Edmond Agoua left 'Union Fait la Nation'. He joined the presidential majority on 30 November and was later followed by fellow MP Cyriaque Domingo, in line with a common opportunistic strategy adopted because being part of the majority allows Beninese politicians to run for office and gain privileges. These political transfers further strengthened Boni Yayi's position, and he was able to press ahead with reforms. The Assembly passed bills on referendums, strike action and corruption, while also adopting the 2012 budget. The **referendum bill** was meant to allow for a revision of the December 1990 constitution, which had never been amended since its adoption. However, on 21 October, in a rare show of independence, the constitutional court declared the referendum law unconstitutional, specifying that article 6 would need to be amended to ensure that the fundamentals of the constitution would be respected. The court's response came as a surprise, for it had in the past frequently shown itself ready to support the president. On 9 December, parliament amended and passed the referendum bill again and the 2012 budget was unanimously approved on 22 December.

According to the Economist Intelligence Unit's **democracy index**, Benin ranked 76th out of 167 countries, a drop of four places since the previous year, placing it in the list of states considered to be "flawed" democracies. Among sub-Saharan countries, Benin fell three places, to 9th position. The decline in overall and regional ranking resulted in a reduction in its score for political participation. According to 'Reporters sans Frontières', Benin came 91st of 179 countries worldwide (after previously being ranked between 70th and 74th). It now ranked 31,00 as compared with 19,00 in 2010, indicating an important decline in **press freedom**. 'Reporters sans Frontières' was surprised at the closure of the newspaper 'Le Béninois Libéré', ordered by the HAAC on 8 December, and warned of the risk of further abuses of the press. Several other newspapers were also forced to cease publication.

Foreign Affairs

The government expanded its cooperation with traditional financial partners (the EU, IMF, World Bank, and bilateral partners such as France, Germany, Belgium, the Netherlands, Denmark, Switzerland, Finland, the USA, Canada and Japan). It also engaged in South-South cooperation (with Brazil, China, India, South Korea, South Africa and Nigeria) and maintained its ties with Arab countries (Kuwait and Saudi Arabia), hoping to improve infrastructure and development. Various donors provided aid for the victims of the previous year's floods. Boni Yayi attended the **inaugurations** of newly elected Presidents Mahamadou Issoufou of Niger in Niamey (7 April), Alassane Ouatara in Côte d'Ivoire (21 May) and Goodluck Jonathan in Nigeria (29 May). He also visited South African President Jacob Zuma on 23–26 November and received him in Benin on 10–11 December. Cooperation agreements with South Africa notably concerned financial and technical support for airport infrastructure in Parakou, Cadjehoun and Abomey-Calavi. The president also received his counterpart from Togo on 2 February, who came to Parakou for the inauguration of the electrical grid connecting northern Togo and Benin. Benin also received the presidents of Chad (6–7 July), Niger (18 July), Côte d'Ivoire (14 November) and Mauritania (8 December).

On 22 November, European Commissioner for Development Andris Piebalgs arrived in Benin for a one-day visit, during which he met with Boni Yayi and several key ministers. The Commissioner announced **EU** funding for decentralisation and the strengthening of local government, as well as financial support for the development of small and medium enterprises. By contributing € 377 m in assistance, the EU remained the country's principal financial partner. On 13 February, Boni Yayi and Chinese Ambassador Geng Wenbing inaugurated the Parakou hospital (newly built by China at a cost of CFAfr 6 bn). **China** also funded various other projects, including the Cotonou-Bohicon road (with a grant of CFAfr 144 bn) and the construction of an office block in Cotonou (with a loan of CFAfr 15.6 bn from the Chinese bank Eximbank). Benin attended the Economic Forum in Dalian, China, on 12–17 September. On 21 December, China and Benin signed an agreement for the construction of an airport at Natitingou, in the north. According to the Chinese embassy, 100,000 Chinese were living in Benin in 2011 (compared with 1,000 in 2008).

On 6–7 October, representatives of Niger, Burkina Faso, Côte d'Ivoire and Benin met in Cotonou for a workshop focusing on the **railway project** that was to connect Cotonou, Niamey, Ouagadougou and Abidjan. The project was meant to accelerate sub-regional integration and development.

On a three-day visit to Benin on 18–20 November, **Pope** Benedict XVI met with Boni Yayi and other government leaders. He delivered a message of peace and reconciliation, condemning abuse of citizens, corruption and injustice. The pope also visited Ouidah, considered a stronghold of Voodoo practice and a centre of celebration during the nation's

National Voodoo Day on 10 January. The pope called for respect for traditional beliefs but also issued a warning against witchcraft. Benin's Catholic community has been growing steadily in recent years.

On 7–12 November, Boni Yayi went to **France** to meet the French president and several ministers. He discussed in particular security issues in the Gulf of Guinea and appealed for assistance to combat piracy. An ECOWAS meeting to reinforce the fight against **piracy** and armed robbery took place in Cotonou on 28–29 November. According to the International Maritime Bureau, pirates were continuing to attack vessels in Nigerian and Beninese waters, which it described as "piracy hotspots".

Socioeconomic Developments

With a Human Development Index of 0.427, Benin ranked 167th of 187 countries, compared with 134th in 2010 – a significant fall. With a per capita income of $ 750 in 2011, Benin remained a low-income country. **Growth** was estimated at 3.1%, lower than expected as a result of a slowdown in port activities, among other things, which hampered commercial activity. The economy was also dragged down by the global economic decline and by the increase in the price of imported petrol from Nigeria. Despite the rise in non-traditional exports, the external current account deficit, excluding grants, deteriorated slightly because of higher international fuel prices. **Inflation** remained under control, however, at less than 3% at year's end. The overall balance of payments registered a small deficit (0.1% of GDP). Revenue performance was weaker than expected: by 22 December, only 82% of target revenue had been realised. In order to preserve the stability of the government finances, the authorities reduced spending. The budget deficit was estimated at 4.3% of GDP.

On 29 January, the official purchase price of **cotton** rose from CFAfr 200 to CFAfr 250 per kg for first grade cotton and from CFAfr 140 to CFAfr 200 per kg for second grade. The price of fertiliser was reduced from CFAfr 240 to CFAfr 220 per kg in order to boost output. Production of cotton – one of Benin's most important cash earners (representing about 25%–40% of overall exports) – reached 300,000 tonnes (compared with 137,000 tonnes in 2010), according to statistics released by the ministry of agriculture, livestock and fisheries. The area planted increased to 200,000 ha, representing an increase of nearly 15% over the previous season. Other priority sectors also received significant support, including rice (with the commissioning of two large factories in Malanville and Glazoué), off-season crops, cassava and maize, as well as palm oil and cashew nuts.

On 27 January, Issa Badarou, the minister of maritime economy, launched the one-stop-window at the **port of Cotonou**. Together with the installation of a scanner and the implementation of an enhanced programme of import value verification, the one-stop-window was expected to improve revenue collection and the port's efficiency. These reforms met with opposition from customs officials.

The government issued statements on transparency, **corruption** and abuse of privilege and took various measures to address them. Boni Yayi announced that the fight against corruption was a top priority of his administration. On 18 May, Godefroy Tchékèté, the director of the national electricity company, was fired, following the results of a commission of enquiry regarding company management. On 25 May, the general manager of the customs service, Isaac Inoussa Issiaka, was replaced by Théophile Soussia, previously tax receiver at the port of Cotonou. Jules Hessou, prefect of the Atlantique-Littoral region, was also replaced, following his role in a financial scandal the previous year (the 'ICC-Services' affair). On 31 August, Boni Yayi gave a speech declaring that bribe takers would be punished and, on the same day, the National Assembly passed a new anti-graft bill, ordering the country's top administrators to disclose personal assets upon assuming and leaving office. The government also made vigorous efforts to strengthen customs and tax administration capacity and controls to improve revenue collection.

In retaliation, **customs agents** started a strike on 13 September, demanding protection against violence by civilians. On 26 September, parliament passed a law against strikes in the military and paramilitary services (including customs officials). On 27 September, civil servants in the finance ministry announced a 72-hour strike in support of customs agents. On 28 September, Boni Yayi asked former customs agents and temporary workers to help the government against the strikers. The strike action in the customs sector led to daily losses of CFAfr 5 m and impacted negatively on traffic to neighbouring countries, such as Niger, Burkina Faso, Nigeria and Mali. On 8 December, in the context of the 6th national day against corruption, the government and UNDP presented a report highlighting public sector corruption, with customs officials singled out as the most corrupt, followed by the judiciary, gendarmerie-police and public (procurement) contracts. However, on 12 December, Justice Minister Marie-Elise Gbèdo created a storm when she openly said that the judiciary was corrupt.

The World Bank reported that, although the government had taken some important steps to address issues of **mismanagement**, much remained to be done. According to TI's corruption index, Benin's position worsened to 100th out of 183 countries (compared with 96th in 2010). In an open letter to the government on 25 October, private investors and users of the port of Cotonou deplored blockades and appealed for urgent action if Benin wanted foreign companies to maintain their activities and prevent their departure to other ports in the sub-region. On 27 October, Niger's parliamentary speaker Hama Amadou, while on a working visit to Benin's National Assembly, expressed criticism of the functioning of Cotonou port (vital to the economy of landlocked Niger) and of the harassment that Nigérien transporters had to endure.

Several strikes took place in the education, health and finance sectors, among others, paralysing government activity. Prime Minister Pascal Irenée Koupaki said it would be difficult to meet the demands of workers because of the lack of resources. On 2 May, civil servants in the finance ministry ended their ten-month strike after an agreement was reached on a 25% wage increase. They continued to demand clarification of the previous year's mysterious disappearance of one of their colleagues – and opposition member – Urbain Dangnivo. On 1 July, the prime minister met with labour unions, which were protesting against the non-payment of salaries arbitrarily deducted in the course of previous strike action. Attempts at negotiation were marred by distrust and escalating demands on both the government and foreign donors – the latter putting pressure on the government. On 18 July, unions representing state employees expanded their industrial action, striking for four days a week instead of three. For the first time, teachers and nurses were involved. Workers were demanding a 25% pay increase backdated to 1 January. This was agreed to by the government on 5 August, on condition that the unions would not engage in further strike action to press wage-related demands before 2014. Nevertheless, new industrial action was announced by the 'Confédération des Organisations Syndicales Indépendantes du Bénin' on 19 September and by the 'Union Nationale des Syndicats des Travailleurs du Bénin' on 21 September, in response to the government's anti-strike law. At year's end, however, this bill had not yet been put before parliament. Moreover, government action to avoid slippages in public expenditure by cancelling bonuses to civil servants was countered by new threats of strikes. On 14 November, the cabinet had to renounce its proposed measures.

Regarding **human rights**, various problems continued, including the use of excessive force by the police and vigilante groups that operated with impunity. Arbitrary arrests and detentions also took place, especially during the election period.

Eric Komlavi Hahonou

Burkina Faso

Widespread public protests, by military rank and file, struggling farmers and ordinary citizens alike, dominated the political headlines. Countrywide social unrest after a high-school student was allegedly tortured to death by police soon turned into demands for broader economic and social reforms. Military mutinies resulted in a government reshuffle and a political reform process. Political developments in Côte d'Ivoire and Libya led to a deterioration in the country's political standing in the sub-region. Macroeconomic forecasts projected solid growth.

Domestic Politics

In the first half of the year, some of Burkina's most important socio-political and economic problems led to violent protest and unrest in the military. It was not the occurrence of the protests as such, but their scale, that surprised observers. The chain of events could be traced back to long-standing unease about the rising cost of living and the regime's political impunity. Escalation started on 20 February with the **death** of Justin Zongo, a high-school student, in the country's third largest town, Koudougou. The young man had been summoned to the police station at the turn of the year following a complaint by a female classmate with whom he had apparently clashed earlier. According to the student's family, Zongo died from the effects of police torture, but according to the police version, which was initially accepted by the authorities, his death was caused by meningitis.

The case immediately provoked **mass protests** by students and pupils in Koudougou and its surroundings. The event was the last straw for the protesters, who had grown weary of the culture of impunity that they perceived to protect the rich and government officials. Some demonstrations turned into violent riots and the police used force to put down the protests. The media reported that at least four protesters and one police officer were killed in clashes on 22–24 February.

The government's reaction was prompt. All **schools were closed** on 25 February, and the regional governor and the regional police chief were sacked. On 27 February, a delegation of four government ministers was sent to Koudougou to show compassion for the victims and to signal that the central government took the event seriously and was in control of the situation. However, the ministers of territorial administration, health, justice and security did not take one side or the other. By contrast, the previous day, opposition party leader Hermann Yaméogo came out in support of the protesters in his home town and political stronghold Koudougou. The government failed to calm tempers. Protests continued and spread throughout the country. The demonstrations revived long-standing issues such as the rising cost of living, inequality and impunity. The 'Coalition Contre la Vie Chère' (CCVC) backed the students and also renewed non-violent protest marches. One of the largest nation-wide demonstrations was organised on 8 April. However, violent incidents recurred over several weeks, including an attack on state media journalists on 11 March at the university campus. On 23 August, in the aftermath of the protests that followed Zongo's passing, a court sentenced three policemen to eight to ten years in prison for manslaughter.

In a parallel development, the same underlying parameters – impunity, monopolisation of power and economic malaise – fuelled troubles in the country's barracks. On 22 March, a judge sentenced five soldiers to 12 to 15 months imprisonment for cruel treatment of a civilian. One month before, the prosecutor had called for only six-month sentences. The judge's verdict caused unrest among the soldier's fellow servicemen, who mutinied. They began firing wildly around their camp and in the centre of Ouagadougou, where they plundered businesses and officials' private homes. One day later, the sentenced soldiers were released pending their appeal. No information was available on the development of proceedings. Individual mutineers later deplored the lootings and said gangsters had exploited the opportunity. The military leadership attempted to explain the revolt by blaming the mismanagement of recruitment in 2008 and 2009 due to the rise in demand for soldiers in UN missions abroad. The rank and file were poorly educated and neither understood the verdict nor demonstrated discipline. The ambiguous confession and feeble excuses of the arrested soldiers convinced neither the magistrates nor the robbed merchants. The judiciary went on strike, seeking protection for its offices. The traders expressed anger by violently attacking associations that supported the head of state. On 16 April, they torched the headquarters of the ruling party. Burkinabè journalists drew parallels with the civil unrest in 1998, after the infamous murder of Norbert Zongo, an investigative reporter who was allegedly killed on the orders of the president's brother, François Compaoré. The incident was never forgotten and still counted as one of the president's major faults. Meanwhile, **soldiers' mutinies** spread around the country. The provincial garrison towns of Banfora, Gaoua and Tenkodogo all experienced similar events. On 28 March, soldiers freed a fellow serviceman from jail in Fada-Ngourma, a private who had been convicted for rape.

The president's initial response to the mutinies was ineffectual. Although he convened delegations of all the security services, the uprisings were escalated on 14 April by the **presidential guard**. Members of the 'Régiment de la Sécurité Présidentielle' (RSP) started firing with light and heavy weaponry and rioted in the capital until dawn. According to the BBC, President Compaoré fled the scene and was evacuated from his nearby presidential palace Kosyam – first to the centre of Ouagadougou and later to his home village of Ziniaré. Economic malaise was one explanation for the RSP mutiny. That same day, CCVC marches took place, protesting that the World Bank had warned of surging prices due to disrupted supplies from Côte d'Ivoire. No direct reference had been made to this in the military uprisings, but the soldiers cited unpaid housing allowances before they went on the rampage. Against the purely economic argument was the fact that the RSP was one of the best equipped and funded units of the military. Another argument therefore circulated that it was issues first of military leadership, and second of unequal opportunities to generate illegal supplementary income, that initiated the unrest among the presidential guard, and the RSP soldiers were also said to be unhappy with their commander. This fitted with the fact that one of Compaoré's first reactions to the RSP mutiny was to replace the commander, Lieutenant General Gilbert Diendéré, whose house was burnt down that same night. Diendéré and his brother, General Dominique Diendéré – the Army Chief of General Staff, who was sacked some days later – had often been cited as alleged co-perpetrators of the Sankara murder in 1987. Meanwhile, trafficking in all sorts of illegal goods – particularly drugs – had been on the increase for several years. It was assumed that government or security officials must have been involved in organising this lucrative business. Technically, it was the Air Force that had the equipment useful for this kind of activity, but no hard evidence was furnished to support these suspicions.

Besides sacking the RSP commander, Compaoré immediately dissolved the government and on 15 April replaced more generals. Further military leaders were replaced in the following days. The outgoing prime minister, Tertius Zongo, whose house was also torched in the course of the events, and most of his ministers, had only been reappointed in January, following the previous year's presidential election. Three days later, Compaoré appointed as prime minister Luc-Adolphe Tiao, a former journalist who had previously served as Burkina's ambassador to France. The number of ministers was slightly reduced. Compaoré, already head of state and commander-in-chief, appointed himself minister of defence. Compaoré's brothers in arms, Djibril Bassolé, a former Gendarmerie colonel who returned to the head of the foreign affairs ministry, and Arsène Bongnessan Yé, a former minister and head of parliament with the rank of colonel, became the most powerful figures in the **new cabinet**. Tiao's government promised civilian protesters that they would cancel the much criticised municipal development tax, lower the rate of income tax and the price of staple food, electricity and fuel, cancel several health charges, introduce special allowances for teachers, and withdraw the recently created special university units of the police. There were no reports of major concessions to the military, beyond the change of leadership and the staggered payment of arrears in soldiers' pay.

The soldiers were clearly not satisfied. By 17 April, the insurrection had spread to elite units in Pô (Parachuting Training Centre, Military Academy) and Tenkodogo (Infantry Commando), as well as to military bases in Dori, Kaya and Koudougou. If soldiers and civilians had allied against the government, it could have seriously jeopardised the president's political grip, but the mutineers alienated the civilian population with their looting. Throughout the following weeks, civilian protests (such as an unlimited teachers' strike starting on 23 May) accompanied new soldier riots in Pô (15 May), Ouagadougou (23 May), and Dori, Kaya and Tenkodogo (29 May). Meanwhile, the **teachers' strike** provoked student unrest, which culminated in the looting of the ministry of education. A new climax in the **mutineers' violence** occurred on 31 May in Bobo-Dioulasso, Burkina's second largest town. This time, the government reacted with force. On 3 June, special units of the armed forces (RSP; 'Régiment para-commando'; 'gendarmerie mobile') ended the Bobo riots, which led to serious physical injuries and material damage. At least seven soldiers were killed, and about 20 people were wounded and 57 arrested. The signal was understood and all protests – including civilian marches – stopped. On 8 June, the government decided to replace all regional governors.

Long promised institutional reforms were accelerated. A Consultative Council on Political Reforms ('Conseil Consultatif sur les Réformes Politiques' – CCRP) was constituted on 23 June, headed by Minister Yé, a minister of state for institutional reforms and one of Compaoré's closest allies. However, the council's 68 members did not include any members of the opposition. The latter boycotted the structure because they feared it would bring in constitutional changes that would allow Compaoré to stand for a fifth term in 2015. Article 37 of the constitution set a presidential **two-term limit**, to run from Compaoré's 2005 re-election. Compaoré could not therefore stand for re-election in 2015. However, the ruling 'Congrès pour la Démocratie et le Progrès' had already indicated in August 2010 that it wished to remove the term limit, which it considered undemocratic. In contrast to his democratic counterparts in Mali and Benin, Compaoré did not publicly declare his opposition to an abolition of the limit. All in all, the CCRP tended to represent a rather conservative position, but it did not take a clear stance on the most sensitive issues, such as the presidential term limit. The CCRP's final report was handed to the president on 21 July. Apart from minor adjustments and the non-decision on Article 37, it advanced three proposals: the creation of a second chamber of parliament, the introduction of an upper age limit for the presidency, and consideration of the role of traditional leaders in politics. The CCRP's proposals were to be discussed in regional public meetings and a final national convention.

On 26 September, the opposition reaffirmed that it considered the reform process to be illegal and called for a boycott of the regional and national conferences. The government argued that the conferences would allow the broader public to participate in the debate, and thousands of citizens did indeed attend regional meetings in all the major towns around the country. However, it is not clear who was actually entitled to attend. Opposition forces were divided over whether the process should be boycotted. The so-called 'Collectif des Organisations Démocratiques de Masse et de Partis Politiques', which united the strongest opposition parties and civil society organisations, had no confidence in the government's intentions. By contrast, intellectuals such as Professor Augustin Loada (founder of the influential think-tank 'Centre pour la Gouvernance Démocratique') regarded the process as an opportunity to influence the reform outcome and therefore criticised the boycott. On 8 November, the radical opposition failed in its attempt to make the Conseil d'État decide on the legality of the composition of the CCRP. This supreme administrative court declared the case inadmissible.

Eventually, 1,510 delegates participated in the **national reform conference** in Ouagadougou on 7–9 December. Most of the CCRP proposals were approved and some details emerged. The Senate would represent non-political actors and consist of about 90 members. Its duties were not specified. It was proposed that the number of seats in the lower chamber should be increased to provide for at least two seats per province. (Fifteen of the provinces currently had only one parliamentary representative.) If these new rules were fully applied to correct under-representation, it would increase the number of seats to almost 400. The upper age limit for presidential candidates was set at 75. (Compaoré is 60.) Concerning the political activities of traditional leaders, the national meeting stated that no consensus could be arrived at, thus disappointing those who had advanced the idea of a stricter distinction between the role of traditional leaders and modern public office. Article 37 remained untouched, but it became more likely that a referendum on the term limit would be held.

Meanwhile, a second politico-institutional conflict led to the early replacement of the 'Commission Électorale Nationale Independante' (CENI). In January, opposition leader Bénéwendé Sankara resurrected the opposition's long-standing unease with CENI president Moussa Michel Tapsoba when he asked for the early replacement of the commission. Although Tapsoba sat on the CENI on a civil society ticket, he was considered too close to the ruling elite because of his previous government membership under the so-called revolutionary regime of the 1980s. Shortly after the mutinies and protests had stopped in early June, three opposition members of the CENI quit their posts in line with Sankara's call for a temporary boycott of the **electoral commission**. Tapsoba refused to resign. However, on 5 July, the National Assembly unanimously passed a bill to dissolve the CENI before the end of its term in September. This was an opposition victory. On 14 July, Tapsoba died. The coincidence of his death with his dismissal days earlier gave rise to speculation that he might have died of unnatural causes. Regardless of the truth of such speculation, it exemplified the deeply rooted distrust that characterised Burkina politics. On 1 August, the new commission elected as Tapsoba's successor Barthelemy Kéré, a lawyer who had sat on the outgoing commission to represent the Catholic Church.

Foreign Affairs

The situation in **Côte d'Ivoire** continued to be central to foreign affairs. Compaoré continued to mediate in the Ivorian crisis, despite being considered partisan by the Gbagbo camp. He held or participated in meetings in Ouagadougou on 19–20 January, in Nouakchott on 19–20 February and 4 March, and in Addis Ababa on 9–10 March. Although the country had diversified import routes in recent years, it remained highly dependent on the port of Abidjan, energy from Côte d'Ivoire and employment opportunities for Burkinabè citizens in the south. Hence, the Ivorian crisis continued to affect Burkina's development, although the relationship with its southern neighbour improved significantly after Alassane Ouattara's takeover in April. By this time, however, the economic consequences of the crisis had already contributed to political problems in Burkina Faso. Commodity prices had surged due to insufficient supplies, and the restoration of peace in Côte d'Ivoire was slow in coming, as was the normalisation of trade and the improvement of immigrant worker conditions. As the largest group of foreigners in the country, Burkinabè citizens continued to be stereotyped as Ouattara partisans and remained the target of xenophobic attacks.

Political developments in **Libya** posed a serious economic and security threat. Burkina and – more personally – Blaise Compaoré were strongly linked to Kadhafi. At the height of Libya's civil strife, Compaoré received high-ranking officials representing Kadhafi's regime: on 21 April, the minister of African affairs and on 23 June the secretary general of CEN-SAD. A few weeks later, rumours abounded that Burkina had offered asylum to the Libyan autocrat, while the government had changed position and was anxious to emphasise its support for Libya's new National Transitional Council (NTC). Even though the NTC declared that it was committed to continue to support development in Burkina, it was widely expected that the new Libyan government would look northwards and decrease Libya's financial assistance to sub-Saharan Africa. The proliferation of Libyan weaponry worsened the security situation in the Sahel. As radical Islamists of **al-Qaida** in the Islamic Maghreb benefited from the influx of arms, they were able to expand into areas south of the Niger River, which endangered northern Burkina. Western development workers were evacuated.

Burkina Faso remained the preferred cooperation partner of Western countries in security issues, particularly **France** and the **US**. Both continued and apparently increased military cooperation and anti-terrorism operations. US AFRICOM commander, General Carter Ham, visited Ouagadougou on 26 October. In parallel, Compaoré followed up several **mediation efforts** concerning Guinea, Guinea-Bissau and Sudan/Darfur. Young-Jin Choi, the UN special envoy to Côte d'Ivoire, visited Burkina on 18 August, and Jean Ping, the president of the AU Commission, did so on 29 December. Like other foreign visitors, they paid tribute to Compaoré's mediation efforts.

Burkina Faso continued to recognise the government of Taiwan as the only diplomatic representative of **China**. Hence, Compaoré was one of the few foreign heads of state to attend the celebrations of the 100th anniversary of the Republic of China on 8–12 October.

Socioeconomic Developments

Over the first half of the year, the country suffered from a scarcity of supplies from Côte d'Ivoire, but recovered from these shortages before the year's end. The IMF projected solid GDP growth (just below 5%) and moderate consumer price inflation of 1.9%. However, the national poverty reduction strategy was based on an optimistic 10% annual real GDP growth until at least 2015. The IMF completed the second and third review under the Extended Credit Facility and approved a total of $ 20.3 m in aid. At the same time, no clear information was to hand about how much the government's promises, made to calm this year's protests, would cost. Several taxes were repealed and subsidies for staple food were increased, while investments and assistance from Libya were expected to decrease.

Cotton exports, the largest in Africa, increased from 385 tonnes in 2010 to 420 tonnes in 2011, and world market prices almost doubled in 2010. However, the minimum purchase price from farmers was only raised by 35% to CFAfr 245 per kg on 25 April, compared with the CFAfr 500 they initially demanded. Later in May, producers reduced their demand to CFAfr 255. Cotton growers also asked for the cancellation of a 38% increase in state-controlled fertiliser and pesticide prices. The conflict over the cotton price linked into the general unrest in May. Farmers' protests quickly escalated, leaving at least one person dead. In response, Compaoré fired the CEO of Sofitex, the largest state-owned cotton company, and suspended plans to seek foreign investment and privatisation. By year's end, cotton companies were optimistic enough to increase seasonal production, even though farmers' protests delayed sowing, and pests and a lack of rain also gave cause for concern.

Gold had become the primary export commodity since 2010, and **gold production** was forecast to rise by a third in 2011 to reach 33.7 tonnes, worth $ 1.5 bn to 2 bn, depending on market prices. Record gold prices on the world market pushed up Burkina's income from the mining sector. Iamgold Corporation's Essakane mine remained the largest gold plant and was forecast to triple the previous year's output to 360,000 ounces (more than 11 tonnes). Pinsapo Gold started operations in August in Peleguetenga (Passoré Province) and in only one month extracted 18 kg of gold, with a value of about $ 1 m. However, in September demonstrations erupted over the environmental consequences of mining. Bloomberg reported that about 300 local residents attacked the Pinsapo industrial gold mine in protest over the use of cyanide. Pinsapo Gold condemned the violence as criminal and reported that 18 people had been injured and about $ 2 m worth of damage caused, which took three months to repair. The company stated that the assailants had been artisanal miners who had their own interests at heart. By contrast, the daily newspaper 'Le Pays' had a reporter on site who reported that locals of all ages, including women, led the protests over environmental and employment concerns. Two days later, police arrested 18 people after the riot units had apparently fled the scene.

Alexander Stroh

Cape Verde

In February Prime Minister José Maria Neves became the first Cape Verdean head of government to win three consecutive absolute majorities in parliament. In August, however, the candidate of the ruling party surprisingly lost the presidential election to Jorge Carlos Fonseca, an independent candidate backed by the opposition. Consequently, for the first time since the democratic transition in 1991, the president and the prime minister now came from different political parties. As a result of the turmoil in North Africa, the archipelago's tourism sector benefited from a significant increase in the number of foreign visitors, but the approval of two reduced budgets nevertheless reflected the impact of the international financial crisis on Cape Verde.

Domestic Politics

In the **legislative elections** on 6 February, the 'Partido Africano de Independência de Cabo Verde' (PAICV) of Prime Minister José Maria Neves won 52.4%, i.e. 38 of the 72 seats in the National Assembly, providing it with a parliamentary majority of two, three less than in the 2006 elections, although the percentage of votes remained almost unchanged. During the campaign, the PAICV stressed its achievements in improving infrastructure and education and health services. The main opposition party, the 'Movimento para a

Democracia' (MpD), headed by Carlos Veiga, succeeded in increasing its number of seats from 29 to 32, although its share of total votes fell from 44% to 42%. In its campaign, the MpD blamed the government for the high unemployment rate and the frequent power cuts that particularly affected the capital, Praia. The small party 'União Caboverdiana Independente e Democrática' (UCID) increased its share of the vote from 2.6% to 4.4%, retaining 2 MPs, but failing to achieve its goal of increasing its number of seats to six. For the first time since the introduction of multiparty democracy in 1990, the PAICV secured a majority of votes in Santo Antão, which had been a stronghold of the MpD in previous elections, while the opposition party won only the islands of Sal, Maio and São Nicolau. Despite his defeat, opposition leader Veiga declared that he would continue as party leader and promised to put up strong opposition in parliament. The total number of registered voters was 298,562, and voter turnout was 76%.

On 21 March, the **new government** headed by Prime Minister Neves took office. In his speech, Neves declared that his new executive faced conditions in which the transformation of Cape Verde into a competitive and innovative economy could be consolidated. He further promised to combat poverty and all forms of social exclusion, as well as crime, especially juvenile delinquency. The formation of the new government, comprising 17 ministers and three secretaries of state, included the creation of new ministries and the appointment of new office-holders. Janira Hopffer Almada, the former youth minister, became head of a new ministry of youth, employment and human resources, created to address the problem of unemployment. Finance Minister Cristina Duarte was reappointed, but several other ministers changed portfolios or lost their jobs. Former justice minister Marisa Morais moved to internal administration, while foreign minister José Brito was replaced by Jorge Alberto da Silva Borges. José Carlos Lopes Correia became the new justice minister and Humberto Santos de Brito was appointed minister of industry, tourism and energy. Eva Ortet became minister of rural development and Cristina Fontes Lima received the health portfolio.

On 21 August, the lawyer Jorge Carlos Fonseca, the independent candidate supported by the opposition party MpD, surprisingly defeated Manuel Inocêncio Sousa, the official candidate of the ruling PAICV, in the run-off for the **presidential elections** with 54.2% of the votes (97,103 ballots). Voter turnout was 59.7%. Fonseca, a former minister in the MpD government (1991–1993) and known locally as 'Zona', benefited from a division within the PAICV. Aristides Lima, the former president of the National Assembly and known as a close ally of outgoing President Pedro Pires (2001–2011), decided to run as an independent candidate after he failed to receive the party nomination in mid-March. The nomination was won by Sousa, a former minister of infrastructure, who was supported by Prime Minister Neves. When Lima decided to stand as an independent candidate, Neves accused him of violating the rules and of disloyalty to the party. Lima's candidacy revealed a split and provoked tensions within the ruling PAICV. In view of Neves' unconditional support for Sousa, the latter's defeat was also a personal blow for the prime minister.

In the **first round** held on 7 August, Fonseca won with 37.4% of the votes, while Sousa qualified for the run-off with 31.8%. Lima obtained 27.5% of the ballots and Joaquim Monteiro, a largely unknown outsider, received 2%. Voter turnout was only 53.2%, considerably less than in the legislative elections. Immediately after the first round, Felisberto Vieira 'Filú', the minister for social development and family, who had supported Lima, resigned from his post. Although Fonseca, who had left the MpD in 1994 to found the 'Partido da Convergência Democrática' (PCD) – which he abandoned in 1998 – was the winner of the first round, his election in the run-off was considered a surprise. Besides the split within the PAICV, he apparently capitalised on popular discontent over high unemployment and rising fuel and consumer prices. Neves and Fonseca both declared that they would work together constructively.

Foreign Affairs

On 24 February, Cape Verde joined the Centre for Development of the **OECD** in Paris, becoming the 39th member state of this centre, which was created in 1962, and its fifth African member state after Egypt, Morocco, Mauritius and South Africa. Foreign Minister José Brito declared that his country's membership was a reason to celebrate as it provided new economic opportunities as well as the sharing of development experiences. He considered membership to be a sign of recognition for his country's development and an opportunity to confirm the country's status in a forum where important international decisions on development were debated.

On 23 June, a delegation of 40 **Chinese businessmen** headed by the vice-minister of trade, Jiang Yao Ping, arrived for a two-day visit to strengthen bilateral trade. The delegation also included the secretary for economy and finance of the government of the Special Administrative Region of Macao, Tam Pak Yuen. During the visit, which also served to promote the role of Macao as an economic and commercial platform for the eight CPLP countries, various agreements were signed in the areas of trade, solar energy, water, education and health. Secretary of State for Foreign Affairs José Luís Rocha, announced the signature of an agreement on a Chinese grant of Yuan 80 m (ca. $ 14 m) to finance projects in these areas.

On 5 July, **East Timor**'s President José Ramos-Horta was received for a two-day visit by President Pires. The same day, Ramos-Horta participated as special guest in Cape Verde's 36th anniversary of independence. Ramos-Horta and Pires awarded each other their countries' highest honours. Ramos-Horta appreciated Cape Verde's contribution to the capacity building in Timor's institutions and promised to strengthen friendship and cooperation between the two countries. Pires declared that he shared Ramos-Horta's position with regard to the current composition of the UNSC, which did not reflect global political changes.

On 19 November, President Fonseca participated in the Ibero-American Summit in Salvador, Bahia, Brazil, to commemorate the International Year for the People of African

Descent (Afro XXI). During the meeting, which was attended by the heads of state and representatives of 14 Latin American, Caribbean and African countries, Fonseca was received by **Brazil's President** Dilma Rousseff. The summit approved the Declaration of Salvador, which included guidelines for the fight against racism and for affirmative action for the emancipation of people of African descent. On his departure, Fonseca announced the visit to Cape Verde in 2012 of a delegation of businessmen and politicians from Bahia, to be headed by the local governor, Jaques Wagner.

On 26 November, Neves arrived for a five-day visit in **Guinea-Bissau**. During a meeting with his local counterpart, Carlos Gomes, both prime ministers expressed the hope that the next summit of the CPLP in July 2012 in Maputo would allow the entry of **Equatorial Guinea**, a former Spanish colony, as a full member state of the Lusophone organisation. The full membership of Equatorial Guinea, an associate CPLP member since 2006, was controversial due to its poor human rights record and the excessive corruption of the regime of Teodoro Obiang Nguema.

Socioeconomic Developments

On 5 January, Cape Verde was the first country to be granted a second Compact by the **Millennium Challenge Corporation** (MCC). The MCC based its decision on satisfactory use of the $ 110 m funds granted under the first five-year Compact, which were spent on infrastructure improvement and agriculture, and the results achieved, as well as on the country's positive performance in the categories of good government, economic liberties and investment in human resources. The second Compact was worth $ 66.2 m and was intended for reform of the water and sanitation and land management sectors, which had been identified as constraints to economic growth.

On 9 January, the local company Fast Ferry inaugurated a **new inter-island maritime service** linking the Sotavento (leeward) islands of Santiago, Fogo and Brava, operated by the catamaran 'Kriola' built by the Dutch Damen shipyard in Singapore. In May, Fast Ferry received a second catamaran from the same shipyard called 'Liberdadi', destined to operate in the Barlavento (windward) islands. The ships were expected to improve maritime transport in the archipelago and consequently also increase inter-island tourism. Fast Ferry financed the investment with bonds worth CVEsc 1.5 bn (€ 13.6 m) through the local stock exchange Bolsa de Valores de Cabo Verde, and with a state subsidy of € 1 m.

From 18 to 31 May, an **IMF mission** visited the archipelago to review implementation of the 15-month policy support instrument (PSI) approved in November 2010. The mission stated that economic recovery was continuing at a steady pace, thanks to a growing tourism sector and the implementation of the public investment programme (PIP). The IMF praised the government's efforts to create growth by public investment, while maintaining sustainable debt levels, but recommended that the government gradually reduce public debt ratios to support private-sector-led growth. Furthermore, the mission supported the government policy of passing on international price increases in energy and food to domestic consumers, but also encouraged the executive to protect poor and vulnerable groups from the consequences of international price shocks. A second and final IMF mission to Cape Verde, from 15 to 29 November to review the PSI, concluded that the economy had expanded at a more moderate pace and warned about the negative impact of the financial and economic turmoil in Europe. The mission appreciated the government's commitment to reducing the public deficit and recommended that the government reduce the external public debt to GDP ratio to below 50%.

On 17 May, the government submitted the **budget** to the National Assembly. Totalling CVEsc 103.4 bn (€ 937.2 m), it involved a 4% decrease in expenditure to CVEsc 59.4 bn (€ 538.4 m), of which CVEsc 27.5 bn (€ 248.2 m) was destined for the PIP. Education represented 23% of total expenditure, while energy, housing and health accounted for 11.5%, 9% and 8% respectively. The budget included revenue of CVEsc 44 bn (€ 398.8 m), of which CVEsc 29.9 m (€ 271 m) was generated by tax receipts. The budget deficit of CVEsc 15.4 bn (€ 139.6 m) corresponded to 10.3% of GDP, less than the 13.6% of GDP in 2010. Finance Minister Cristina Duarte expected a fall in the budget deficit as a proportion of GDP to 9.2% in 2012 and 6.7% in 2013. However, she admitted that these ambitious goals would depend on sustained economic growth. On 6 December, the Assembly approved the 2012 budget with 37 PAICV votes in favour to 25 opposition votes against. The budget envisaged expenditure of CVEsc 57.1 bn (€ 517.5 m), 3.8% less than in the previous year, and revenue of CVEsc 40.7 bn (€ 368.9 m), a reduction of 7.5%. The PIP accounted for spending of CVEsc 24.8 bn (€ 224.8 m). Current expenditure accounted for CVEsc 32.3 bn (€ 292.8 m), of which 36.6% was for public administration, 22.8% for education, 13.1% for social security and 9.7% for health. Concessional loans from foreign donors (AfDB, World Bank, EU, Portugal, Spain, China, Luxemburg and France) were expected to finance the 9.8%-budget deficit of CVEsc 16.4 bn (€ 148.6 m).

New major investments in the **tourism sector** further increased hotel bed capacity. On 7 May, Neves inaugurated the five-star Mélia Tortuga Beach Resort & Spa in Sal, the first hotel of Mélia Hotels in the archipelago. The 220-room hotel was expected to create 300 new jobs. The next day, RIU Hotels & Resorts inaugurated the five-star hotel RIU Touareg in Boavista. This new 881-room hotel represented an investment of € 120 m and was the fifth hotel owned by the Spanish company in Cape Verde. On 27 May, Neves reopened the **airport** of São Filipe in Fogo, which had been closed for three weeks for the extension of the 1,500 m. runway. The work included the modernisation of the cargo and passenger terminals and the construction of a new parking area and an access road to the town of São Filipe. The extension of the runway enabled the airport to receive bigger airplanes and created hopes that international flights could be accommodated in the future.

The dominant tourism sector benefited from the political unrest in North Africa. In the first half of the year, Cape Verde registered the arrival of 219,000 tourists, a considerable increase of 47,000 (27.5%) in comparison with the same period the previous year. The majority of tourists came from the UK, followed by France, Italy, Germany and Portugal. The average hotel bed occupancy rate was 55%, a 10% increase on the first half of 2010, with the islands of Boa Vista and Sal registering the highest visitor rates, with 37.7% and 35.6% of the total, respectively. Over the whole year, the country's air traffic increased by 179,044 passengers (11.2%) to a total of 1,783,111 passengers. In mid-September, the cooperative **vineyards** in Fogo, which started production in 1989, announced that wine production had reached 106,000 l, exceeding 100,000 l for the first time. White wine continued to account for approximately 70% of production, while the share of red wine increased to 30%.

Gerhard Seibert

Côte d'Ivoire

The year started in a complete stalemate with two governments and two presidents: the president-elect, Alassane Ouattara, recognised by the international community and trapped in an Abidjan hotel under UN protection, and his defeated but defiant predecessor, Laurent Gbagbo, who had refused to step down and controlled the country's southern half with the support of the military. This unsustainable situation ended in an open war in Abidjan, the defeat of Gbagbo's camp in April and the conquest of the whole country by pro-Ouattara troops, followed by a return to legality after eight years of crisis. Then began the long and challenging process of reconciliation, the reconstruction of crumbling infrastructure and the rebuilding of the economy. This gradual normalisation was reinforced by the election of a new parliament in December.

Domestic Politics

Charles Blé Goudé, leader of the pro-Gbagbo Young Patriots, 'minister of youth and employment' in the government of Gilbert Aké (appointed 'prime minister' by the obstinate Gbagbo), called for a **march** on the Golf Hotel – Ouattara's headquarters – on 1 January. Following warnings by the international community, notably UN Secretary-General

Ban Ki-moon, and because of the high risk of bloody clashes, the march was finally cancelled to give renewed negotiations with international mediation a chance. However, while Gbagbo continued to play games, the situation continued to deteriorate. On 3 January, 33 people were killed in Duekoue (600 km west of Abidjan), during confrontations between groups backing Gbagbo and the *dioulas* – northern Ivorians supporting Ouattara. This added to the more than 170 reported dead by the UN since the 28 November 2010 election. The 'Forces de Défense et de Sécurité' (FDS – the new name of the pro-Gbagbo army) carried out a **pre-dawn raid** on the headquarters of the 'Parti Démocratique de Côte d'Ivoire' (PDCI) on 4 January, which resulted in the death of an 'activist' and 63 arrests.

On 11 January, Youssoufou Bamba, the new Ivorian ambassador to the UN, told the BBC that Ouattara still favoured the formation of a **unity government** including members of Gbagbo's party, the 'Front Populaire Ivoirien' (FPI), if the latter stepped down first, an offer immediately rejected by FPI head and former prime minister Pascal Affi N'Guessan, who said that Gbagbo's victory over Alassane Ouattara was "non-negotiable". Parallel to intense international diplomatic activity, Ouattara attempted on 18 January to increase pressure on Gbagbo through a nationwide strike, but this failed to create much momentum, with participation limited to Abidjan neighbourhoods that supported Ouattara. On 25 January, following UEMOA's decision to definitely cut Gbagbo's access to the **sub-regional central bank**, 'Banque Centrale des États de l'Afrique de l'Ouest' (BCEAO), his government seized the BCEAO's offices and took control of its staff. Gendarmes and armoured vehicles were deployed around BCEAO offices in Abidjan.

From the end of January, **clashes** between FDS forces and Ouattara supporters started to increase in intensity and there were daily killings, notably in Ouattara's stronghold of Abobo, a northern neighbourhood of Abidjan. In reaction to permanent harassment by the security forces, residents organised protests, which were systematically suppressed, raising the death toll and diminishing chances of any de-escalation. Ouattara's Prime Minister Soro declared on 18 February from Dakar, Senegal, that the people of Côte d'Ivoire would have to stage a revolution, following the example of Tunisia and Egypt, to remove Gbagbo from power. On 21 February, pro-Gbagbo militias attacked supporters of the coalition of opposition parties, 'Rassemblement des Houphouëtistes pour la Démocratie et la Paix' (RHDP), who had gathered at crossroads in Koumassi and Treichville to welcome the heads of state of the AU mediation panel. Rockets were launched and five were killed. **Intense fighting** occurred on 23 and 24 February in Abobo. When pro-Gbagbo reinforcements entered the neighbourhood, hundreds of residents fled with their belongings and 1,800 people were reported to have taken shelter in a Catholic mission in Anyama, a city north of Abidjan. This worsening of the situation was echoed by violence escalating in the west and hostilities resuming across the north-south ceasefire line, which had been largely quiet since the events of 2002–2003. On 25 February, Blé Goudé announced the formation of a vigilante committee to support the FDS, and called for resistance against those seeking to depose Gbagbo. This resulted in the looting of shops owned by foreigners in the Plateau district on 1 March and attacks on and robbery of UN staff during that week. On 6 March, the 'Forces Nouvelles' (FN, ex-rebels, now fighting on behalf of the new president, Ouattara) announced that they had captured the town of Toulepleu, near the border with Liberia, a major escalation in the fighting that showed the hostilities were taking a new direction.

The confirmation of Ouattara as the president-elect by the AU panel on 10 March removed the last obstacle to a **return to full civil war**. While Gbagbo's forces were putting pressure on pro-Ouattara districts in Abidjan, with an assault on Abobo on 12 March, pro-Ouattara forces made major gains over the weekend, seizing several localities in the west. In parallel, in Abidjan on 13 March, fighters from neighbourhoods loyal to Ouattara (although the president-elect denied formal links with them), who had called themselves the 'invisible commando', made incursions for the first time into southern districts, towards Gbagbo's presidential palace. Gbagbo troops fired six missiles on the Abobo market on 17 March, killing 30 people and injuring many. In the meantime, Ouattara made a decisive move when he decided to unify Côte d'Ivoire's security forces. A decree created the 'Forces Républicaines de Côte d'Ivoire' (FRCI), a new army comprised of members of the national armed forces and the FN, and which officially gave Ouattara command over the ex-rebels' firepower. Ouattara forces continued their progress in the western region, putting pressure on Duekoué and seizing Bloequin on 21 March. The same day in Abidjan, answering a call from Blé Goudé, Young Patriots converged on the Adjamé military camp to enlist in Gbagbo's forces. On 26 March, a massive 24-hour rally in front of the presidential palace demonstrated the strength of Blé Goudé's forces. The crowd carried Ivorian flags and placards with slogans such as "I am ready to free my Côte d'Ivoire".

While Gbagbo was digging in in Abidjan, Ouattara forces seized the strategic western city of Duekoue on 28 March, opening the way for an all-out offensive. They captured Yamoussoukro, the administrative capital, on 30 March and the same day entered San Pedro, the country's second port. They reached Abidjan on 31 March and swept into the northern districts, demanding that Gbagbo hand over power. On 1 April, with the embattled former president remaining silent, the **battle of Abidjan** began in earnest, with heavy artillery and machinegun fire resounding in deserted streets. FRCI troops seized control of the pro-Gbagbo state radio and television. In the meantime, General Mangou, chief of staff of the FDS, had taken refuge on 30 March in the residence of the South African ambassador.

Following the determination of the international community to restore the rule of law (as expressed by the UNSC on 31 March), troops of the 'United Nations Operation in Côte d'Ivoire' (UNOCI) and French 'Licorne' forces engaged in direct military operations in an unprecedented escalation of their efforts to oust Gbagbo. In order to facilitate the protection and evacuation of 1,500 foreigners, mainly Westerners (who were gathered in the French military camp), on 3 April, the Licorne force took over the airport, which had been under UNOCI control since the defection of its military commander on 31 March. On 4 April, a group of soldiers from the 'Garde Présidentielle' (Gbagbo's elite troops) and militias kidnapped some foreigners at the Novotel hotel in downtown Abidjan. They included two French nationals – Yves Lambelin, the executive manager of SIFCA, the largest company in Côte d'Ivoire, and the Novotel director – as well as two SIFCA staff from Benin and Malaysia. It was learned a few weeks later that they were executed, most probably in the presidential palace. The same day, Licorne and UNOCI provided air support and opened fire with **attack helicopters** (Mi24s, Gazelles and Pumas) on three strategic garrisons and on Gbagbo's residence. This created the momentum for a last attempt to negotiate. On 5 April, French Foreign Minister Juppé said that the international community demanded a document from Gbagbo, and signed by him, formalising his resignation. This fell on deaf ears and the following day FRCI forces began an assault on the **former president's bunker**. This met with unexpected resistance, however, and Ouattara felt obliged to appear on television on 7 April to announce a blockade. He called on his troops to restore order in Abidjan, where roaming militias had been engaged in looting and random attacks. (A few days earlier, Ibrahim Coulibaly, alias IB, a key figure in the 1999 coup and the 2002 uprising, told 'Radio France Internationale' that he had returned to Abidjan and was leading the pro-Ouattara 'invisible commando'.) Surprisingly, on 9 April, Gbagbo forces broke through the security perimeter around the presidential compound and were able to attack the nearby Golf Hotel and fire on French helicopters, showing that they had used the interlude created by the last-ditch mediation effort to regroup and deploy heavy weapons. In retaliation, the UN Secretary-General ordered an attack, which led to missiles being fired into Gbagbo's compound on 10 April. FRCI forces were finally able to enter the residence and they **captured Gbagbo**, his wife, son, and staff on 11 April. Desiré Tagro, former interior minister in Gbagbo's government and key negotiator of the 2008 Ouagadougou Peace Agreement, was wounded in the course of this operation and died the following day. Defeated army chiefs, including General Mangou, now publicly backed Ouattara. In a televised address, Ouattara urged his troops to show restraint and announced the "dawn of a new era of hope".

The government ordered civil servants to resume work on 18 April, but violence continued in two districts of Abidjan. FRCI forces attacked 'invisible commando' fighters led by IB in Abobo on 20 April, as the 5,000-strong militia refused to join the national army and was asking for recognition of its role in the liberation of Abidjan. FRCI forces simultaneously fought to remove **militias** loyal to Gbagbo in Yopougon, involving five days of heavy fighting. On 25 April, reviving old rivalries among former rebels, IB accused Prime Minister Soro of taking Ouattara hostage, insisting that the new president had no army. The stalemate between the two camps led to new fighting on 27 April, when IB was killed.

On 5 May, the constitutional council, after the negotiated return of its chairman, Paul Yao N'dre from Ghana, where he had fled following the collapse of Gbagbo's regime, declared Ouattara president of Côte d'Ivoire. Ouattara decided to introduce a 'Martyrs' Day' on 12 May to pay tribute to the 3,000 people who had died during the crisis. He was sworn in as president in an **investiture ceremony** in Yamoussoukro on 21 May and, on 1 June, a **new cabinet** was announced. In order to facilitate the transition, Guillaume Soro remained prime minister and defence minister. Among the 36 ministers, 14 were members of Ouattara's 'Rassemblement des Républicains' (RDR), eight were from Konan Bédié's PDCI, five from the ex-'Forces Nouvelles', including Soro, and the remaining portfolios were taken by smaller parties and civil society representatives. Gbagbo's FPI decided not to participate, a condition being the release of arrested comrades.

On 25 July, **constitutional council** president Yao N'dre was dismissed and replaced by Francis Wodie, founder of the 'Parti Ivoirien des Travailleurs' and a presidential candidate in 1995, 2000 and 2010.

Parallel to the start of criminal investigations against Gbagbo, his wife and 100 members of his inner circle, Ouattara announced that former prime minister Banny would head a 'Commission Dialogue, Vérité et Réconciliation' (CDVR). He was encouraged on this course by the **'Group of Elders'** – a group of independent global leaders brought together by Nelson Mandela in 2007, who included South African Nobel laureate Archbishop Desmond Tutu (former president of the post-apartheid reconciliation commission), former UN Secretary-General, Kofi Annan, and former Irish president, Mary Robinson. On 1–2 May, these three travelled to Abidjan and then Korhogo, where Gbagbo was under house arrest. Gbagbo acknowledged his defeat and the election of Ouattara. Later, at a news conference, he urged his supporters to drop political quarrels and work for the revival of the country. The CDVR was officially created by presidential decree on 5 September. It had 11 members, including one Christian and one Muslim religious leader, one representative of traditional chiefs, and seven representatives of the country's major regions and the diaspora (including Chelsea footballer Didier Drogba). Ouattara inaugurated the CDVR in Yamoussoukro on 28 September.

Against a background of growing international pressure, on 15 June, the government announced a national **commission of inquiry** to shed light on human rights violations during the post-electoral crisis. Ouattara also asked the ICC to investigate the most serious violations. On 23 June, ICC prosecutor Luis Mariano-Ocampo requested court judges to open a formal investigation and the ICC's deputy prosecutor, Fatou Bensouda, made a preliminary visit to Côte d'Ivoire on 28 June. Fifteen ex-Gbagbo ministers, who had been held without charge since the former president's arrest, were indicted on 27 June for crimes against the state, embezzlement and other offences. They included former prime minister Ake, former foreign minister Djedje, and former BCEAO governor Dacoury-Tabley. On 3 July, Côte d'Ivoire issued an international arrest warrant for Blé Goudé, under UN sanctions since 2006, and reportedly on the run since 11 April. Ouattara confirmed on French television on 13 September that Gbagbo would be judged by the ICC in order to guarantee a fair and impartial trial and, on 3 October, the ICC's prosecutor received the official go-ahead to commence his investigation. Laurent **Gbagbo** was finally **transferred to The Hague** on 30 November.

On 27 October, the FPI announced that it would boycott planned **legislative elections** in protest at the continued detention of Gbagbo and other party leaders. It was also concerned that the outcome might be unfairly affected by continuing lack of security. On 21 November, the 'Commission Electorale Indépendante' (CEI) announced that 1,182 candidates vying for the 255 seats in the National Assembly had registered for the election scheduled for 11 December and that a total of 25,000 troops, supported by UNOCI peacekeepers, would be deployed. Mamadou Koulibaly, FPI's interim leader since the imprisonment of Affi N'guessan and speaker of the National Assembly (itself de facto on hold), had announced on 13 July that he was leaving the FPI to create a new party. Koulibaly said a party could not have the release of its leader as its sole policy. The new party, named 'Lider' ('Liberté et Démocratie pour la République'), was formally launched on 11 August.

Polling day was peaceful but turnout was low (although, at 36.5%, it was higher than at the 2000 election). The final results were released by the CEI on 16 December and Ouattara's RDR won a majority in the National Assembly with 127 seats. The PDCI won 77 seats (30%) and 35 candidates running as independents (most of them Gbagbo supporters trying to escape the FPI boycott) were also elected. Small parties under the umbrella of the RHDP coalition (the 'Union pour la Démocratie et la Paix en Côte d'Ivoire', 'Union pour la Côte d'Ivoire' and 'Mouvement des Forces de l'Avenir'), and candidates running under the RDHP coalition banner itself, won the other seats. Mamadou Koulibaly, the former speaker running for his new Lider party, lost his seat in Koumassi, a southern district of Abidjan. Many candidates disputed the results and filed complaints with the constitutional council. Despite the rhetoric from the FPI camp about Ouattara monopolising power and some political fever in Abidjan districts and other major cities, the campaign went smoothly on the whole. However, it was marred by a **rocket attack** during a rally in the costal town of Grand Lahou (100 km west of Abidjan) on 7 December, when three people were killed, and by the murder of an RDR candidate in Logouale (western region).

Foreign Affairs

Presidents Koroma of Sierra Leone, Boni Yayi of Benin, and Pedro Pires of Cape Verde, representing ECOWAS, travelled to Abidjan on 3 January. They had conveyed a message to Gbagbo on 28 December 2010, threatening military action, and the defeated president had in return issued threats to the millions of **West African migrants** living in the country. The three leaders were accompanied by Kenya's Prime Minister Raila Odinga, newly appointed as AU mediator to replace South Africa's former president, Thabo Mbeki. They met with Ouattara and Gbagbo on 4 January, when the latter allegedly agreed to negotiate a peaceful end to the crisis without preconditions and pledged to lift the blockade around the Golf Hotel. But nothing changed and Gbagbo's government again called on the UN peacekeepers to leave.

On 6 January, Raila Odinga, returning to Kenya from Abidjan, said that Gbagbo would be offered an amnesty if he stepped down and that he would be able to stay in the country. In parallel, West African military chiefs said they had set in motion plans to oust Gbagbo if negotiations failed. On 8 January, former Nigerian president, Olusegun Obasanjo, started a **new mediation attempt** at the request of ECOWAS chair, Nigerian President Goodluck Jonathan. He met the two rivals on 9 January and warned Gbagbo of the international community's determination, offering the defeated head of state the option of foreign exile and a monthly stipend.

Following the establishment of a curfew in pro-Ouattara neighbourhoods, Gbagbo forces tried to get UN peacekeepers out and fired at and wounded three UN soldiers on 12 January. FDS forces also seized UN food trucks meant for Ouattara's Golf Hotel headquarters. The UN Secretary-General condemned the action and said UNOCI was determined to stay in any of Abidjan's troubled districts. **Harassment of UN forces** continued over the following days, with vehicles stoned and burnt.

On 14 January, the **EU** decided to freeze the European assets of the two main ports in Côte d'Ivoire to prevent funds reaching Gbagbo's illegitimate government. EU-registered vessels were also forbidden to engage in new financial deals with the ports. Christian Preda, head of the EU election observers, presented his report on 25 January, which confirmed Ouattara's victory by 400,000 votes.

Earlier, on 17 January, AU mediator Odinga travelled to Abidjan again after meeting the Nigerian president. No progress was made and the AU envoy cut short his trip. Goodluck Jonathan said later that ECOWAS would not change its stance. After several new acts of aggression against UNOCI peacekeepers on 18 and 19 January, the UNSC agreed, after postponements imposed by Russia, to send 2,000 **extra peacekeepers** (Resolution 1967) to assist the existing 9,150 UNOCI personnel, who had already been increased by Resolution 1942 of 29 September 2010. It also decided to transfer three armed helicopters from the UN Mission in Liberia. That same day, Gbagbo's foreign minister told a press conference that Odinga had failed in his mission and would no longer be welcome.

On 23 January, a UEMOA summit held in Bamako, Mali, put pressure on **BCEAO**'s Ivorian governor, Dacoury-Tabley, to step down. Being close to Gbagbo, he had been facilitating the latter's cash supply, despite a decision in December 2010 to give Ouattara control of Ivorian assets lodged with the bank. Gbagbo's spokesman, Ahoua Don Mello, said the government would find new partners and alternative ways to deposit and access funds.

With the deadlock continuing, on 25 January, Ugandan President Yoweri Museveni and South African President Jacob Zuma called for an independent African enquiry into the registration of voters and the polling and counting processes – a move criticised by UN Secretary-General Ban Ki-moon, who said in Davos, Switzerland, on 28 January that he was concerned by **African divisions** concerning the Ivorian crisis. Ban Ki-moon reaffirmed his position a day later when speaking to African leaders in Addis Ababa, Ethiopia, ahead of the AU Summit, asking for joint efforts by the AU and the UN. The summit was preceded by a visit by the AU chair, Malawian President Mutharika, to Côte d'Ivoire on 27 January, when he met the presidential rivals, and by a meeting of the AU Peace and Security Council on 29 January. AU Commission Chairperson Jean Ping briefed the Council on the conclusions of AU special envoy, Raila Odinga, who had submitted his report and recommendations earlier that day. Due to a division between member states about whether or not military intervention was opportune, the Council decided to appoint a panel of five African leaders tasked with finding a binding settlement within a month. At the end of the summit on 31 January, Ping announced that the AU panel would include the presidents of Mauritania, South Africa, Burkina Faso, Tanzania and Chad.

While Ouattara's prime minister, Guillaume Soro, said on 2 February that the new **AU panel** was the last chance for a peaceful resolution, Gbagbo's foreign minister declared that his government would not accept any finding that questioned Gbagbo's legitimacy as 'president'. The day before, Blé Goudé announced that the Young Patriots rejected Burkina's President Blaise Compaoré's membership on the panel, claiming that Burkina was a belligerent and provided a base for the (former) rebels. The AU panel, without Compaoré, travelled to Abidjan, where it met with Gbagbo, Ouattara and their staffs from 6 to 10 February. However, tensions between AU member states were brought to light when ECOWAS commission chair James Gbeho told journalists on 8 February that solidarity was fast being eroded by countries siding with Gbagbo. He explicitly pointed to **South Africa** for sending a warship to Abidjan. South Africa's ambassador to Nigeria objected that the vessel could serve as a neutral negotiation venue, referring to a similar situation at the end of ex-president Mobutu's regime in the former Zaire. The AU panel returned to Abidjan on 21 February, while bloody clashes took place between Gbagbo's and Ouattara's forces. The mediators met again with both sides but information released by the South African government on 22 February that the discussed option was to form a power-sharing interim government to run the country until new polls were held provoked angry reaction from Ouattara backers, who violently confronted Zuma, demonstrating with placards against his alleged support for Gbagbo.

The intensification of fighting during the panel visit and following days put all **diplomacy on hold**. On 24 February, Nigerian Foreign Minister Ajumogobia said that an air and naval blockade was necessary and that the UN should endorse any use of force to remove Gbagbo. FDS forces opened fire on 28 February on UN sanctions experts checking the observance of the international arms embargo. The UN Secretary-General reacted strongly and expressed fears that Côte d'Ivoire could be sliding back into civil war. The same day, the AU Peace and Security Council extended the panel's mandate to the month of March. Consequently, the **panel met again** in Nouakchott, Mauritania, on 4 March, with the participation of Blaise Compaoré, and Jean Ping travelled to Abidjan on 5 March to convey a message from the panel to Gbagbo and Ouattara, including an invitation to Addis Ababa, where they could have direct talks and discuss the panel's recommendations. Gbagbo turned down the proposal because of the deterioration of the security situation. FPI leader Affi N'Guessan and 'foreign minister' Djedje went in his place. Ouattara travelled to Addis Ababa on 9 March, while 'Fraternité Matin' published an interview with Djedje naming seven countries allegedly backing Gbagbo: Uganda, South Africa, Ghana, DRC, Gambia, Equatorial Guinea and Angola. However, on 10 March, the AU panel released its conclusions, confirming the election of Ouattara, and asking him to form a broad-based government and provide an honourable exit for the former president. Gbagbo's camp rejected the AU's decision straightaway.

The long-awaited outcome of continental diplomacy immediately led to an escalation of fighting, both in Abidjan and along the ceasefire line, while Gbagbo's government decided to ban UN and French peacekeeping aircraft from flying over or landing in the country. On 15 March, French Foreign Minister Alain Juppé said financial sanctions would take time and that Gbagbo was gradually being strangled. He reaffirmed support for Ouattara, even though international news and attention were at that time fully focused on the situation in Libya. On 22 March, UNOCI raised the alarm about the increasing use of heavy weapons against civilians, and the next day Goodluck Jonathan, addressing the 39th ordinary **ECOWAS** summit in Abuja, Nigeria, pointed to the risks that the Ivorian crisis posed to the entire sub-region. ECOWAS formally called on the UN to force Gbagbo to step down. When the AU came back with a new mediation attempt on 26 March, appointing Cape Verde's former foreign minister Jose Brito – a proposal accepted by Gbagbo and rejected by Ouattara – UNOCI urged the UNSC to strengthen its mandate. Following reports of massacres in Duekoue by Ouattara's troops, Ban Ki-moon called Ouattara on 3 April, asking him to take immediate action against the perpetrators. Ouattara said he would order an investigation – a decision that was obviously postponed by the events.

On 30 March, the **UNSC** unanimously passed a **resolution** prepared by France and Nigeria (Resolution 1975) ordering new sanctions on Gbagbo and his closest associates, asking the FDS to yield to the authority of Alassane Ouattara, calling on Gbagbo to step down, and reiterating UNOCI's authorisation to prevent the use of heavy weapons. A clear and deeper engagement of UNOCI and French troops followed, including an increase of the Licorne force from 1,200 to 1,650 on 3 April, with new French troops arriving from Gabon (a first increase of 200 had occurred in February), and direct engagement on military targets. This culminated in massive overnight raids by combat helicopters on 10–11 April.

On 13 April, Ouattara made his first foreign visit to Senegal and, on 25 April, the AU lifted all sanctions imposed on Côte d'Ivoire and the country was reinstated as a full member of the organisation. The investiture ceremony of the new president in Yamoussoukro on 21 May was witnessed by 23 heads of state, including French President Nicolas Sarkozy, Goodluck Jonathan, Blaise Compaoré, Gabon's Ali Bongo, and Ban Ki-moon. Ouattara was invited as a special guest to the Deauville **G8 Summit** in France on 26–27 May, along with eight other African leaders, including the newly elected presidents of Niger, Mamadou Issoufou, and Guinea, Alpha Condé – a tribute to emerging African democracies. In the meantime, on 25 May, **AI** accused Ouattara of reacting passively to massacres committed in the west during the war and the following weeks, notably in May. International pressure continued with an HRW report released on 2 June, which accused FRCI forces of targeting ethnic groups seen as loyal to Gbagbo and warning the new regime about one-sided justice.

France's Prime Minister François Fillon arrived for a two-day visit on 14 July with the objective of revitalising bilateral cooperation. He visited the Licorne forces, which were cut back to their 2010 level of 900 troops. He also announced another reduction by the end of the year to 450 personnel, as well as a revision of the bilateral defence protocol with Côte d'Ivoire. Ouattara visited the **US** on 27–30 July, where he met President Obama, and the presidents of the IMF and the World Bank, and the UN Secretary-General. On 27 July, in its seventh and last resolution on Côte d'Ivoire for 2011 (Resolution 2000), the UNSC renewed its support by extending UNOCI's mandate for one year and targeting its assistance on disarmament and preparations for legislative elections. Due to continuing insecurity in Côte d'Ivoire's western region and reported killings by suspected mercenaries from Liberia, the government, together with UNOCI and other members of the MRU (Guinea, Liberia, and Sierra Leone), decided on 18 September to deploy soldiers in the common border region and intensify patrols. Ouattara also took part in the 66th session of the UN General Assembly in New York. In his speech on 22 September, he thanked the international community and the UN for their strong support during the crisis. In the following days, he met in Washington with officials of the World Bank, the US Council of Foreign Relations, the US Congress' Black Caucus, and several think-tanks.

Resuming the joint cabinet meetings that had existed before the emergency and the deterioration of bilateral relations, **Burkina Faso**'s President Compaoré hosted Ouattara on 18 November, when the latter thanked him for his personal involvement in resolving the crisis.

Gbagbo's transfer to the ICC on 30 November was broadly welcomed internationally. Human rights groups, however, emphasised that the court would have to investigate both sides. The year ended with repeated warnings by UNOCI of risks of renewed political violence in the aftermath of the parliamentary polls and in relation to difficulties in restructuring the armed forces.

Socioeconomic Developments

The year was the worst in the country's 50-year history as an independent state. With heavy weapons used in the final battle for the liberation of Abidjan, thousands dead, hundreds of thousands of people fleeing the fighting, lack of food and sporadic water and electricity provision, the population paid **a heavy price** for Gbagbo's refusal to step down. Excesses by militias and armed forces, including muggings and killings, usually along ethnic lines, led to a climate of terror that put heavy pressure on social cohesion. Being rapidly confronted with a shortage of **cash**, Gbagbo's camp, after seizing BCEAO reserves, took control of the electricity company. When major foreign banks decided to close their operations, causing long queues of customers rushing to withdraw their money, Gbagbo's people announced on 17 February that they would be nationalised. On 7 March, they said that full control would be taken of the cocoa sector, the heart of the economy. Private companies were asked to pay their taxes directly to Gbagbo representatives.

After the fall of the regime, parallel to the progressive resumption of basic services, it took several weeks before security was restored and refugees had returned home (according to UNHCR 300,000 people were still displaced by mid-June). The impact of the five-month economic-institutional paralysis on business was severe and translated into a worsening macroeconomic situation. GDP had been lower than expected in 2010 due to the events in November and December that year (2.4% instead of 3.6%) and, unsurprisingly, it plummeted to **negative growth** (–4.7%) in 2011.

It could have been even worse (the initial forecast was –5.8%), but **recovery was quicker** than anticipated due to a favourable combination of factors including higher commodity prices (the cocoa sector saw a record harvest), increased revenue collection, and donors' budget support. The World Bank and EU quickly announced they would lift sanctions and the freeze on credit – the EU released emergency support to the tune of € 500 m, as did France, for a similar amount. The AfDB disbursed $ 150 m in May, while discussions began for the bank's return to its old headquarters in Abidjan – it had been in Tunis in recent years as a result of the Ivorian crisis. In September, the IMF agreed to allocate a $ 600 m loan under the ECF. In addition, fiscal stimulus measures, tax breaks for affected firms and payment of domestic arrears helped the private sector to begin to recover and regain confidence, as did the first infrastructure repairs and the government's fight against illegal roadblocks and racketeering. A debt relief agreement was concluded with the Paris Club in November, the consequence of which should be a strong reduction of debt service by nearly 80% for the next three years. Reform of the cocoa sector was taken up again with the implementation of the new Coffee-Cocoa Council and a forward-selling mechanism, with the objective of enabling producers to earn a 60% FOB (Free On Board) price.

However, in spite of this rapid recovery, which confirmed the resilience of the Ivorian economy, it would be a long and steep upward path to reach the 'emerging status' claimed by President Ouattara. Over the previous decade, the population had grown by almost 3.2 m (7.3 m since 1990), while GDP per capita fell by an average of 2.1% annually. **Education** remained deeply stricken, with recurring interruption of classes. With a yearly cohort of about 450,000, only 20% of young people were reaching middle school, 10% high school, and a mere 2% university.

Bruno Losch

Gambia

On 24 November, Yaya Jammeh, president since 1996, was re-elected for another five-year term, having received 72% of the votes. This happened in the midst of growing international concern over Jammeh's involvement in arms and drug-trafficking and over the country's poor human rights record. Throughout the year, Gambian on-line media based abroad spread rumours about Jammeh's divorce from his second wife, his assumed pancreatic cancer, and his connections with the arms dealer Victor Bout, but without in any way undermining his firm grip on the country. Relations with Senegal were tense during the first part of 2011, following an arms scandal with Iran in the latter part of 2010. Drought led to dramatic crop failure and the increased economic vulnerability of large sections of the population.

Domestic Politics

At the beginning of the year, the death of Dembo Sisi (who was tortured by security men stationed in his village after he was accused of having stolen a motorbike) and of Ello Jallow (one of the plain-clothes officers attached to the First Lady Zeinab Suma Jammeh) reopened debate on the latitude enjoyed by security forces under Jammeh's regime and Gambia's poor **human rights record**. While Sisi's murder led to a death sentence for the two officers involved by the end of the year, Jallow's death remained a matter of speculation. Officially, he died in a fatal car accident, but rumour pointed to his adulterous relationship with the First Lady, which would have prompted the president to order his assassination.

January witnessed minor cabinet reshuffles and growing rumours on the connection between Jammeh and Victor Bout, the Ukrainian arms dealer known internationally as the "merchant of death" because of his alleged ties with terrorist groups. Bout was extradited from Thailand to the United States in 2010, and his trial raised the expectations of Gambians abroad that there would be revelations about Jammeh's involvement in **arms trafficking** in the sub-region. In February, the Iranian authorities disclosed that an arms container seized in Nigeria in October 2010 was destined for Gambia. The shipment was the last of three arranged in the context of a confidential agreement signed between the two countries in 2007.

Registration of voters for the 2011 **presidential elections** started on 2 May. For the first time, computer technology was used thanks to a government investment of GMD (dalasi) 65 m. According to officials, registration was not extended to expatriate Gambians because of budgetary constraints, but the opposition spoke of a deliberate government plan to exclude them. (Jammeh has never won the support of the Gambian diaspora, as people were often forced to leave the country because of intimidation and repression.) The opposition parties proved unable to unite, except in pointing to irregularities in the registration system and advocating change. The major defection of supporters from the ruling Alliance for Patriotic Orientation and Reconstruction (APRC) to the United Party (UP) in the district of Sami in February remained an isolated case. Most Gambians showed support for the president, and suggestions that they would stay away from the polls never materialised. Jammeh won all 48 constituencies, including those that were traditional opposition strongholds. Ouseinou Darboe, a human rights lawyer and leader of the UP, and Jammeh's principal opponent since 1996, stood as presidential candidate for the fourth and last time. Darboe was already 63 years old and the 1997 Constitution fixed 65 as the age limit for the office of president. The other candidate was Hamat Bah, leading a coalition of small political parties (National Reconciliation Party, Gambia Party for Democracy and Progress, National Alliance for Democracy and Development, and the People's Democratic Organization for Independence and Socialism), which was formed at the end of October under the campaign slogan: "Own yourself, own your country/ save yourself, save your country".

ECOWAS denounced the elections and withdrew its team of observers a few days before the polls on the grounds that the electorate had been intimidated. A Commonwealth team of experts remarked that the campaign period of 11 days was too short to create a level **playing field** and challenge the position of the incumbent. It also noted the blurring of state and party lines as far as the president's campaign was concerned. Jammeh's propaganda had unofficially started in July with a 'Dialogue with the People Tour'. On that occasion, gifts of rice and sugar were distributed and Jammeh warned his opponents that he could withdraw government development assistance from the communities they represented. As this had happened in the past, when opposition strongholds such as MacCarthy Island experienced deteriorating and badly managed services, the warning was taken seriously.

Also in July, prosecutors charged Ndey Tapha Sosseh (former president of the Gambia Press Union) and three others, including Amadou Janneh (former minister of communication and a US citizen), with treason for plotting against the government. Sosseh was in exile in Mali but Janneh was arrested by plain-clothes policemen in June. In May, Sosseh, Janneh and two other activists had distributed what the prosecutors called "seditious T-shirts" bearing the words "Coalition for Change The Gambia, End to Dictatorship Now".

Talks about Yaya Jammeh's intention to turn the country into a monarchy, which started in the latter part of 2010, continued in the first months of 2011. They stopped before the start of the May registration of voters, only to resurface after the elections. **On-line media** based abroad (including 'Freedom Newspaper', 'The Gambian Echo' and 'Senegambia News') waged an intensely negative campaign against Jammeh by unveiling details of his connections with the Kadhafi regime and his divorce from his second wife, Alima Sallah, spreading rumours that he had pancreatic cancer and, more importantly, discussing his relationship with Victor Bout. The effects were modest. First, those living in the country knew the risks of opposing Jammeh; second, they had minimal internet access, not only because internet facilities were limited to the major urban centres but also because of government attempts to block opposition websites and punish those who spread that kind of information.

Two months before the polls, and a few days after Kadhafi's death, the death of **Baba Jobe**, former APRC parliamentary and majority leader, led to more talk about Jammeh's dealings. Jobe was serving a nine-year sentence for fraud in Miles II Prison, which, since the 1994 coup that brought Jammeh to power, had become a national symbol of repressive policy. After the 1994 coup, Jobe helped Jammeh and the junta to restore diplomatic relations with Libya, which had been severed for almost 13 years. Jobe had lived in Libya, and Libya helped to train many members of the 22 July movement that he had created on the eve of the 1996 elections to support Jammeh's candidature. In 2001, a UN investigation team pointed to Jobe's involvement in the 'blood diamond' trade from Sierra Leone and Liberia. Gambia is not a diamond producer, but its diamond exports rose abruptly in the second part of the 1990s, in parallel with the Liberian and Sierra Leonean civil wars. In 2003, the government arrested Jobe on allegations of fraud, thus closing down further international investigations, which, if pursued, would probably have led to Jammeh himself.

Foreign Affairs

In February, following growing international concern over the revolution in **Libya**, Jammeh urged Kadhafi, his long-term financial supporter, to step down immediately. This clearly demonstrated his ability to manipulate the international community by severing ties with allies should the need arise. In 2009, Kadhafi had been a special guest at the annual celebration of the anniversary of the 1994 military coup, while that same year Jammeh had attended the anniversary celebrations in Tripoli of the 1969 takeover that brought Kadhafi to power. In April, Libyan property in Gambia was confiscated and the Libyan diplomatic corps expelled. These were the only notable consequences of the 'Arab Spring' in Gambia, apart from the sudden repatriation of Gambians who had been working in Libya and other North African countries.

Throughout the year, Gambia's foreign affairs were dominated by tension with neighbouring **Senegal**, whose government has long suspected Jammeh of supporting the Casamance rebellion, while Gambia protests that Senegal provides sanctuary to Gambian political dissidents. Complaints by Senegalese drivers about the imposition of exorbitant fees and harassment by Gambian customs officers caused an informal border closure in the first part of the year, which compromised commerce and seriously affected the re-export sector, a pillar of the Gambian economy. Relations with Senegal remained volatile in spite of the continuous exchange of visits by top officials of the two countries.

Nigeria, Venezuela and Taiwan continued to support Jammeh's government. In October, the eight foreigners who had been arrested in 2010 following the seizure of cocaine worth $ 1 bn, were sentenced to 50 years' imprisonment. Jammeh's compliance with the Western **anti-drug crusade** is one of the factors that have helped him to withstand international pressure concerning his human rights violations.

Socioeconomic Developments

Although the IMF had praised the capacity of the Gambian economy to achieve robust growth with low-to-moderate inflation in spite of the global economic crisis, reports showed that average incomes had not risen since 1995. Close to 59% of the population still lived below the poverty line. Agriculture continued to provide employment for 75% of the population and accounted for 25% of GDP. The scarce and poorly distributed **rains** in July, August and September therefore dealt a major blow to the economy and the livelihood of large sections of the population. Expectations of growth were high at the beginning of the year, immediately after the IMF released its 2010 report on the country's performance and after the launching of the Programme for Accelerated Growth and Employment (PAGE). PAGE was meant to boost infrastructural development and increase the proportion of land under cultivation and the quality of crops through support irrigation schemes. By October, however, it was clear that the country was to face a **major**

subsistence crisis. The year saw a 70% reduction in the total harvest of millet, rice and groundnuts, the last of which being the major export crop since colonial times. The impact of the poor harvest was exacerbated by rising global food prices and by a fall in the flow of migrants' remittances because of the recession in Europe and North America. The European crisis also affected the tourist sector, which accounts for one-fifth of GDP. By year's end, rural households began to reduce the frequency of meals, sell livestock and borrow increasing amounts of money. The outstanding domestic debt increased (8.6%), and in September the National Assembly approved a supplementary budget of $ 7.2 m, which, according to external observers, was used to support the president's patronage politics in the campaign for the upcoming elections. Inflation, which was high at the end of 2010, slowed down in the first part of the year, only to increase again when news of crop failure and food shortages started to circulate.

Economic development continued to be supported by **international donors**. In June, for instance, the government signed a financing agreement worth $ 52.5 m with the Islamic Development Bank in order to strengthen power plants in the peri-urban areas around the capital of Banjul and improve telecommunications with the installation of 817 km of fibre-optic cables. This agreement demonstrated the increasing support of the Islamic Development Bank and the commitment of the government to realise its 'Vision 2020', whose development goals were established during the 1996 democratic transition.

Alice Bellagamba

Ghana

Flourishing oil sales in the first year of commercial drilling propelled GDP into double figures, even though the national debt also increased. There was single-figure end-of-year inflation for the second time in two years. Two petroleum related acts of parliament were passed, and a national gas company was formed. Petrol price increases were very well managed. Citizens were also rewarded with other real benefits of cocoa, apart from foreign exchange. Ghana continued to negotiate sensitive foreign policy curves with neighbours and others abroad. Sufficient funds were committed for the prosecution of a competent election in 2012, and the nation progressed with the agenda of bridging the gap in development between the north and the south.

Domestic Politics

On 1 January, President John Atta Mills declared a "year of action". Despite the previous intensive debate on the **Petroleum Revenue Management Act** and crude oil as collateral for loans, the government expedited action for a $ 3 bn loan from the China Development Bank but on terms of doubtful benefit to the national interest, according to the opposition, citing the potential granting of the right to 90 crude oil liftings of 950,000 barrels per lifting at $ 85 a barrel over 20 years. The Revenue Management Act was passed on 2 March, and the Petroleum Commission Bill also passed into law on 1 June. Subsequently, the government presented arguments against IMF and World Bank reservations regarding the Chinese loan, such as the unwillingness of the West to fund the infrastructure Ghana needed.

A **Petroleum Security Co-ordinating Committee** was set up in January and four new armoured speed boats were subsequently added to the Western Naval Command closest to the oil waters. Two Airbus Military C295 transports, an Embraer 190 and two Diamond DA 42 surveillance aircraft were also ordered. A CASA C-295-M twin-turboprop transport aircraft was commissioned to replace the Fokker 27 that had been in use for 37 years. The ministry of food and agriculture (MOFA) funded two 46 m. patrol vessels for fisheries surveillance and combating piracy and towards the general drive to modernise the navy and beef up maritime security against external threats.

Following the July report of the National Task Force on Gas chaired by Dr Kwesi Botchway, the president authorised the formation of the National Gas Company. The **Tema Oil Refinery** faced financial challenges, and the price of petrol went up in December. However, all actors including government, the banking sector, road transport operators, legal institutions and the refinery itself acted amicably to avoid chaos. A Petroleum Commission Board was set up in November by the minister of energy to execute cost efficiency and sustainability measures. The New Alpha Refinery-Ghana, the Ghanaian subsidiary of the South African company, undertook feasibility studies for establishing a tank farm, an oil refinery and a gas turbine power-generation plant, which would have the capacity to process 200,000 b/d of crude **oil**, well over the 45,000 b/d currently produced by the existing refinery.

The National Tripartite Committee increased the minimum wage from GHS 3.11 to GHS 3.73 from 15 February. There were frequent demonstrations by civil service labour unions about distortions in the migration of salary structures onto the single spine salary scheme being administered by the Fair Wages and Salaries Commission. On 8 October, public health doctors of the Ghana Medical Association (GMA) embarked on **strike action** for over two weeks, causing the president to abort his October trip to the Commonwealth Heads of Government Meeting in Australia. There were reports that some middle-level government officials earned more than doctors, who worked sacrificial hours to save lives, but the ruling of a compulsory arbitration panel to which the case was referred did not address all the concerns of the GMA.

Laureta Vivian Lamptey was sworn in on 1 August as head of the Commission for Human Rights and Administrative Justice, replacing Anna Bossman, who resigned to take on an international assignment. While the television industry progressed with the digital switchover project, some key sackings rocked the **media**. On 15 April, the general manager of the Ghana News Agency (GNA) was sacked by the National Media Commission (NMC). William Ampem Darko, the director-general of the Ghana Broadcasting

Corporation, who had also been sacked by the NMC, was effectively replaced in mid-October by Berifi Appenteng. The existing board of the Electricity Company of Ghana (ECG) was dissolved on 1 December, and another reconstituted later.

Strong demands from the opposition parties for the verification of voters on election day to complement the biometric registration of voters generated intense debate between the Electoral Commission and its Inter Party Advisory Committee. The crucial nature of the **2012 elections** required that the electoral process be satisfactory to all parties, so the finance minister committed sufficient funds to cover such verification.

The government did not bow to pressure from the US and UK governments over **gay rights issues**, regardless of whether this might be tied to aid. Parliament rejected the legalisation of homosexuality and resolved to maintain the country's criminal code in line with the constitution.

On 23 December, Ghana announced that it would review the ECOWAS protocol on **Fulanis**. The herdsmen had encroached on areas of land in Agogo to graze their cattle, assuming the territory to be available so that they could pursue their nomadic life-style. It was alleged that the herdsmen also struck up relationships with the wives of some Agogo townsfolk. The consequent unrest led to the intervention of a combined military and police force, which escorted the nomads to a new area allocated to them.

Foreign Affairs

A great deal occurred on the **ECOWAS** front. Minister of Environment, Science and Technology Sherry Ayittey was appointed on 17 May to the board of the ECOWAS Regional Centre for Renewable Energy and Energy Efficiency. On 30 August, the ECG led on the West African Power Pool (WAPP) project, and signed a GHS 3.6 m deal with its Togolese counterpart 'Communauté Electrique du Benin', to supply power to communities in neighbouring Togo. Under WAPP, the Volta River Authority (VRA) is also expected to supply to Burkina Faso and Côte d'Ivoire with a minimum 2 MW of electricity each.

A mutiny and military clashes in **Burkina Faso** during April caused the closure of both sides of the Burkinabè/Ghanaian border. Ghana's ambassador to Burkina Faso was also attacked. At the beginning of July, after a three-day conference to strengthen trans-border cooperation and peaceful coexistence, the governor of Central East Burkina Faso, the district chief executive of Savannah Region of Togo, and Ghana's Upper East regional minister signed a joint communiqué. On 14 August, the Ghanaian Police and Togolese Gendarmerie conducted a joint operation against suspected criminal hideouts along the Ghana-Togo frontier at Aflao, which led to the arrest of 33 suspects. It was reported on 26 September that Ghana and **Togo** had agreed to settle outstanding claims of CFAfr 36 m incurred between the two countries under the ECOWAS Brown Card Insurance scheme. On 3 October, a six-member delegation on a three-day working visit from

Togo's constitutional court called on Ghana's Chief Justice Georgina Wood in Accra, and discussed mutual court structures and jurisdictional roles with Ghanaian colleagues.

On 21 June, a four-man transport delegation from **Liberia**, led by their deputy minister of transport, Ebenezer Kolliegbo, visited Accra to make strategic decisions. In September, 40 Liberian immigration officers graduated from the Ghana Immigration Academy and Training School in Assin Fosu. It was noted in mid-December that over 11,000 Liberian refugees were due to return to a now stable Liberia in 2012.

On 18 July, the West Africa Network for Peace Building revealed that weapons from the **Côte d'Ivoire** crisis had appeared in Ghana. On 10 September in Abuja, Nigeria, a mini summit of ECOWAS heads of state from Senegal, Nigeria, Ghana, Côte d'Ivoire and Liberia discussed arms proliferation. On 6 October, Ivorian President Alassane Ouattarra held closed-door talks with President Mills in Accra, and on 7 October, the Ghanaian president held another closed-door session with the ECOWAS chair, Nigerian President Goodluck Jonathan, in Accra. Consequently, Ghana, Côte d'Ivoire and UNHCR signed a tripartite agreement on 7 October on the voluntary repatriation of 18,000 Ivorian refugees. The two countries agreed to engage UNHCR to repatriate refugees identified as ex-combatants to a third country that did not border on Côte d'Ivoire. Relations between Côte d'Ivoire and Liberia, which share a common border, became strained because of Ivorian (or former president Gbagbo's) support for the Movement for Democracy in Liberia during the second Liberian civil war of 1999–2003. An attempt was made in 2010 by Liberian President Ellen Johnson-Sirleaf to repair the relationship, but sensitivities remained in certain Ivorian quarters. On 7 December, the new Ivorian government sent warrants to Ghana for the extradition of alleged Ivorian ex-combatants, coinciding with the Ivorian government's 29 November unveiling of a new and controversial **maritime border** with Ghana, which sought to incorporate a substantial area of Ghana's Jubilee Oilfields. Taking into account the indisputable accuracy of modern GPS technology, and the ongoing discussions between the two countries in accordance with the UN Convention on the Law of the Sea (which followed the ECOWAS agreement that had resulted from a ministerial meeting on 13–14 February 2009), this new development on oil boundaries seemed politically motivated.

On 7 February, the Australian High Commissioner announced scholarship awards to 26 Ghanaian students, to pursue Masters degrees in **Australia**. On 9 April, an 11-member delegation from private sector organisations of the Energy Chamber of **Trinidad and Tobago** arrived in Accra on a week-long visit to explore opportunities in the energy sector, and seek joint venture partners. On 25–27 April, Trinidad and Tobago's Minister of Energy Affairs Carolyn Seepersad-Bachan discussed Ghana's Gas Infrastructure Development Project with Energy Minister Joe Oteng-Adjei and government officials. The National Gas Company of Trinidad and Tobago was then invited to conclude joint venture negotiations with the Ghana National Petroleum Corporation.

In May, the **US** Embassy handed over the American Corner Research Library to the Legon Centre for International Affairs and Diplomacy (LECIAD), to serve as a nerve centre for studying US foreign policy, educational system, culture and history. The director of LECIAD, Professor Kwame Boafo-Arthur, reiterated that the library provided opportunities for researchers. At the beginning of June, US Senators Johnny Isakson of Georgia and Chris Coons of Delaware visited Ghana to assess the state of projects under phase one of the Millennium Challenge Account.

On 2 June, Ghana's Vice President John Mahama and cabinet colleagues, and the EU Ambassador to Ghana Claude Maerten and eight EU ambassadors based in Accra, met in Accra under the framework of political dialogue defined in the **Cotonou Agreement**, to take stock of issues of mutual interest in both Europe and Ghana.

On 8 September, Sharon Bar-Li presented her Letters of Credence to the president of Ghana in Accra, to mark the first posting of an **Israeli** ambassador to Ghana for three decades.

Accra saw a variety of other **international events** and visits. On 15 March, a delegation from the UN Industrial Development Organization came for a two-day conference on diversifying African economies. On 30 March, **Spain**'s Secretary of State for Foreign and Iberoamerican Affairs Juan Antonio Yya Fez-Barnuevo commenced an official visit to Ghana and, in April, the third symposium of the African Forum for Agricultural Advisory Services was held. On 16 August, President Ian Khama of **Botswana** held bilateral talks with President Mills and, on 27 October, the UN Fund for Population Activities launched the 2011 edition of the World Population Report. In addition, Minister for Tourism the Honourable Akua Dansua was appointed to the advisory board of the Institute for Cultural Diplomacy in Berlin on 1 April, and President Mills visited **Canada** in November, and held closed-door discussions in Ottawa with Canadian Prime Minister Stephen Harper.

Socioeconomic Developments

According to the Ghana Statistical Service, Ghana earned $ 444,124,724 from 3,930,189 barrels of crude oil, propelling **GDP** to 14.4%, far above the 5.1% target. A non-oil GDP target of 7.6% was set for 2012. The economy also experienced single digit **inflation**, ending at 8.6% (the same as in 2010). An 8.5% target was set for 2012. Total public debt at the end of the year stood at $ 14 bn or 44.2% of GDP (a rise of 34.1% compared with the previous year). Overall fiscal operations saw revenue and grants amounting to GHS 10.7 bn, compared with GHS 7.5 bn in 2010, but total expenditure was GHS 12.7 bn, compared with GHS 9.2 bn in 2010. Public service wage and salary increases shot up from just over GHS 2 bn to GHS 5.2 bn. The Bank of Ghana announced that the "narrow" budget deficit arising from wage increases was financed by issuing domestic bonds. A sum of GHS 30 m was allocated from the Oil Fund to support the Forestry Commission for plantation development and afforestation. On 24 January, the British High Commission announced a £ 36 m DFID grant for Multi-Donor Budget Support (MDBS). Also under MDBS, the EU disbursed € 26.4 m on 14 August, in the context of the MDG contract. On 2 March, Ghana and Japan signed two budget support agreements: $ 2.4 m for Ghana's health sector, and $ 12 m for food aid for victims of the 2010 flood.

On 22 January, the **World Bank** approved a $ 215 m Poverty Reduction Support Credit, to help consolidate fiscal stabilisation and promote development objectives of the Ghana Shared Growth and Development Agenda, which is the medium-term development policy framework for 2010–2013. On 16 March, the World Bank, in partnership with DFID, the European Commission and the Danish International Development Agency (DANIDA), signed a memorandum of understanding to pool a $ 60 m grant over four years for the implementation of the Ghana Integrated Financial Management Information System. In June, the World Bank and the Canadian International Development Agency voted $ 17 m to assist combating desertification and drought. In July, the World Bank announced an offer of $ 3.86 m to the Accra Metropolitan Assembly in support of its Millennium City Project. In August, the government acquired $ 40 m from the World Bank to provide technical and financial support for the Ghana Statistics Development Plan: $ 30 m came from IDA Credit and $ 10 m from the Statistics for Results Facility Catalytic Fund. In October, an **IMF** team led by Christina Daseking conducted the fifth economic review under the ECF arrangement since June. It was reported that this review had implications for Ghana's authority to proceed with a $ 3 bn loan application with China. In December, the World Bank announced that it was committing $ 50 m to the second phase of Ghana's Land Administration Project.

The Ghana Investment Promotion Centre announced **FDI** worth $ 7.68 bn, of which $ 2.5 bn attributed to the beleaguered STX project and $ 3 bn from the Asanteman Home Group Ltd were yet to be realised. The $ 2.18 bn already in the bag, was well over the set target of $ 1.5 bn, which had been exceeded by the third quarter of the year. Altogether, 514 new projects were registered, of which China continued to dominate with 79, followed by India with 77, Nigeria 39 and Lebanon 36. With regard to amounts invested, the high value of STX meant that South Korea topped the list with $ 4.77 bn, followed by Bermuda, the value of whose investments was recorded as $ 300 m. Following the official listing of Tullow Oil Plc in July, the Ghana Stock Exchange became the third largest capital market in sub-Saharan Africa, after South Africa and Nigeria.

The Chamber of Mines reported a 3% rise in **gold** production in the first half of the year from 1,455,234 ounces in the previous year to 1,497,023 ounces. Gold revenues in the same period increased by 31% from $ 1,683 m to $ 2,205 m. Ghana sold a 1.3% stake in AngloGold Ashanti for $ 43.97 a share, which generated $ 215 m in government revenue. **Diamond** revenues in the first half of the year also increased by 42%, from $ 6.9 m in 2010 to $ 9.7 m, despite an 8% decline in production. A divestiture of the former Ghana

Diamond Company resulted in a Ghanaian owned company now known as the Great Consolidated Diamond Ghana Limited.

The **cocoa** harvest for the full 2010/2011 season increased from 944,000 tonnes in 2010 to 1,024,000 tonnes. The Bank of Ghana reported that cocoa had already earned $ 1,900 m by the end of November. In response, the government announced an increase in the producer price of cocoa in October, from GHS 3,200 per tonne to GHS 3,280 for the 2011/2012 season. Cocoa farmers would then earn GHS 205 per bag of 64 kg, up from GHS 200. A series of other benefits arose from cocoa. On 25 July, the Cadbury Cocoa Partnership presented 10,000 household solar lanterns valued at GHS 600,000 for distribution to cocoa farmers in 160 communities. On 8 September, COCOBOD inaugurated a 64-Slice CT Scanner for the Cocoa Clinic in Accra. On 8 October, Clement Bugase, the chief executive officer (CEO) of the Community Water and Sanitation Agency, announced that all residents of cocoa growing areas in the country would receive drinking water from solar water machines by the end of 2013. The GNA also announced on 22 December a COCOBOD release of $ 200 m to the ministry of roads and highways, under the Cocoa Roads Improvement Project (Tranche II), to carry out maintenance on 4,000 km of road and spot improvements on 2,000 km, and to surface 750 km of feeder roads with bitumen.

On 27 April, the VRA revealed that plans were in place to increase access to **electricity** from 60% to 90% of the population. On 29 August, the Public Utilities Regulatory Commission announced a 7% increase in electricity tariffs and a 6.7% increase in water tariffs from 1 September to 30 November. A subsequent 3% increase in the electricity tariff, and a 1.1% increase in the water tariff were introduced on 1 December. The Sunon Asogli power plant produced 15% of total electricity generated.

On 20 March, the government announced it had secured $ 80 m to undertake infrastructural development in polytechnics, with the aim of generating skills to sustain Ghana's middle-income economy status. On 17 June, the government announced the release of GHS 2 m for bursaries and scholarships for over 5,000 qualified applicants to second-cycle vocational, technical and tertiary institutions under the Mathematics, Science and Technology Scholarships Scheme for the 2011/12 academic year. On 22 July, the minister of education announced the introduction of an annual free apprenticeship programme for junior high school graduates unable to continue their **education** to enable them to acquire employable skills. The pilot scheme would sponsor 5,000 beneficiaries through informal apprenticeships. The temporarily suspended school feeding programme resumed on 19 September. A total of 791 students from less affluent schools were admitted to the University of Cape Coast for the 2011/2012 academic year, representing 18% of total admissions to the university. On 13 July, The Netherlands provided € 2 m for the implementation of the 'Girl Child Project', to be carried out by four civil society organisations, the Sissala Literacy and Development Programme, the Centre for the Alleviation of Poverty and

Child Support, the Ark Foundation, and the CRESCENT organisation. They signed a memorandum of understanding to implement the project over five years and announced that it sought to empower young schoolgirls aged ten to 17 and young women aged 18 to 24 who did not attend school.

On 18 January, Ghana signed an agreement with OPUS 7 SRO Satov of Austria for the construction of 12 district hospitals and technical training institutions, and the supply of two air ambulances, 200 ambulance cars, 50 mobile clinics and ten educative mobile units. In March, an Oxfam report that criticised the operations of the National **Health** Insurance Authority was described by the authority's CEO as unsubstantiated and inaccurate. Also in March, President Mills ordered the release of GHS 5 m to fight a cholera outbreak. In July, the World Bank commended the Northern Regional office of the Ghana AIDS Commission and its social partners for successfully implementing the Multi-Sectoral HIV/AIDS Programme, funded by the World Bank over five years and aimed at building collaboration between social partners in the fight against HIV/AIDS through capacity building and other interventions. Through measures adopted by the Regional AIDS Commission, civil society organisations and NGOs, the Northern Region had consistently reduced HIV/AIDS prevalence, and now had the lowest prevalence rate (0.7%) in the country. On 28 July, former US president, Jimmy Carter, issued a press statement from the Carter Center in Atlanta to congratulate Ghana on stopping the transmission of Guinea worm. WHO would monitor this over a period of three years before declaring the country totally free of infection. In August, the government distributed 161 ambulances to district hospitals. As part of National Family Planning Week, on 28 September, DFID announced support for family planning measures that would benefit 690,000 Ghanaians over a year. Starting from October, the Ghana Health Service was to receive the first part of a delivery of 2.5 m doses of injectable contraceptives and 66,350 doses of implant contraceptives provided by UKaid. It was estimated this would avert 178,000 unintended pregnancies.

Agricultural developments continued. Among other things, on 4 April, the University of Ghana Research Centre at Okumening publicised findings on preserving fresh oranges for 60 days in the open. On 16 May, Japan donated 125 agricultural tractors with matching implements, ten rice mills, 35 rice threshing machines, 35 rice reapers, two combine harvesters and 40 irrigation pumps worth $ 5.1 m, under a scheme for grant assistance for underprivileged farmers. MOFA directed that the equipment be sold to farmers at reduced prices. On 11 August, the ministry of trade and industry announced that Ghana's banana exports had reached 65,000 tonnes per year. On 17 November, Ghana and IFAD signed a $ 31.5 m agreement to scale up the first and second phases of the Rural Enterprise Project.

The effects of **climate change** have regular environmental and economic impact. It was reported on 30 May that more than 6,000 buildings, including schools, were destroyed by rainstorms in the Upper East Region alone. On 11 July, a team of 75 US army personnel, including 20 doctors, began a ten-day joint medical outreach with colleagues from Ghana's 37 military hospitals and the National **Disaster Management** Organisation (NADMO). This operation took place under the Medical Field Logistics Assistance Group programme to promote interoperability between the two sides, and involved undertaking medical, dental and veterinary outreach services in three communities in Dangbe West, as well as classroom instruction, field training and mass casualty exercises. On 26 October, **floods** from torrential rain exposed the poor drainage system in Accra, leaving 14 people dead and 43,087 affected in other ways. NADMO responded on 31 October by distributing relief items to victims. It was estimated that the flood insurance claims amounted to $ 20 m.

Continual gestures were made to bridge the **north/south divide** through development. The Millennium Development Authority (MiDA) invested over $ 5.3 m in the Tamale Water Extension Project for the Tamale metropolis and other districts in MiDA's intervention zone in the Northern Region. On 30 March, the president launched a GHS 90 m rural electrification project for the Upper West Region at Siiriyiri. A similar project in the Northern Region also began a few weeks later, to support the plans of the Savannah Accelerated Development Authority to transform the area. On 13 May, the Ghana Airport Company announced that Tamale Airport would be upgraded into an international airport. The government announced on 18 June that 129 senior high school girls from the three northern regions were to benefit from a GHS 74,000 scholarship scheme to guard against drop-out. On 22 June, the Environmental Protection Agency announced in Tamale that the three northern regions were to benefit from a $ 15.23 m sustainable land and water management project to reduce land degradation and enhance biodiversity. On 13 April, the GNA reported that the US had provided $ 1.5 m for a 7.5 km road linking Wa East to Nadowli, involving the construction of a steel bridge and two concrete bridges, to be completed in seven months by PW Ghanem Construction.

On 12 April, Crown Prince Haakon and Crown Princess Mette-Mariti of Norway visited Accra, and announced a grant of $ 6.5 m to the Ministry of Environment, Science and Technology, to address environmental challenges in oil exploration. On 13 April, a $ 350,000 agreement was signed in Accra between the Bank of Ghana and the Swiss government, representing the latter's support for the development of a web-based collateral registry facilitating access to credit for **small and medium-sized enterprises** (SMEs). The agreement was part of $ 1.25 m support from the Swiss government to the IFC, which is implementing the Secured Transactions Project with the Bank of Ghana, to ease access to finance for SMEs. The facilitation follows on from Ghana's Borrowers and Lenders Act 773, which was passed in 2008 to establish the collateral registry currently hosted by the Bank of Ghana. On 10 August, a € 3 m agreement was signed in Accra for DANIDA to support the advocacy project for SMEs through the Business Sector Advocacy Challenge (BUSAC) Fund Phase II. DANIDA, which had already committed $ 8 m to the advocacy project, is the leading organisation under BUSAC II, together with USAID, which recently contributed $ 3 m as co-donor.

On 16 July, Ghana and France signed three financing agreements in Accra during French Prime Minister Francois Fillon's two-day official visit, to support various sectors of the Ghanaian economy. The agreements were for a loan of € 40 m, and a grant of € 500,000 for the Ghana Urban Management Pilot Programme. Agreements were also signed for the funding of two local banks: CAL Bank ($ 10 m) and Fidelity Bank Limited ($ 8 m).

Ghana was the second largest export market for **South African goods** in West Africa, after Nigeria. During President Mills's visit to South Africa on 23 August, the host officials stated that exports of goods and services from South Africa to Ghana had grown from about $ 138 m to $ 416 m in ten years.

On 20 October, Ghana and Turkey signed a $ 1 bn trade agreement to strengthen bilateral trade. The two countries set themselves three years to achieve targets set by the Ghana-Turkey Joint Economic Commission in trade, agriculture and tourism. Turkey would assist Ghana to build capacity and infrastructure in these and the petroleum sectors. This followed the first meeting of the joint commission in March, when President Gül of Turkey visited Ghana with a delegation of 108 officials.

On 23 October, during a four-day official visit by Cuban Vice President Estaban Lazo Hernandez, Ghana signed a memorandum of understanding with Cuba for the training of 250 Ghanaians as **medical doctors**. The medical students were to be selected from deprived districts, where they would be appointed on completion of training.

On 21 December, Ghana signed a pre-feasibility studies contract with Inekon Group of the Czech Republic to undertake a three-month comprehensive study on potential **tram routes**. The studies carried potential for awarding contracts for tram links in a number of Ghanaian cities.

Adverse reports about Chinese companies generated public concern. It was reported on 9 September that the Tesano Divisional Police were investigating Chinese staff at the Chinese furniture company Bedmate for almost killing a Ghanaian co-worker, and it was reported on 2 October that the China Jiang International Construction Company, which was building a road at Akatsi, had been ordered to stop because the company was failing to comply with Ghana's **labour laws**. In December, the minister of lands and natural resources ordered a halt to developments that had encroached on the Ghana Atomic Energy Commission site, including one by the Chinese company Anainia, which had laid claim to a 164-acre plot at Dome-Kwabenya, where the nuclear facility is situated.

Mish Aviation Flying School, the first private **aviation** school in West Africa, was established in Tema Community 22 at the beginning of July to train senior high school graduates as full commercial pilots, using Cesna 172 aircraft. The institute would use the Federal Aviation Administration syllabus of the US Department of Transport. It was estimated that training would cost $ 58,652 per student for a maximum two-year training period.

Michael Amoah

Guinea

Guinea experienced a year of relative calm, welcome after many years of economic degradation and political tumult. At the end of 2010, Alpha Condé became the country's first president elected in contested elections, and he named his government by early 2011. Among his first initiatives was a re-evaluation of the mining code, which had never been favourable to Guinea. Despite a relative improvement in the country's stability and lessening of the levels of abuse of civilians by the security forces, many Guineans remained dissatisfied. Ethnic Fulbe accused the new president of singling them out for anti-democratic repression and excluding them from influential positions. Both opposition parties and ordinary Guineans were unhappy that legislative elections that had been slated for mid-2011 were postponed until 2012. On the international front, Guinea's relations with African (sub-)regional bodies and the rest of the world began to be normalised.

Domestic Politics

2011 was characterised by two dynamics: the naming and early functioning of the **new government** and the debate over legislative elections. At the end of 2010 and beginning of 2011, Alpha Condé named his government, headed by Mohammed Said Fofana. Many Guineans were surprised by its composition, which was skewed strongly toward Maninka co-ethnics and those who had supported Condé in the bitter electoral struggle against Cellou Dalein Diallo. The 2010 elections, which included candidates from nearly every ethnic group and marked an end to a disastrous two-year period of military rule, had not initially been ethnically polarised. However, in the five-month period between the first and second rounds of the election, the two second-round candidates, Alpha Condé (an ethnic Maninka) and Cellou Dalein Diallo (an ethnic Fulbe) became increasingly embroiled in pitched battles between these two ethnic groups/constituencies, each of which makes up roughly one-third of the population.

Many thus expected that Condé, in naming his government, would make special efforts at reconciliation, and that he would at least continue the tradition, which stretched back to independence, of naming ministers and secretary generals within the ministries in proportions such that the ethnic representation in these posts roughly mirrored the proportion of each ethnic group to the general population. Even if Sékou Touré had been accused of favouring his Maninka co-ethnics and Lansana Conté of favouring his Sosso people, they had still largely respected this unwritten rule. Dashing these hopes, Condé chose a government comprised overwhelmingly of ethnic **Maninka ministers**.

The government, which was still in place at the end of 2011, included 24 ministers from the related Maninka and Sosso ethnic groups, six from the Forest Region ('Région Forestière' – a slightly higher percentage than the 16% of the population that live in the region), and only seven ministers who were **ethnic Fulbe**, less than 19% of the ministerial posts, or roughly half the proportional representation many Guineans had expected. The choice of the Fulbe ministers was also characterised as being in repayment of political debts. Among the ethnic Fulbe who received ministerial posts, Ousmane Bah was named as cabinet minister of transport and public works. Bah had been the one Fulbe politician to have backed Condé in the second round of the presidential elections. Meanwhile, Christian Sow, appointed minister of justice, had been Condé's personal lawyer for 20 years, representing him in his treason trial in 1999–2000 and in various other matters in which he had opposed the Conté government. A third Fulbe minister, Sanoussy Sow, received the poisoned chalice of the ministry of youth and youth employment, where he was called upon to solve the intractable youth problem.

A fourth Fulbe minister, General Mamadou Korka Diallo, who became minister of animal husbandry, was one of the **outgoing junta members** who received a position in the new government. This was a separate but equally worrying problem. Other figures recycled from the Moussa 'Dadis' Camara period included El Hadj Papa Koly Kourouma, considered one of the most corrupt and nakedly ethnonationalist members of the Dadis regime, Mamadouba 'Toto' Camara, former number three within the junta, General Mathurin Bangoura, and Aboubacar Sidiki 'Idi Amin' Camara, a key figure in the December 2008 putsch, who had later fallen out of favour with Dadis and been jailed. Two other junta hard men, Claude 'Coplan' Pivi and Moussa Tiegboro Camara, were also made members of the Condé government. Both stood accused of being centrally involved in the 2009 massacre and in gang rapes of anti-government protesters in Guinea's main football stadium, among a variety of other illegal and abusive practices during the period of military rule.

Guineans understood the necessity of Condé's **managing the military**, which could stage another coup if it felt disrespected or excluded. The fact that Condé succeeded in handling this delicate issue was evidenced by the 1 November announcement that 4,000 soldiers would be retired from the army. This was a first but important step toward drawing the armed forces back down to a reasonable size. At Lansana Conté's death in 2008, estimates of the army's size hovered around 15,000, but between 2008 and 2010 this at least doubled. Nevertheless, both Guineans and international human rights observers signalled their dismay that Tiegboro Camara and Claude Pivi had been included in the government, given their atrocious track records. When combined with the government's ethnic imbalance, many observers and opposition figures complained that all signs pointed to Condé's desire to exercise uncontested autocratic power. Opposition figures such as Sidya Touré were scathing in their criticism of Condé as having abandoned all of the democratic ideals he claimed to have been fighting for during his decades in the opposition camp.

The same issues were debated between the administration and the opposition in the context of **legislative elections**, which were supposed to take place by June, as agreed within the parameters of the January 2010 Ouagadougou Peace Accords. Over the course of the year, these elections were pushed back to December, and by year's end had been postponed yet again. According to the Condé administration, existing electoral rolls were so flawed that a new list had to be drawn up. Opposition and civil society actors claimed that this was an attempt to rig future legislative elections, and also complained that the head of the 'Commission Electorale Nationale Indépendante' (CENI), was biased toward Condé's party, the 'Rassemblement du Peuple Guinéen'. CENI head Louceny Camara had been elected president of the commission to replace Ben Sékou Sylla in 2010. Both Camara and Sylla were indicted for electoral fraud during the first round of the 2010 presidential elections. Sylla died shortly after the accusations were brought but Camara – despite being sidelined in favour of a Malian interim CENI head for the second round of the 2010 elections – returned to his top spot in 2011. Most leaders of opposition parties demanded that Camara be removed before they would agree to participate in legislative polls. At the end of 2011, these differences had yet to be resolved.

The Condé administration was unequivocal in blaming such political blockages on opposition figures, both in Guinea and in the diaspora, who exaggerated and encouraged differences in pursuit of political advantage. Adding to the administration's sense of embattlement, on 19 July, assailants attacked Condé's residence, hitting it with rocket-propelled grenades. Condé called the attack an attempted assassination rather than a coup, as no efforts were made to take over the national television and radio stations, military bases or other strategic institutions. Several army officers were arrested immediately after the attack but, within days, opponents of the Condé government began to suggest that the attack was a set-up, created as a theatre piece (as many Guineans believe some of the 'plots' regularly discovered by the earlier Sékou Touré administration had been) in order to justify the arrest of perceived opponents. There was little evidence to support this conspiracy theory, but the overall **climate of mistrust** was an undeniable and important dynamic in Guinean politics.

Over the course of the year, there was a series of **violent clashes** in the capital, Conakry, between security forces and demonstrators. On 3 April, supporters of presidential election runner-up Cellou Dalein Diallo massed to greet him at the airport. The government had banned any such "demonstration" the day before, but many of Diallo's supporters ignored this. Security forces violently broke up the crowd, firing live bullets and reportedly wounding many. Unconfirmed reports claimed up to three supporters may have died. On 27 September, the day before the anniversary of the 2009 stadium massacre (also the anniversary of Guinea's vote for independence, so now a potently symbolic date), thousands marched and again clashed with security forces, leaving three dead.

Nevertheless, towards the end of the year, the country had stabilised considerably as compared with the previous five years, but most people's expectations of the new administration outstripped what any government could deliver in the circumstances. **Ethnic polarisation**, which had begun during the 2010 election campaign, also showed no signs of lessening, with Condé seemingly uninterested in attempting reconciliation and his opponents apparently promoting a cynical reading of anything the government did.

Foreign Affairs

The sanctions and bans of the previous two years were lifted. No longer ruled by putschists, the country was once again **eligible for assistance** from the UN, World Bank, and United States, and was reinstated by ECOWAS and the AU. On 16–17 February, the International Contact Group on Guinea held its final meeting in Conakry. The group, which had met over the course of 2009 and 2010, had accomplished its work in accompanying Guinea toward the election of a civilian government. In July, the same members (including representatives of ECOWAS, the AU, the US, France, the EU and the UN Office for West Africa) formed a Group of Friends of Guinea to serve in a more informal informational and support role. While many donors jump-started their assistance to the country, the EU continued to insist it would not release its next aid envelope before Guinea held parliamentary elections.

With politics less tempestuous than in recent years, many international visits appeared to have business motives. In February, **China**'s Foreign Affairs Minister Yang Jiechi visited Guinea, promising a grant and interest-free loan worth Yuan 170 m ($ 26 m), and more scholarships for Guinean students. In March, **former Brazilian president** Lula da Silva visited Guinea to celebrate the start of Brazilian mining company Vale's operations in the country. Three months later, as Anglo-Australian company Rio Tinto dug in to defend its mining rights in the same Simandou mountains where Vale operates, the UK's former prime minister, Tony Blair, visited Condé.

For his part, Condé visited heads of state around the world. This began the process of making up for the fact that Lansana Conté almost never left the country during the last decade of his rule, while the putschists who succeeded him were not recognised or invited to international gatherings. Condé thus had much work to do in order to raise **Guinea's international profile** in Africa and beyond. In January and early February, he made visits to Burkina Faso, Libya (still ruled by Kadhafi), Angola, and to the AU's heads of state gathering in Addis Ababa. In Addis, Condé met with his African peers as well as UN Secretary-General Ban Ki-moon. He also travelled to France in March, Turkey in May, Washington in late July, and to the UN General Assembly in New York in September.

Over the course of the year, **former junta head** Moussa Dadis Camara remained in Ouagadougou, Burkina Faso. It was not clear whether the Condé government wanted him to return any time soon. A large number of irregular fighters recruited and trained by Dadis' government in 2009 were let go and mostly returned to Dadis' native Forest Region. This area, adjacent to Côte d'Ivoire and Liberia, had long been a zone marked by smuggling and recruitment of young men interested in fighting in the Mano River Region's wars. Many of these young men had lived and sometimes fought in several of the countries that meet around Guinea's Forest Region, and some of them remained loyal to Dadis. Reports indicated that he was fully recovered from his gunshot wound to the head, and lived near the Burkinabè presidential palace. Meanwhile, the junta's original number two and Dadis' eventual successor, Sékouba Konaté, took up his position as AU High Representative for the operationalisation of the African Standby Force.

Guinea is a member, along with Sierra Leone, Liberia, and Côte d'Ivoire, of the **MRU**. On 2 July, the Union's Secretary-General, Guinean diplomat Habib Diallo, was killed in Sierra Leone in a car accident. Two weeks later, the MRU held its 20th summit in Monrovia. This was the first time Alpha Condé and Alassane Ouattara had visited Liberia as presidents of their countries. The four heads of state pledged to concentrate on patrolling the countries' porous borders and to look for regional opportunities for economic development.

Socioeconomic Developments

By now, Guineans had survived more than a decade of cross-border attacks, disastrous mismanagement and theft during the late Conté years, and two years of chaotic and criminalised military pillage before the Condé administration took over. Condé and his government received their highest marks from international players for beginning to restore order and predictability in the government, and for beginning to bring revenue into the state's coffers. Ordinary citizens were able to pursue the business of survival without constant fear of violence. However, real provision of services such as electricity, water, health care and education remained poor, and citizens' expectations largely outstripped the government's ability to deliver.

The **exchange rate** hovered between 6,400 and 7,400 Guinean francs (GF) to $ 1, remaining relatively stable over 2011. Black market exchange rates floated closer to GF 8,000 to $ 1. The Condé government attempted to shut down foreign exchange bureaus in order to exercise greater control over the exchange rate. Meanwhile, the IMF increased the holdings of foreign currency in Guinea's central bank in order to stabilise the Guinean franc. **Inflation** was estimated at between 16% and 20% for the year, down from the previous year's 20.8%. The Economist Intelligence Unit estimated 2011 economic **growth** at 4% (up from 2010's 2% – earlier estimated at 3% – which represented a per capita decline). GDP was estimated at $ 4.54 bn by the IMF.

Guinea's ranking in TI's **corruption** perception index was somewhat improved. At 164th of 182 countries, respondents still described Guinea as "highly corrupt", but it was no longer among the three lowest-ranking countries in the world, as had recently been the case. Similarly, in the World Bank's 'Doing Business' ranking, Guinea was placed 179th out of 183 countries. Trying to address these problems, the new government banned no-bid contracts and publicly committed itself to the guidelines suggested by the Extractive Industries Transparency Initiative. The audit of mining and other contracts signed during the period of junta rule began to connect words and deeds. Guineans and others were all watching to see whether this would primarily serve the purpose of pushing the last government's favourites out in order to make room for those of the new government, or whether all businesses would receive equal scrutiny.

In March, the IMF began negotiating a new relationship with the government, and advised Guinea on the way forward toward the completion point in the HIPC programme, at which international donors would begin erasing its **international debts**. International bankers remained happy that Kerfalla Yansané, a highly competent Conté-era central banker who took over as finance minister in early 2010, remained in place when Condé named his new government. The World Bank gave the government $ 78 m in budgetary support, which helped to jump-start ministries that had effectively lain dormant during the period of military rule, and assisted the government in managing its most pressing debts. The smash-and-grab approach of the junta had pushed Guinea's overdue internal and external debt up from $ 36 m at the end of 2008 (when Lansana Conté died and the junta took power) to $ 375 m at the end of 2010.

The Condé government focused much of its attention on rewriting the country's mining code. George Soros offered Condé the assistance of the International Senior Lawyer's Project and Revenue Watch Institute to help draft a new code. The new code raised the ceiling on Guinean equity in mining projects, boosting it to at least 30% from its former limit of 20%. It also increased taxes and royalties accruing to the government. The new code was approved by the acting legislative body, the National Transitional Council

('Conseil National de Transition') in September. Parallel to the reworking of the mining code, the cast of characters in Guinea's **mining sector** continued to shuffle and jockey for position. Russian Rusal, with bauxite operations in Friguia, much improved relations with the Condé government. Rusal had experienced poor relations with the two successive military-led governments in 2009 and 2010, as had Anglo-Australian giant Rio Tinto. Rio Tinto lost half of its Simandou iron ore exploration rights in 2009, when the Dadis Camara government revoked them and gave them to Benny Steinmetz Group Resources (BSGR), a Geneva-based company headed by Israeli diamond heir Steinmetz, who specialises in political arbitrage of mining deals in volatile settings such as Guinea, Sierra Leone and the DRC. BSGR soon sold half of its interest in Simandou on to Brazilian mining international Vale for a reported $ 2.5 bn. Vale and Steinmetz found themselves criticised by Minister of Mines Mohamed Lamine Fofana, who suggested the two companies would come under particular scrutiny in the context of a review of all mining licences. Given the consistent suggestions of illegal practice on the part of the junta, and specifically its minister of mines, Mahmoud Thiam, this was not surprising. Thiam had gone in three short years from his job as a Manhattan banker to Guinean minister of mines under the junta and New York representative of the China International Fund, the secretive Hong Kong-based fund that specialised in opaque mining-for-infrastructure deals in Angola and Guinea.

Vale publicly floated the possibility of pulling out. The reasons seemed to be both that the rewritten mining code gave foreign companies smaller possible profit margins, and that the issue of a **trans-Guinean railway** again complicated discussions. At the beginning of the year, the plan was to exfiltrate iron ore via the nearby Liberian railway that leads from Nimba County to the port of Buchanan, Liberia. At year's end, however, Vale and BSGR had once again signed up to a plan to build a 700 km trans-Guinean railway from the country's south-eastern corner to a deep-water port just south of Conakry. This infrastructure, called for by Guinea for nearly 40 years, remained a sticking point in the negotiations. It was estimated that the railway and port would cost at least $ 10 bn.

In September, Australian mining giant BHP Billiton hinted that it was suspending work on an alumina refinery it was building in partnership with Canadian and Middle Eastern investors. It was unclear what roles the new mining code, political instability and declining Chinese demand for aluminium played in the suspension. While BHP's and Vale's fortunes looked worse, Rio Tinto's improved significantly, not least as a result of a **$ 700 m settlement** paid to the government to make amends for not having moved to the active mining stage, and to solidify Rio's claims on Simandou iron ore blocks 3 and 4. Mohamed Diaré, the minister for the budget, said that $ 250 m of this sum would be held in an account destined to improve electricity production and distribution to the population. The government used part of these funds to give Guinean soldiers pay rises that had been promised by the outgoing Konaté government, and the rest was slated for infrastructure, education and other sectors.

If revenues continued to increase and were applied effectively by the government, citizens could begin to see changes in 2012 and 2013. Still, it remained likely that, as in neighbouring Liberia and Sierra Leone, the devastation of the past 15 years would place a drag on the rhythm of change, leaving many angry and dissatisfied at the government's performance.

Mike McGovern

Guinea-Bissau

Macroeconomic developments and political reform efforts were encouraging. Security sector reform made progress but still had a long way to go. An alleged coup attempt that rocked the country in late December was a set-back, leading to the arrest of the naval chief of staff and other officers. The EU temporarily froze parts of its assistance programme in response to the April 2010 coup attempt, which was allegedly undertaken by the acting army general chief of staff and the naval chief of staff, who were also among several high ranking officers accused of drug-trafficking. In mid-year the opposition organised protest rallies against the 'Partido para a Independência da Guiné e Cabo Verde' (PAIGC) government.

Domestic Politics

On 26 December, residents of Bissau's Santa Luzia neighbourhood reported machine gun fire and rocket blasts from nearby army headquarters, after mutinous soldiers had apparently tried to arrest the army general chief of staff, António Indjai. Movements of army units, some of them allegedly originating from the town of Mansôa, about 60 km east of Bissau, could be observed around army bases in the capital. Soldiers reportedly erected barricades in some areas of Bissau, with some demanding an increase in pay.

Rumours spoke of a **coup attempt** by naval chief of staff José Bubo NaTchuto, who – after publicly denying involvement – was arrested in the course of the day. He was subsequently detained in the Mansôa barracks in conditions that were said to be difficult. He had for years been considered one of the main destabilising figures in the county. In the run-up to these events NaTchuto and Indjai accused each other of involvement in drug-trafficking: on 19 December a plane had reportedly landed on a road linking Mansôa and Bambadinca – close to a village where Indjai allegedly owns a house – to unload drugs. Other high-ranking officials arrested were Watna NaLaie, vice chief of the army, Cletch NaGhanha, and more than 20 soldiers.

Prime Minister Carlos Gomes Junior was reportedly brought to safety by units of **MISSANG** ('Missão de Cooperação Técnica de Segurança Angolana na Guiné-Bissau') and his residence was secured by police. A couple of days later, Gomes denied that he had fled to the Angolan embassy after opposition politician Victor Pereira accused him of selling out to Angola, dismissing MISSANG as foreign 'occupation force'. While Indjai spoke at a press conference on the day of the coup attempt, the minister of education initially tried to downplay the events, portraying them as an attack on a military arms depot, but government and army officials convened immediately. The residence of former minister Robert Cacheu was destroyed by rockets. Cacheu was an opponent of Gomes within the PAIGC and had been accused of involvement in a 2009 coup attempt. He and some members of parliament (including former ministers Francisco Conduto de Pina and Marcelino Cabral) were suspected of being involved in the present uprising. Cabral gave himself up to the authorities. **Search operations** in army barracks in Bissau led to exchanges of gunfire and left one soldier dead and another wounded. A retired police officer, Iaia Dabó – a brother of Baciro Dabó, who was assassinated in 2009 – was killed on 27 December by members of the Rapid Intervention Police, although he had allegedly wanted to surrender. He had been accused of killing a police officer earlier that day.

The **international community**, among them the UN secretary-general, the representative of the EU in Bissau, European ambassadors and the AU Commission President Jean Ping – the latter visiting Bissau on 28 December – condemned the events and confirmed their continued support for the government. After a meeting in Burkina Faso on 30 December, Ping asked Burkina Faso's President Blaise Campaoré to mediate in the crisis. On 29 December, Indjai presented to the media two soldiers, who confessed their involvement in the coup and spoke about the poor state of soldiers' living quarters. They gave up a large cache of arms, which they had stored in their residences, and confirmed that Indjai and Gomes had been the targets of the coup plotters. If the coup had been successful, they would have been temporarily replaced by NaLaie (as interim army general chief of staff) and Cacheu (as interim prime minister). Among the reasons for the coup attempt, observers advanced opposition to Gomes within the ruling PAIGC, the strengthening of state governance, which was feared by some army officials, and Indjai's possible inability to continue with security sector reform in the face of NaTchuto's interests.

On 31 May, the public prosecutions office announced the partial closure of files related to the **2009 assassinations**, including the investigations against Cacheu and Conduto de Pina. A week later, the office let it be known that the cases of Baciro Dabó and Helder Proença would be transferred to the military prosecutions office, but this led to a dispute over jurisdictions when the superior military court returned the cases to the public prosecutions office on 21 July. Attorney General Amine Saad was dismissed on 2 August, accused of negligence, and Edmundo Mendes succeeded him. Early in November, Joseph Mutaboba – head of the UN Integrated Peacebuilding Office in Guinea-Bissau (UNIOGBIS) – proposed handing over the investigations to the ICC. Apparently due to pressure by some politicians and army officials, the judicial authorities were reluctant to investigate the cases, thus risking further destabilisation.

On 14 July, there was a series of peaceful **demonstrations** organised by a dozen extra-parliamentary opposition parties led by the 'Partido da Renovação Social'. They criticised the government for the high cost of living and called for its dismissal and clarification of the 2009 assassinations – inter alia of late President Vieira and the army general chief of staff NaWaie. The PAIGC organised counter-demonstrations.

The repeated absences of **State President** Sanhá for undisclosed health reasons led to speculation, especially by his rivals, Gomes Junior and parliamentary speaker Raimundo Pereira, about his successor and about the possibility of an institutional power vacuum. On 22 November, Sanhá was hospitalised in Dakar, Senegal, from where he was taken to Paris on 26 November. He had not returned to Bissau by year's end.

The position of the **media** remained critical. On 20 April, the government cancelled a decision taken two days earlier that had ordered the closure of the weekly 'Última Hora' for slandering the country's image and condemning the government record. The paper had referred to a US State Department report that accused Indjai of being behind the murder of State President Vieira in 2009. Instead, the government only reprimanded the media. It was reported in November that state-owned national radio continued to suffer from lack of finance and appropriate equipment. The problematic **human rights** record was echoed by the resignation of the head of the judicial police, Lucinda Barbosa, on 13 May. She gave as her reason death threats she had received in the wake of anti-drug-trafficking investigations. On 8 June, parliament passed a law prohibiting **female genital mutilation**, a practice widespread in the country's Muslim regions; the first prosecution was brought in October.

Reports by the landmine removal group HUMAID in May said that the country would become free of landmines in 2012. The landmines were left over from the war for independence in the 1960s–70s, the military conflict of 1998–99 and the Casamance conflict.

On 25 July, the prime minister presented a new national plan to fight **HIV/AIDS**. The prevalence rate was estimated at 3.6% (about 52,000 infected persons). The government was to receive $ 19 m over three years from the Global Fund for this programme.

Drug trafficking remained a problem. The prime minister called for vigilance at all the country's airstrips and planned to make inoperative one particular airfield (out of 24), which was often used by drug-traffickers. Indjai threatened to shoot down illegal aircraft. On 10 February, police burnt 76 kg of cocaine and 800 kg of cannabis seized in 2007. On 22 February, the public prosecutor issued a circular calling for better investigation of drug-trafficking. In late September, two Portuguese nationals of Bissau-Guinean origin were arrested at Belfast airport, Northern Ireland, for attempted drug-trafficking and, on 26 October, for the first time ever, a Cape Verdean was sentenced in Bissau for drug-trafficking. The government's plan to tackle drug-trafficking and organised crime was to come into operation from 2011 to 2014.

Foreign Affairs

Security sector reform remained a major issue. A peace mission by the AU, ECOWAS and CPLP announced on 6 January and due to start in February did not take place. Several meetings of ECOWAS and CPLP discussed issues concerning Guinea-Bissau, such as security sector reform and maritime security. Following an intervention by Portugal, the EU postponed a decision to freeze bank accounts and ban the entry of high-ranking officials – inter alia Indjai and NaTchuto, who were accused of drug-trafficking and plotting a coup in 2010. However, EU assistance was suspended and the government tried to avert more far-reaching sanctions. The EU consequently opened consultations on democratic progress in line with the Cotonou Agreement, and this resulted on 19 July in the restoration of cooperation subject to compliance with democratic principles. On 25 February, the UNSC also appealed for security sector reform and for further efforts to combat drug-trafficking and the culture of impunity. On 21 March, it became known that Angola would send about 200 soldiers as part of MISSANG to train the country's security forces over a period of two years. The soldiers were accommodated in a former five-star hotel in Bissau that had been bought by Angola. Co-financed by the UN Peacebuilding Fund, the EU and Guinea-Bissau, security sector reform should start in September, with the goal, reported on 30 June, of reducing security force numbers from 7,000 to 4,000. On 23 September President Sanhá reaffirmed the military's commitment to reform, but in late November Defence Minister Baciro Djá and the UN, including the secretary-general, called for international assistance, lamenting that pension funds for former military personnel had almost dried up. However, on 1 December Indjai threatened to resign if ECOWAS sent a peace mission and, on 12 December, 350 young adults went to Angola for a six-month security training programme. On 21 December, the UNSC extended the UNIOGBIS mandate until 28 February 2013. At year's end the long expected signing of a memorandum of understanding with ECOWAS and CPLP was still pending. It would potentially involve implementation of a roadmap for security sector reform agreed earlier in the year, in particular with regard to the operationalisation of the pension fund.

On 12 March, a Guinea-Bissau-**Libya** friendship organisation held a pro-Kadhafi rally in Bissau. The government condemned the NATO airstrikes on Libya that took place on 4 May. On 16 September, the state president withdrew the offer of asylum previously made by the prime minister to Kadhafi – Guinea-Bissau is not a state party to the ICC. Kadhafi had in the past supported Guinea-Bissau financially, including in the course of presidential election campaigns, and personally mediated in the 2009 crisis. Libya's fruitless involvement in a hotel complex in Bissau was criticised for serving merely to avoid taxes, and the regime was blamed for incompetence and inefficiency. In October, the government removed the rebel National Transitional Council flag from Libya's embassy.

On 31 August, Guinea-Bissau and **South Africa** signed an agreement on development and democracy cooperation, which also included the opening of a Bissau-Guinean embassy in Pretoria. Relations with **Cape Verde**, which were once very close but deteriorated after a coup d'état in Guinea-Bissau in 1980, improved after a visit in late November by Prime Minister José-Maria Neves of Cape Verde to Bissau, promising the upgrading of the new consulate to the status of embassy.

On 21 November, Bissau-Guinean **veterans** who fought on the Portuguese side during the war for independence accused the former colonial power of not having paid their pensions, in contravention of existing treaties.

Socioeconomic Developments

Crucial progress was made with regard to **economic performance, reforms and debt relief**. On 26 January, the AfDB announced that Guinea-Bissau had benefited from debt relief worth $ 60.4 m plus exceptional additional debt relief to the tune of $ 23.7 m. The first agricultural credit bank was launched – with Senegalese capital – in Farim on 16 March. Assisted by the World Bank, UNDP, EU and AfDB, a centre opened in May for the accelerated registration of business enterprises, leading to a sharp decrease in the time and formalities required to start a business. The Paris Club agreed on 10 May to cancel debts of $ 256 m and an additional $ 27 m owed on a bilateral basis. The debt that remained totalled $ 280 m. The media reported on 24 May that Portugal had cancelled a further $ 108 m of debt and, on the same day, following the second review of Guinea-Bissau's economic performance under a three-year extended credit facility arrangement launched in 2010, the IMF authorised the country to draw $ 3.85 m. The World Bank granted $ 6.4 m for public finance management reform on 21 June. In July the government endorsed the second National Poverty Reduction Strategy Paper (DENARP II), to be implemented in the period 2011–2015. The foundation stone of the first UEMOA office was laid in Bissau on 16 August. On 20 September, the IMF gave a positive assessment of economic performance in its third review. Owing to a good cashew harvest, higher prices, improved fiscal income and buoyant construction activity, the IMF expected a GDP growth of 5.3% and inflation of 4.8%, making positive predictions for 2012 if the government continued prioritising oversight of spending, revenue mobilisation, reduction of arrears, and reforms. This progress was symbolised by the installation of the country's first traffic lights – as part of a first phase $ 300,000 UNIOGBIS project to light up streets and initiate police patrols – and the re-opening in March of the country's only brewery, now owned by a Moroccan company. On 5 December, the IMF authorised another disbursement worth $ 3.77 m, bringing disbursements to $ 23.6 m of a total $ 33.3 m. Corruption remained an issue, however, and employees in the public transport sector threatened strikes over police abuse in mid-December.

In the field of **South-South cooperation**, Angola announced in December a credit line of $ 25 m for economic development. This followed an initial credit of $ 600 m in February. Negotiations focused, among other things, on the intensification of economic exchange, including exploration for bauxite in Guinea-Bissau. Critics questioned the Angolan commitment in view of that country's own socioeconomic needs. China financed the reconstruction of the presidential palace, which had been destroyed in 1999, and work began on 20 October.

As in previous years, several **strikes** took place in support of demands for better working conditions and the payment of overdue or higher salaries. Despite improvements in public sector pay, the strikers included judges and judicial employees, health workers and school teachers. In April, the government increased public transport fares because of rises in fuel prices. On 11 May, various consumer associations protested against the high price of basic consumer goods.

The country attracted various foreign investments and migrants' **remittances** made a moderate contribution to GDP (3.9%).

The significance of the **fishing sector** was clear and, on 31 March, the World Bank approved an $ 8 m loan to improve the country's ability to control and manage the fishing sector. In addition, a new one-year provisional fishing agreement with the EU was reached on 15 June, after Guinea-Bissau had asked for higher payments in previous and protracted negotiations. Although the first commercial fishing port, funded by the AfDB at a cost of € 10 m was inaugurated in mid-September, the country's revenue from fishing shrank as a result of illegal catches and overfishing.

The Cape Verdean Airline TACV considered offering a link between Bissau and Lisbon in July and, on 26 September, an airlink was announced between Bissau and Casablanca.

On 17 May, the World Bank approved a $ 2.2 m grant to improve the **water supply and electricity** sector in Bissau, complementing a 2010 grant. The capital suffers from structural deficiency in the supply of energy. Three new generators (producing a total of 3 MW) worth € 1.25 m arrived on 6 October, and the AfDB promised to finance three more generators (producing a further 15 MW) in 2012. The World Bank emergency **food security** support project, in place since 2008 and phasing-out in September, provided about 14,000 student meals. It also improved paddy rice production. It was strengthened by the EU food crisis rapid response facility trust fund, which was active from October 2010 until August 2011 and provided 28,000 meals for students. In February, it was announced that follow-up multi-donor funding had been arranged with ECOWAS, including $ 7 m for Guinea-Bissau. Despite these efforts, the country had to import 30,000 tonnes of rice in mid-year, owing to a three-month shortage, which led to a sharp increase in prices. On 18 April, the government signed a contract with UNICEF and the EU to provide wells and sanitation in the south of the country in the next three years.

The Luso-Bissau-Guinean oil company Petromar and the Portuguese 'Instituto Camões' renewed a teacher training agreement on 6 June. In June, there were media reports of secondary **education** reform.

Christoph Kohl

Liberia

Preparations for the presidential and parliamentary elections in October dominated the socio-political landscape. Incumbent President Ellen Johnson Sirleaf was easily re-elected after a controversial second-round poll, which the main challenger, Winston Tubman, boycotted. Though her record for combating widespread graft was decidedly mixed, Sirleaf remained the darling of the donor community and an international superstar. On 7 October, amidst local concerns about nepotism and the lack of a coherent policy of reconciliation, Sirleaf was awarded the Nobel Peace prize along with Leymah Gbowee (a Liberian peace activist) and Tawakkoi Karman (a Yemeni pro-democracy activist). The prize, however, probably had little impact on Liberian voters, though it was an indisputable boost for Sirleaf's supporters, many of them women. Sirleaf had previously signalled that she was determined to combat corruption head-on by sacking her entire cabinet, but by year's end she had re-appointed many of the ministers – noting that corruption in the country was "systemic" and that it would take more than "naming and shaming" to combat it. Events in neighbouring Côte d'Ivoire had an adverse effect in the first half of the year. Unemployment remained high despite massive foreign investment in the iron ore and other extractive sectors, and despite an economic growth rate of 7.3%. On 16 September, the UNSC adopted resolution 2008, extending the mandate of the UN Mission in Liberia (UNMIL) until 30 September 2012. UNMIL personnel included 7,782 troops,

1,288 police and 130 military observers, and the mission cost $ 525.6 m a year – more than the national budget.

Domestic Politics

On 24 January, Sirleaf delivered her annual **state of the nation** message under the theme "Our nation is heading in the right direction". She noted that the October elections would be a crucial test of Liberia's nascent democracy and hard-won peace, and drew attention to the ongoing post-election violence in Côte d'Ivoire. "We are at a crossroads in our country's history," she said. "We only have to look across the border to know we could go backwards as easily as we could go forward." Sirleaf's anxiety reflected wider concerns about the rising tensions in the country ahead of the polls.

The main opposition party, the Congress for Democratic Change (CDC), called for a boycott of the constitutional **referendum** to be held on 23 August, disputing, among other things, the neutrality of James Fromayan, the chairman of the National Elections Commission (NEC). On that day, voters had to decide on several constitutional revisions, including the date when presidential elections should be held, the residency requirement for presidential candidates and the majority required to win the election. Voter turnout was low (34.2%) and none of the key referendum proposals – including reducing the minimum residency requirement for candidates from ten years to five, raising the retirement age for judges to 75, and moving the election date to November – was endorsed.

Four linked issues were seen to contribute to a tense electoral atmosphere: youth unemployment, lack of education, weak security and the need for national reconciliation. Some 60% of Liberians were said to be under the age of 35, while 64% of the population lived below the poverty line. The **electoral process** began in earnest with voter registration from 10 January to 6 February. The NEC had projected that 2.1 m people, out of Liberia's population of 3.5 m, would register, and 1,780 registration centres were set up across the country. The government declared 6 February a public holiday to allow the maximum number of people to register, and a one-week extension was granted by the NEC. Nevertheless, only 1.7 m people registered. When registration for the October elections began on 10 January, UNMIL quickly mobilised support to transport registration materials by helicopter to remote areas. In January, the UN Peace Building Office in the country rolled out the three-year Liberia Priority Plan, designed to strengthen the security sector and to support the rule of law and national reconciliation.

There was heightened concern for much of the first half of the year about the negative impact of the **Ivorian crisis**. In April, Liberian security personnel announced the arrest of Isaac Chegbo (aka Bob Marley), a notorious Liberian former warlord, who was accused by the UN of organising massacres while fighting in Côte d'Ivoire as a mercenary on the side of former president Laurent Gbagbo. In June, a UN Panel of Experts report estimated that 4,500 Liberian mercenaries had been "hired and deployed" by Gbagbo during the conflict in Côte d'Ivoire, and that many of them might have returned to Liberia, posing a significant threat there. Also in June, 88 suspected Ivorian combatants were arrested and detained in a local prison after crossing the border into Liberia. On 14 June, Liberian security agencies seized a significant number of weapons and ammunition from a cache in River Gee County, believed to have been hidden by a group of Ivorian fighters who had entered the country. UNMIL destroyed the weapons and ammunition in July and the Liberian authorities arrested 37 people in connection with the arms seizure.

Liberia continued to experience serious **violence** related to **land disputes**, a perennial security issue since the end of the civil war. Triggered by the return of more than 100,000 refugees, some of whom found that their land had been occupied illegally, land disputes continued to pose threats to long-term stability. In March, about 50 people, allegedly from Maryland County, armed with cutlasses and single-barrel shotguns, attacked a village in Grand Kru County, setting two houses ablaze. The national police and UNMIL intervened and brought the situation under control, and officers of the Emergency Response Unit of the Liberia National Police (LNP) were subsequently deployed to maintain the peace. There was also serious violence in connection with **labour disputes**, which the UN projected would continue, given the presence of large plantations, the importance of timber and the activities of extractive industries generally. On 26 May, 30 workers of the Cavalla Rubber Corporation in Maryland County raided a local court, where four of their fellow workers were to appear. Elements of the Emergency Response Unit, the paramilitary police, shot and killed one of them. Subsequently, a group of residents burned down two of the plantation buildings. In late March, protests in Monrovia regarding teachers' salary arrears escalated into violent clashes between students and LNP Support Unit officers, resulting in the temporary closure of the city's schools.

In June, **communal tensions** between the Mano and Krahn ethnic groups in Sowaken Village, Grand Gedeh County, resulted in a group of about 20 members of the Krahn ethnic group attacking and destroying several houses and looting belongings of members of the Mano and Gio ethnic groups. As usual, UNMIL police assisted the weak and inefficient police to restore calm. In September, the UN reported that there had been six incidents of **mob violence** against police authorities and infrastructure since the beginning of the year.

Political manoeuvring intensified in the run-up to the polls. On 30 April, Winston Tubman, a former UN diplomat and nephew of Liberia's longest-serving ruler, William Tubman, won the CDC presidential primary in Kakata, Margibi County. He polled 118 votes, to win from former CDC presidential candidate and popular football star, George Opong Weah, who received 111 votes. Sirleaf's Unity Party co-opted leading figures from the regime of former president Charles Taylor (discredited, but still-popular), such as Edwin Melvin Snowe and Lewis Browne. Sirleaf made maximum use being the incumbent, including having her banners placed on major government and private buildings. The opposition complained but to no avail. In August, one minor political party, the

Movement for Progressive Change, started legal proceedings before the supreme court, challenging the right of six candidates, including Sirleaf, to stand in the presidential elections on the grounds that they did not meet the 1986 constitution's ten-year residency requirement, but the case was dismissed. Campaigning was marked by less than edifying **posturing**. On 10 September, as a sign of her political power and popularity, Sirleaf held a mass rally in Monrovia, which attracted some 500,000 people and where she called the opposition candidates "ugly baboons". Tubman for his part claimed that "the only way we'll lose is if we are cheated", while Dew Tuan Wreh Mayson of the National Democratic Congress called the president a "419-er" (shorthand for fraud) for going back on her decision to stand for only one term.

At the **presidential elections** on 11 October, 16 candidates, including Sirleaf, ran, but none received more than 50% of the votes, which would have avoided a run-off. Sirleaf led with 43.9%. Second-placed Tubman, who won 32.7%, claimed that the polls had been rigged and announced that he was withdrawing from the run-off slated for 8 November. A day before the second round, Tubman's supporters clashed with the LNP, who opened fire, killing at least one protester. The run-off was conducted on schedule, but turnout was predictably low, probably due to the opposition boycott and pre-election violence. Sirleaf, backed by Prince Yormie Johnson of the National Union for Democratic Progress, who had won third place in the first round, received 607,618 votes (or 90.7% of the total votes cast) and was declared re-elected for another six-year term. In the elections for the 73-member House of Representatives, only 33% of sitting MPs were re-elected. Female representation dropped substantially, from 12.5% to 7%. On 18 November, the UNSC issued a statement praising the election as "free, fair and transparent".

Issues relating to **drug trafficking** and organised crime remained salient. The UN Secretary-General noted in his report on Liberia in August that the country continued to be "vulnerable to drug trafficking. Hard drugs, including heroin and cocaine, transit through Liberia in limited amounts." The report also noted that domestic production of marijuana "is flourishing and in many areas is thought to be replacing other agricultural activities, with large amounts crossing into neighbouring countries. There are also reports of human trafficking using similar routes." Liberia is a member of the West Africa Coast Initiative, a sub-regional action plan to address the growing problem of illicit drug trafficking and organised crime.

Foreign Affairs

On 10 February, Foreign Minister Togo McIntosh announced that events in **Côte d'Ivoire** threatened to upend the upcoming elections. Thousands of Ivorians were fleeing to Liberia amidst post-election violence in their country, and the UN predicted in January that the number of Ivorian refugees would reach 100,000 by April. In this respect, Sirleaf continued to play a lead role in ECOWAS and the MRU. She was actively engaged in mobilising the MRU to support the ECOWAS stance on Gbagbo, though she expressed public opposition to military intervention by the sub-regional bloc (probably for fear of the immediate repercussions on the security of her fragile country).

The **US**, which leads on Liberia in the UNSC, continued to be Liberia's key international partner and promoter. Sirleaf visited the US several times during the year, including in September (a month before the elections), where she was fêted by US Secretary of State Hillary Clinton, with whom she maintains a personal friendship.

Sirleaf visited **Nigeria** twice in September, soliciting assistance for the elections. Nigerian President Goodluck Jonathan promised to provide 600 police officers to help maintain order during polling, but Liberian opposition politicians were very critical of this. Sirleaf also travelled to oil-rich **Angola** on 11–12 September, and there were reports that, while she was there, the Angolan government asked her to help mend fences with the new Ivorian President Alassane Ouattara. Angola had supported Gbagbo during the electoral stand-off in Côte d'Ivoire, helping to have the AU block the ECOWAS plan on military intervention.

Socioeconomic Developments

On 4 and 7 February, a joint meeting in New York of the executive boards of UNDP, the UN Population Fund, UNICEF, UN-Women and WFP decided on a programme of humanitarian relief and longer-term development assistance to Liberia. On 27 September, the country's economic prospects brightened when the revived ArcelorMittal, in its iron ore concessions area in Nimba County, made its first shipment of **iron ore** in 20 years. The chief executive officer of ArcelorMittal, billionaire UK businessman Lakshmi Mittal, attended the occasion of the first shipment.

There were also reports of substantial deep-water oil off Liberia's coast, and African Petroleum, a UK-based company, bought several blocks for **exploration**. Thirteen offshore blocks were demarcated and auctioned in 2011. The other companies that won licences were Repsol, Chevron, Anadarko and Woodside Petroleum. In fact, in January, the Africa Governance Initiative (Tony Blair's foundation) estimated FDI in Liberia since 2006 at over $ 16 bn, perhaps the highest FDI per capita in the world.

However, government revenue from these investments was still small, since most of the companies had not started making profits and were therefore not paying royalties or income tax. The UN reported in August that revenue from the commercial **forestry sector** was "short of expectations", with operators paying only $ 2.1 m of the $ 13.5 m owed during the fiscal year 2010–2011. Sirleaf's government established a task force to review the tax regime and assess whether easing some requirements might improve company compliance. The Forestry Development Authority also issued procedures for community forestry development committees to access and manage funds on behalf of affected communities legally entitled to benefit-sharing.

In May, the National Legislature passed the annual **budget** to the tune of $ 458.9 m for the fiscal year 2011/12, which was 26% higher than the previous year's budget. It set a minimum wage for civil servants at $ 100 a month, one of the highest in the sub-region. Formal sector employment, however, remained at about 15%, and inflation was at a high 8.1%, compared with 7.2% in 2010. This reflected vulnerability to global **price increases** of fuel and food (Liberia imports about two thirds of its food supply).

Lansana Gberie & Aaron Weah

Mali

Rising security threats in the northern regions increasingly preoccupied Malian citizens and international observers. The influx of thousands of well-armed Tuareg soldiers from post-Kadhafi Libya significantly altered the already fragile power balance in the north to the advantage of the Tuareg separatist agenda. Moreover, kidnappings conducted by the al-Qaida in the Islamic Maghreb (AQIM) extended southwards and a Salafist movement ('Ansar Aldine') rapidly gained influence in the Kidal region. Economically, the country was dealt a serious blow by the poor and erratic rainfall, which seriously affected the agricultural sector and led to a doubling of prices for staple foods. By the end of the year, millions of Malians faced severe food insecurity. Regional cooperation slowly increased to combat the shared security challenges. Various donors also augmented their financial assistance, enabling the government to increase socioeconomic and security investment in the northern regions.

Domestic Politics

An attack on the French embassy on 5 January, conducted by a Tunisian man trained by AQIM but acting independently of that organisation, marked the start of a troubled year characterised by increased levels of **insecurity**, which was fuelled by four principal factors. A first notable security threat in the northern region stemmed from a former Algerian Salafist group that had rebranded itself in 2007 as the local branch of **AQIM**. Two French youngsters whom they had abducted in Niamey, Niger, tragically died on 8 January in a failed liberation attempt on Malian territory near the Niger border. Three of the seven hostages abducted by AQIM in Arlit, Niger, in September 2010 were released in Mali on 24 February. A joint operation by Mali and Mauritania against an AQIM basis near their mutual border on 24 June was marked by a serious lack of coordination, causing severe collateral damage. After three weeks of fighting, the Malian army gained control over the area on 19 July, but reports released on 9 August indicated that AQIM had retaken control of the territory. On 24 November, two Frenchmen, Philippe Verdon and Serge Lazarevic, were kidnapped at their hotel in Hombori, which marked a significant shift southwards of the **kidnapping threat**. The next day, three tourists (a Dutchman, a Swede and a South African) were taken from a hotel in Timbuktu, while a fourth (German) tourist was shot dead when he resisted his abductors. On 13 December, the government said it had arrested four alleged kidnappers of the two Frenchmen, who appeared to have been handed over to AQIM.

Alongside the AQIM threat, the northern regions became more heavily involved in the Libyan conflict as many (Tuareg) youngsters joined pro-Kadhafi forces in the first months of the year, allegedly being paid $ 10,000 to sign up. In the second half of 2011, **thousands of Tuareg soldiers** who had served in the Libyan army returned to Mali after the fall of the regime. This significantly altered the fragile balance of power in the northern regions. The influx, in which former Tuareg rebellion leader Ibrahim Ag Bahanga played an important facilitating role, involved well-trained soldiers and senior officers who brought heavy weaponry with them. On 25 August, approximately ten heavily armed pick-up trucks coming from Libya and passing through Niger were witnessed entering the country. On 14 October, the UN released an alarming statement warning of the return of hundreds of former Kadhafi allies and, two days later, around 80 vehicles transporting 400 well-armed Tuaregs, mainly from the Chamanamasse, Ifoghas and Imghad tribes, arrived in the north. Only the last group attended a welcoming ceremony organised by the governor of Kidal on 18 October. A diplomatic source in Bamako indicated that a total of some 2,000 men had returned by that date, but stated that the real number could be well above 4,000. A ministerial delegation travelled to Kidal, Gao and Timbuktu, trying to persuade the returning fighters to join the army. A group of roughly 300 Imghad Tuaregs are believed to have taken up the offer.

Despite the death of Bahanga in a road accident on 26 August, the majority of Tuareg factions established on 15 October the 'Mouvement National de Libération de l'Azawad' (MNLA), together with Tuareg youngsters calling themselves the 'Mouvement National de l'Azawad', and this helped to establish a **united Tuareg front**. The group published an essay through the press association 'Toumast', which contained a detailed analysis of both national and international political factors, concluding that the establishment of an independent country, 'Azawad', should take place "now or never". Unity was not preserved, however, as Iyad Ag Ghali, an Ifogha Tuareg most influential in the Kidal region and converted to the Salafist movement by Pakistani preachers, broke ranks. Being refused the leadership of the MNLA, the former diplomat established the **Ansar Aldine movement** aiming to introduce Sharia law in northern Mali and beyond.

A fourth destabilising factor in the north concerned the rapid spread of **transnational smuggling networks** (engaged in trafficking cocaine, weapons, people, cigarettes, etc.) in which both Tuareg and AQIM, as well as government employees, were involved. Tensions between the state and the smugglers increased and there were also conflicts between competing smuggling groups. A group linked to the militia of a Fulani arms smuggler, Sadjo Diallo, attacked the Ouatagouna army base, near Gao, on 22 March. On 10 September, a group of Malian smugglers clashed with a Sahrawi group near Timbuktu, both groups taking members of the other group and local people hostage.

The government tried to respond to these threats by continuing with its divide and rule strategy, not only aiming to incite conflicts between al-Qaida and the Tuareg but also encouraging intra-Tuareg disputes. The executive discouraged public debate on the government's strategy and policies (whether in parliament or by political parties), revealing the authoritarian nature of Malian consensus democracy and frustrating the channelling of popular discontent. On 3 April, President Touré announced a **cabinet reshuffle** following the resignation of Prime Minister Modibo Sidibé on 30 March. Former defence minister and director of the intelligence service Soumeylou Boubèye Maiga, a heavyweight of the 'Alliance pour la Démocratie au Mali' (ADEMA) and himself born in Gao, was appointed minister of foreign affairs. His principal task was to enhance regional cooperation in combating the mounting security threats. Other major changes concerned the appointment of Mali's first **female prime minister**, Kaidama Cissé, and the cooption of two of the three parliamentary opposition parties into the government (the 'Rassemblement pour le Mali' and the 'Parti pour la Renaissance Nationale'). The latter was a notable exception amidst the political silence on the northern troubles and brought together 30 MPs, hundreds of representatives from civil society and political representatives from the region on 10–11 December to discuss the challenges. Earlier, on 9 August, Touré had launched the 'Programme spécial pour la paix, la sécurité et le développement dans le nord du Mali' (at a cost of CFAfr 32 bn), which was meant to increase investment in local development programmes and build up military capacity. Meanwhile, Touré tried to combat the rising Tuareg threat by working closely with an Imghad militia that was frustrated by the Ifoghas dominance over other Tuareg groups and by training and arming local civic groups in northern towns. The government also actively tried to recruit Tuareg returnees from Libya, offering senior army positions to their leaders. On 3 December, Touré received a delegation of returned Imghad Tuareg, led by two senior officers, at the presidential palace and on 22 December he received a delegation of Ifoghas Tuareg. But when he called for an extraordinary session of the National Defence Council, on 6 December, he must have been aware of the increased difficulty of buying off various Tuareg leaders, observing the increased cooperation between the various Tuareg factions.

Another matter that dominated politics was the second reading of the Malian **Family Code** in parliament on 2 December. The National Assembly had adopted a fairly liberal version of the family code during its first reading in 2009, raising the minimum age for marriage and improving women's rights within marriage and in inheritance matters. However, following street protests organised by Islamic institutions, Touré had sent it back for a second reading. The balance of power had now clearly turned in favour of these Islamic organisations, as MPs agreed upon a very conservative code. The obedience clause (of women to their husbands) was reinstated, the marital age reduced to 16 years (in some cases 15) and inequality of inheritance was further institutionalised. When Touré seemed to be delaying its promulgation, Islamic organisations (again) mobilised tens of thousands of people in Bamako to put pressure on the executive.

The lengthy **constitutional revision process** also entered its last stage. On 2 August, an overwhelming majority of MPs (141 to 3) adopted the Constitutional Revision Act, paving the way for a referendum during the first round of the presidential elections in 2012. Major changes would include the establishment of a senate, the introduction of a mixed electoral system and the improvement of some parliamentary oversight mechanisms – but also the further expansion of an already powerful executive. On 3 April, Touré anticipated the outcome of the referendum by nominating Daba Diawarra as minister of state reforms. Much more controversy arose over the drawing up of an **electoral register**. As the extensive biometric registration process was unfinished and costly to adapt for use with the existing register, the much more restricted census for elections would be used, which angered opposition parties.

As usual, political parties proved unable to agree upon the establishment of the **electoral commission,** an organ that urgently requires restructuring. When the 21 July deadline failed to be met, controversies continued, fuelled by the question of allocation of seats between opposition and ruling parties. On 7 September, the government unilaterally adopted a decree granting but one seat to an extra-parliamentary opposition party (which had in fact realigned itself with the ruling majority) and nine seats to parties supporting the ruling bloc. The political tinkering was obvious, though in a legal sense not forbidden as the government had altered the electoral code in favour of the ruling coalition in 2008.

The two major parties, ADEMA and the 'Union pour la République et la Démocratie' (URD), approved the **presidential nominations** for the 2012 elections – Dioncounda Traore and Soumaila Cisse. Other senior candidates included the son of former president Traoré, and Mountaga Tall on behalf of the 'Congrès National d'Initiative Democratique'. Former prime ministers Ibrahim Boubacar Keita, Modibo Sidibe and Soumano Sacko were expected to announce their candidature early in 2012.

Foreign Affairs

Regional diplomatic efforts concentrated heavily on the rising security threats in the north. The need to strengthen regional cooperation between the four countries bordering the Sahel-Sahara strip (Algeria, Mauritania, Niger and Mali) had been on the agenda for many years, but progress on the ground was only slowly achieved. A joint military base was established in southern Algeria in April 2010 to counter the rising influence of AQIM and illegal smuggling networks in the area. On 20 May, the ministers of foreign affairs of these countries outlined a number of joint strategic operations. Mali and Algeria in particular continued opposing the direct involvement of external forces. Furthermore, mistrust between Algeria and Mali persisted, with the former complaining that Mali's response to the northern threats was far too weak, although cooperation between them improved somewhat over the year. On 29 April, Touré met with the chief of staff of the Algerian army, General Salah and, on 15 October, the Algerian minister of African Affairs visited Bamako to discuss the security threats. On 24 October, the Malian president left for Algeria for an official four-day state visit to discuss security threats, as well as political, economic (oil) and cultural cooperation.

On 13 June, the Malian president met with his new Nigérien counterpart, Mahamadou Issoufou, and, on 17 August, with the vice president of **Niger**'s National Assembly to further discuss economic and security ties between the two countries. On 7–8 September, the first (US-backed) international conference on the terrorist threat in the Sahel took place. A month later, the **United States** provided the Malian government with additional military equipment. On 21 October, the Committee of Joint Chiefs (CEMOC) released a warrant for the arrest of 26 alleged drug traffickers and exactly one month afterwards, Bamako hosted a CEMOC meeting during which Algeria was selected as the principal hub for regional security operations. On 9 December, a UN delegation met with Touré to discuss the rising security threats in the wake of the Libyan war.

Other regional events included the 15th ordinary conference of UEMOA in Bamako (22 January), during which Alassane Ouattara was recognised as the legitimate president of **Côte d'Ivoire**. Touré later attended his swearing-in ceremony on 21 May. In his turn, President Ouattarra visited Mali on 20 October to re-launch commercial activities along the Bamako-Abidjan axis and reinforce overall diplomatic ties.

The ECOWAS summit on 23–24 March discussed sub-regional economic integration and cooperation with the EU. On 15–16 April, Touré and his wife visited Senegal to open the headquarters of the 'Organisation pour la Mise en Valeur du Fleuve Senegal', an institution established by Senegal, Guinea, Mali and Mauritania. On 25 April, the president visited Liberia, mainly to discuss commercial, industrial and infrastructural cooperation with a specific interest in the exploitation of Liberia's port. On 18 October, Bamako hosted a regional conference bringing together over 1,000 participants to discuss the exploitation of the Niger River. The presidents of Burkina Faso, Niger and Mali agreed on 24 November to revitalise their regional cooperation in the Liptako-Gourma region, a dormant network established in the early 1970s.

Cooperation with the **EU** further intensified when Commissioner Piebalgs visited Mali and announced on 22 November that the EU would provide the Malian government with € 50 m to increase the state's presence in the northern regions. The following day, an additional € 12.5 m was granted to civil society organisations. Former EU commissioner Louis Michel was honoured by being made a 'Commandeur de l'Ordre National of Mali' on 25 February. A day after his accreditation to Mali on 16 March, the new French ambassador signed a financial agreement with Touré worth CFAfr 27 bn, mainly focusing on urban development projects, private sector development and the Malian Security and Development Programme in the northern regions. The negative travel advice for Mali issued by the **French government** to its citizens soured relations as it was believed to be linked to the Malian government's refusal to sign an agreement to facilitate the repatriation of Malian migrants from France. During a brief visit to Paris on 12 July, Touré, rather questionably, emphasised that Mali was safe enough for Western tourists to visit.

Other significant diplomatic contacts with EU member states were an official three-day state visit by Touré to the Netherlands on 28–30 November and a visit to Bamako by the speaker of the German Bundestag on 8 December to celebrate 50 years of German-Malian cooperation. A visit by the new general of the US Africa Command (AFRICOM) on 22 April marked the increased concern of the **United States** regarding Mali's commitment and capacity to confront its security threats, clearly revealed by the diplomatic cables revealed through Wikileaks. Mali was also selected by the Obama administration as one of the eight eligible countries under the Global Health Initiative, and investment in various infrastructural programmes continued under the Millennium Challenge Cooperation. Furthermore, the US made funds available for the irrigation of an additional 16,000 ha of land managed by the 'Office du Niger'. Mali's increased cooperation with **China** was marked on 22 September by the inauguration of the 'bridge of Malian-Chinese friendship' over the Niger River in Bamako – entirely funded by Bejing and built by a Chinese company. Trade between the two countries in the first half of the year was 50% higher than in the same period in 2010.

Socioeconomic Developments

While GDP was estimated at 5.3%, actual growth was only 2.3%. Inflation, after years of relatively low levels (1.3% in 2010), rose to 3.1% (on average consumer prices). Overall domestic revenue remained limited and but some progress was achieved towards increasing revenue levels in the course of the year.

Tourism was seriously hit by the unrest and rising insecurity (the north being one of the country's more important tourist attractions). The government constantly tried to convince tourists that Mali was predominately safe, even launching a specific campaign to that effect on 13 July, but tourism nevertheless collapsed in both Mopti and Timbuktu, with the number of annual visitors falling by more than 50%.

Agricultural output had been expected to fuel growth. FAO reports confirmed that agricultural policies had put in place a good framework for achieving increased production and the 2010/2011 results lived up to expectations, attaining 98.6% of the objectives set. The ministry of agriculture provided 400,000 farmers with a fertiliser subsidy. Ambitions for the 2011/2012 season were high, with a total production target of 9 m tonnes (8.9 m tonnes of cereals and 500,000 tonnes of cotton), but the results were in fact an estimated 12% below the 2006–2010 average. Cereal production was as much as 20% lower than the year before. This was mainly caused by insufficient, erratic and unevenly distributed rainfall. By the end of the year, WFP identified 159 local communities that were at risk of food insecurity. Between October and December, grain prices rose significantly, the price of millet and maize almost doubling compared with prices at the end of 2010. Moreover, livestock was also heavily affected, particularly in the Segou and Gao region. Together with mounting security issues, the poor agricultural production severely challenged food security for millions of citizens. On 30 December, the government announced that 45,000 tonnes of cereals would be distributed free of charge in the regions of Kayes, Ségou, Mopti and Timbuktu.

Mali's **healthcare** challenges remained paramount, as illustrated by the country's child mortality rate, which is still one of the highest in the world. On a positive note, UNICEF reported that the percentage of children sleeping under mosquito nets had risen from 27% in 2000 to 70% (one-third of children under five die of malaria), and an extensive meningitis A vaccination campaign was completed by the end of the year. A cholera outbreak affected over 1,200 people and had caused 51 deaths by the end of December. The ten-year 'Programme de Développement Sanitaire et Social', which guides cooperation between Mali and its international partners, was extended by one year, and ran till the end of 2011.

The **education sector** was confronted with a series of strikes, starting with one by university teachers (February-May). During the last months of the year, primary and secondary teachers followed their example. They stopped work sporadically throughout October but on 25 November a fully-fledged strike was called and this was still ongoing by the end of the year. Malian pupils also face serious problems with regard to quality of teaching. An external evaluation of primary school teachers concluded that more than half lacked sufficient qualifications and skills.

Levels of **corruption** remained high. The country's gold sector failed to qualify for the Extractive Industries Transparency Initiative when the government was unable to account for almost 4% of total gold revenues. On 3 June, Minister of Health Ibrahim Oumar Touré was arrested on suspicion of involvement in a $ 4 m corruption scandal. Mali fell two places on TI Corruption Perception Index, now ranking 118th on a list of 182 countries.

More positively, a number of **infrastructural improvements** were achieved. On 18 September, President Touré opened the upgraded airport in Kayes. On 5 December, the prime minister inaugurated the entirely new administrative and ministerial area in Bamako, largely funded by the fallen Libyan regime of Muammar Kadhafi. In addition to the third bridge crossing the Niger River, an improved road between Bamako and Kangaba was opened on 27 December, and later that month construction of a hydro-electric dam began in Djenné.

On a **cultural note**, the seventh 'Festival sur le Niger' in Ségou, which traditionally takes places during the first weak of February, drew many visitors and Malian and West African artists. On 1 November, the national museum launched a major biennial photography exhibition focusing on the quest for a sustainable world. Lastly, Malian artist Fantani Touré was awarded the UNESCO Grammy Award for best African Artist 2011.

Martin van Vliet

Mauritania

In the wake of the 'Arab Spring', a new protest movement, 'Coordination de la Jeunesse du 25 Février', emerged at the beginning of the year. The previously contested election of President Abdel Aziz in 2009 was regarded as a *fait accompli* and, instead of regime change, the protesters mainly focused on tangible social issues and constitutional amendments. The government responded by launching a series of social programmes and initiated a national dialogue with the opposition in September. Severe criticism from the opposition concerning lack of information and coordination as regards the election process, as well as serious allegations from minority rights groups concerning the national census, eventually forced the government to postpone the parliamentary and municipal elections. Activities of the terror network al-Qaida in the Islamic Maghreb (AQIM) constituted a regional destabilising factor and led to an increase in military spending. Despite certain tensions in the mutual relationships with Algeria, Mali, Mauritania and Niger, these countries continued military cooperation in accordance with the Tamanrasset agreement of 2010. Joint efforts with the EU to reduce illegal immigration from West Africa continued.

Domestic Politics

On 17 January, Yacoub Ould Dahoud, a 40-year-old Mauritanian, set fire to himself in front of the presidential palace in Nouakchott, obviously inspired by similar actions in Tunisia and in Egypt. In order to calm down the protests that followed, on 20 January, President Aziz announced an extensive programme that included food subsidies, recruitment of more civil servants and the building of new homes. However, the protests resulted in the formation of a **new youth movement**, the 'Coordination de la Jeunesse du 25 Février', mainly consisting of educated, urban, middle-class youngsters. As in North Africa, social media such as Twitter, YouTube, Facebook and mobile-phone text messages played a key role in circulating demands for far-reaching change, including a reduction in the president's power and reform of the electoral system.

Demonstrations were initially tolerated by the authorities but, on 8 March, the police prevented demonstrators from gathering in the main square in Nouakchott, the 'Place des Blocs', and in other towns protests were also broken up and demonstrators arrested. 'Coordination de la Jeunesse du 25 Février', with its diffuse leadership and a relatively narrow membership base, failed to develop a critical mass and was sidelined in main policy debates. The movement's major march in Nouakchott on 24 May – 'Journée du rejet' – attracted only a few hundred people. Activists accused the government of using social media to spread false information about the time and place of demonstrations. On 13 February, the main unions – the 'Confédération Nationale des Travailleurs de Mauritanie', the 'Confédération Générale des Travailleurs de Mauritanie' and the 'Confédération Libre des Travailleurs de Mauritanie' – organised demonstrations in Nouakchott, Nouadhibou, Zouérate and Aleg. The government responded with minimal wage increases for public-sector workers, food and fuel subsidies and increased public sector investment.

On 2 February, Mauritanian soldiers fired on a car packed with explosives 12 km south of Nouakchott, killing three suspected AQIM members. The suspects had apparently intended to assassinate Aziz, accusing him of "opening the Mauritanian territory to France". Several trials of other suspected AQIM members continued and, on 16 March, a court convicted three individuals for the murder of a US citizen two years earlier in Nouakchott. All three denied the charges. On 22 November, the security forces arrested 19 suspects on **terrorism** charges, including two well-known Salafi preachers, Salem Ould Mohamed Lemine ('al-Majlissi') and Hamahoullah Ould Hannena.

Parliamentary and municipal elections were scheduled for September and October. In June, parties united in the 'Coordination de l'Opposition Démocratique' (COD), a platform calling for official dialogue on a series of political issues, including election standards. Several senior COD members, among them the president of the National Assembly, Messaoud Ould Boulkheir, representing the 'Alliance Populaire Progressiste' (APP), raised the possibility of boycotting the **scheduled elections**. Meanwhile, the opposition took advantage of public discontent and, at the end of August, Prime Minister Laghdaf announced that elections would be postponed until spring 2012. No new date was fixed.

Identification problems were closely connected to this. Plans for a new system for conducting a census and the replacement of old identity papers with biometric identity cards raised concerns among **Afro-Mauritanians**. Small but violent protests were organised in August and September by the movement 'Touche pas à ma nationalité'. On 25 September, a 19-year-old Afro-Mauritanian, Lamine Mangane, was killed and several other protesters injured, detained or arrested near Kaedi in southern Mauritania and, on 28 September, 56 people were arrested in Nouakchott. Mohamed Diop, a journalist with the 'al-Akhbar' news agency, was detained on 2 October for six hours while covering a demonstration. The controversies surrounding the census also gave new life to the 'Coordination de la Jeunesse du 25 Février' and the movement now attracted a more diverse group of urban youth and Afro-Mauritanians.

In August, Aziz initiated the 'Dialogue national'. These **talks with the opposition** took place from 17 September to 17 October. In late September, however, the COD announced a boycott of the dialogue process. Four opposition parties, the APP, 'El Wiam', 'Sawab' and 'Hamam', continued the talks. At the same time, splits became apparent within the president's ruling 'Union pour la République' and its parliamentary coalition, the 'Coalition des Partis de la Majorité' (CPM), as small parties began to announce their intention of running with the COD rather than the CPM. The national dialogue resulted on 19 October in a wide-ranging agreement, including restrictions on participation in politics by military personnel and plans to amend the constitution in order to make the government accountable to parliament. An independent national commission for elections was also established. However, the absence of the main opposition parties, including the 'Rassemblement des Forces Démocratiques' (RFD), the 'Union des Forces du Progrès' and 'Tawassoul', left the dialogue process open to criticism.

Although **slavery** was abolished in 1981 and was made a criminal offence in 2007, the national dialogue agreement contained an explicit rejection of the phenomenon, as well as of torture and all forms of humiliating and degrading treatment. Both local and international NGOs estimated that nearly 600,000 people continued to work in bonded labour, but slavery trials were unusual. On 17 January, a Mauritanian woman was sentenced to six months' imprisonment for keeping two children aged 10 and 14 in slave-like conditions. On 4 August, police violently dispersed an anti-slavery demonstration in Nouakchott and four activists belonging to an anti-slavery NGO, 'Résurgence du Mouvement Abolitionniste en Mauritanie' (IRA Mauritanie)', were given six-month suspended sentences.

Media laws were liberalised and, on 20 November, the 'Haute Autorité de la Presse et de l'Audiovisuel' authorised two new television channels ('Mauri-Vision' and 'Wataniya Television') and five new radio stations ('Sahara FM', 'Radio Cobenni-MAPUCO', 'Mauritanides FM', 'Radio Tenwir' and 'Radio-Nouakchott'). 'Reporters sans Frontières' ranked the country's **press freedom** index at 67th out of 179 countries, a considerable improvement from the ranking of 95th in 2010. Internet access was unrestricted, but the estimated number of users remained low.

Foreign Affairs

Mauritania continued to play an active role in regional politics. On 20 February, Aziz chaired the AU High-Level Panel of Heads of State on the Ivorian crisis. The AU meeting on **Libya** on 19 March, hosted by Mauritania, to discuss a no-fly zone over Libya was regarded as a failure and also probably resulted in the dismissal of the minister for foreign affairs, Ms Naha Mint Hamdi Ould Mouknass, who was replaced by the minister of defence, Hamadi Ould Hamadi. In May, Aziz started to distance himself from the Libyan leader Kadhafi, obviously as a result of pressure from donors. The main opposition party, the RFD, recognised Libya's National Transitional Council (NTC) as early as 30 May. In July, Foreign Minister Hamadi met with representatives of both the Kadhafi government in Tripoli and the NTC in Benghazi. The special envoy of the UN Secretary-General to Libya, Abdel Ilah Al Khatib, visited Mauritania on 28 August and Mauritania officially recognised the NTC on 25 November.

On 5 June, Foreign Minister Hamadi met several African, Arab and Western ambassadors to discuss a bid for a non-permanent seat on the **UNSC**. Mauritania was eventually one of the final candidates but failed in the third round of the elections held on 21 October at the UN Headquarters in New York, when Togo was elected.

Diplomatic ties with Mali had been suspended in 2010 in protest against the latter's allegedly soft line on AQIM. Following the **counter-terrorism** summit in Bamako on 19 May, the participating countries agreed on joint operations, and an offensive against AQIM in the Wagadou forest in western Mali took place on 24 June. On 5 July, AQIM attacked a military base in Bassiknou, near the Malian border. Tension on the Malian border remained high and, on 20 October, an aerial bombardment near the Wagadou forest region killed Teyeb Ould Sidi Aly, a high-ranking AQIM official who was accused of being behind a number of attacks in Mauritania, including the failed plot to assassinate Aziz at the beginning of the year. The head of the US Africa Command (AFRICOM), General Carter Ham, visited Nouakchott on 11–12 July to discuss intensified security cooperation and French Foreign Minister Alain Juppé also visited Nouakchott on 11 July. Mauritania participated in an international summit on terrorism in the Sahel hosted by Algeria on 7–8 September in Algiers, where the risk of arms proliferation from Libya and its potential to destabilise the region were discussed.

Spain and Mauritania boosted cooperation against illegal **migration** and **drug trafficking** from West Africa to Europe. During a meeting in Nouakchott on 26 April, Spanish Secretary of State for Security Antonio Camacho confirmed continued support for strengthening border control mechanisms, including a contingent of Spanish national police and Civil Guards stationed in Nouadhibou.

Several high-level meetings with **Algeria** took place during the autumn. A visit by Aziz to Algiers in early December resulted in a joint statement on improved cooperation. This was regarded as a sign of rapprochement between Algeria and Mauritania after a period of tension following Algerian reluctance to provide the Mauritanians with intelligence and other support during confrontations with AQIM in northern Mali in June. On 14 February, **Morocco**'s Foreign Minister Saad-Eddine Al-Othmani visited Nouakchott for talks on bilateral cooperation and inter-Maghreb relations. However, Mauritania's closer collaboration with Algeria contributed to a certain tension in relations with Morocco, due to the dispute over Western Sahara, occupied by Morocco since 1976, in which Algeria supported the POLISARIO liberation movement. Both Mauritania and Algeria continued to participate in talks on **Western Sahara** under UN auspices, together with the parties to the dispute. Two rounds of informal talks took place during the year, on 21–23 January and 19–21 July in New York.

Cooperation with **Gambia** was strengthened, especially following the bilateral ministerial conference and the state visit of Aziz to Banjul on 1–4 June. Voluntary repatriation of the remaining 5,000 Mauritanian refugees in **Senegal** continued and, on 20 October, a tripartite meeting with the governments of Mauritania, Senegal and UNHCR resulted in an agreement to repatriate 1,000 refugees by the end of 2011.

Iran's President Mahmoud Ahmadinejad visited Nouakchott on 25 September and discussed cooperation between the two countries, which, since 2008, had been under increasing scrutiny from Western and Arab countries, as tensions over Iran's nuclear programme took on more prominent international dimensions. UK Foreign Secretary, William Hague visited Nouakchott on 19 October to discuss Iran and Libya, as well as the potential for an expanded economic relationship between Britain and Mauritania and increased trade between Europe and the Maghreb region. An anti-terrorism accord with Saudi Arabia was signed on 30 November, when Interior Minister Mohamed Ould Boilil visited Riyadh. The accord was seen as an effort to check perceived Iranian influence in Mauritania.

Bilateral relations with **China** became closer and Aziz visited China on 19–23 September, signing several economic and military assistance deals.

Socioeconomic Developments

A number of **social programmes** were launched during the year in order to contain public protests. On 24 February, the government announced a large-scale and long-term housing programme to provide low-cost housing for 100,000 families. Several youth employment projects were launched during the year. In August, the government decided to intensify the dialogue with detained militant Islamists and offered them loans to start up small businesses as part of a reintegration programme. On 1 September, the minimum public-sector wage was increased from $ 75 to $ 108 a month. GDP growth was estimated at 5.2% (compared with 4.7% in 2010) and the current account deficit was estimated at 7.4%. Average consumer price inflation was estimated at 6.5% (compared with 6.3% in 2010), but the country continued to be vulnerable to price shocks on international markets. Income from tourism remained low as a result of the ongoing fight against terrorism.

Mauritania continued to be a food-deficit country and highly dependent on grain purchased on the international market. On 20 January, Aziz announced a food subsidy scheme, 'Opération solidarité', under which daily rations of imported rice or wheat, sugar and oil were sold at below market price in a total of 600 government-established shops, 250 of which were in the capital. A longer-term programme to reduce **food insecurity** was launched in August, aimed at wheat farming and mechanisation for large-scale production, and 125 unemployed university graduates were trained in farming techniques on the M'Pourié plain, on the banks of the Senegal River, near the city of Rosso. On 3 November, IFAD provided a $ 17.9 m loan and grant to improve the living conditions of poor rural households in the Aftout South and Karakoro regions.

On 6 June, parliament ratified an agreement with a Chinese fishing company, Poly Hon Done Pelagic Fishery, for a 25-year offshore fishing licence in exchange for $ 100 m of investment in fish-processing infrastructure. The deal was controversial because it allowed the company to hire 30% of its labour from outside Mauritania. Just a month before, the European Parliament had adopted a resolution regarding renewal of the EU-Mauritania Fisheries Partnership Agreement, due to expire on 31 July 2012, warning that Mauritania's offshore **fish stocks** were either fully exploited or over-exploited. The EU recommended the reduction of fishing quotas and a more sustainable long-term fisheries agreement.

On 22 June, the IMF executive board completed its second review of Mauritania's ECF, which resulted in the disbursement of $ 17.6 m. On 22 July, the 'Société Mauritanienne d'Électricité' received a $ 61 m loan from the AFD. On 13 September, the Kuwait Fund for Arab Economic Development granted a loan of $ 37.4 m for a drinking water distribution network. On 18 September, a Chinese military delegation led by Admiral Sun Jianguo visited Nouakchott, bringing a grant of $ 3.1 m for the army. In Rabat, Morocco, on 26 September, Mauritania, Gabon, Morocco and Senegal signed a memorandum of understanding with UNDP aiming at enhanced bilateral cooperation for local sustainable **development** and poverty reduction.

There was continued interest among foreign investors in the country's uranium and other **mineral resources**. On 14 July, Australia's Aura Energy announced that it had discovered around 50 m lb of uranium in Reguibat province and, on 27 September, Australian-based Forte Energy announced that it been granted new uranium exploration permits in Hasi Baida and Gin Ouissat in the north. General interest in Mauritania's oil and gas sector had been flagging as a result of problems in the Chinguetti field but, on 31 October,

Anglo-Irish Tullow Oil announced a new production-sharing contract for exploration in an offshore area covering 10,725 km^2.

Despite the tough rhetoric on fighting corruption, the country's corruption ranking remained low, 143rd out of 182 countries, according to TI's corruption perceptions index. At the beginning of the year, misuse and fraud related to grants from the Global Fund were reported. The country was placed on the Fund's list of additional safeguards countries. Several MPs reported that corruption had hindered the 'Opération solidarité' programmes and that stores had sold the family rations for profit. Mauritania's HDI ranking was 159th out of 187 countries.

Claes Olsson & Helena Olsson

Niger

Presidential and legislative elections concluded a successful return to civilian rule. The new president, long-time opposition leader Mahamadou Issoufou, gained a precarious hold on power as it would be difficult to keep all the promises made on the economic front and sections of the military remained unruly. In the summer, there was another coup threat, followed by several arrests. At the start of the year, a kidnapping incident involving two young Frenchmen rocked the capital and underlined the deterioration of security in the Sahelian region, made worse by the violent overthrow of the Kadhafi regime in Libya. A catastrophic harvest further complicated the country's food security and presaged famine for 2012. General economic prospects for 2012 were boosted by the beginning of oil production and the start-up of a new uranium mine.

Domestic Politics

Ahead of the parliamentary and presidential elections scheduled to finalise the transition to civilian rule, the party alliance, 'Coordination des Forces pour la Démocratie et la République' (CFDR), came apart. The CFDR had been formed in 2009 to oppose the continued hold on power by President Tandja – deposed in 2010 by the military for his constitutional putsch the previous year – and that of his party, the 'Mouvement National pour la Société du Développement' (MNSD). **Local elections**, delayed into 2011 as a result of logistical problems, preceded the general contest on 11 January. While 80% of council seats were taken by the country's four principal parties, the results signalled an end to the dominance of the MNSD, essentially in place since the end of the Cold War. The opposition 'Parti Nigérien pour la Démocratie et le Socialisme' (PNDS) of Mahamadou Issoufou gained the largest number of council seats. The MNSD lost half its usual vote and came second and, surprisingly, the new 'Mouvement Démocratique Nigérien' (Moden-Lumana) of one-time MNSD colleague and rival of Mamadou Tandja, Hama Amadou, came third, cutting deep into the western region, from where the new MNSD leader – Tandja confidant Seyni Oumarou – hailed. The 'Convention Démocratique et Sociale' (CDS) of former National Assembly chair Mahamane Ousmane trailed behind.

The relative decline of the MNSD sealed the fate of the CFDR pact. On 25 January, before the legislative elections and the first round of the presidentials – to be held on 31 January – Hama Amadou and Mahamane Ousmane broke with the PNDS and formed a new alliance with the MNSD called 'Alliance pour la Réconciliation Nationale' (ARN). They and Seyni Oumarou promised to support whichever of them would make it to the presidential run-off. Isolating Mahamadou Issoufou, this **reversal of alliance** was meant to limit the damage to Ousmane's CDS and maintain Hama Amadou's influence, but it was condemned in the media – the MNSD had, after all, become tainted by Tandja's 2009 constitutional coup.

The local elections had already shown that, despite its decline, the MNSD could not be completely written off, and the general elections on 31 January confirmed this. In addition to Mahamane Issoufou, Seyni Oumarou, Hama Amadou and Mahamane Ousmane (all but Oumarou long-time established figures), six more people joined the race, including civil society activist Bayard Mariama Gamatié, Niger's first female presidential contender. PNDS leader Mahamadou Issoufou gained the upper hand with 36.1% of the vote, followed by Seyni Oumarou with 23.2% and Hama Amadou with 19.8%. Mahamane Ousmane, whose activism had declined in the course of Tandja's putsch, gained 8.3%, and the other candidates still less. In the **parliamentary polls**, the PNDS won a clear 34 seats (out of 113), doubling the number of its MPs in the National Assembly, followed by the MNSD and the new Moden of Hama Amadou. The CDS was practically annihilated. The remainder of the seats were shared between a couple of lesser parties.

With turnout hovering around the 50% mark, the parliamentary landscape had been thoroughly redrawn, making Hama Amadou into **kingmaker**. As member of the ARN coalition, he should have given his support to Seyni Oumarou, but he made another U-turn, possibly also because of the negative reaction by Moden members to the alliance with the MNSD. On 9 February, the Moden leader declared his support for Mahamane Issoufou in the presidential run-off, thus creating – together with three lesser parties – a **two-thirds majority** in the National Assembly (78 seats). In August, the PNDS-led majority was boosted to 84, when some minor parties agreed to join what was now called the 'Mouvance pour la Renaissance du Niger'.

In the **presidential run-off** on 12 March, Issoufou took 57.9% of the votes and Seyni Oumarou 42.1%. Turnout was 48%. On 16 March, Oumarou conceded defeat, opening the way for Issoufou's accession to the highest office. Nicknamed 'Zaki' (lion), the 59-year-old mining engineer had twice been runner-up. This experience had had a sobering effect on a man known not only for his leftist convictions (he was active in the Socialist International and is a friend of fellow 'eternal' opposition leader-turned president, Alpha Condé of Guinea) but also for his fierce temper. It was essentially Tandja's ill-judged attempt to hang on to the presidency that paved the way for his success. Issoufou is also one of the few leading politicians without a military background. With the new president sworn in on 7 April, the textbook transition begun with the 'republican' coup of junta leader Salou Djibo the previous year came to an end.

Issoufou appointed Brigi Rafini, a technocrat and Tuareg from the northern town of Iferouâne, as **prime minister** – an appointment calculated to appease Niger's chronically malcontent Tuareg community, while harmlesss for Issoufou as Rafini was not part of his inner circle. Foreign affairs went to Bazoum Mohamed, a member of that inner group; Foumakoye Gado, also a presidential confidant, got the important ministry of energy and mining; and Issoufou's ally, Karidjo Mahamadou, became minister of defence. Marou Amadou, a human rights campaigner prominent in the struggle against Tandja, became minister of justice. The **cabinet** included five women. In a minor **reshuffle** on 12 September, intended to accommodate the disappointments of the government's Moden partner about their ministerial posts, mining was made into a separate ministry, together with industrial development, and awarded to Hamidou Tchiana, an ally of Hama Amadou. The Moden leader himself had been elected chair of the National Assembly on 19 April, taking over from Mahamane Ousmane. In a break with the past, President Issoufou invited Seyni Oumarou to join a government of national unity, but the MNSD leader declined.

The happy end to the crisis of the previous years went hand in hand with an **ambitious government programme**. Issoufou pledged to work for strong republican institutions and vast investment in agriculture, irrigation, water supply and livestock improvement (the right to education, drinking water and an adequate diet was inscribed in the constitution). The entire five-year development plan would require funds to the tune of € 9 bn, to be supplied by fiscal revenues and development aid and to be undergirded by a projected growth rate of 7%. The agricultural part of Issoufou's plans would be allocated a prospective € 1.8 bn.

In May, the National Assembly passed a bill granting amnesty to the former junta – a sine qua non for a smooth beginning of the '7th Republic'. The **armed forces** had already, on 7 March, signed a republican pact with political parties, the media and civil society groups, vowing to respect the new constitution. In reference to the previous two years, the pact noted that Niger was sick and its consciousness needed to be enhanced with regard to respect for democratic and constitutional principles. However, if the army came out of the transition with its republican reputation reinforced, this did not apply to all sections of the military, for many officers still harboured sympathy for Tandja. On 22 July, several officers were detained on suspicion of plotting to kill the new president. They were said to have conceived a **coup plan** for 16 July, when Issoufou would be assassinated. Those arrested included a major and a lieutenant, a member of the presidential guard and a captain formerly responsible for the security of Salou Djibo. On 9 September, Colonel Abdoulaye Badié, Salou Djibo's former secretary who had already been detained over similar rumours in October 2010, was re-arrested and another top military man was arrested two days later. It was alleged that the rebellious military were angered by Issoufou's efforts to stamp out corruption, which had led to several dismissals. However, this could hardly be expected to be the end of the matter, as the prospective start of oil production would make the country less dependent on foreign aid and thus less susceptible to the corrective pressure of donors.

On 7 January, a **kidnapping incident** sent shockwaves through Niger's Western community. Members of al-Qaida in the Islamic Maghreb (AQIM) snatched two young Frenchmen from a restaurant in the capital Niamey, 700 m. from the presidential palace. This blatant act was clearly intended to intimidate Niger's Western partners, and the victims – one an NGO worker about to marry a Nigérien girl, the other his friend who had come over for the wedding – were taken towards the border with Mali. The French government, in close consultation with the Niger and Mali authorities, dispatched helicopters from a base in Ouagadougou, while Nigérien gendarmerie pursued the kidnappers on land. One party of gendarmes fell victim to an AQIM ambush (with four taken prisoner), but French special forces caught up with the kidnappers, reportedly just across the border in Mali. Violent clashes took place in which two French military, including one of the helicopter pilots, were wounded. Eight people were killed: four kidnappers, three Nigérien gendarmes and the two hostages, one of whom was executed by the AQIM men, and the other caught in the cross-fire (his body was later found badly burned).

If the swift response was the proper answer to the **AQIM challenge**, the incident did not fail to increase concern over security. US Peace Corps volunteers were withdrawn, and Niamey's security industry received a new boost. Issoufou's government vowed to fight AQIM and trans-border crime. In late February, three hostages who had been kidnapped from the uranium town of Arlit in September 2010 were released from an AQIM hide-out in Mali: one Togolese, a Malagasy and a French woman sick with cancer; this left four Frenchmen from Arlit in AQIM hands. On 23 March, AQIM demanded a € 90 m ransom. It was unknown whether money had been paid for the freed hostages. In June, 80 km north of Arlit, Niger soldiers clashed with men coming from Libya who were alleged to be on their way to an AQIM hide-out. Their vehicles were carrying explosives and detonators of Czech manufacture. One soldier and one militant were killed and six soldiers wounded. As a result of the crisis in Libya, the armed forces were put on maximum alert. In September, another clash took place in the Agadez region, in which three AQIM militants were killed and arms were recovered, along with 50 young men who were being recruited, either forcibly or with the promise of cash. In comparison, the threat posed by ordinary Tuareg rebels was insignificant. In July, members of former rebel forces surrendered weapons, vehicles and ammunition. Prime Minister Rafini, himself a Tuareg, appealed for the loyalty of his people. Security in the border region with Mali continued to be problematic. In April, 24 pastoralists were killed and several wounded in a cattle camp when armed men from Mali staged an attack.

Issoufou seemed determined to continue the clean-up started by the junta in the wake of Tandja's overthrow. A 'cour des comptes', established in 2010, produced a damning report in March about **financial irregularities** between 1996 and 2009, most of them involving false or inflated procurement invoices. A total of 3,000 people had by now come under scrutiny, and reported embezzlements totalled CFAfr 77 bn. The Ibrahim Index of African governance rated Niger's performance as very poor (ranking 39th out of 53 countries and in sixth place among the eight-member UEMOA). One of Tandja's sons, arrested in 2010, still awaited trial, together with a former mining minister, for corruption involving mining licences.

On 16 January, **former president Tandja** was moved from house arrest to a state prison, having been charged with financial malfeasance (the previous year the ECOWAS court of justice had ruled his detention without charge illegal). However, in May, an appeals court dismissed all charges, arguing that it was constitutionally impossible to try a head of state after he had left office. Although this provided an unsatisfactory conclusion to the clean-up campaign, the law had been designed in this way to prevent politically motivated cases against former leaders. Tandja left jail on 10 May. However, an audience granted by Issoufou to Seyni Oumarou on 12 May was said to mark the end of Tandja's long-standing influence.

The insurrection and regime change taking place in Libya created a huge **refugee crisis**. By April, almost 60,000 sub-Saharan Africans had made their dangerous way across the desert and found themselves in overstretched camps. Most having worked for years in menial jobs in Libya, they found themselves the target of racist and revenge attacks by rebel militias, being accused of connivance with Kadhafi's regime – West African Tuareg fighters had been paid huge sums of money to defend the maverick leader against the rebels. Many Nigériens struggled to receive family members while having to cope with a drop in remittances. By the summer, some 210,000 Nigériens were said to have returned home.

Although the 2010 Human Development Index ranked Niger as the third poorest country in the world (two places higher than in 2009), **social unrest** was limited. On 1 August, police broke up demonstrations in the capital where people were protesting against blackouts due to disruptions in the electricity supplies from Nigeria (the source of 80% of the country's power). Several people were wounded and some were arrested. Top police officials were sacked in the wake of clashes between police and demonstrators in Niger's second city, Zinder, on 6–7 December.

Foreign Affairs

With the return to civilian rule, the country's membership rights in ECOWAS and the AU were restored. At the end of May, Issoufou participated in the Africa outreach session at the G8 summit in Deauville, which signalled continuing close relations with France. Together with three other sub-Saharan heads of state, Issoufou visited the White House on 29 July (a particularly gratifying experience for a politician who had been so long in the wilderness).

Relations with France and the US were expected to remain dominated by **concerns over security**. Cooperation in this area also included West African countries, as well as Algeria. On 20 May, a get-together began in Bamako, involving Niger, Mali, Mauritania and Algeria, to discuss terrorism and trans-border crime. While Mali had called for a regional approach and the training of tens of thousands of troops to tackle the AQIM challenge, Algeria remained lukewarm, despite the fallout of the Libyan crisis (it had consistently opposed the involvement of France in this issue). Nevertheless, Mali and Niger vowed to strengthen their cooperation. This pattern repeated itself on 7–8 September at a meeting in Algiers. The Algerians claimed that Algeria and its West African partners needed to develop their own security capabilities and that foreign troops should be kept out, while Niger warned that the region had been turned into a powder keg. Relations with **Nigeria** were reinforced, strengthening cooperation to counter the threat of terrorism and banditry (AQIM in Niger were reported to have had contacts with the Boko Haram group in the Nigerian city of Maiduguri). On 9 August, the two countries held talks on the issue and vowed to strengthen border patrols.

The government had to tread cautiously with regard to the deteriorating **crisis in Libya**. In July, Issoufou warned against arms proliferation and the risk of fundamentalists taking power in Tripoli. While other West African states were distancing themselves from Kadhafi or had already recognised the rebel-dominated transitional government, Issoufou stressed Niger's neutrality. On 6 September, as the Libyan regime was falling apart, more than 30 members of Kadhafi's inner circle made their way to Niger, together with one of Kadhafi's sons, Saadi, and the government felt compelled to host them on humanitarian grounds. Niger's stance was complicated by: the fact that the Kadhafi regime had made substantial gifts to the country; the impossibility of patrolling the common border; the violent treatment of Niger migrant workers by anti-Kadhafi forces; and the fallout of the regime change for security and the Tuareg community. Aghaly Alambo, former leader of the rebel 'Mouvement des Nigériens pour la Justice', had taken up residence in Tripoli after he had made his peace with the Tandja government (brokered by Kadhafi). Upon the latter's fall he travelled back to Niger, together with Libyans loyal to the old regime. Things became more sensitive when the US State Department called on Niger to arrest those senior figures who might become the target of international prosecution, and Libya's rebel forces threatened action if Niger helped Kadhafi himself to escape. While Issoufou promised full cooperation with the ICC, to which Niger is a signatory, the government was much relieved when it turned out that the Libyan leader had remained in his country to meet his maker. Earlier, on 27 August, Issoufou recognised Libya's transitional government, ahead of AU policy on this point, obviously to protect Niger's interests.

Socioeconomic Developments

Early in the year, there was a temporary let-up in the previous year's food shortages, themselves caused by the disappointing 2009 harvests. However, rainfall, though it improved in July and August, proved erratic and the autumn harvests were catastrophic, auguring badly for the situation in 2012. Cereal prices began to rise after the harvest, which is unusual, and in December the UN Emergency Response Fund said it would allocate $ 6 m to help people cope with **food shortages**. By then some 750,000 people in various parts of the country were already food insecure, especially as they had not yet recovered from the previous year's difficulties. The 2010 harvest, better than in 2009, had not fully eradicated **malnutrition**, and the overall 2011 harvest was 11% lower than the average of the five preceding years. UNICEF reported on 21 July that more than 15% of children were suffering from acute malnutrition. The civilian government, like the preceding junta, was open about the country's problems (in contrast to the Tandja years). In May, it put the number of people facing severe food shortages at 1.2 m (this was before the autumn harvest!), with another 1.4 m suffering moderate shortages.

Issoufou called for international help. His € 1.8 bn **agricultural programme** aimed to increase production by 7.4% annually, but this target was unlikely to be met in 2011. Government revenue was prioritised to the agricultural and livestock sectors (besides education), which together accounted for nearly 85% of the work force and 40% of GDP. On 24 August, the government launched an irrigation pilot project worth CFAfr 10 bn aimed at the production of 1 m tonnes of various types of food crops (the Kandadji dam on the River Niger was still under construction). The ADF provided a $ 33.8 m grant to finance irrigation projects in the country's central-eastern regions.

Meanwhile, numerous people were leaving for **the cities**, with urban residents hard pressed to assist rural relatives – the refugees coming from Libya did not ease the situation. The capital alone had witnessed a population growth of 6% annually for the five preceding years. Housing projects during the Tandja years had hardly taken off, but the new civilian government committed itself to constructing 1,000 social housing units annually in the north-west of the city during the next five years.

Much-needed **foreign aid** began to flow again. At the beginning of the year, the 'Banque Ouest Africaine de Développement' granted a loan of CFAfr 22 bn for road construction and irrigation projects (and later lent $ 107 m for energy programmes). The OPEC Fund for International Development gave loans totalling more than $ 18 m for road upgrading and rural development. China gave a grant for the extension of the second bridge across the River Niger in the capital. An IDA loan of $ 52 m was to help overcome institutional bottlenecks hindering road maintenance and rural development, among other things. The EU released € 25 m in budget support in July, the first tranche since the accession of Issoufou to the presidency and marking the full resumption of ties. If all went well, € 450 m worth of European aid would be disbursed in the next five years.

Towards year's end, the **IMF** awarded an ECF facility to the tune of $ 123 m, intended to help in absorbing the fall in remittances and the disappointing harvest. The **World Bank** provided assistance for a social safety net for vulnerable households that should cover 1 m people over five years by way of regular transfers of small amounts of money paid out to women. Health and water were also targeted in the programme, which totalled $ 280 m. In May, the government reduced the national **budget** by 6.6% to cope with delays in aid transfers and various administrative problems. While the overall budget declined, at some CFAfr 65.9 bn, it was expected that the government would still aim to increase spending on food security and the military – the latter in order to confront the country's growing security threats. The 2010 growth figure according to the national statistical agency appeared higher than first expected (7.5% as against ca. 3%). By contrast, optimistic figures for 2011 were later toned down to 3.8% as a result of the catastrophic harvest.

The start of Chinese **uranium** mining at Teguidan Tessoumt (Azélik) at the end of 2010 was followed by the official opening on 17 March. Salou Djibo had already received the vice-president of the China National Nuclear Corporation, which together with a South Korean firm controls two-thirds of the mine's capital (and Niger a blocking one-third). A third of the mine's expected yearly 700 tonnes production (out of a national total of 3,000 tonnes) would be to the benefit of the national budget. Representing around half of the country's exports, the importance of the yellow cake was expected to grow further, despite the nuclear disaster in Japan. Australian, Canadian and Indian firms remained active in exploration. French Areva, which had security for its personnel reinforced after the kidnappings that had taken place in 2010, remained dominant. According to the World Nuclear Association, Niger's uranium production increased in 2010 by 29.4% to 4,198 tonnes, becoming the world's number five.

Oil production also began. Extraction from the Agadem block near the Chadian border started in September. Chinese construction of the 460-km pipeline connecting the block to a refinery in Zinder was also completed. With oil production coming on stream in 2012, growth could rise to 14%, boosting domestic revenue. The refinery could produce 20,000 b/d, destined for the domestic market to ease local consumption (7,000 b/d), although transportation might become a problem. In any case, it could cut the country's import bill. In the meantime, the Chinese would construct another pipeline, probably to link up with the Chadian-Cameroonian one, for the transportation of their 60% share of the crude. Daily total production could grow to 100,000 barrels. However, disagreement arose over the costs of the refinery, which was officially opened on 28 November but whose revenue could possibly not be enough to cover the government's share in its capital outlay, advanced by the Chinese. The China National Petroleum Corporation (CNPC) demanded a higher share of Agadem's output and claimed that the deposed Tandja had agreed to this. Typically for the latter's opaque dealings with Chinese firms, the new minister of finance disputed the existence of such an agreement. NGOs asked the government to review the CNPC contract. On 2 March, Niger was declared compliant with the Extractive Industries Transparency Initiative. The new constitution reserves 15% of revenues in this field for the communities where mining or production takes place.

Klaas van Walraven

Nigeria

The April elections at federal and state levels dominated the political scene and confirmed the incumbent Goodluck Ebele Jonathan as president, giving him a very strong political mandate. An improved election commission conducted the most credible elections yet in Nigeria's history, despite continuing widespread shortcomings and lapses. However, the country experienced an unprecedented wave of political and sectarian violence, evoking the political turmoil and ethnic violence on the eve of the civil war. Although the political class had demonstrated its willingness and ability to continue to stabilise democratic institutions, it failed to understand the dynamics and structures underlying sectarian violence, suicide bombings and organised crime, so that the president and his government gave the impression of being rather helpless. Furthermore, they continued to ignore the microeconomic level as well as the persistent, grinding poverty in the far north. Thus, the government somehow managed to return to the brinkmanship politics of the past, exacerbating the north-south dichotomy and the nationwide youth violence.

Domestic Politics

Over the course of the year, the most striking issues were the **general elections**, scheduled for 2 April (National Assembly), 9 April (presidential) and 16 April (gubernatorial and state assemblies), and the threat of Boko Haram. All eyes were fixed on the run-up to the elections, in which the incumbent President Goodluck Ebele Jonathan, a Christian from the Niger Delta, eventually emerged as the front runner of the ruling People's Democratic Party (PDP). On 13 January, almost 80% of the more than 3,500 delegates voted in favour of the incumbent at the PDP primaries in Abuja, thereby, in all probability, heralding a strong mandate. While Goodluck Jonathan kept his vice president, Namadi Sambo, a Muslim from the north as running mate, the former military dictator and twice presidential candidate, Muhammadu Buhari, was endorsed by the Congress for Progressive Change (CPC) as the main challenger.

At the start of the year, however, it became obvious that the **Independent National Electoral Commission** (INEC) would not meet the deadline for completing the electoral register. Reacting swiftly, the National Assembly on 25–26 January amended the electoral act No.6 of 2010, reducing the time INEC had to complete the registration of voters before a general election from 60 to 30 days. In the end, the electoral register comprised 67 m eligible voters, and the lists went on display at the 120,000 polling stations in mid-February. In early March, however, INEC updated the number to about 73.5 m.

Twenty presidential and dozens of gubernatorial candidates, as well as more than 50 parties, contested the elections. Soon after parts of the electorate had cast their vote in the parliamentary election on 2 April, and to the consternation of most Nigerians, the well respected INEC chairman, Attahiru Jega, aborted the whole exercise at the eleventh hour after it turned out that voting materials had failed to arrive on time in large parts of the country. As a result, the elections were postponed for one week.

To the surprise of many Nigerians, as well as international observers, the delayed ballot for the bicameral National Assembly on 9 April passed off with far fewer hitches and some notable improvements, despite the chaotic run-up, which was marred by legal wrangling and localised violence that left some 100 people dead. Despite its successes, INEC had to postpone parliamentary polls for 15 senatorial and 48 federal constituencies, where ballot papers had printing errors or had already been used during the aborted election. The PDP maintained its grip on power and won a two-thirds majority in the 109-member senate and an absolute majority in the 360-member house of representatives. The Action Congress of Nigeria (ACN) did reasonably well and came second in both chambers, winning more than a dozen seats in the senate and some 60 seats in the house of representatives, thus confirming its strong stand in the ethnic Yoruba dominated south-west. As in previous elections, several results were subsequently challenged at the **election tribunals**; some were reversed while others were annulled and fresh elections conducted. A small number of cases were still pending in the appeal courts at year's end.

Given the fact that Jonathan had a level of resources no other candidate could hope to match, the ACN and the CPC tried to form an alliance to unseat him. This strategy failed, however, making the result of the **presidential election** a foregone conclusion. Jonathan polled close to 59% of the some 38 m valid votes cast and the runner-up, Buhari, almost 32%. However, against the background of the run-up to the election, local observers and even members of Buhari's inner circle had had no expectation that Buhari would achieve such a respectable result. Interestingly, apart from securing the majority of votes, only Jonathan fulfilled the second constitutional requirement for winning an election, that is to say, to win at least a quarter of the votes cast in 24 states and in the Federal Capital Abuja (FCT). In fact, since Jonathan exceeded this requirement, with 32 states and the FCT, the electorate had given him a mandate stronger than any previously elected head of state or government. Shortcomings and lapses notwithstanding, most international observers and Nigerians saw the poll as the **most credible** in Nigerian history. When the head of INEC officially declared Goodluck Ebele Jonathan the winner on 18 April, he immediately accepted the mandate. Buhari for his part rejected the poll result but refrained from challenging it at the election tribunal. Instead, his party, the CPC, went to the tribunal, but the petition was dismissed on 1 November and, on 28 December, in a unanimous decision, the supreme court confirmed the tribunal's verdict.

However, in some northern parts of the country, a wave of violence unparalleled since the eve of the civil war erupted in the aftermath of the elections. No sooner was it known that Jonathan would definitely win the election than organised gangs, mostly of youths angered by the incumbent's victory, went on the rampage in northern urban centres, particularly in the cities of Kaduna, Kano, Bauchi, Yola and Azare. The apparently well orchestrated protest gathered momentum in the days that followed, and threatened to spiral out of control. Polling stations and INEC offices were vandalised, churches, mosques, houses and police stations set ablaze, up to **1,000 people killed** and thousands of innocent citizens forced to flee their homes before security forces finally checked the spreading violence. According to the national Muslim and Christian leaders, the vast majority of those killed were Muslims, but some 200 Christians suffered a similar fate.

Kaduna state, which on 18 April imposed a two-day 24-hour curfew, suffered the greatest level of destruction and recorded the highest number of deaths. A less rigid curfew in the state lasted until 26 July. Against this background, it emerged that, in the run-up to the general election, INEC's chairman, Attahiru Jega, had sidelined large numbers of staff and had instead entered into close partnership with the **national youth service corps**, which comprised tens of thousands of youths completing their one-year national service outside their home states. This move was aimed at avoiding, or at least significantly reducing, malpractices at the polling stations, an operation which the corps members were able to implement quite successfully. However, ten of them, all but one from southern states, fell victim to the violence in Bauchi state and, soon after, several hundred members originating from the South were evacuated from the North back to their respective states. The slain corps members were given a national burial and the families generously compensated by the government.

On 21 April, Jonathan addressed the nation and vowed that, despite the violent incidents, the final round of elections would go ahead as planned. He also indicated his reluctance to declare a state of emergency in any part of the country.

At the state level, all assembly seats were contested, but of the powerful **gubernatorial mandates** only 26 of the 36 eventually went to the vote. Apart from five sitting governors – three affiliated to the ACN; one to the All Progressive Great Alliance (APGA), and one to the Labour Party (LP) – whose tenure had not yet expired, the legal end of the tenures of five sitting PDP governors in Adamawa, Bayelsa, Cross River, Kogi and Sokoto states was highly contentious. All had reclaimed their governorships in a 2008 re-run, after their victories the previous year had been annulled, so their tenures had started later than all the other duly elected incumbents. In 2010, a constitutional amendment had resolved the contentious tenure issue, and it was on the basis of this amendment that INEC tried to push through the implementation of gubernatorial elections in the five states in question. For their part, the governors argued in court that the case came under pre-amendment regulations. On 15 April, after a fierce legal battle, the appeals court affirmed the judgement of a lower court, which had made the point that constitutional changes could not be applied retrospectively and barred INEC from holding the said ballots. In the case of the re-run in Delta state on 6 January, however, the amended rules were applied, although an appeal by INEC to the supreme court was still pending at year's end. Emmanuel Uduaghan reclaimed his governorship by a considerable margin and abided by the appeals court's verdict, contesting the gubernatorial elections held on 26 April.

Uduaghan and 17 other PDP front runners finally triumphed, while the ACN and the All Nigeria Peoples Party (ANPP) won three and the APGA, LP and CPC one governorship each. In other words, the PDP, despite minor losses, continued to dominate politics at state level. The ACN consolidated its power in the south-western Yoruba region, ANPP kept its position in the north-eastern Kanuri area and the APGA in the Igbo heartland in the south-east. At year's end, all **elected governors** were still in power. Most petitions had been dismissed with only very few exceptions, such as in Borno state where, on 23 December, the appeals court ordered that the petition by the PDP candidate be heard afresh at a different tribunal. The incumbent ANPP governor, Kashim Shettima, challenged this verdict at the supreme court, which was now entitled to deal with the outcome of gubernatorial elections. On 3 December, Kogi state was the first of the five controversial states to conduct a gubernatorial election in accordance with the appeals court's verdict of 15 April. This election was eventually won by PDP candidate Wada Idris.

Thanks to the amended deadline of 21 days for filing petitions and another 180 days for the tribunal's verdict, only some 400 cases involving election disputes were reported, compared with more than 1,200 after the previous general election. However, on 11 May, in the immediate aftermath of the election, a 22-man **investigation panel** on election violence and civil disturbances was inaugurated. The panel was chaired by Sheikh Ahmed Lemu, former Grand Khadi of Niger state, with retired supreme court judge Samson Uwaifo as vice chairman. The report was submitted to the president on 10 October, alerting the nation to the existence of politicians' private armies, widespread unemployment and a security situation that might escalate into unprecedented social unrest. Earlier, on 29 June, the committee on security in the north-east was set up, which in some way officially acknowledged the reality of a deep North-South divide. Its findings were still pending at year's end.

Jonathan was sworn in on 29 May. At the senate's inaugural session on 6 June, PDP-senator David Mark, from Benue state, once again emerged as senate president, while Ike Ekweremadu (PDP), from Enugu state, was re-elected as his deputy. On the same day, Waziri Aminu Tambuwal (PDP) was elected speaker of the house of representatives and Chukwuemeka Nkem Ihedioha (PDP), from Imo state, became deputy speaker. However, these appointments did not meet the party's primary zoning formula, and thus the distribution of power among the top three positions in the Nigerian political system was not as balanced between the six **geo-political zones** as it had been in the past, since it excluded the south-west and the north-east.

In successive steps during July, Jonathan formed his **new cabinet**, reappointing several ministers from his previous government. Diezani Allison-Madueke kept her petroleum resources portfolio, while outgoing finance minister Olusegun Aganga took over the new ministry of trade and investment. In his place, Ngozi Okonjo-Iweala, a managing director of the World Bank, took over the finance ministry for the second time – she had served former president Olusegun Obasanjo in 2005, when Nigeria had settled huge foreign debts with the Paris Club. The career diplomat Olugbenga Ashiru became foreign minister, engineer Bart Nnaji was appointed minister of power, former acting PDP-chairman Bello Harillu Mohammed emerged as the new defence minister, and the well-known editor of 'The Guardian' (Lagos) newspaper, Reuben Abati, was named government spokesperson. Thirteen women were appointed in the new cabinet of some 40 ministers.

In October, the new president dissolved dozens of **federal parastatals** and agencies and assigned their responsibilities to new personnel. Key bodies such as the petroleum product pricing regulatory agency and the department for petroleum resources were assigned to Reginald Chika Stanley and Osten Oluyemisi Olurunsola respectively. In August, Jonah Otunla had already been appointed as the new accountant-general of the federation, and Dahiru Musdapher was named the chief justice, succeeding Aloysius Katsina-Alu, who had reached the mandatory retirement age of 70. In June, two appeals court judges advanced to the supreme court, among them Mary Peter-Odili, bringing the number of **female judges** to two. On 2 December, a total of 144 promoted generals from the three branches of the armed services were awarded their new ranks, and on 14 December, the police force followed suit to the benefit of more than 1,200 police officers of middle and upper ranks. Towards year's end, 25-year-old Blessing Liman became the first female fighter pilot.

Jonathan signed **several acts** into law, including an amended National Minimum Wage Act (22 March), an amended Pension Reform Act (7 April), the Nigeria Sovereign

Investment Authority (Establishment) Act (26 May), which inter alia created the controversial Sovereign Wealth Fund, an amended 2011 budget (27 May), and the Freedom of Information Act (28 May). Soon after the president had been sworn in, he signed the Terrorism (Prevention) Act and an amended and more rigorous Money Laundering (Prohibition) Act, which came into force on 3 June. Prior to that, on 4 March, the president had signed the Constitution of the Federal Republic of Nigeria (Third Alteration) Act, 2010, which altered the constitutional provision for the establishment of the national industrial court.

In the previous year, the **constitutional amendments**, which included significant alterations to executive powers and the electoral law, had been a serious bone of contention. Backed by a federal high court, legal experts insisted that the constitutionally passed amendments be signed by the president, but the National Assembly rejected this argument and challenged it in court. Despite the fact that the appeals court's verdict on this controversial issue was still pending, the president signed the amended constitution into law on 10 January and gave his assent to two new amendments to the electoral act, thus avoiding unpredictable legal wrangling both before and after the general election.

The second half of the year saw a clear deterioration in the already **precarious security situation**, particularly in the North where it reached a nadir, mainly due to clashes between factions of the Islamic sect 'Jama'atu Ahlis Sunna Lid Da'awati Wal Jihad', better known as Boko Haram (meaning 'Western education is forbidden'), and the security forces. In the first half of the year, politicians and Muslim clerics had been assassinated, as had members of the royal family in Borno state. These included ANPP gubernatorial candidate Modu Fannami Gubio and Goni Sheriff, brother of the then ANPP governor, who were killed on 28 January, Abba Anas Umar, younger brother of the Shehu of Borno, killed on 30 May, the cleric Ibrahim Birkuti, killed on 6 June, and several policemen and civilians. The violence culminated in a wave of bomb attacks, suicide bombings, assaults and several deadly raids on police stations, barracks, state security offices and banks in large parts of the northern region. At year's end, at least 500 people, including many northerners of Christian faith, had fallen victim to the assaults. Given the fact that many of these attacks took place in areas with limited means of communication, it was almost impossible to verify the number of assaults and casualties. Although alleged Boko Haram speakers claimed the group's responsibility for most of the attacks, there were plausible indications that sophisticated criminal networks from the South were also at work. Over the years, they have shifted their deadly activities, particularly bank robberies, northward, and exploited the serious sectarian crisis there.

The **bomb attack** on a police headquarters on 16 June, in which at least eight policemen lost their lives, along with the bombing of the UN headquarters in the capital Abuja on 26 August, which cost the lives of 24 civilians, half of them UN staff, marked a clear watershed. At this point, if not before, the federal government showed that it was largely incapable of understanding the multidimensional causes and ramifications of the violence, as well as the threat it posed to the political system as a whole. A modest attempt by former president Obasanjo to establish some form of dialogue with **Boko Haram** was immediately shattered. On 15 September, two days after his meeting with Babakuru Fugu, a brother-in-law of the executed leader Mohammed Yusuf, Fugu was killed. In the wake of these bombings and killings, the worst political and strategic blunder was the direct involvement of the military, which, instead of enforcing and coordinating intelligence for all the security agencies, itself became part of the problem. Moreover, the president hinted that backers and sympathisers of Boko Haram might even have penetrated the state machinery, thereby hampering any effective response. On two occasions alone, on 9 and 25 July, more than 50 suspected **Islamic militants** were shot dead in the course of large-scale military actions in Maiduguri. The forthright criticism by top members of the Islamic establishment, including the Sultan of Sokoto, of the military's brutal behaviour was tantamount to an official acknowledgement of its contentious role. Despite such criticism, the government did not learn from its mistakes. Worse still, it continued to ignore the fact that radical Islamist thinking had gained the hearts and minds of many in the Muslim north. Moreover, it reminded the public of the extra-judicial killing of the Boko Haram leaders in 2009. In this regard, and despite damning footage, five policemen, who had allegedly conducted the execution in cold blood and who were charged in court, were eventually released on bail on 19 July.

In many cases, Boko Haram chose to target civilians at popular drinking spots in north-eastern urban centres such as Maiduguri, where, on 26 June alone, two dozen were killed. Attackers created **carnage** amongst the citizens of Yobe state capital Damaturu on 5 November, killing about 150 people, including some 20 soldiers. Shortly after, the minister for youth development ordered that no new youth service corps members be posted to Borno and Yobe states, while those who had already been posted should be redeployed to other states. On 27 November, the divisional police headquarters, the First Bank and the council secretariat in Geidam, the home of the governor of Yobe state, were bombed and a number of churches and market stalls destroyed. Four policemen lost their lives during the assault. On Christmas Day, two bombs targeting churches killed 44 people. One was set off at St Theresa's Catholic Church in Madalla in Niger State, not far from Abuja, killing 43 people, and another at the Mountain of Fire and Miracle Church in Jos, Plateau state, killing one. In addition, four state security officers lost their lives in a suicide bomb blast in Damaturu.

Despite several arrests and charges being brought against alleged Boko Haram militants and the indictment of Borno state PDP-senator Mohammed Ali Ndume for having **links to the sect**, the federal and various state governments could not contain the violence. The senator, who was arrested along with one Sanda Umar Konduga on 21 November, was charged with terrorism, but pleaded not guilty. On 10 December, Ndume was granted bail on stringent conditions, while Konduga was sentenced to three years' imprisonment on 6 December. The latter admitted that he had been a spokesman for the group under the name of Usman al-Zawahiri, but maintained that he had been expelled on suspicion of being a government agent.

On New Year's Eve, an allegedly exasperated but hesitant president declared a **state of emergency** in 15 local government areas in four states – Borno, Niger, Plateau and Yobe – while on the same day an Islamic school in the city of Sapele in Delta state was attacked, causing the exodus of the small Muslim community of ethnic Hausa-Fulani, although no one was killed. Prior to that, on 11 December, a bomb had been set off in a mosque in the same city and shortly thereafter one injured person died. On 6 December, 20,000 Muslims had joined a peaceful demonstration in Kaduna staged by Ibrahim Zakzaky's Muslim Brethren to mark Ashura day. Towards the end of the year, on 21 December, two factions of the purist Izala movement reunited, having been split for about 20 years.

Against the background of party primaries and the forthcoming elections in the eastern part of the **Middle Belt**, particularly Plateau and Bauchi states – for years a centre of sectarian clashes – conflicts continued unabated, leaving a relatively large number of people dead. In January, attacks and counter attacks in and around the city of Jos by members of both faiths cost dozens of lives. Once again, some of the worst incidents occurred in Barkin Ladi local government area, close to the capital Jos. Over the course of the year, this area alone experienced at least eight deadly attacks, with more than 60 people killed, the worst assaults taking place in mid-August and on 24 November. During the latter, a local Christian councillor lost four children.

The police in neighbouring Bauchi, capital of the state of the same name, foiled a bomb attack in a church on 31 January, days after **sectarian youth violence** had caused the death of some 20 people. The town of Tafawa Balewa, home of Nigeria's first prime minister of the same name, became another epicentre of violence. There, on 26 January, trouble broke out between a Christian billiard table owner and a Muslim player in a dispute over money. Soon after, mosques and dozens of houses were set ablaze with at least four people killed and more than 4,000 displaced. On 6 May, a further 16 people were killed when several houses were set on fire in a revenge attack, and a further dozen people lost their lives when a bomb blast rocked a popular drinking place inside an army barracks on the city's periphery on 29 May.

The security forces were limited in their ability to quell the sectarian violence. The seizure of a truck with bomb-making devices on the Kaduna-Jos road on 11 March was one of their rare success stories. The military was increasingly blamed for taking sides and even for shooting innocent citizens. On 24 January, for example, villagers hurled stones and burned the tents of **military personnel** whom they blamed for killing five locals in Farin Lamba, not far from Jos, a few days earlier.

Over the course of the year, news of the serious crisis in the North somewhat overshadowed volatile incidents in the **Niger Delta**, as well as the unabated spread of organised crime throughout the country. On 11–12 May, militants believed to be loyal to self-proclaimed 'General' John Togo and his Niger Delta Liberation Force fought a gun battle with soldiers of the joint military force near the Ayakoromo community in Delta state. In another encounter on 17 November, nine soldiers and an unknown number of the gang were killed. In addition, piracy was on the rise, though not on the scale seen off the coast of Somalia. On 30 October, for example, pirates seized the Maltese oil tanker MT Halifax off the coast of Port Harcourt. The ship was released the following week after part of the cargo had been siphoned off, but no crew members were harmed. On 10 November, a former lieutenant commander, Lawrence Adesanya, who was thought to have abused his former position within the petroleum task force, was paraded alongside four other suspected pirates. They were accused of having hijacked on 7 October and 3 November two vessels carrying tonnes of premium motor spirit and gas oil.

On 21 October, however, a federal court in Delta state sentenced two Ghanaians and seven Nigerians to ten years for illegal oil trade and conspiracy. This was one of the rare occasions when oil thieves were arrested and convicted. **Kidnappings** remained common in the area, although the overall numbers decreased. On 12 May, a British and an Italian construction worker were taken hostage in Birnin Kebbi, and their fate was still unknown at year's end. On 9 June, five members of the national youth corps, deployed in Rivers state, were abducted outside Port Harcourt and their captors quickly demanded a ransom of Naira 100 m, which they later reduced to Naira 10 m. The hostages were eventually freed by police on 20 June, but it was not clear whether any ransom had been paid. Michael Obi, father of the famous Chelsea midfielder Mikel Obi, suffered a similar fate, being captured on 12 August in Plateau state and released ten days later. Two soldiers attached to the joint military force in Jos, along with six others, were arrested in connection with the kidnapping. Months later, two Catholic clerics, Sylvester Chukwura in Edo and Chijioke Amoke in Enugu state, were abducted on 3 October and 2 November respectively. The first was freed by security forces on 16 October and some of the kidnappers were arrested, while the second regained his freedom on 9 November. As in most cases, no information was available as to whether a ransom had been paid.

Despite ongoing criticism of the 2009 amnesty programme, the federal government continued its programme for the rehabilitation and reintegration of some 26,000 **ex-militants**. However, it eventually emerged that the government had put even more emphasis on sending youths abroad for various vocational training courses in Africa, Asia, the US and the Middle East, with some 2,000 benefiting from this costly exercise. Moreover, those who had successfully passed through the non-violence and reformatory training in the Obubra camp in Cross River state, were to be paid a transitional safety allowance of an unknown amount over and above the so-called monthly stipend of Naira 65,000. Prior to that, in May, the then minister for petroleum had announced that 12,000 teenagers were to be employed to protect oil and gas pipelines. On 25 May, almost 4,000 guns and several rocket-propelled grenades recovered from the militants were publicly destroyed.

Raids on banks across the country ran into dozens and, almost out of the blue, southwestern Ogun state became a centre for **armed robberies**. A police officer and three civilians were killed in Ilaro, when four banks were robbed on 11 August. In one day, on 10 November, a gang of 20 robbed five banks on the Olabisi Onabanjo University campus in Ago Iwoye and made off with millions of naira. This was one of the rare cases where no one was killed. On 23 November, four banks were raided in the Sabo/Akarigbo area of Sagamu and almost a dozen people killed; on 13 December, the police paraded some 17 suspects, allegedly responsible for this crime. On 14 December, a gang blocked the busy Ota-Idiroko road for some two hours, robbing traders and passers-by of hundreds of thousands of naira. By pure chance, some armed air force personnel on their way to an exercise ran into the robbers and engaged them in a shoot-out, which forced the bandits to flee. Again in early December, in protest against the incessant attacks, almost all the banks in the state abandoned their services for a few days, bringing business to a virtual standstill. On 15 November, about 20 people died in the Sango-Ota area, when opposing factions of the National Union of Road Transport Workers clashed over the control of car parks in the state. This occurred in the aftermath of the gubernatorial election, in which the PDP lost the governorship to the ACN.

The deteriorating general security situation, exacerbated by long-standing corruption within the upper echelons of the police force, was matched by a worsening **human and civil rights record**. Nevertheless, the courts discharged several suspected criminals for lack of evidence, while governors commuted prison terms and death sentences. On 17 January, for example, a Lagos court acquitted Lucky Igbinovia and Effong Elemi Edu, who were standing trial for the 1995 murder of Alfred Rewane, a leading critic of the then military regime. The two had been in detention for 16 years. Five other accused died while awaiting trial. On 4 February, the supreme court overruled a court martial judgement that had convicted and demoted then rear-admiral Francis Agbiti in 2005 for alleged fraud and related matters. Among other things, the unanimous judgement stated that the entire proceedings were invalid, as the court martial was not properly constituted.

On 18 October, six suspects accused of involvement in the January crisis in Plateau state were acquitted and, on 13 October, an appeal court confirmed the verdict of a lower court, which the previous year had discharged retired Major Hamza Al-Mustapha, a notorious chief security officer of the late dictator Sani Abacha, and three others, who were accused of the attempted murder of the celebrated newspaper publisher Alex Ibru. However, Al-Mustapha and one Lateef Shofolahan were remanded in custody pending another trial related to the much publicised murder of Mrs Kudirat Abiola in 1996. The judge eventually moved the date for the verdict of this controversial case to early 2012. To mark the 51st anniversary of Independence, the Ondo state governor commuted five death sentences to life imprisonment and empowered the prison authority to discharge six prisoners who had served part of their sentence. On 24 November, a high court judge in Lagos awarded more than $ 155,000 compensation to the ethnic Yoruba comedian Babatunde Omidina, alias Baba Suwe, for the flagrant abuse and infringement of his fundamental human rights by the national drug law enforcement agency. On 12 October, he had been detained on suspicion of drug-trafficking, but after more than three weeks in custody and some 20 bowel movements, no drugs were excreted and on 4 November the actor was released on bail. The agency appealed the ruling.

On 29 November, the senate introduced a rigorous bill **banning same sex marriage**, a bill backed by leading clerics, both Muslim and Christian. By year's end it had not yet passed into law. As for the internationalisation of jurisprudence, on 18 January, the ECOWAS court of justice in Abuja dismissed any objections by the federal government and the oil companies, asserting its jurisdiction over a case brought by a registered NGO involving both violation of human rights and oil pollution in the Niger Delta. Thus, the court concurred with its vice president, Benfeito Mosso Ramos, who had maintained in December the previous year that disregarding the court's verdict was tantamount to a violation of the ECOWAS treaty.

The **anti-corruption campaign** produced few positive results. Most charges by the Economic and Financial Crime Commission (EFCC) against politicians, such as the outgoing speaker Dimeji Bankole and deputy speaker Usman Bayero Nafada, and several bankers, were either dismissed outright in court or the accused were granted bail. In a rare case, on 2 March, a federal high court granted the EFCC an asset forfeiture order to seize properties of former Edo state governor Lucky Igbinedion over an alleged Naira 3.2 bn fraud case. He had already been convicted and fined in 2008, but the EFCC had appealed that verdict. After fresh evidence of embezzlement and money laundering, Igbinedion was declared wanted, but the case was still pending at year's end and showed that the EFCC's record was at best mixed. The subsequent sacking of the chairman, Farida Waziri, did not come as a surprise and, on 23 November, Ibrahim Lamorde, director of operations, was appointed acting chairman in her place. Much earlier, on 9 February, the senate had rejected the president's nomination for the Independent Corrupt Practices and other Related Offences Commission, maintaining that the nominee was too old. Soon after his inauguration as president, Jonathan nominated Francis Ugochukwu Elechi, which drew scorn from civil society groups. On 29 November, at the eleventh hour, Jonathan suspended the swearing-in after receiving disturbing calls and reports, and eventually appointed board member Ekpo Una Owo Nta as acting chairman.

On 20 November, the 66-year-old founder, chairman and publisher of 'The Guardian' (Lagos) newspaper, Alex Ibru, passed away. A few days later, on 26 November, 78-year-old Chukwuemeka Odumegwu Ojukwu, the leader of the breakaway state of **Biafra**, died after a protracted illness.

Foreign Affairs

Good relations with the **US**, Nigeria's most important crude oil and liquefied gas customer, were to some extent shaped by the Boko Haram complex. On 29 September, Secretary of State Hillary Clinton, at a joint press conference with her Nigerian counterpart,

Olugbenga Ashiru, in Washington, assured Nigeria that the US would stand by the nation as it faced serious security issues. At the start of the year, the first FBI agents were already deployed to Nigeria to help investigate previous bombings. Other agents arrived after the deadly attack on the police headquarters in June and, soon after, the then inspector-general of police Hafiz Ringim went to the US for a five-day working visit. In addition, in November, Nigerian soldiers received training in counter terrorism tactics in the US, at a time when experts warned a congressional hearing on 30 November that Boko Haram posed an emerging threat to US interests and the US homeland. During a four-day visit in mid-August, the head of US Africa Command, General Carter Ham, had set the agenda when he made a broad reference to a potential alliance between al-Qaida in the Maghreb and Boko Haram, al-Shabaab and other alleged militant groups, fuelling rumours of a worsening security situation and the threat of international terrorism in West Africa. On 13 May, at a handover ceremony in California, the Nigerian navy took over a US coast-guard ship, donated by the US government, to patrol the Niger Delta region. For its part, Nigeria paid some $ 8 m for the refurbishment of the vessel. In June, both sides signed an in-flight security agreement, involving the deployment of security officers on international flights.

Earlier, on 17 February, USAID had signed a $ 50 m partnership with Chevron's Niger Delta partnership initiative to try to help develop local businesses and boost community relations in the restive oil and gas producing area. This may have been in anticipation of a pending lawsuit against Shell, in which, on 17 October, the US supreme court eventually decided to consider the potential liabilities of corporations under the long-standing Alien Tort Claims Act. The Nigerian plaintiffs, relatives of the Ogonis who were hanged in 1995 after a show trial, charged Shell with complicity in torture, extra-judicial executions and crimes against humanity. On 11 October, the trial of Umar Farouk Abdulmutallab, accused of trying to blow up a US-bound flight on Christmas Day 2009, began with a guilty plea. Both **law suits** were still pending at year's end. On 13 October, 42-old Nigerian-born Bidemi Bello was sentenced to almost 12 years imprisonment by a US court on human trafficking charges. Her US citizenship was revoked and, besides being ordered to pay compensation, she was to be deported upon completion of her sentence. Nevertheless, Nigeria retained its good ranking in the eyes of the State Department because of its genuine efforts to combat human trafficking.

In a move aimed at strengthening political and economic ties, the newly elected Goodluck Jonathan was given a warm welcome in the White House on 8 June. Earlier, on 10 March, high profile US companies, led by the Assistant Secretary of Commerce Suresh Kumar, had paid a visit to Nigeria to explore **investments**, particularly in the ailing power sector. In August, a working group of the bi-national commission in Abuja reaffirmed its commitment to the implementation of power sector reform and, in December, a Nigerian trade mission, accompanied by US Ambassador Terence McCulley, attended a power trade show in Las Vegas. Last but not least, the US government institution, the Overseas Private Investment Corporation, approved $ 250 m to finance two US firms helping to revitalise Union Bank of Nigeria to enable it to reach the many people in Nigeria who do not have a bank account.

During a high-ranking meeting between Britain's Prime Minister David Cameron and the Nigerian president and key ministers from both sides in Lagos on 19 July, Cameron assured Jonathan of **British support** for Nigeria's efforts in restructuring its anti-terrorism security. During a visit to Nigeria in late June, Secretary of State for International Development Andrew Mitchell announced that Britain was to spend £ 50 m on family planning and nutrition in the states most affected by malnutrition. However, Nigeria's relations with Britain were shaped more by legal issues, involving members of the large **Nigerian diaspora**. The prisoners' transfer deal, which would permit Britain to transfer Nigerian offenders to Nigerian prisons, was still high on the agenda. The corresponding Nigerian bill had not yet been become law at year's end, but in late October, it was reported that both governments had signed a so-called Prisoner Exchange Agreement.

On 18 March, Lucy Adeniji, was jailed in Britain for 11½ years, having been found guilty of **trafficking children** into the UK for domestic servitude. She had entered the UK on a false passport in the mid-1980s and had become a pastor of the evangelical church TLCC Ministries. On 7 July, 32-old Anthony Harris, who was alleged to have several aliases and believed to be a key player in a sophisticated network of West African human traffickers, was sentenced to 20 years. Although refused asylum after his arrival in 2003, he was later granted indefinite leave to remain. Two girls from southern Nigeria, controlled by Juju magic rituals, had been imprisoned in his home in Stratford and were about to be sent to Greece and Spain as prostitutes. On 20 May, four Nigerian women, who came to Britain during their childhood, were awarded £ 5,000 each after a court verdict stated that the Metropolitan Police Service had failed to investigate allegations of slavery. On 18 December, a stewardess of the Nigerian airline 'Arik Air', Chinwendu Uwakaonyenma Ogbonnaya, was arrested at Heathrow Airport on suspicion of smuggling cocaine into Britain.

The most prominent lawsuit concerned James Ibori. The former Delta state governor had sought refuge in Dubai, where he had been arrested at the request of Britain's Metropolitan Police for various **money laundering** offences the previous year, and on 15 April he was eventually extradited to Britain. The court case was still pending at year's end, but his UK lawyer, Bhadresh Gohil, had already been given a seven-year sentence in March.

The dynamics of increasing economic cooperation with **China** almost came to a standstill, particularly in the energy sector. Nigeria's state-run oil company, the Nigerian National Petroleum Corporation, and the oil states concerned had failed to fulfil their obligations concerning the already planned and badly needed construction of three oil refineries, thereby postponing the project indefinitely. In February, diplomats and politicians celebrated the 40th anniversary of diplomatic relations in a rather low-key way. However, on 19 December, the China Great Wall Industry Corporation successfully launched the Nigerian communications satellite NIGCOMSAT-1R into orbit.

The 'Arab Spring' in North Africa did not fail to have an impact on Nigeria, which in late August recognised **Libya**'s National Transitional Council as that country's legitimate government. Apart from the fact that a number of Nigerians had served as mercenaries in Kadhafi's army, several thousand civilians were living and working in Libya and Egypt. An unknown number of Nigerians died during the uprising and, in the course of the year, a few thousand were evacuated, with several managing to return home across the desert, among them an undisclosed number of mercenaries whose presence strengthened Boko Haram in the north-east. In the light of security threats in the region, the ECOWAS committee of chiefs of defence met in Abuja on 3–5 October. Earlier, on 11 March, Nigeria and **Cameroon** had agreed to jointly exploit any cross-border oil and gas reserves in the Bakassi peninsula. And in May, the West African Gas Pipeline Project Company WAPCo finally started its commercial activities, if only on a rather limited scale.

On 1 February, Jonathan travelled to **Turkey** on a two-day state visit, after attending the AU summit in Addis Ababa. He joined the second AU summit in Equatorial Guinea on 30 June to 1 July, and received German Chancellor Angela Merkel in mid-July. It was the first visit by a German head of government for 25 years. Soon after, on 21 July, the president paid a visit to Liberia, and in early October he went for a two-day working visit to **Rwanda** in anticipation of the December launching of direct flights run by RwandAir between Kigali and Lagos. On 9 August, Jonathan received his Niger counterpart, Mahamadou Issoufou. However, when President Jacob Zuma of **South Africa** attended the annual Shehu Musa Yar'Adua memorial lecture in Abuja on 10 December, he was only welcomed by the vice president. Jonathan addressed the UN General Assembly in New York on 21 September, joined the 21st Commonwealth summit in Australia at the end of October, and in late November opened an international investors' council meeting in Paris, coordinated by Baroness Lynda Chalker. Prior to that, on 12 November, French Foreign Minister Alain Juppé met his counterpart in Abuja, offering France's assistance in tackling terrorism. The president rounded off the year on 19 December by welcoming the new managing director of the IMF Christine Lagarde, who attended an economic forum in Lagos the following day.

On 17 January, Babatunde Osotimehin was sworn in as executive director of the UN Population Fund by Secretary-General Ban Ki-moon, who paid his first official visit to the country on 22–23 May. In December, a Nigerian, Chile Eboe-Osuji, was elected to serve on the bench of the **ICC** for the first time.

Socioeconomic Developments

In the course of the year, oil and gas prices remained high and Nigeria benefited strongly from its high quality crude, which was sold at $ 95 a barrel at the start of the year and close to $ 110 at year's end.

However, the **2011 budget**, totalling Naira 4.48 trillion ($ 28 bn) based on a benchmark of $ 75 per barrel and an exchange rate of Naira 150 to $ 1, was not signed by Jonathan until 27 May, and only after a series of deliberations with lawmakers. Earlier, on 16 March, the National Assembly had covertly inflated the initially proposed budget of Naira 4.2 trillion to Naira 4.9 trillion, which had prompted the president to send it back. On 13 December, Jonathan presented his 2012 budget proposal of Naira 4.75 trillion, emphasising the need to create jobs, particularly for young people, and to address the rising domestic debt profile. Interestingly, the sensitive issue of fuel subsidies, which accounted for up to $ 7 bn annually, was omitted. In fact, not long before, the senate had revealed that some 100 companies were the real beneficiaries of the heavily subsidised fuel import contracts, and that the latter were not unrelated to corrupt practices.

Against the background of Boko Haram and increasing youth violence in large parts of the country, however, the government finally acknowledged the existence of a "ticking time bomb". Regarding **demographic development**, it was suggested that the population had doubled to more than 160 m over 20 years, with some 40% aged under 15, and at least 20 m young people were jobless, posing a genuine danger to the political and socioeconomic system. Local observers estimated that the number was far higher.

As in previous years, the central banks issued bonds and treasury bills with varying maturities almost monthly, this year worth more than $ 12 bn. In addition, on 21 January, Nigeria issued a $ 500 m debut Eurobond, which was heavily oversubscribed. Towards the end of the year, the **debt management** office announced that external debt stood at an acceptable $ 5.6 bn, while Nigeria's domestic debt amounted to more than $ 34 bn, a steep increase of some 20% within a year.

While the promised wide-ranging reforms to the oil and gas industry were put on hold, to be considered by the new National Assembly the following year, the government, together with the central bank, continued to restructure and stabilise the **banking sector**. Thus, the court of appeal upheld the verdict of a lower court, which had ruled that the governor of the central bank had the power to hire and fire directors of any bank found to be in a serious financial predicament. In addition, in late November, the bank declared 82 of the 104 licensed finance houses to be unhealthy and undercapitalised. These institutions had been assigned the task of offering financial services to small and medium-sized enterprises. On 20 June, the central bank granted the first Islamic banking licence to Jaiz Bank International, run by well-known bankers and businessmen such as Umaru Abdul Mutallab, Falau Bello and Aminu Alhassan Dantata. Soon after, on 4 July, the Nigerian branch of South African Standard Bank was given approval to set up an Islamic banking division.

Nigeria's phenomenal growth in the **telecommunications sector** continued apace as the number of mobile phones in use rocketed to more than 80 m. In Africa's biggest and fastest growing telecoms market, demand was still outstripping supply. In the light of these developments, the UAE-based company, Etisalat, signed agreements on 10 March for a $ 650 m syndicated loan with local banks. The following day, the leading provider, MTN Nigeria, an arm of the South African MTN Group, announced that it was to spend $ 1 bn in the following year. And on 7 June, the indigenous company Globacom signed another long-term contract with Shell, to provide a high-speed broadband link, connecting Shell's operational hubs in Lagos and the Niger Delta. According to the science and technology ministry, Nigeria spends some $ 450 m annually on importing foreign bandwidth and $ 100 m on services, so the long-awaited launch of the communication satellite NIGCOMSAT-1R in December was a real boost for Nigeria's ICT. Earlier, on 17 August, two Nigerian earth observation satellites had already been successfully sent into orbit in Russia.

The spread of **HIV/AIDS** continued unabated and it was reported that the number of infections had passed the 7 m mark. Compared with previous years, progress in the fight to eradicate **polio** suffered a minor setback, indicated by the fact that 60 cases were reported towards year's end. The figure of more than 3,000 deaths and some 18,000 injured in over 2,200 road **traffic accidents** proved Nigeria's poor road safety record once again. In this respect, it was hardly surprising that, according to the Federal Road Safety Commission, some 60% of driving licences in Delta state were fake, indicating a serious and widespread problem.

The federal government continued to further the commercialisation of **education** when, on 2 March, it approved licences for four new private universities in Kwara, Edo and Osun state and the Federal Capital Territory. The overall number of universities thus increased to 118, comprising 36 federal, 37 state and 45 private universities.

On 3 April, the German, Uli Beier, passed away in Australia, aged 89. He had arrived in Nigeria in 1950 as a lecturer at the University of Ibadan, Nigeria's only university at the time. In the decades to come, Beier recognised the creative spirit and verve of **Nigerian literature** and arts, particularly in the Yoruba-speaking area, and enthusiastically represented their interests in other parts of the world. On 2 May, the US-based 2009 winner of the 'Caine Prize for African Writing', E.C. Osondu, was announced as one of the winners of the 'Pushcart Prize' for his short story "Janjaweed Wife".

While the U-20 soccer team won the sixth Africa youth championship final against Cameroon on 1 May, the Nigerian 'Super Eagles' failed for the first time in 25 years to qualify for the 2012 **African Cup of Nations**, after the last game in Abuja, on 8 October against Guinea, ended in a 2–2 draw, handing Guinea the ticket to the finals.

Heinrich Bergstresser

Senegal

Senegal went through a bumpy year politically, wholly preoccupied with the presidential election due in March 2012 and President Abdoulaye Wade's controversial candidacy. While the opposition failed to unite behind a single candidate, it put up powerful resistance to the regime's manoeuvres. Tensions resulted in urban unrest. The political context resulted in a boost in public expenditure, which aggravated the state deficit but counterbalanced a catastrophic rainy season.

Domestic Politics

Wade's candidacy and his **potential succession** by his son Karim remained the main political issue. For some time, the country had been living with the idea that Wade was paving the way for Karim to take over by means of what critics called a "monarchical devolution". The handshake between Karim and Barack Obama arranged by French President Nicolas Sarkozy at the G8 Deauville summit in May 2011 fed into the controversy.

That perspective caused much frustration, beginning in Wade's 'Parti Démocratique Sénégalais' (PDS) itself. A former Wade associate and prime minister, Idrissa Seck, had never hidden his ambitions to replace Wade at the head of the PDS. He had already been excluded from the party in August 2005 and had run on his own in the 2007 president elections, only to return to the PDS. As Seck kept pushing his own candidacy against Wade's, he was expelled from the party for a second time on 22 April.

Frustration was no less among the general public, in a context of deteriorating living conditions, especially in Dakar and its suburbs. In January, a **new movement** appeared alongside 'Bennoo Siggil Senegal' (BSS, 'United to boost Senegal', in Wolof), the coalition of the main opposition parties: journalist Fadel Barro and rap artists Malal Talla, Thiaat and Simon created 'Y'en a marre' ('Enough is enough'), a youth movement calling for peaceful political change, strongly criticising the Wade regime independent of all political parties and calling for a 'nouveau type de Sénégalais', i.e. a committed and attentive citizen, conscious of his rights and duties. The challenges presented by 'Y'en a marre' and BSS prompted heavy-handed reactions from Wade's regime, some of them clumsy. On the very evening of 'Y'en a marre''s first meeting, held on 19 March to mark the 11th anniversary of Wade's coming to power, Justice Minister Cheikh Tidiane Sy announced that the BSS youth wing, student movements and some opposition leaders had been preparing a coup. Although some activists were interrogated by the police, the accusations petered out, ending in ridicule.

A turning point came on 23 June, when the National Assembly, an institution where the ruling PDS had an overwhelming majority, examined a spectacular two-tier **constitutional reform**. The reform proposed that the vice president – a position created by an earlier constitutional revision, but to which no one had ever been appointed – would be elected with the president on the same ticket. Many suspected that Wade would put his son on his ticket and resign soon after if he were to win, thus passing on the presidency to Karim. The other major proposal, couched in suspiciously innocuous tones, was the 'quart bloquant': according to this provision, the candidate who came first in the first round of the presidential election would be deemed to have won the election if he received at least 25% of the votes, a project which many thought revealed the regime's loss of electoral confidence and its desperate attempt to win regardless.

On 23 June, the day of the debate in the Assembly, BSS and 'Y'en a marre' called for protests. The demonstrations were important and by and large peaceful, but for some incidents in which civil society activist Alioune Tine was assaulted by PDS militants and the properties of several leading PDS hardliners were attacked. Even within the PDS, where many seemed unhappy at the prospect of Wade's candidacy and his son's succession, dissent was acute, and several PDS representatives in the Assembly declared their opposition to the reform. The **regime backpedalled**, withdrawing the project. Only a few days later, on 27 June, persistent power cuts provoked a new spate of riots in Dakar and Mbour. This did much to energise Wade's adversaries, who created the 'Mouvement du 23 juin' (M23), dedicated to opposing Wade's candidacy on constitutional grounds: the constitution, which Wade had got adopted in 2001, clearly stated that a president could only remain in post for two terms, and Wade's argument that, since he had been elected under the older constitution, his first mandate did not count, failed to convince many. On 14 July, Wade reacted to critics who pointed out that he himself had previously insisted that he would not run for a third term. His phrase on that day, "maa waxoon waxeet" ("I spoke, and I am going back on my word", in Wolof) became a symbol for critics.

As M23 was trying to keep up the momentum, organising rallies, and 'Y'en a marre' was busy setting up cells throughout the country (the so-called 'esprits'), the judicial controversy continued. After an M23-sponsored gathering of constitutional experts declared Wade's candidacy unconstitutional on 23 August, **Wade counter-attacked**, hiring a US law firm and mobilising lawyers linked to the French right, who pronounced in his favour on 21 November. In addition, on 15 December, Wade announced the creation of an additional public holiday to celebrate the 'magal', the religious festival of the influential Murid brotherhood. He had already made gestures to mollify interest groups and potential middlemen, announcing on 19 July that village chiefs would soon start receiving a salary from the state, and meeting with the 'Collectif des Associations des Écoles Coraniques' on 28 September. He also targeted smaller strategic groups, granting pay raises to senior magistrates, including members of the Constitutional Council, who were expected to decide on the validity of his candidacy, and the state auditors.

When the time came for the composite movement that had been fighting Wade to decide on a candidate, things did not go well. Idrissa Seck had made it clear on 30 June that he would be running, and another of Wade's former prime ministers, Macky Sall, had been preparing for this himself since his fall from grace in 2008, touring the Senegalese heartland to develop networks of supporters, while BSS had to deal with the ambitions of its large and varied membership. Debates became so tense that, on 6 September, some of the smaller parties of BSS, civil society organisations and independent individuals created a new structure, 'Bennoo Alternative 2012', to decide on the criteria by which a candidate should be chosen. 'Bennoo Alternative 2012' designated star journalist Abdou Latif Coulibaly as its candidate on 15 December, but several other **presidential candidates** declared themselves, including Mansour Sy Djamil and Amsatou Sow Sidibé. As for BSS, on 1 December, a majority of member organisations designated Moustapha Niasse, the leader of the 'Alliance des Forces du Progrès', giving him 19 votes against 14 for Ousmane Tanor Dieng. Dieng's 'Parti Socialiste' (PS), which had ruled Senegal from 1960 to 2000, rejected the decision. The PS had earlier proposed that votes be allotted according to the number of representatives sitting in local councils – a means of ensuring that their strong presence on local authorities would win them the vote. On 10 December, Macky Sall was unsurprisingly nominated by the party he had created, the 'Alliance pour la République'.

As for Wade, he was nominated on 23 December by the PDS and its coalition, the 'Forces Alliées pour la Victoire en 2012'. In speeches on 14 September and 26 November, singer and media businessman **Youssou Ndour**, who the previous year had created a civil society movement of his own, announced that he too would enter the political arena, leading many to suspect that he was considering running for president. At the end of

December, about 30 people had declared their intention of running for the highest office (though they had not yet submitted their candidacy to the Constitutional Council), and more names were being aired in the press, including those of renowned former international civil servants Jacques Diouf and Lamine Diack.

On 9 November, Wade offered cabinet positions to both Ousmane Tanor Dieng and Moustapha Niasse, a possible indication of his vulnerability but also of the growing strength of Macky Sall. Both men flatly refused. As tension mounted, politics ended up in court. On 18 October, Malick Noël Seck, the leader of a PS substructure, appeared before a court about a letter that he had brought to the president of the Constitutional Council, pressing the latter to reject Wade's candidacy. He was found guilty of death threats and contempt of court and began serving a two-year prison sentence – the decision of the court of appeal was due in early 2012. On 19 December, it was Alioune Tine, the M23 coordinator, who was interrogated. On 22 December, the mayor of a Dakar district and leader of the PS youth wing, Barthélémy Dias, shot at a group of PDS **party thugs**; one of them was killed and three more wounded. Dias was arrested but pleaded self-defence. This episode led to a tense debate over the intimidation strategies of the PDS and over 'nervis' – thugs some parties recruited for the campaign, often from wrestling teams. The media reported that Baye Moussé Bâ, a Wade bodyguard, had been involved in the recruitment of the men involved in the Dias incident.

The campaign also led to controversy over **opinion polls**: the publication, on 22 November, of the supposed and contradictory results of unspecified polls in two different newspapers stirred trouble, and the editors of the newspapers involved were questioned. On 5 December, the 'Commission Nationale des Sondages', supposedly in charge of vetting all opinion polls, confirmed that the publication of polls would not be allowed during the campaign.

Controversy also raged over the organisation of the election itself, despite the fact that a few specialists, including constitutional lawyer Ismaila Madior Fall, insisted that the electoral system was generally satisfactory. The US, Germany and the EU financed a mission to scrutinise the electoral list and its report was published on 2 February. A 'Comité de veille et de suivi des recommandations' was set up on 11 January, but tensions between the majority and the opposition made it difficult to designate a chair. On 14 March, Abdoul Mazid Ndiaye, the experienced and respected head of a leading Pan-African NGO, was appointed. **Voter registration** was exceptionally prolonged, taking until 31 July, and the electoral code was revised in September. Distrust was so high that, for the first time in Senegal's history, it was decided to have an international observation mission and, in October, the authorities asked the EU and US to provide observers. The deposit that was required from presidential candidates was substantially increased in August (from CFAfr 25 m to CFAfr 65 m), which caused another outrage. On 12 December, a decree set the date for the first round of the election on 26 February 2012. It did not help that a leading minister, Khouraïchi Thiam, said on 10 December that the supposedly neutral regional governors were committed to Wade's victory and would support his campaign. Some opponents demanded the resignation of the governors, but to no effect.

Minor cabinet reshuffles took place, though it was not clear whether these were about sanctioning the ministers less active in the campaign or those less competent. Moustapha Sourang lost the ministry of education only to return to the ministry of defence in December, replacing Bécaye Diop, considered too soft and demoted to urban planning and sanitation. Khadim Guèye, the minister of agriculture, was replaced by the controversial Amath Sall, and took over the portfolio of civil service and employment from Abdoulaye Makhtar Diop, who took over the ministry of sports.

In the **Casamance region**, separatist guerrilla groups of the 'Mouvement des Forces Démocratiques de Casamance' (MFDC) continued their offensive. By March 15, government soldiers had been killed in various incidents. Most notable were direct assaults on army camps in Karongue on 20 February and Goudomp on 3 March. In February, drawing on the South Sudanese precedent, a moderate member of the MFDC civilian wing, Ansoumana Badji, called for a referendum on self-determination in a letter to the UN and AU; his proposal was turned down by the authorities. In March, the armed forces declared themselves to be in a "situation of war" and the chief of staff, Abdoulaye Fall, said he would stop listening to politicians calling for temporisation. With reinforcements coming in, the army launched a large-scale operation in the districts of Sindian and Diouloulou, which ended on 22 March with the loss of four more soldiers. Things stayed relatively calm until August, which saw a multiplication of armed robberies launched against vehicles along the Ziguinchor-Senoba road and villages along the Guinea-Bissau border.

In a speech on Independence Day, 4 April, Wade called for peace, insisting that the government would guarantee the security and reintegration of the **separatist militants** who turned themselves in, but that those who persisted would be fought and that no concessions could be made regarding the country's territorial integrity. In May, the authorities secured the release of a number of MFDC moderates imprisoned in Gambia on suspicion of involvement in a coup attempt in that country. On 16 August, Wade visited Gambia, calling on President Jammeh to help him to achieve peace in Casamance. Jammeh insisted that "solving the crisis in Casamance is in the best interest of the two countries" and that "Gambia will never be a safe haven for Senegalese dissidents". **Violence** nevertheless increased towards the end of the year. On 21 November, ten woodcutters were killed in Diagnon. While some MFDC figures denied involvement, blaming local villagers instead, MFDC fighters apparently wanted to show that trespassers on 'their' territory would be punished. On 5 December, another group of woodcutters was threatened and robbed near Toubacouta. Possibly to re-establish their credentials as a force at war against the Senegalese troops, MFDC fighters attacked military positions in Kabeum and Diégoune on 13 and 18 December, respectively. In all, nine soldiers were killed, nine others wounded, and six were captured by the MFDC, their first acknowledged prisoners since 1982. Human rights groups demanded that the Red Cross be granted access to these men. New reinforcements moved in from north Senegal and the government obtained new reassurances from Gambia's President Jammeh about border controls.

In a **conciliatory gesture**, Wade announced on 15 December that he was busy securing the return of the bodies of two Casamançais once involved in resistance against French colonialism, prophetess Aline Sitoé Diatta, deported by the French and buried in Timbuktu, and priest-king Sihalébé Diatta, whose body lay preserved at the 'Musée de l'Homme' in Paris. With the approaching elections, civil society initiatives multiplied to put the Casamance conflict on the agenda. The 'Plateforme des Femmes pour la Paix en Casamance', a Ziguinchor-based women's association, held a prayer meeting in January and went on an advocacy tour in September. On 29 August, 'SOS Casamance', a French-based NGO, called for negotiations and subsequently sent questionnaires to the presidential candidates to inquire about their views on the conflict. Opposition politicians expressed harsh criticism of Wade's failure to solve the dispute, insisting on the need for **dialogue** and negotiations. In November, the controversial MFDC moderate-turned-federalist Jean-Marie Biagui announced that he would organise the movement's congress in Ziguinchor in mid-December. Meanwhile, the external wing of the MFDC seemed to be getting stronger under the influence of the 'Cercle des Universitaires et Intellectuels du MFDC', a small but influential diaspora group led by Ahmed Apakéna Diémé. Some pro-MFDC websites were revived. While the influential 'Comité des Cadres Casamançais', an organisation of loyalist Casamançais professionals and high-level civil servants led by Pierre Atépa Goudiaby, urged the government and the MFDC in December to accept the mediation of Sant'Egidio, an Italian Catholic mediation organisation, the 'Cercle des Universitaires et Intellectuels du MFDC' also pleaded for international intervention, putting forward conditions for dialogue that included the withdrawal of all Senegalese troops to their peacetime positions and an agreement on a mediator and a negotiation venue.

Foreign Affairs

The approaching elections made Senegal's **Western partners** increasingly nervous. On TI's Corruption Perception Index, Senegal dropped from 71st in 2007 to 112th in 2011 (out of 182 countries). Economic and financial governance thus remained a point of contention with Western donors. Tensions were particularly high over the new code of public tenders, as donors were intent on securing the reversal of a September 2010 law that put tenders relating to state security and the presidency beyond proper control. Neither the 6 January decree nor the new code made public on 27 July satisfied donors. The equally controversial reduction of the power of the 'Cour des Comptes' stood uncorrected. The authorities did not go through with the legislation transferring to the ministry of justice the power to decide on the opening of investigations into **financial crimes** reported by the 'Cellule Nationale de Traitement des Informations Financières', but donors remained concerned.

American criticism was particularly strong. The powerful Senegalese diaspora in the **US** was mobilising against Wade. In March, a Republican congressman for California, Ed Royce, denounced Wade's government, referring, among other things, to the new 'Monument de la Renaissance Africaine', and called into question the $ 540 m programme for Senegal under the Millennium Challenge Corporation (MCC). MCC boss Daniel Yohannes insisted that governance in Senegal was carefully monitored and that the US and other donors had forced Wade to recall certain controversial legislation. On 14 December, a bipartisan group of US congressmen sent a letter to Wade telling him his candidacy would be damaging "for Senegal and African democracy".

Even with **France**, which had striven to maintain close relations with the Wade presidency, relations seemed to become progressively less easy as the year went by. The French newspaper 'L'Express' revealed that during the 27 June riot in Dakar, Karim Wade had asked Robert Bourgi, a Franco-Lebanese lawyer with a family history in Senegal and an informal advisor to President Sarkozy on African affairs, about a potential French intervention. Karim Wade denied this, but Bourgi confirmed it, insisting that Abdoulaye Wade should not run for the presidency and that his son had nothing to do with politics. It was not clear how far this reflected France's official stance. Bourgi asserted on 12 September that Karim Wade had donated significant sums in cash in 2001 to support the re-election campaign of Jacques Chirac, in an obvious attack on Chirac's close associate Dominique de Villepin, who was then challenging Sarkozy for control of the French right. The Senegalese presidency reacted strongly, threats of prosecutions were made, and Bourgi quickly pulled back. As agreed in the new defence agreements yet to be signed between Paris and Dakar, the 1,200-strong 'Forces Françaises du Cap Vert' were transformed on 31 July into a smaller 300-strong 'Eléments Français au Sénégal', a military presence engaged essentially in support for French air and naval operations, as well as military cooperation with West African armed forces.

With the election approaching, Wade's abandonment of Kadhafi and his early recognition of **Libya**'s Transitional National Council in May and subsequent trip to Benghazi on 9 June gave the appearance of a gesture to placate crucial Western and Arab Gulf partners, but it caused controversy in Senegal and throughout the African continent, and Wade was again attacked as a pawn of the West.

Wade remained embroiled in the case of former Chadian president Habré, a long-time guest of Senegal, wanted since 2005 by a Belgian court for war crimes. As Senegal had failed to act since 2006, when the AU had given it a mandate to try Habré instead of extraditing him, Belgium reiterated its demand for **Habré's extradition** on 15 March. The Senegalese authorities refused to extradite him, and the AU decided on 23–24 March to create an ad hoc international court. On 30 May, however, the government announced that it had put an end to talks with the AU over the court. When the AU insisted at the Malabo, Equatorial Guinea, summit in July that Senegal must either try Habré quickly or extradite him, Senegal threatened to expel Habré to Chad, a country whose judiciary is the object of severe criticism but, under international pressure, Senegal suspended this decision. Belgium reiterated its demand on 11 July, but its request was turned down by a Senegalese court on 18 August. Belgium made a new attempt on 5 September, but at year's end the court of appeals had still not given a judgement.

In the **Côte d'Ivoire** crisis, Wade was a committed supporter of Alassane Ouattara, whose final victory over his rival Laurent Gbagbo was clearly one for Senegal too. On 12 May, Ouattara paid a visit to Dakar. Following an assault on **Guinea**'s presidential residence on 19 July by some rebel soldiers, President Alpha Condé accused Senegal and Gambia of having played a part – Wade's sympathy for Guinea's opposition figure Cellou Dalein Diallo, and the influence in Senegal of a substantial Guinean Peul trading diaspora supportive of Diallo, remained points of friction. While the Guinean authorities had never accused Diallo of involvement, they pointed the finger in the direction of associates of his and accused Senegal of allowing them to operate from its territory. Dakar denied involvement. As for **Guinea-Bissau**, the deteriorating health of President Malam Bacai Sanhá, who was evacuated to a Dakar hospital in August and then again in November, was not a good sign: while Senegal had been able to establish strong links with Sanhá, Guinea-Bissau's Prime Minister Carlos Gomes Junior was known to be a less amenable partner and closer to Angola and Portugal. Armed raiders from Guinea-Bissau kept preying on cattle in Casamance, and the two countries agreed on 22 June to organise joint patrols. This proved to have little impact, since new raids led villagers in Balantacounda to close the border on 19 July and to subsequently protest against the withdrawal of troops. The December 2010 scandal over Iranian weapons imported by **Gambia** but widely suspected to be destined for MFDC rebels forced Gambia into playing the reconciliation card. Both Senegal and Gambia broke diplomatic relations with Iran and, in August, Wade paid a trip to Banjul. There were renewed tensions with **Mauritania**. In October, 33 Senegalese were arrested in Nouakchott for participation in protests against a census deemed to be discriminatory against the country's black minority. On 13 December, Senegalese fishermen fought with Mauritanian coastguards in the border region, and one Senegalese was wounded. The Senegalese arrested in Nouakchott were released on 21 December, and discussions over a fishing agreement resumed.

Socioeconomic Developments

According to the national statistical agency, **growth** reached only 2.2%, down from 4.1% in 2010, and well below the forecasts and the demographic growth rate (2.5%). This was essentially caused by a slump in the primary sector (–12.6%) as a result of insufficient rainfall, though the global economic downturn and power cuts did not help. The secondary and tertiary sectors maintained growth above 4%. Inflation stood at 3.4%. While economic prospects seemed good, the short-term was uncertain, with electoral competition leading to a boom in public expenditure.

The poor rainy season affected **agriculture** profoundly. Millet production for 2011/2012 fell to 480,000 tonnes, compared with 813,000 tonnes in the previous year, and rice production from 604,000 to 439,000 tonnes. The situation for export crops was no better: groundnut production fell from 1,286,000 to 527,000 tonnes. Experts were warning of an impending **food crisis,** and UNICEF figures indicated that, by the end of the year, acute global malnutrition had reached alarming proportions in a number of regions. Food items, particularly fish, along with cement and phosphoric acid, remained a major element in exports, which grew by 17%. The structural deficit in the balance of trade remained, with exports totalling $ 2.5 bn while imports stood at a little above $ 5 bn. As usual, the trade deficit was covered by transfers, aid and remittances. Remittances grew slightly, reaching $ 1.4 bn from $ 1.3 bn in 2010.

The uneasy situation paved the way for **protests**. Most spectacular were the tensions in the educational sector, where state high schools and universities were affected by strikes and protests by students and academic staff – the boom in registered students was simply not matched with the necessary resources, causing recurring tensions. The 'Université Cheikh Anta Diop' did not operate at all in the first months of the academic year 2011–2012.

Senegal continued to attract **investors**, however. IBM, which had left the country in the 1990s, opened shop in May, and so did Hewlett Packard in September. Agroindustrial projects were also in progress, though the one developed in Fanaye by the Tampieri Group (an Italian company) in the Senegal River Valley caused trouble: two people were killed and 20 more wounded on 26 October during clashes between the local authorities and adversaries of the project. In March, for the first time in its history, Senegal saw its Moody's rating rise to B1, an indication of its stable economic outlook. A month later, Standard & Poor's gave Senegal a satisfying B+, but warned that the electoral campaign could mean instability and an increase in the budget deficit. The electoral campaign did indeed have an impact on the management of the economy and the public finances, as it had done in 2007. As a result of an increase in investment spending and civil service recruitment (about 5,000 civil servants more), the **fiscal deficit** increased substantially, reaching 7.1% of GDP while the IMF's medium-term fiscal deficit target stood at 4%. On 9 November, in a move to appease donors, the National Assembly adopted a rather tight budget for 2012 (CFAfr 2,200 bn revenue and CFAfr 2,300 bn expenditure).

The elections and mounting discontent did much to speed up the completion of major infrastructural projects, if not to bring about a solution to the structural **shortage of power**. The state electricity company Senelec had difficulty paying its bills. It proved incapable of modernising its infrastructure to deal with fast-growing consumption, and power cuts became more frequent, costing an estimated 1.4% of growth. On 21 January, Karim Wade announced the launch of a special $ 1 bn plan called Takkal (meaning "restart" [the machines] in Wolof), aimed at improving oil supplies, renting generators and modernising infrastructure. Takkal, which received financial support from the World

Bank, the West African Development Bank and the ADF, also planned the building of a coal-fuelled power plant by the South Korean company Kepco, with coal to be procured in South Africa, as well as an oil-fuelled power plant to be constructed by the Lebanese company Matelec, which had already set up the Kounoune plant. These efforts did bring cuts to a stop from December, but critics were concerned that much of Takkal's money had been used for short-term solutions aimed at courting public opinion in preparation for the presidential election. And, despite Wade's declaration in May that new buildings would have to source 60% of their energy from solar panels, Takkal was also criticised for its lack of environmental friendliness.

Transport infrastructure saw some progress. A new road was built to supplement the two-lane road through the city of Rufisque, which used to be the only way in and out of Dakar, and part of the new highway that would connect Dakar to the new airport was inaugurated. On 19 September, Karim Wade, as minister of transport, energy, infrastructure and international cooperation, signed a € 406 m deal with ten banks, securing funding to complete the new Blaise Diagne international airport being built 45 km to the south-east of the capital by the Saudi Bin Laden Group, under the management of the German airport management group Fraport. However, the construction of the airport, initiated in 2007, would not be completed in 2012 as planned. On 7 December, a three-year CFAfr 46 bn plan for the development of airports and airfields in the hinterland was announced. Air transport was also in for a big shake-up with the first flight, on 25 January, of 'Senegal Airlines'. This company, set up by private Senegalese investors with a technical partnership with the aviation company Emirates, was to replace Air Senegal International, which had closed down as a result of the withdrawal of its Moroccan investors. After the failure of previous national airlines, the project, placed under the oversight of Karim Wade, aimed to make Dakar a sub-regional hub. The government's decision to grant the company a monopoly on flights to other sub-regional capitals led to disputes with Brussels Airlines and Mauritania Airlines, but agreements were eventually reached. Senegal's bid to increase its influence as a major sub-regional trade hub also involved repair works on the Dakar-Bamako railway, starting with the 70-km stretch between Dakar and Thiès. Mali and Senegal were still looking to complete the financing of the $ 1.6 bn needed for the upgrading of the aged and badly maintained railway, now operated by the Belgian group Transrail.

In May, to cover the budget deficit, Senegal successfully issued a $ 500 m Eurobond, thus reaching the IMF-agreed ceiling for non-concessional borrowing. Attempts at increasing fiscal pressure were continued. On 10 August, President Wade announced a tax on incoming phone calls. Due to come into effect on 1 October, this **new tax** was expected to generate CFAfr 60 bn (€ 91 m) annually. In an unexpected alliance, trade unions and the management of Sonatel, the country's main mobile phone company and a hugely profitable subsidiary of France Télécom's Orange network, led the resistance to the new tax.

In October, the government also proposed a law that would ensure that the state received at least a 35% share in all telecommunications companies operating in the country.

Another controversial measure was the 18 August law replacing all existing **waste collection companies** by a monopoly managed by the 'Société pour la Propreté du Sénégal', a new company in which the state would have a majority share. While the government explained that a national monopoly was the only way to collect and process enough waste to sell it profitably and insisted it was dealing with an American company that would buy the recycled waste, the law raised an unsuccessful outcry among the often opposition-controlled and underfunded municipal authorities, which stood to lose one of the few cash-generating sectors they controlled.

Vincent Foucher

Sierra Leone

Sierra Leone celebrated its 50th anniversary of independence from the United Kingdom. On the political front, the parties were gradually preparing for the 2012 presidential and parliamentary elections. In July, the main opposition party elected its somewhat controversial presidential candidate. Large foreign investments took place in the iron ore mining sector and a new railway link to transport the ore came into operation. Meanwhile, the government continued to revise its deals with the extractive industries. The Special Court for Sierra Leone had its final trial – that of the former Liberian president Charles Taylor – concluded, with a verdict expected in 2012.

Domestic Politics

At the end of July and in preparation for the presidential and parliamentary elections, scheduled for 17 November 2012, the main opposition party – the Sierra Leone Peoples Party (SLPP) – chose its **presidential candidate** at its party congress. The SLPP candidate – Julius Maada Bio – was selected by 238 of the 600 or so delegates and not without controversy: Bio was among the group of young officers who ousted the All Peoples Congress (APC) president and authoritarian leader Momoh in 1992 and subsequently established a military council – the National Provisional Ruling Council (NPRC) – which ruled for four years. In 2010, it was announced that an investigation would be started into the summary executions of nearly 30 Momoh loyalists by the NPRC regime. Although the investigation was later shelved, it was expected that it would help discredit Bio's candidature. As a relatively young candidate, Bio might be able to attract support from disaffected youths, as the NPRC regime had done 20 years earlier.

Following a series of **violent incidents** between supporters of the ruling APC and the opposition SLPP in the south and east of the country, the police announced a three-month ban on all political rallies. Violence erupted in the Kono district – the diamond mining centre – on 3 September and in Bo – traditionally an SLPP stronghold – on 9 September, following a visit by Maada Bio. On 12 December, four of the six political parties registered thus far signed a memorandum of understanding pledging to take all necessary measures to prevent their supporters from engaging in violence.

There were some **minor cabinet reshuffles**. On 18 July, Mamoud Tarawali – deputy minister of labour and social security – became deputy minister of health and sanitation, and Daniel Gaima, deputy minister of youth employment and sports, was transferred to the ministry of labour and social security to replace him. On 28 October, the president appointed Stephen J. Gaojia as the new minister of social welfare, gender and children's affairs, replacing Dr Dennis Sandi, who had been relieved of his duties in early August. On 2 July, the family of El-hadj Habib Diallo, the executive secretary of the MRU since May 2010, announced that he had been killed in a car accident, at the age of 65. Condolences were offered to his family by all four MRU countries during an extraordinary summit of heads of state and government on 17 July in Monrovia, Liberia.

On 17 January, the **army** started to address some of the problems caused by overcrowded barracks, which held as many as 20 times more people than they were originally designed for. Soldiers sub-letting their rooms to civilians seemed to be a common practice, but under new army regulations even relatives of soldiers were no longer allowed to stay in the barracks. On 21 January, the army paid out nearly $ 1.5 m to the families of soldiers who lost their lives in the 1991–2002 civil war. According to the army, just over 1,600 soldiers went missing in action, but other sources put this number higher. More controversially, the army also paid the country's former military leader Captain Strasser, who seized power in 1992 in a military coup and ruled the country up to 1996, a 'service benefit' of Le 6.5 m, although the government turned down his demand to be paid salary arrears from his time as president. On 2 May, Chinese Ambassador Kuang Weilin presented military equipment worth $ 4 m to the army, including anti-aircraft guns, mortars and rocket launchers, to further increase its defence capabilities. Six Chinese military experts led the training of army personnel in the use of these weapons, and 11 officers received training in China, all meant – in the words of Defence Minister Paolo Conteh – to make the military a force capable of performing its mission and tasks.

On 13 May, the Anti Corruption Commission (ACC) presented its 2010 annual report to the president. ACC Commissioner Joseph Kamara added that the Commission had prosecuted 17 cases, involving eight convictions and two acquittals, in 2010. Le 2.5 bn (nearly $ 600,000) in recovered cash was presented, which would be transferred to the Consolidated Revenue Fund. On 20 October, the ACC commissioner presented a cheque for nearly Le 900,000 m to President Koroma as part of fines levied against individuals found guilty of **corruption**, but the level of corruption still remained disturbingly high.

Foreign Affairs

In April, the president attended the inauguration of President Boni Yayi of **Benin**. Koroma and Yayi were earlier part of a three-man ECOWAS presidential delegation that aimed to resolve the political stalemate in **Côte d'Ivoire** and encourage former Ivorian president Gbagbo to stand down. The following month, Koroma attended the inauguration of the new Ivorian president, Alassane Ouattara, in the capital Yamoussoukro. During discussions President Ouattara expressed his interest in the Sierra Leone Truth and Reconciliation Commission and its functioning. Later in the month, on 28 May, Koroma visited **Nigeria** with a five-man delegation to attend the inauguration of President Goodluck Jonathan. The visit was aimed to further consolidate the ties between the two countries and to facilitate discussion of further collaboration. The Nigerian government was supporting Sierra Leone through its Technical Aid Cooperation programme, focusing on medical doctors, teachers and lecturers.

On 13 October, Koroma visited neighbouring **Guinea**. His minister of foreign affairs accompanied him and signed a joint communiqué with his Guinean counterpart, covering issues such as security and bilateral trade. In the same month, the president was in New York and attended a special lunch with US President Obama and **UN Secretary-General** Ban Ki-moon. He also addressed the 66th Session of the UN General Assembly. In his capacity as chair of the AU's committee of ten heads of state on UNSC reform, the president called for "the increasing need for the Security Council to be more representative, inclusive, and democratic as well as the need for an improvement on its working methods and its relations with the General Assembly".

In February, the last contingent of what was once a 17,500 strong UN peacekeeping mission left the country. The 150 Mongolian troops – assigned to provide protection for the Special Court for Sierra Leone – handed over to the national police force on 17 February. The Court, created to try those most responsible for war crimes and crimes against humanity during the decade-long civil war, saw its last case end on 11 March with the closing arguments of the final trial briefs. Earlier in the year, on 8 February, the trial was adjourned (again) for a few days when **Charles Taylor** and his lawyer, Courtenay Griffiths, boycotted closing arguments. A verdict by the judges on the 11 charges, including the use of child soldiers, rape and murder, was scheduled for 26 April 2012. If found guilty Taylor, would be the first African head of state to be tried by an international court and would serve his prison sentence in the UK. Taylor was indicted in March 2003 and his trial started in 2007.

In September, the UNSC extended for another year the mandate of the UN Integrated Peacebuilding Office in Sierra Leone, mandated to help the country to consolidate peace and stable governance. The **British**-dominated International Military Assistance Training Team – 55 members strong – continued to provide instruction to the new Sierra Leone army, which was downsized from 20,000 straight after the war to its current size of around 8,500. On 27 June, the UK's DFID announced the commitment of $ 30 m over a three-year period to further boost the security and justice sector, a key investment area for the British since the end of the civil war.

On 3–5 October, the ECOWAS' Committee of Chiefs of Defence met in Abuja, Nigeria, to find solutions to the problems of terrorism, piracy and the proliferation of weapons in the sub-region. Among the key outcomes was the expansion of the membership of its sub-committee on maritime security from five to ten, including Sierra Leone. A key issue for **maritime security** was the significant problem of drug trafficking between Latin America and Europe, using the West African coastal zone as a transit point. Towards the end of September, the AU announced that it expected to receive 3,000 troops from Sierra Leone and Djibouti to support its 9,000 soldiers guarding the Somalian capital, Mogadishu, against the Islamist insurgents of al-Shabaab.

Socioeconomic Developments

In January, the European Commission approved € 10 m in budget support under its so-called Vulnerability FLEX mechanism. The global economic downturn caused the government to revise its growth projections downward, but the support would enable it to continue spending in priority areas, such as its free health care initiative.

An Investment Climate team, including DFID, donors from Norway, the Netherlands and Ireland, and the World Bank, published their Rebuilding Business and Investment in Post-Conflict Sierra Leone Report in March. The report reflected on the results of a seven-year programme to build a strong regulatory environment, mainly by removing administrative barriers. Such an environment could foster private sector growth, increase employment and attract **investment**. During the period under review the number of local and international businesses registered more than doubled, 25,000 new jobs were created, and the number of taxpayers increased from 4,650 in 2008 to 6,593 in 2010. Agribusiness and tourism were the two sectors in which the report saw ample opportunities, with investments totalling $ 150 m expected to be made into the latter. In August, one of the main cocoa export companies announced that, for the first time since the early 1990s, a profit was made, totalling about $ 50,000, partly due to the world price for cocoa, which was at a 30-year high, and political violence in Côte d'Ivoire.

On 19 July, a $ 61 m project, funded by the AfDB and the OPEC Fund for International Development, was launched to improve three water stations supplying pipe-borne water to the three provincial capitals. The four-year project was expected to improve the national provision of **water** from 33.5% to 75%.

Between 23 August and 6 September, an IMF team visited the country to discuss the second and third review of the programme supported under its ECF. According to the mission, the country's gross international reserves remained at a comfortable level and real GDP had increased from 3.2% in 2009 to 5% in 2010 with good prospects for 2011, reflecting continued **growth** in agriculture, manufacturing, mining and construction. The main challenges, the mission concluded, remained in accelerating investment in social services and basic infrastructure while maintaining macroeconomic stability and reducing domestic fuel subsidies. In September, the AfDB approved a grant of $ 15.7 m, to be disbursed over two years, from its Fragile States Facility, to pay for the second Economic Governance Reform Programme. The grant would focus on good governance and state building projects.

In early February, the Sierra Leone Exploration and Mining Company announced that it had discovered **bauxite** deposits in the Port Loko and Kambia districts totalling 140 m tonnes. The company's chairman, Alieu Mohamed Sesay, expected that exploitation of the reserves would bring development and benefits to the communities in the area. Also during February, Sierra Rutile Ltd announced its resource estimate for its mining operations in the country totalling 600 m tonnes, including measured (4.4 m tonnes), indicated (436.6 m tonnes) and inferred (163.9 m tonnes) categories. In addition to **rutile, ilmenite and zircon**, some rare-earth mineralisation in tailings were also identified. Pala Investments (38%) and M&G Securities (20%) are the major shareholders in Sierra Rutile Ltd, which has produced rutile since 2006.

The opportunities for **iron ore mining** gained a significant boost when, on 1 June, China's Shandong Iron and Steel Group announced that it was finalising the terms on its $ 1.5 bn investment in African Minerals Limited (AML), the British company exploiting the deposits in the Tonkolili district. Earlier in the year, on 23 February, African Minerals paid the government a $ 10 m expatriate tax for the year 2010, covering the tax obligations for the expatriates working for the company in Sierra Leone. AML announced in 2010 that it had discovered an estimated 10 bn tonnes of nearly 30% grade ore and the railway between Marampa and the deepwater port at Pepel came into operation in 2011. In November, African Minerals sold its first shipment of 40,000 tonnes to China. The government was expected to earn hundreds of millions of dollars in taxes when the mine produced its envisaged 3 m tonnes a year, with a potential capacity of up to 15 m tonnes. Protests by local people continued, however, as they complained that the operations brought few jobs, with the companies mainly hiring European and Asian expatriates.

On 20 July, the government, civil society groups and mining companies committed themselves to higher returns to the people by signing a memorandum of understanding (MoU), following the launch of the Work Plan of the Sierra Leone Extractive Industries Transparency Initiative. A representative from the Initiative, based in Oslo, described the Sierra Leonean Work Plan and MoU as a global best practice guide meant to keep in tune with transparency and accountability, as well as to ensure inclusive participation in the entire process. On 1 September, the president announced that talks had been concluded on the revision of a mining agreement between the state and the London Mining Company Ltd, raising the company's cooperate tax from 6% to 25%. Earlier, Koidu Holdings also saw its **mining agreements revised** and brought in line with the 25% tax level. Other mining companies, including Sierra Rutile, Sierra Minerals, Koidu holdings Tongo Fields and Cluff Gold, would be next to have their agreements brought in line. Earlier in the year, in April, the government obtained a grant of $ 4 m to boost its capacity to further improve and regulate the extractive industries sector.

In June, the National Democratic Alliance (NDA) – a leading opposition party – raised the alarm concerning major **land deals** signed between the government and international investors. According to the NDA, about 10% of the country's arable land was leased out to foreign companies. The NDA expressed its concern that these deals would seriously affect the livelihood of farmers in the affected areas. Just days before, the Swiss energy group Addax & Oryx signed a $ 368 m deal for a renewable energy project that included a sugarcane plantation, ethanol refinery and biomass power station near the Makeni area. The group claimed to have held elaborate consultations with affected populations over a two-year period.

In August and September, more than 500 km of coastline was affected by an unusual amount of washed up seaweed. The Freetown Peninsula beaches, considered as among the most beautiful in Africa, were also covered. The Sierra Leone Tourist Board expressed its concerns, as the phenomenon affected the country's reputation as an emerging tourist destination. In the first half of the year, the tourism industry earned $ 19 m. Local fishermen were particularly affected by the seaweed invasion. Some good news for them followed in August, when Sierra Leone signed an agreement with the Dutch firm Precon, which would facilitate access to European markets. It also received $ 28 m grant from the World Bank to develop its **pelagic stocks**.

In early December, the government opened the Gola Rainforest National Park, one of the last remnants of primary tropical rainforest left in the country, and part of the Upper Guinea Forest Ecosystem which extends over a number of countries in the region. The 71,000 ha park is particular rich in birdlife, while there are a number of smaller and larger mammals, including pygmy hippos and chimpanzees. Bordering Liberia, the area was used as a rebel base for many years during the civil war, but the flora and fauna survived reasonably well. The World Travel and Tourism Centre projected that Sierra

Leone's **tourism industry** would experience an annual growth of nearly 6% for the next ten years.

In February, about 4,000 students of Fourah Bay College – the main university in Sierra Leone and oldest Western-style university in West Africa – had their first semester examinations delayed by two weeks because there was not sufficient classroom furniture. Further embarrassment for the university came when the same **students** saw their final exams postponed because of a shortage of paper. The University's principal, Professor Thomas Yormah, blamed a combination of low student fees and lack of government support. On 21 May, the British-born author Aminatta Forna won the Commonwealth Writers' Prize for the African region for her book 'The Memory of Love'. Forna was raised in Sierra Leone and had previously published 'The Devil that Danced on the Water', which was shortlisted for the Samuel Johnson Prize in 2003. Both books are about Sierra Leone and the armed conflict.

In early August, 11 Sierra Leone scouts, mostly teenagers, who were participating in a 12-day World Scout Jamboree in Sweden, absconded. Sierra Leonean athletes had made off before while participating in events in the West, as happened during the 2002 UK and 2006 Australian Commonwealth Games. The scouts apparently found their way to neighbouring Denmark. On 17 March, the Youth Employment Support Project was launched, funded by the World Bank and aiming to help over 30,000 young people throughout the country by empowering them and increasing their chances of finding or creating a job. Koroma earlier identified **youth employment** as one of the three most significant threats to the security and peace in the country.

On 22 December, the police announced that they had seized a significant quantity of **drugs**, hidden in a 40 ft container shipped from Ecuador. The cocaine was concealed between nappies. Five people, including some foreigners, were subsequently arrested in a series of raids in the capital. Strangely, the container had duty-free concessions. The UK's Serious Organised Crime Agency was called in to help with further investigations.

Krijn Peters

Togo

The coalition government continued on the path to establishing democracy, good governance and the rule of law. Its efforts were honoured by the international donor community with growing commitments and the cancellation of foreign debt. Domestic politics were dominated by simmering confrontations within both the opposition and the ruling Gnassingbé clan. The president successfully followed the divide-and-rule strategy of his late father, Eyadéma. The radical opposition remained isolated and its MPs excluded from parliament, despite a ruling of the ECOWAS Court of Justice to the contrary. The showdown between the president and his rivals within the Gnassingbé clan culminated in the conviction of Kpatcha Gnassingbé and his followers as ringleaders of the 2009 coup attempt.

Domestic Politics

President Faure Gnassingbé and his 'Rassemblement du Peuple Togolais' (RPT), controlled by the Gnassingbé family, continued to consolidate their positions after the presidential elections of 2010. Consequently, politics was dominated by the coalition government, formed with the entry of Gilchrist Olympio's 'Union des Forces du Changement' (UFC) into the cabinet as junior partner.

However, Olympio's shift of allegiance and the resulting schism within the major **opposition** party complicated the political scene. Only nine of the 27 UFC MPs followed Olympio in supporting the coalition government. Nine others, who broke away in order to continue in opposition with the newly created 'Alliance Nationale pour le Changement' (ANC), were suspended from parliament, as were the remaining nine who refused loyalty to Olympio, even though they did not join the ANC. By contrast, on 13 May, André Johnson, a leading figure within the former UFC, who had become the ANC's deputy secretary general, returned to the UFC, denouncing ANC tactics. That same month, another critic of the Eyadéma regime, the lawyer and human rights activist Jean Yaovi Degli, returned to Lomé after 17 years in exile. He was invited by the powerful Minister for Territorial Administration Pascal Bodjona to assist in drafting a new law on political demonstrations. At the same time, Degli created a new front of pro-government parties ('Front-Sage') to counteract the influence of the opposition umbrella group, the 'Front Républicain pour l'Alternance et le Changement' (FRAC).

The ANC protested against what it saw as repression. Together with the FRAC, it held regular demonstrations, against, among other things, a bill on the right to freedom of association (adopted on 17 March). The law was introduced as part of the coalition agreement to replace colonial regulations used to suppress opposition. It was drafted with the assistance of the Office of the UN High Commissioner for Human Rights and largely corresponded to international standards. However, although the bill permitted **demonstrations** without prior permission, they could still be banned if they gave rise to disturbance. The National Assembly approved the bill with 50 RPT votes and 18 from the UFC, in the absence of 13 members of the opposition parties (notably of the 'Comité d'Action pour le Renouveau' (CAR) and of nine ANC MPs. Earlier in March, the coalition and 12 smaller parties adopted a new electoral code, drafted with American and UNDP assistance. The FRAC boycotted the signing of the code because, among other reasons, the nine ANC members were still suspended from the National Assembly following a ruling of the Constitutional Court in November 2010. The ECOWAS Court of Justice in Abuja, Nigeria, found on appeal on 7 October that the verdict of the Lomé court constituted a violation of human rights, and asked the government to reinstate the nine ANC legislators and pay them compensation. Already in June the human rights committee of the Inter-Parliamentary Union in Geneva had condemned the exclusion in a note to the government. Although the ministry of finance paid compensation of CFAfr 3 m (€ 4,573) to each of the MPs, the government still opposed their return to the Assembly. On 7 November, the opposition and the 'Ligue Togolaise des Droits de l'Homme' condemned the government's attitude.

On 15 September, the **trial** of the alleged plotters of the thwarted 2009 coup brought the long-expected showdown between rivals in the **Gnassingbé clan**. The key person in the trial was the younger half-brother of the president and former defence minister Kpatcha Gnassingbé. Kpatcha, a full Kabyè, rooted in the Eyadéma fief in the north and well connected with the military and RPT mandarins, denied the charges. Ten of the 33 suspects had already been released from jail in mid-April, among them another half-brother of Faure, Essolizam Gnassingbé, and two of the president's cousins. The Supreme Court sentenced the three ringleaders, Kpatcha, the retired army chief General Assani Tidjani, and Abi Atti (a gendarmerie commander), to 20 years. The same sentence was given, in absentia, to the alleged financer of the coup attempt, Bassam El-Najjar, a Lebanese citizen. Eight others, including Esso Gnassingbé, a cousin of the president, were sentenced to between two and 15 years, and 21 remaining suspects were acquitted, among them a third brother of the president, Rock Gnassingbé, a young career officer. AI and the UN Human Rights Commission were concerned about accusations of torture. The outcome of the trial was seen as another sign of the strengthening of the power of the president, who had successfully styled himself as a reformer. All accused military personnel were demoted.

During the presentation of the military's annual report towards year's end, senior officers of the Army ('Forces Armées Togolaises' – FAT) were accused of inciting violence and undermining reconciliation. As a precaution, the president rotated key posts in the security forces. In February, Colonel Dokissima G. Latta was appointed minister of security in a minor cabinet **reshuffle**. His predecessor, Atcha Mohamed Titikpina, had been promoted chief of general staff three months earlier. Outgoing chief of staff General Ayéva Essofa was nominated as minister of water and sanitation.

On 15 September, the 'Cadre Permanent de Dialogue et de Concertation' (CPDC) resumed its work. It was to propose **institutional reforms**, notably of the 2002 revisions of the 1992 constitution that had served to perpetuate the rule of the late president, Eyadéma, as well as of the electoral law. However, the former prime minister and leader of the opposition 'Organisation pour batir dans l'union un Togo solidaire', Agbéyomé Kodjo, withdrew from the CPDC in December, denouncing it as biased in favour of the government, and also because opposition demands to limit the presidential term to two five-year periods, which would have implied the withdrawal of Faure Gnassingbé from the presidential race in 2015, were allegedly rejected. Other opposition parties, including the CAR and ANC, boycotted the debates for similar reasons. At the end of the year, it was rumoured that the RPT would be dismantled in favour of a new party to bring about a break with the past. This would probably imply a clash between RPT barons and the young architects of Faure's success, while it would also enhance the president's standing as a reformer. The first congress of the new party was scheduled for early 2012. The upcoming local elections were again postponed for one year to be held together with the legislative elections in October 2012.

On 17 November, the 'Commission Vérité, Justice et Réconciliation' (CVJR) finished its hearings, which had started in September. It had considered 508 out of a total of 20,011 depositions. Its final report was awaited anxiously, although the CVJR did not have the power to prosecute and its recommendations for compensation would have to be implemented by the government, which had the right to make final decisions.

Though the **human rights** situation had further improved, there were continuing concerns on press freedom and the closure of four private radio stations, as expressed by Togolese watchdogs, the International Federation of Journalists and Reporters sans Frontières. The Coalition for the International Criminal Court urged Togo to become a member of the ICC in order to strengthen its commitment to international justice and the rule of law.

A report on Togo by the inter-governmental action group against **money laundering** in West Africa, published in May, considered the risk of money laundering and terrorist financing in the light of Togo's political environment, the predominant role of the informal sector (including alternative money transfer systems) and its geographical location (sea access and Togo's transit function for Sahelian countries). The report concluded that, although the country had a legal system in place to counter terrorist financing, the law still contained major loopholes. In addition, enforcement of provisions was rated as poor.

Togo continued to be used as a hub for **drug trafficking**. At the end of June, the authorities made two important seizures of cocaine from Brazil, in addition to considerable amounts of cannabis derived from Nigeria, both in transit to Europe. Shortly before, 48 kg of cannabis had been seized at the airport en route to China. On 21 December, the US made public accusations about a network of money couriers involving a Lebanese resident in Lomé. He allegedly collaborated with a Hezbollah operative, who was said to have transported tens of millions of US dollars and Euros in drug money from Benin to Lebanon through Togo and Ghana.

The threat of **piracy** increased dramatically and reportedly damaged the economy by causing a fall in shipping and higher insurance rates. Togo joined Benin and Nigeria in trying to combat the spread of piracy in the Gulf of Guinea. Up to November, 53 attacks were reported for the 177 km of shared coastline of Benin and Togo, as compared with 47 in 2010. Four of them took place off the Togolese coast and 22 off Benin, neither of which had reported incidents the previous year. The International Maritime Organization suspected the real figures to be considerably higher as many attacks probably went unreported. Trans-border cooperation started with joint sea patrols by the Benin and Nigerian navies, a naval alliance which Togo and Ghana also wanted to join. However, UN investigators underlined that combating pirates would be useless without accompanying measures on shore, notably the rule of law and anti-corruption measures.

Foreign Affairs

In February, a Togolese delegation headed by Prime Minister Gilbert Fossoun Houngbo visited Brussels and, on 2 March, the Netherlands. Louis Michel, co-president of the **ACP-EU** joint parliamentary assembly, commended the "remarkable progress" of the government since the 2010 elections, following EU recommendations. Later in the year, Togolese human rights organisations castigated Michel for his support of the ruling elite in its stand against the ECOWAS court of justice ruling on the ousted ANC MPs. The FRAC opposition group staged a major demonstration in Lomé on the occasion of the ACP-EU summit on 23 November.

EU Development Commissioner Andris Piebalgs met the president and prime minister in Lomé on a West African tour in November in order to officially launch resumed economic cooperation, which had been suspended from 1993 to 2008 because of the human rights situation. Piebalgs used the occasion to participate in the 22nd Joint Parliamentary ACP-EU Assembly in Lomé on 20 November. In stark contrast to public talk of EU-African partnership, a report of the confederation of European development NGOs, CONCORD, criticised EU policies. On 24 November, ACP-EU parliamentarians expressed concern about the threat posed by the proliferation of arms from **Libya**, where rebel forces had toppled the Kadhafi regime. In mid-September a member of the new Libyan revolutionary council had expressed concern about mercenaries from Chad, Niger and Togo, which had supported the old regime's forces.

Towards the end of May, an extraordinary **UEMOA summit** in Lomé welcomed the return of peace in Côte d'Ivoire, underlining the need to find sustainable solutions to violent crises in the sub-region.

On 21 October, Togo was elected a non-permanent member of the **UNSC** for the 2012–2013 term, along with Morocco, Guatemala and Pakistan. Thus Togo and Morocco replaced outgoing Nigeria and Gabon in the three-member African grouping, to join South Africa, whose term ended at the end of the year. In the first and second round of elections, Lomé had failed to attract the votes required to secure a seat. Only in the third round did it reach the two-thirds threshold, with 131 votes. This was the second time since 1982 that Togo had been on the UNSC. In view of simmering tensions concerning the Syrian crisis and other questions between the two blocs in the Council (Russia and China on the one hand and the Western powers on the other), Togo was expected to continue to back the latter. This expectation was borne out in another context when Togo, as representative of 22 mainly francophone African countries in the administrative council of the **IMF**, backed the candidature of Christine Lagarde as new director general, proposed by the seven EU administrators, against the five administrators from non-aligned states, including Lesotho which represented another 21 African states.

The support of **key donors**, including the EU, IMF and World Bank, continued to grow. The three-year IMF-assisted reform programme (ECF), which had started in 2008, ended in August after the sixth review on 18 June, with a $ 14 m final instalment of a total of $ 151 m, though two of the six key reform demands had not yet been met: the privatisation of four state-owned banks, and improved conditions for private sector investment (including the ailing phosphate sector). At the end of March, the **World Bank** granted a further $ 93 m for structural reforms, private sector development, urban infrastructure and agriculture. France and other Western donors wrote off most of Togo's debts within the framework of the HIPC initiative, for which the country had already reached the completion point in December 2010. On 12 May, **France** cancelled all bilateral debts, which amounted to € 101 m, and in November granted an additional € 2 m to clear domestic commercial debt. Italy, Switzerland and Japan followed suit. The IMF and Germany had already approved the cancellation of debts in the previous two years. Because of the write-off, the debt burden fell from 52.7% of GDP (2009) to 17.2% (2010), or 32.3% including debts of parastatals. **Germany**'s Minister for Economic Cooperation Dirk Niebel visited Lomé on 7 December to announce the official resumption of bilateral aid to the tune of € 27.5 m for the next two years. Earlier, the West African Development Bank had signed a loan agreement with Lomé for three development projects totalling $ 108 m or CFAfr 49 bn.

On 15 February, **China**'s Foreign Minister Yang Jiechi met the president in the northern town of Kara. Both visited the neighbouring village of Pya, the spiritual centre of the Gnassingbé clan where the president, as well as most of the elite of the army and security services, was born. China and Togo agreed to further deepen cooperation in bilateral and international fields. Apart from considerable economic cooperation, Beijing reinforced its socio-political links through, among other things, the activities of its news agency, Xinhua. With its network of correspondents, it now offered an array of up to 1,000 news items a day, embedded in a comprehensive information service to propagate the Chinese view on global and African affairs. This service also involved advantageous agreements and win-win deals with Togolese journalists. Thus, the informal neo-colonial network of Françafrique continued to be replaced, piece by piece, by an equally opaque system of 'Chinafrique'.

The repercussions of the Ivorian civil war continued, though on a diminishing scale. On 14 November, Ivorian President Alassane Ouattara visited Lomé to sign an agreement with Togo and the UNHCR concerning the repatriation of 5,000 **Ivorian refugees** living in Togo, more than half of them settled in the Avepezo camp on the outskirts of Lomé. However, it was doubtful whether all the old barons of the defeated regime in Abidjan and their families would be willing to return. Many of them had moved from Ghana to Togo just two months before, either for security reasons, as their hideout had been discovered by the media and Ivorian intelligence services, or because of similar repatriation agreements between Accra and Abidjan.

Socioeconomic Developments

A fourth general **population census**, whose preliminary results were presented on 3 May, revealed that the population had more than doubled over the previous 29 years. It was the first census for almost 30 years and had been conducted in November 2010 as part of the fulfilment of the comprehensive global political accord of 2006 and the 2010 coalition agreement between the RPT and UFC. Minister of Planning Dede Ahoefa Ekoué explained the rapid growth by reference to high birth rates (2.58% p.a.) and a decline in the mortality rate, and said its impact on economic development might lead to increased unemployment, poverty and vulnerability, especially among the most fragile sectors of the population. She therefore proposed counter-measures to be taken by the government, civil society and the donor community. There were considerable regional variations in population growth, however. Most affected were the Savannah (2.96%) and the already densely populated Marine (2.88%) region, whereas Plateau (2.33%) and Kara (1.81%) remained below the national average, the latter probably because of the semi-official promotion in the past of emigration of ethnic Kabyé (to which the Gnassingbé clan belongs) to the more prosperous south, where about 42% of Togolese live. More than one-third (37.4%) reside in urban areas, including the capital Lomé with 750,757 (13%) inhabitants, against 62.6% in rural areas. These results were expected to inform development planning and influence future elections, because of the necessity to compile a reliable electoral register and adjust constituency boundaries (biased in favour of the RPT). The adjustment of constituencies was controversial in view of regional and ethnic political affiliations.

The National Employment Agency, the 'Agence National Pour l'Emploi', created at the end of April 2009 with joint representation of the government, employers and trade unions, estimated the rate of **unemployment** at year's end at about 33%. In September, the government, assisted by UNDP, officially launched a new programme of national volunteers, directed particularly at the approximately 50% of young graduates most seriously affected by unemployment, to improve their chances of integration into the labour market by offering them their first job experience in various professions for a period of up to 12 months (also renewable). Up to December, about 700 of the 1,000 volunteers that had responded to the government call had been integrated into the programme. On 21 December, the 'Conseil National du Dialogue Social' signed a collective agreement between workers, employers and government on an increase of the minimum wage from CFAfr 28,000 to CFAfr 35,000.

The 2012 draft **budget** was presented in cabinet on 17 November and adopted in parliament on 31 December. It forecast a high growth rate of 4.5%, accompanied by decreasing inflation (from 2.1% in 2011 to 1.2% in 2012). The estimated increase in revenue for 2012 (CFAfr 638.2 bn, an increase of 18.9% over 2011) appeared to be rather optimistic as the national economy continued to be vulnerable in view of the global financial crisis, climate change, fluctuation of commodity prices, high unemployment and low productivity. Revenue included rising income from internal sources, notably of customs and duties, besides extraordinary revenue to the tune of CFAfr 298.5 bn (mostly donor-financed), compared with CFAfr 235.6 bn the year before. The latter was meant to finance an estimated deficit of CFAfr 310.2 bn. Total government spending was up by 18.4%, including CFAfr 295.2 bn in primary spending and CFAfr 17.2 bn in debt interest, which was 30.5% higher than in 2011. Investment spending increased by 22.4% to CFAfr 281.7 bn. The opposition rejected the budget because it held that the investments would be too dependent on external resources.

University students took part in violent protests throughout the year against the new licence-master-doctorate system, suspended scholarships and the expulsion and persecution of student leaders. The universities were closed up to the end of the year. In November a series of **occult murders** of young girls troubled the population of Agoé and Adidogomé, two suburbs of Lomé. The perpetrators apparently wanted to profit from the sale of body parts and human blood for occult practices. In the same vein, a ritual murderer in East-Mono, who had killed his sister-in-law and her child, was lynched by an outraged mob in Kpékplémé.

Dirk Kohnert

V. Central Africa

The "super election year" for the sub-region, with presidential elections held in five out of eight countries and legislative elections in four, did not bring any surprises. The autocratic regimes confirmed and sometimes tightened their grip on power and the single democracy of the sub-region continued its tradition of balancing representation between different political currents within the legislative and executive branches of government as a result of presidential elections. There were no spectacular changes with regard to economic and social developments. Sub-regional organisations were particularly passive during the year and held no major summits.

Democracy and Elections

Democracy remained rare in the sub-region and – with one exception – all elections confirmed or strengthened authoritarian regimes (in Cameroon, the CAR, Chad, the DRC and Gabon). The single exception was once again **São Tomé and Príncipe**, where Manuel Pinto da Costa, a well-known politician running as an independent candidate, became the third democratically elected president of the country. The winner's score – 52.9% against 47.1% for the candidate of the ruling 'Acção Democrática Independente' – was further proof of a respectable democratic standard in a sub-region where incumbent presidents with less than a two-thirds majority are rare. Still heading in the opposite direction, **Equatorial Guinea**'s Obiang Nguema decided to change the Constitution to give himself even more power: already the longest-serving president of the continent after 32 years at the helm of the country, he would be entitled under the proposed amendment to serve two more seven-year terms and to appoint the person of his choice to the new position of vice president. In addition, the establishment of a senate was envisaged as a second parliamentary chamber. The constitutional referendum took place on 13 November under familiar conditions – partly in public, many voting for absent or ill relatives, etc. – and produced an official result of 97% in favour.

Presidential elections in **Cameroon** continued to attract less and less popular attention, though a period of high social tension preceded the vote on 9 October. Surprisingly, the government found it necessary to curtail the powers of a rather well-controlled electoral commission and allocate them to the administration. Turnout figures varied, from official rates of 65%, to estimates of about 30% by some NGOs. Unsurprisingly, long-time President Paul Biya (competing with 21 opponents) received 78% of the votes cast. Both the party in government and the unconvincing opposition looked strongly out of touch with the masses.

Legislative and presidential elections were held in **Chad**. The ruling 'Mouvement pour le Salut de la Patrie' and its allies took 125 of the 188 seats in the parliamentary elections held on 13 February. The presidential election held on 25 April was boycotted by the three most important opposition candidates, so Idriss Déby easily won with a large majority officially put at 83.6%.

Legislative elections in **Gabon** were held after a long discussion on the need to have biometric voter cards. The main opposition parties boycotted the elections when the government declared it did not have the resources to implement this technical innovation. The former single-party, 'Parti Démocratique Gabonais', consequently won close to all the seats in the National Assembly (114 out of 120), marking a de facto return to one-party politics. This followed considerable turmoil subsequent to presidential elections in 2010, when opposition candidate Mba Obame had declared himself president. His party was dissolved and he took refuge in the UN compound, together with 20 supporters, on 27 January.

Presidential and parliamentary elections were also held in the **CAR**. Incumbent President Bozizé was re-elected with 66% of the votes in the presidential elections held on 25 January, although the four opposition candidates cried foul for a number of serious shortcomings. After calls for a boycott of the second round of parliamentary elections on 27 March (the first round was held in parallel with the presidential polls), the outcome would surprise nobody. Most long-established parties now had at best a symbolic parliamentary representation. Bozizé's Kwa Na Kwa (KNK) party directly controlled 62 seats (out of 105), but with most of the 28 officially 'independent' candidates solidly anchored within its camp, plus 11 seats for small KNK-affiliated parties, the majority was overwhelming. (The two former ruling, now opposition parties of the 1990s took only three seats between them.) A good number of close relatives of the head of state were elected to the National Assembly.

The **DRC**'s National Assembly and Senate approved an important revision of the Constitution in January. This paved the way for presidential elections held in a new simple plurality system, i.e. one round of elections with the winner being the candidate who receives most votes, with no absolute majority required. It was clear to everybody that this system would be favourable to incumbent President Joseph Kabila. Even more controversial was the attribution to the president of power to dissolve provincial assemblies and dismiss governors, amounting to a reversal of the decentralisation policy that was meant to be a cornerstone of the post-war order. And in March an electoral law was passed that changed the electoral system for parliamentary elections from pure proportional representation to a mixed system that favoured bigger parties. As a consequence, the stage was set for a reinforcement of the regime when elections took place on 28 November. They were overshadowed by widespread violence and credible allegations of manipulation. Kabila officially received only 48.9% of the votes (meaning he would have been forced to go to a second round under the old system, with a rather uncertain outcome), but the results were contested to the point that veteran politician and rival Etienne Tshisekedi declared himself president. The results of the legislative elections were not announced before year's end. Internal rifts within one of the main opposition parties and an announced dialogue process ahead of the legislative elections in 2012 marked the political year in the neighbouring Republic of **Congo**.

A somewhat underrated factor in the sub-region's political development was the impact of the **death of emblematic figures of the opposition** not only in 2011, but also in recent years. In October, Pierre Mamboundou, arguably the most important opposition figure in Gabon died of a heart attack. This had an impact that was deemed more important than the death in 2009 of Bernard Kolélas, an important opposition figure in neighbouring Congo. More spectacular were the circumstances surrounding the passing of the CAR's former president, Ange-Félix Patassé, who died in a Douala hospital in March after the authorities had several times refused to allow him to leave the country for medical treatment. This followed the death of his predecessor as head of state and equally important opponent

André Kolingba in 2010 (and the disappearance of long-time opponent Abel Goumba a year before). The implication was that highly personalised political parties were experiencing a succession crisis and that political systems as a whole needed a new generation of political opposition leaders, but not all the countries of the sub-region were producing new challengers to the regimes in power.

Instability, War and Peace

Compared with previous years, and with the notable exception of the DRC, relatively few major armed conflicts were recorded. However, in the **CAR**, on-going confrontations between rebel movements that were mostly officially part of an all-encompassing peace arrangement, as well as between government forces and rebels, resulted in the continued displacement of civilians and made it impossible to lead a normal life in large parts of the country. Demobilisation eventually began, focussed on one particular rebel movement.

The **DRC** continued to be most seriously affected by armed violence. Arguably the single most dangerous act was the armed attack on President Kabila's Kinshasa residence on 27 February by about 50 gunmen, which resulted in nine deaths. This was at first portrayed as a coup attempt, allegedly conducted by Bemba supporters. Transnational connections obviously played a major role in the reconfigurations of the conflict zone in the East. In South Kivu, local Mai-Mai groups cooperated with the Burundian rebel movement 'Forces Nationales de Libération' and staged an attack in the border area. More surprisingly, an alliance between the 'Forces Démocratiques de Libération du Rwanda' (FDLR), which was opposed to the government in Kigali and usually portrayed as a Hutu movement, and supporters of the arrested Tutsi rebel leader Laurent Nkunda under the umbrella of the 'Forces Patriotiques pour la Libération du Congo' (FPLC) was formed in **North Kivu** province. It figured now under the name FPLC/FDLR Soki. The Security Sector Reform process was characterised by the privileged integration into the national army of former rebels, particularly those from the 'Conseil National pour la Défense du Peuple' (CNDP), once led by Nkunda, later by Jean-Bosco Ntaganda, who had negotiated the peace agreement with the government in 2009, and another small rebel group. Discontent with privileged access for former rebels increased within the army, and parallel command structures impeded the creation of a truly united force. In the course of this power-struggle, about 170 men deserted from a training centre in June.

This was a rather calm year in **Chad**, despite some anxiety about the direct and indirect effects of the Libyan crises. President Déby, visibly interested in ameliorating relations with neighbouring Sudan, propagated reconciliation and issued amnesties to some former rebel leaders arrested in the preceding year. The demobilisation of about 16,000 rebel combatants had not yet started and remnants of Chadian rebel movements were active in the CAR. There was good news of a decline in the notorious highway banditry in the east.

With the end of the UN peacekeeping mission to Chad and the CAR, only the United Nations Organization Stabilization Mission in the Democratic Republic of the Congo (MONUSCO) remained as a major international peacekeeping operation within the sub-region. It continued to struggle with limited legitimacy as a result of its equally limited performance with regard to the protection of civilians. In addition, the CEEAC countries still maintained a small peacekeeping mission in the CAR. But two Western countries maintained or stepped up their presence in the area. While France remained solidly anchored in Central Africa with a permanent base in Libreville, Gabon, and forces stationed in Chad (though Déby announced that he wanted to renegotiate their presence) and the CAR, the US government deployed about 100 special forces personnel towards the end of the year to all relevant countries (i.e. the DRC and CAR, plus Uganda and South Sudan) affected by the raids of the **Lord's Resistance Army** (LRA), which was originally based, but no longer active in Uganda.

In **Cameroon**'s Bakassi peninsula, bordering Nigeria, a number of skirmishes between official security forces and local rebels continued, particularly in February. It became increasingly difficult to draw a line between fighters for autonomy and criminal gangs, as the most vocal organisation (Africa Maritime Commando) openly blackmailed oil companies operating in the area. A spectacular bank robbery in the middle of the economic hub of Douala in March, during which five civilians were killed, was further proof that the official security forces could not protect citizens – and that not only in outlying regions. Above all, it became more obvious that there was some complicity between criminal gangs and military officers.

The sub-region still contained important numbers of **refugees** who had to cross borders to find safety. The most important contingents were Sudanese refugees in Chad (about 278,000), and DRC citizens in Congo (124,000), with substantial numbers of CAR citizens residing temporarily in both Cameroon and Chad. Probably worse was the situation of **IDPs**, whose numbers were particularly high in the DRC (1.7 m), but a similarly high proportion of IDPs to the general population was attained in the CAR with 105,000 individuals. Chad had a substantial 126,000 IDPs at year's end, but this amounted to a lower proportion of the population than in either of the other seriously affected countries.

Human Rights

Some regimes responded nervously to the 'Arab Spring' in North Africa, fearing repercussions in their own countries. This was particularly evident in the case of the most authoritarian of all regimes in the sub-region, Equatorial Guinea, where civil rights and freedom were further curtailed. Foreign media were particularly targeted and could not report freely, including on the first AU summit to take place in Malabo. The fact that Obiang Nguema was at its head was a visible sign that the continental organisation was out of tune with the African population. Security forces in Cameroon dealt heavy-handedly with public demonstrations in an election year, despite the absence of any serious opposition alternatives.

Cameroon once again had a bad human rights record. Journalists and homosexuals were harassed, arrested and sentenced to prison terms. Both AI and HRW called upon the government to end discriminatory anti-homosexuality laws that provide for the severe punishment – up to five years' imprisonment – of private homosexual activity. Furthermore, people accused of homosexuality were reportedly often abused by other detainees or prison guards. At least four men were sentenced to prison terms late in the year because of their sexual orientation and up to six others remained in custody. At year's end a draft bill was prepared that would make legislation even harsher, with penalties of up to 15 years' imprisonment.

The human rights situation was obviously even worse in areas directly affected by conflict, i.e. in northern and eastern CAR, and particularly in eastern **DRC**, where the army trainee deserters already referred to committed mass rapes and killings. But the elections, too, were preceded, accompanied and followed by numerous human rights violations. The UN Joint Human Rights Office counted 188 cases of human rights abuse between 30 September and 1 November alone. On election day (28 November), the capital, Kinshasa, as well as Lubumbashi and Kananga, were sites of violent clashes. The controversial outcome of the elections, announced with some delay, led to further violence, with barricades erected, government buildings looted by angry mobs and acts of retaliation against opposition headquarters. In Northern Katanga (home and stronghold of Kabila), ethnic hatred flared against people originating from Kasai (home and stronghold of Tshisekedi). Army deserters also committed serious human rights violations, including rape.

The **ICC** proceeded with its cases in the CAR and DRC. The trial of Jean-Pierre Bemba (for crimes against humanity and war crimes committed by his military movement in the CAR) continued with the hearing of witnesses. It became clear that the trial had a direct impact on domestic politics, as Bemba was unable – despite his intentions – to stand as a candidate in the DRC presidential elections. (Similar effects were expected to be felt in Kenya and by its top politicians Uhuru Kenyatta and William Ruto.) In the five cases concerning the DRC, three accused and one suspect were in the custody of the ICC, while warlord Bosco Ntaganda (CNDP) remained at large. On 16 December, the relevant pre-trial chamber declined to confirm the charges of war crimes and crimes against humanity against Callixte Mbarushimana and released him from custody on 23 December.

Socioeconomic Developments

The IMF's 'World Economic Outlook' (published in April 2012) again showed a somewhat variable picture of the sub-region for the year, with Equatorial Guinea scoring highest on GDP growth rates with 7.1% (after depressing negative figures in the previous year). With its abundance of and dependence on oil and gas (the sector accounted for 99%

of exports), the country remained exceptional in terms of its basic economic structure. All other oil-producing economies were more diversified, which meant that they would not profit as much from the current world market prices. Gabon achieved 5.7% GDP growth, Congo 4.5% and Cameroon 4.1%, ahead of Chad (1.6%). Chad's modest growth came mainly from the non-oil sector, as the old wells were now becoming less productive and new ones were not yet on stream. The non-oil economies of the DRC and CAR, the two countries experiencing most violence, were able to achieve intermediate growth rates of 6.9% and 3.1% respectively, but started from very low levels. The respectable score of São Tomé and Príncipe (4.9%) was based on the expanding construction sector and trade.

The moderate **inflationary trend** of the previous year increased slightly in five out of eight countries (Cameroon, the CAR, Chad, Congo, Gabon – all with inflation rates between 1.6% and 6%), but declined somewhat from rather high values in both the DRC (17%, down from 23.1%) and São Tomé and Príncipe (12%, down from 14.4%), with Equatorial Guinea in between (7%, from 8.2% in 2010). From a consumer's perspective, it clearly remained difficult to profit from high growth. In addition, income distribution remained uneven, particularly within the oil economies.

The unfolding crisis within the European Monetary Union had some effect on the sub-region, with the CFAfr pegged to the Euro at a fixed rate and being the currency of six of the sub-region's eight countries; the DRC and São Tomé and Príncipe maintained their own currencies. However, there was little public discussion of the issue. The prospects of a CFAfr devaluation were similar to the major 1994 devaluation: potentially beneficial for exports, but detrimental to conditions for borrowing – and making imports of crucial goods from outside the Euro zone (e.g. China) more expensive.

UNDP's **HDI** was differently calculated compared with previous editions of the Index, but the overall picture of the sub-region hardly changed. Gabon ranked best (106; HDI value 0.66). A second group with rather similar aggregate values was headed by Equatorial Guinea (ranked 136), Congo (137), São Tomé and Príncipe (144) and Cameroon (150). The worst ranking was again reserved for the CAR (179), Chad (183) and the DRC (187), with values of 0.33, 0.32 and 0.28 respectively. With 187 countries surveyed, the DRC was at the very bottom end of the list.

No major change was recorded with regard to the UN-sponsored **MDG monitor** as 2015, the closing date, moved nearer. Gabon and Equatorial Guinea remained the best performers with most development goals "on track" or still within reach. Chad still lagged behind with five out of eight MDGs again considered "off track". Somewhat surprisingly, Cameroon presented a worse picture than the poor, conflict-ridden CAR, with three MDGs "off track" compared with the latter's two. With six countries likely to achieve goal no. 2 (universal primary education) and only the DRC off track in this regard, it was clear which sector had received the highest attention from the sub-region's governments over the past years.

Sub-regional Organisations

CEMAC became increasingly mired in crisis. The grandiose declarations of past years and apparent major achievements, such as the opening of the CEMAC Parliament in 2010, were not followed by concrete action. The merging of the two stock exchanges in Douala and Libreville did not materialise as planned. The common biometric CEMAC passport project did not progress. The regional development plan was not developed and the long-term dossier to create a regional airline (Air Cemac) slowed down when South African Airways, the future airline's preferred technical partner, had diverging views on some strategic elements. Even worse, though foreseen in the statutes, the heads of state failed to meet for the entire calendar year. The current secretariat team was less and less respected. At a CEMAC ministerial meeting on 19 December in Brazzaville, CAR Finance Minister Sylvain Ndoutingaï directly asked Cameroonian Antoine Ntsimi to vacate the CEMAC commission presidency as soon as possible.

BEAC's banking commission COBAC (Commission Bancaire de l'Afrique Centrale) was relocated to Libreville, Gabon, in the framework of a new dispensation of the sub-organisational headquarters. The inauguration ceremony on 8 August was attended by Gabon's President Ali Bongo.

CEEAC was similarly passive. The 15th summit of heads of state and government, originally planned for 2010 in N'Djaména, Chad, then re-scheduled for February 2011, was further postponed (to January 2012). The mandate of the secretary-general, Louis Sylvain Ngoma (Congo), expired on 31 October, but he remained in office until the next summit. CEEAC sent an electoral observer mission to Gabon's legislative elections. Unsurprisingly, the mission issued a moderately positive statement on the conduct of the elections on 19 December. The MICOPAX ('Mission de Consolidation de la Paix en République Centrafricaine') peacekeeping mission in the CAR had to step up its presence after the departure of UN troops and opened a base in Ndélé.

Similarly, the **Gulf of Guinea Commission** held no summit and was almost non-existent, despite the pressing issue of piracy in the area. Initially planned for Bata, Equatorial Guinea, in May, the organisation's third summit was postponed and invariably presented as pending until year's end. The UNSC, with resolution 2018 on 31 October, called on ECOWAS, CEEAC and the Gulf of Guinea Commission to cooperate in the prosecution of alleged perpetrators, including facilitators and financiers of piracy. It welcomed the intention (read: urged) to convene a summit of Gulf of Guinea heads of state to consider a comprehensive strategy.

Andreas Mehler

Cameroon

The presidential election was without doubt the most important event of the year, although it took place against a background of general indifference. Unsurprisingly, 78-year-old President Paul Biya, already one of Africa's longest serving presidents (29 years), was re-elected against competition from 22 other candidates (a record) for a further term of seven years, receiving 78% of the votes, according to official figures. The leader of the Social Democratic Front (SDF), John Fru Ndi, seen as Biya's main opponent, received only 10% of the votes, his lowest ever result. NGOs and opposition political parties reported widespread fraud and described the organisation of the polls as chaotic. Throughout the year social tension was high, and the authorities maintained a high security force presence in public spaces.

Domestic Politics

The 9 October vote was preceded by a long period of political and social tension. In June, **a football match** played in Yaoundé between the national teams of Cameroon and Senegal escalated into **riots** after the match ended in a draw, preventing Cameroon from qualifying for the 2012 African Cup of Nations. Supporters clashed with police for several hours, and local newspapers reported that between one and four people were killed during the violence, although there was no official confirmation. In July, five people were killed, including four by lynching, and dozens injured in clashes between residents and criminals in Douala.

Spectacular acts of violence were also reported. In March, a bank robbery perpetrated by heavily armed men took place in the district of Bonabéri in Douala. The gang controlled the area for two hours and killed five people before escaping by boat on the Wouri River with their booty (CFA fr 200 m – about € 305,000). A few weeks later, several soldiers and a navy captain were arrested, suspected of involvement in the case, which reinforced the impression of a high degree of **criminality in the Cameroonian security forces**.

As in the past three years, violence continued on the **Bakassi** peninsula (bordering Nigeria). In February, three attacks were recorded in less than a week. On 6 February, 13 people, including a sub-prefect, were kidnapped. They were released for a ransom after ten days of captivity. On the night of 6–7 February, the police station in Mbonjo was attacked and, according to the government, two policemen were killed. These two attacks were the work of the Africa Marine Commando (AMC), the most active armed group in the Bakassi region. According to the private daily newspaper 'Le Jour', the AMC was demanding that the five oil companies operating in Bakassi each pay a monthly tax of Naira 6 m (around € 150,000). Following these attacks, Paul Biya returned urgently from Switzerland, where he makes extended private visits, and ordered the establishment of a crisis committee. Only a few days later, another attack occurred at Isangele (Bakassi): a soldier and a civilian were killed.

On the political level, tension was particularly high in early February, when several small **opposition parties** (including the 'Union des populations du Cameroun' and the 'Mouvement Africain pour la Nouvelle Indépendance et la Démocratie' – Manidem), and the SDF MP of Wouri (Douala) Jean Michel Nintcheu, announced that they would organise **demonstrations**. Their aim was to celebrate the 'martyrs' of the riots of February 2008 and also to ask Biya not to stand in the elections. The anxious authorities publicly threatened opponents with reprisals, and cut the Twitter service for several days. Although the popular mobilisation was almost zero, a consequence of the widespread disinterest in politics among Cameroonians, a large number of security forces were deployed in Douala to prevent the coalition of parties from holding a meeting, scheduled for 23 February. On that date, they arrested the organisers of the meeting and transported them to the outskirts of Douala, where they were released. Nintcheu was beaten by the police but not arrested. A correspondent of 'Agence France Presse' who covered the event was arrested and detained for nearly 48 hours. No other demonstrations were attempted after this event, seen by some observers and citizens as a way for the opposition to put pressure on the government to extort money from it in return for withdrawing its threat to cause disturbances. Nevertheless, the authorities, who seemed to be frightened by the revolutions in

Arab countries, maintained their tight control of both opposition moves and the media during the following weeks.

Thus, in March 2011, the National Assembly adopted a bill authorising the president to have telephones tapped without making a request through parliament. During the same period, the number of soldiers in the 'Brigade d'Intervention Rapide' (a special unit of the army, directly linked to the presidency) was revised upwards with the recruitment of 3,000 new members. In April, the long-time opposition activist, Mboua Massok, was arrested on several occasions, and the first edition of an International Human Rights Film Festival, organised in Yaoundé by several associations and funded by the EU, was banned by the authorities: only a few hours before the first screening, the authorities sent the riot police authorised by a prefectural ban mentioning a threat to public order. At the end of April, the authorities also banned a private screening in Yaoundé of the documentary 'The Big Banana', which is very critical of the activities of the Franco-American company 'Plantations du Haut-Penja'.

There was also perceptible **tension inside the ruling party**, the Cameroon People's Democratic Movement (CDPM). In June, a controversy erupted, fueled by disgruntled, but anonymous members of the ruling party, about the Biya's eligibility to stand for election for another term,. The assertion was that the Constitution, revised in 2008, would not allow Biya to stand in another election, because his mandate began in 2004 under a constitutional clause that limited the number of presidential terms, and that he could not take advantage of rules introduced after that date.

At the beginning of September, the publication by **Wikileaks** of numerous cables issued by the US embassy in Yaoundé generated new tension within the ruling party. For several days, newspapers re-published parts of this material, describing interviews between several prominent officials and US diplomats. According to one of the cables, Minister of State for Territorial Administration Marafa Hamidou Yaya admitted that he had ambitions to become president after Biya's term ended. Another cable detailed the ethnic theory supported by Deputy Prime Minister and Minister of Justice Amadou Ali, in a discussion with the US Ambassador. According to the source, Ali said the struggle for Biya's succession should be viewed through ethnic and regional lenses. He explained that the foundation of Cameroon's stability would be the detente between Biya's Beti/Bulu ethnic group (in the south), and the populations of Cameroon's northern region. Ali claimed that the north would support Biya for as long as he wanted to be president, but would not accept a successor who was either another Beti/Bulu, or a member of the economically powerful Bamileke ethnic group (originating from the west). "Ali's analysis and his willingness to speak so frankly about such a sensitive topic reinforced our conviction that Cameroon's political elite is increasingly focused on jockeying for the post-Biya era," the cable concluded, reflecting the fear of most observers that the tribalisation of Biya's regime would one day degenerate into inter-communal violence.

In September, the **CPDM held an ordinary congress**, which should normally be held every five years and be the time to revise the membership of the central committee, although the last congress had been held in 1996. The meeting, eagerly expected for a long time by the party's 'reformers', had in recent years been repeatedly announced and then postponed. By holding it, Biya seemed to want to prove to his foreign partners – who discreetly criticised his long tenure of power – that he still had the support of the CDPM, which de facto controls elections. Internally, a lot of members were waiting for a rejuvenation of the party leaders, wondering whether the president would try to stop the clan war raging in his party and his entourage about his heritage. There was finally no surprise: Biya was re-elected unopposed as the head of the party, silencing the rumours that had suggested he might hand over to a successor. The changes introduced by Biya were insignificant: the number of members of the Central Committee, the party's governing body, was increased (from 250 to 350, much more than the party rules allowed), as was the political bureau (from 23 to 30). Some individuals who were positioning themselves as 'renovators' or 'reformers' were appointed by Biya to the Central Committee and thereby silenced.

Until the very end, Biya remained vague about the **election**: he fixed the election date at the last moment and left many guessing about his candidacy. The date of the election (9 October) was in fact only announced on 30 August and Biya registered his candidacy on 4 September, the closing day for submissions, without any prior public statement. His candidacy documents were submitted at Elecam (the office charged with organising elections) by party officials, almost through the back door and the incumbent candidate hardly campaigned,attending only three meetings (in Maroua, Douala, Kribi), all in the week before the election.

His challengers were unable, however, to take advantage of this low-key public campaigning. The **opposition was again strongly disorganised**: in addition to Biya, 22 candidates were approved by Elecam (out of 52 submissions), which was a record. John Fru Ndi, the president of the SDF, was also silent for a long time about his own intentions, and it was only on 3 September that he was officially selected by his party to be their presidential candidate. In August, Fru Ndi had called on Cameroonians to register as voters just days before the registration deadline, which was seen as an important change in his attitude: in September 2010, he had encouraged Cameroonians not to register as voters and had also threatened to prevent the elections. He was at that time protesting on behalf of **Elecam**, demanding reforms to guarantee it more independence. The government did indeed introduce reforms, but not in that direction: in April, a new amendment, passed in a special session of the Parliament, took away Elecam's right to announce the provisional election results, which became the prerogative of the Supreme Court, acting on behalf of the Constitutional Council (one of the key institutions foreseen in the current Constitution, but not yet created). This was probably the Cameroonian authorities' reaction to the post-election crisis in Côte d'Ivoire in late 2010, which resulted from a conflict between the Independent Electoral Commission and the Constitutional Council. Other changes, introduced a few weeks later, gave more power to the ministries of justice and territorial administration in the organisation of elections.

At the end of September, a few days before the presidential elections, a bizarre incident occurred in Douala: **gunmen** wearing military uniforms and holding placards saying "Biya must go" blockaded the bridge over the Wouri, shooting at police for some hours. There was no clear explanation of this episode. Many Cameroonians suspected that the authorities were behind it, creating a pretext to militarise the country before the election, and security measures were in fact greatly enhanced in the days following the incident.

The presidential election was held on 9 October without major incident, although the SDF claimed that, an SDF party worker was killed in the western region of Bandjoun by supporters of the ruling party, and a previously unknown armed group called the 'Commando Alliance Brotherhood of Cameroon' claimed responsibility for the killing of two soldiers at a polling station in Isangele. Even though the voting took place without major violence, it was marked by widespread voter apathy: observers and NGOs, including Transparency International Cameroon, estimated the real rate of participation at less than 30%, although the official figure was 65.8%. The organisation of the polls itself attracted much criticism from the opposition, observers and some foreign partners. The SDF spoke of a "complete mess" and an "electoral farce", as some polling stations did not even open, the counting in others took place by candlelight, some voters received several voter registration cards, etc. The team of Commonwealth observers considered that voting had been free from coercion, but stressed that there were "many complaints" about its organisation. A US statement was also very critical. During the days that followed, seven candidates, led by Fru Ndi, summed up the problems, denouncing many fraudulent practices. They announced that they would not recognise the results and called for the cancellation of the election. The ruling party, however, urged the public not to yield to the "provocation" and used the state media to call for calm, and the Catholic Church also called for the acceptance of the results.

The tension gradually subsided after arrangements were made behind the scenes. The Supreme Court rejected a request by the opposition to annul the elections, paving the way for the results to be announced, and they were published three weeks after polling day, by which time interest in the elections had faded.

In December, Biya carried out a **government reshuffle**, which gave the impression that he wanted to end the ambitions of some top figures in the regime. Several ministers changed portfolios. The influential Minister of Justice Amadou Ali became deputy prime minister in charge of relations with parliament, a ministry without power or resources. The powerful Minister of Territorial Administration and Decentralisation Amadou Marafa lost his job and was replaced by CPDM Secretary General René Sadi, often presented as a potential successor to Biya. At the same time as the reshuffle, in an indication the he did not distinguish between his party and the state administration, Biya appointed former minister of agriculture and rural development Jean Nkuete to be secretary general of the Central Committee of the CDPM. This appointment was announced on state radio as an extension of the statement about the government reorganisation. In December, the president chaired a cabinet meeting for the first time since July 2009.

There was no progress in the cases of the former ministers detained in **Operation Sparrow Hawk**, but some of them spoke openly for the first time. In July, the former minister of health, Urbain Olanguena Awono, accused of corruption, issued an open letter denouncing a settling of scores against a background of political manipulation by the state apparatus. In October, Polycarpe Abah Abah, the former minister of economy and finance, declared in court that he had been in prison for almost four years on the basis of evidence that consisted of slander, lies and defamation. In December, the former secretary general of the presidency, Jean-Marie Atangana Mebara, published a book critical of Operation Sparrow Hawk, which spoke of an "abusive remand" and a "biased examination". All three had been detained since 2008 and each accused ministers of having plotted to kick them out of office, but no one dared to accuse Biya himself, which illustrated the fear that the president still inspired.

With regard to the fight against **corruption**, in November, the 'Commission Nationale Anti-Corruption' (CONAC) delivered its first report since its creation in 2006, focusing on just a few ministerial administrations. The results showed diversion of money at the national treasury and at the ministry of agriculture. CONAC also observed that, if the state put an end to the corrupt practices at the ministry of public works, three times as many roads could be built. The report pointed out the responsibility of several high officials, recommending prosecution, but no legal action was taken.

Foreign Affairs

The presidential election led to a cooling of relations between Cameroon and some of its main international partners, who seemed to want Biya not to stand for election. Several weeks before the elections, the **United States** caused offence by making statements hinting at a repudiation of the regime. On the occasion of the celebration of Cameroon's National Day on 20 May, US Secretary of State Hillary Clinton in a message to the Cameroonians urged the authorities to hold a free and fair presidential election. At the end of June, Assistant US Secretary of State for African Affairs, Johnnie Carson, paid an official visit to Cameroon and he also urged "free, fair and transparent elections". CPDM Secretary General Rene Sadi responded at a meeting in Kribi, saying that only Cameroonians would have the last word on the fate of their country. At the same meeting, the secretary general at the prime minister's office, Jules Doret Ndongo, also had harsh words for Cameroon's foreign partners. In July, the bishops of Cameroon, known for being close partners of the regime, recommended in a pastoral letter that the international community show greater respect for Cameroon's sovereignty.

Meanwhile, **France** remained silent in this debate, which was seen as a distancing from Biya, which was taken badly in Yaoundé. However, most Cameroonians had no doubt that Paris was still supporting Biya. French Minister of Cooperation Henry De Raincourt made a statement to the press during an official visit to Yaoundé on 1 July that France had no candidate for the elections.

Some tension and confusion were perceptible after the presidential elections. US Ambassador in Yaounde Robert P. Jackson made a statement noting irregularities at all levels on election day, which had given free rein to multiple voting. He also called on Elecam to demonstrate its independence from the ruling party, the CPDM, and for public resources not to be used in future for CPDM campaigns. This was in strong contrast to French Foreign Minister Alain Juppé's statement shortly after the polls that the elections had taken place "under acceptable conditions". Given the US position and the negative judgment of the Commonwealth on the organisation of the elections, Paris was obliged to re-examine this view and, a few days later, Bernard Valero, spokesman of the French foreign ministry, was less positive. He said that France had taken note of the result announced by Cameroon's Supreme Court confirming Biya's re-election, but that many irregularities had been found. "France hopes that steps would be taken to ensure that irregularities do not occur in the legislative and municipal elections of 2012," Valero added in his statement. In contrast to France, the US did not send any message of congratulation to Biya.

Biya replied to these criticisms in a speech delivered at the publication of the results: he claimed that the people of Cameroon had decided "freely and transparently" to assign him once again the responsibility of President of the Republic. In his end-of-the-year speech, he made a small concession by acknowledging some "shortcomings", but insisted that they had not been such as to jeopardise the outcome of the ballot, and that they would be corrected before the next elections.

Amid speculation about the cooling of relations with Washington and Paris before the election, Biya seemed to show his independence by making an official visit to **China** on 20–22 July, at the invitation of his Chinese counterpart Hu Jintao. Seven cooperation agreements (in the areas of health, education, vocational training, public lighting, culture and media) were signed on this occasion. Biya also had talks with several Chinese businessmen interested in investing in Cameroon, and several senior Chinese officials visited Cameroon later. Chinese Deputy Prime Minister in charge of Agriculture Hui Liangyu had already made an official three-day visit to Cameroon in January.

In June, tensions erupted on the border with **Gabon**: at least two people died and more than 2,000 crossed the border into Cameroon after being forcibly driven from the gold mining site in Minkébé (northern Gabon). Of those registered, 1,551 were from Cameroon and the rest from West Africa (Benin, Burkina Faso, Côte d'Ivoire, Guinea, Ghana, Mali, Niger, Senegal) and Chad. The expulsion order was made as a result of security issues and because, according to the Gabonese authorities, many workers had no identity documents. The Gabonese authorities further claimed that, in addition to criminal activity (poaching and illegal gold mining), Minkébé had also become a centre for illegal drug trafficking. Gabon President Ali Bongo said that, if there had been any wrong-doing during expulsion of the migrants' expulsion, it would be punished.

There were also incidents in late November on the border with the **Central African Republic** (CAR). The border was closed for four days at Garoua Boulaï (300 km east of Yaoundé) after an argument between a CAR soldier and a Cameroonian moto-taxi driver, which escalated into a shoot-out between CAR soldiers and Cameroonian police, although there were no casualties. The prefect of Nana Mambéré division, based 200 km away in Bouar, in west CAR, stayed in Garoua Boulaï for 72 hours to resolve the issue.

At the very end of the year, **Nigeria** decided to close the border with Cameroon because of the threat from Boko Haram, which was reported to have infiltrated northern Cameroon. A few days later, Cameroonian media reported that there had been calls for calm, tolerance and co-existence by imams in the mosques in the far north of Cameroon. They also reported that intelligence agencies believed that Islamic schools were being used for radical Islamic indoctrination and that surveillance was being undertaken by the Cameroonian authorities.

Socioeconomic Developments

There were no major economic events during the year. In January, the **IMF** office in Cameroon summed things up well in a document titled "Time for the lion to wake up?", which drew a portrait of the country's contrasts: although it has plentiful resources, its economic results do not match its economic potential because of the government's reluctance to adopt reforms. The IMF particularly underlined the lack of infrastructure, citing road transport tariffs in the order of $ 0.13 per ton-kilometre, compared with $ 0.05 in southern Africa and well below $ 0.04 in much of the rest of the developing world. The IMF estimated that the impact of improved infrastructure on real per capita GDP growth would be about 4.5%, and also noted the weakness of the **telecoms sector**: the two mobile operators charged very high prices and provided a poor quality of service for consumers. According to the IMF, if the quality and prices of telecoms services in Cameroon rose to match that found in Mauritius, real growth in GDP per capita would increase by 1.3% per annum, thus closing one-third of the gap between the country's current economic performance and its aspirations (Vision 2035) would be covered.

The 2011 budget was very similar to that of the previous year: it was set at CFAfr 2,571 bn (more than € 3.9 bn). The government targeted a GDP growth rate of 3.8% and an inflation rate of 3%, and predicted an oil price of $ 80 per barrel. The state intended to raise CFAfr 1,552 bn (€ 2.3 bn) in tax revenue, compared with CFAfr 1,440 bn (€ 2.1 bn) in 2010, and to earmark 59.1% of expenditure for public services, 26.5% for investment and 14.4% for debt repayments. It was counting on issuing government securities, on foreign borrowing and, of course, on oil revenue.

However, **oil production** continued to decline to an estimated 58,000 b/d, against 65,000 b/d in 2010. But there was some good news: the minister of mines said in November that heavy investment made in the previous three years, including in exploration, should increase oil production by 17% in 2012 to an expected 68,000 b/d. A few months before, in May, the Scottish group BowLeven, which holds an exploration licence covering a total area of 2,300 km^2, made a major discovery of oil off Douala, the economic capital and, in July, the state-owned 'Société Nationale des Hydrocarbures' announced the discovery by China's Yan Chang Logone Development Holding Company Ltd (a subsidiary of Shaanxi Yan Petroleum Group Corporation) of a field in the Zina and Makary blocks of the Logone Birni basin, in the Extreme North.

There was some small degree of progress on **infrastructure development**. Biya, who spent the entire election and post-election period in Kribi, in southern Cameroon, laid the cornerstone for the construction of the **deepwater port of Kribi** (which had been announced in 2000) on 8 October, just one day before the election. In January, the government had announced that it would borrow € 316 m from the Chinese bank Eximbank to finance the construction of the port (whose total cost was expected to be CFAfr 282 bn, about € 430 m), and construction work began at that time. A veteran of construction in Africa, the French company Razel, was responsible for the earthworks, and the China Harbour Engineering Company began the gigantic port engineering, including the construction of an embankment nearly 3 km long to guard against potential waves. In April, the works were halted for several days by angry villagers demanding compensation and relocation.

In the **mining sector**, some NGOs expressed concern about the mining law, asking the government to introduce regulations to control the use of local mineral royalties. There was also suspicion of fraud in connection with the diamond deposit at Mobilong (eastern Cameroon). In South Korea, the authorities opened an investigation into alleged corruption involving senior Korean officials and the Korean company C&K Mining, which had received a permit from the Cameroonian government to exploit the mine in 2010. The investigation was thought to hinge on the size of diamond deposits at the Mobilong field and on whether the mine's potential value had been intentionally exaggerated, as claimed by activists and experts, to cause a significant rise in the value of C&K Mining shares. Two Cameroonian NGOs demanded the suspension of C&K Mining activities in the country and a parliamentary investigation into the issuing of the mining permit. The South Korean investigation was expected to be concluded by the beginning of 2012.

In October, Cameroon was downgraded for the second time by the Council of the **Extractive Industries Transparency Initiative** (EITI) and failed to earn the status of compliant country. The Council estimated that the data from Cameroon in the EITI reports were under discussion, with questions being raised about their quality, and concluded that the EITI Secretariat, supported by the World Bank, should conduct further investigations.

The embarrassment of the Council was apparent as it had to create a new status of "candidate close to compliance" specifically for Cameroon.

The crucial problem of **unemployment** persisted, despite a promise by the president that was headlined throughout the year. In February, Biya promised to create 25,000 jobs in the public sector for young graduates in the coming year, but there was no doubt that the promise was directly related to the election. The government made efforts implement it and about 300,000 people applied for the jobs, but many of them complained about the lack of transparency and organisation and the commitment was ultimately not met. In early July, a strike by 2,500 health workers, recruited in 2007, exposed the real status of employment in the public sector: the workers were demanding payment of two years' unpaid wages and their integration into the Civil Service.

In May, the **Moroccan Attijariwafa Bank** bought 51% of the 'Société Commerciale de Banque Cameroun', the fourth largest bank in the country. The remaining shares (49%) were still held by the state of Cameroon. The Moroccan group said that it wanted to increase the rate of use of the banking system, which was very low (only 7% in Cameroon against 50% in Morocco).

In early July, Cameroon and France signed a second **'development contract debt (C2D)'**, amounting to € 326 m (about CFAfr 214 bn) over a period of five years (2011 to 2016). Initiated by France, the C2D is intended to cancel the debt of some countries by converting it into grants to finance development. As part of this programme, Cameroon had already received € 536.6 m (CFAfr 352 bn) for the period from 2006 to 2011. Cameroon was the first recipient in 2011 of French financial aid of France in sub-Saharan Africa and, according to French authorities, was the largest recipient of the C2D; 60% of the total C2D budget would benefit agriculture and rural development.

The **agricultural sector** received attention from the authorities during the agro-pastoral show held in January in Ebolowa (in southern Cameroon). Once a major rural affairs event, the show had not been held for 24 years and had been postponed several times in 2010. It brought together several hundred farmers, ranchers and companies for several days, and was, once again used by Biya as part of his election strategy: he visited it several times, accompanied by large numbers of attendants and many senior officials and media representatives. Recognising the exponential growth of food imports (for example, the expenditure of CFAfr 500 bn on imported flour, rice and fish in 2009 was seven times more than in 1994), he made many promises to the rural community, but no concrete measures were taken to solve the sector's pressing problems.

Cameroon was not immune to **land grabbing**, even though it went unreported in the media. In August, Biopalm Energy, a subsidiary of Siva Group of Singapore, launched a CFAfr 900 bn ($ 1.974 bn) palm oil project in southern Cameroon to be developed on 200,000 ha. It was claimed it would increase the annual production of palm oil to 80,000 tonnes over the first five years of production. Another agricultural company, Herakles Farm, based in New York, was also planning to develop some 60,000 ha of palm oil plantations in the south-west, but the project raised the ire of several environmental groups, among them the Australian Rainforest Rescue, which launched an online petition to put pressure on the Cameroonian government to reconsider the project, which it claimed was threatening some parts of Cameroon's unspoiled rainforest and the livelihood of the local population. There was no reaction from the government.

Fanny Pigeaud

Central African Republic

For most Central Africans this was another painful year during which they endured widespread violence. Armed clashes continued, particularly in the periphery of the country. Democratic standards declined, not least because of suspect elections for the presidency and the National Assembly. Not surprisingly, both were won by the regime in power. All available data on the social situation presented a miserable picture. President Bozizé tried to diversify his international ties, both in the sub-region and beyond.

Domestic Politics

The **presidential election**, postponed from 2010, had been set for 25 January. All the main candidates were allowed to run, although the outsider, Innocent Justin Willité, was disqualified in early January because the cheque for his registration fee bounced. Nevertheless, the opposition complained about the preparation for and conduct of the election. In fact, it was virtually impossible for the opposition to tour the country with all the restrictions on free travel that were in place. Another major problem was that the electoral register was published only one day before the poll, which made any correction impossible. This criticism culminated in the resignation of seven opposition members from the

34-strong Independent Electoral Commission ('Commission Electorale Indépendante', CEI) in protest against irregularities detected two days after the poll. The CEI, now completely controlled by the regime, announced its results on 1 February, giving incumbent President François Bozizé a two-thirds majority (66.1% of the votes), outstripping former president Ange-Félix Patassé, who ran as an independent, with 20.1%, Martin Ziguélé, candidate for the strongest opposition party 'Mouvement pour la Libération du Peuple Centrafricain' (MLPC), with 6.5%, and Emile Gros Raymond Nakombo of the 'Rassemblement Démocratique Centrafricain' (RDC), with 4.6%. Jean-Jacques Démafouth, a former defence minister, standing as the candidate of the 'Nouvelle Alliance pour le Progrès' and not officially for his politico-military movement 'Armée Populaire pour la restauration de la République et la Démocratie' (APRD), received a mere 2.7%. On the basis of these figures, Bozizé won the election easily, but criticism continued. The four opposition candidates claimed *inter alia* that the CEI had not taken into account the votes cast at 1,262 out of the 4,612 polling stations and lodged a complaint for election-rigging against the CEI president, Joseph Binguimalé.

In the parallel **legislative elections**, the 'Kwa Na Kwa' party (KNK), supporting Bozizé, won 26 seats in the first round. Among those directly elected were the president himself, his wife Monique, his sister Joséphine Kéléfio and two of his sons. All the opposition presidential candidates also stood as candidates for the National Assembly, but had to face crushing defeats. Irregularities were potentially more important in these elections than in the presidential race. In the course of the unfolding investigations, three electoral commissioners were arrested on 9 February and the votes had to be recounted in two electoral districts. On 12 February, the Constitutional Court generally confirmed the results of the presidential election, lowering Bozizé's vote insignificantly to 64.3% (with Patassé on 21.4% and Ziguélé on 6.8%).

In light of the numerous shortcomings, as well as organisational weakness, the opposition decided on 15 February to **boycott the second round of the legislative elections**, which still took place on 27 March. The results could not but confirm Bozizé's grip on power: KNK won a total of 63 out of 105 seats in the National Assembly, but most remaining seats went to "independents" – in fact, candidates equally close to the president. The Constitutional Court subsequently annulled close to 20% of the results in both rounds of the legislative elections, a margin that did not challenge the presidential majority. Finally, by-elections were held in 14 constituencies on 4 September, again boycotted (for the most part) by the opposition. This produced the following final overall composition in the National Assembly: KNK – 62 seats; independents – 28 (most of them pro-KNK); KNK-affiliated parties – 11; MLPC – 2; RDC – 1. This represented an overwhelming majority sympathetic to Bozizé. A further by-election in Bouar was deemed necessary by a ruling of the Constitutional Court on 26 October.

The **opposition**, in particular the country's main parties, the MLPC and RDC, showed remarkable firmness in rejecting the electoral masquerade. Civilian parties, i.e. excluding the APRD, formed the 'Front d'Annulation et de Reprise des Elections de 2011' (FARE-2011), but were in fact in a weak position. The split in the MLPC, between a majority supporting former prime minister and party president Ziguélé and a minority who would still side with Patassé, was palpable and became more critical with the distance between the two candidates' election results, which humiliated Ziguélé. Both men tried to downplay the split and officially reconciled in early February. Worse was to come, when Bozizé initially refused to grant permission to Patassé to leave the country for medical treatment. When he belatedly did so, it was all too late and the former president died on 5 April at the age of 74 in Douala, Cameroon, on his way to Equatorial Guinea. The controversial and charismatic Patassé had been a major threat to Bozizé, who probably preferred being criticised for his handling of the affair to continuing to be nervous about the manoeuvres of the man he had removed by military force in 2003. But constant rumours had it that Bozizé himself was seriously ill, consulting traditional healers and visiting Nigeria in November mainly for medical treatment.

Bozizé re-appointed Prime Minister Faustin-Archange Touadéra on 22 April as the head of a **new government**. Despite the fact that the 2009 'inclusive political dialogue' had concluded with agreement that all the parties to the dialogue would be represented in future governments, this did not happen. Three members of the opposition were appointed to relatively minor positions in the government, but their parties suspended them immediately. The government of the war-torn country clearly lacked inclusiveness. Ten ministers survived the change in government, most significantly Jean-Francis Bozizé, one of the president's sons, as defence minister, and the donors' darling Sylvain Maliko as minister of planning. The controversial mines minister, Sylvain Ndoutingaï, was shifted to the finance ministry. Fidèle Gouandjika, the former minister for communication and reconciliation, lost some clout by being shifted to the agriculture portfolio and losing the prestigious title of minister of state.

The president himself seemed uninterested in the peace process and considered that the **on-going rebel activities in the periphery** hardly challenged his rule in the capital, Bangui, and the surrounding area. The army ('Forces Armées Centrafricaines', FACA) nevertheless conducted operations against the 'Convention des Patriotes pour la Justice et la Paix' (CPJP) in the north-east. Clashes between them in early February near Bria, in March near Ndélé, and again on 10 April close to Birao, resulted in government victories – at a heavy price. The clashes in Ndélé resulted in mostly civilian casualties, and 500 people were displaced, but the majority of the CPJP declared a ceasefire thereafter and officially signed a ceasefire agreement with the government on 12 June in Ndélé, followed by the dissident CPJP faction on 17 July in Nzacko. This did not amount to creating peace in the region, however, as non-government groups continued to fight each other. One confrontation involved the CPJP and the 'Union des Forces Démocratiques pour le Rassemblement' (UFDR) in the Bria area between August and October, apparently motivated by desire for control of diamond production there. Both movements were also associated with separate ethnic identities (the UFDR with the Gula, and the CPJP with the Runga). Various contradictory sources claimed that the fighting displaced between 4,500 and 15,000 people and claimed 50 lives. On 8 October, both movements signed a ceasefire agreement and left Bria. However, the CPJP still remained outside the formal Libreville Comprehensive Peace Agreement signed by most other rebel movements in 2008. The other major confrontation took place in June around Kaga Bandoro between the APRD, mostly recruiting in Patassé's strongholds in the north, and a formerly Chadian rebel group, the 'Front Populaire pour le Redressement' (FPR). This strangely coincided with the start of a major demobilisation campaign targeting APRD fighters. On 13 June, FPR leader Babba Laddé had signed an agreement with Chadian and CAR mediators that was meant to facilitate the return of his fighters to Chad, but he later renounced the agreement and openly declared that he was pulling out of peace negotiations on 22 July. FPR fighters subsequently occupied a village between Bambari and Kouango. The overall security situation in the north, with competing rebel movements and the FACA engaging in battles that jeopardised the lives of civilians more than those of combatants, was replicated in the south-east, where combined forces fought off the formerly Ugandan-based **Lord's Resistance Army** (LRA), which staged an attack on Nzacko, far further north than its troops were believed to be. The porosity of borders was as evident as the inner weakness of the state's security forces.

In July, the minister for **disarmament**, General Yangongo, said that 1,439 rebels (out of 8,800) had been demobilised. The process was looking untransparent and disorganised when Bozizé finally took a personal interest in moving it on by mid-year. Towards year's end, new and somewhat promising figures, apparently focusing mostly on APRD combatants, were issued (4,770 men demobilised and 3,500 – mostly handmade – weapons collected). Most rebel movements expressed concern about the pace and inclusiveness of the disarmament process.

Several ministers and top officials were involved in **corruption** scandals, some of them truly embarrassing. A series of articles in 'Les Collines de l'Oubangui' pinpointed Defence Minister Jean-Francis Bozizé as being involved in the embezzlement of EU funds earmarked for a demobilised soldiers' pension fund. The editor, Faustin Bambou, was arrested without a warrant and indicted for "inciting violence and hatred", but later released by order of the court, together with another newspaper editor. Elie Ouéfio, secretary-general of both the president's office and the ruling party, lost both positions on 14 November after being accused of embezzling part of the KNK's electoral campaign budget. The general director of the 'Société Centrafricaine de Stockage des Produits Pétroliers' was arrested for embezzling close to € 3 m.

Interreligious violence erupted in Bangui on 31 May to 1 June. A mosque was burnt down by Christians, the police shot at demonstrators and a curfew was imposed. Seven deaths were officially reported.

Foreign Affairs

External reactions to the fraudulent elections were rhetorically harsh, but otherwise ineffective. On 16 May, the **EU** ambassador presented a highly critical report by international election experts to the press, using expressions such as "massive fraud" and "terrorisation of voters... by state officials and security forces". This was a significantly strong statement by the most important sponsor of the elections. Furthermore, on 27 March, EU High Commissioner Ashton criticised the on-going restrictions on freedom of movement, clearly aimed at opposition candidates. However, the EU did not threaten to cut development aid and remained one of the CAR's major donors. Paris had already urged the opposition to accept the election result on 14 February.

The **UN**'s Integrated Peacebuilding Office in the CAR (known by its French acronym as BINUCA) acquired a new leader when Ethiopian Sahle-Work Zewde was replaced by the very experienced Margaret Vogt of Nigeria. In an extended resolution on 21 December, the UNSC took positions on a number of recent urgent issues (i.e. disarmament, ceasefires, elections), but more concretely decided to extend the BINUCA mandate, on the recommendation of the UN Secretary-General, until 31 January 2013. The UN Peacebuilding Commission held several meetings with ministers and Bozizé, but on-going violence in several parts of the country made it clear that it could hardly be considered to be in a post-conflict situation. After the closing down of the UN peacekeeping mission in November 2010, **CEEAC**'s 'Mission de Consolidation de la Paix' (MICOPAX) moved in and, following fresh violence, opened a military base in Ndélé on 26 April.

The announcement by **US** President Barack Obama on 14 October that some 100 special forces troops would be sent to the sub-region to combat the LRA and train soldiers from the four affected countries (Uganda, the CAR, South Sudan and the DRC) was well received in Bangui. It was foreseen that only a small contingent of the commandos would be stationed in the CAR. Some troops arrived in December.

Bozizé fostered ties with **China**, when Vice Foreign Minister Zhai Jun was received in Bangui on 7 April. The president also made a two-day visit to **Qatar** on 21–22 November.

Only three presidents of the **sub-region** attended the re-elected president's investiture on 15 March (Idriss Déby of Chad, Ali Bongo of Gabon and Obiang Nguema of Equatorial Guinea). A trilateral meeting was held in Khartoum, Sudan, on 23 May between Déby, Bozizé and President al-Bashir of Sudan. On the agenda were issues of common security and a project to link the CAR by road to Port Sudan. Visiting Nigeria on 6–7 November, Bozizé called for stronger economic ties between the two countries and opened a consulate in Abuja. Senegal's President Abdoulaye Wade visited Bangui on 28 March.

The case against former **DRC** vice president Jean-Pierre Bemba for crimes against humanity committed in the CAR continued at the **ICC** in The Hague with the hearing of witnesses. The trial was increasingly unpleasant for the regime, as one witness, a former member of the Presidential Guard, alleged that it was the rebel army under the control of Bozizé, rather than Bemba's troops, that was raping and killing civilians in 2003. Concerns were voiced with regard to the intimidation of some prosecution witnesses whose identity had apparently been revealed, even though the chamber had put in place measures to protect their identities.

Socioeconomic Developments

According to the IMF, growth rates were expected to decline from 3.3% in 2010 to 3.1% – well below expectations. The government presented a second-generation **poverty reduction** strategy (for 2011–2015) costing $ 9.8 bn at a donor meeting in Brussels on 16–17 June and received moderate commitments. The AfDB was the most generous, promising to double its portfolio to $ 180 m and the World Bank promised a 20% increase in its allocation. An IMF delegation visited in July and the official Article IV consultations were held in November. Leaked information had it that the IMF remained critical regarding budget execution in 2010 and the resulting public debt increase. A new IMF programme was seen as crucial for initiating a new round of donor commitments more generally, as some donors had suspended their budget aid over the previous year. But controversial Finance Minister Sylvain Ndoutingaï could not attend the IMF annual meetings because of fears that he might be prosecuted in the US for charges dating back to 2005–2007, when he had ordered the Presidential Guard to attack civilians in an area controlled by the APRD.

The French **uranium** giant Areva dealt the government a heavy blow when it announced the suspension of exploitation at the Bakouma mine for one or two years. The project had given rise to high hopes for augmenting GDP growth rates and bolstering government revenues. The announcement came after the Fukushima disaster in Japan, which had a measurable impact on the price of uranium on the world market. The government thereafter threatened Areva with renegotiation of the contract, as the French firm had committed itself to launch operations in earnest by 2010.

The cumulative effect of such bad news was that observers began to fear that the debt-service ratio would rise in parallel to the government's growing inability to service its internal **debt**. In this context, the old problem of salary arrears again became a prime issue of concern. University professors went on strike, demanding their salaries, and only returned to work after lengthy negotiations on 23 September. Seven retired soldiers and gendarmes took the EU ambassador and the national mediator hostage for some hours to secure payment of 31 months of pension arrears.

On the other hand, better news came from the **mining sector** when the Extractive Industries Transparency Initiative granted the CAR "compliant" status. The government and operating mining companies now produced similar information on the level of taxes paid/received. The government wanted to put pressure on artisanal producers of diamonds, who would receive titles to their plots in exchange for regular information on sales and registration with the government. This was intended to end the illegal export of diamonds. Bozizé visited the oil exploration site in Boromata in the north-east in April to give a boost to further exploration activity. He announced that minimum security requirements were in place, but this was contradicted by ensuing clashes between the UFDR and the CPJP in the region. The government also hoped to increase gold production after the announcement of several successful explorations by foreign firms.

Meanwhile, the **misery** of the population continued, mostly linked to violence and inadequate public health services. In November, 'Médecins sans Frontières' published an alarming report on extremely high mortality rates in the western city of Carnot, and the UN's Office for the Coordination of Humanitarian Affairs put the number of IDPs at 103,000 and returnees in precarious situations at 66,500. Apart from rebel operations and the army's retaliation, local conflicts between herders and settlers were responsible for additional displacements. About 17,750 refugees from neighbouring countries were resident in the CAR. Heavy rainfall on the night of 15–16 July caused floods and significant damage in Bangui.

Andreas Mehler

Chad

The year was marked by the parliamentary and presidential elections, which took place without major incident. The security situation remained calm throughout the year, as relations with Sudan remained cordial. There was some worry over the unrest in Libya, with Chadian nationals returning to the north of Chad. The economy showed moderate growth, helped by high oil prices and an almost normal agricultural season after the bumper crop of 2010 and the drought of 2009.

Domestic Politics

Politics in Chad were dominated by the parliamentary and presidential elections, which took place on 13 February and 25 April, respectively. The **parliamentary election** was the first in ten years, having been postponed several times since 2006, and was the result of prolonged negotiations with the opposition within the 'Commission Électorale Nationale Indépendante' (CENI), which was established on 13 August 2007 after an agreement between the government and the 'Coalition des Partis Politiques pour la Défense de la Constitution'. More than 100 political parties participated in the election, indicating the complete fragmentation of the opposition in the face of the ruling party and allies of President Idriss Déby Itno. Despite allegations of preferential treatment of the ruling party by the authorities, the election itself was apparently held in a reasonably fair and free atmosphere. The ruling party, the 'Mouvement pour le Salut de la Patrie' (MPS), and its allies won a majority in parliament, with 125 seats out of 188. The major opposition parties, the 'Union Nationale pour la Démocratie et le Rénouveau', 'Union pour le Rénouveau et la Démocratie' and 'Rassemblement National pour la Démocratie au Tchad' took nine, seven and seven seats, respectively, the remaining 40 being divided among a spectrum of small political parties, often with a local and regional character. Observers said that the election did not give the opposition a real chance, since the MPS had more resources at its disposal and was helped by the administration. Others, such as the head of the EU observer delegation, Louis Michel, welcomed the election, since it opened "an unseen road to a democratic phase after decades of conflict".

The **presidential election** was held on 25 April, after being postponed from 3 April because of technical difficulties. It was marred by a boycott by the three major opposition candidates, Saleh Kebzabo, Wadal Abdelkader Kamougué and Ngarlejy Yorongar, when demands for new voter identification cards and numbered and secured voting slips were refused. The opposition also withdrew its participation from the CENI, which thus lost its decision-making quorum. As a result, Déby was re-elected without any serious competition and took 83.6% of the votes. The two remaining opposition candidates, Albert Pahimi Padacké and Nadji Madou, took 8.6% and 7.8%, respectively. Turnout was officially given at 55.7%. Déby was sworn in for his fourth term on 8 August. In line with the constitution, a new government was appointed consisting of 40 members, with Emmanuel Nadingar re-appointed as prime minister. Despite a number of changes, some of the key figures in the government returned, including Moussa Faki Mahamat as minister of foreign affairs. Among the 40 cabinet members, five were from the 'Rassemblement pour la Démocratie et le Progrès' of former president Lol Mahama Choua (who served for four months in 1979), now an ally of Déby, and four were from another ally of the MPS, the 'Rassemblement National Démocratique Populaire', led by Nouradine Kassire Koumakoye. Both parties were thus rewarded for their support for the MPS in the parliamentary election.

Minister of State AbdelKader Kamougué, a former minister of defence and presidential candidate, one of the most prominent Southern leaders in Chad, died on 9 May, while campaigning for his wife in a parliamentary by-election in the south of Chad.

During 2011, the process **of reconciliation with former rebel leaders** continued. The president issued an amnesty ahead of the celebration of the 50th anniversary of Chad's independence for all rebels who were being held as prisoners of war. He also granted amnesty to a number of former rebel leaders, including Taher Guinassou, Taher Wodji, Djougourou Hemichi, Ahmat Djibrine Azene, prominent members of Mahamat Nouri's 'Union des Forces pour la Démocratie et Développement', who had been in prison since November 2010. Another rebel, Colonel Djibrine Dassert of the 'Mouvement pour la Paix, la Réconciliation et le Développement', was captured in the south of the country in

January. By April, the majority of about 16,000 combatants belonging to the armed opposition had returned to Chad. There were no reports of armed clashes associated with their return, despite the fact that they were not yet demobilised, but concerns about security remained as long as the former combatants had not been either demobilised or re-integrated in the national army. The number of incidents of banditry in the east also decreased, with the exception of the region around Kyabé, Daha and Gore. There were also reports of remnants of Chadian rebel groups being active outside Chadian territory, which posed some security challenges in the south of the country, and of security incidents involving the regular security forces because of lack of discipline.

After the departure of the 'Mission des Nations Unies dans la République Centrafricaine et Tchad' (MINURCAT), the **special police force** put in place by the Chadian government and the UN, the 'Détachement Intégré de Sécurité' took over patrolling the area, escorting aid organisations' convoys and securing refugee camps in the east of Chad. Though the security situation improved, the capacity of these forces was too limited to guarantee security over the whole area.

Despite the relative calm in the east of Chad, there still remained approximately 2.5 m people, out of a population of 11 m, in need of **humanitarian assistance**, in addition to 131,000 internally displaced Chadians, 264,000 Sudanese and 64,000 refugees from the CAR in refugee camps in the east and south-east of Chad, assisted by some 54 international humanitarian organisations. To help bring eastern Chad back on track again, the Chadian government launched a special programme for the regeneration of the region, which is to be part of the national poverty reduction and economic growth strategy. There were signs of increasing willingness among internally displaced Chadians to return to their home areas, but few actually did so, owing to the persistent insecurity and fear of banditry.

Foreign Affairs

Relations with **Sudan** remained cordial over the year. Sudan's President Omar Hassan al-Bashir could not attend Chad's celebration of its 50th anniversary of independence in January because of the ICC's arrest warrant issued against him for alleged war crimes. During its June summit, the AU cleared Chad and other countries of any wrongdoing in receiving al-Bashir following its own resolution. Later, al-Bashir flew to N'Djaména to attend the inauguration of President Déby on 8 August, his second visit to Chad. The Chadian government's decision to welcome the Sudanese president was severely criticised by the EU spokesperson for the High Representative of the Union for Foreign Affairs and Security Policy. She stated that it was important for all members of the UN to abide by the UNSC's resolutions in this respect and that the ICC was a valuable instrument in the fight against impunity for serious crimes against humanity. Sudan and Chad continued to collaborate in security matters at their joint border and to stop rebel groups from intruding into each other's territory, in particular by maintaining a joint border patrol whose command alternated every six months. In January, joint patrols were stepped up after movements by "elements of outlaws" were detected. Its field of operation was also extended to the **CAR** to keep close watch over the potential presence of rebels from the 'Front Populaire pour le Redressement' (FPR), led by Chadian warlord Babba Laddé, in the lawless border zone. A joint offensive by the armies of both countries against the FPR is on record for the month of January. A two-day summit of all three countries was held on 23 May in Khartoum, Sudan, to discuss economic and political cooperation. As a result, Sudan launched the construction of a 158-km road between Nyala in south Darfur and the CAR and agreement was also reached to construct a route between Port Sudan on the Red Sea and N'Djaména. A contract was signed for a loan with a Chinese bank to construct a railway from Nyala into Chad and to upgrade its own railway network. Chad signed a $ 7 bn contract with the China Civil Engineering Construction Cooperation to start work on a railway line to connect Chad to Sudan and Cameroon.

Chad and Sudan also continued to collaborate on the issue of **banning rebel groups** from their territories. Prior to the tripartite summit, the Sudanese government arrested several members of the armed Chadian opposition, including Adoum Erdimi in Khartoum, and the deputy chief of staff of the 'Union des Forces de la Résistance' (UFR), Colonel Daoud Ali Bouyeneou, in El-Fasher in north Darfur. The Sudanese government allegedly handed over two leaders of the armed opposition to Chad. According to opposition leader Timan Erdimi, residing in Doha, Qatar, they were tortured while in Chadian custody. On 27 September, Déby dispatched a special envoi to Khartoum to affirm his commitment to the security cooperation agreement between the two countries after Khalil Ibrahim, the leader of the Justice and Equality Movement, the leading Darfur opposition movement, re-entered Darfur from Libya after being expelled from Chad. There were allegations of Chadian complicity in his return to Darfur and the involvement of the French authorities and members of Déby's family. Despite this incident, Khartoum remained firmly committed to its support for bilateral cooperation. On 27 November, the second vice president of the UFR, Abdelwahid Aboud Makaye, was arrested in Khartoum. On 5 December, Déby arrived in Khartoum for consultations. He declared that the time had come to conclude peace in Darfur and expressed his support for the Doha Document for Peace in Darfur, brokered in Qatar. He also held discussions with Darfur opposition leader Tijani el-Sissi on this issue. In addition to all this, on 30 December the marriage was announced between Déby and Amani Musa Hilal, daughter of the notorious Janjaweed leader Musa Hilal. According to Chadian sources, Déby had to pay a dowry of $ 25 m to her father and a further $ 1 m to the bride in gold and jewelry.

Political unrest in **Libya**, resulting from the civil war that started in February between opposition forces and the Kadhafi regime, was a matter of concern. On 12 January,

Kadhafi was present at the 50th anniversary celebration of Chad's independence on what turned out to be his last foreign visit. Initially, Déby remained loyal to Kadhafi, a long-time mediator in the conflicts with the Chadian armed opposition and Sudan. Even after Déby's other major ally, **France**, had recognised the Libyan National Transitional Council (NTC) as the only legitimate representative of the Libyan people on 10 March, the Chadian government maintained that the troubles in Libya should be resolved through dialogue, and even welcomed Kadhafi's representative at Déby's inauguration on 8 August. It also declared that it would not collaborate with the ICC in bringing members of the Libyan government to justice. There were accusations that Chad's presidential guard was fighting alongside Kadhafi's troops and that mercenaries were recruited by the Libyans in Faya and N'Djaména. Behind the scenes, the NTC maintained contact with both the Chadian armed opposition and the government. There was fear that the conflict would lead to new unrest in the north of Chad, given the relations between the Toubou in south Libya and north Chad, and 5,000 troops of the Chadian army were deployed to secure the border region with Libya. Finally, and only on 24 August, the Chadian government recognised the TNC. In the end, the tensions that arose between the NTC and the Chadian government because of Déby's continued support for the old Libyan regime had to be repaired by Sudanese President el-Bashir, who mediated in this conflict.

Because of the unrest and negative attitudes of the Libyan opposition towards African migrants, an estimated 78,000 **Chadian migrants** returned to the North of Chad, some of whom had to be airlifted from the south of Libya, since they were stranded there without transport, food or water. The negative attitude towards Chadian migrants was caused, among other things, by the fact that the Kadhafi regime had made widespread use of Chadian soldiers as mercenaries in its security forces, although this was denied by the Chadian government. Another immediate consequence of the conflict in Libya was that the 3,000-km supply route used by WFP through Libya to reach Darfur refugees and Chadian IDPs was cut off. This corridor had provided 40% of all the food aid for these refugees and supplies had to be re-routed to Port Sudan, which caused considerable delays.

On 28 January, the governments of Sudan and Chad signed an agreement to collaborate in the voluntary **repatriation of Sudanese refugees to Darfur**. This document was drafted without consultation with UNHCR, which had offered technical advice. The agreement underlined the voluntary nature of the repatriation and, given the continued fighting in Darfur and consequent insecurity, the Darfurian refugees were unwilling to return. Renewed fighting in the CAR led to a new inflow of approximately 2,000 refugees in February and March.

The **UNSC** remained worried about the security situation in eastern Chad and, in a report released in May, a UN-mandated panel of experts recommended an arms embargo against Chad and Sudan, to be upheld until both the Sudanese and Chadian governments had provided conclusive evidence that weapons sold to their respective national armies were no longer finding their way into conflict areas such as Darfur, or to Chadian and Darfurian armed opposition groups.

On 8 July, President Abdoulaye Wade announced that **Senegal** would expel former Chadian dictator Hissène Habré to Chad. He annulled this decision two days later, however, because of concerns over Habré's eventual treatment in Chad, where he was to have faced trial and probable execution for of crimes against humanity. Chad expressed regret over this decision, stating that every measure had been taken to ensure Habré's safety and fair trial. On 22 July, Chadian Secretary of State for Foreign Affairs Mahamat Bechir Okoromi issued a statement requesting Habré's extradition to Belgium, where an international arrest warrant was issued in 2005 for violations of international humanitarian law.

Socioeconomic Developments

According to standard indicators, the economy developed satisfactorily with a growth rate of 3%–3.5%, mainly fueled by the non-oil sector (+3.6%), despite higher oil prices than in the preceding year. A new oil field near Bongor came into production, yielding 20,000 b/d. With the declining productivity of the old wells, total **oil production** stood at 120,000 b/d, translating into negative growth in the oil sector (–1.8%). Local consumer prices for fuel fell after the opening of a new oil refinery, which increased the supply to the markets, The overall supply became increasingly erratic, however, apparently because imports decreased when they were no longer competitive with the new cheap fuel. Electricity capacity was increased when a new fossil-fuel power plant came into operation. This is expected to give a boost to economic growth, since the erratic electrical supply had long been a major impediment to sustained economic growth. In addition, a new cement factory reinforced the country's industrial capacity.

Despite these new developments, the economy and exports remained highly dependent on oil, which accounted for 90% of export earnings. There was also concern about the **banking sector**, as most banks were undercapitalised and highly dependent on government spending, particularly on infrastructural projects, and on a small number of enterprises associated with the oil industry. Inflation in the first five months was negative, but picked up later and was expected to average 2% over the year.

The projected government budget amounted to CFAfr 1,260 bn. Spending procedures improved, but halfway through the year it was estimated that real spending would exceed the budget by CFAfr 180 bn. Non-oil GDP was estimated at CFAfr 2,912 bn, and GDP including oil at CFAfr 4,476 bn. Spending on social infrastructure (health, education and infrastructure maintenance) lagged behind. Ninety per cent of the budget set aside for extraordinary security spending – estimated at 5.3% of non-oil GDP – had already been spent by May because of the uncertain situation in Libya. On 26 September, parliament approved a law to allocate an extra budget of CFAfr 309 bn to provide for security in the north and to help repatriate Chadian refugees. Of this amount, CFAfr 200 bn were allocated to the ministry of defence and security and the rest was destined to facilitate the settlement of the refugees. Emergency measures had to be undertaken around Faya in northern Chad to settle approximately 78,000 returnee migrants fleeing from Libya, most of whom were returning completely empty-handed.

The conflict in **Libya** impacted the Chadian economy in a number of other ways. Libya was an important investor in Chad, and the ending of these investments affected the economy. Some Chadian banks were part-owned by the Libyan government, and the political unrest in Libya therefore contributed to the fragility of the Chadian banking system. In a number of regions, particularly in the north, the decline in trade with the south of Libya had negative repercussions. In addition, the flow of remittances from Chadian migrants in Libya completely dried up; in some areas, including, for example, Kanem, already a backward and very food insecure region, these remittances constituted a major proportion of people's income.

At the beginning of the year, large parts of the country were still recovering from the **2010 famine** conditions, despite the bumper harvest of the 2010–2011 agricultural season. Despite a fall in malnutrition rates for small children, malnutrition levels remained high, especially in Kanem and Bahr el Ghazal. The government maintained cereal price ceilings at nearly half the nominal five-year average and this kept prices in local markets at 13%–30% below the five-year average. These price ceilings were maintained until the end of the presidential campaign, which led to a fall in stocks and caused difficulties in supplying food-deficient areas in the north. Pasta imports from and livestock exports to Libya were interrupted because of the unrest. Livestock exports were also banned in view of the elections, leading to lower livestock prices and unfavourable terms of trade for livestock owners who needed to buy cereals. Wages in the east of the country fell because of the departure of MINURCAT. For poor households, **food insecurity** remained high, because their production fell when they had to engage in non-agricultural wage labour to cover food needs during the 2010 season, and a substantial part of the harvest went into the servicing debts and the replacement of assets that had been were sold because of the 2010 famine.

The **agricultural season** started late, especially in the north, leading to a late return of livestock to the north because the pastures were insufficient, and a high demand for labour in the south at the peak of the agricultural season. Despite the fact that the rains picked up in late July and early August, yields had already been affected by the erratic rainfall. At the end of the year, pastoralists moved south earlier than usual because of the lack of pasture in the north. In the central and eastern parts of the country, harvests were affected by plagues of grasshoppers and grain-eating birds. In the Guera in particular, harvests were 40% below average. Overall, the 2011 harvest was estimated to be 85% of the five-year average. By the end of the year, livestock prices were expected to drop again after the feast of Tabaski, and malnutrition rates were expected to increase.

A **cholera epidemic** raged through the country, affecting more than half of Chad's health districts. In total, more than 16,000 cases were reported, resulting in 433 deaths. Suppression of the epidemic was hampered by lack of surveillance, the vastness of the country, large-scale population movements and lack of health infrastructure, especially in remote areas. Polio continued to be a problem because of major flaws in vaccination campaigns; Chad had the highest number of cases of polio in the world, with 68 reported in the first half of the year. Most cases occurred in the east of Chad and there was concern that the epidemic would spread towards Sudan, with the movement of people for Hajj and Ramadan.

Han van Dijk

Republic of Congo

There was little movement in Congolese domestic politics, with President Denis Sassou-Nguesso continuing to dominate the political scene. In foreign affairs, however, the Congo suffered a major rift with its largest neighbour, the DRC, although the issue was nominally resolved by the end of the year. Congo's economy, and its national budget, again grew at a healthy pace, as it had over the previous several years, fuelled by rising oil production and world petroleum prices. Few of the macro-economic gains trickled down to Congo's impoverished masses, however. Meanwhile, government corruption and lack of vision for the country's post-petroleum future continued to be major stumbling blocks to sustainable development.

Domestic Politics

The major public political event of the year in Congo was the Sixth Extraordinary Congress of the ruling **'Parti Congolais du Travail' (PCT)** that took place from 21 to 25 July. Some 1,350 delegates attended. The major theme of the Congress was 'ouverture' (opening), which referred to the desire of many party leaders to gain more support for the party from beyond the country's northern regions. Within the PCT, a contest continued behind the scenes between those who favoured continued domination by northerners (the 'Katangais', who wish to 'inherit' power) and those who wanted to open the party to broader, national constituencies. President Sassou had sided with the latter group since the mid-2000s, and intervened in the party's internal politics to put them in charge. In the year leading up to the Congress, some 30 small parties were pressured to merge with the PCT, which thus absorbed many of the minor parties of the 'Rassemblement de la Majorité Présidentielle' (RMP), the broader coalition supporting the president, though not the most important of them.

Despite the presidential rhetoric and superficial opening, the PCT remained largely unreformed in significant ways. The party's new secretary-general, Pierre Ngolo, an Mbochi from the Gamboma district of Plateaux region, the heartland (along with Cuvette) of the northern leadership, had been a Sassou loyalist since 1998, serving as first secretary of the transitional legislature (1998–2002) and then of the new National Assembly (2002 to the present). Northerners, and especially ethnic Mbochi cadres, were heavily over-represented in the new 471-member Central Committee and 51-member Politburo. Four of President Sassou's children were on the Central Committee, and his son Denis-Christel stayed on the Politburo. In the indirect Senate elections held for six of Congo's 12 regions in October, PCT candidates won all 12 seats in the northern departments of Cuvette and Sangha, but none in four southern departments, confirming the PCT's regional character, although most of the winners in the southern regions were from RMP parties.

Intriguingly, some of the RMP parties that refused to merge with the PCT were led by regime insiders, suggesting that these political actors wanted to maintain an appearance of independence from Sassou. Three such parties included the 'Mouvement pour la Solidarité et le Développement', headed by René-Serge Blanchard Oba, the 'Club 2002-Parti pour l'Unité de la République', led by Wilfrid Nguesso, a nephew of the president, and the Comité d'Action pour la Défense de la Démocratie – Mouvement de Jeunesse, led by André Okombi Salissa. These actors played a 'double game', benefitting from their family connections and proximity to presidential power, while also maintaining some distance from the regime.

A central political preoccupation within the regime remained the **presidential succession**. Sassou-Nguesso, who turned 68 in November, and would be 72 at the end of his (second) term in 2016, apparently wished to remain president for as long as he was able. This would require a change in the constitution, which limits presidents to two seven-year terms, and requires that they be not older than 70 when they declare their candidacy. Public discussion of constitutional change had picked up during the previous year, stimulated by Sassou loyalists. Meanwhile, senior figures in the PCT, the National Police and the army were discretely positioning themselves to take power in the event of the president's unscheduled demise. Following the examples of the deceased presidents of Togo and Gabon, Sassou was apparently grooming his son Denis Christel to replace him, in the face of strong opposition from many quarters. The younger Sassou-Nguesso had in the past been accused of diverting funds in his post at the national oil company, the 'Société Nationale des Pétroles du Congo'.

The only substantive domestic **opposition** party was the 'Union Panafricaine pour la Démocratie Sociale' (UPADS), led by former president Pascal Lissouba, which held 11 Assembly seats, although it had previously posed no great challenge to Sassou because of its long-term disunity. In 2011, the party made its best effort in years to re-unify itself ahead of the 2012 legislative elections, but it ultimately failed. At an 'extraordinary' meeting of its leadership on 10–11 May, the party finally replaced Lissouba, now gravely ill, as its official leader, and briefly presented a unified front to the Congolese people. Pascal Gamassa, as a compromise candidate, was elected leader of a 'council of vice presidents' at the meeting. His two first vice-presidents were stalwarts of the Lissouba regime, Victor Tamba-Tamba and Christophe Moukouéké. The arrangement was allegedly encouraged by former Congolese first lady, Jocelyne Lissouba. The party was then to hold an extraordinary Congress by the end of the year. By August, however, it became clear that the party was still divided. In that month, Gamassa attempted to launch the work of a preparatory committee of the party to organise the forthcoming Congress, but a party faction led by Tamba-Tamba and another member of the UPADS politburo, Clément Mouamba, separately established their own preparatory committee. In the end, the party remained divided, and the Congress had not taken place by year's end.

The star of Ambroise Hervé Malonga, a lesser known opposition figure, continued to rise during the year. Malonga led a small party, the 'Convention des Républicains', which held no seats in the Assembly, but he succeeded in irritating the regime by his stalwart legal defence of Mathias Dzon following the 2009 presidential elections. During 2011, he continued to denounce the low quality of previous elections, and to call for a neutral elections commission.

In contrast, the standing of Frédéric Bintsamou, alias Pasteur Ntoumi, continued to fall. Bintsamou had led the last serious rebellion against the government, which officially ended in 2003. Although Bintsamou had agreed to come into Brazzaville from the bush in late 2009, and take up a government post created especially for him, he had played no meaningful role in government in 2011, as in the year before, but rather moved around between several residences in the Pool region, and rarely spent time at his Brazzaville office. His failure to win a seat in the Assembly when he ran against the formidable Adélaïde Mougany in a 2010 by-election had also revealed his lack of popularity, even within the Pool region. Many residents of Pool believed that he had received support from forces in the government during his long period as a regime opponent, and they resented the exactions of his followers from the citizens of Pool. Consequently, Bintsamou now had few friends, either inside or outside of government. The government's 'Opération Kimia' (literally: 'peace'), designed to disarm 'bandits' in the Pool region, was successfully completed during the year.

On 21 November, Minister of Interior Raymond Zéphirin Mboulou announced the beginning of a dialogue process on the organisation of the 2012 **legislative elections**. Included would be parties of the RMP, opposition parties and civil society organisations. Most of the opposition reacted with scepticism, given the failure of a similar initiative in 2007 to produce elections, although Bintsamou did respond favourably to the dialogue. In general, the initiative revealed the government's preoccupation with ensuring that the 2012 elections would be perceived as fair by the international community, if not by the Congolese themselves.

Foreign Affairs

Congo suffered a rupture of relations with its most important neighbour, the **DRC**, beginning in March. The problem began in January, when Republic of Congo authorities arrested General Faustin Munene in Pointe Noire at the request of DRC officials. Munene had been implicated in a rebellion in the Bas-Congo region of the DRC in 2010, and was under indictment in the DRC. As of January, the DRC demanded the extradition of both Munene and Mangbama Udjani, the leader of the 2010 rebellion in the DRC's Équateur region, who had also been under arrest in Congo since May 2010. Following the coup attempt against DRC President Joseph Kabila on 27 February, the DRC authorities implicated Munene in the attack on Kabila's residence, and escalated their demands for his extradition. Congo's authorities refused, and Sassou himself justified the decision by publicly citing the case of Pierre Mulele (Munene's uncle), who had been executed by Mobutu Sese Seko following his extradition from Congo-Brazzaville in 1968. Following this comment, published in the Paris-based weekly 'Jeune Afrique', the DRC announced the severance of diplomatic relations with Congo and recalled its ambassador, Esther Kirongozi, on 25 March.

Neither country wanted the rupture to last for very long, however, and diplomats from the two Congos were soon in discussions on how to restore relations. After some preparation, Sassou flew to Kinshasa, where he met with Kabila on 15 April. Officially, the two leaders discussed issues of security and mutual assistance, but the focus of conversation was clearly on the Munene and Udjani cases. Following this meeting, there was a resumption of generally normal relations between the two states, though no agreement on the issue in question was announced. It was only on 4 November that the DRC send a new ambassador to Brazzaville, whose credentials were accepted by Congolese Foreign Minister Basile Ikouébé, and, by the end of the year, neither Munene nor Udjani had yet been extradited to the DRC.

Congo also suffered a major international embarrassment when it attempted to host the Pan-African Music Festival (FESPAM), after months of preparation and intense publicity. During the opening event on the night of 9 July, a stampede occurred when Congolese police and gendarmes failed to control a crowd of spectators, who rushed into a sports stadium for the opening musical act. Seven Congolese were killed and 30 others injured in the melée, leading Congolese authorities to cancel the remainder of the festival the following day.

On the other hand, Congo maintained excellent relations with its two key international allies, **France** and China. Franco-Congolese relations could hardly have been warmer. France's current ambassador to Congo, Jean-François Valette, was an unapologetic supporter of the Sassou regime. In February, the ambassador, authorised by French President Nicolas Sarkozy, presented Sassou's closest adviser and supporter, Jean-Dominique Okemba, with the French Legion of Honour at a grand public ceremony. Okemba, the secretary-general of Congo's National Security Council, and unofficially called Congo's 'vice president', was thought to be a leading candidate to succeed Sassou in the event of his demise. Perhaps to balance this overtly partisan act, the same award was presented in April to Roger Bouka Owoko, the executive director of the Congolese Observatory of Human Rights. Critics pointed out, however, that Owoko, once a strong critic of the Sassou regime, had recently been more cautious in his statements about the Congolese government. French financial support for civil aviation improvements, environmental programmes, and military training initiatives was also in evidence during the year, leaving most Congolese with the strong impression of firm French support for the Sassou regime.

Despite France's obvious efforts to maintain its influence in Congo, it became clearer than ever that **China** had overtaken France as Congo's most important international partner. Most significantly, in May the new Imboulou hydro-electric plan on the Lefini River north of Brazzaville at last came on-line, doubling Congo's electricity output. Throughout the remainder of the year, electricity was introduced to several towns and villages in the Cuvette, Plateaux and Pool regions. Even parts of northern Brazzaville began to receive power from the new source. Meanwhile, Chinese cooperation assistance to Congo was evident in nearly every possible domain: new Chinese fellowships for Congolese students were announced; Chinese firms began work on the second terminal of Maya Maya International Airport in Brazzaville, and on the new headquarters of the Autonomous Port of Pointe Noire; new Chinese-funded agricultural research stations were opened; new Chinese-run factories to produce goods such as solar panels were discussed; construction began on new public housing and hospitals, carried out by Chinese firms with Chinese economic assistance; and, most importantly, Chinese-led work continued on the upgrading of the section of National Route no.1, linking Pointe Noire and Dolisie. The Chinese government even invited PCT militants to China for political training, symbolising the overlap in the governing visions of the Sassou regime and one-party China. Meanwhile, China's economic interest in Congo was clear. In July, a Chinese company, Evergreen Resources, took over the operations of MagIndustries, a Canada-based firm that had been developing Congolese potash, magnesium and forestry products since 1997. China was already the second leading importer, after the United States, of Congolese petroleum.

Socioeconomic Developments

Congo's macro-economy continued to boom, driven by rising international **oil** prices, which were pushed higher at the beginning of the year by the uprising in Libya. Congo's economy grew at a rate of some 5% during the year, reaching a nominal level of almost CFAfr 8,000 bn (more than double that of Congo's 2007 GDP). Nearly all of Congo's growth was attributable to rising petroleum income, driven by modestly higher output and price increases of about 20% in 2011. Some 90%–95% of the value of Congolese exports was from oil, with timber accounting for most of the remainder. Congo's exports reached $ 12.6 bn, more than double the 2009 level, and the country enjoyed a healthy trade surplus of over $ 7 bn. As a result, Congo was able to increase its foreign exchange reserves to some $ 5.9 bn, compared with $ 4.5 bn the previous year. Meanwhile, most of Congo's debt had been cancelled by multilateral and bilateral donors in 2010.

Congo's national **budget** continued to balloon, though not as rapidly as in recent years. In the budget passed at the end of 2010, revenues were projected at CFAfr 3,001 bn, or about $ 6 bn. Expenditure was put at CFAfr 2,780 bn, leaving a projected surplus of CFAfr 230 bn. The large majority of government income was to come from petroleum revenues and a much smaller amount from foreign aid, with only about CFAfr 800 bn to come from domestic taxation. As in previous years, the details of the budget were opaque, and it was in any case impossible to tell to what extent the government actually followed the budget. Expenditure in the Congolese budget had risen six-fold since the late 1990s, when it stood at about CFAfr 500 bn, and had doubled since only 2009. For 2011, the budget for capital investment rose by over 50% to more than CFAfr 1,000 bn.

In small, incremental ways, life continued to get better for most Congolese. The country's HDI score inched up to .533, the highest it had yet attained. It had now risen every year from 2000 to 2011. The score mostly reflects rising per capita income, which has been raised by increasing oil revenues in recent years. Life expectancy also rose slightly to 57.4 years, a full two years longer than the figure for 2006 (and more than six years longer than in Cameroon and nine years longer than in the DRC). The government continued to spend less than 2% of GDP on health and the same on education, even though GDP rose rapidly, as noted above. Gender equality, measured by the ratio of female high school graduates to male high school graduates also reached an all-time high at 9:10, but the average number of years of schooling for all Congolese remained well below the high level of the 1980s. Electricity continued to be in short supply in Brazzaville, where more than one-third of the country's population (now over 4 m) live, though power from the new Imboulou dam began to reach northern Brazzaville late in the year.

Employment and wages in Congo presented a mixed picture. One reason for the ongoing improvement in the quality of life was that some of the oil wealth was passed on to government workers in pay raises, announced in December 2010 and implemented in 2011. The lowest paid government employees saw their monthly salaries rise from

CFAfr 50,000 to CFAfr 64,000 during the year. Although only (the few) Congolese employed in the formal economy benefited directly from this increase, some of this wealth was passed down to informal sector workers. Unemployment remained high, estimated at some 29%, despite the economic boom.

John F. Clark

Democratic Republic of the Congo

The year was marked by the preparation and organisation of presidential and parliamentary elections. The run-up to the elections was plagued by various logistical problems and violence between the camps of the main competitors, Joseph Kabila, Etienne Tshisekedi and Vital Kamerhe. A change in the constitution abolishing the second round in presidential elections made it possible for the incumbent president, Joseph Kabila, to win the elections with just under 50% of the votes, a result that was immediately contested by the opposition. Violence in the eastern part of the country continued throughout the year and little progress could be observed with regard to security sector reform (SSR) or the fight against the various remaining rebel groups in the Kivus. The year also saw a quasi breakdown of mining activity in many parts of the country as a result of the announced Dodd-Frank Act, which requires companies publicly quoted on the US stock market to certify that their mineral imports are conflict-free.

Domestic Politics

For the second time since the completion of the peace process in 2002, the Congolese were called to vote in **presidential and parliamentary elections** on 28 November, later than the constitution envisaged.

The run-up to the elections was marked by serious political tensions. In January, the government **revised the constitution**. Presidential elections were reduced to one round of voting, the president was given the authority to dissolve provincial assemblies, remove governors and call referenda, and the prosecutor's office was subordinated to the ministry of justice. In short, the amendment significantly strengthened the presidency. Despite a boycott by over 100 opposition members, the revision was passed within days by the National Assembly and the Senate – institutions which often take months to pass minor laws. There was an 80% majority in favour of the amendments, which gave rise to allegations of bribery. Two amendments were particularly controversial. The first was the reduction of presidential elections to one ballot, which was justified by the claim that it would lower costs and reduce the political polarisation that would be caused by a second round of voting between the two winning candidates in the first round. Although these arguments cannot be entirely dismissed, it is clear that the abolition of the second round served mostly to enhance Kabila's chances of winning the election. The second controversial amendment provided for the dissolution of provincial assemblies and the removal of governors. This further strengthened the presidency to the detriment of local democracy. The aborted decentralisation process now seemed even more unlikely to resume, and in September, the ministry of decentralisation was abolished. Decentralisation was still widely acknowledged as an indispensable step towards more political stability in the vast country, but the government's objective was nevertheless to centralise and secure power in Kinshasa.

In March, the ruling 'Parti du Peuple pour la Reconstruction et la Démocratie' (PPRD) proposed a new **electoral bill**, containing significant modifications to the electoral system, including changes to the procedure for the election of deputies whereby proportional representation would only apply in districts where no single party list received an absolute majority; this would clearly favour big parties, such as the PPRD and rule out independent candidates. Against the expectation of the ruling party that the legislature would rubber-stamp the new bill within days, parliament discussed it for three months. Finally, both the National Assembly, controlled by the ruling 'Alliance pour la Majorité Présidentielle' (AMP), which includes the PPRD and smaller coalition parties, and the Senate, controlled by opposition parties, adopted the bill only after making significant amendments to the original proposition, including the rejection of the amendment on the election of deputies. This meant that the electoral law was roughly similar to that applied during the 2006 elections, thereby increasing the chances of re-election for the many independent MPs. This move by the legislature could also be assessed as a demonstration of its ability to object the executive's efforts to centralise power in the hands of the ruling party, and furthermore attests to the growing disappointment of non-PPRD members of the AMP.

Election preparations were plagued by logistical problems. Voter registration was slow and fraught with severe tensions; many citizens complained that they were not able to register. The results of the registration are highly important as they determine the number of parliamentary seats to which each province or commune is entitled. In addition, they act as a census, as the government has scant knowledge of how many citizens live within the Congolese borders. Furthermore, in the absence of a functioning bureaucracy, voter cards are used as ID cards, and so even those who are not interested in voting were eager to register if they had not done so in 2006. The voter registration process was officially closed on 18 July. Total numbers were around 32 m, 7 m more than at the previous elections. In some Kabila strongholds, such as Katanga, voter registration was much higher than in 2006, securing the province three additional seats in the National Assembly. In contrast, Kinshasa, where opposition parties were strong, lost seven seats. However, there was no clear pro-Kabila bias overall.

Annexes to the election law presenting the new distribution of legislative seats resulting from voter registration figures had to be adopted by parliament. There was a short period of doubt as to whether elections would have to be postponed, as the president of the 'Commission Electorale Nationale Indépendante' (CENI), Daniel Ngoy Mulunda, urged parliament to pass the amendment within less than two weeks, or CENI would decouple the presidential and parliamentary elections. The law was urgently passed and promulgated by Kabila on 17 August. The short time frame meant it was not possible for the voter registration results to be independently audited, and accusations of fraud were rampant.

Of the 12 registered presidential candidates, the three main contenders were Etienne Tshisekedi, Vital Kamerhe and Joseph Kabila. The runner-up in the 2006 elections, Jean-Pierre Bemba, was refused permission to register as he was still on trial before the ICC in The Hague. Despite some talks between the opposition parties, they had not been able to agree on a single candidate. Over 19,000 candidates registered for the parliamentary elections, including 5,351 candidates for the 51 seats in the capital Kinshasa alone. Official election campaigning began on 28 October and most demonstrations were concentrated in Kinshasa.

Violence before, during and after the elections was widespread. On 9 November, the UN Joint Human Rights Office released a report documenting 188 cases of human rights abuses linked to the election process between 30 September and 1 November. The 'Union pour la Démocratie et le Progrès Social' (UDPS) complained about acts of vandalism against their headquarters in Lubumbashi, Mbuji Maji and Kinshasa, as well as the looting of a radio station belonging to an ally of Tshisekedi and the killing of UDPS activists by PPRD militants. The PPRD in turn accused UDPS militants of setting fire to their premises in Kinshasa. The Republican Guard opened fire on demonstrators in Kinshasa's Maina district on 27 September, killing five, and at Kinshasa's N'djili Airport on the following day, killing 12 UDPS supporters. The leader of the 'Movement de Libération du Congo' (MLC) faction in the Kinshasa provincial assembly, Marius Gangale, was killed on 23 November. Numerous clashes on election day were reported in Kinshasa, Lubumbashi and Kananga (Kasai Occidental). In the weeks after the election, violence became even more apparent, with clashes between the various camps, barricades, shootings, looting of police stations and other government premises opposition parties' buildings in Kinshasa, and attacks on people from Kasai Oriental and Kasai Occidental provinces in Northern Katanga.

CENI announced preliminary **election results** four days late, on 9 December. According to their announcement, the incumbent president won the election with 48.9% of the votes. The result was immediately contested by the opposition. Kabila was sworn in as president on 20 December. The only head of state to attend the ceremony was Zimbabwe's Robert Mugabe. Tshisekedi declared himself president during a ceremony at his home a few days later.

A joint statement by the AU, SADC, ECCAS, the International Conference of the Great Lakes Region and COMESA welcomed the "successful holding of the elections", while the EU and the Carter Center, a US-based NGO, denounced the presidential election process and result as seriously flawed.

Incriminating irregularities included missing essential election material such as ballot papers and voter lists, and the loss of polling station results. Furthermore, there were inconsistencies in voter turnout and numbers of invalid ballots for the presidential and parliamentary elections in the same constituency. According to the Carter Center, 28,110 more votes for the presidential election were counted than for the parliamentary election in Walikale. In Kinshasa, 10% of the ballots for the parliamentary election were invalid as compared with only 3.6% in the presidential election. Overall, voter turnout was 58%, compared with around 80% in 2006. Strikingly, turnout figures reached almost 100% in some Kabila strongholds, such as several Katangan constituencies, with almost all the votes going to Kabila, as compared with 50%-60% in the Tshisekedi strongholds in the two Kasai provinces.

During the days before the announcement of the presidential election result, SMS services were shut down throughout the country, making it almost impossible for observers from civil society and churches to coordinate their reaction. Furthermore, observers from political parties claimed they were denied access to polling stations. Neither international nor national observers had access to the national processing centre, where results were consolidated and verified before the announcement.

The results of the parliamentary election were not announced before the year's end. Elections for provincial assemblies were set to be held in March 2012, followed by elections for the Senate in June and elections of governors in July. Local elections were scheduled for 2013.

A minor **cabinet reshuffle** was announced in September, filling posts that had been vacant for months. François-Joseph Mobutu Nzanga, son of the former president, Mobutu Sese Seko, former minister of labour and social affairs and one of the three deputy prime ministers, was fired in March after being accused of negligence in his duties. He was replaced by Simon Bulupiy Galati, previously telecommunications minister, in September. A few days after sacking Mobutu, Minister for Rural Development Philippe Undji was fired following corruption charges. In May, Transport Minister Laure-Marie Kawanda Kayena had to resign after various fatal boat accidents on rivers across the country. She was replaced by Joseph Martin Gasagisa in September. Jean-Pierre Daruwezi, former head of the intelligence service and known for his loyalty to the president, became the new economy minister, replacing Jean-Marie Bulambo Kilosho. Louis Alphonse Kayagialo was appointed deputy prime minister and minister for post, telephones and telecommunications. Decentralisation Minister Antipas Mbusa Nyamwisi resigned and the ministry of decentralisation was abolished in September.

The firing of Mobutu caused his 'Union des Démocrates Mobutistes' (Udemo) to pull out of the AMP. Udemo had been the only group within the coalition with a support base in Equateur province, where Kabila traditionally enjoys very little popularity. By appointing Kayagialo as deputy prime minister, Kabila kept a symbolic representative of Equateur, as Kayagialo comes from the same area as Mobutu. Furthermore, probably expecting that the ICC would not allow Jean-Pierre Bemba to run for election, Kabila did not fear the same electoral defeat in Equateur province as in 2006, when Bemba's MLC took a clear majority of the votes. On 15 March, the AMP was officially dissolved and reborn as the 'Alliance Présidentielle' and member parties had to re-join the alliance. Aubin Minako, formerly leader of the PPRD faction within the AMP, became the new secretary general.

On 27 February, **Kabila's residence in Kinshasa and the Kokolo military camp were attacked** by armed men, who allegedly included some of Bemba's former bodyguards and other MLC militants. Nine people died and some 80 were arrested. The minister of information called the assault a coup attempt, while Kabila himself spoke of the incident as a terrorist attack. It remains unclear whether the attack was part of a wider plot against government buildings or whether it was a staged attack to serve as a pretext for government forces to hunt down opposition members.

The two **Kivu provinces** were once more the theatre of both efforts to establish some form of peace and on-going violence. A reconfiguration of the 'Forces Amées de la République Démocratique du Congo' (FARDC) in North and South Kivu slowly made some – albeit ambiguous – progress. The various brigades were regrouped and trained in 'regiments' of 1,400 soldiers. The aim of this regimentation strategy was to weaken parallel command structures by mixing battalions from different former rebel groups and national armies. In addition, it was intended to lead to better management of the army and a reduction in corruption. This process was agreed upon without discussion with two significant international partners – the UN Stabilization Mission in the DRC (MONUSCO) and an EU **advisory and assistance mission for security reform** (EUSEC). This lack of communication between the government and international actors has long been deplored by international partners and the result has been parallel and uncoordinated bilateral SSR programming in the absence of a national plan. Despite the attempt to improve matters through the restructuring of the FARDC, it has been characterised by increased power and privileges for the former rebel groups within the army, 'Conseil National pour la Défense du Peuple' (CNDP) and 'Patriotes Résistants Congolais' (PARECO), which in many parts have led to discontent among army officers who are not part of the CNDP. In spite of an arrest warrant from the ICC for the former CNDP Chief of Staff General Bosco Ntaganda, he was able to further strengthen his military and economic influence in the Kivu Provinces. It was clear that the significant compromises Kabila had to make in the peace deals of 2009 continued to affect SSR programmes, to the benefit of the CNDP. Parallel command structures continued to exist, with Ntaganda at the top of a hierarchy that monopolised military decision-making in the Eastern Provinces. Ex-CNDP commanders were put into key positions and CNDP units were deployed in strategic areas. The UN Group of Experts further stated that parallel structures in Masisi territory continued, with a police force composed of ex-CNDP and ex-PARECO officers loyal to Ntaganda. The military command justified the privileges of ex-CNDP officers by citing the need to reduce tensions and reassure ex-CNDP elements so that it would be possible to station them outside of their heartland in the East.

Furthermore, the withdrawal of troops into training camps cleared the way for the 'Forces Démocratiques de Libération du Rwanda' (FDLR) and Mai Mai militias, which took over large parts of north-eastern territories in South Kivu and parts of Walikale territory in North Kivu.

The restructuring of the army did not, by year's end, lead to reduced corruption or to an end to illegal activities among the FARDC. The FARDC's stocks of arms, ammunition and uniforms continued to be uncontrolled and as a result were a source of supplies for armed groups throughout the country.

A new alliance was apparently forming in North Kivu between the FDLR, i.e. armed opponents to the government in Kigali, and ex-CNDP elements loyal to Laurent Nkunda. Nkunda had been arrested and put under house arrest in Rwanda in 2009 following a peace agreement between the Congolese government and former CNDP rebels under the command of Bosco Ntaganda. The 'Forces Patriotiques pour la Libération du Congo' (FPLC), formed in early 2010 by CNDP elements angry with the arrest of their leader, attracted many defectors from the newly integrated CNDP, as well as from the Rwandan Defence Force. The alliance now went by the name **FPLC/FDLR Soki** (after the name of its commander). The group's operations and attacks were confined to the Rutshuru and Masisi territories and along the border with Uganda and thus far posed a rather minor threat to security in the province, as their fighting force was limited.

The FPLC/FDLR-Soki was an example of an improbable alliance of former enemies, the FDLR being predominantly Rwandan Hutu and the CNDP being predominately Congolese Tutsi as far as the officer corps was concerned. One of the official raisons d'être of the CNDP under Nkunda was the protection of Tutsi against FDLR attacks in North Kivu. However, the faction loyal to Nkunda came to be defined more by their anti-Kigali position than by their ethnicity. The eastern provinces of the Congo are famous for ever-shifting rebel alliances based more on temporary interests than on long-term ethnic or political antagonisms.

In South Kivu, the **Mai Mai militia Yakatumba**, already linked to the FDLR, fostered its alliance with the Burundian **'Forces Nationales de Libération' (FNL)**, which had returned to hide in Congo after the Burundian elections of 2010. On 4 October, an attack against a vehicle was launched south of Sange in the region bordering Burundi. Five Congolese aid workers and two other civilians, all of them Banyamulenge (Congolese Tutsi living in South Kivu), were killed during the assault. The FNL alone had not previously posed a serious threat to the Burundian government. However, the renewal of its historical alliance with the FDLR and recently also with the Mai Mai Yakatumba created a powerful group of mainly Hutu rebels in the southern parts of South Kivu close to the Burundian border, which was almost entirely beyond the control of the Kinshasa government. The groups further profited from the withdrawal of FARDC soldiers following the regimentation strategy.

In January, negotiations with the **'Forces Républicaines Fédéralistes' (FRF)** resulted in the integration of the FRF into the FARDC. This small Banyamulenge rebel group, which established itself in the High Plateau of Minembwe in South Kivu in 2005, had never posed a significant military threat to the Congolese government. However, fighting between the FARDC and the FRF had a serious impact on the humanitarian situation in the area. The record of the integration process was mixed. FRF officers complained about the non-recognition of ranks and delayed payments. The group managed to remain in the area of the High Plateau despite regimentation, which led to tensions with other ethnic groups and Mai Mai militias in Minembwe. In June, struggles for control of the 43rd sector of the 10th military region in South Kivu between General Masunzu and a former PARECO commander, Colonel Kifaru, led to the desertion of around 170 men from the Kananda training centre in Fizi territory, where the newly formed regiment was trained. Kifaru accused Masunzu of favouring FRF soldiers during the regimentation process. The deserters allegedly looted the villages of Nyakiele, Abala und Kanguli and raped more than 100 women on their way.

On 14 March, Kabila announced that a peace deal with the **FDLR** was being struck which would include the relocation to Maniema province of the latter's headquarters, including 1,500 troops from Walikale territory in North Kivu, in exchange for material advantages. Rumours had it that Rwandan President Paul Kagame had urged Kabila to strike the deal in order to push the FDLR away from the Rwandan border. The FDLR had already been active in Maniema and were believed to be moving not with the intention to disarm but rather to increase their influence in mineral rich Kabambare, the border region between Maniema, South Kivu and Katanga. The FDLR, which still included Rwandan 'génocidaires' (involved in the 1994 genocide), had always been a serious threat to the local population in the Eastern provinces, despite efforts by the FARDC and the Rwandan army to break up the group. Clashes between the FDLR, Mai Mai militias and the FARDC in South Kivu continued to displace thousands of people, but the effective strength of the FDLR had nevertheless decreased considerably over the previous years.

Some disturbing news came from other provinces. In June, **Matata Banaloki**, the leader of the 'Front de Résistance Patriotique de l'Ituri' (FRPI) abandoned the process of integrating his rebel group and went back to Ituri, Orientale Province. On 20 October, the town of Gety was taken by the FRPI, forcing some 30.000 people to flee. On 4 February, between 20 and 30 unidentified armed men launched an **attack on Luano airport** at Lubumbashi, the capital of Katanga province. As in the past, rumours were rife that secessionist groups were at work, and had apparently left behind the flag of the Katanga Tigers, a notorious secessionist movement that emerged around the time of independence (in 1960). In late June, gunfire in an industrial area in Lubumbashi was reported. The government claimed that the attackers had meant to break into a mining company, while other sources stated that the neighbouring army weapons depot was the target. Kinshasa was reluctant to speak of political violence in Katanga, as this mineral rich province had so far been considered one of the most stable parts of the Congo.

Human rights violations continued to be a serious concern. On 23 July, four policemen were sentenced to death by the military court Kinshasa-Gombe for the murder of human rights activist Floribert Chebeya. The director of the organisation "La-Voix-des-Sans-Voix" was killed in early June 2010 on his way to a meeting with the then inspector-general of police, General John Numbi. Those convicted of his murder included the deputy chief of police intelligence, Colonel Daniel Mukalay. Despite the notable fact that the court held policemen accountable, many observers found the trial ambiguous. The fact that it was referred to an ordinary military court and not the High Military Court precluded the possibility of charging officers with the rank of general, as they would be hierarchically superior to the judges. Numbi only appeared as a witness before the court, despite being accused by Chebeya's widow of being linked to the assassination. On 6 July, the **UN Joint Human Rights Office** released a report following investigations into mass rapes and other human rights violations committed in 13 villages in the Kibua-Mpofi axis, Walikale territory, North Kivu, from 30 July to 2 August 2010. The report described a general lack of accountability of various actors in Walikale territory, and further found that MONUSCO had experienced significant difficulties in fulfilling its mandate to protect civilians. Since the attacks, logistics and interactions with the population were said to have improved. MONUSCO had already come under criticism in previous years for its failure to protect the local population.

Foreign Affairs

The DRC remained a focus country for the entire UN system. On 28 June, the UNSC adopted Resolution 1991, and thereby **extended the MONUSCO mandate** for one year, conditioning its withdrawal on improved security in the east. MONUSCO's mandate included the provision of logistical support for elections as well as reporting on human rights violations during elections. France, which chaired the UNSC in June, wanted to take this further and mandate MONUSCO to be the guarantor of the elections, including certification of results. This was strongly opposed by both the Congolese government and MONUSCO itself, the latter fearful of further endangering its tense relations with the government. According to the UN Secretary General, the **security situation** in most of the DRC had improved and the dismantling of foreign and Congolese armed groups in the east had made progress. These developments reportedly resulted from: improved military operations in accordance with MONUSCO's conditionality policy; effective programmes to disarm, demobilise and repatriate foreign ex-combatants; efforts to extend state authority; and the DRC's improved relations with neighbouring Great Lakes countries. Just before the new year, the **UN Group of Experts released their final report** on the DRC. The main findings of the report were that the Dodd-Frank Act had had ambiguous consequences (see below), that the unrecorded gold trade was booming, and that trade in non-mineral natural resources was helping to finance armed groups and criminal networks. Furthermore, armed groups had benefited from the support of national and provincial politicians during the election period and had formed links with international (mainly Burundian and Rwandan) opposition figures in Congolese exile. Finally, the CNDP – specifically Ntaganda – was found to have strengthened his military and economic empire despite the restructuring of the army and the ICC arrest warrant. The UN Group of Experts' mandate was renewed by Resolution 2021 on 29 November.

Investigations into the FDLR leadership in exile achieved some progress. Hearings against three leaders of the FDLR took place in a court in Stuttgart, Germany, and the ICC in The Hague. The trial began in May of Ignace Murwanashyaka and Straton Musoni, former president and vice-president of the FDLR, who had been arrested in Germany in 2009. According to the indictment, both men were accused of being responsible for 39 war crimes and 26 crimes against humanity, committed by FDLR soldiers between January 2008 and November 2009. They were charged with initiating a strategy that involved systematic attacks on the civilian population in the Kivus in order to precipitate a humanitarian catastrophe, with the aim of forcing the Rwandan government into negotiations with the FDLR. The third suspect, the Rwandan Calixte Mbarushimana, arrested in France in 2010, was released from ICC custody in December for lack of evidence. After months of investigations in the Kivus, the Confirmation of Charges hearing was held on 16–21 September. Mbarushimana had acted as vice-president of the FDLR since the arrest of Murwanashyaka and Musoni. The arrests of the heads of the FDLR significantly reduced the morale of the militia, but the opening of the trials did not seem to have much influence on FDLR operations because leadership functions had long been taken over by others.

Two more Congolese cases were dealt with by the ICC. The closing statements in the case against the alleged founder and president of the 'Union des Patriotes Congolais' and the FPLC, Thomas Lubanga Dyilo, took place on 25–26 August and the verdict was expected in early 2012. In the case of Germain Katanga, alleged commander of the FRPI, and Mathieu Ngudjolo Chui, alleged former leader of the 'Front des Nationalistes et Intégrationnistes', closing statements were scheduled for May 2012.

Relations with **Angola** remained tense throughout the year, mainly because of disputes over the common maritime border and DRC claims to oil fields off the Atlantic coast, currently exploited by Angola. This dispute had started in May 2009, when the DRC claimed a portion of Angolan territory under the UN Convention on the Law of the Sea (the Montego Bay Treaty), a claim that has been consistently opposed by Angola. Since then, thousands of Congolese have been violently expelled from Angola and vice versa. Nonetheless, a cautious rapprochement between the two countries became apparent in 2011. On 4 August, Kabila and Angola's President José Eduardo dos Santos met for talks in Luanda, followed by renewed contacts between government officials in late August and October. Discussions revolved around possibilities for sharing the offshore oil blocks, but in order for an agreement on a zone of common interest to be ratified, the exact border had to first be officially established. Angola is definitely the stronger party to the dispute, being militarily superior to the DRC. This became obvious in the cautious reactions of the Kinshasa government towards Angolan operations in the provinces of Bandundu and Bas-Congo – reportedly against separatist rebels from the Angolan province of Cabinda – and to the expulsion of Congolese citizens from Angola, and Angola's involvement in the disputes with the Republic of Congo.

Tensions with the **Republic of Congo** (ROC) revolved around the Congolese government's request for the extradition of General Faustin Munene, who was arrested in the ROC in January. The former FARDC commander was allegedly implicated in the attack on Kabila's residence in February (see above). Kinshasa furthermore accused Angolan troops of protecting Munene on ROC territory. Udjani Mangbama Mambenga, another significant western rebel leader, was also detained in the ROC, but not extradited. In March, the Kinshasa government withdrew its ambassador from Brazzaville. Talks took place between government officials of the two countries, but without any real rapprochement. The DRC government was cautious with respect to its small neighbour, as the ROC's President Denis Sassou-Nguesso maintained close ties with Angola's President dos Santos.

After a meeting of the defence ministers of the DRC and **Uganda**, FARDC held direct talks with the Uganda People's Defence Force (UPDF) in Kasese, Uganda. The two army leaderships discussed the ongoing strategy against two Ugandan rebel groups operating on Congolese territory, the Lord's Resistance Army and the Allied Democratic Front-National Army for the Liberation of Uganda. The UPDF was allowed continued access to Congolese territory in order to pursue these armed groups.

Rwanda backed Kabila in his election campaign, in stark contrast to the elections of 2006, when Kabila won a majority in the Kivu provinces for campaigning against Rwandan influence in the eastern provinces. Because of the strengthening of the FPLC/ FDLR-Soki (see above), which could one day pose a serious threat to the Rwandan government, Rwanda's President Kagame pursued his strategic alliance with Kabila. This alliance is highly unpopular with a majority of the population in the eastern provinces and led to strong support during the election campaign for Vital Kamerhe, who represented the anti-Rwandan position.

Relations with **Kenya** revolved around the increase in gold smuggling from Congo. Most gold is smuggled through neighbouring Kenya and Uganda. A dubious case of smuggling brought against five men related to the US company CARMAC (see below) apparently also involved some Kenyanss. On 3 March, Kabila held talks with Kenya's President Mwai Mbaki in Nairobi and agreed on appointing a joint investigation team into gold smuggling issues, in cooperation with Interpol's regional office in Nairobi.

Socioeconomic Developments

While some macro-data showed positive trends, the population faced true challenges, the **humanitarian situation** remained disastrous, especially in the east of the country, with continued violence against civilians, including sexualised violence, torture and looting. The number of IDPs remained as high as in the previous year at an estimated 1.7 m as of October, including roughly 1 m in North and South Kivu, 500,000 in the Uélé districts of Orientale province, and the rest in northern and central Katanga and Maniema.

Year-on-year **inflation** was recorded at 17.7%, indicating that the government's goal of single digit inflation was far from being met. Rising food and fuel prices added to the population's dire economic situation, which was, however, not as drastic as in 2009, when inflation stood at 46%.

The IMF expected **real GDP growth** to continue to 6.5 % (from 5.1% in 2010 and 2.7% in 2009), mainly due to mining output and infrastructural programmes related to booming Sino-Congolese cooperation. The Congolese economy thus found itself in line with a general trend in many African countries, which were recovering much faster from the effects of the global economic crisis than many in Europe. Agriculture still made up the largest share of GDP, although the mining sector also heavily influenced GDP growth and it remained to be seen how the breakdown of mineral exports in many parts of the country as a result of American legislation (see below) would impact real GDP growth over time.

The implementation of economic reform programmes attached to the three-year arrangement under the **Extended Credit Facility (ECF)** arrangement with the IMF continued to be a government priority. The ECF was a $ 561 m loan programme to promote economic growth and reduce poverty. The IMF evaluated Congo's economic performance as broadly satisfactory and disbursements were paid as planned (around $ 80 m in the reporting year). However, the interests of Kabila and his entourage, especially in the area of resource deals, were becoming increasingly contradictory to the reform programmes and so the environment was becoming even less investment friendly than before.

In late September, the IMF asked the state-owned copper mining company **Gécamines** to publish contracts from sales of stakes in the Mutanda and Kansuki mining projects worth $ 800 m, which had probably been sold at below-market prices. The stakes were sold to companies related to Israeli business man Dan Gertler, a close ally of Kabila said to have helped finance his 2006 election campaign. The company refused to publish its sales figures. It was unclear where the proceeds had gone and accusations of corruption were rife. Gécamine's reluctance to move on the issue delayed the fourth ECF review, scheduled for September. A cause of great concern dating back to 2009 was the cancellation of the granting of a licence held by the Kingamyambo Musonoi Tailings in Kolwezi, Katanga, to Quantum Minerals (FQM). The latter had already invested in the project but was nonetheless deprived of the licence. Metakol, a company linked to Gertler, had acquired the licence from the government in dubious circumstances and sold it to a company based in Kazakhstan, the Eurasian Natural Resources Corporation (ENRC). A court on the British Virgin Islands upheld FQM's $ 2 bn claim against ENRC in September. FQM has also taken the case to the international arbitration tribunal of the Chamber of Commerce in Paris. In August, 'Bloomberg Businessweek' revealed that the state-owned mining company Sodimico had sold its 30% stake in the Frontier and Lonshi copper mining projects, valued at $ 480 m, for only $ 30 m.

In early October, a draft of the **2012 budget** reached the National Assembly, which did not manage to discuss it. Its adoption has therefore been de facto handed over to the new parliament for discussion in 2012.

The **mining sector** attracted particular attention. In July 2010, the US Congress adopted a financial reforms bill that included legal regulation of mineral exports from the Congo. Section 1502 of the **Dodd-Frank Wall Street Reform and Consumer Protection Act** requires companies listed on the US stock exchange to certify that their imported minerals are "conflict-free" by disclosing their delivery and production chains. Although the provisions of what is nicknamed by the Congolese "Obama's Law" were not yet implemented, it had widespread consequences for the Congolese mining sector – none of which was a reduction in violence. Kabila had already in September 2010 imposed a ban on all mining activities in the eastern provinces of North Kivu, South Kivu and Maniema, arguing that most mines were controlled by armed groups. This ban was not lifted until March, but was soon followed by a de facto embargo of Congolese minerals as a result of the Dodd-Frank Act. Companies were already acting cautiously, paralysing the export of minerals in many parts of the country. One important company was the Malaysia Smelting Corporation, which had previously purchased up to 80% of the tin from eastern Congo and stopped all imports in April. Although it was unquestionable that the working conditions of artisanal miners did not meet human rights standards, work in the mines was often the only way to secure a livelihood. The ban on Congolese minerals therefore had devastating consequences for millions of Congolese – both artisanal miners and their families and workers in other parts of the production chain. The lack of income for large parts of the population spread to most other parts of the eastern Congo economy and heavily reduced tax revenues from the region. Moreover, violence continued to threaten the now even more fragile communities in the east. The UN Group of Experts found that there were some positive developments, such as: increased awareness in the affected industry with regard to the necessity for due diligence in relation to conflict zones; increased production and improved governance in the zones where mines were not militarised; and a reduction in the income of rebel groups. However, they also stated that the result of Kabila's ban and the Dodd-Frank Act were not necessarily a reduction in armed violence, but rather that Congolese rebel groups turned to other sources of revenue, such as the timber trade and drug smuggling. Furthermore, the gold trade continued to boom, not yet being touched by efforts to control production chains, and provided resources for both rebel groups and networks within the FARDC.

Despite the negative consequences for the local population, a mechanism to reduce the influence of rebel groups on mines seemed indispensable. Various organisations and international companies engaged in the development of certification mechanisms. The International Tin Research Industry advanced their Tin Supply Chain Initiative, begun in 2010, which was financed by numerous electronics companies, including Apple, Microsoft, Nokia, Philips and Sony. On 25 May, the OECD agreed on renewed guidelines for responsible international business, including a section of guidance on how to limit the use of conflict minerals.

In early February, two Americans, two Nigerians and a French citizen were arrested in Goma for **smuggling gold** and released in late March after having confessed and paid a $ 3 m fine in Kinshasa. They were trying to smuggle more than 400 kg of gold worth around $ 20 m, which they had allegedly bought from networks led by Bosco Ntaganda for a bargain price of around $ 6.8 m. The gold turned out to be fake. The deal involved the head of the US-based oil and gas company CARMAC International, Kase Lawal, who was appointed to a trade committee by US President Obama in 2010, and a former basketball star of the American National Basketball Association, who was leading CARMAC's Nigerian operations. According to the felons, the deal was initially planned to take place in Nairobi, but they had been ordered to Goma to get the gold. A month before the incident, a leading Kenyan government tax investigator was killed in Nairobi, perhaps in relation to the CARMAC deal. This case led to bilateral efforts between Kinshasa and Nairobi to stop the illegal gold trade.

These events revealed that international businessmen had not refrained from buying gold from rebel groups, and even from ICC indicted individuals such as Ntaganda, despite efforts to carry out due diligence with regard to the sources of trade. Aside from smuggling, regional scam networks also formed an important part of Ntaganda's financial empire in the east. Much of the gold was smuggled through neighbouring Uganda to the Arabian Peninsula. The UN Group of Experts uncovered a discrepancy of more than 3 tonnes of gold between import statistics from Dubai and export statistics from Kampala. The involvement of Ugandan business men in illegal gold trading and scams remained a sensitive issue in relations between the two countries.

Whereas the unofficial gold trade was booming and increasingly providing income for rebels and criminal networks, legal **gold production** remained insignificant, although this may change in coming years. The first new industrial gold mine for over 50 years was opened in South Kivu, with concessions held by Banro, a company listed in New York and Toronto. The $ 209 m Twangiza mine project was expected to produce 1 m troy ounces of gold within seven years. The Twangiza mine was the first of several planned mines on a 210 km-long belt in South Kivu. Randgold Resources proceeded with their Kibali mine project in Orientale province, which they expected to produce around 400,000 troy ounces a year from 2014, which would make it one of the largest goldmines in Africa. For the project to succeed, several thousand villagers would have to be resettled in newly built towns, and at year's end, 15,000 people had already been relocated. On the one hand, the project offered local residents work opportunities and good infrastructure, such as schools and hospitals, in the new towns, but, on the other, it was an example of increasingly aggressive international investment politics in Congo.

On 8 July, a **Hewa Bora Airline plane crashed** close to Kisangani airport while trying to land in bad weather, leaving 74 people dead. The incident gave rise to renewed discussion of security concerns regarding Congolese airlines and the desperate lack of transport in this vast country. On 14 July, The transport ministry banned Hewa Bora from operating.

Claudia Simons

Equatorial Guinea

Political and social processes during the year in Equatorial Guinea were strongly linked to external and transnational events. The 'Arab Spring' gave rise to fear of social unrest; the government reacted by strengthening its control over the population and at the same time proposing formal constitutional reform. President Obiang gained new international prominence as the new president of the AU, which held its summit at the end of June. But the new position also made him more exposed to criticism. The abject poverty of the population and the state's efficient repression apparatus facilitated the grip on power of the ruling 'Partido Democrático de Guinea Ecuatorial' (PDGE).

Domestic Politics

The year began with a **partial reshuffle of the cabinet**, which included four members of political parties different from PDGE. The second deputy prime minister in charge of political affairs and democracy, Demetrio Eló Ndong Nsefumu, also became minister of public works and infrastructures. Francisca Tatchoup Belope was appointed minister of economy, the first woman to occupy such an eminent position. Celestino Bacale Obiang, who had been the presidential candidate of the major opposition party, the 'Convergencia

Para la Democracia Social' (CPDS) in 2002, was appointed delegate minister of economy and consequently expelled from the CPDS.

In March, the parliamentary session resumed in the presence of the only opposition deputy returned in the legislative elections in 2008, Plácido Micó Abogo of the CPDS. On this occasion, the 'Cámara de los Representantes del Pueblo' approved the Constitutional Court Law, the law on state attorneys, and the Equato-Guinean nationality law, which established very strict requirements for the acquisition of Equato-Guinean citizenship by foreigners. During the second round of the parliamentary session, in September and October, the national budget was approved, and **parliament** adopted Portuguese as a national language, along with Spanish and French.

Political revolts in Tunisia, Egypt and Libya in March, and their echoes in many African countries, encouraged some political groups in Equatorial Guinea to cautiously mobilise the population. The authorities responded by forbidding demonstrations set for International Women's Day and those organised by the CPDS and 'Unión Popular' (UP) for 20 and 23 March respectively. A strong military and police presence throughout the country was the government's first reaction to the 'winds of change' blowing from North Africa.

In addition, President Obiang Nguema announced a constitutional reform and, on 1 April, convoked, for the first time since 2008, the 'Comisión de Vigilancia y Seguimiento del Pacto Nacional' (created in 1993), on which all nine legal political parties were represented. A **constitutional reform commission** was created by the president and met on the remote island of Annobón on 18–24 May in order to formulate a draft text. Only members of the PDGE government and allied political parties participated, as opposition parties (the CPDS, UP and 'Acción Popular de Guinea Ecuatorial') decided not to attend because of what they saw as the total absence of crucial democratic conditions from the process. On 15 July, Obiang himself presented the conclusions of the 'Annobón agreement' in parliament, and they were set to be put to a referendum in November. He also toured the country in August and September to campaign for the reforms, although the text was not widely distributed until some days before the vote.

The proposed reforms included the creation of a senate as a second parliamentary chamber, the limitation of the presidential mandate to two seven-year terms, and the establishment of a court of auditors and an ombudsman. The most controversial measure was the establishment of the office of vice president, to be filled at the president's discretion. This move was interpreted by many observers as an attempt to assure an automatic official succession by Obiang's eldest son, Teodoro Nguema Obiang (aka 'Teodorín'). The CPDS and the proscribed 'Movimiento para la Autodeterminación de la Isla de Bioko' (MAIB) campaigned against the reforms, while the UP called for abstention.

Subsequently, the government encouraged internal splits within opposition parties and increased the familiar harassment of their activists. In September, five members of the

CPDS Executive Committee publicly supported the reforms and, as a consequence, were expelled from the party. Similarly, three UP members claiming to represent the party campaigned for the government. Other CPDS, UP and MAIB members were briefly detained during the year, particularly on the eve of the referendum. They included UP Secretary General Daniel Darío Martínez Ayécaba, accused in September of complicity in unlawful party funding, and CPDS member of the national electoral committee Marcial Abaga Barril.

The **referendum** on constitutional reform, which took place on 13 November, was flawed, according to some human rights organisations: people were encouraged to vote publicly as well as to cast ballots on behalf of absent relatives, and military forces were seen in and around some polling stations. Opposition members were harassed and the CPDS withdrew its polling station monitors. The government initially claimed that 99% of votes were in favour of the reform ('reduced' some days later to 97%).

Apart from political activists and their families, other social groups suffered **violations of human rights** at the hands of the government and its security service, in the context of government fears of contagion from the revolts in the Arab world, the AU summit in the capital, Malabo, at the end of June, and the organisation of the referendum. Freedom of information was severely compromised during the year, as the government prohibited reporting about the Arab revolts: a public television journalist was suspended in March for simply mentioning the situation in Libya. In June, a television crew working for the German television station ZDF, who were reporting on women's football and the general situation in Equatorial Guinea, were detained, had some of their material confiscated, and were expelled from the country.

A strong military and police presence was felt in cities and on the roads during most of the year. Schools were closed on 30 May, one month in advance of the AU summit, in order to avoid student demonstrations during the summit. Students and foreigners were detained indiscriminately, and some were tortured in police stations. In spite of a formal complaint on 31 May by all CEMAC ambassadors regarding the mistreatment of their citizens, 23 Cameroonians and 37 Malians, plus 150 employees of the French company Bouygues (including Cameroonians, Gabonese and Ghanaians, among others) were expelled from the country shortly afterwards, accused of having entered the country on false documents.

On the occasion of the president's birthday on 5 June, 22 political prisoners were pardoned. AI deplored the fact that 30 other people had been in jail without trial since October 2010, simply because they were family members of two escaped political prisoners. On 1 August, eight people from Aconibe district, relatives of a political exile in Spain, were also detained. Human rights abuses during the year were the subject of various reports by organisations such as AI and HRW.

Foreign Affairs

The 'Arab Spring' affected the country's foreign relations as much as its domestic politics as it coincided with the beginning of Obiang's mandate as AU president and the celebration of an **AU summit** in Malabo from 30 June to 1 July. Obiang proved to be one of the strongest supporters of Muammar Kadhafi's regime in the AU and presided over its commission on Libya. By contrast, he changed his initial support for Laurent Gbagbo into support for the new Ivorian president, Alassane Ouattara, who was backed *inter alia* by France.

In the **regional context**, oil interests and security concerns led to the reinforcement of military cooperation between the governments of the Gulf of Guinea, including Equatorial Guinea, and those of the United States, France and Spain. On 31 October, the UNSC condemned the frequent acts of piracy and armed robbery committed at sea in the Gulf of Guinea, and encouraged ECOWAS, ECCAS and the Gulf of Guinea Commission to develop a comprehensive strategy to combat them.

Dialogues on border questions were conducted between Equatorial Guinea and neighbouring governments. However, conversations in New York and Geneva at the beginning of the year between the Equato-Guinean and Gabonese governments about the territorial dispute over Mbanie Island proved inconclusive. A February meeting of the bilateral Committee on Consular and Border Affairs between Cameroon and Equatorial Guinea failed to lead to a reopening of the border at Kye-osi. The establishment of the CEMAC regional passport and the consequent free movement of people, which should have been implemented in 2010, continued to be a fiction.

Oil revenues continued to strengthen the government of Equatorial Guinea in its **bilateral relations** with consumer countries. Whereas the main foreign companies continued to be based in the US, the Obama administration avoided over-friendly gestures towards the autocratic regime. US Deputy Assistant Secretary for African Affairs Susan Page visited the country in May, when she met not only with the government but also with opposition leaders, and attended the ground-breaking ceremony for the new US embassy building. European countries, such as Spain and France, continued to strengthen their bilateral relations with the government. President of the Spanish Parliament José Bono and Spanish Minister of Foreign Affairs Trinidad Jiménez visited the country at different times, during a year in which Spanish business groups acquired an increased presence: in May, a Spanish investment mission arrived, and a 'First Business Forum Spain-Equatorial Guinea' took place in July.

However, the government showed more interest in its bilateral relations with strong African (South Africa, Angola) and non-Western (Israel, China, Russia) countries, especially in the sphere of security. **South African** Deputy Minister of Police Maggie Sotyu visited Equatorial Guinea in March, in order to strengthen cooperation on security issues related to events such as the AU summit and the Africa Cup of Nations, scheduled to be held in Equatorial Guinea in 2012. In October, Obiang paid a visit to South Africa. He also made a high-level visit to **Russia** in June, during which the two countries signed an agreement on military technology, and Gazprom Neft and the Equato-Guinean state-owned company GEPetrol reached an agreement to develop two off-shore blocks in Equatorial Guinea. In his capacity as AU president, Obiang looked for a strong ally in Dmitri Medvedev for his stance on the Libyan conflict. Morocco and Israel continued to be reliable supporters of the government, the latter selling two offshore patrol vessels and arms worth about $ 100 m to Malabo.

During the year, external pressures on the dictatorial government continued. Malabo's efforts to make **UNESCO** reverse its decision not to create a prize in Obiang's name were met by a campaign within UNESCO; a final decision was postponed to 2012. The **CPLP** again refused Equatorial Guinea's acceptance as a full member on the basis of its non-compliance with the organisation's guiding principles.

The judicial initiatives in France and the US against the president's eldest son, designated vice president under the amended constitution, were a severe blow to the regime. In September and October, the French police seized up to 18 luxury cars belonging to Teodoro Nguema Obiang, as part of an ongoing investigation into illegal assets. In October, he was sued by the US Department of Justice for more than $ 70 m in a corruption and money laundering case – the consequence of an investigation that started in 2007, following a 2004 US Senate report. Finally, another French court ruled in favour of the NGO 'Comité Catholique contre la Faim et pour le Développement-Terre Solidaire', which had been accused by President Obiang of defamation for a report on misappropriation of oil revenues. In reaction to these cases, the government appointed Teodoro Nguema Obiang as deputy envoy to UNESCO and FAO.

The government's repressive politics had spread to the region during recent years and was the cause of other judicial and non-judicial initiatives in neighbouring countries. In May, members of the military and the police in Cameroon were charged with the kidnapping in 2008 of a political refugee, Cipriano Nguema Mba, who had been handed over to the Equato-Guinean embassy. In Calabar, Nigeria, the Nigeria-Malabo Boat Operators Association demanded $ 158 m compensation for the attacks upon their members, including torture, detention and killing, by agents of the Equato-Guinean government in 2009 and 2010.

Intense international attention was also paid to the construction of the Sipopo luxury resort complex.

Opposition parties' foreign relations continued to languish, although a CPDS-UP delegation visited the US at the invitation of the State Department in June, and the CPDS was invited to participate as an observer in proceedings of the German Social Democratic Party in December.

Socioeconomic Developments

According to the IMF, real **GDP** was estimated to have grown by 7.1% (far below the 21.4% in 2007, but recovering from almost negative growth in 2010). The oil and gas sector accounted for more than 90% of GDP, 99% of exports and the 86% of government revenue. Inflation continued in high figures, reaching 7.3%. The IMF did not publish the conclusions of the 2011 Article IV Consultation with Equatorial Guinea, which took place in April. The year before, the IMF had identified lack of competition in the retail sector, rising public sector wages and strong domestic demand as the main causes for the decline of growth rates.

In the oil and gas sector, the American Energy Information Administration estimated that Equatorial Guinea's total liquid supply was about 320,000 b/d in 2011. Production was expected to rise again in the near future, thanks to the Aseng oil and gas-condensate field, which came on stream in November. American KRB was awarded a contract to provide a preliminary study for the building of a refinery at Mbini, on the mainland Rio Muni coast. Natural gas production grew to 238 bn ft^3 in 2010, and was expected to increase as new projects developed in the short and medium term from the Aseng and Alen fields. In January, Noble Energy (US) announced the official approval of its development plans for the Alen condensate/gas-recycling project.

The **construction sector** continued to attract numerous foreign companies from Europe, the Arab world, China and other Asian countries, which entered into joint ventures with local partners associated with members of the president's family. Small local entrepreneurs without such connections could not benefit. Agriculture and the rest of the primary sector continued to decline, representing a mere 3% of GDP. Food continued to be mainly imported from neighbouring countries. Immigrants came from the sub-region and also from more distant countries, notably China, although precise numbers were not available.

The government's commitment to economic and **human development** was highly debatable, despite formal programmes such as the National Economic Development Plan (Horizon 2020) launched in 2007, whose objective was to turn the country into an emerging economy by 2020. Much public spending was devoted to prestige 'white elephant' projects such as the lavish resort of Sipopo, whereas education and health continued to be underfunded. Personal ambitions for quick enrichment through access to public funds dominated over macroeconomic considerations. Moreover, the well-being of the majority of the population, and a consequent growth of political awareness and independent thinking, was clearly contrary to the political elite's interest in remaining in power as long as possible.

The country's failure to diversify the economy and lower its reliance on the exploitation of oil and gas was therefore not a new phenomenon but the result of government policies since the onset of the oil boom in the 1990s. The country's dismal **poverty** record, with almost 80% of the population living below the poverty line, and a very poor level of social services, was due to one-sided decisions and ill-conceived government policies. Whereas per capita GDP (in current US $) in 2010 stood at $ 20.009, i.e. over eight times higher than in 2000, health indicators were extremely poor when compared with countries with similar per capita income. Average life expectancy had barely increased, from 49 years in 2000 to just over 51 in 2011, and less than 50% of the population had access to drinkable water. Equatorial Guinea was the eleventh worst place in the world to be a mother, according to the annual report by Save the Children. The UNDP's Human Development Index presented Equatorial Guinea as the country with the biggest gap (–91) between its gross national per capita income ranking and its HDI ranking (136th of 187 countries).

Alicia Campos

Gabon

Legislative elections occupied much of the political calendar this year, with the political opposition eventually boycotting the polls, leaving the ruling 'Parti Démocratique Gabonais' (PDG) with a virtual monopoly of seats in the National Assembly. On-going allegations of widespread corruption continued to haunt the Bongo family dynasty. Nevertheless, high commodity prices and increased oil production allowed for modest economic growth.

Domestic Politics

Following the November 2010 broadcast of a French documentary, 'Françafrique', in which a former French presidential advisor, Michel de Bonnecorse, had very publicly accused Ali Bongo and his ruling PDG of fraudulently stealing the 2009 presidential elections – allegedly won by opposition leader Andre Mba Obame – the year opened with a dramatic political crisis. Bonnecorse later disavowed his allegations, claiming his words had been taken out of context, but the effect of the broadcast was to cause the intense resurgence of popular suspicions that the presidential elections had been stolen, with the complicity of the French. Inspired by the popular uprisings of the 'Arab Spring' in Tunisia, Egypt and Libya, Obame returned to Libreville, after a prolonged stay in France for medical treatment, and was enthusiastically greeted by several thousand supporters at the airport. On 25 January, he declared himself the true 'president elect'. Calling on the Gabonese people and the international community for support, Obame vowed to form a parallel government.

In reaction, the **government dissolved the 'Union Nationale' (UN) party** on 25 January, followed by unofficial statements that Obame would be tried either for treason or for insurrection. Fearful of more violent government reprisals, Obame then fled to the Libreville offices of the UNDP. The following day, on 26 January, a demonstration by his supporters outside the building was quickly broken up by security forces using tear gas. Another protest in the capital three days later was also broken up by police. Unfortunately for Obame, there was little international support for his manoeuvres. Not only were his allegations impossible to buttress with any evidence (given the regime's tight control on all information), but also the international community had already officially recognised Ali Bongo's electoral victory. France and the United States recognised Bongo as the country's only rightful president. In addition, the AU, presided over by Jean Ping (the former minister of foreign affairs under Omar Bongo and a long time loyalist of the Bongo family), refused to give the slightest credibility to accusations of electoral fraud. Finally, no vast popular protest in the streets ever materialised to support Obame's bid for a central African version of the 'Arab Spring'; he had been a high-ranking PDG minister in the former government, and was therefore perceived by many as unlikely to lead a popular uprising against a regime he had served for so long.

The real opposition leader in the country, Pierre Mamboundou, who had officially come second in the 2009 presidential elections, spent much of the year in closed-door negotiations with the Bongo regime. Mamboundou, leader of the 'Union du Peuple Gabonais' (UPG), based in the southern oil-capital Port-Gentil with electoral support coming principally from the Punu-Eshira ethnic group, was rumoured to have accepted a power-sharing deal with the regime. In exchange for recognising Bongo's legitimacy and supporting his policy agenda, Mamboundou had pressured the regime to introduce a biometric electoral roll in advance of the upcoming legislative elections. It was hoped that the introduction of biometric voting cards would reduce the likelihood of certain kinds of electoral fraud (in particular the massive participation of 'ghost voters', whose numerical increase on recent electoral lists far exceeded the population growth in their corresponding districts). On 14 April, it was reported that Mamboudou had met with the president of the Constitutional Court, Marie Madeleine Mborantsuo, to discuss the logistics of introducing the new biometric voting system.

In order to implement this technological innovation, Bongo had requested the Constitutional Court to validate a postponement of the legislative elections until the following year. On 15 June, the Court held that there were insufficient legal grounds for such a delay. On 7 September, the government declared that it would not be able to introduce biometric voter cards before the elections. It tried to give assurance that the elections would nevertheless be transparent and would be conducted in a credible manner. Incredulous, most of the **opposition decided to boycott the elections,** but this boycott was not followed by Mamboundou's UPG. On 9 October, several thousand people gathered in the capital to demand the introduction of the biometric voter registration ahead of the legislative elections. Although this gathering was authorised by the interior ministry, it was not allowed to hold a march afterwards, and the protest was monitored by a large police presence. The protest was organised by a new civil society movement called 'Ça Suffit Comme Ça!' (That's enough!).

Suddenly, during the night of 15 October, **Pierre Mamboundou died of a heart attack**. Having spent the better part of his life opposing the Bongo family dynasty, he was probably the last opponent of the regime with any stature left in the country, the other opposition leaders having either been compromised, co-opted, or just threatened into silence. Mamboundou's death left a vacuum in the Gabonese political world. It also left the UPG to face the legislative elections without a familiar face. But since many in his party had been opposed to Mamboundou's rapprochement with the regime, and since they wanted to hold on to their seven seats in the National Assembly, they decided in the end not to boycott the legislative elections.

Meanwhile, the PDG, certain of a landslide victory, did not even bother to negotiate with the opposition parties or traditional allies and chose instead to field candidates in every electoral district in the country. Before the December elections, the PDG held 82 seats (out of 120) in the National Assembly, and Mamboundou's UPG held seven, but few of the other parties in the assembly were real opposition parties. For example, the Fang leader of the 'Rassemblement Pour le Gabon', Paul Mba Abessole, had joined the Bongo regime, bringing his seven seats into an alliance with the ruling PDG. The 'Alliance Démocratique et Républicaine' (Adere) of the former vice president, Didjob Divungi Di Ndinge, held one seat, and the 'Centre des Libéraux Réformateurs' of Jean Boniface Assélé held two seats in the legislature. Both were long-time supporters of the Bongo family dynasty. Assélé is actually a brother of former first lady Josephine Kama and thus an uncle of President Ali Bongo.

With Obame facing charges of treason, and with Mamboundou dead and buried, the reality was that there was nothing to stop the PDG from sweeping the legislative elections, which is what they did. On 17 December one-third of the electorate went to the polls, and the **PDG won 114 out of 120 (or 95%) of the seats in the National Assembly.**

On 14 January, there was a **cabinet reshuffle**, the second since Ali Bongo came to power. Despite reported disagreements between the president and Prime Minister Paul Biyoghé Mba, the Fang prime minister was retained. Negotiations with Mamboundou ended with no ministerial portfolios being offered to either the UPG or any of the other opposition parties. There were five changes of portfolio, and six new or returning ministers. When comparing the total composition of the key ministers in the cabinet from January to December, it could be observed that certain members of the government were becoming well-established. Communications Minister Laure Olga Gondjout, for example, survived both cabinet reshuffles. (She is a daughter of the late Paul Gondjout, former president of the Constitutional Court and the National Assembly.) Foreign Affairs Minister Paul Toungui also remained in place. (He is the ex-husband of Ali Bongo's sister, Pascaline Bongo.) One of the notable changes in the cabinet was the shuffling of Julien Nkoghé Bekalé from strategically important minister of mines, oil and hydrocarbons to transport. His replacement by the economist Alexandre Barro Chambrier was a small but positive sign that merit could still be rewarded in an otherwise dynastic regime.

Foreign Affairs

In June, Bongo made an official visit to New York during Gabon's presidency of the UNSC. During his visit to the United States, on 9 June, **Bongo was invited to the White House** where he met with President Barack Obama, who urged his counterpart to make further progress on fighting corruption and improving public accountability. Pressed on the wisdom of inviting the Gabonese ruler, White House Spokesman Jay Carney said Bongo was "making reform efforts" which the Obama Administration supported: While he admitted that Bongo had a "less than sterling" record, Carney touted Gabon as an important ally in dealing with mutual interests in Libya, Ivory Coast and Iran. The two leaders reportedly discussed strategic regional and bilateral topics of mutual importance, including the latest developments in the areas of security, democracy and economic growth.

As part of his US public relations tour, Bongo announced the creation of a new prize at the New York Academy of Sciences, which would provide $ 1.3 m for a biennial African Research Award for Young Scientists to be awarded to young African researchers. Bongo would be identified as the founder and honorary president of the prize, in exchange for providing the funding.

Charges of grand corruption against the Bongo family continued to disturb relations between Gabon and France. On 10 June, police officers working for the 'Office Central Pour la Répression de la Grande Délinquance Financière' reported that they had established that Ali Bongo had acquired a € 200,000 Bentley a few months before being elected president in 2009, as well as an € 18 m mansion in Paris with the fortune of his now deceased step-mother, Edith Sassou-Nguesso Bongo (daughter of neighbouring Congolese President Denis Sassou-Nguesso). These new revelations, which added to a long list of embarrassing accusations concerning the Bongo family fortune, followed a surprise re-opening by the French 'Cour de Cassation' in November 2010 of the so-called 'biens mal acquis' ('ill-gotten gains') investigation.

When combined with the charges made in the French media that Ali Bongo had stolen the presidential elections, the effect of continued scandalous accusations was a **cooling of otherwise warm diplomatic relations with France**. Bongo maintained very good personal relations with, for example, French President Nicolas Sarkozy. But even these have been tainted by media rumours and scandals, as new revelations were made in the French press that former president of Gabon, Omar Bongo, had made illegal contributions to Sarkozy's 2007 presidential campaign. In mid-September investigative journalist Pierre Péan released his new best-seller: 'La République des Mallettes' ('The Republic of Suitcases'), which contained many stories of attaché cases stuffed with cash being transported from French Africa to Paris in an occult system of political lobbying. In early December, another book published in Paris on the ill-gotten gains scandal by Xavier Harel and Thomas Hofnung, included revelations by Robert Bourgi, an advisor to former president Jacques Chirac, that tens of millions of francs had been provided by a number of African leaders to influence French policy. These accusations were confirmed by a former prime minister of Gabon, Jean Eyeghé Ndong, who admitted that it had been common practice for the late president Omar Bongo to hand over suitcases of money to important French politicians.

Pascaline Bongo, the president's sister, released a statement that rejected the accusations. But this troubled relationship with France explained, in part, Ali Bongo's aggressive efforts to cultivate his country's **economic relations with China**, which had soured slightly following delays to the giant Bélinga iron ore project. Negotiations were reported to have re-started in 2011, with China National Machinery and Equipment Company. The $ 3 b mega-mining project at Bélinga had been on hold since late 2007 because of the global economic downturn, as well as delays caused by such things as administrative inefficiency and environmental complaints on the part of certain Gabonese ministers. On 10 July, a manganese agreement was signed with Huazhou Mining (CICMHZ) to transport manganese from Gabon's manganese mines in the Moyen-Ogooué province. CICMHZ would provide two new locomotives and 88 new wagons, to be operated by the 'Transgabonais' railroad company. As these two examples suggest, relations cultivated with China were mainly related to minerals-extractive industries. While Chinese loans increased with prestige projects such as the construction of the Grand Poubara Hydroelectric Dam and the Stadium of Sino-Gabonese Friendship for the 2012 Africa Cup of Nations, and while China was Gabon's second largest customer after the US, Chinese products represented a small percentage of total Gabonese imports.

Relations with **Cameroon** were strained this year when 4,700 clandestine gold diggers were expelled by the army on 31 May from the Minkébé gold mines in the northern region of Ogooué Ivindo. According to the testimony of some of these clandestine workers, they were held for two days in a tiny, windowless cell. Three of them, who had been detained in a centre in Bitam, died from the treatment they received from their jailors. The charges were denied by the authorities, who claimed that the prisoners had died of cholera. On 14 June, the Gabonese Council of Ministers announced that there would be an investigation into the affair, and the following week Cameroonian President Paul Biya sent an emissary to meet with Bongo to resolve any misunderstanding arising from these unfortunate events.

Socioeconomic Developments

The economy was boosted by record exports, estimated at around $ 10.9 b, resulting from **high oil prices** (averaging over $ 100 per barrel) and **increased oil production**. The increase in oil production came principally from the new Koula oil field, which had been inaugurated in late 2010, and is estimated to contain around 40 m barrels of oil reserves. Koula produced on average more than 60,000 b/d and was operated by Shell Gabon in partnership with the Chinese oil companies Sinopec and Addax. The field was estimated to be capable of producing around 80,000 b/d in a few years' time, which would make it the leading producing oil field in the country.

Another French oil firm, Maurel and Prom, announced in January that it had drilled two test wells in the Onal prospecting block, located a little inland from Port-Gentil, and by the end of the year the company was producing over 20,000 b/d. Throughout the year, the government was in the process of creating a **new state oil firm, Gabon Oil Company**, in order to increase its share of revenues generated by the oil sector, and to wrest some control of the logistics and infrastructure from the large integrated foreign oil companies that have historically dominated the largely offshore industry.

On 27 March, Turkish President Abdullah Gül visited Gabon as part of an economic-promotion tour on behalf of his country. Accompanied by 120 Turkish businessmen, the president was received with full honours by Ali Bongo in Libreville. Before 1998, Turkish trade relations with Sub-Saharan Africa were almost non-existent, but they have been growing since then at a rate of 10% a year, increasing from $ 1.5 b in 2011 to $ 20 b in 2011. The Turkish president was especially interested in Gabonese fisheries, and the businessmen who accompanied him on this tour were interested in acquiring major construction contracts for some of Gabon's newest infrastructural programmes. A photograph of President Gül speaking with fishermen on the beach at Libreville drew attention to this new foreign actor in Gabon.

During the year, Gabon inaugurated the Nkok industrial zone, a much-vaunted project in Ali Bongo's economic strategy of 'Gabon Emergent', designed to increase the amount of value-added industrialisation in the essentially raw-materials-exporting economy. In mid-April, a leading Indian firm, Tata Chemicals, acquired a stake in a project of the Singaporean company Olam International to build an ammonia factory near Libreville at Nkok. The first phase of the project would start producing 2,200 tonnes of ammonia per day, to double by 2014, for use in fertilisers, for which demand is growing rapidly in India.

This ammonia factory was only one of a series of large investment projects set up by Olam, which was developing a special economic zone to process timber in Nkok and a vast plantation in the south-east to produce palm oil. The government announced its intention to overtake Nigeria as Africa's largest producer of palm oil within a decade. Relations with Singapore had started in the previous year when Bongo visited that country and became inspired to turn Gabon into "the Singapore of Africa".

Striking energy workers in Gabon shut down half the country's crude oil output in April and then briefly brought the remainder to a halt. The union began its strike over what it said was the industry's failure to hire enough local workers. As a result of the strike, Shell and Total, the two biggest oil producers in the country, decided to stop all oil production in order to ensure the safety of their sites. To end this potentially crippling industrial action, the government promised to assess the number of foreigners working illegally in the petroleum sector, estimated to be over 2,800 by the trade union 'Organisation Nationale des Employés du Pétrole' (ONEP). By late September, the police were involved in heavy-handed spot checks of workers' permits near several major oil fields operated by Shell Gabon. Police demanded that workers produce their documentation in the street, despite never before having required this. Some companies reported that workers who failed to produce the necessary documents were being threatened with deportation. ONEP gave the government a deadline of 15 October to resolve these problems, threatening another strike if the government failed to find satisfactory solutions.

Douglas A. Yates

São Tomé and Príncipe

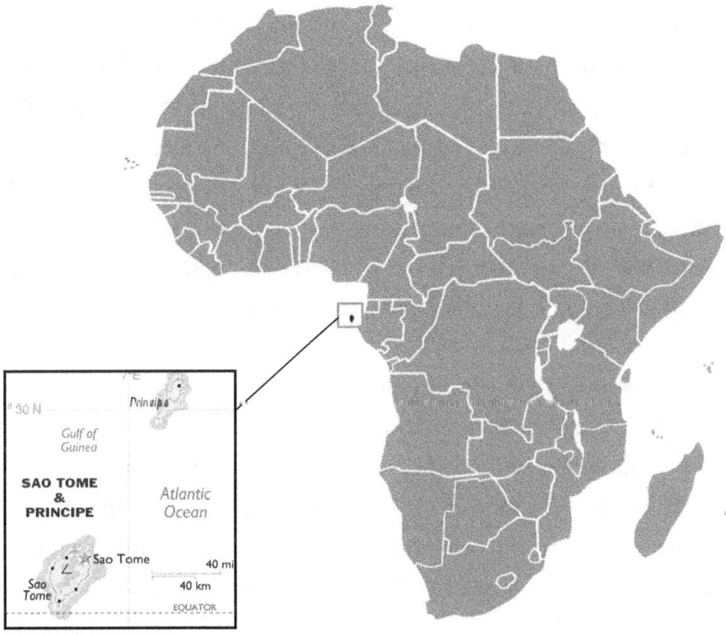

In August, Manuel Pinto da Costa, the country's first president, in office from 1975 to 1991, became the third democratically elected president. Foreign tourism investments in Príncipe provoked a conflict between the island's regional government and the central government. The Angolan oil company Sonangol took control of São Tomé's harbour and airport, while the country's oil sector made little progress.

Domestic politics

On 7 August, 74-year old Manuel Pinto da Costa, the country's first post-independence head of state during the socialist one-party regime (1975–91), won the run-off in the **presidential elections** and became his country's third democratically elected president, succeeding Miguel Trovoada (1991–2001) and Fradique de Menezes (2001–11). Pinto da Costa, ex-leader of the 'Movimento de Libertação de São Tomé e Príncipe/Partido Social Democrata' (MLSTP/PSD), ran as an independent candidate. He defeated Evaristo Carvalho, president of the National Assembly and candidate of the ruling 'Acção Democrática Independente' (ADI) with 52.9% against 47.1% of the votes. Pinto da Costa owed his victory to the absence of a charismatic rival candidate and the local electorate's traditional preference for having a prime minister and a president from different parties. He returned to the presidency after a lean period of 20 years and two failed attempts to return to the highest office through the ballot box, in 1996 and 2001 respectively.

Altogether 14 contenders registered their candidature for the presidential elections scheduled for 17 July, but most of them were predicted to stand no chance. Ten candidates eventually ran for the presidency, since one withdrew and three others were excluded by the Supreme Court because they had dual nationality, which is prohibited under the electoral law. Besides Evaristo Carvalho, two other candidates were endorsed by political parties: Aurélio Martins, the leader of the MLSTP/PSD, and Defim Neves, vice-president of the 'Partido de Convergência Democrática' (PCD). The nomination of Martins, who had been elected as the new party chairman with 73% of the votes in January, was fiercely contested as irregular by two other aspirants for the party nomination: Maria das Neves, a former prime minister, and Elsa Pinto, a former minister of defence, who both dedided to run as independent candidates.

Pinto da Costa won the **first round** with 21,457 votes (33.9%), while Carvalho came second with 13,125 votes (20.1%). Delfim Neves and Maria das Neves received 13.7% and 13.4% of the ballots respectively. Three candidates received less than 5% of the votes, while the other three got less than 1%. Elsa Pinto obtained only 4.2% of the ballots, but still more than her party's official candidate, Aurélio Martins, who received 3.8%. Martins was the greatest loser in these elections, since he received the worst result of the four competitors coming from the MLSTP/PSD, even though he was the official party candidate. The turn-out was 68.4% of a total of 92,638 registered voters.

On 8 December, anonymous protesters in Príncipe burnt the national flag in front of the seat of the island's Regional Government. They spread pamphlets with anti-government slogans and demanding independence for the small, 142 km² island, an autonomous region within the twin-island nation since 1995. The action was immediately condemned by Defence Minister Carlos Stock and Nestor Umbelina, secretary of infrastructure of Príncipe's Regional Government, who promised to take all measures to find the culprits. While the burning of the flag in Príncipe took everybody by surprise, its timing was by no means arbitrary, since it occurred while José Cassandra, head of the Regional Government since 2006, was staying in São Tomé to renegotiate with the Trovoada government the terms of a **development project for Príncipe**, signed in February between the Regional Government and the South African computer software entrepreneur Mark Shuttleworth.

The central government contested the legality of several terms of the € 70 m investment agreement with Shuttleworth's company HBD Boa Vida (HBD stands for "Here be Dragons", referring to unexplored territory), including the concession of tax exemptions, arguing that they were subject to national legislation since they would surpass the competences of Príncipe's Regional Government. In addition, the deal with HBD ignored a previous agreement on the production of palm-oil signed by the central government with the Belgian company SOCFINCO in 2010. Under this agreement SOCFINCO's local subsidiary, Agripalma, received a 25-year concession to develop 5,000 ha of oil-palm plantations on two estates in São Tomé and on the Sundy estate in Príncipe. In mid-December the local population in Príncipe announced demonstrations against the dead-lock in the negotiations between HBD Boa Vida and the government. However, no agreement was signed by the end of the year.

Foreign Affairs

On 20 April, Prime Minister Patrice Trovoada arrived for a 24-hour visit to Luanda, Angola. The principal objective of his trip was to speed up the privatisation of his country's harbour and international airport to the 'Sociedade Nacional de Combustíveis de Angola' (Sonangol). Trovoada declared that São Tomé and Angola maintained a consolidated relationship that favoured additional opportunities for Angolan investors. The seventh session of the joint bilateral commission with Angola was held in São Tomé from 30 May to 1 June. After the meeting, São Tomé Foreign Minister Salvador Ramos again stressed the **importance of Angola** for his country's development.

Gabon's Prime Minister Paul Biyoghé Mba arrived with a delegation of businessmen from his country for a two-day visit to São Tomé on 2 May to strengthen bilateral economic relations between the two countries and to intensify **regional integration**. Biyoghé Mba, who was received by Trovoada and President Menezes, visited the Agostinho Neto estate, the fuel installations of the 'Empresa de Combustíveis e Óleo' (ENCO) and the Rosema brewery. He also participated in a workshop for businessmen from both countries organised by the local Chamber of Commerce, Industry, Agriculture and Services. On his departure, the Gabonese prime minister pledged a credit of $ 5 m in support of São Tomé's national budget. Trovoada announced the establishment of a branch of the private Gabonese BGFI Bank and a supermarket in São Tomé.

On 18 April, Trovoada attended the Maritime Piracy Summit in Dubai and used his visit to the UAE to look for funds to finance his country's national budget and the construction of the € 260 m. deep-sea port in Fernão Dias. The French consortium 'Compagnie Maritime d'Affrètement' and 'Compagnie Générale Maritime', which had signed the agreement for the port in 2008, failed to obtain the necessary finance. In early October, a seven-member **delegation from Dubai**, headed by the emirate's Sovereign Wealth Fund's director Mohamed Al Shaibani, paid a two-day visit to São Tomé to explore investment opportunities in the archipelago. On 9 December, Dubai's prime minister and UAE Vice President Sheikh Mohammed bin Rashid Al Maktoum received Trovoada to discuss possibilities of enhancing bilateral cooperation.

On 2 November, Trovoada initiated a three-day **visit to Washington DC**, where he held talks with the World Bank, the IMF and the US Millennium Challenge Corporation in an attempt to mobilise funds for his country's national budget. The prime minister claimed that his vision of São Tomé as a service platform in the Gulf of Guinea had been well received by his hosts. On his return, he was received in Lisbon, on 7 November by

Portuguese Prime Minister Pedro Passos Coelho and Foreign Minister Paulo Portas. After the meeting, Trovoada declared that, despite Portugal's financial crisis, Lisbon's support in the health, education and justice sectors were guaranteed.

On 17 November, Trovoada returned from a visit to Havanna, where the Cuban authorities promised to strengthen their country's cooperation in the health and agriculture sectors. A planned visit to Venezuela to discuss the financing of a medical school staffed by Cuban teachers was cancelled for unknown reasons.

Socioeconomic Developments

In February, the South African investor Mark Shuttleworth purchased the Bom Bom Island Resort in Príncipe from the Dutch businessman Rombout Swanborn, director of the tour operator Africa's Eden. In May, the Regional Government granted Shuttleworth's company, HBD Boa Vida, the concession of the Sundy estate. Shuttleworth, who is known in Príncipe as 'homem de lua' (man in the moon), since he had become the world's second space tourist, promised to invest in the small impoverished island in **sustainable development based on luxury eco-tourism**, agriculture and agro-forestry. HBD Boa Vida also received a concession for the beach Praia Uva and acquired the Paciência estate and two tourist complexes at Praia Macaco and Praia Boi from foreign concessionaires.

On 27 April, Minister of Public Works and Natural Resources Carlos Vila Nova and Sonangol Industrial Investments's administrator Batista Sumbe signed a 30-year concession agreement on the management and exploitation of the **port of Ana Chaves** and the country's **international airport** by the Angolan state oil company. The agreement included the establishment of a private management company owned by Sonangol (80%) and the Santomean state (20%) to run the two facilities. Sonangol, which already owned a 78% stake in the fuel company ENCO, promised to invest $ 5 m in the upgrading of the port and another $ 7 m in the modernisation of the airport, including a 300 m. extension of the runway. It was expected that, after the upgrading works, which started in late November and were scheduled to last for seven months, the airport would be removed from IATA's black list. While this agreement further strengthened São Tomé and Príncipe's relationship with Angola, it also revealed the country's inability to properly maintain and run its principal infrastructures.

A new three-year **fisheries partnership agreement** with the EU for the period from 2011 to 2014, signed on 13 May, allowed 40 trawlers (28 tuna seiners and 12 surface longliners) to operate in the archipelago's waters. In exchange, the EU promised to pay a total of € 2.05 m, of which € 455,000 per year for an annual reference tonnage set at 7,000 tonnes for 40 vessels and € 227,500 per year for the support of the fisheries policy in the archipelago.

On 23 May, the government, the 'Companhia Santomense de Telecomunicações' (CST) and Africatel Holding, the Amsterdam based subsidiary of Portugal Telecom, signed an agreement on the country's connection to an **optical fiber submarine cable**, which was expected to improve the speed and quality of communications with the archipelago. Under a second agreement, a new company called STP Cabo, jointly owned by CST (74.5%) and the government (25.5%), was established for the management of the submarine cable. The new cable, which connected Africa with Europe and Latin America, arrived at Praia Melão on 15 November.

From 26 August to 8 September a team from the IMF visited São Tomé to review the Fund's economic programme supported under an ECF. The IMF expected economic growth to increase from 4.5% in 2010 to almost 5% in 2011, with construction and trade as principal growth sectors. Central government spending stayed in line with the budget, but the regional government and some municipalities accumulated arrears on their utility bills, although they had received financing from the central government to pay for these services. The IMF asked the government to solve the recurrent problem of arrears accumulation beween the Treasury, the water and elecricity utility EMAE, and the fuel company ENCO. Despite the debt relief received in 2007, which reduced debt from $ 359 m to $ 110 m, the country remained at high risk of returning to unsustainable debt burdens (which had risen again to $ 172 m) due to increased borrowing and a weak export and production basis.

On 15 December, the National Assembly approved the **2012 national budget** of Dobras 2.716.856 m ($ 152 m) with the 26 votes of the ruling ADI and the vote of the deputy of the 'Movimento Democrático Força de Mudança' MDFM, while the oposition MLSTP/PSD and PCD abstained. The public sector wage bill represented 44.3% of current expenditure (34.8% of the total), while transfers and goods and services accounted for 25% and 24.6% respectively. Capital expenditure (65.2%) depended largely on donor financing.

The first licensing round for seven of the 19 offshore blocks of the country's **Exclusive Economic Zone (EEZ)**, started in March 2010, proved to be another setback for the country's oil sector. On 2 May, the government awarded the exploration licence for Block 3 of the EEZ (4,228 km^2) to the Nigerian company Oranto Petroleum, while the other six blocks were not awarded to any of the other five third-tier oil companies that had submitted bids. EEZ Blocks 4 and 11 had previously been allocated to the Nigerian Houston-based company ERHC Energy, and EEZ Blocks 5 and 12 to Equator Exploration, under preferential agreements. In October, the government signed a 28-year production sharing contract with Oranto. Under the agreement, Oranto had to pay a signature bonus of $ 2 m and would conduct research in the first eight years, while oil production was expected to begin from the ninth year of the licence. In the first four production years, Oranto would receive 80% of the oil income to recover its investments. On 8 November, Trovoada declared that new licensing rounds of EEZ blocks would not be held until at least 2015, the year in which the anticipated start of oil production in the Joint Development Zone (JDZ) with Nigeria was expected to draw the attention of major oil companies to the country's EEZ.

In early December, during a meeting with the Joint Development Authority (JDA) in São Tomé, Total announced an investment of $ 200 m in **exploration drillings** in two wells in JDZ Block 1, scheduled for the first quarter of 2012. In 2010, Total had acquired its 45.9% stake in JDZ Block 1 from Chevron, which had withdrawn from the JDZ after exploration drillings in early 2006 had produced disappointing results. At the meeting, Olegário Tiny, one of São Tomé's directors at the JDA, known for his optimistic affirmations, claimed that within three years the effective production process would start since everything pointed to the existence of commercially viable oil.

Gerhard Seibert

VI. Eastern Africa

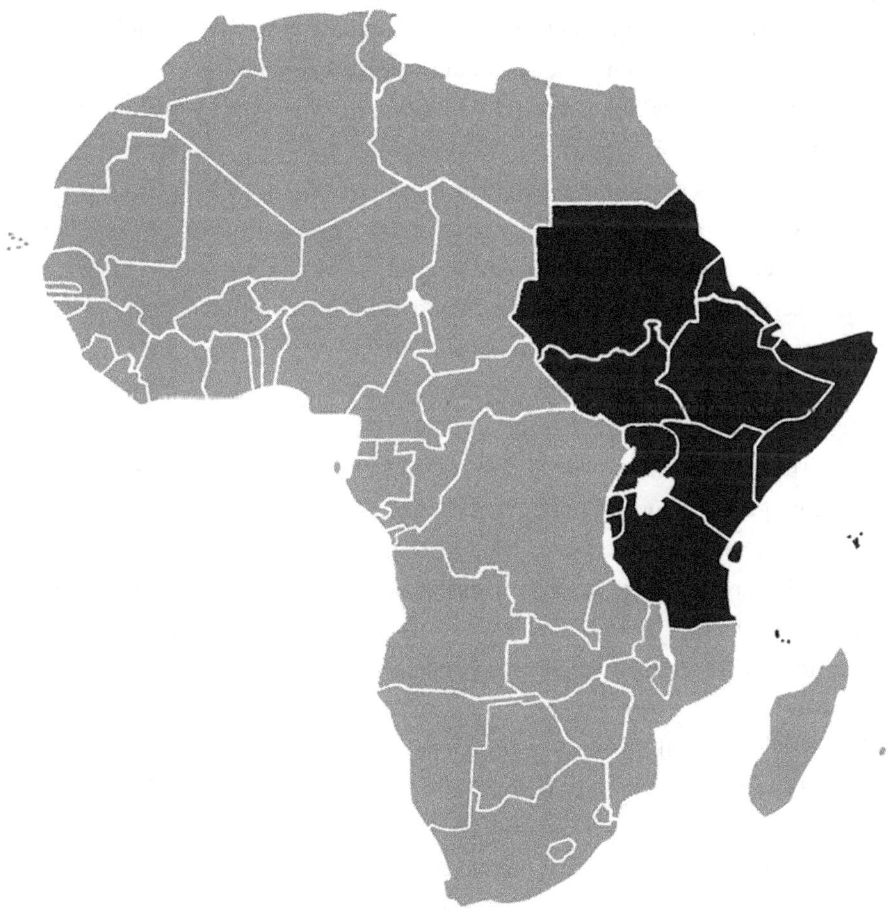

The creation of a new independent state, the Republic of South Sudan, was undoubtedly the most important political event in the sub-region. Although celebrated peacefully, this threatened to contribute to new conflicts and to changes in the sub-regional power configurations. Tensions quickly arose between Sudan and South Sudan and UN peacekeepers had to be deployed in the border area. The Darfur region of Sudan was still not pacified, but the level of violence remained somewhat subdued. This was not the case in the southern parts of Somalia, where radical Islamist groups continued to impose their control by the use of force over large areas and to launch attacks against the fledgling transitional state authorities. With the strengthening of the AU peacekeeping forces and the additional involvement of Kenyan and Ethiopian troops, the Islamist militias were forced to retreat somewhat, but they were by no means defeated. Otherwise, external attention continued to be mainly focused on international efforts to contain the unrelenting threat from Somali pirates to international shipping in the Indian Ocean and the Gulf of Aden. On-going concerted anti-piracy activities by both sub-regional and external forces were of only limited effect and were not able to significantly curtail the threat. The ICC continued to investigate the cases of the alleged perpetrators of the post-election violence in Kenya in early 2008, but no decisions about formal charges were made.

The year saw practically no changes in the prevailing political situations in the countries of the sub-region. Elections were held in only three countries (Djibouti, Seychelles and Uganda). In all cases, the incumbent presidents and parties managed to take full advantage of their privileged positions in the face of generally much weaker opposition forces, and were confirmed in power. In Comoros, a new president took office half a year after his election in December 2010. The mandate of the transitional authorities in Somalia was extended by another year until August 2012.

Large areas of the Horn of Africa (particularly Somalia and parts of Ethiopia, Djibouti and Kenya) were affected by a severe drought, by some accounts the worst for about 50 years. The threat of large-scale famine led to the belated mounting of substantial international emergency aid operations and to extensive media attention, although early warning signals that had been noted since late 2010 had been largely ignored for some time. In Somalia, all aid efforts were severely hampered by the civil war situation and the hostile attitude of the Islamists. Between 50,000 and 100,000 people were estimated to have died from famine, mostly children under five years old.

The macroeconomic performance of the sub-region was quite mixed and, considering the persistent global financial and economic crisis conditions, relatively satisfactory. Eritrea and Rwanda were the best performers, with GDP growth rates of almost 9%. Most other countries achieved moderate growth rates in the range of 4%–7%, with Comoros trailing with only about 2%. The only exception was Sudan, with an estimated GDP contraction of about 4%, due to problems with oil production after the secession of South Sudan. Most countries were hit by significantly higher than usual inflation rates, which fuelled growing popular discontent.

South Sudan was quickly admitted as new member of IGAD, but an application to join the EAC was deferred until a comprehensive assessment was made. Sudan's application for EAC membership was rejected, as was Eritrea's application for re-admission to IGAD. The EAC made further routine progress in many integration areas and was widely regarded as the most advanced regional economic community in Africa. Plans continued to be pursued for an extensive envisaged tripartite FTA (made up of COMESA, EAC and SADC), but no firm commitment was reached. The long-overdue conclusion of a full EPA between the EU and the EAC was again deferred. After years of Egyptian obstruction, some optimism emerged that a consensus would finally be reached on a new agreement on the sharing of the water resources of the River Nile between upstream and downstream riparian states, but no treaty was signed by year's end.

Political Developments

For **Sudan**, 2011 was a momentous year. Fifty-five years after independence, it finally had to accept the secession of its southern provinces as the result of a long civil war and the 2005 Comprehensive Peace Agreement. In January, the population of the South took part in a referendum, and almost 99% of those who voted were in favour of full independence, to be obtained in July. After long hesitation, the Sudanese government finally accepted the inevitable and declared itself ready to deal with the South thereafter on equal terms and in accordance with international practice. A number of important separation issues, including the demarcation of the common border, still needed to be resolved. For Sudan, the loss of about two-thirds of its oil industry was the most difficult sacrifice, with the considerable uncertainty this implied for the rest of the economy. No permanent peace solution was yet in sight for the crisis-ridden Darfur region, which had suffered since 2003 from the extremely complex interplay of politically-motivated rebel activities, government reprisals and violent actions by disparate criminal groups. The level of outright fighting was relatively low, but there was a general lack of security. A large hybrid AU-UN peacekeeping force continued to be tasked with protecting the civilian population. New localised conflicts emerged in areas near to the new border with South Sudan, with local population groups rebelling against Khartoum. President al-Bashir continued to be subject to an ICC arrest warrant on charges of crimes against humanity in Darfur, but again received signs of solidarity from many African and Arab governments. The political opposition to al-Bashir tried to forge a new alliance, but failed to mount a strong challenge.

South Sudan celebrated its independence on 9 July but, despite its oil resources, was severely handicapped as one of the poorest countries in the world, land-locked, and with practically no modern infrastructure and an extremely low level of education. An abundance of aid organisations descended on Juba to initiate the same processes that other African states had experienced decades ago. President Salva Kiir and his former liberation movement controlled all political institutions, but there was clear evidence of growing internal disagreements and of sharp rivalries along ethnic and regional lines. Traditional cattle raids between different ethnic groups repeatedly led to hundreds of casualties and many thousands of IDPs.

No change was discernible with respect to the domestic political situation in **Eritrea**. The authoritarian regime remained in undisputed control, continued with its harsh repression of all potentially dissenting voices and showed no sign of permitting even limited public debate on political issues. There was a continuing refugee exodus from the country, but the various exiled opposition groups failed to make any noticeable impact on the internal situation because of the draconian measures taken by the state security apparatus.

Similarly in **Ethiopia**, the repressive political climate and the authoritarian nature of the regime remained unchanged. In a de-facto one-party state with absolute control over the parliament and the regional assemblies, Prime Minister Meles Zenawi and his ruling party saw no need for more transparency, open political discourse or a conciliatory approach towards the fledgling opposition. The state's executive authorities were paramount, and all dissenting voices were harshly suppressed. The government continued to appease the general population by pursuing a dedicated modernising development strategy, although the results remained very unevenly distributed between regions and societal groups.

In **Djibouti**, President Guelleh was easily re-elected in April in a sham contest with a former close associate, while the opposition parties once again decided to boycott the elections in protest against the extremely uneven playing field and constant harassment by the security apparatus of the authoritarian regime. Guelleh was able to further consolidate the influence of his own family clan, but also brought a new generation of young technocrats into government positions. The opposition groups that were tolerated remained resigned to their ineffectiveness and made no noticeable impact on Djibouti's political situation.

Large parts of **Somalia** again saw hardly any improvement in the violence-ridden and chaotic situation that had by now prevailed for two decades, but two distinct geographical entities in the north managed to remain aloof from the turmoil and civil war in the southern regions. The internal situation in **Somaliland** remained generally stable and allowed for the normal administrative functions of a regular state to be carried out, and a move was initiated to broaden the political order into a full multi-party system. However, again no progress was made with respect to Somaliland's desire for full international recognition as an independent state. **Puntland** also maintained its status as a semi-autonomous state in practice, but without any declared intention of becoming fully independent. The authority of the existing governmental structures remained relatively limited, with only little control exercised over pirate groups who were installed along the Puntland coast and made their raids on the Indian Ocean from there. The situation in **Southern Somalia** saw some very modest improvement with respect to a consolidation of the authority of the struggling transitional political institutions physically installed in Mogadishu since 2009. Under the precarious protection of a further expanded AU peacekeeping mission, the transitional government at least gained practical control over Mogadishu and the immediate vicinity following the withdrawal of the Islamist militias. A new prime minister assumed office in June and drafted a road map towards achieving an end of the transitional period, which was again extended by mutual consent until August 2012. New permanent authorities were by then expected to be installed. Several radical Islamist groups continued to subject large parts of the population to their draconian rules and regularly launched armed attacks against all representations of formal state institutions. In some areas, however, clan-based local leaders were able to establish a limited semblance of political order in defiance of the Islamist extremists.

Kenya experienced another year full of political excitement, rumours about changing political alignments and possible strategies for the next elections, due in late 2012, but stability ultimately prevailed and the power-sharing grand coalition of the two main political camps, created under pressure in early 2008, still held together. All political actors within and outside of parliament were largely occupied with transforming the many requirements of the new 2010 constitution into legislative practice and with creating and/or staffing various key public institutions. Typically of Kenya's volatile political scene, speculation was rife about the ambitions of all the leading politicians and about the possible creation of new, mostly ethnically-oriented political parties and/or alliances, but no decisive steps were taken. Throughout the year, most public attention was centred on the case of six individuals (including four prominent politicians) who had in late 2010 been identified by the ICC as primarily responsible for the 2008 post-election violence. A decision about their possible indictment, with consequences for their political future, was expected in December, but then postponed to January 2012.

As usual, **Tanzania**'s political landscape remained quite stable, but nevertheless experienced freshly invigorated public debates. In the first year of his second term, President Kikwete and his long-ruling government party were still in undisputed control of all political institutions, but they were confronted with a stronger and more outspoken opposition than in the past. This clearly manifested itself in parliament and in the media. The government was even openly criticised by some of its own MPs, thereby demonstrating a continuation of factional feuding between opposing wings of the ruling party (defenders of old privileges vs. reformers). The initiation of a constitutional review process dominated the political agenda. After many years of sometimes vicious confrontations, politics in the semi-autonomous **Zanzibar** archipelago was calm and peaceful after a government of national unity had been formed between the two major political parties and politicians from the long neglected Pemba island had been elevated to leadership positions.

February elections in **Uganda** convincingly confirmed President Museveni and his ruling party in their dominating position, although the opposition parties complained of a very uneven playing field and alleged fraudulent conduct of the polls. The opposition had, however, failed to agree on a credible united front against the incumbent president and his camp, thus decisively weakening their chances. As a result of fast-rising consumer price inflation and generally worsening living conditions, the government was later faced by growing public discontent and sympathy for opposition protest demonstrations, which were harshly suppressed by the security forces. The government thus lost much credibility, but clearly was able to maintain full control over all public affairs.

The authoritarian domestic political situation in **Rwanda** remained unchanged. President Kagame and his ruling party exerted absolute control over all aspects of public life and firmly suppressed all potentially dissenting voices. Despite the outward appearance of exemplary stability and unity in the political system, clear signs of internal dissension and cracks in the inner circles of the regime that had emerged in 2010 continued to be in evidence. Several former high-ranking Kagame collaborators who had formed an opposition alliance in exile were convicted in absentia in a military court and given long prison sentences, and a potentially credible opposition candidate in the 2010 presidential elections, who had been prevented from standing, continued to be held in prison on charges of having supported a foreign-based terrorist group.

Political life in **Burundi** was still largely influenced by the aftermath of the contested 2010 elections. No reconciliation was yet in sight between President Nkurunziza and his ruling party on the one hand and the alliance of opposition parties that had boycotted the presidential and parliamentary contests on the other. The opposition parties were left in a weak extra-parliamentary position, with their most prominent leaders remaining in exile, while the government secured its position by using the strong-arm tactics of harassment and, allegedly, even the extra-judicial killing of suspected opponents. The general security situation deteriorated, but there was no return of identifiable politically-motivated guerrilla activities, as rumours sometimes had it.

The **Seychelles** had a rather turbulent political year, with noticeably increased confrontation between the government and opposition camps. President Michel was convincingly re-elected in May, but the opposition leader then underscored demands for substantial amendments to the electoral laws by a partial boycott of regular parliamentary work. Surprise early parliamentary elections in October were boycotted by the traditional opposition parties, leaving the field open for an easy win by the long-ruling government party against a fledgling, newly-registered opposition group. Towards the end of the year, however, a more conciliatory climate seemed to re-emerge.

The political scene in **Comoros** was unusually calm and peaceful, after it had for years been habitually fluid and characterised by tensions between the leaders of the three constituent islands of the Union. The rotating presidency cycle had been completed by the election in December 2010 of Ikililou Dhoinine from Mohéli as the new president, but he did not assume office until May in order to allow his predecessor, Ahmed Abdallah Sambi, to complete a five-year term. For the first time in many years, a relatively cooperative style began to emerge.

In the entire **Eastern Africa sub-region**, there were no changes in **Freedom House**'s annual assessment of **political rights** and **civil liberties** in 2011; South Sudan was added as a new entry. While none of the 13 sub-regional countries (plus Somaliland as a separate entity) scored top points (on a scale of 1 at the top to 7) in the 'free' category, seven countries were now listed in the 'not free' category (Djibouti, Eritrea, Ethiopia, Rwanda, Somalia, South Sudan and Sudan). Eritrea, Somalia and Sudan remained among the lowest-rated countries in the world (with scores of 7 for both political rights and civil liberties), while Djibouti, Ethiopia, Rwanda and South Sudan were only slightly better (with scores of 6 for political rights and 5 – or 6 in the case of Ethiopia – for civil liberties). Six countries (plus Somaliland) were categorised as 'partly free' (with both political rights and civil liberties in the 3–5 point range). Among these, Seychelles and Tanzania were again judged the best (with 3 points in both categories), followed by Comoros (3 and 4), Kenya (4 and 3), Somaliland (4 and 5), Uganda (5 and 4) and Burundi (5 and 5).

TI's **Corruption Perceptions Index** for 2011 once again revealed wide discrepancies between the countries of the sub-region. Of the 183 countries listed, Rwanda achieved an outstanding top position with an overall ranking of 49 and a score of 5.0 points (out of 10), thus making a remarkable leap within two years from ranking 89th. The Seychelles remained practically unchanged at 50 with 4.8 points. By contrast, Somalia was again rated as the worst country (ranked 182nd with a score of 1.0), while Sudan (ranked 177th with 1.6 points) and Burundi (172nd with 1.9 points) were also at the very bottom of the list. The remaining countries, like most African countries, ranged somewhere between 3.0 and 2.2 points in the following order: Djibouti and Tanzania (=100th), Ethiopia (120th), Eritrea (134th), Comoros and Uganda (=143rd), Kenya (154th).

Similar divergences between countries were discernible with regard to **press freedom**, as indicated in the 2011 Press Freedom Index by **Reporters Without Borders**. Of 179 listed countries and territories, Eritrea for the fifth year took the last position (scoring 142). Sudan (ranked 170th), Somalia (164th), Djibouti (159th), Rwanda (156th) and Uganda (139th), with scores ranging from 101 to 64, were also judged to be general offenders against the principle of freedom of the media. Djibouti and Uganda fell dramatically by 49 and 43 ranks, respectively. The relatively best marks for press freedom, based on noticeable improvements, were given to Tanzania (ranked 34th, score 6) and Comoros (45th, score 13), while the Seychelles (ranked 73rd), Kenya (84th), South Sudan (111th), Ethiopia (127th) and Burundi (130th) were somewhere in between. Generally speaking, the gap between good and bad performers was widening.

Freedom House's similar **Press Freedom Report** 2012, covering all events in 2011, showed comparable results, but with some notable variations for specific countries. Out of a total of 197 listed countries, six Eastern African countries appeared in the category 'partly free': Comoros (ranked 95th), Tanzania (97th), Kenya (52nd), Seychelles (122nd), Uganda (123rd) and South Sudan (130th). The press situation in the remaining countries was judged to be 'not free', ranking in the following order: Burundi (161st), Djibouti (164th), Sudan (170th), Ethiopia (175th), Rwanda (178th), Somalia (182nd) and Eritrea (194th).

Transnational Relations and Conflict Configurations

Again, no substantial progress was made towards bringing the **Darfur** conflict in **Sudan**, on-going since 2003, closer to a sustainable solution. A peace agreement signed in Qatar between the government and just one rebel faction had no validity for the other groups, and limited fighting continued to occur throughout the year. Over 2 m people were still forced to remain in IDP camps. The large hybrid UN-AU Mission in Sudan (**UNAMID**) was tasked with protecting the civilian population and performing a peacekeeping role, but its effectiveness remained limited and it was not able to suppress continued belligerent activities. New conflict zones emerged after the independence of **South Sudan** along the uncertain border. In the oil-rich **Abyei** area, where a promised referendum to determine its future status was not held, a UN Interim Security Force for Abyei (**UNISFA**) was quickly deployed to prevent the outbreak of full hostilities. In parts of Southern Kordofan and Southern Blue Nile states, local population groups who preferred to be linked with the new South started rebel activities against the authority of Khartoum.

In **South Sudan**, a wave of violent clashes, often traditional cattle raids, between ethnic groups, causing very heavy casualties, threatened to destabilise the new state. The renamed UN Mission in South Sudan (**UNMISS**) was restricted in its mandate and effectiveness and could do little to prevent or suppress these hostilities.

The population in very remote areas in the triangle between **South Sudan**, the **CAR** and the **DRC** continued to be victimised by small remnant groups of the **Lord's Resistance Army** (LRA), which had for many years terrorised large parts of northern **Uganda**, but had now been completely driven out from there. The LRA was no longer a domestic Ugandan issue, but the Ugandan military was still pursuing LRA leader Joseph Kony and his fighters in the CAR and DRC. In November, about 100 American military advisers were deployed to logistically support the national armies in those countries, while the AU also launched an initiative for a concerted effort against the LRA. No tangible success was reported up to the year's end.

Eritrea remained seriously isolated in the sub-region and at loggerheads with all other governments, with the partial exception of **Sudan**. There was still no permanent solution in sight for the border conflicts with either **Ethiopia** (dating from the full-scale 1998–2000 war) or **Djibouti** (partially resolved with Qatari mediation in 2010). There were no open military confrontations along the disputed borders, but still no agreement on mutually accepted frontiers. The Eritrean government continued to be suspected of supporting the radical Islamist groups fighting against the transitional national authorities in **Somalia** and was sceptical of the general international recognition of these authorities. Eritrea's application for re-admission to IGAD, after it had unilaterally suspended its membership in 2007, was rejected.

All neighbouring countries continued to be significantly affected by the on-going insecurity and turmoil in the south-central part of **Somalia**. The Transitional Federal Government (**TFG**) in Mogadishu attempted to slowly widen the scope of its effective authority, but remained fully dependent on security protection by the AU peacekeeping mission (**AMISOM**) and still exerted no real clout over most of Somalian territory, although some modest progress was made. Several radical Islamist groups controlled large parts of the countryside, imposed strict Islamic rules on the population and repeatedly launched armed attacks on installations and representatives of the TFG. Their ultimate aim was to expel the TFG and install an Islamist style of government. With EU and US support, units that would constitute a new national police force and army continued to be trained in neighbouring countries, but had yet to become an effective force against al-Shabaab and other groups. The numerical strength of AMISOM was further increased, with a small contingent from Djibouti augmenting the troops from Burundi and Uganda. In a new move, **Kenya** and, on a much smaller scale, **Ethiopia** also got directly involved by sending troops into Somali territory. **IGAD** repeatedly discussed the Somalia problem at ministerial meetings but, other than eliciting general support for the TFG, was unable to have any significant positive influence.

The threat by **Somali pirates** to international shipping in the Gulf of Aden and along the East African coast remained at an alarmingly high level, but was nevertheless considerably restricted by further intensified and coordinated international anti-piracy activities. Most of the pirates operated from the territory of Puntland, with others based in places in Southern Somalia. The Puntland authorities tried with only limited success to contain piracy activities from their shores. Piracy statistics differed between sources, but clearly indicated a substantial decline. According to some accounts, there were altogether 151 attacks in 2011 (compared with 127 in 2010), but only 25 were successful (compared with 47). By early 2012, ten ships with 159 crew members were reported to be held. It was estimated that $ 146 m were collected in ransoms in 2011 and that about 3,000–5,000 people were operating as pirates. About 1,000 pirates had been captured over the previous five years and were prosecuted in about 20 different countries. About 25 military vessels from EU countries, under NATO command and from China, India, Korea, Japan and Russia, participated in the coordinated anti-piracy surveillance, supplemented by air patrols. **Djibouti, Kenya** and the **Seychelles** were of key importance as support bases for these operations in the sub-region. Kenya and the Seychelles played a valuable role as countries where apprehended pirates could be prosecuted and imprisoned, since there was no trustworthy judiciary in Somalia, although both found this responsibility difficult to fulfil.

Burundi was still affected by the aftermath of the disputed 2010 elections and continuing rumours about the possible return of armed rebel activities, although these were never fully substantiated. The leader of the last former rebel movement was reported to be hiding in the neighbouring **DRC** and to be forging new alliances in preparation for renewed rebel assaults in Burundi. This remained unconfirmed throughout the year, while the government declared a heightened number of ambushes to be simply criminal activity.

The **Great Lakes Region**, with its wide-ranging significance across several national borders, continued to witness the complex interplay of many groups and interests from various countries in the sub-region. On the whole, inter-state relations remained relatively unproblematic, as in 2010, and clearly less tense than had been the case for well over a decade. The governments of the **DRC**, **Rwanda** and **Uganda** maintained quite normal and warm diplomatic relations and managed to cooperate relatively closely in their common attempts to contain the activities of the various militant groups that were a continuing source of insecurity for both state structures and the civilian population. Bilateral relations between Rwanda and Uganda also remained free from renewed set-backs. Belligerent groups, such as the Rwandan *Democratic Forces for the Liberation of Rwanda* (FDLR) and the Ugandan LRA and Allied Democratic Forces (ADF), had long ago retreated into hideouts in the vast, practically uncontrolled territory of the eastern DRC. They remained a potential threat to their countries of origin, although they had lost almost all political motivation and had become brutal criminal gangs. The official Congolese army was still not able or motivated enough to put an end to these rebel activities, so Ugandan and Rwandan military units continued to be allowed, albeit on a very limited scale, to pursue rebels on Congolese territory, although ultimately without lasting success.

UN peacekeeping activities in the sub-region again faced severe constraints. The continued presence in the eastern DRC of the large UN Stabilization Mission in the DRC (**MONUSCO**) had some limited effect in containing an overspill of rebel raids (FDLR, ADF, LRA) into neighbouring East African countries and in stabilising the internal Congolese situation. The gradual reduction of MONUSCO's strength continued. The UN Mission in South Sudan (**UNMISS**) was tasked with monitoring the internal security situation in South Sudan, prior to and after the attainment of full independence. The large hybrid UN-AU Mission in Sudan (**UNAMID**) continued its struggle to satisfactorily fulfil its peacekeeping role in the embattled Darfur region. A new UN Interim Security Force for Abyei (**UNISFA**) was deployed to prevent the outbreak of open hostilities in this border area between North and South Sudan. There was again no serious international support for setting up a UN Mission for Somalia, although this was repeatedly said to be desirable.

The indictment of Sudanese President al-Bashir for crimes against humanity in the Darfur conflict, issued by the **ICC** in 2009, had few practical consequences and only partially restricted his international travel. Most African and Arab governments condemned the ICC move as unjustified and an expression of a one-sided persecution of alleged African perpetrators. Al-Bashir was able to travel to several Arab and African countries without being arrested. The ICC conducted elaborate pre-trial hearings in the cases of six Kenyans (including senior politicians) who had been identified as alleged key culprits of Kenya's 2008 post-election violence, but no decision on formal charges was declared before the year's end.

Socioeconomic Developments

The **macroeconomic performance** of countries in the sub-region was again quite diverse, but on the whole relatively satisfactory. They had, by and large, weathered the effects of the continued global financial and economic crisis better than had initially been feared, although generally experiencing some slow-down. The still relatively limited integration of most countries into the global economic system, particularly the complex financial networks, had proved to be a blessing in disguise. The slow-down nevertheless further retarded progress with respect to most poverty reduction goals, with growth rates well below the scale needed to lay the foundations for a more dynamic economic acceleration and substantial employment generation. Growth rates achieved about the same levels as in 2010.

According to preliminary IMF figures for April 2012, the **2011 GDP growth rate** for sub-Saharan Africa was 5.1% (against 5.3% in 2010). This was again somewhat surpassed by the EAC block (five countries) with a GDP growth of 6.2%, the best EAC performance since 2007. Of all Eastern African countries, Rwanda (8.8%) and Eritrea (8.7%) managed to achieve particularly outstanding growth. Ethiopia (7.5%) experienced just a slight slow-down, but had nevertheless an eighth consecutive year of exceptional growth. Tanzania and Uganda (both 6.7%) also performed quite well, and clearly better than had been projected. Another group of countries was just slightly below the African average: Kenya (5.0%), the Seychelles (4.9%), Djibouti (4.5%) and Burundi (4.2%). Clearly lagging behind, as in most previous years, was Comoros (2.2%). Sudan suffered an absolute GDP decline (-3.9%) as a result of the loss of about two-thirds of its oil production after South Sudan's secession. No reliable GDP figures were available for Somalia and South Sudan.

Most countries officially announced cautious monetary policies and comparatively modest **inflation** targets but, as a result of a new global surge in food prices and oil costs, practically all countries experienced significant average consumer price increases, which in most cases accelerated steeply towards the year's end. The IMF's preliminary estimate of the 2011 average sub-Saharan inflation rate was 8.2% (compared with 7.4% in 2010). The EAC as a group was only slightly above this figure with 9.4%, but by the year's end inflation had jumped to 14.6%. Not surprisingly, the track records of individual countries differed widely, with some far exceeding the continental average. Top of the list with double-digit annual average inflation rates were Ethiopia and Sudan (both 18.1%), Burundi (14.9%), Kenya (14.0%) and Eritrea (13.3%). A clear exception, with only 2.6% inflation, was the Seychelles, where prices in 2010 had even fallen after two years of hyperinflation. The remaining countries had acceptable inflation rates in the 5%–7% range. By the end of 2011, some countries were hit by particularly steep inflation rises: Ethiopia (38.1%), Kenya (18.6%), Uganda (15.7%) and Tanzania (10.9%).

Most countries in the sub-region (except Eritrea and Sudan) had a considerable negative **current-account** balance, in contrast to the only slightly negative sub-Saharan average of –1.8% of GDP (due to surpluses on the part of major oil and mineral exporters, which strongly skew the average). The Seychelles had by far the highest current-account deficit of 21.6% of GDP, with most other countries having a deficit somewhere in the range of 9%–13% of GDP. Eritrea and Ethiopia had an almost balanced account, while Sudan showed a surplus of 2.1% of GDP due to its oil exports.

A good measure for the intensity of domestic development efforts, without simply relying on the inflow of aid funds, is the volume of **government revenue** (excluding grants and expressed as a percentage of GDP). Most of the countries in the sub-region remained somewhat below the yardstick of the sub-Saharan 2011 average of 27.5%. The EAC as a group achieved only 19.0%, which was nevertheless a continuing improvement over previous years. The Seychelles (37.9%), in line with a long-standing past record, Djibouti

(28.5%) and Kenya (24.5%) were able to demonstrate high domestic revenue generation. In contrast, disappointingly low rates obtained in Uganda (13.3%), Ethiopia (13.7%), Eritrea (14.2%), Rwanda (14.6%), Sudan (15.1%), Burundi (15.4%), Comoros and Tanzania (both 16.5%). All these countries (except Eritrea) relied to a large extent on the influx of external funds (in very different forms) to meet governmental expenditure.

UNDP's 2011 **HDI** again clearly highlighted considerable variations in the sub-region in respect of general socioeconomic development levels. With the exception of the Seychelles, all other Eastern African countries (out of a total of 187) appeared in the low human development category. The Seychelles, with an HDI value of 0.773 and ranked 52nd, was by far the highest-ranked African country in the high human development category. Kenya (HDI value 0.509, 143rd) and Tanzania (152nd) had a somewhat higher HDI value than the sub-Saharan average of 0.463, while Uganda (161st), Comoros (163rd), Djibouti (165th), Rwanda (166th), Sudan (169th), Ethiopia (174th), Eritrea (177th) and Burundi (185th, the third-lowest) showed a lower-than-average HDI value. Somalia and South Sudan were not listed in the 2011 HDI.

Sub-regional Cooperation and Sub-regional Organisations

The **EAC** held its 9th extraordinary **summit** on 19 April in Dar es Salaam. Upon the expiry of Juma Mwapachu's five-year term as secretary-general, Richard Sezibera from Rwanda was appointed as new head of the EAC secretariat after several months of excited media discussions about a fierce Kenyan challenge for the post. Enos Bukuku from Tanzania was appointed as new deputy secretary-general. The main topics of discussion were food security, climate change and the Somalia problem. A report by a team of experts on fears, concerns and challenges facing the political federation was found inadequate with regard to practical recommendations, and the team was asked to submit a revised report to the next summit. A parallel EAC Investment Forum attracted over 900 participants.

At the 13th ordinary **EAC summit** on 30 November in Bujumbura, the rotating chairmanship passed from Burundi's President Nkurunziza to Kenya's President Kibaki. Important discussions centred on the possible enlargement of the EAC. Sudan's membership application, submitted on 10 June, was rejected because Sudan did not meet several key requirements. Prior to the summit, it had become clear that Tanzania and Uganda were opposed to the admission of Sudan, while Rwanda supported it. South Sudan's application of 11 November was in principle welcomed, but a decision was deferred until the conclusion of a formal assessment procedure by the council of ministers. The undeniable progress of the EAC also seemed to make membership, or at least observer status, attractive to several other neighbouring countries. Ethiopia, Somalia, Comoros and the DRC were occasionally mentioned as showing an interest, but this was as yet far from official.

Tanzania caused some consternation ahead of the **Bujumbura summit**, when its delegation declined at the last moment to sign a report already agreed by the council of ministers on the future course of integration and progress towards a political federation. Sensitive issues were land ownership, defence cooperation and the use of passports and/or ID papers for intra-regional travel. Only after some amendments agreed by the presidents at the summit was Tanzania eventually willing to sign up to compromise formulations. This incident reaffirmed the widely held perception that Tanzania was the most reluctant member of the EAC and was responsible for constantly slowing down moves towards faster integration. Tanzanian politicians, however, stressed their continued full support for the EAC, but warned against too much fast-tracking and advocated a cautious, gradual approach.

A particularly ambitious goal remained the establishment of a **Monetary Union** as the next stage in integration. A high-level task force was launched in January with a mandate to prepare the technical ground for such a move by mid-2012 but, as time went by, a growing number of sceptical voices warned against making a precipitous decision. The East African Business Council, as well as many other critics, repeatedly pointed out the slow progress on the concrete implementation of the requirements of both the **Customs Union** and the **Common Market** Protocols. Many of the relevant regulations had still not been transformed into national legislation, and bureaucratic hurdles and a host of non-tariff barriers continued to prevent the formation of a genuine Common Market. Despite these obvious shortcomings, the EAC was generally regarded as a role model for Regional Economic Communities in Africa, far ahead of other organisations.

The new **EAC budget** for 2011–12, amounting to $ 110 m showed a steep 41% increase over the previous approved budget. Of this sum, 46% were allocated to the EAC secretariat in Arusha, 40.5% to the Lake Victoria Basin Commission, 10.5% to the East African Legislative Assembly and 3% to the East African Court of Justice. About two-thirds of the total were expected to come from contributions from external development partners. In September, a joint EAC-US **military exercise** was conducted in Zanzibar. Again no substantial progress was made on the protracted issue of signing a full **EPA** with the **EU**; a resumption of technical-level discussions in September still did not lead to a satisfactory conclusion of this long-expected trade pact and full negotiations were further postponed into 2012.

The 14th **COMESA** summit was held on 14–15 October in Lilongwe, Malawi. Malawi's President Mutharika assumed the rotating chairmanship from Swaziland's King Mswati III. Lilongwe had been COMESA's birthplace, where the PTA, with Mutharika as general secretary, had in 1974 been transformed into COMESA. Other than the host, only five heads of state attended the meeting, and no member state offered to host the next summit in 2012. Prior to the summit, the 30th ministerial council and other policy organs met to deliberate on the wide range of COMESA's cooperation activities. The main focus was on progress during the three-year transition period for the attainment of the **COMESA Customs Union** by mid-2012. All 19 member states were expected by then to have aligned their national tariffs with a common external tariff. The DRC became the twentieth member of the **PTA Bank**, which had still not relocated its headquarter from Nairobi to its official location in Bujumbura.

The ambitious plan of creating a **Grand Tripartite FTA** made up of all 26 member states of COMESA, EAC and SADC, stretching from the Cape to Cairo, received further high-level political backing through a second summit on 12 June in Johannesburg, a follow-up to an earlier 2008 summit in Kampala. The summit adopted a roadmap for the establishment of an eventual **single FTA**, with detailed negotiations expected to begin in early 2012 on the basis of preliminary studies that had already been carried out by a number of expert groups. The various overlapping memberships of individual countries in different sub-regional organisations made the intended move extremely difficult. It was estimated that the first preparatory phase would extend over 24–36 months. The longer-term goals centred on three distinct pillars: trade and services, infrastructure and industrialisation. A Tripartite and IGAD infrastructure investment conference on 28–29 October in Nairobi was also regarded as a step in that direction.

The **International Conference on the Great Lakes Region (ICGLR)** held its 4th ordinary summit and a special session on sexual and gender-based violence on 15–16 December in Kampala. Uganda's President Museveni assumed the chairmanship from Zambia's President Sata for a two-year term, and Ntumba Luamba from the DRC was appointed as the new executive secretary upon the expiry of the term of the Tanzanian Liberata Mulamula. The well-attended summit adopted a declaration against all forms of sexual violence and discussed proposals for the establishment of an intelligence fusion centre in Goma, DRC, to enable better coordination of joint efforts against all "negative forces" in the crisis-prone region. Reviewing her five years in office, Mulamula pointed out that the security situation had significantly improved, although many problems undoubtedly still existed. An expected membership application from South Sudan had so far not been made.

Little tangible progress was made towards the revitalisation of the **'Communauté Économique des Pays des Grands Lacs' (CEPGL)**, which had been on-going since 2007, mostly with support from Belgium and the EU. A meeting of the Burundian, Rwandan and Congolese foreign ministers in late July in Bujumbura was considered as an important step in the reinvigoration of the CEPGL, but a tentatively planned summit, the first since 1994, did not materialise. The ministers gave priority to the need for better cooperation with regard to energy and infrastructure. A conference of parliamentary presidents from the three member countries and Belgium in mid-March in Kigali emphasised the question of peace and security in the region. High-ranking defence officials from the member states met occasionally to compare strategies against the so-called "negative forces" present in the east of the DRC.

IGAD's top organs remained mostly occupied by deliberations on the political situations in Somalia and Sudan, but also dealt with the exceptional drought situation and with Eritrea. Summit meetings were held on 31 January, 4 July and 25 November in Addis Ababa. At the last, South Sudan was officially admitted as a new member. In July, Eritrea made an attempt to break out of its isolation and to seek re-admission to the organisation, which it had left unilaterally in 2007. First reactions from the IGAD secretariat were positive, but this was quickly reversed. On 24 August, an Eritrean diplomat was ejected from a ministerial council meeting in Addis Ababa, and it was decreed that the application for re-admission should follow appropriate rules and procedures. The antagonistic attitude towards Eritrea on the part of Ethiopia, which held the IGAD chairmanship, had clearly prevailed. IGAD repeatedly expressed full support for Somalia's struggling transitional government, endorsed Kenya's operation against the al-Shabaab militia and attempted to have a moderating influence on the rising tensions between Sudan and South Sudan.

Moderate further progress was made towards the establishment of the **Eastern Africa Standby Force (EASF)** as a component of the AU's envisaged African Standby Force. The 11th policy organs meetings of the chiefs of defence and the council of ministers were held in mid-September in Victoria, Seychelles. The political chairmanship of the 14-member grouping (with four countries, including Eritrea and Tanzania, not actively participating) was passed on from Djibouti to Ethiopia. Guided by its Nairobi-based Coordinating Mechanism (EASFCOM), plans were pursued to achieve full capacity (with military, police and civilian elements) by 2015. EASFCOM provided some technical assistance to AMISOM in Somalia.

The **IOC** held its 27th ministerial council meeting on 6 October in Port Louis, Mauritius, where the rotating presidency was assumed by the Seychelles. The IOC's activities remained very modest, mostly concentrating on some technical cooperation programmes with EU support. The current focus was mainly on the piracy problem. A new regional anti-piracy unit was to be set up in the Seychelles with EU funding.

The Seychelles was re-admitted as the nineteenth member of the **IOR-ARC** during its 11th ministerial council meeting on 15 November in Bangalore, India, subsequent to its withdrawal from the organisation in 2003 due to foreign exchange shortages. India maintained the two-year chairmanship and provided a new secretary-general. India and Australia in particular appeared interested in giving some new impetus to this almost moribund organisation, with its rather disparate membership. Piracy and maritime security were main topics of the ministerial deliberations, with other focus areas identified as environmental cooperation, fisheries, tourism, academic exchange and trade and investment.

There was still no formal conclusion of the protracted negotiations for a new consensus treaty on the shared utilisation of the water resources of the Nile river system by all riparian states. The water ministers of the **Nile Basin Initiative (NBI)** member states held their 19th council meeting on 28 July in Nairobi, again stressing the urgency of concluding the outstanding issues for agreement on a Cooperative Framework Agreement (CFA) that would provide for the intended establishment of a fully-fledged Nile River Basin Commission. South Sudan was seeking to change its observer status to regular NBI membership. On 28 February, Burundi had become the sixth country (out of nine NBI members) to sign the CFA text that had been agreed by five upstream countries in May 2010; although in principle expected to do so, the DRC had still not signed the text by the year's end. With Burundi's signature, the way was cleared for the ratification of the CFA by the national parliaments and thus the loss of Egypt's power of veto against changes to the historical water rights formulated in colonial-era treaties in 1929 and 1959. All upstream countries had long been adamant that they would no longer be constrained in making fuller use of the water resources. The post-Mubarak Egyptian government pursued a more conciliatory approach in its discussions with the upstream countries – particularly with Ethiopia, in view of its huge dam construction plans on the Blue Nile.

Rolf Hofmeier

Burundi

The year was marked by the aftermath of the 2010 elections. Political developments and rising insecurity were closely related to the continued contestation of these elections and their impact on the functioning of several political parties. Attempts at consolidating the dominant position of the ruling 'Conseil National pour la Défense de la Démocratie-Forces pour la Défense de la Démocratie' (CNDD-FDD) gave rise to a further restriction of the political space for opposition parties and civil society movements. New self-proclaimed rebel movements did not constitute a significant threat for the incumbent government's control over Burundian territory. The UN presence in Burundi was extended for another year. Burundi continued and increased its engagement with the AU Mission to Somalia. The year also saw the launch of the activities of the Independent National Human Rights Commission and the Office of the Ombudsman. The number of extrajudicial executions was on the rise. Further steps were taken to prepare the establishment of a national Truth and Reconciliation Commission in early 2012. Hunger levels remained alarming. Burundi considerably improved its ranking in the World Bank's Doing Business Report. The recently established Burundi Revenue Office contributed to a significant increase in domestic revenue collection.

Domestic Politics

While control of the legislative and the executive branches of government by the **CNDD-FDD** – a direct outcome of the party's overwhelming victory at the 2010 general elections – resulted in a fair degree of stability within the institutions, most of the political debate was relocated and taken out of the regular political institutions, with political opposition parties requesting a political dialogue with the government and self-proclaimed rebel movements announcing renewed armed insurgence "in order to liberate the country from a dictatorial regime".

The **government** of President Pierre Nkurunziza continued to be composed in a manner that was fully in accordance with the Constitution, reflecting the country's ethnic diversity and including members of all three political parties represented in parliament. However, this – formally speaking – coalition government, made up of 21 cabinet members, was strongly dominated by the CNDD-FDD, leaving little room for 'Union pour le Progrès National' (UPRONA) with one vice-president and three ministers, and 'Front pour la Démocratie au Burundi Nyakuri' (an offshoot of the 'original' FRODEBU, led by its former chairman Jean Minani) with one minister, to have an influence on government policy. Nevertheless, as noted below, UPRONA did publicly express a divergent opinion on a number of occasions. The government was reshuffled in early November, with the appointment of eight new ministers. Important newcomers were Minister of Foreign Affairs Laurent Kavakure and Minister of Public Security Gabriel Nizigama. However, continuity prevailed as their predecessors were appointed to crucial positions in the president's office. Former foreign affairs minister Augustin Nsanze became the president's senior advisor on political and diplomatic affairs, while former public security minister Alain Guillaume Bunyoni became the president's civil chief of staff, replacing Clotilde Niragira who was appointed minister of national solidarity, human rights and gender.

Parliament convened in regular sessions, conducting legislative work but – not surprisingly, in light of the fact that the CNDD-FDD had more than two-thirds of the seats in both the National Assembly and the Senate – there was little significant parliamentary control over government action. As the three parties represented in parliament were also included in the government, there was no parliamentary opposition.

Of all of the legislation adopted in parliament, the **law on political parties** was no doubt among the most controversial. As of early 2011, a total of 44 political parties had registered, some 23 of which had participated in the 2010 local elections while several others presumably only existed on paper. According to the government, legislation was needed in order to rationalise the party political landscape and to reduce the number of political parties. According to the (extra-parliamentary) opposition, the hidden objective of the government was to undermine and starve the opposition and to isolate opposition party leaders in exile from their constituencies, thus contributing to the de facto return to one-party rule. In one of the contested provisions, the new law stipulated that coalitions between political parties were only possible at the time of elections, not outside that period. Furthermore, public funding of political parties by the State was henceforth limited to those parties represented in parliament. Also, all parties must have at least 20 registered members in each of the 17 provinces of Burundi and the party leadership must be resident on Burundian territory. In case of serious violations of these and other provisions by a political party, the Supreme Court might dissolve it at the request of the minister of internal affairs. The law required that all political parties submit a declaration of conformity to the minister of internal affairs by early 2012. Because all opposition parties felt targeted by the new legislation, they announced they would not meet this requirement.

Within the **CNDD-FDD**, the position of President Nkurunziza – directly elected by the Burundian population – and a group of army generals loyal to him had clearly been reinforced as a result of the 2010 elections. Nevertheless, the party faced important internal dissension at a very senior level. In February, Manassé Nzobonimpa, the executive secretary of the party's Council of the Wise, the most important advisory group to Nkurunziza, and a member of the East African Legislative Assembly, denounced widespread corruption and embezzlement of public goods by senior party officials. He also revealed the existence of death squads within the presidential police. More specifically, he accused the party chairman, Jeremie Ngendakumana, Minister of Finance Clotile Nizigama, the then Minister of Education Saidi Kibeya and leading party member, Mohamed Rukara, who in the meantime had been appointed as Ombudsman, of transferring $ 13 m into their personal bank accounts in 2007. They had allegedly received this money from the Ugandan government when it reimbursed a debt to Burundi. In June, Nzobonimpa narrowly escaped death after a violent assault in Kampala, Uganda. The internal dissension did not spread within the party, however, and central control over the party was re-established by the end of the year.

In a rare demonstration of political independence vis-à-vis the dominant party, **UPRONA**, CNDD-FDD's main partner in the coalition government, requested a parliamentary commission of inquiry into the allegations made by Nzobonimpa. However, new internal divisions that had come to light one year after a reunification congress of the party in August 2009 continued to undermine and weaken the party. The conflict between, on the one hand, party members loyal to party chairman Bonaventure Niyoyankana and former president Pierre Buyoya – both of whom insisted on the need to collaborate as smoothly as possible with the ruling party – and, on the other, a wing ('le Courant de la Réhabilitation') that wished to see the party develop into a critical opponent of the dominant party, further escalated. In August, three senior 'dissident' executive committee members of the party were suspended. In December, one party member died during a violent confrontation at the party premises in Bujumbura. Despite these internal difficulties and the chairman's desire to align himself with the CNDD-FDD, UPRONA expressed divergent opinions vis-à-vis CNDD-FDD on transitional justice and on the strategy to curb rising insecurity (see below).

The question of whether or not to have a **political dialogue** between the government and the opposition dominated the political landscape throughout the year. After the May 2010 municipal (or communal) elections, a group of 12 opposition parties – including the 'Forces Nationales de Libération' (**FNL**) of Agathon Rwasa (leader of the former FNL rebel movement) and **FRODEBU** – had set up an 'Alliance des Démocrates pour le Changement au Burundi' (**ADC-Ikibiri**). This opposition alliance continued to function throughout the year, despite clear difficulties, both within the individual ADC-Ikibiri parties and at the level of the coalition as a whole. The debate around the need for a political dialogue or political negotiations largely amounted to a shadow game, both parties to the debate playing 'hide and seek' as part of their political strategy. On the one hand, ADC-Ikibiri, both in Burundi and through their diaspora representatives, regularly insisted on a political dialogue with the government. However, it was not exactly clear what its demands or expectations were. Initially, it had insisted on the annulment of the elections, but it gradually came to realise that, without the support of the international community, such a demand stood no chance. ADC-Ikibiri denied that it was simply asking for political posts for opposition party leaders. It also denied any intention to engage in a renewed armed conflict against the government. At the same time, however, it attributed the rising insecurity (see below) to an armed insurgency against the government which, in its view, would only cease its activities if a genuine political dialogue took place between the government and the extra-parliamentary opposition. This somewhat contradictory position – alleging the existence of a nascent rebellion and its political motivation, but denying any involvement with it, yet arguing that political talks were needed with ADC-Ikibiri to reduce insecurity – was received with great scepticism by the government and by Burundi's international partners. It was probably also related to divergent strategies advocated within the ADC-Ikibiri by its political leaders who had, after all, been political opponents until the 2010 local elections but 'suddenly' found themselves setting up an alliance with fellow 'enemies' of their common 'enemy'.

In November, a report of the UN Group of Experts on the DRC identified a number of opposition politicians in exile as political leaders of a renewed FNL rebellion operating on Congolese territory. On the other hand, as far as the position of the government was concerned, there was an almost constant denial of the existence of an **armed rebellion** with a political agenda. Yet again, the government rejected engaging in a political dialogue with opposition parties it openly accused of establishing and/or supporting an armed rebellion. Furthermore, the government felt that the opposition was itself to blame. Had they participated in the legislative elections, opposition parties would have been able to conduct political activity in parliament. The government therefore rejected any kind of dialogue that might give rise to a renegotiation of the results of the 2010 elections. At the same time, the government's position was also somewhat contradictory. For instance, while Nkurunziza publicly called on opposition leaders in exile to return to the country, an arrest warrant against one of them, Alexis Sinduhije ('Mouvement pour la Solidarité et la Démocratie',

MSD) was issued in January, accusing him of endangering the security of the state. Also, in May, Nkurunziza warned that all those responsible for post-election violence were to be brought to trial. Furthermore, especially when facing demands from international community representatives for some kind of talks with the opposition, the government referred to the existing framework of the 'Political Parties Forum', which the opposition rejected as mere window-dressing, the Forum in their view being fully controlled by CNDD-FDD. In November, the president launched a campaign for the promotion and reinforcement of democratic culture in Burundi and called upon all political actors to look forward and to prepare for the 2015 general elections. In line with its earlier successful attempts at internally dividing the opposition, the government also further organised the hand-over of the **FNL** leadership from Agathon Rwasa to Emmanuel Miburo. Probably at the instigation of the CNDD-FDD, the 'Union pour la Paix et le Développement' (**UPD-Zigamigamba**), one of the ADC-Ikibiri coalition members, was also internally divided, in particular around the question of political dialogue. In May, a leadership conflict arose between Chauvineau Mugwengezo and Zedi Feruzi, the latter announcing the party's withdrawal from the ADC-Ikibiri opposition coalition.

It was hard to deny that the political tension and the lack of political dialogue were reflected on the ground, with **insecurity rising considerably**, particularly from May to September. However, this was exactly what the government tried to do most of the time. Breaches of security, the factual occurrence of which it could not deny, were attributed to armed banditry, poor disarmament of former rebel combatants and land conflicts. An exceptional 'slip of the tongue' by Minister of Defence Gaciyubwenge (UPRONA), acknowledging the existence of pockets of armed insurgency in Bujumbura Rural province, was not endorsed by the government in later statements. The **National Security Council**, an advisory body in charge of assisting the president on a variety of public security related issues, convened and issued public statements in August and September. Also, quite exceptionally, in October the government published a 45–page memorandum on the security situation, which denounced certain media and civil society groups for presenting an excessively negative picture of the security situation and, in so doing, even exacerbating political tension. The memorandum also outlined the measures the government had already taken to reduce insecurity (arrests of armed bandits, sensitisation of the population, continued disarmament of former rebels). In early September, the human rights organisation 'Association pour la Protection des Droits Humains et des Personnes Détenues au Burundi' had accused the government of launching an extermination plan called *Safisha* ('to clean' in Swahili) against its opponents. This was based on evidence that FNL and MSD party members throughout the country were targeted and either arrested, killed or made to disappear. On several occasions, corpses had been found floating on rivers.

Insecurity reached its climax when 36 civilians were killed by gunmen at a bar in the village of **Gatumba**, near Bujumbura and close to the border between Burundi and the DRC. This new Gatumba massacre led to general fear among people in the capital city, not least because it symbolically reminded people of the earlier Gatumba massacre of August 2004, when at least 150 Congolese refugees, mostly ethnic Tutsi (Banyamulenge), were assassinated. No one had ever been brought to justice for that massacre. Again, although a trial of 21 suspected perpetrators was opened in November, there was little hope that truth of the new Gatumba massacre would ever be told. Speculative explanations ranged from a government-led operation, to a failed attempt at arresting Agathon Rwasa, to an operation of a revived FNL rebellion, and a first raid by a new rebel movement based across the border in eastern DRC.

At least **two armed insurgencies** announced a war against the government, in particular against the intelligence service 'Service National de Renseignements' (SNR) and the CNDD-FDD youth division (or, in their perception, 'youth militia') Imbonerakure. It remained very hard, however, to confirm the existence of these movements on the ground, with little evidence of clashes between government forces and insurgents to prove their alleged capacity to topple the regime. In May, one rebel movement identified itself as the 'Front National pour la Révolution au Burundi' (FRONABU-TABARA) and was allegedly based in eastern DRC. A French television ('France 24') documentary interviewed the self-proclaimed leader of the rebel movement, 'General' Moïse, which nearly led to a diplomatic incident between Burundi and France. The government immediately rejected what it considered to be pure manipulation based on information provided to the journalist by opposition leaders in exile. In November, a second rebel movement identified itself as the 'Forces pour la Restauration de la Démocratie' (FRD-Abanyagihuhu), under the leadership of Colonel Kabirigi, a former CNDD-FDD rebel, and with its base in the eastern Cankuzo province, near the Tanzanian border. It published a memorandum and launched a website in order to 'prove' its existence. On the ground, despite some attacks on police stations for which they claimed responsibility, neither of the two armed movements constituted a significant security threat to the national security forces.

The **human rights** record of the government continued to receive strong domestic and international criticism, despite some positive developments. In January, the minister of internal affairs lifted the 2009 ban on the 'Forum pour le Renforcement de la Société Civile'. However, throughout the year, some **civil society** groups were targeted by the government and the intelligence service. After having submitted the names of top officials it considered most responsible for corruption to the G8 summit, asking the participants at the summit no longer to grant visas to those listed, the corruption watchdog 'Observatoire de Lutte contre la Corruption et les Malversations Économiques' was threatened with suspension by the minister of internal affairs. 'Net Press' journalist Jean-Claude Kavumbagu, who had been arrested on charges of defamation and treason in July 2010, was acquitted in May. Nevertheless, while **media** freedom remained generally safeguarded, some restrictions were imposed that particularly targeted radio stations critical of the CNDD-FDD dominated government. In the aftermath of the Gatumba massacre in September, a media black-out was imposed on all radio stations for one month. On a number of occasions, **lawyers**, some of whom were seen as siding with the opposition, were intimidated and arrested.

As far as institutional safeguards for human rights protection were concerned, the establishment of the **Independent National Human Rights Commission** in May was widely welcomed, including by the opposition, civil society and Burundi's international partners. After a lengthy parliamentary debate, the National Assembly appointed seven commissioners representative of Burundi's ethnic and regional diversity and a chairman, Father Emmanuel Ntakarutimana, whose expertise, independence and impartiality was widely recognised. However, this institutional progress was not immediately reflected on the ground. Both the final report of the UN Independent Expert on the human rights situation in Burundi – whose mandate was ended in September by the UN Human Rights Council – and the December report of the UN Secretary-General on the UN Office in Burundi expressed great concern at the high number of politically motivated killings and urged the government to urgently take all necessary steps to bring to justice the members of the defence and security forces and others suspected of having perpetrated gross human rights violations. HRW and other international human rights organisations particularly criticised the role played by the SNR. In a remarkable joint note addressed to the minister of foreign affairs in early June, most diplomatic missions – some representing countries (Netherlands, France, Belgium) that collaborated with the police and the army – expressed concern at the rising number of reported **extrajudicial executions**.

In the field of **transitional justice**, some progress was made. A high-level delegation visited the UN High Commissioner for Human Rights in Geneva in May. In June, the president set up a Technical Committee charged with preparing for the establishment of transitional justice mechanisms. This was met with great scepticism by civil society organisations, who saw the Committee – chaired by Laurent Kavakure who soon after became minister of foreign affairs – as an instrument of the president's office. The Committee submitted its report in October, including a bill on the establishment, mandate and functioning of a Truth and Reconciliation Commission (TRC). Contrary to demands by the UN and civil society organisations, the Committee proposed the establishment of a strictly national commission (with an international consultative council rather than foreign commissioners), a position not shared by UPRONA. The Committee also suggested delaying the establishment of a Special Tribunal for Burundi until the TRC had completed its activities. It was proposed the TRC should be established in early 2012 in order to complete its activities before the 2015 electoral campaign. In his Address to the Nation on 31 December, Nkurunziza announced that 2012 would be marked by three special events, including the establishment of a TRC, as a final step marking the end of Burundi's peace process.

In January, the office of the **Ombudsman** started operating. Despite criticisms related to the close links between Ombudsman Mohammed Rukara, a member of the

CNDD-FDD Council of the Wise, and Nkurunziza, his initial interventions solving a dispute between the authorities and motorcyclists taxi-drivers were generally appreciated.

Foreign Affairs

As requested by the government and in accordance with a UNSC Resolution adopted in December 2010, the UN downsized its presence in Burundi from January onwards, reducing its international staff from around 450 to some 60 in-country personnel. The **UN Office in Burundi** ('Bureau des Nations Unies au Burundi', BNUB) was led by UN Secretary-General Special Representative (SGSR) Karin Landgren. In contrast to the experience of her predecessors, relations between the UN SGSR and the government were remarkably smooth. On 20 December, the UNSC extended the BNUB mandate until 15 February 2013. Two new components were added to the BNUB mandate: support for the socioeconomic development of women and youth, in particular conflict-affected populations, and support for Burundi's regional integration.

The **UN Peace-building Commission** (PBC) continued its engagement with Burundi. In April, the PBC produced the Outcome Document of the fifth review of the implementation of the Strategic Framework for Peace-building in Burundi. In November, the chair of the PBC's Burundi configuration visited Bujumbura. The PBC committed itself to continued support in a number of areas, including the organisation of a stocktaking exercise to draw lessons from the 2010 elections, and support for the implementation of the zero tolerance policy against corruption, the socioeconomic reintegration of vulnerable groups and regional integration.

After an international conference on Somalia had been held in Bujumbura in November 2010, Burundi increased its contribution to the **AU Mission to Somalia** (AMISOM). In March, an additional 1,000 troops were sent, raising the number of Burundian peacekeepers to around 4,500. This was part of a wider effort by the AU to increase the contingent to 12,000 by the end of the year. Following combat against militia in Mogadishu in October, and after considerable confusion about the number of casualties, the minister of defence announced that ten Burundian soldiers had been killed and some 18 others wounded.

Relations between Burundi and its neighbouring countries remained generally friendly. Nkurunziza met his counterpart President Kagame of **Rwanda** on several occasions. The 13th ordinary summit of the **EAC** heads of state convened in Bujumbura in November. On that occasion, the government established an inter-ministerial committee on the integration of Burundi into the EAC. Nkurunziza handed over the chairmanship of the EAC to Kenya's President Kibaki. In July, a meeting of the ministers of foreign affairs of the member states of the 'Communauté Économique des Pays des Grands Lacs' **(CEPGL)** was held in Bujumbura. Burundi continued to be a member of the **Peace and Security Council (PSC)** of the **AU**, having started its mandate in April 2010. In August, Burundi took over the chairmanship of the PSC.

South Africa's President Jacob Zuma visited Burundi for three days in August, signing a number of cooperation agreements in the education, agriculture and energy sectors. Burundi intensified its relations with **China**. In February, an important delegation of the CNDD-FDD visited Beijing. In June, additional cooperation agreements were signed, increasing China's support for the education sector. The **UK** Department for International Development announced it would end its bilateral cooperation programme by the end of 2013. In December, the government announced that Burundi was about to open a new embassy in **Iran**. Although a mid-term review of its cooperation programme with Burundi was due before the end of the year, **Belgium** did not make a decision on the release of a € 50 m incentive tranche (amounting to an extra 33% on top of its regular aid budget), the payment of which depended on a number of political governance conditions, including the adoption of a national governance strategy. During a visit in June, the Belgian minister of foreign affairs expressed concern that some of the conditions might not be met. The government invited the king of Belgium – Burundi's former tutelage authority – to attend the celebrations of the country's 50th anniversary of accession to independence on 1 July 1962.

Socioeconomic Developments

In the 2011 **Global Hunger Index**, Burundi was listed 80th out of 81 countries ranked on the basis of three key indicators (calorie deficiency, underweight children under five, child mortality rate). Burundi was one of the four countries where hunger levels were rated as "extremely alarming".

In July, Nkurunziza launched **Vision 2025**, which presented a road map for sustainable development through accelerated growth and comprised eight pillars (governance, human capital, economic growth, regional integration, population growth, social cohesion and land use planning). Preparations continued for the adoption of a second **Poverty Reduction Strategy Paper**, which was to include the Strategic Framework for Peace-building, but no final text was adopted.

In the World Bank's 2012 **Doing Business Report**, Burundi rose from 177th place to 169th. The improvement was particularly due to improved protection for investors and the adoption of a new companies act. A **Land Code** was adopted in April. This provided for an increased decentralisation of land use policy. With the support of UNDP and UN Habitat, the policy of the creation of villages ('villagisation') was further refined.

Judges and other justice sector personnel went on strike in February and in September and October, protesting against low salaries and lack of judicial independence. A new **justice sector** policy document was drafted by the minister of justice.

In September, a national plan of action against the proliferation of **small arms and light weapons** was launched, including a programme of accelerated disarmament of the civilian population.

In December, the national **budget for 2012** was adopted in the National Assembly, including a 32% increase in capital expenditure. While tax levels were left unchanged, the budget provided for an increase in revenue by over 18% compared with the 2011 budget. This was, in part, based on the expected benefits generated by the continued good performance of the 'Office Burundais des Recettes', which led to a 30% increase in domestic revenue collection over 2010.

Macroeconomic performance was marked by a small increase in real **GDP growth** to 4%. Consumer price **inflation** for the year averaged at 9.6%. A sharp increase in the price of electricity and water was likely to increase inflation in 2012.

Stef Vandeginste

Comoros

After years of political unrest and uncertainty over the institutional structure of the 'Union des Comores', 2011 turned out to be relatively calm and restored an unaccustomed degree of political normalcy. Ikililou Dhoinine from Mohéli island had been elected as new president in December 2010, but only took office in late May after an unusually long interim period that allowed his predecessor, Ahmed Abdallah Sambi, to hang on to power. The smooth handover exemplified an undisputed continuity between representatives of the same political camp. The contentious Mayotte issue and ambivalent relations with France continued to dominate the foreign policy front. There was a modest improvement and stabilisation of the economic situation, but no progress on substantial structural reforms.

Domestic Politics

On 13 January, the Constitutional Court officially confirmed the results of the **presidential and gubernatorial elections** held on 26 December 2010, despite noting some irregularities, specifically in Anjouan. Four external observer missions also judged the elections to have been "generally free and fair". **President-elect Dhoinine** was to be the third Union president under the 2001 Fomboni constitution, thus bringing the rotation principle between the three islands to its conclusion and ending fears in Mohéli, the smallest island, of being bypassed. **Outgoing President Sambi** had finally succeeded in his goal of harmonising the election calendar for the Union presidency and the island governors. New governors aligned to Sambi's political camp had also been elected in Anjouan and Ngazidja (Grande Comore), thus raising prospects for more amicable cooperation in future between Union and island authorities, which had in the past been severely marred by constant quarrelling. Only in Mohéli had the sitting governor and opponent of Sambi been re-elected, but he subsequently pledged support for Dhoinine as the island's favourite son.

In accordance with the June 2010 agreement on an interim government of national unity, Sambi and Dhoinine were to decide within 15 days on the date of the actual **handover of power** (also of the governors). Their amicable agreement "in the best interest of the country" to set the handover for **26 May**, the latest possible date, confirmed the widely-held perception of Dhoinine as a mere disciple of the still dominant president. This allowed Sambi a full five-year term instead of his original four-year mandate and led to speculation about emerging tensions and Sambi's true ambition to remain an influential background force. The expression of such sentiments and criticism of the extra costs were met by an official crackdown, including charges against two journalists for alleged "false reports" and the dismissal of the editor of the leading newspaper 'Al-Watwan'. Sambi thus stayed in full control for five months after election day, while Dhoinine remained in the background and in February undertook a private visit to France to meet members of the large Comorian diaspora, but the **long interim period** nevertheless led to symptoms of standstill in some areas of public administration. Popular protests in the capital Moroni in March over demolitions and land rights in connection with port extension works led to the removal of the mayor and the withdrawal of the French contractor.

Dhoinine's **presidential inauguration** on 26 May turned out to be a relatively low-key event with only one foreign head of state, from Madagascar, in attendance and with somewhat deficient protocol arrangements. Three days earlier the **new island governors**, Anissi Chamsidine in Anjouan and Mouigni Baraka in Ngazidja, were at last installed in their posts, while Mohéli's re-installed governor Mohamed Ali Said promised to support Dhoinine, despite having been in the opposition camp during the election campaign. These ceremonies completed the long-disputed full election cycle of the Comorian Union and seemed to augur well for more continuity and stability in conformity with the constitution and for fewer inter-island disputes than in the past.

On 30 May, Dhoinine presented a **cabinet** to prove his independence and to contradict the allegations that he was simply following in Sambi's footsteps. The three vice-presidents (one from each island) were given responsibilities for the key portfolios in a cabinet of ten ministers and four deputy ministers (including three women). Only two members of Sambi's team were retained, but some of his close associates from Anjouan were given posts as advisors. The new governors similarly appointed their own administrative heads for the islands. As a first visible demonstration of fresh initiative, Dhoinine in mid-June promulgated **anti-corruption legislation** that had been passed by parliament in 2008 but had not been signed by Sambi. New anti-corruption commissions for the Union and the islands were quickly installed in August. In July, first signs of tensions within the political alliance of Sambi's and Dhoinine's baobab camp and the orange camp in Ngazidja emerged, but remained largely inconsequential. At the root of this deterioration was the earlier dismissal of 'Kiki', the strongman of the orange camp, from his post as director of customs.

A first major test for the new government emerged in late September over the issues of fuel price increases, fuel and power shortages and a general deterioration in the felt standard of living. Anger over the poor performance of relevant state agencies and the increase of hitherto unsustainably low petrol prices turned into widespread **popular protests**, supported by opposition parties, trade unions, employers' associations, a consumer protection agency and a so-called 'indignant movement'. This climaxed on 10/11 October in a **general stay-away** ('ville morte') in Moroni, but was eventually contained without major political upheavals. The directors of the 'Société Comorienne des Hydrocarbures' (SCH) and the public power company Ma-Mwe were replaced.

An amateurish **putsch attempt** on 11 November in **Anjouan** by apparent cronies of the former secessionist leader, Mohamed Bacar, was easily quashed, but was nevertheless indicative of remaining elements of unrest. A disarmament programme to collect small arms left from the secessionist attempt of 2007/08 and the subsequent military invasion was only marginally effective. In April, former army chief General Salimou Amiri, after seven months of house arrest, was cleared by a court of charges of plotting a **rebellion**, but the state prosecutor appealed against this ruling. Amiri continued to be held in his residence under surveillance for his alleged complicity in the assassination of Colonel Combo Ayouba in June 2010. Neither case was concluded before the year's end. In mid-September, opposition leaders from the 'Convention pour le Renouveau des Comores' filed legal charges against Sambi for misappropriation of funds during his presidency, but no apparent action was taken. In June, the French-Comorian opposition lawyer, Said Larifou, publicly accused an influential businessman, Bashar Kiwan, well connected with Arab financiers, of mafia-style corruption and money laundering. Towards the end of the year, a move towards a controversial **ban on all alcohol sales** gathered some momentum. Strong demands for it had been made by Islamic ulema, and Dhoinine was perceived to have assented in a move to please his predecessor. The second-highest religious leader was caught trying to obtain an illicit exclusive import licence for a leading commercial enterprise and the case was deferred to January 2012.

Foreign Affairs

The long-standing conflict with **France** over the status of **Mayotte**, the archipelago's fourth island, continued to receive most attention. In consequence of a March 2009 referendum, on 31 March, Mayotte officially obtained the status of France's 101st Département and a peripheral territory of the EU, although all Comorian governments had always insisted that Mayotte remain an integral part of the Comoros under international law. The advent of the crucial date precipitated new political tensions and a **diplomatic mini-crisis** in Comorian-French relations that lasted for about two weeks. Anti-French demonstrations protesting against Mayotte's illegal occupation were held on 26 March by civil society organisations and with government support. In mid-March, the Comorian authorities went against previous practice and started to refuse re-entry to any Comorians expelled from Mayotte who did not have proper identity papers, allegedly out of concern for security. France immediately retaliated by stopping the issue of visas for Comorian citizens. A new accord on practical procedures was agreed, after heated exchanges, on 1 April, with a de facto Comorian retreat. A planned Sambi visit to Réunion was cancelled as expression of French disapproval of his rigid stance.

Subsequently, Dhoinine started to take a somewhat **more conciliatory approach** towards France, albeit without foregoing the legal claim on Mayotte as part of the Comoros. In his maiden speech in the UN General Assembly on 22 September, he naturally raised the Mayotte issue, but refrained from using aggressive language. The AU summit at the end of June in Equatorial-Guinea once again formally backed the Comorian legal claim, but without any practical consequences. Bilateral **Comorian-French relations** continued to be characterised by considerable ambivalence, ranging from conflict over Mayotte to substantial dependence on France as major traditional donor. In January, the French cooperation minister announced the resumption of activities of the bilateral 'Groupe de Travail de Haut-Niveau', which had been formed in 2007 to foster a pragmatic form of cooperation, but had been suspended by Sambi in 2009. Despite a quick government denial that activities had resumed, a range of assistance programmes did in fact continue to operate.

Generally speaking, the government continued to pursue an **open-door foreign policy** within the limited scope available to it, and attempted to maintain similarly cordial relations with Western powers (particularly France and the USA) and with China, Iran and most Arab countries, in the expectation of attracting aid or commercial investment from these diverse sources. In November, Dhoinine undertook a first foreign tour to Sudan and Saudi Arabia. A small **Libyan military contingent** of about 50 soldiers, who had been attached to the presidential guard for a year and had created some political anxiety, departed in mid-March upon the emergence of the rebellion in Libya. In September, the government recognised the transitional Libyan authorities despite having been strongly supported by Khadafi. To the great relief of the government, Abdullah Fazul, a notorious Comorian Islamist terrorist who had been unsuccessfully pursued internationally since 1998, was killed in Somalia in June. On 5 December, Comoros, Mozambique and Tanzania signed an agreement in Maputo on their common maritime borders, which formally rejected the French illegal presence on Mayotte.

Socioeconomic Developments

The apparent political stabilisation and guarded optimism with regard to a continuation of Sambi's various reform measures had a noticeable, although still rather modest, impact on the limited further improvement of the general **macroeconomic performance**. Broadly favourable assessments were made by the IMF, which nevertheless underscored the continuing urgent need for more far-reaching structural reforms. The **GDP growth rate** was expected to have modestly increased to about 2.5%, slightly higher than in 2010, and clearly better than earlier annual averages of around only 1%. Robust agricultural production and good harvests contributed to this result. The inflation rate of about 4% was largely due to the restraining effect of membership of the franc zone, whereby the franc comorien remained pegged to the euro. Substantial remittances from the numerous Comorian diaspora (equal to about 25% of GDP) and higher inflows of aid funds remained essential to counterbalance the traditional enormous **structural trade deficit**. Increased export revenues of about $ 20 m (practically all from cloves, vanilla and ylang-ylang) covered just one-tenth of the ever-increasing import bill of around $ 220 m, due inter alia to the unchanged heavy dependence on the import of food staples. A somewhat reduced current account deficit of around 7% of GDP indicated a slight improvement. Foreign exchange reserves of $ 145 m (in September) provided a relatively comfortable safety cushion.

IMF missions in March, August and October reviewed the country's performance under the three-year ECF approved in 2009, and concluded that the programme targets had by and large been met. The macroeconomic outlook was considered as moderately positive, but major emphasis was again, as in previous years, placed on the need to improve the **fiscal situation**, where considerable slippages and a higher than anticipated deficit were observed. Priority attention still needed to be addressed to containing the large civil service wage bill but, in view of the severe shortage of any jobs outside of the public sector, a personnel reduction was politically extremely difficult to realise. A civil service census had identified the existence of 11,672 budgeted positions. The government, contrary to frequent earlier experiences of considerable salary arrears, nevertheless managed on the whole to pay its staff regularly and even to make up for some arrears, although a backlog of four months still existed in October. A teachers' strike over pay conditions in April led to the temporary closure of most schools. Another area of concern continued to be the unsatisfactory management of parastatal companies, particularly key public utilities (electricity, water and telecoms). New directors were installed in October for the SCH and Ma-Mwe, the power company, but no substantial progress was made with regard to their intended privatisation, as was also the case for 'Comores Télécom'. The assessment of the country's general business environment in the World Bank's Doing Business Report 2012 showed no improvement, with the country ranked 157th. Some further cancellations of old external debts were agreed during the year, and the **completion point** under the **HIPC initiative** was now expected to be reached by December 2012.

An **investment forum** on 23–24 February in Moroni was intended as a follow-up to a March 2010 conference in Doha, Qatar, where funding pledges of $ 540 m for Comoros had been made. Representatives from Qatar, UAE, the Islamic Development Bank and other Arab countries and institutions reiterated pledges to an increased volume of over $ 600 m, but very few concrete signs of implementation became evident during the ensuing months, probably largely due to the rising general unrest und uncertainty throughout the Arab world. Comorian expectations of very substantial investment inflows were thus severely disappointed. Outgoing President Sambi, in his farewell speech on 20 May, had again raised expectations with the announcement of an alleged gift of $ 2 bn from an unspecified Dubai foundation, apparently already signed over in November 2010, but the reliability of this sudden promise remained questionable.

A revised **fisheries accord** with the **EU** was approved by the European Parliament in early April. The permitted reference tonnage was reduced, as was the EU's financial contribution. In December, a company from the French Bolloré group was awarded a ten-year concession for the management of the port of Moroni, after the previous contract with Gulf-Com port management was terminated in September after recurrent complaints of poor services.

Rolf Hofmeier

Djibouti

President Guelleh was re-elected for a third term in a nominal election contest boycotted by all opposition parties. A short flare-up of violent social discontent was quickly suppressed and the authoritarian regime was able to remain in undisputed full control of public affairs. A rejuvenated cabinet did not alter the dominating influence of the president's family circle. The government successfully took advantage of the country's strategic location in a conflict-prone region and was spared any harsh foreign criticism of its human rights record. Djibouti remained a crucial hub for international efforts to fight Somali piracy activities. A severe drought impacted strongly on deteriorating living conditions for large parts of the population. Ambitious plans for further major infrastructural projects aimed to transform Djibouti into a leading service centre.

Domestic Politics

A constitutional amendment in April 2010 had lifted the presidential two-term limit and thus cleared the path for **President Ismail Omar Guelleh** (widely dubbed **IOG**) to run again for his own succession in presidential **elections**, scheduled for 8 April. On 20 January, at a large convention of the governing **'Union pour la Majorité Presidentielle' (UMP)** coalition, he was unanimously elected as their presidential candidate. Within this alliance, Guelleh's own 'Rassemblement Populaire pour le Progrès' (RPP) wielded the real power and was generally perceived to represent the interests of the Somali Issas, the major population group. Three other political parties, including the internal wing of the 'Front pour la Restauration de l'Unité et de la Démocratie' (FRUD) as representatives of the Afars, were relegated to subsidiary positions in the coalition. The other minor UMP members were the 'Union des Partisans de la Réforme' (UPR) and the 'Parti Social Démocrate' (PSD), which in April elected the daughter of its founder as Djibouti's first female party leader.

All existing **opposition parties** once again, as in recent years, decided to **boycott the elections**, since they did not trust the independence of the Election Commission and saw no chance for a fair contest. Thus Guelleh only had to face one **independent candidate** without party affiliation – Mohamed Warsama Ragueh, a former president of the Constitutional Council (2005–2009) and thus a leading figure in the regime, who had been sacked for alleged forgery. To many observers this seemingly futile candidacy smacked of being a ploy to give at least some semblance of credibility to the election. The official results showed a 70% participation rate and an overwhelming win for Guelleh, with 80.6% of the votes. A joint statement by foreign observer groups (from the Arab League, AU, IGAD, OIC, OIF) declared the elections to have been calm and peaceful, but did not raise the serious flaws in the general pre-election environment.

Encouraged by the popular protest movements in Tunisia and Egypt, various opposition groups had in late January started **demonstrations** calling for a postponement of the elections and expressing general disapproval of the regime. In contrast to earlier disunity in the opposition ranks, the main **opposition alliance**, the 'Union pour l'Alternance Démocratique' (UAD), consisting of three separate parties, now joined forces with the 'Parti Nationale Démocratique' (PND), led by Aden Robleh Awaleh, which had in 2010 still been part of the governing UMP, and the 'Parti Djiboutien pour le Développement' (PDD), which had been expelled from the UAD in 2004. An officially permitted demonstration on 18 February, in which an estimated 20,000–40,000 people took part, got out of control and resulted in vicious **street violence**, with two policemen killed and a number of people wounded. The opposition leaders were briefly arrested for failing to control the crowd. Applications for further demonstrations on subsequent Fridays were turned down by the authorities, forcing the opposition leaders to abandon their campaign. On 11 March, they confirmed their boycott of the coming elections.

A **US-funded project** to support a transparent **electoral process** and generally improve conditions for open political dialogue, operated by a small NGO 'Democracy International' (DI) since mid-2010, also fell victim to the tense political atmosphere. In January, DI made recommendations for the good conduct of the elections, but also noted that money and khat were distributed by alleged governmental agents to win electoral support. DI was subsequently accused of supporting anti-government protesters and its activities were obstructed; in March, it was finally expelled, without an apparent protest reaction from the US government.

Guelleh's **inauguration** for a new five-year term, supposedly his last, on 8 May, was attended by several high-ranking politicians from neighbouring countries, including Sudan's President al-Bashir, despite the ICC warrant for his arrest. On 12 May, Guelleh announced a remarkably changed new **cabinet**: 13 of the 23 ministers were practically unknown young technocrats. Prime Minister Dileita Mohamed Dileita, the loyal leading representative of the Afar minority, kept the post he had held since 2001. The delicate balance between ethnic and clan groups was generally maintained, with nine portfolios going to Afars. Several of the previous ministers were not reappointed on account of their perceived unsatisfactory performance, while former interior minister Yacine Elmi Bouh was apparently side-lined because of his apparent ambition to be a future presidential candidate. Most of the released ministers were quietly rewarded with posts as advisers or ambassadors. On 8 October, the new education minister, Ali Hassan Adawa, was unexpectedly sacked after it was discovered that he had secretly met an opposition figure while on an official trip in Canada. He quickly fled to Ethiopia to seek exile.

The installation of a new government team had little effect on the strong direct influence exerted by **IOG** and his **extended family clan** on most political and economic developments in the small, close-knit Djiboutian society or on their energetic pursuit of their family interests. Guelleh's wife, Kadra Mahamoud Haid, was generally considered a very powerful figure, despite having no official role, while her brother was governor of the Central Bank. One of Guelleh's daughters was given a key position as his chief-of-staff, and other members of the family also held important public offices.

Most of the current opponents of the regime had at one time been part of the system and been associated with Guelleh, but had fallen out with him for various reasons. These close personal links and a well-functioning state intelligence service made it very difficult to mount a strong and viable opposition to the long-entrenched power formations. This enabled the continuance of an **authoritarian regime**, characterised by a high level of corruption and the absence of an independent judiciary and media. In August, a civil rights activist was arrested for revealing information about political detainees and, in November, a judge and two journalists were arrested for encouraging illegal demonstrations, tortured and then released. New social unrest in November about difficult living conditions was contained by a deterrent police presence. New applications by the PND and PDD in late December for permission to hold legal demonstrations were again turned down. The illegal external wing of the FRUD mounted hardly any guerrilla actions in the Afar-populated north during the year, but nevertheless remained a latent threat. Nominations for the coming local elections in January 2012 closed in mid-December. Other than the UMP, only a few independent lists were submitted, but again no candidates from the opposition parties.

Foreign Affairs

Most attention focussed on relations with neighbouring countries in the conflict-prone Horn of Africa region. The border situation with **Eritrea** remained calm and without any open hostilities, thanks to the 2010 Qatari mediation and the deployment of a military peacekeeping group, but no progress was made towards a final demarcation of the border and relations remained frosty.

The government continued to take a close active interest in the complex and highly fluid political developments in **Somalia**, its ethnically closely linked and crisis-ridden neighbour. Full political support for Somalia's struggling Transitional Federal Government (TFG) was maintained, underscored *inter alia* by Guelleh's visit to Mogadishu in mid-August. Several TFG leaders came to Djibouti for consultations. In September, special training got underway, with French assistance, for about 850 Djiboutian soldiers who were to join the AU peacekeeping mission in Somalia; this had initially been contemplated in early 2010, but had not been implemented. The first contingent of 250 soldiers was finally deployed to Mogadishu in mid-December. The president of the self-declared Republic of **Somaliland** was in Djibouti in late November for an official three-day visit that served to underline Djibouti's close cooperation and friendship with this fledgling political entity, which was still denied formal international recognition. Djibouti thus served as a crucial link to the outside world for Somaliland. Guelleh stressed his desire that Somaliland's authorities should participate in any future Somali reconciliation talks and not remain completely aloof.

Relations with **Ethiopia**, Djibouti's large neighbour and hegemonic player in the subregion, remained by and large unproblematic. Most questions related to the management and possible improvement of the infrastructural and trade links on which both countries depended, although in very different ways. Ethiopia accounted for about 85% of Djibouti's port traffic and was thus crucially important for the economy, but Ethiopia itself also depended on the port as its primary lifeline to the outside world. The threat, sometimes raised by Ethiopia, that traffic would be diverted through Somaliland's port of Berbera was not realistic in the short term. There was still no progress in sight for the repeatedly planned upgrading of the dilapidated Ethio-Djiboutian railway line. On 5 October, a long-delayed power line connection, operative on a trial basis since May, was officially inaugurated and allowed to import up to 35 MW from Ethiopia, thus somewhat easing Djibouti's constant energy problems.

The long-established **French military base** remained a crucial pillar of Djibouti's economy, bringing in annual rents of € 30 m to the government plus substantial further income generation. The longer-term future of the base, however, continued to be somewhat uncertain in view of changing geo-strategic priorities. With the departure of 700 soldiers, the troop strength had been reduced to about 2,100. Bilateral relations with **France** had considerably improved since 2010, after having been strained for years due to an old judicial affair dating back to 1975. After lengthy discussions, Guelleh and French President Sarkozy signed a new defence treaty on 21 December in Paris, substantially different from the 1977 treaty. Djibouti's request to have all its officers trained in French military academies was turned down, but military and police training was to be provided by the French in Djibouti.

The **US** also continued to greatly value their **military base**, manned by about 2,000 personnel under the Combined Joint Task Force-Horn of Africa. Visits by the new AFRICOM commander, General Carter Ham, in March and October and by Defence Secretary Leon Panetta in December underscored the importance attached to this strategically-located military installation. The government was nevertheless unhappy about not getting more direct military assistance from the US. During an October visit to **Russia**, the foreign minister apparently sounded out possibilities of technical military cooperation. On 5 July, **Japan** officially opened its new **military base**, the country's first foreign military installation intended as a permanent base for participation in international anti-piracy activities in the Indian Ocean. Despite having a personnel strength of only about 200, Japan paid an annual rent of $ 40 m, higher than either France or the US. The **EU** naval anti-piracy forces also used Djibouti as their main base, although without a permanent installation.

A ceremony at the end of August for newly appointed ambassadors was indicative of Djibouti's ambitions to become a more active presence in the world. Five **new embassies** were opened, bringing the total to 14. Particularly close links were maintained with the Arab Gulf states, although efforts were made to loosen somewhat the close commercial links with Dubai, whose phenomenal growth still served as something of a model for Djibouti. Guelleh represented his country at various international forums, such as AU and Arab League summits, the UN General Assembly and an OIC Economic Forum in Kazakhstan in June. Djibouti continued to receive pledges of aid and to attract private investments from various sources, and it was by and large spared any open criticism by Western governments of its authoritarian regime and civil rights violations, all due to its valuable geostrategic location in an international conflict zone.

Socioeconomic Developments

The macroeconomic environment was difficult in a year that was marked by probably the worst **drought** in 60 years in the Horn of Africa region, as well as by high international food and oil prices. The overall economic performance was, therefore, a mixed one. The **GDP growth rate** was estimated at 4.6%, an improvement over a (revised) 3.5% rate in 2010, driven by a recovery in port activity and trade with Ethiopia. **Inflation** increased markedly to an average 5.1%, and stood at 7.6% at year's end. The **current-account deficit** deteriorated sharply to 12.6% of GDP (from 5.8% in 2010). Foreign reserves nevertheless remained high at $ 228 m, with the Djibouti franc remaining pegged to the US dollar under a currency board arrangement. Exports (in fact mostly re-exports) of $ 80 m continued to be dwarfed by imports of $ 415 m, thus maintaining the traditional huge structural trade deficit. The **budget** outturn for 2011 was a modest deficit of 0.8% of GDP, the result of surprisingly stern fiscal discipline on the part of the government. Djibouti slipped further down in both the **HDI** (to rank 165th out of 187 countries) and the World Bank's 'Doing Business' (to rank 170th out of 183). These ratings were indicative, respectively, of comparatively low social living standards and a very restrictive business climate.

During 2011, the **IMF** conducted the fourth and fifth reviews of the September 2008 three-year ECF arrangement, which was extended to June 2012 to allow for a full disbursement of the credit line. The IMF assessments stressed that the short-term challenge continued to be maintaining price stability and budget discipline, while the medium-term challenges centred on tackling the deep economic disparities, spreading the benefits of growth among the population at large, and addressing the high unemployment (estimated at around 60%). The 2012 budget envisaged a surplus of 0.5% of GDP, reflecting an expected strengthening of tax revenue and tight control on expenditure.

In late 2010, early-warning signals of a looming exceptional **drought crisis** had already been discernible. In mid-July the government launched an international appeal for famine relief, which, however, received no substantial response due to the fact that most international attention was focussed on the disastrous situation in Somalia, Ethiopia and Kenya. In March, WFP started the construction of a large logistical centre, the first of its kind in Eastern Africa (and second in Africa).

Port operations, after a disappointing decline in 2010, showed a good recovery, although the transhipment figures for the Doraleh container port still remained far below the original expectations. Nevertheless, plans remained in place for a second-stage expansion at an estimated cost of $ 330 m, although there was no firm completion date. This was again envisaged in partnership with Dubai Ports World, despite intermittent disagreements over its management performance in the Doraleh port. In December, finance agreements were signed with the Kuwait and Saudi Development Funds for the construction of an entirely new port at Tadjourah, which would serve as the closest access point for Ethiopia upon construction of a new railway link. This also raised longer-term visions of possible transport (and pipeline) links with newly-independent South Sudan. In October, a first **geothermal** project was launched as a pilot for exploiting a much larger potential. A private financial group, with mostly Arab resources, started operating a new airline, **Djibouti Air**, in March. The remarkable recent expansion of the **banking system** continued, with the opening of two new foreign-owned banks, from Iraq and Tanzania, in December, bringing the total number of banks to 12. This faced the central bank with the challenge of strengthening supervision and enacting a regulatory framework.

Djibouti's **economic prospects** thus continued to oscillate between highly ambitious plans to become an international service centre and maritime hub in imitation of the Dubai model and the reality of a country with a high level of social discontent and unemployment, reliant on the skills of foreign workers, and lacking a dynamic indigenous private sector.

Rolf Hofmeier

Eritrea

Eritrea celebrated 20 years of independence without its government envisaging political and economic reforms. The state retained its autocratic political system without an independent judiciary; the human rights record remained precarious and civil liberties were lacking. The government denied that the country was affected by the drought prevailing throughout the Horn of Africa, but satellite pictures and refugee reports indicated that at least parts of Eritrea suffered from drought and famine. The Warsay-Yikealo Development Campaign and the mass exodus of the younger generation continued unabated. Hundreds of refugees fell victim to human traffickers, who held them hostage in the Sinai Peninsula to extort money from relatives or even to remove and sell their organs. In reaction to a report by the Monitoring Group on Somalia and Eritrea in July, which presented extensive evidence that the government had supported armed opposition groups in Somalia and other countries in the Horn, the UNSC passed resolution 2023 (2011) in December, thus expanding the sanctions on Eritrea. The border conflicts with Djibouti and Ethiopia remained unsolved. In February, a Canadian company started mining gold at its Bisha Project.

Domestic Politics

On 24 May, Eritrea celebrated **20 years of** (de facto) **independence**. Yet, the autocratic political system remained unchanged and the leadership showed no willingness to introduce political or economic reforms. The **People's Front for Democracy and Justice** (PFDJ) remained the only permitted political party in the country and there were no government plans to hold elections in the near future. No changes to the cabinet were made during the year and the impact of the ministers on the political decision-making process remained weak. Eritrea had a **duplicate administrative structure** with two parallel administrative systems: there were five regional (Zoba) administrations, each headed by a civil administrator directly appointed by **President Isaias Afewerki**, and four military command zones, each headed by a high-ranking military figure. Major General Tekle "Manjus" Kiflai, who had gained far-reaching influence during recent years, was appointed commander of the western military zone and the border units. It was unclear exactly when he obtained this position, but he had been involved in smuggling activities between Eritrea and the Sudan for the past couple of years and was able to strengthen his power base decisively. Major Generals Teklai Habteselassie, Samuel Haile "China" and Filipos Woldeyohannes were able to maintain their power base, while Gerezghier Andemariam aka "Wuchu" lost much of his former power. He had been involved in a failed assassination attempt against the head of Internal Security, Colonel Simon Ghebredengel, in 2007. Simon recovered and was promoted to the rank of general, while Wuchu officially retained his rank, but lost considerable influence. Generally, the **military zone commanders** controlled significant economic assets and had executive powers over military prisons in their respective zones and administrative structures that paralleled the civic administration.

The **judicial system** remained in the same poor state that had characterised it since independence. The formal court system was still not able to provide efficient services and was institutionally weak and unable to act independently from the government. The 'special courts' headed by military lay judges maintained their jurisdictional power in cases of corruption, in which defendants still had no right to a lawyer or to appeal against verdicts. **Corruption** was widespread and clandestinely tolerated by the government, unless an individual involved in corrupt practices fell out of favour with the president and consequently had to face trial. Thus, the selective use of the 'special courts' was used as a tool by the power elite to enforce political allegiance, while leaving opportunities for personal enrichment to middle- and high-ranking members of the military and loyal businessmen. Community courts continued to handle civil cases and criminal cases of minor importance based on customary law. They were headed by lay judges appointed by the government; the population generally preferred to avoid the formal court system and to settle any disputes with the involvement of respected elders and mediators, who were skilled in the application of customary law. The **members of the G15**, a group of high-ranking members of the PFDJ who had been arrested in September 2001 after demands for political reform, as well as the **journalists of the free press** who had been jailed at the same time, remained in custody without formal proceedings. The government did not react to allegations that several of them had died in prison as a result of the extremely harsh conditions to which they were subjected, or that they were in poor health. **Dawit Isaak**, a journalist with dual Eritrean-Swedish citizenship who was among those arrested in 2001, continued to be held without charge or trial. On 13 October, he was awarded the **Golden Pen of Freedom Award** of the World Association of Newspapers and News Publishers in absentia. His brother Esaias Isaak accepted the award on his behalf in Vienna.

Eritrea was ranked **last in worldwide press freedom** by Reporters Without Borders for the sixth consecutive year. More than 30 journalists were held in detention without charge or trial. In February, the radio journalists Nebiel Idris, Ahmed Usman and Mohamed Osman were arrested, followed by sports journalist Tesfalidet "Topo" Mehbratu of EriTV, who was imprisoned in March.

Religious freedom remained severely curtailed and only members of permitted faiths (Orthodox, Catholic and Lutheran Christians and adherents of Islam) were allowed to practise their religion, while persecution of Pentecostal Christians and Jehovah Witnesses continued. In April, a 28–year-old woman reportedly died at the Sawa military camp after two years of detention in a shipping container because she had participated in a Bible study group. In October, some 40 adherents of the Full Gospel Church were arrested in the Southern Region (Zoba Debub). Throughout the year, Muslims were detained in various parts of Eritrea, particularly in the towns of Keren, Ghinda, Adi Keyeh, Senafe, and the capital Asmara. They were arrested either because of alleged religious extremism or because they were suspected of sympathising with militant ethnically-based opposition movements such as the Read Sea Afar Democratic Organisation (RSADO) or the National Democratic Front for the Liberation of the Eritrean Saho (NDFLDS), who operated from Ethiopia. The government continued to suppress Muslims who followed the Wahabi school of Islam, who were regarded as critics of certain government policies, although they did not promote violence in any form.

Eritrea remained one of the most highly militarised societies worldwide and no demobilisation of the army took place. The so-called **Warsay-Yikealo Development Campaign**, introduced in 2002, remained in place. This military and national service programme forced Eritreans aged between 18 and 50 to work for pocket-money for unspecified periods of time on farms controlled by military commanders and enterprises owned by the PFDJ. National Service recruits were also hired out to the Canadian Enterprise Nevsun, which started the extraction of gold at its Bisha mine in Zoba Gash-Barka. The ongoing Warsay-Yikealo Campaign further accelerated the **mass exodus** of young Eritreans that had been taking place for the past ten years – about 2,000 people per month crossed the borders to neighbouring countries. According to the UNHCR, in early 2011 the number of Eritrean refugees had reached 220,000, about 5% of the population, not including thousands of Eritreans who had left their country and settled in third countries without being in touch with UNHCR. The number of unaccompanied children among the refugees increased considerably, some of them being as young as six years old. This was due to the fact that parents wanted to get their children beyond the reach of government control as soon as possible. In its report of July 2011, the UNSC monitoring group on Somalia and Eritrea revealed that high-ranking Eritrean military personnel, most prominently Major General Tekle "Manjus" Kiflai, were involved in **human trafficking**: they charged about $ 3,000 for a border-crossing and for smuggling the escapees to Egypt through the Sudanese desert. Israel became a major destination for Eritrean refugees, given the dangers of crossing the Mediterranean in overcrowded boats. Hundreds of them fell into the hands of human traffickers from the Rashaida ethnic group, who cooperated with agents of both the Eritrean and the Sudanese governments. The escapees were held hostage in the **Egyptian Sinai Peninsula**, where they were subjected to severe physical abuse and maltreatment, while ransom payments of about $ 20,000 were extorted from family members residing in the diaspora in return for allowing them continue their journey to Israel. Some of them fell victim to illicit '**organ harvesting**' operations organised by Rashaida traffickers and corrupt Egyptian doctors. The human rights organisations New Generation Foundation for Human Rights (Egypt) and Every One Group (Italy) reported that hundreds of victims had their organs removed by the doctors and were subsequently left to die in the desert. A CNN report presented photographs of human bodies as evidence. Nevertheless, the number of Eritreans who entered **Israel** reached at least 22,000 in 2011. The Israeli government did not consider them as refugees, but rather as 'infiltrators'. In December, the Knesset passed a "law to prevent infiltration", which allowed the detention of asylum seekers, including children, without trial for up to three years.

A further **accentuation of political polarisation** became apparent among the Eritrean **diaspora**. While government supporters continued to be mobilised by campaigns related to the "resolute national rebuff" against the international sanctions imposed on Eritrea, the events of the 'Arab Spring' that unfolded in 2011 had a noticeable impact on the diaspora youth, who organised themselves into movements for change and developed new and creative methods of anti-government protest. The **Young PFDJ** continued its activities as a purely diaspora-based branch of the PFDJ, which was involved in the political organisation of government supporters and pressured them to donate money. When Isaias visited New York on 25 September, thousands of Eritreans from across the US travelled there to attend his 'seminar', wearing T-Shirts with his portrait and cheering him loudly, giving the event the appearance of a pop concert. At the same time, his close adviser **Yemane Ghebreab** (dubbed "Yemane Monkey"), who had accompanied him on his journey, was confronted by a group of anti-government youth activists while sitting in a bar. They asked him about the whereabouts of the G15 and other prisoners and documented his reaction – he left hastily without giving a response – with a mobile camera. The video was widely distributed on the internet. One of the new youth movements was **Eritrean Youth Solidarity for Change**, which claimed to consist of some Eritreans operating underground within the country and others operating openly in the diaspora. They demanded Isaias' immediate resignation, the release of all prisoners of conscience and an end to the Warsay-Yikealo Development Campaign. Another group was **Eritrean Youth for Change** (EYC), founded in the Californian Bay Area, which was committed to the democratisation of Eritrea and to assisting Eritrean refugees worldwide. Using Facebook as medium of communication, EYC extended its activities worldwide throughout 2011.

The established opposition parties and several civil society groups in the diaspora held an **Eritrean National Conference for Democratic Change** in Awassa, Ethiopia, on 21–30 November. They discussed a roadmap to democratic change and elected a 127-member National Assembly. In addition, a 21-member executive committee was elected; seven of its members came from Eritrean Democratic Alliance (EDA) member organisations, five from non-EDA political organisations, and eight were representatives of independent civil society organisations. Unlike in the past, the participants of the conference engaged in constructive work, and there were no party splits or walkouts during the event. This was probably due to the considerable pressure that had been put on participating organisations by journalists and anti-government activists in the diaspora.

The ethnic-based **militant opposition** movements based in Ethiopia continued their acts of insurgency on a small scale, among them RSADO and NDFLDS, who reportedly launched attacks in the Southern Red Sea Region and in the area around the mountain of Amba Soira, Southern Region (Zoba Debub). In mid-June, the **Nabo volcano** erupted in the Danakil Depression in the Southern Red Sea Region. RSADO called for international support for the affected inhabitants of the region, mostly ethnic Afar.

Foreign Affairs

In pursuance of the sanctions that had been imposed on Eritrea in December 2009 (UNSC resolution 1907/2009), the **Monitoring Group on Somalia and Eritrea** delivered its report to the UN Secretary General on 18 July. One of its main findings was that the PFDJ controlled functions normally discharged by the state and that power and resources were concentrated in the hands of a small number of individuals (senior party, military and intelligence officials) and were largely managed outside government institutions and channels.

The group found firm **evidence** that Eritrea had **supported armed opposition groups** in Djibouti, Ethiopia, Somalia and Sudan. Moreover, it had been involved in the planning of a (failed) bomb attack to disturb the AU summit meeting in Addis Ababa in January 2011, had given support to individuals with links to al-Shabaab in Somalia, and had received weapons deliveries in **violation of UNSC resolution 1907**. The report also confirmed that Eritrean generals were involved not only in contraband trade, but also in the smuggling of arms and people over the Sudanese border. The group's report stated that Eritrea ran two economies: a formal one managed by the state, and another informal network of companies and individuals that engaged in illicit activities. In addition, several hundred million dollars in tax collected from the diaspora were controlled by the PFDJ's head of financial affairs. These funds were not invested in Eritrea's ailing economy, but spent to support armed groups throughout the Horn of Africa. As usual, the **government denied** all accusations levelled against it.

Following the publication of the Monitoring Group, Ethiopia and other **IGAD** member states lobbied for the tightening of UN sanctions, supporting in particular the targeting of Eritrea's mining sector. At the same time, Eritrea made an unsuccessful effort to rejoin IGAD. It had unilaterally suspended its membership in 2007 in protest against Ethiopia's military engagement in Somalia. On 23 September, Isaias attended the 66th General Assembly of the UN in New York, but did not elaborate on the sanctions issue in his speech, which was characterised as 'subdued' by various media outlets.

On 5 December, the UNSC **expanded the sanctions** against Eritrea, although the original suggestions by several East African states were watered down. The text was sponsored by Gabon and Nigeria and 13 council members voted in favour of the sanctions; Russia and China abstained. **UNSC Resolution 2023 (2011)** demanded that "Eritrea cease all direct and indirect efforts to destabilise States" and resolve its border conflicts with its neighbours. It confirmed the intention to apply targeted sanctions against individuals and entities (i.e. the PFDJ and military elites and their enterprises) that violated the sanctions in place. Another important point was that Eritrea was told to stop using its '**diaspora tax**' to destabilise the Horn of Africa region and not to use coercion to collect the money. The resolution called upon member states to monitor financial services under their jurisdiction, not to help Eritrea to violate the sanction resolutions. With regard to the mining sector, it called upon UN member states to be vigilant that profits earned through mining activities in Eritrea were not used to sponsor terrorist groups in the region, and demanded that the Eritrean government show transparency in its public finances (which it had never done since independence).

The political stalemate between **Ethiopia** and Eritrea following the border-impasse prevailed, but the situation at the border remained calm. Both governments resorted to supporting their adversary's opposition in exile – Ethiopia sponsored armed ethnically-based Eritrean opposition movements that operated from its territory and hosted the Eritrean National Conference in Awassa, while Eritrea sponsored the Oromo Liberation Front, the Ogaden National Liberation Front and other armed Ethiopian opposition groups.

Eritrea's border conflict with **Djibouti** was not resolved. The agreement between the two governments signed in June 2010 with the mediation of **Qatar**, which referred to the settlement of the border conflict, the demarcation of the border and the release of prisoners of war, was not implemented. When Isaias was asked about the results of Qatari mediation between Djibouti and Eritrea in an interview with the Egyptian newspaper 'Al-Ahram' in June, he replied: "There is no Qatari mediation. The emir of Qatar had offered to mediate, but it wasn't necessary because the situation between Djibouti and Eritrea returned to normal." This position was a clear **breach of UN resolution 1907/2009**, which required that Eritrea acknowledge its dispute with Djibouti and actively engage in dialogue and diplomatic efforts leading to a settlement of the border issue. In addition, the UN Monitoring Group on Somalia and Eritrea reported that Eritrea supported FRUD-C, an armed splinter group of the 'Front pour la Restauration de l'Unité et de la Démocratie' (FRUD), which carried out limited guerilla operations in the north of Djibouti.

Relations with **Sudan** remained close, despite some tensions along their common border. On 19–21 October, Isaias visited Sudan and met President al-Bashir. On 26 October, he attended the inauguration of the new Kassala–Al-Laffa road linking the two countries. Prior to the independence of **South Sudan**, the Eritrean president had declared that he considered this independence "a mistake" in his June interview with 'Al-Ahram'. Since 2009, Eritrea's relations with the Sudan People's Liberation Movement/Army (SPLM/A) had been strained and SPLA officials accused the Eritrean government of having supported an insurrection against it. Isaias nevertheless attended the independence celebrations of the Republic of South Sudan in Juba on 9 July. On that occasion, he met with UN Secretary General Ban Ki-Moon, who lauded his contribution to peace and stability in the Sudan and his role in the Darfur peace process.

With the Libyan Revolution and the death of **Muammar Khadafi** in October, Isaias lost one of his few permanent allies and financial supporters. The only remaining country that gave continuous **financial support** to Eritrea was **Qatar**. Isaias visited Doha on 30 January and 30 June; he also met the emir of Qatar during his trip to Sudan in October. It was unclear how the Qatari government reacted to Isaias' repudiation of the mediation agreement in the Djibouti-Eritrea conflict, which it had sponsored.

Eritrean authorities held four **British nationals** in custody for five months for alleged 'espionage' without granting them access to consular support. They had been arrested on 24 December 2010 after a dispute over non-payment for fuel. The ex-Royal Marines were employed by the **security company** Protection Vessels International (PVI), which was engaged in protecting ships from piracy in the Indian Ocean. On 5 April, Britain warned Eritrea that it would take "robust action" if no consular access to its nationals was granted, and complained that it had not received any response to demands for contact with them. Eritrea released the British nationals in early June, followed by a lengthy press release by the ministry of foreign affairs which claimed that they had offloaded "countless amounts of arms" on an Eritrean island and intended to carry out acts of terrorism and sabotage. It also claimed that the men had fully admitted their crimes. According to PVI, the men had carried weapons as standard equipment for anti-piracy operations and were forced to land in Eritrea because of technical problems. In spite of their 'crimes', they were unconditionally released after an informal intervention by Qatar. The incident worsened the already **frosty relations** between **Great Britain** and **Eritrea**.

A somewhat obscure incident took place in August, when the Eritrean authorities held two pilots from **Israel** in custody for ten days. The Israelis had allegedly entered Eritrea to deliver a mechanical spare part, but were arrested after a security check because they were carrying weapons and ammunition for a German-owned ship for use against Somali pirates, according to an Israeli newspaper. It remained unclear, however, why the ship had docked in Eritrea at all.

Relations between Eritrea and the **United States** remained poor. The US strongly supported the tightening of UN sanctions. In reaction to the hostile rhetoric employed by the Eritrean government against the US, the US Embassy in Asmara warned US citizens to postpone travel to Eritrea or to be extremely cautious because of possible hostilities against US citizens.

Socioeconomic Developments

Eritrea's **economy** remained largely under the control of the PFDJ and the military and its performance was weak, despite the commencement of gold mining by the Canadian company Nevsun Resources. **Basic consumer goods** remained scarce and kerosene for cooking purposes was in very short supply throughout the year. During September and October, there were frequent blackouts in Asmara, an indicator of a **lack of fuel and spare parts** needed to operate the only electrical power plant of the country in Hirghigo, near Massawa. The government denied that Eritrea was affected by **drought** and **hunger**, as was the case for the entire Horn of Africa region, but did not grant international agencies access to its countryside to assess the situation on the ground. In an interview with the 'Voice of America' on 27 September, Isaias claimed that Eritrea did not face food shortages and needed no humanitarian assistance, and that he was willing to send modest amounts of food aid to assist hungry Somalis. These claims were, however, doubtful, as satellite photographs showed that Eritrea had been affected by the drought and there were reports of numerous Eritreans fleeing to Ethiopia because of **malnourishment and destitution**. Some of them were interviewed for a report screened by German television on 15 August. According to the Ethiopian refugee administration authority ARRA, between 1,200 and 1,500 Eritreans arrived in Ethiopia every month, many of them ethnic Afar. The 2011 Global Hunger Index ranked Eritrea among four countries with 'extremely alarming' levels of hunger. The report indicated that more than 50% of Eritreans were malnourished. **UNICEF** applied for $ 14 m for its children's emergency programme in Eritrea, while donor response to its plea for $ 24.8 m the previous year had been low. It did not give statistical details about the nutritional situation of children in Eritrea.

Generally, availability of data remained extremely poor as a result of continuous lack of transparency and independent financial monitoring. The ruling PFDJ and the military controlled the business sector and there was an absolute lack of financial monitoring. Both party-owned and military-controlled businesses were exempted from tax payments and continued to use the unpaid labour force of national service recruits. **Inflation** was estimated at 20%, while the **GDP growth** was expected to attain 8.2% due to the beginning of gold extraction. For the same reason, the **current-account balance** improved, but was still negative at $ 77.5 m. Foreign reserves had risen to an estimated $ 164 m. The UNDP ranked Eritrea 177 out of 187 countries with an HDI of 0.349.

The **Bisha project** (in Gash-Barka region) of the Canadian company Nevsun Resources started commercial production in February. The mine was meant to produce low-cost **gold** for two years, and high-grade **copper concentrate** and zinc for its remaining life. The Eritrean state owned a 40% share in the mine which, according to Nevsun, would be paid for over time out of Bisha cash distributions. Labour conditions at the project were appalling. Several workers who eventually escaped to Ethiopia were extensively interviewed by Human Rights Concern Eritrea, which published an audio version of their reports in July. About 400 foreign workers from South Africa and Zimbabwe were employed by Nevsun and paid and housed according to international standards, while Eritrean workers were subject to exploitation and hazardous work conditions. Nevsun had given subcontracts to **PFDJ-owned construction companies** such as Seghen Construction, which employed local workers for monthly salaries of 1,500 Nakfa (about $ 40), while National Service recruits received 400 Nakfa ($ 9). Their camps were separate from the housing facilities of the foreign workers and they received food of poor quality, while having to work for up to 16 hours a day. They were also denied safety equipment by Seghen. The state security had spies and informers among the workers in order to prevent them from complaining about their situation. Nevsun officials turned a blind eye to these conditions.

Australian-based **Chalice Goldmines** announced on 27 December that it had agreed to sell its remaining 60% stake in the Zara mining project to the **Chinese SFCEO Group**, a subsidiary of Shanghai Construction Group. Chalice had sold a 30% share to the government-owned Eritrean National Mining Corporation in July, in addition to the 10% share owned by the Eritrean state. Overall, 14 companies were exploring mineral resources throughout the country.

On 15 November, the **EU Commission** announced that the Eritrean government had **terminated** all on-going programmes under the 10th EDF. This included programmes in support of the agricultural sector (€ 37 m), Community Courts (€ 5 m), training of public servants (€ 3.4 m) and the rehabilitation of Asmara's National Heritage (€ 5 m). A further available amount of € 68.3 m was also rejected by the government, which argued that it intended to "fully review and finalize the country's five-year National Development Plan" before re-engaging with the EU. As usual, the Eritrean media remained silent about this step. The **AfDB** approved an ADF grant of $ 19.2 m to Eritrea on 30 November to improve the quality of technical vocational education and training.

In an interview for state media on 4 March, Minister of Transport and Communication Woldenkiel Abraha stated that **Eritrean Airlines** and the privately-owned **NasAir** Company had merged. NasAir had started to operate in Eritrea in 2006 and provided local and regional flights.

Nicole Hirt

Ethiopia

Ethiopia saw an intriguing combination of economic growth (although uneven and full of uncertainties), progress on MDGs, and a harsh and repressive political climate. De facto power in all political, economic and social domains was in the hands of the sole party in government and in parliament, the Ethiopian Peoples' Revolutionary Democratic Front, now in its twentieth year in power, and still led by Prime Minister Meles Zenawi. Independent private media, NGO activities, open political debate, academic freedom, respect for human rights and economic freedoms were under pressure. Many opposition politicians and independent journalists were put behind bars on charges that were difficult to take seriously. Nevertheless, Ethiopia's prominence, regionally in the Horn of Africa and on the wider world scene, increased. It was courted by traditional donors (the EU and USA), as well as by new emerging powers, such as India and especially China, both major investors in the country. Ethiopia's leaders, notably the prime minister, were present at major world forums. Incidents of religious and ethnic violence occurred, reflecting deep divisions in the population, and several low-key armed rebellions also continued in peripheral areas. No consultative political processes with opposition forces of any kind were in evidence.

Economic dynamism and growth were substantial, leading to continued high GDP growth, advances in health and education coverage, and substantial infrastructure investment, sustained by international aid flows. Domestic and international controversy over large-scale commercial land acquisitions by foreigners and mega-dam construction grew in intensity, as their social and environmental costs were denied by the government and debates about these schemes were criminalised. Ethiopia suffered from a huge budget deficit, excessive government spending and high inflation, and there was little critical scrutiny of its non-economic record. A serious drought in the south and east caused pockets of famine and malnutrition, which led to several thousand deaths and was combated with the help of humanitarian aid from Western donors and UN agencies.

Domestic Politics

Ethiopia remained a **highly constrained political environment**, marked by entrenched authoritarianism and one-party rule dominating all sectors of society, from political processes to economic life and civic and social structures. The country scored low on all available indexes of governance and freedoms. Its redeeming features in the eyes of Western donors and Asian investors, however, were its economic growth, openness to foreign investment and general improvement on MDG criteria. Ethiopia was notable both for its relatively high GDP growth rate, public spending in education, infrastructure outlay and healthcare, and its investments, notably in extractive industries and land commercialisation. The growing economic confidence of the regime was not, however, reflected in political or social confidence; the lack of political and socioeconomic freedoms, the stifling public space and the serious lack of trust in the solidity, legitimacy and performance of governmental institutions remained a hindrance to inclusive development and sustained the high level of distrust and dissatisfaction felt towards the government by the general population.

The **ruling party**, the **Ethiopian Peoples' Revolutionary Democratic Front (EPRDF)**, led by Prime Minister Meles Zenawi, who entered his twenty-first year in power, governed with the support of 546 of the 547 MPs in the House of People's Representatives and thus faced **no parliamentary opposition**. The ruling party's virtual monopoly meant there could be no serious public debates, and virtually all the executive's proposals were unanimously approved.

Extremely **restrictive laws** regarding NGO activities, civic political activity, media freedom and public order had their effect and, combined with the intimidating behaviour of police and special forces, bred distrust, fear and self-censorship among citizens. They affected the media, business life, civil society activities and even university research and teaching programmes. Political parties were recognised in law, but existed only outside the parliament (apart from a single non-EPRDF member, from the Medrek party) and were under constant pressure. They were thus marginalised and had no impact on policy formulation.

The **independent press** – or what was left of it – was the only place where some shades of debates on national policy were reflected and some cautious criticisms appeared, but in the course of the year several of these publications were harassed and closed, among them the weeklies 'Addis Neger' and 'Awramba Times'. A shrinking number of non-governmental journals remained, including 'The Reporter' and 'Fitih', and some economic weeklies. Journalists were hindered and threatened and a number of them again left the country, alleging intimidation and threats to their safety.

The ruling party seemed to fear all criticism, divergent opinion and policy debate, and increased its grip on the country by implementing close surveillance and widespread party recruitment drives. A continued process of **fusion of state administration** with the **EPRDF** and its cadres thus occurred at the national, regional and local levels and it became difficult to see any distinction between the state and the party. The combined police, army and security services backed up this authority structure with surveillance and selective coercion. A process of 'democratisation' (already nominally on-going for more than 20 years and with no end in sight) was evident only in government rhetoric and hardly at all in reality. The government saw its record on economic growth indicators as sufficient ground for its legitimacy, and regarded itself as indispensable and irreplaceable. This was the reason for a redefinition of national policy aims whereby the 'developmental state' model advocated by the ruling party and Zenawi marginalised any political democracy, freedoms and human rights discourse.

The EPRDF also wielded power by keeping office holders on their toes with demotions, sudden dismissals and 'evaluation sessions' (called *gimgema*). For example: in February, Tamiru Ambelo, chairman of the local administration in Gambella Region, was fired for protesting against foreign land acquisition schemes in his area; on 12 November it was announced that the minister and state minister of trade had been dismissed; on 13 November the Addis Ababa land administration deputy-manager was sacked. Deviation from the party line was the usual cause of such dismissals and demotions, which were daily political practice throughout the country, as were regular EPRDF training sessions for public servants, teachers, etc., to keep them ideologically in line with the party's developmental model. In June, seven army generals, 240 colonels and nearly 500 commissioned officers were removed. In January, the long-serving former foreign minister Seyoum Mesfin took up a new post as ambassador to China. On 28 May, the **EPRDF marked its twentieth year in power**, with public celebrations.

Domestic peace was still not achieved, with on-going armed rebel movements defying the government. Examples were the tenacious Ogaden National Liberation Front (ONLF) in the Somali-inhabited Ogaden area, and actions in parts of the Oromo areas, where remnant Oromo Liberation Front units were active, and in Gambela, where the Anywa people were hard hit by displacement due to externally-driven land lease schemes and the expansion of neighbouring groups, and suffered on-going precarious living conditions, and there were rumours that some Anywa youngsters had taken up arms. Army units also clashed with Afar rebels in November, near the village of Derrab and local conflicts about territorial borders continued to occur between certain ethnic-based communities. For example, on 2 January, five people were killed and 11 injured in clashes between Guji Oromo and Sidama people in the southern Wondo Genet district, and in December the Borana and Gabbra peoples in the Ethio-Kenyan border area fought several battles over pasture and water resources, resulting in 15 people killed and more than 6,000 displaced.

The government kept the lid on the escalating **religious tensions**, which nevertheless led in some places to clashes and attacks, notably between Christians and Muslims, and between Pentecostal-Evangelical groups and traditional believers, as well as internally between denominations within the Christian and Muslim communities. On 29 November, hundreds of Muslim students, aided by Muslim police officers, burned down an Orthodox church in the village of Qoto Baloso, in the predominantly Muslim Silte zone, after a controversial court ruling that it had been built without legal authorisation. In the Muslim town of Besheno (in Alaba district) in January, Evangelical Christians were harassed after Muslims posted notices on the doors of Christian homes saying they should convert, leave the city or face death. In March, there were reports that radical Muslims had killed one Christian and burned down eight churches, a Bible school and 17 Christian homes in the town of Asendabo after a false rumour that Christians had "desecrated the Qur'an". In the same month, Muslims in the Goda district of Jimma were reported to have burned down ten Christian homes, leaving 80 Christians homeless. In several places in the south, Evangelical or Pentecostal Christians were reported to have destroyed places of worship belonging to traditional religions.

On the national level, some disquiet emerged within Ethiopia's Muslim community in response to attempts by the government, in an apparent effort to discourage 'Wahhabist extremism', to impose a particular form of Islam (i.e., that of the 'al-Ahbash' movement, seen as non-political and non-Wahhabist). On 8 October, Minister of Federal Affairs Shiferaw Teklemariam issued credible warnings about illegal underground activities of 'Wahhabists', but Ethiopian Muslims were, on principle, loath to accept any government imposition in matters of faith.

Some internal political **controversy** emerged on the nature and scope of the **massive land acquisitions** by foreign and domestic investors, as many of these commercial schemes appeared to damage the interests of local communities, causing alarm among local farmers and the public at large. In February, it became known that even Ethiopia's (ceremonial) President Girma Wolde-Giorgis had expressed sympathy for some of these concerns, agreeing with a delegation of the Majangir people who pleaded for a halt to the lease of an extensive part of their area to an Indian company. However, even support for this call from the state's Environmental Protection Agency (EPA) produced no result. In November, the newly-installed sultan of the Afar people, Hanfareh Ali Mirah, son of Sultan Ali Mirah, who died on 25 April, indirectly referred to the potentially harmful effects of foreign land leases and major industrial developments in Afar territory, which would consume huge amounts of water to the detriment of local people. The government held no consultations with local stakeholders and gained substantial revenue from land lease fees, declaring that the benefits in terms of food security, knowledge transfer and agrarian development would become obvious. It acted against the local protesters who opposed these deals and arrested hundreds of people. In addition, the government pursued its **resettlement schemes**, moving people from allegedly overpopulated, drought-stricken areas to new sites, which regularly led to clashes with local people, many of whom were injured and killed by the police and security forces. State **villagisation** programmes, notably in Gambela Region, also met with resistance. In August, the BBC screened an impactful, critical documentary on the political use the government was allegedly making of foreign aid packages, penalising citizens perceived as critical of government policies. As usual, the British government and its aid agencies, like other Western donors, did not want to know and were dismissive of these findings.

Domestic repression of free debate and media continued, including the arrest of, among many others, journalists Reeyot Alemu and Woubshet Taye (of the 'Awramba Times') in early June, Sileshi Hagos in early September, and Eskinder Nega, a popular blogger, on 11 September. There were many other examples. In March, more than 200 members of the Medrek opposition party were arrested in the Oromiya region. On 29 August, Legesse Deti Dhaba, former secretary-general of (Oromo) Mecha-Tulama Self-Help Association, was put in prison. On 8 September, the popular actor Debebe Eshetu was detained for alleged contacts with an exiled opposition party, and members of opposition parties, such as Unity for Democracy and Justice executive members Andualem Arage, Natnael Mekonen and Asaminew Berhanu, and the All-Ethiopia Democratic Party's secretary-general Zemenu Mola were also arrested. No credible charges were produced against them, but the 2009 'Anti-Terrorism' law allowed virtually any critic of government policy to be charged and tried by state prosecutors. On 11 November, 24 people, among them six journalists, were charged with 'terrorism'. Some of the accused stated before the court that they had been abused and tortured in custody.

There were **no public protests** in Ethiopia, apart from occasional university student demonstrations. On 25–28 November, students at Gondar University protested over badly spoilt food that had caused health problems for many students. This turned into a wider demonstration for academic rights and freedom in general. It was suppressed by federal police, with one student killed and others arrested. In January, some 340 Addis Ababa University Oromo students were arrested and abused for protesting against the Oromia regional government's decision to move its capital from Addis Ababa to Adama (Nazreth).

The government tried to prevent news about the 'Arab Spring' from reaching mass audiences in Ethiopia and none of the state media reported on it in any detail. Occasional acts of protest occurred, but did not spark mass movements. On 11 November, Yenesew

Gebre, a 29-year-old school teacher from the southern town of Waka, set himself on fire, apparently in protest against Ethiopia's repressive politics. Proper medical care was not given and he died of his injuries. This was not reported by any media except opposition diaspora websites (difficult to access in Ethiopia).

Local human rights organisations could no longer operate, their accounts being frozen and their field investigators harassed. Only a government-instituted human rights council was tolerated but it produced no reports during the year. The annual reports of HRW, AI, the Committee for the Protection of Journalists, Reporters without Borders, etc., were highly critical of the regime's overall record, registering no improvement over previous years. The 2011 US State Department's annual human rights report also referred to a depressing catalogue of serious human rights problems.

Foreign Affairs

Foreign policy was the sole prerogative of the top echelons of the EPRDF, which rejected all other opinions or debates questioning the party's approach. Opposition parties, civic groups and the media had no impact on policy, and even ran the risk of being prosecuted for expressing their criticism.

In the **Horn of Africa region**, Ethiopia maintained cooperative relations with Kenya, Djibouti, Somaliland and Puntland, including in the fields of security, regional policy and economic relations, but these relations were characterised by an underlying fragility and volatility. Sudan was important as a growing oil supplier. There was some tension with **Egypt** over the implications of the Blue Nile dam, constructed by Ethiopia without any prior consultation with Egypt. In a surprising comment to parliament, Meles said on 4 April that Ethiopia should build a defence capacity to repel any "Egyptian threat". During the 35th session of UNESCO's World Heritage Committee in June in Paris, a call was made on Ethiopia to "immediately halt all construction" of a second mega-dam, Gibe-3, due to its potential damage to world heritage sites and to Lake Turkana.

Ethiopia continued to support **Somalia**'s transitional federal government (TFG) in Mogadishu against the radical insurgency of the Islamist al-Shabaab movement and cooperated with some local Somali militias allied with the TFG. In December, Ethiopia carried out military operations near its border with northern Somalia to back efforts by the TFG and the AU Mission in Somalia (AMISOM) to combat al-Shabaab, which was on the retreat after the Kenyan military invasion in October. Ethiopia continued to play an important role in **IGAD**, the **AU**, and various international donor forums.

In July, Ethiopia deployed troops to the contested **Abyei** area in **Sudan,** as major part of the UN Interim Security Force for Abyei.

Relations with **Eritrea** remained as tense as ever. There were no signs of a solution to the border dispute, and the government kept a large military force in place near the border.

Economic links were also absent. Government rhetoric against the Eritrean leadership and plans for its removal continued. In his performance report to parliament in April, Meles announced a more assertive policy towards Eritrea, abandoning the so-called "passive defensive attitude". In addition to diplomatic pressure, support for Eritrean opposition groups in exile was also stepped up. In April, the completion was announced of the installation of power transmission lines to Sudan and Djibouti, intended for the future export of energy from the mega-dam hydropower stations.

Internationally, relations with **China** and **India** (the largest foreign investors in Ethiopia) as well as other Asian countries grew in intensity, driven by the economic logic of easier loans, investments and the absence of any political conditions. The government also strengthened its relations with emerging countries such as Turkey and Malaysia. On 23 August, Turkish Foreign Minister Ahmet Davutoglu visited Addis Ababa for economic cooperation talks and a visit to the AU.

Ethiopia also continued to enjoy the economic support of the **traditional donor countries** – mainly the EU and the USA – who had no qualms about the political stagnation and repression in the country and did not insist on respect for constitutional rights and accepted political and media freedoms. Ethiopia continued to be perceived as a **security partner** of Western and Middle Eastern countries in the wider Horn of Africa against Islamist terrorism in Somalia and the spread of al-Qaida-like groups from Yemen and other areas. This largely 'immunised' it from serious criticism of its domestic political record.

During the year, a large number of confidential US embassy cables (from the Addis Ababa embassy and covering the years 2006–2010) was released by **Wikileaks** and revealed **strongly critical views** on the Ethiopian government, often in stark contrast to official US State Department policy.

In July, **two Swedish journalists** were **arrested** in the Ogaden area and charged with "illegal entry" (via Somaliland) and "**support to a terrorist organization**" – the rebel ONLF on which they were making a news report. They were charged and faced the prospect of long prison sentences. International journalist associations, the Swedish and other foreign governments and the Ethiopian opposition called for their release. In an unprecedented trial in December, they were sentenced to 11 years in prison, although negotiations on their release started soon afterwards.

Ethiopia was **visited** by a number of **world leaders**. On 13–14 June, US Secretary of State Hillary Clinton attended for talks with the government and at the AU. Egypt's new Prime Minister Essam Sharaf visited in May, former US President George Bush, whose humanitarian charity ran a health programme in the country, in December, and UN Secretary-General Ban Ki-moon on 25–27 May to attend the AU summit and visit some health extension projects in northern Ethiopia. In January, French President Nicolas Sarkozy visited at the head of a business delegation for talks with the government and to attend an AU summit. Even Bill Gates, as philanthropist and head of his Gates Foundation, visited the country on 27–28 March for talks with the government on health policy and agriculture. Various high-level politicians from the UK (Ethiopia's major European donor) also visited, including: in July, Minister for Africa Henry Bellingham; in August, **Mark Lowcock**, Permanent Secretary of DFID (this institution was a major Ethiopia cheerleader); and in June, Simon Fraser, a permanent under-secretary at the Foreign and Commonwealth Office.

Prime Minister Meles made several **foreign diplomatic trips**. On 27 January, he was at the World Economic Forum in Davos, Switzerland; on 30 June, he attended the 17th AU summit in Malabo, Equatorial Guinea, giving a keynote speech on 'youth empowerment'. He also chaired meetings of the Committee of Heads of State and Government on Climate Change, held at the Malabo summit, and, on 16 November, at the AU in Addis Ababa. In May, he attended the G-8 summit in Deauville, France. In September, he went to the US, where he was invited by Columbia University to give a speech on his "developmental state model", and was there met with vociferous objections from the large Ethiopian diaspora audience present. On 10–11 October, he attended the large international 'Energy for All' conference in Oslo, Norway. He also paid a visit to Cairo for talks with the Egyptian government in September, where an agreement for a 'trilateral committee' (Egypt, Sudan and Ethiopia) to manage the Nile issue was signed.

Relations with **Egypt** thus seemed to be improving slightly after an earlier row over the planned building of the Blue Nile Dam, when Ethiopia's minister for water resources had in April even ruled out granting permission for an Egyptian representative to visit the site of the dam. On 12 November, a 25–member Egyptian delegation arrived in Addis Ababa on a working visit to discuss economic cooperation and the dam issue, which remained a delicate subject.

Cross-border migration of people and goods across Ethiopia's rather porous frontiers continued, and there were also substantial flows of **contraband goods** into the country, both with and without bribes, from Djibouti, Somaliland, Puntland and Kenya.

Socioeconomic Developments

The year was marked by another very serious **drought** and food shortages in southern and eastern Ethiopia – extending to south-central Somalia, and particularly evident in the Oromo, Afar and Somali-inhabited areas. While Ethiopia needed regular additional food aid for some 3–4 m people, as in previous years, this year's drought presented an added emergency, although not an acute famine endangering the lives of millions, as some media and NGO reports claimed. The severe drought, said to be "the worst in 60 years", demanded extra relief food assistance for some 4.5 m people (or $ 398 m). Several thousands died but a major famine disaster was averted via domestic and especially international resources (from the USA, WFP and UNHCR).

Ethiopia made some progress in **increasing food production** through incentives, new land exploitation and more use of fertilisers. The absolute number of those in need remained more or less constant, despite the 3% annual population growth rate. The economy overall maintained a **high rate of growth**, although skewed toward donor-funded infrastructure outlay and growth in services, rather than in productive capacity.

Ethiopia's **population** increased this year by almost 2 m people, reaching an estimated 85 m. Population density thus increased, impacting strongly on resource use and complicating livelihoods, access to land, food security and ecological sustainability. In **urban areas**, notably the capital, Addis Ababa, urban 'renewal' went ahead full-speed, with the destruction and replacement of old, popular neighbourhoods in the city centre and the transfer of the population to the outskirts of town, into new three- and four-storey 'condominium housing' complexes. The plan was to turn Addis Ababa's city centre into a massive business district without "slum neighbourhoods". Many complaints were heard among displaced persons about the new, substandard facilities, the delays in delivery, the disruption of solid social networks, and the loss of employment and income. On 28 November, a controversial new 'Urban Lands Lease Holding Proclamation' was gazetted, which in effect nationalised urban land and eliminated all remaining forms of transferable and inheritable urban private property: such property would have to be held on lease so that everything could eventually be redistributed and expropriated at will by the authorities.

The **environmental impact** of large-scale land acquisitions and investments – many of them monocultures of sugar cane, rice, maize or bio-fuels over vast areas, destined for export – was not seen as an issue of concern in government policy.

The economy of **pastoral societies** on the southern and eastern fringes of the Ethiopian highlands was again under pressure from government sedentarisation and land alienation policies that privileged cultivators over herders, accompanied by a civilisational discourse labelling pastoral people as "primitive" and "backward" (e.g., in a speech by Meles on 25 January). There were no successful compensation schemes for displaced or dispossessed pastoralists – who were without territory rights as they formally lived on state land and whose customary rights were rarely recognised – making these people increasingly vulnerable and marginalised.

More land was cultivated for agrarian production by both smallholders and new investors, and the government seemed to step up the incentivisation of the country's farmers. However, parts of existing national parks were also handed over to domestic and foreign agrarian investors. The enforcement of existing environmental laws was lax, and the EPA was notable for its lack of impact and activity; it usually supported all government measures. The EPA did not pursue its role of demanding environmental impact assessments and implementation clauses from new agrarian investors. Neither national policies on ecological sustainability nor meaningful respect for the customary use rights of locals –

notably pastoralists – were in evidence, as the gospel of quantifiable economic growth was put above all.

Some **mining** companies, both foreign and domestic, started up new mining exploration ventures (prospecting for potash, gold, tantalum, nickel) in eastern and southern Ethiopia.

The economy showed a **GDP growth** of 7.5% to a total volume of $ 95 bn. The **per capita GDP** rose to $ 380. Government spending made up some 20% of GDP. Domestic tax revenue grew by almost 20%, most of it from dues on imported goods. **Export** proceeds increased by an estimated 30% to about $ 2.5 bn, and growth was chiefly in newer sectors such as gold mining, flowers, horticulture, hides, skins and leather products, and *ch'at* (the stimulant Catha edulis), while income from the country's traditional export product, coffee, stagnated. The main export destinations were China and Germany. Imports came primarily from China, the US and Saudi Arabia.

Manufacturing growth occurred (in textiles and leather), but was limited and below potential, as overall investments went mostly into infrastructure (particularly dams and road building) and services. Job growth occurred notably in the service sector, which yielded 43% of GDP. Agriculture contributed 44% to the national GDP and grew in absolute terms but hardly in relative size. Some 80% of Ethiopia's working population were engaged in agriculture, and 6% in industry. The **private business sector** remained weak, with state and party-affiliated businesses (notably the ruling party-linked EFFORT business empire) taking the lion's share of economic activity and protecting their access and interests. The major private player (although closely linked to the government) was multi-billionaire Saudi-Ethiopian tycoon al-Amoudi, who made many new investments in commercial agriculture. **Unemployment** remained very high, although exact figures were not available and calculations differed. Estimates varied from 24% to 50%. Youth unemployment remained alarming, with estimates as high as 60%–70%. The higher education institutions kept on expanding and producing graduates, but they found no jobs.

Economic growth did little to alleviate the employment and poverty problems. With regard to ICT, the **mobile phone market** expanded in tandem with population growth, but lagged behind growth rates and coverage in most other African countries. The **sole Internet provider** remained the Ethiopian Telecommunications Corporation, which, despite technical innovations and extension of services and coverage, did not allow full demand-driven expansion and information freedom. The state also maintained its **ban on foreign banks** entering the domestic market, but this was a move widely supported by the population. Ethiopia continued its membership negotiations with the WTO. The country maintained its huge **trade balance deficit**, with imports exceeding exports by $ 5 bn, or 250%. **Remittances** from Ethiopians abroad to relatives and friends in the country were only partly registered, but reached an estimated $ 1.5 bn.

Another worrying sign amidst the news of economic growth was the jump in **foreign debt**: although Ethiopia had significantly reduced its debt in 2008 under the HIPC initiative, when it fell to $ 2.7 bn, it reached $ 12 bn (or ETB (birr) 200 bn) in December. Most of this was due to huge loans and investments in infrastructural schemes, including the Renaissance Dam, Gibe-3 Dam, new railway plans and agrarian state plantation outlays. Some 47% of the foreign debt was now owed to China (which in 2011 lent the state-owned Commercial Bank of Ethiopia $ 300 m in one go); other substantial lenders were India and the Kuwait Fund. Although figures differed with regard to their source and calculation method, the public debt reached an amount between 29% and 42% of GDP; foreign debt was half of this sum. Total international aid to the country (including loans and grants) amounted to about $ 3 bn., the largest in Africa. According to UNCTAD's Investment Report, however, **foreign direct investment** had declined compared with the previous year to $ 184 m.

The national **budget** for the budget year July 2011–June 2012 was ETB 117.8 (or $ 6.8 bn), a 39% rise compared with 2010. Some 59% of government spending was on capital expenditure, i.e., on infrastructure, energy supply, state housing complexes, state companies, education, health facilities, etc. About 39% was allocated to the regional governments.

The economy was marked by **very high inflation**, which hit the middle classes and the poor very hard: the annual rate computed in December was 35%, with food inflation reaching 46%, the highest in Africa. Non-food inflation was 21% on an annual basis. This high rate – also reflected in the higher state budget – was explained by the government's expansionist monetary policy, and, as the government emphasised in order to shift the blame, by external, world market factors. The IMF and World Bank contended that, at the most, only 15% of the 35% rate could be explained by such external factors. In January, the government tried to combat inflation with enforced price controls and threats to the nation's traders, but this was a total failure, as the policy did not address the root causes of the problem.

The **very ambitious investment programmes** under the 2010 Growth and Transformation Plan caused the World Bank head in Ethiopia in July to issue warnings that these plans were unrealistic, unsustainable, and far beyond Ethiopia's means. A row between the government and the World Bank followed. The underlying assumption of the regime appeared to be that the global donor community would again in due course have to cough up the costs or issue debt forgiveness, as a 'reward' for its economic growth policy. For the 5,250–MW Renaissance Dam, under construction since early 2011 in a gorge 40 km from the Sudanese border, the government raised ETB 7 bn ($ 408 m) domestically via government bonds, with the general public constantly urged to buy them. Civil servants were forced to acquire them 'voluntarily' by handing in one month's salary.

According to the World Bank's Global Business Report, the **business climate deteriorated** somewhat, despite all the news about growth figures. Ethiopia dropped seven places on the 'Doing Business' index, mainly due to additional restrictive regulations, bureaucratic complexity, lack of trust, judicial insecurity and corruption. **Corruption**, however, was still significantly lower than the African average. On TI's global 'Corruption Perception Index', Ethiopia was ranked 116th out of a total of 178 countries, but its ranking did not fall either, despite judicial action against dozens of officials. Notably problematic were the top levels of government, regional governments and parastatal entities. Anti-corruption drives were selective and often seemed politically motivated. The growing restrictions on doing business also showed the naivety of foreign investors and company owners, who did not count on the ultimately politically conditioned business environment, where state directives could suddenly change the rules of the game and force those who had already invested a lot to just go away and take the losses.

An estimated 29% of the population remained below the **poverty line**, which was nevertheless a reduction of 5%, and on this score, as on health, child mortality and education enrolment indicators, Ethiopia performed comparatively well on the UN MDGs. Life expectancy and the general educational level (and literacy) rose. On other world indexes measuring wider human development, such as the Multidimensional Poverty Index or the Legatum Prosperity Index, Ethiopia did not do well.

In 2011, Ethiopia hosted more than 290,000 **refugees** from neighbouring Eritrea, Sudan and Somalia. Up to 55,000 **Eritreans**, mainly young males, continued to flee to Ethiopia to escape national (army) service, unemployment and repression in Eritrea. The drought and famine in south-central Somalia caused an estimated 130,000 **Somalis** to enter UNHCR camps in Ethiopia (mainly Dolo Ado). More than 27,000 **Sudanese** refugees from the Blue Nile Region entered Ethiopia in September-October after violent clashes that began on 1 September between the Sudanese army and rebels from the Sudan People's Liberation Movement North, later followed by another 19,000. On 8 December, Ethiopia became a member of the International Organization for Migration, which allowed it to seek more international assistance and cooperation on migration and refugee issues.

Out-migration roughly comprised two groups: poorer migrants in search of work in neighbouring countries and the Middle East (via Djibouti, Kenya and Bosaasso port in Puntland), and the more educated – often professionals, intellectuals and political dissidents. Figures for both remained relatively high, running into many thousands. The first group also comprised the many hundreds of children given for adoption and the victims of child and woman trafficking. The latter out-migration, of educated people, put Ethiopia among the global top-20 of countries affected by 'brain drain'. A special group of migrants were the about 3,000 'Falash Mura' people, descendants of Ethiopian Jews or Beta Israel, who were able to move to Israel, their preferred destination.

Wood being the chief source of household energy in the countryside, **deforestation** went on unabated in the wake of high population growth. The problems of **pollution** by industry, horticulture (flower industry chemicals) and consumer waste (e.g. huge amounts of batteries and plastic bags scattered in the landscape) was not addressed. Environmental sustainability was a remote ideal. The government announced plans to invest in solar and wind energy with the help of donor country funding. The construction of mega-dams for hydro-energy was also claimed to contribute to solving Ethiopia's long-term energy supply problems, but the possible local environmental and economic damage caused by these mega-schemes (also intended for future 'energy export' to Sudan, Djibouti and Kenya), in contrast to that of existing micro-dams, loomed large.

Jon Abbink

Kenya

The case against six prominent Kenyans at the ICC continued to dominate the headlines, as political leaders sought to manipulate the proceedings for their own benefit ahead of the next elections. Towards the end of the year, the government's decision to invade Somalia, and the threat of reprisals by al-Shabaab, transformed Kenya's foreign affairs. Relations between the government and Kenya's own Muslim population subsequently deteriorated and the popularity of separatist groups in Coast Province increased. However, despite consistent reports of corruption and a dip in tourist numbers following a series of high-profile abductions close to the Somali border, the power-sharing government managed to deliver economic growth and relative political stability.

Domestic Politics

Domestic political developments continued to be overshadowed and shaped by the **ICC** investigation into six prominent Kenyans accused of crimes against humanity. The charges stemmed from the role they were alleged to have played in the post-election violence, which left over 1,000 people dead and 660,000 internally displaced in early 2008. The clashes, triggered by the controversial re-election of **President Mwai Kibaki** in late 2007, pitted state forces and gangs aligned to Kibaki's Party of National Unity (PNU) against militias allegedly organised by members of the Orange Democratic Movement (ODM), an opposition alliance led by **Raila Odinga**. To end the violence, a power-sharing government was established in February 2008. The political settlement allowed Kibaki to retain the position of president and created the post of prime minister to accommodate Odinga. In May 2008, the Committee of Investigation into the Post-Election Violence, better known as the **Waki Commission**, was established to investigate the violence. Fearing that the government would whitewash the report, the Commission gave an envelope containing the names of six high-profile suspects to former UN Secretary-General **Kofi Annan**, who in turn promised to give the envelope to the ICC unless a credible domestic tribunal was established. Following the failure of the Kenyan government to make significant progress towards the arrest of the suspects, the ICC publicly named the accused and made an application for summonses to be issued against them on 15 December 2010.

To avoid politicising the process, the list was designed to include an equal number of individuals from each political camp. The **accused** therefore included **three allies of Kibaki** – Deputy Prime Minister Uhuru Kenyatta; Permanent Secretary to the President and Secretary to the Cabinet Francis Muthaura; and Mohammed Hussein Ali, former police chief – along with **three allies of Odinga** – former minister for industrialisation Henry Kosgey, former education minister William Ruto, and Joshua Arap Sang, a radio executive. However, much had changed since the chaotic days of early 2008. Most notably, having realised that both of their names were on Annan's list, **Uhuru Kenyatta** and **William Ruto** had formed a new 'anti-prosecution' alliance. This unlikely backdoor coalition between two former rivals was widely believed to have the backing of Kibaki and to have enlisted the services of Vice President Kalonzo Musyoka. The main short-term consequence of this political realignment was a rapid deterioration in relations between Odinga and Ruto and the collapse of the ODM.

Following the formation of the informal **'KKK'** alliance – so-called because Kenyatta, Musyoka and Ruto were leaders from the Kikuyu, Kamba, and Kalenjin communities, respectively – Odinga and Kibaki began to adopt very different approaches to the ICC process. The 'anti-prosecution' camp around Kibaki became increasingly strident in its criticism of the ICC, seeking to halt the international process in favour of domestic court cases that it could more easily control. On 23 December 2010, Isaac Ruto, a close ally (but not a relation) of William Ruto, introduced a motion in parliament to withdraw Kenya from the ICC's **Treaty of Rome**. The motion was passed but was ultimately an empty gesture for two reasons. First, actually removing Kenya from the Treaty would involve complicated constitutional changes that would have required significant time and energy to effect. Second, active ICC cases were not halted when a country voted to leave the Treaty. Nonetheless, the vote sent a clear signal that Kibaki and Kenyatta intended to use their positions within the government to fight the proceedings.

In January, the KKK alliance redoubled its efforts. **Kalonzo Musyoka** was dispatched by Kibaki to build support around Africa for an appeal to defer the investigation for

12 months under article 53(4) of the Rome Statute, which allows prosecutions to be halted "in the interests of peace and security". Kibaki's hope was that a deferral would give the government sufficient time to establish a domestic tribunal. If such a local process were seen to be credible by international actors, the accused could be tried locally with the ICC taking on an oversight, rather than a prosecuting, role. Initially, Musyoka's mission appeared destined for success. Following positive meetings with South African President Jacob Zuma, Ugandan President Yoweri Museveni, and Ethiopian Prime Minister Meles Zenawi, the **AU** officially endorsed Kenya's request on 1 February.

While Musyoka was performing shuttle diplomacy, **Raila Odinga**, the main rival of the KKK, found himself in a difficult position. He obviously stood to gain if Kenyatta and Ruto were prevented from contesting future elections. However, Odinga also recognised that, if he openly supported the ICC process, he would leave himself open to accusations that he was a lackey of the West prepared to sell out Kenyan sovereignty for his personal benefit. Odinga therefore went to great lengths to argue that he was not using the ICC process for political ends, and distanced himself from the campaign to support the ICC action at a rally in Bungoma on 8 February. But as the debate heated up, Odinga emerged as an important and influential proponent of prosecutions at The Hague. In response to Musyoka's success with the AU, Odinga's allies lobbied the **UN Secretary-General** and the **UNSC** to reject the appeal. A petition submitted by the Network for Global Justice listed 15 reasons "why the Kenyan cases at the ICC must neither be deferred nor referred". These included the fact that the prosecutions did not pose a real threat to peace and security, that local trials would be used to "shield the suspects from justice", and that the prime minister, a signatory to the power-sharing agreement, "does NOT support deferral" (emphasis in the original text).

Although Musyoka had won many of the battles along the way, the KKK lost the war. Key UNSC members, including **Great Britain** and the **USA,** let it be known that they would not support a postponement, forcing the government to abandon its efforts at the UN in favour of a direct appeal to the ICC. The case was heard on 30 August and, although one judge sided with the Kenyan government, the majority rejected the appeal. In delivering his summary, the presiding judge, Daniel David Ntanda Nsereko, explained that "for the cases to be inadmissible, a national investigation must be ongoing and must cover the same individuals and substantially the same conduct as alleged in the proceedings before the ICC". Furthermore, the ICC Appeals Chamber considered that the Pre-Trial Chamber made no error when it found that the government of Kenya had failed to provide sufficient evidence to substantiate that it was investigating the six suspects for the crimes alleged in the summonses issued against them.

During the long wait for the appeals process to reach its conclusion, the prosecution process had rolled on. On 8 March the accused – known locally as the **'Ocampo Six'** after the ICC's Prosecutor Luis Moreno Ocampo – were officially indicted by the ICC's Pre-Trial Chamber II and summoned to appear before the Court. Many of the accused hired lawyers with considerable experience of international tribunals. Kenyatta acquired the services of British lawyers Steven Kay and Gillian Higgins, who had previously defended Slobodan Milosovic during the Tribunal for the former Yugoslavia, while Muthaura recruited Karim Ahmad Khan, who had defended Liberia's Charles Taylor. The announcement that the Kenyan government would pay the legal costs of Muthaura and Ali, because the charges against them related to a period in which they were employed by the state, generated widespread criticism. On 7 April, the initial hearing to decide whether the accused would have to face formal charges began. The prosecutor effectively decided to run two separate cases, one against Kosgey, Ruto and Sang, and one against Ali, Kenyatta and Muthaura. The former group were charged with murder, deportation or forcible transfer of a population, and persecution. The latter group were also charged with these crimes, but were additionally accused of rape and other forms of sexual violence and inhumane acts.

The proceedings of the Pre-Trial Chamber made the top billing in Kenyan television shows and newspapers for months, playing into and transforming domestic political dynamics. The presentation of evidence linking Kosgey, Ruto and Sang to the organisation of violence against Kikuyu, Kamba and Kisii groups in Rift Valley Province exacerbated ethnic tensions. Moreover, the allegation that Ali, Kenyatta and Muthaura had co-opted the leadership of the notorious **Mungiki** gang to keep Kibaki in power at all costs, and that Muthaura and Ali had deliberately instructed the police not to protect Kenyan citizens targeted by the group, further eroded confidence in the state. The response of the accused did not help to calm the situation. Kenyatta and Ruto came out fighting, declaring that they intended to stand for the presidency at the next elections, whatever the outcome of the ICC process. During and after the Pre-Trial sessions, the two leaders held joint '**prayer meetings**' at which participants criticised the ICC, lambasted Odinga, and prayed for the safe return of the Ocampo Six from The Hague. This, and the sense that foreigners were meddling in Kenyan affairs, contributed to the emergence of a siege mentality within Kenyatta's and Ruto's home areas of Central Province and Rift Valley Province, respectively. For example, following a prayer meeting held in Bomet on 2 April, 30 MPs declared that they would "stand with Uhuru and Ruto to the bitter end". As a result, the ICC investigation simultaneously made the accused more popular among their core support group and less palatable to the wider population.

As Kenyatta, Odinga and Ruto jostled for position ahead of the next elections – which Kibaki was unable to contest, having served two terms in office – Kibaki and Odinga used **cabinet reshuffles** to strengthen the positions of their allies. Under the power-sharing deal, the two leaders were given full control over the ministries allocated to their parties. In a reshuffle on 8 August, Odinga moved to dismiss former allies who had rejected his leadership or otherwise disappointed him. Ruto was replaced as higher education minister by Professor Margaret Kamar, while nominated MP Musa Sirma replaced Professor Hellen Sambili as EAC Minister and Voi MP Dan Mwazo replaced Aden Duale as livestock minister. Odinga's intention was to regain the political initiative, but some of his decisions smacked of desperation. Having sacked some of the ODM's most powerful figures from the contested Rift Valley Province, he sought to replace them with individuals of dubious character and influence. Most notably, by appointing Kamar, Odinga aligned himself with her husband, **Nicholas Biwott**, a man whose reputation as one of the most corrupt and vicious of Kenyan politicians during the particularly corrupt and vicious regime of Daniel arap Moi was well deserved. Odinga's willingness to associate himself with the Biwotts called into question his commitment to reform Kenyan politics. At the same time, critics suggested that Biwott's influence in the Rift Valley had waned to such an extent that the appointment of Kamar had been futile. Indeed, shortly after accepting her position, the new minister was forced to speak out against the suggestion that, by aligning herself publicly with the prime minister, she had committed "political suicide".

While Odinga's reshuffle grabbed the headlines, Kibaki used the opportunity to quietly reinstate **Foreign Affairs Minister** Moses Wetang'ula, following his earlier suspension on corruption charges. Wetang'ula's reappointment served as an important reminder, if one was needed, that anti-corruption efforts had stalled. Following his appointment as director of the **Kenyan Anti-Corruption Commission (KACC)** in 2010, Patrick Lock Otieno Lumumba (popularly known as PLO) had impressed Kenyans and donors alike by launching investigations into a number of prominent individuals. In addition to Wetang'ula, Industrialisation Minister Henry Kosgey and Education Minister William Ruto were all forced to resign their posts pending the outcome of corruption investigations. But as had happened so often in the past, anti-corruption efforts floundered due to a lack of political will. As a result, none of the KACC's major investigations led to prosecutions, and one by one those accused of corruption were allowed to return to government.

Frustrated by the lack of progress, **Lumumba**, like his well-known predecessor John Githongo, went public with evidence that elected politicians had deliberately blocked his efforts. On 22 August, he accused Cecily Mbarire of offering him a $ 1,000 bribe to slow down an investigation into the minister of water and irrigation. Mbarire replied that the money had been a charitable donation that Lumumba had solicited, and filed a lawsuit for defamation. Lumumba's gambit was remarkable because, in contrast to Githongo, who left the country after revealing details of the Anglo-Leasing scandal, Lumumba stood his ground. The response of Kenya's political elite was predictable. Charity Ngilu, now water and irrigation minister but formerly the minister for justice and controversial affairs, said that Lumumba's appointment had been a "big mistake".

Those threatened by the KACC's activist stance did not have to wait long for an opportunity to undermine the organisation and its director. The new Kenyan constitution, promulgated on 27 August 2010, envisaged a new anti-corruption framework, which required new legislation to be passed by parliament. The resulting **Ethics and Anti-Corruption Bill** represented the perfect opportunity to remove Lumumba and undermine the KACC. According to Chairman of the National Council of NGOs Ken Wafula, the proposal finally put before the legislature was little more than a personal attack on Lumumba. Wafula campaigned against the legislation, arguing that it would "greatly undermine the fight against corruption", but to no avail. When Kibaki signed the new legislation into effect with unusual efficiency on 28 August, Lumumba and his four deputies were effectively sacked. The post of director and the four posts of deputy directors were left vacant, pending the outcome of a political appointment process. This decision effectively stalled anti-corruption investigations for the rest of the year and a new Ethics and Anti-Corruption Commission remained to be created.

The disembowelling of the KACC encouraged the abuse of public office by a political class that systematically misused state funds. A Food Assistance Integrity Study conducted by **TI** in late 2011 (in partnership with the UN and the government of Kenya) found that much of the **food aid** intended for the 3.75 m Kenyans suffering shortages resulting from the **drought** crisis in parts of the country was diverted to the supporters of political leaders, local elites, and those in charge of local relief committees. The investigation also provided evidence that in some cases rations were looted and sold on, instead of being given freely to those in need. Executive Director of TI Kenya Samuel Kimeu, noted that food aid was particularly susceptible to corruption as a result of its scale and the difficulty of tracking its ultimate destination. He added that the organisation was concerned at the "internal pressures to employ relief staff from certain communities and there were also risks and challenges in transporting the food due to political influence in procuring trucking companies, and transportation costs not being adequately resourced by the government".

The Anti-Corruption Bill was only one of the pieces of **legislation** that had to be considered by parliament as a result of the new constitution. Partly because the draft was put together fairly quickly (notwithstanding numerous previous constitutional review processes), and partly because it would have been unfeasible to build consensus on the minutiae of every point, the constitution delegated responsibility for many of the details to the legislature. As a result, constitutional experts estimated that the new constitution would not fully come into force until 49 separate pieces of legislation had gone through parliament. In 2011, parliament passed a phenomenal amount of legislation including the Commission on Administrative Justice Act, the Kenya National Commission on Human Rights Act, the Commission on Revenue Collection Act, the National Police Service Act, the Political Parties Act, the Industrial Court Act, the Kenya Citizen and Immigration Act, and many others. The speed with which these laws were enacted, and the lack of debate over many of them, led to concerns that Kenya's Second Republic would inherit a poorly drafted legal framework that would fail to eradicate the loopholes and ambiguities that had plagued the First Republic.

On 12 September, Kenya suffered a further domestic tragedy when a **petrol pipeline explosion** in Nairobi killed over 100 people and injured 100 more. According to reports from the scene, the blast was caused by someone throwing a cigarette butt into a sewer that had filled with fuel following a leak in the Mombasa-Nairobi pipeline. The pipeline runs through the Sinai slum and, because many residents had rushed to collect the leaking fuel, they found themselves at the heart of the explosion. The accident had a deleterious effect on national morale and, in the days that followed, it seemed that everyone was looking for someone to blame. The media criticised the **Kenya Pipeline Company (KPC)** for not investing more to prevent leaks, and the government for failing to regulate the industry and the slow response time of the emergency services. For their part, the politicians were happy to deflect criticism on to the KPC. On the day of the tragedy, three MPs and their supporters, led by Gideon Mbuvi, better known locally as Mike Sonko (meaning boss or rich person in Sheng, the dialect spoken by many young people in Nairobi), stormed the KPC headquarters. The mob overpowered security officers but were unable to meet with the management to press their demand of full compensation for the victims and their families.

The decision to send **troops into Somalia** on 16 October, and the resulting threat of reprisals by the radical Islamist group, al-Shabaab, had significant domestic consequences. Most notably, the threat of terrorist attacks within Kenya led the police to crack down on Somali communities, which in turn placed greater strain on Christian-Muslim relations. The relationship between Kenyan Somalis and the state had always been problematic. In the run-up to the end of colonial rule, many Somalis expressed their wish to join a greater Somalia rather than to be subsumed within the Kenyan nation. The resulting **'Shifta War'** ended in 1968, when the government finally put down the uprising, but over the next 40 years successive regimes treated the Somali communities living in North-Eastern Kenya with both suspicion and contempt.

The growth of the Somali community in the Eastleigh neighbourhood of Nairobi over the last decade shifted the focus of concern to the capital city itself. Chatham House estimated that Eastleigh, or **'Little Mogadishu'** as it is commonly known, had so far received over $ 1.5 bn in investments from Somali businessmen. As a result, the area had grown rapidly in economic and political influence, inspiring both jealousy and fear among rival communities. Significantly, many Somali networks, including those related to the Transitional Federal Government and the al-Shabaab rebellion, were said to be run from, or to run through, Eastleigh. In response, the government placed the area under increasing scrutiny, a policy shift that was epitomised by a set of police raids intended to root out **illegal immigrants** on 6 December 2010. A total of 346 people were arrested, mostly of Somali or Ethiopian origin. Following a series of al-Shabaab inspired grenade attacks on the capital in late October, the state's presence on the ground in Eastleigh increased dramatically. But despite the government's concerns, many Eastleigh residents were ambivalent about the invasion, while many of those who had fled Somalia to escape al-Shabaab explicitly supported the war. However, this did not stop the government from launching "the mother of all operations" on 20 October to root out supporters of the terrorist organisation. The crackdown included stop-and-search programmes, a strong police presence and routine demands for Kenyans of Somali appearance to show their identity papers. Unsurprisingly, this combative approach led **Somali human rights groups** to accuse the government of racial profiling and of creating a repressive atmosphere that would make it easier for al-Shabaab to recruit new members.

The government's relations with non-Somali Muslims also deteriorated after **Elgiva Bwire Olicacha** confessed to having participated in a grenade attack on Nairobi in late October. Bwire's involvement played to the worst fears of the Christian elite, because he had enjoyed an ordinary Kenyan upbringing before converting to Islam. Bwire's involvement in the attacks therefore exacerbated concerns that Kenya's non-Somali Muslim population sympathised with, and might in some instances actively support, al-Shabaab. The government responded by instigating a further crackdown on Kenyan Muslim organisations accused of having links to Somali groups. This exacerbated tensions between the PNU and Muslim communities in Coast Province, which had deteriorated after Muslim leaders supported Odinga in the 2007 elections. Kibaki's victory, and his introduction of anti-terror legislation that made it easier to target Muslim groups, reinforced a long running sense of injustice and marginalisation. Partly as a result, groups such as the **Mombasa Republican Council** (MRC) appeared to have won new converts in their campaign for the secession of the coastal region. The MRC was banned in 2009, but continued to operate covertly. On 21 May, 30 MRC members were arrested and charged with organised criminal activity. Over the following months, the court case raised the profile of the group, as blogs and newspapers ran sensationalised stories that the MRC was recruiting youths who had allegedly been radicalised by the governments "anti-Muslim stance". The government provided official backing for this story on 1 November, when Coast Provincial Commissioner Ernest Munyi, said that the MRC was known to be "working closely with al-Shabaab associates" and "recruiting youth for training on military activities". However, in reality religion played a secondary role in the formation of the MRC, which had always been keen to portray itself as an inclusive regional movement, and the authorities may well have exaggerated its size and radical leanings in order to justify a heavy-handed response.

Foreign Affairs

A number of **abductions and kidnappings** in the second half of the year demonstrated the porous nature of the Kenya-Somalia border and triggered Kenya's first serious deployment of troops on foreign soil. On 11 September, a gang that had travelled down from Somalia abducted a British woman from a coastal resort, killing her husband during the attack. A second kidnapping followed on 1 October, when Somali gunmen took a wheelchair-bound Frenchwoman hostage in the popular tourist resort of Lamu. Although the British woman was later released, the French woman died in captivity. These incidents were followed by the abduction of two Spanish doctors and two local Kenyan staff from the Dadaab refugee camp on 13 October. Just three days later, around 3,000 **Kenyan**

troops invaded Somalia. The official justification for the operation was to push back the Islamist militants the government accused of perpetrating the kidnappings. However, there were two good reasons for doubting that the abductions were the work of **al-Shabaab**. First, al-Shabaab was known for taking credit for its attacks, but vehemently denied any involvement in the abductions. Second, some of al-Shabaab's most important economic network flowed through Nairobi and many injured al-Shabaab fighters went to Nairobi to receive treatment. Given this, the group had more to lose than to gain by unnecessarily antagonising the Kenyan state.

The precise motivations behind the invasion remained unclear. Kenyan officials initially claimed that they had been asked to deploy troops by Somalia's **Transitional Federal Government** (TFG), but this account was contradicted by the TFG itself. The confusion over exactly why Kenya had gone to war inspired the country's vibrant media and blog scene to advance alternative explanations. Some suggested that **Minister of Internal Security George Saitoti**, and **Foreign Minister Moses Wetang'ula** had promoted the invasion as a way of raising their own profiles ahead of the next presidential elections. While Kibaki largely stayed out of the limelight after October, his ministers rushed to make political capital out of the invasion. Others argued that the Kenyan military had for years been itching to move against Somali groups traversing the Kenyan border, while the political elite had become increasingly sympathetic to the idea of an intervention as a result of the growing political and economic significance of Somali networks in Nairobi. In other words, the abductions simply offered a useful cover for an operation that had already been planned. A third camp pointed out that Kenya's long-term development vision, Vision 2030, rested on the creation of a corridor from Lamu to Ethiopia and South Sudan, through which resources could be transported to and from a new port near Lamu. Because the abductions shook investor confidence, they threatened to undermine the government's ability to fund the project, forcing Kibaki to act to address the security situation in the region. Finally, still others pointed out that some of the territory occupied by Kenyan troops was thought to be resource-rich. By invading, the Kenyan government guaranteed itself a more prominent seat at the table for the next round of international negotiations on the rebuilding of Somalia, and the role that external states should play in the process.

There may be truth in some or all of these rumours, but there is currently not enough evidence for a clear explanation to be given. The high levels of secrecy and misinformation deployed by both sides also made it difficult to assess which party had the better of the fighting. The Kenyan government made reaching and securing the strategically important port of Kismayo its number one priority, using a combination of direct combat and targeted bombing. On 18 October, the military claimed that it had killed 73 al-Shabaab members in **air strikes** and that it was making steady progress. But a sign of things to come soon followed when a Kenyan convoy came under attack between the towns of Tabda and Bilis Qoqani on 28 October. According to the Kenyan government, nine al-Shabaab fighters were killed while two Kenyans were wounded, one critically. This account was rejected by an al-Shabaab spokesperson, who said that 20 Kenyans had died in the incident. As the fighting continued, the disagreement over casualties escalated into a bizarre war of words conducted over Twitter. After the Kenyan Army spokesman, Emmanual Chirchir had tweeted to warn Kenyan **donkey traders** not to sell to al-Shabaab, threatening that animals close to the border would be bombed, the militants responded, "Your eccentric battle strategy has got animal rights groups quite concerned, Major."

In addition to winning the battle of wits, al-Shabaab used various channels to threaten reprisals for the invasion and undermine Kenyan morale. Operating through international reporters, spokesman Sheikh Ali Mohamud Rage sent a chilling message to the Kenyan population: "Kenya has peace, its cities have tall buildings and business is booming there, while Somalia is in chaos. If your government ignores our calls to stop its aggression on Somali soil, we will strike at the heart of your interests." These were not idle threats. On 24 October, a **grenade attack** on a nightclub in the centre of **Nairobi** injured 12 people. The same day, there was a similar attack on a bus stop, which killed one person and wounded another 28. It was unclear to what extent the attacks were actually coordinated by al-Shabaab, but those subsequently arrested declared themselves to be supporters of the group. As the fighting continued, Kenya appealed for international assistance, with considerable success. The governments of the **USA** and the **UK** initially attempted to dissuade Kenya from invading, but had little choice but to tacitly support the operation once it had begun. For their part, the **AU** and **IGAD** both offered their official support.

France also provided logistical support, using its planes to transport military equipment and Kenyan soldiers. More significantly, the **Israeli government** received Odinga on 12–13 November and responded positively to the prime minister's request for assistance. According to Odinga's office, Prime Minister Benjamin Netanyahu declared that "Kenya's enemies are Israel's enemies" and pledged to build a "coalition against fundamentalism" with Kenya, Ethiopia, South Sudan and Tanzania. Meanwhile, Israel's President Shimon Peres promised to "make everything available" so that Kenya could secure its borders. This "security pact" had an immediate impact on the conflict. On 24 November, Israeli assassination drones launched from a Kenyan military base killed an estimated 17 people in southern Somalia. The Israeli government also supplied 13 "trainers" to assist the Kenyan army with technical matters and provided anti-terrorism experts to help Kenyan security agencies protect major towns and cities from attack. The Kenyan offensive received another boost on 20 November, when it was reported that **Ethiopian troops** had re-entered Somalia, opening up a new front against al-Shabaab. But despite the range of international actors lined up against the militants, Kenyan troops continued to make slow progress towards Kismayo and by the end of the year it remained unclear exactly what the government hoped to achieve, and whether it had a viable exit strategy.

As a result of the war in Somalia and the ICC proceedings, there was a plethora of visits from foreign dignitaries throughout the year. Important visitors included **Chinese Vice Premier Wang Quisham**, who met with Vice President Musyoka on 18 March in Nairobi, and Li Changchun, a member of the Standing Committee of the **Communist Party of China** and the Central Committee's Political Bureau, who visited Kenya the following month. During meetings with the president and the prime minister, Li expressed his opinion that bilateral ties between the two countries were the "best ever". The main focus of the trip was to finalise a cooperation agreement which committed China, among other things, to providing around $ 113 m of preferential loans to support higher education and scientific research. In a speech at Nairobi University on 20 April entitled 'Strengthening China-Africa Friendship and Cooperation to Build A Better Tomorrow', Li also pledged to double the number of annual government scholarships to Kenya from 32 to 64 and to support youth exchanges.

Relations with the **US** government were significantly more variable. The atmosphere at the start of the year was distinctly frosty after a report released by Wikileaks and published by the German magazine 'Der Spiegel' on 9 December 2010 revealed that US officials saw the Kenyan government as a "swamp of flourishing corruption". Government spokesman Alfred Matua claimed that the description was "malicious" and the government swiftly received an apology from US Assistant Secretary of State for African Affairs Johnny Carson. However, it was reported that Carson apologised for embarrassing the government but did not deny the evidence contained in the report. Relations appeared to be improving when an American delegation including US Deputy Secretary of State James Steinberg backed the Kenyan government's plans to initiate a war on drugs on 4 February. However, President Barack Obama's decision on 3 June to freeze the American assets of two Kenyans accused of being narcotics kingpins was unpopular with some factions of the Kenyan government. The source of the controversy was that one of those blacklisted was Harun Mwau, MP for Kilome and a former presidential candidate. Mwau was believed to own a large part of Nakumatt Supermarkets, one of the most successful retail chains in Africa, and to be one of Kenya's richest, and hence most influential, men. In response to Obama's statement, Mwau appealed to the Kenyan government to shield him, claiming that the US government wanted him dead because of the size of his business interests in America, which were thought to amount to $ 750 m. Although the government did not formally respond to this request, Washington grew increasingly frustrated at the lack of prosecutions of Kenyans alleged to be involved in drug trafficking. However, this was rarely publicly expressed, as the US government was painfully aware of Kenya's strategic importance in the war on terror, especially in the wake of the invasion of Somalia.

Relations with **Sudan** also grew tense after the High Court ordered the arrest of Sudanese President Omar Hassan al-Bashir on 28 November. The ruling was the result of a petition filed by the International Commission of Jurists, which demanded that the Kenyan government should arrest al-Bashir if he were to visit the country again. The petition followed a number of incidents in which the authorities had failed to act under its Treaty of Rome obligations to detain al-Bashir, who was the subject of arrest warrants issued by the ICC in 2009. Sudan responded by ordering the Kenyan ambassador to leave within 72 hours. However, the Kenyan government quickly moved to heal the rift, launching an immediate appeal and reaffirming its commitment to the AU's policy that member states would not cooperate with the ICC investigation.

Socioeconomic Developments

Events along the Kenya-Somali border had significant economic consequences. The high cost of Kenya's intervention in Somalia necessitated an unplanned increase in government spending. The normal budget of the **department of defence** was just $ 520 m a year, which barely covered the cost of sustaining the military within Kenya. Funding the war in Somalia therefore required the government to divert resources from other areas. When the government needed to increase military salaries in September, it did so by redirecting funds that were originally intended to go to teachers. At year's end, it remained unclear exactly what the operation in Somalia had cost and how the government had paid for it. Financial support from foreign allies no doubt helped to soften the blow, but as early as November the government asked all departments to draw up spending cuts in order to help finance the war effort.

International news coverage of the abductions resulted in a drop in **tourism** bookings, a significant blow to an economy in which tourism typically contributed 10% of GDP. The government went to great lengths to promote Kenya as a safe tourist destination, flooding the relevant areas with police. Despite this, hotels in and around the normally popular Lamu resort were empty throughout October and November. Tourist levels had only just recovered from the slump that followed the post-election violence in 2008 and were likely to remain low for 2012. However, the tourist industry received a boost on 1 November when Abercrombie and Kent, a leading American travel agent, declared that Kenya was a safe destination following a trip to assess the security situation and a meeting with Tourism Minister Najib Balala. Moreover, the strong growth in the tourist sector prior to the October events, when arrivals increased by 13.6% compared with the first half of 2010, ensured that the **service sector** continued to grow.

The further expansion of **information and communication technology**, which continued to transform the socioeconomic landscape, was more good news for the service sector. Mobile phone subscriptions peaked at 25.3 m at the end of June, more than the current estimated adult population. During the same period, the number of internet users increased by a remarkable 60% to 12.5 m, making Kenya one of the most 'connected' countries in Africa. According to the Portland Communications group, Kenyans used

Twitter more than any other sub-Saharan African country bar South Africa, both in terms of the total number of users and the average number of tweets per person.

The picture was not nearly so rosy in the **agricultural sector. Drought** in North Eastern and Eastern Provinces was estimated to have reduced GDP growth by around 0.2% as a result of livestock mortality. The problems caused by falling production were compounded by falling prices, as the political crises in North Africa and economic crises in Europe reduced demand for cash crops such as coffee, flowers and tea. However, production in the Rift Valley held up and agriculture overall achieved a steady growth rate of 3.5%. Although this was lower than projected, it marked a significant improvement over the figures for 2007 (2.3%), 2008 (–4.3%) and 2009 (–2.5%).

The **drought** also pushed up inflation because the government was forced to meet the country's food deficit by importing **maize**, which increased in price from $ 167 per metric tonne in 2010 to $ 299. Moreover, research conducted by the World Bank suggested that Kenyans actually paid up to $ 530 per metric tonne due to policy distortions in the domestic market. As a result, the cost of transport and food more than doubled between January and October: Kenyans now paid twice as much for sugar as Europeans. The combination of higher food and fuel prices resulted in an average **inflation** rate of 14%. The situation deteriorated further towards the end of the year and, in November, inflation climbed to 19.7% year-on-year; the highest rate recorded since the government changed the way it measured inflation in 2009. The impact of rising prices was particularly severe on the poor. The World Bank estimated that, in October, high-income households experienced inflation of 14.5%, compared with 19.6% suffered by low-income households. As a result, **inequality** continued to increase, raising concerns about political stability.

Kenya's economic difficulties were illustrated by the falling value of the **shilling**, which reached an all-time low against the US-dollar in October. According to the World Bank, the main drivers of this **depreciation** were "high international food and fuel prices, the drought compounded by conflict in the Horn of Africa, the Euro crisis, widening fiscal and current account deficits, and major inefficiencies in Kenya's agriculture sector". The shilling's depreciation made it more expensive for Kenyans to import the goods and services they needed from abroad: in the first three quarters of 2011, the value of exports expanded by just 15%, while the cost of imports expanded by 22.7%, resulting in a record **current-account deficit** of 10.5% of GDP. However, the shilling staged a late recovery, strengthening from KSh 106 : $ 1 in mid-October to KSh 90 : $ 1 at the end of November as a result of a tighter **monetary policy** – although it remained to be seen whether the government would be able to maintain this discipline as political leaders geared up for the next election.

This mixed picture was reflected in a **GDP growth** rate of 4.2%. Although this represented a 1.3% fall on the 5.6% growth achieved in 2010, it was considerably above Kenya's long-term average of 3.7% and the World Bank predicted that growth would bounce back to 5% in 2012. Considering the many difficulties the economy faced in 2011, this represented a solid performance, and one that suggested the country's macroeconomic situation might be stabilising. However, at the year's end, concerns that the government had not revealed the true cost of the Somali invasion undermined confidence in its **balance of payments** estimates.

Nic Cheeseman

Rwanda

Nearly all aspects of political and public life continued to be controlled by President Paul Kagame and his ruling Rwandan Patriotic Front (RPF) party. The government continued to receive international praise for its technocratic governance and sustained economic growth, despite continuing human rights abuses against political opponents and critics of the government. Political violence increased slightly, with four grenade attacks rocking Kigali in the latter part of the year. The government blamed dissident military officers who had fled into exile in 2010 for the attacks, the first since those in rural Rwanda in the run-up to the August 2010 elections. Relations with the international donor community remained cordial, despite Kagame's blunt rebuttal of criticism by US ambassador to the UN, Susan Rice; in November. Rice praised Rwanda's economic growth and prosperity, while noting that this was unsustainable if political liberalisation did not follow soon. Relations with France and neighbouring Burundi and DRC remained cordial, and on the terms of the Rwandan government. The government continued to implement its roadmap to move Rwanda to a middle-income country by 2017. The plan was long on ambition and short on specific resources (human and financial) to implement its goals. The country saw considerable economic growth of 6.8% because of its focus on infrastructure spending and increased agricultural production beyond coffee and tea, the traditional cash crops.

Poverty decreased in urban areas but remained widespread and chronic in rural areas, as public policy favoured the former at the expense of the latter.

Domestic Politics

In the continued absence of an open political environment, the domestic political scene remained in the hands of the **governing RPF**. From the *nymubakumi* (the lowest officer in the administrative hierarchy) to **President Paul Kagame's** inner circle of advisors, the RPF controlled all levels of socio-political life. The president's cabal of advisors decreased in size, but seemingly not in influence, following Kagame's reshuffle of the military leadership in efforts to fill the power vacuum left by the earlier flight into exile of former army chief of staff, General Kayumba Nyamwasa, and Patrick Karegeya, the former head of intelligence. The **military reshuffle** in July resulted in the appearance of a number of new faces in the security services leadership, including Major-General Emmanuel Karenzi Karake as chief of national intelligence and Brigadier-General Richard Rutatina as head of military intelligence. The head of the presidential guard, Colonel Tom Byabagama, moved to the newly created position of head of the anti-terrorist unit. The relative youth of Kagame's new appointees highlighted his difficulty in replacing Nyamwasa and Karegeya, two senior military officers whom he had considered his closest and trusted aides. A **cabinet reshuffle** in early May led to some technocratic changes in the ministerial line-up, with Health Minister Richard Sezibera departing to become secretary-general of the EAC. On 6 October, the loyal non-partisan and long-serving prime minister, Bernard Makuza, was made vice-president of the Senate and replaced by Education Minister Pierre-Damien Habumuremyi. Neither cabinet change appeared to have any impact on the direction of government policies.

The changes to the president's inner circle of military advisors were emblematic of a broader trend that emerged in the course of the year. A growing number of urban, educated and English-speaking ethnic Tutsi resident in the country – the RPF's core constituency – had become **disillusioned with the RPF**. Many in this group felt that the RPF had lost its vision of ethnic unity and economic prosperity for all Rwandans, noting government scapegoating of the political opposition and an increasing tolerance for corruption and nepotism among members of the ruling clique. A TI report on bribery in May found that the Rwandan National Police and representatives of civil society, both of which were dominated by RPF loyalists, were very likely to demand a bribe in exchange for service delivery. Important to note, however, was that many disillusioned ethnic Tutsi were not clamouring for a more politically liberal or inclusive Rwanda, but only that they be allowed to share in the spoils of RPF policies and programmes. They did not therefore represent a threat to Kagame's political strength. Kagame still commanded the loyalty of much of the Rwandan Patriotic Army (RPA), although defections by senior military officers thought to be close to the president made a coup appear to be possible, but probably not imminent. Political opponents of the regime, ethnic Hutu, Tutsi and Twa alike, accused Kagame of **authoritarianism** and of trampling on media and political freedoms. The voices of these critics remained muted as the government continued to **harass and intimidate the political opposition**. The United Democratic Forces-Inkingi (FDU-Inkingi), led by Victoire Ingabire, and the Social Party (PS-Imberakuri), headed by Bernard Ntaganda, issued joint press releases at various times during the year, calling upon the RPF to allow for greater political openness. Together, these parties constituted the **Permanent Consultative Council of Opposition Parties in Rwanda (PCC)**. A third opposition party, the Democratic Green Party of Rwanda (DGP), led by Frank Habineza, continued its boycott of the PCC, stating in June that the FDU-Inkingi's continued calls for violent measures to force the RPF to open up Rwanda's political space ran contrary to the DGP's values.

At the end of the year, **Victoire Ingabire** remained in **prison** on charges that her FDU-Inkingi was funding the Democratic Forces for the Liberation of Rwanda (FDLR) with the intention of committing acts of terrorism in Rwanda. According to the RPF, the FDLR was a terrorist group based in eastern DRC that was seeking to overthrow the Rwandan government by violent means. Ingabire was also accused of making public statements denying that the events that constitute the 1994 genocide took place, as well as remarks aimed at promoting the hatred of ethnic Hutu for ethnic Tutsi (genocide denial, and promoting genocide ideology, in contravention of articles 13 and 33 of the 2003 Constitution). Ingabire, who had been in prison since October 2010, denied any involvement with the FDLR. In November, a Dutch court approved the transfer of evidence regarding Ingabire's alleged involvement with the FDLR from her home in Zevenhuizen to the Office of the Prosecution in Kigali. Ingabire had lived in the Netherlands from 1994 until 2010, when she returned to Rwanda from exile to stand in the 2010 presidential elections. Her husband and adult children still lived in the Netherlands, and lobbied the Dutch government not to support the Rwandan government in what the PCC considered politically motivated charges against Ingabire.

In February, **Bernard Ntaganda** of the PS-Imberakuri was tried and sentenced to four years' **imprisonment**. He was found guilty of endangering national security, ethnic divisionism, and attempting to organise political demonstrations without government authorisation. With Ingabire and Ntaganda both in prison, the PCC parties were rendered toothless. In May, the interim secretary-general of the FDU-Inkingi, Sylvain Sibomana, issued a statement attacking Frank Habineza of the DGP for his party's lack of commitment to the ideals of revolution in Rwanda, perhaps revealing the military intentions of some members of Rwanda's political opposition. Following the unsolved murder in 2010 of their vice-president, André Kagwa Rwisereka, the **Democratic Greens** rarely commented on domestic politics, having distanced themselves from the mandate of the PCC and other perceived or real critics of the government.

Throughout 2011, members of the FDU-Inkingi and PS-Imberakuri, journalists, and other perceived **critics of the government** were **arrested, detained, and tried**, some solely for expressing their views. Others were harassed and intimidated. In April, the government arrested Anastase Hagabimana and Norbert Manirafasha of the FDU-Inkingi in connection with a draft statement by their party criticising the rise in the cost of living. Manirafasha was released without charge in early May. Hagabimana was held in pre-trial detention until the end of August, when he was provisionally released. He was, however, put on trial on charges of endangering state security; judgment in his case was still pending at year's end.

The most dramatic trial took place in January, when four former senior government and army officials, turned outspoken critics and now in exile – Nyamwasa, Karegeya, Gerald Gahima, and Théogène Rudasingwa – were tried in absentia in Rwanda's **military court**. In 2010, the four men joined together to create the **Rwanda National Congress (RNC)**, and issued a 60-page indictment of Kagame's shortcomings as president. As a result, their trial focused on their public criticisms of the government and the president. They were found guilty of endangering state security, destabilising public order, divisionism, defamation, and forming a criminal enterprise. Karegeya and Gahima were each sentenced to 20 years' imprisonment and Nyamwasa and Rudasingwa to 24 years, with the additional charge of desertion from the army. The shuffle of Rwanda's military leadership in July was widely believed to reflect the government's desire to remove from positions of authority those officers with known or suspected ties to the RNC leadership, particularly since Nyamwasa apparently retained a considerable following among the rank-and-file. Rudasingwa, the primary spokesperson for the RNC, scoffed at the *in absentia* rulings in a series of comments made in February, stating that they were not the result of an independent judicial system, and were thus illegitimate. Also in February, the RNC announced its partnership with the **Paul Rusesabagina Foundation**, to the chagrin of the government. Rusesabagina, an ethnic Hutu, outspoken critic of the RPF government and hero of the popular movie 'Hotel Rwanda', was believed to command the loyalties of ethnic Hutu resident both in and outside Rwanda. Ethnic Hutu represent some 80%–85% of the Rwandan population. Also related to the RPF was the September announcement that the **RNC** and the **FDU-Inkingi** had joined forces to 'overthrow Kagame's dictatorship'.

International donors' representatives resident in Kigali began to voice concern about the various restrictions on free speech and lack of political openness. Few considered the FDU-Inkingi or PS-Imberakuri a real threat to the political power of the RPF, and the UK, Rwanda's biggest donor, urged the government to relax its continued suppression of political opponents and critics. Rwanda's insistence that foreign governments should not meddle in its political affairs met a brick wall in May, when the British Secret Intelligence Service (MI6) and the London Metropolitan Police warned that Rwandans resident in the UK who were critical of RPF policies faced threats from representatives of Rwanda's Department of Military Intelligence (DMI). The Rwandan government painted this as resulting from the relationship between the RNC and the Rusesabagina Foundation, citing it as proof of the existence of external forces seeking to remove the RPF from power by violent means. In June, MI6 produced evidence to show that a DMI operative had sought to enter the UK to assassinate at least two Rwandans resident in London. The RPF did not publicly comment on the report. The episode appeared to have negatively impacted Western perceptions of the RPF's human rights record, particularly in the UK, but also in other European donor countries more generally. The Rwandan government received another blow to its public image in October, when Rudasingwa released a statement saying that he had firm evidence that Kagame was personally responsible for the shooting down in 1994 of the plane carrying then-president Habyarimana, further tarnishing the RPF's human rights record. In November, **US ambassador to the UN Susan Rice** remarked in a speech to Kigali's political and business elite that, although Rwanda's economic growth since the 1994 genocide was remarkable, the government should take all necessary steps to open up Rwanda's political culture in order to ensure continued economic prosperity. Rice's statement marked the first public criticism of the government by one of its key donors since the 1994 genocide. Her remarks enraged Kagame, who retorted in a speech in rural Rwanda two weeks later, in early December, that "the government only has 100 or 150 critics" and that he would not allow "these idiots to destroy what we have created". It remained to be seen whether these developments would fundamentally alter the foreign aid and development policies of most Western governments.

Kagame also pointed out in his reaction to Rice's remarks that the government would alter Rwandan political culture as it saw fit, reminding international audiences that "recovering from the ill effects of genocide must respond to the needs of Rwandans, not international donors". Kagame's outrage was perhaps in part rooted in comments he made in his inaugural **State of the Nation address** in February. Here, he urged Rwandans to be proud of the progress the country had made since the 1994 genocide, highlighting the security of the state, and the role of government in building a unified, prosperous and democratic Rwanda. Kagame used the address to inform Rwandans of policy changes his RPF would implement to ensure that "Rwanda remains on the right track". International donors in Kigali reported that Kagame felt that Rice's remarks were unduly harsh and excessively critical, as his government was nudging towards greater political openness. Kagame noted in his February address that Rwanda had made great strides in bringing **women into government**, and that women were the backbone of Rwanda's socioeconomic development. After the 2010 elections, 56% of Rwanda's parliamentarians were women. Kagame also noted that his government was **revising the law on genocide ideology** to limit the scope of the law by requiring that the intent behind the crime be proven, and to define the offence more precisely. The revisions of the law began in August, only three months before Rice's visit, but, much to Kagame's dismay, Rice did not mention in her remarks that the government was revising a law that it considered central to its post-genocide reconciliation and reconstruction strategy. In addition, in July, the government initiated revisions of its 2009

media law, making draft amendments that would lift some of the burdensome restrictions on journalists and introduce self-regulation of the profession.

In the run-up to the 2010 elections, the government had used the genocide ideology and media laws to target political opponents, journalists and human rights advocates critical of the government. The **genocide ideology law** was vaguely worded and arbitrarily applied to anyone who made public statements critical of government policies. In the opinion of international human rights groups such as AI and HRW, the revisions did not go far enough, as vague offences, such as approving of acts of genocide by 'mocking' a person or group on the basis of shared characteristics, were included in the draft revision, and were open to abuse. The new draft law, introduced in June, also proposed a reduction in penalties. International human rights groups slammed the **proposed media law revisions**, noting that they placed control over all forms of media in the hands of the government. The rules for defining professional standards and the rules for media licensing and operation remained squarely the prerogative of the RPF. In addition, the right to free expression was not safeguarded, notably since the law defined 'journalism' broadly to include blogs and social media postings. Under the revised law, anyone involved in disseminating information about the government or its policies was considered a journalist. In addition, the minister for information had total control over which individuals and organisations could operate in Rwanda. Reporters Without Borders (RWB) ranked Rwanda 156th out of 178 countries for press freedoms, an improvement from its 2010 ranking of 169th out of 178. In December, after the revised law was announced, RWB stated that the changes to the media law were a positive development, although much remained to be done before Rwanda could be considered a media-friendly environment.

For the RPF to acknowledge that its genocide ideology and media laws required some revision marked a **profound shift** in its willingness and ability to **accept criticism** from its donor and development partners. Rice's lack of sensitivity to these subtle changes in RPF policy may have affronted Kagame, provoking his strong reaction to her remarks. In December, in Kampala, Uganda, unknown assailants gunned down Charles Ingabire, a respected journalist whose writing was often critical of the RPF. Many Rwandans and Ugandans felt that his murder was in response to Rice's criticism of the RPF, which sent a chill through the press corps.

After years of intimidation and harassment, it was evident that there were almost **no independent Rwandan journalists** operating in Rwanda. Several leading independent journalists remained in exile as the government continued to crack down on independent media. In February, Agnès Nkusi Uwimana and Saidati Mukakibibi, of the newspaper '*Umurabyo*', were tried and sentenced to 17 and seven years' imprisonment, respectively, for publishing articles critical of the government and the president. The court ruled that the two women had incited the public to rise up against the government and found them guilty of endangering state security. Uwimana, the newspaper's editor, was also found guilty of minimising the genocide, divisionism, and of libel.

By the end of 2011, **neo-traditional *gacaca* courts** had nearly completed their work, registering a total of 1.2 m genocide-related cases since 2005. HRW noted in a July report that the courts left a **mixed legacy** of both positive and negative achievements. Critics alleged that the courts violated the right to a fair trail, harassed and intimidated witnesses, and were prone to corruption of judges and government interference. Positive aspects of the *gacaca* process included the speed with which the courts dealt with cases, the broad-based participation of the local population, and the establishment of a record of information about events during the 1994 genocide. In June, the referral chamber of the **International Criminal Tribunal for Rwanda (ICTR)** in Arusha, Tanzania, ruled that the case of Jean-Bosco Uwinkindi should be transferred to Rwanda's national courts. In the past, the ICTR and jurisdictions in other countries had declined to transfer genocide cases to Rwanda because of fair trial concerns. Uwinkindi's appeal against the decision was pending at the end of the year. In October, the **European Court of Human Rights** held that the extradition of Sylvère Ahorugeze from Sweden to Rwanda would not expose him to a real risk of a flagrant denial of justice, and so would not violate the European Convention on Human Rights.

Foreign Affairs

As in previous years, foreign affairs were dominated by Rwanda's presence (critics would say interference) in **eastern DRC**. In October 2010, the UN had released a Mapping Report alleging that the RPA had committed serious and systematic violations of human rights and international law in eastern DRC in the mid-1990s. The RPF government reacted quickly and strategically to minimise the effects of the Report on its internal and regional affairs. Rwanda's donors were much more cautious, with several donors, including the British, Dutch and Americans, debating behind closed doors whether or not to reprimand the Rwandan government. In the end, no substantive policy changes were put forward, but Kagame embarked upon a **European tour** in January. Kagame and Foreign Affairs Minister Louise Mushikiwabo met with representatives of the Belgian, Dutch and Spanish governments, and with Rwandan nationals resident in those countries, to gauge the impact of the UN Mapping Report on foreign relations as well as on domestic and diaspora politics. The official government line was that Congolese and Rwandan nationals resident in Europe "left their countries in difficult circumstances", making it harder for them to praise the RPF. Behind closed donors, analysts noted that Kagame was impatient with European partners who were beginning to insist on accountability for Rwanda's human rights abuses at home and in the DRC. Relations with **France** remained cordial, marking Kagame's pragmatic approach towards the key ally of the genocidal regime of his predecessor, Juvenal Habyarimana. In September, Kagame and French President Nicholas Sarkozy met in Paris, the first diplomatic meeting on French soil between the two countries since the genocide. Relations remained terse as France continued to reject

Rwanda's request for the extradition of Habyarimana's widow Agathe. She was arrested in France a few days after Sarkozy's 2010 visit to Kigali. In May, a Paris court found that there were no grounds for her extradition because there was insufficient evidence of her alleged genocide and war crimes.

At home, relations with the **DRC** remained central to Rwanda's foreign policy. Cooperation with Kinshasa remained warm, with continued collaboration between the Rwandan Defence Force (RDF) and the Congolese armed forces to contain the security threats posed by the Hutu-chauvinist FDLR, and other disaffected armed groups and militias. In March, Congolese President Joseph Kabila announced that his envoy had successfully negotiated with the FDLR president, General Gaston Iyamuremye, to begin negotiations with the Rwandan government on demobilising and disarming the FDLR in exchange for between $ 250,000 and $ 1 m, and the relocation of its bases from the Rwandan border. The Kigali government remained concerned that the FDLR might link up with exiled military officers and the RNC's founding members, Nyamwasa and Karegeya, to launch raids into Rwanda from FDLR bases in eastern DRC. Rumours abounded that Nyamwasa and Karegeya had joined forces with the FDLR, although actual evidence was sparse. Military analysts noted that the Nyamwasa-Karegeya alliance had no financial resources, and it was unclear what proportion, if any, of the estimated 4,500–6,000 FDLR rebels the pair actually controlled. In August, FDLR Commander General Sylvestre Mudacumura defected to the RDF, effectively ending any real or imagined military alliance with the RNC. The bigger thorn in Kigali's side was the **'Congrès National pour la Défense du Peuple' (CNDP)**. Since May 2009, its leader, **Laurent Nkunda**, had been under house arrest in Kigali, despite two extradition requests (in September and November) from the DRC. Nkunda had never been charged with any crime. His CNDP continued to control much of eastern DRC and any peace settlement would require the co-option of Nkunda loyalists.

The sole constant force in eastern DRC was the UN Stabilization Mission in the DRC **(MONUSCO)**. In June, the UNSC adopted Resolution 1991, extending the current mission till 30 June 2012. US ambassador to the DRC, Roger Meece, was appointed as head of mission in October. MONUSCO's mandate remained unchanged: to protect civilians and to assist the Kabila government in disbanding the FDLR and supporting domestic political processes in DRC. The leadership of the FDLR remained in disarray. In May, the trial of Ignace Murwanashyaka, head of the **FDLR**, and his deputy, Straton Musoni, began in Stuttgart, Germany, where both men resided. They were accused of ordering militias to commit mass murder and rape between January 2008 and the date of their arrest in Germany in November 2009. Their trial was on-going at the end of the year. In February, FDLR Executive Secretary Callixte Mbarushimana was extradited from France to face trial at the ICC. He was released in December for lack of evidence. The Rwandan government expressed anger at the decision, and asked France, where Mbarushimana lived as a political refugee, to extradite him to Rwanda, but no formal request for his extradition had been made by the end of the year.

The trial of three Rwandans and three South Africans for involvement in a failed assassination attempt on Nyamwasa in 2010 opened in Johannesburg in June and hearings continued through October. The trial had not concluded by the end of the year. The Rwandan government vigorously denied any involvement in an alleged government plot to kill Nyamwasa, but the trial strained relations between Rwanda and **South Africa**. In June, South African President Jacob Zuma appointed Welile Nhlapo his Special Envoy to the Great Lakes Region. Relations between the two countries remained tense, as Rwanda's requests to extradite Nyamwasa went unheeded. Rwanda's diplomatic ties with **Uganda** continued to improve, as Presidents Museveni and Kagame met four times during the year on matters of mutual interest, including the return of Rwandan refugees living in Uganda, the exploitation of methane gas on their borders with the DRC, and trade and investment. Relations with **Burundi** remained warm, with the two countries cooperating in economic and military matters. The Burundi rebel group 'Forces Nationales de Libération' stated its intention to return to armed struggle in cooperation with the FDLR, making military cooperation between the two countries central to their relationship. Strengthening military ties with regional neighbours was a pillar of Rwanda's security strategy. In October, it hosted 300 military officers from **EAC** partner states to practise interoperability and to conduct training in counter-terrorism and peace support operations. Rwanda's military was also active in various **AU** peace-keeping missions, and RDF troops were deployed as peacekeepers in Darfur and Somalia.

In October, Defence Minister General James Kabarebe visited his Chinese counterpart. The meeting resulted in a pledge to deepen military cooperation between Rwanda and **China**. In November, the Chinese government promised funds for the Rwandan navy to build a floating dock to facilitate patroling Lake Kivu, which borders eastern DRC. China also expressed an interest in securing **minerals**, such as tin, coltan, tungsten and gold, from Rwanda. Mining decrees instituted by the government in 2010 to regulate the mining sector had readied and streamlined it against illegal mining practices. Rwanda led in implementing the Dodds-Frank Act, legislation imposed by the US government on the DRC and its neighbours to prevent trade in conflict minerals. Rwanda's military cooperation with the **USA**, through its US Africa Command (AFRICOM), remained strong, with several high-ranking visits from American officers, and numerous joint military operations during the year. AFRICOM had provided material and resource support for the RPA/RDF since 2007, but expressed concern about Rwanda's increasing military ties with China.

The country remained a model of post-conflict reconstruction and reconciliation, despite negative media coverage of the human rights record throughout the year. In June, Kagame received the Chello Foundation Humanitarian Award for his outstanding leadership and, in November, the International Olympic Committee awarded Kagame its 'Inspiring Youth' award.

Socioeconomic Developments

The government continued to **promote social reconciliation and political harmony** among Rwandans through its policy of national unity and reconciliation. Kagame, in his first **State of the Nation address** in February, lauded his government's achievements in rebuilding the country following the devastation of the 1994 genocide and promoting Rwanda on the international stage as a positive place to live and work. Kagame noted that, since reconciliation had been achieved, his government would now focus on the fight against genocide ideology, promoting national ethnic unity and the rule of law as the continued basis of political harmony, continuing economic development, and building a version of democracy based on different ideas and opinions and the right of choice that accord with Rwandan rather than Western values. Central to the government's socioeconomic achievements was its commitment to **technical governance**. Policy goals were pursued without consultation with targeted populations, and local government officials who failed to meet the top-down directives of the ruling RPF were often punished. The government continued the practice of ***imihigo*** **contracts**, under which local government officials made commitments, in formal meetings with the president, to specific development goals in their jurisdictions. This meant that local officials were contractually obligated to develop their bailiwick in accordance with national policy objectives, but not accountable to the needs of the local populations they were supposed to serve.

When local officials did not perform according to the *imihigo* expectations they had agreed to, they were relieved of their duties by councils of their peers, citing incompetence or inability to fulfil their agreed responsibilities. In June, the government announced the results of a survey conducted by the Civil Society Platform, illustrating that 93% of Rwandans were happy with the contribution of *imihigo* contracts in national development. The results on the ground revealed a different picture. For example, in November, the international NGO Global Integrity announced in its Notebook on Corruption that local officials often cut corners to meet the development commitments made in the *imihigo* process. In rural southern Rwanda, Global Integrity found that schools and hospitals built in accordance with *imihigo* requirements soon became unusable, as local leaders did not take the time required to build solid structures. The government also required that local leaders across the country commit in their *imhigo* contracts to **demolish thatched-roofed homes**. According to UNDP, nearly 60% of Rwandans, notably those living in rural areas, lived in thatched-roofed homes (known as *nyakatsi*). Throughout 2011, the government decreed that thatched-roofed houses represented a health and safety concern, and began demolishing these homes across the country. By December, when the 'End Nyakatsi' campaign ended, at least 80,000 rural Rwandans were rendered homeless by the initiative, as the government did not provide funds for displaced citizens to rebuild the required cement structures and metal-sheeting roofs that the decree demanded.

In November, the World Bank's Worldwide Governance Indicators ranked Rwanda as the **fourth least-corrupt state** in Africa, and the least corrupt in East Africa. In response to the ranking, the acting Ombudsman, Augustin Nzindukiyimana, stated that the Rwandan government considered fourth place to be a "poor showing", citing the unwillingness of "at least 50% of rural dwellers" to report instances of corruption. In December, the **Ombudsman's Office** reported that it had set up anti-corruption committees at district and other local levels, to fight corruption among rural residents. These local committees were another component of an already strong anti-corruption regime. In February, the government hosted Anti-Corruption Week, the highlight of which was the hearing of 85 corruption cases in the Supreme Court. A July study issued by the Rwandan TI office found that 67 of these cases were dismissed as baseless, calling into question the allegations of corruption and the government's commitment to try them. The report further noted that the government's willingness to eliminate corruption among senior government officials was weak, despite an impressive institutional framework consisting of the Ombudsman's Office, the Public Accounts Committee and the Office of Auditor-General. Global Integrity reported the same in its November report, finding that both the Ombudsman's and the Auditor-General's offices prosecuted senior government officials accused of corruption rather selectively.

The government began implementation of its **Roadmap 2017** for an economic and poverty alleviation policy, introduced in December 2010. It remained unclear whether the Roadmap was meant to supplement or supplant the existing policy **Vision 2020** (introduced in 2000). The Roadmap was long on ambitious measures to make Rwanda a middle-income country by 2017, meaning $ 1,000 income per capita per annum. The policy was, however, short on specifics regarding how middle-income status would actually be reached, despite lofty economic and social goals peppering the Roadmap plan. The document outlined the government's plan for modernising the economy through industrialisation and service provision, including developing export strategies for cash crops, increasing national energy production and extending financial services to Rwanda's poorest citizens. Roadmap 2017 also called on Rwandans to redouble their efforts to make the country economically self-sufficient. When international journalists asked Kagame during his February State of the Nation address how feasible the Roadmap was, given the current economic crisis, he said that the country was food self-sufficient and that the number of Rwandans with access to clean water had risen from 41% in 2003 to 80% in 2011. Kagame added that 13% of households now had electricity, compared with 4% in 2000. Further research by the World Bank illustrated that the statistics that Kagame cited represented gains registered in Kigali and other urban centres. The quality and availability of infrastructure and service delivery, including schools, hospitals, water, sanitation and health clinics, continued to vary considerably across the country. The northern region, save the towns of Gisenyi and Ruhengeri, still lacked basic infrastructure. The situation was similar in the south, west and east, where basic services remained limited and were available only close to town centres. Individuals not living within walking distance of principal towns or close to tarmacked roads remained among Rwanda's most economically vulnerable citizens, notably widows, orphans and female-headed households. Rural poverty continued to be shaped by the government's land and mono-cropping policies.

In January, the government introduced a **National Land Use and Development Master Plan** that placed small-holder plots in the hands of the ministry of land and environment with the aim of ensuring that land was used in the most economically effective way possible. The directive displaced countless subsistence farmers, placing control over land use in the hands of local government officials. The Master Plan augmented the government's 2010 mono-cropping policy and shaped the food security and poverty levels of rural households. The policy made it illegal for subsistence farmers to grow crops for their family's nutritional needs. Instead, they were told by local authorities to grow coffee, tea and other export crops that earned foreign currency.

The government intensified its efforts to produce high-quality **coffee** and **tea**. Average commodity prices for both rose again in 2011. The cost of exporting the finished product to Western markets also rose, as global oil prices remained high. The government continued to emphasise a **value-chain approach** to the development of premium coffee and tea. In 2011, coffee earned $ 69 m, up from $ 51 m in 2010, buoyed by a 23% rise in volume and strong commodity prices. Tea revenue remained strong, with receipts of $ 62 m, up 18% from 2010. In order to further diversify its sources of foreign exchange, the government targeted horticulture. Exports in 2011 were valued at $ 3 m, with projected revenue of $ 300 m by 2017. **Mineral receipts** doubled, despite the restrictions instituted by the US Dodd-Franks legislation, thanks to high international demand for cassiterite and coltan, resulting in high commodity prices. Tourist receipts also increased, bringing in revenue of $ 116 m, up from $ 91 m in 2010. Despite these achievements, **foreign aid** contributions accounted for 44% of the government's budget, up from 41% in 2010. In 2011, GDP per capita rose to $ 593 from $ 541 in 2010, still far short of the Roadmap 2017 target.

In April, UNDP reported that Rwanda remained on track to meet **MDG targets** in several key areas, including gender equality in primary and secondary education, primary school enrolment rates, and reduction in HIV and malaria prevalence. UNDP also reported that the country remained unlikely to meet other targets, notably goals to eradicate extreme poverty and hunger, and the equitable use of land.

Finance Minister John Rwangomba released a nearly balanced **budget** in June. The World Bank and IMF continued to praise the government's economic and fiscal policy. An IMF review of Rwanda's Policy Support Instrument found that all quantitative assessment criteria and structural benchmarks had been met, and that the Rwandan economy would weather the global economic downturn. Donors responded positively to the government's increased expenditure on its poverty-reduction strategies, and the commitment to **privatisation** of government-owned industries. By the end of the year, the government had divested 'Brasseries et Limonaderies du Rwanda' and the Bank of Kigali. **GDP growth** remained steady at around 7%, mainly due to increased commodity prices and the privatisation of government industries. **Inflation** rose markedly to 7% (from 3% in 2010), due to increased food and fuel prices combined with the depressed global economy. The ministry of finance announced a new FDI strategy in July, aimed at improving the coffee, tea, horticulture and telecommunications sectors.

Susan Thomson

Seychelles

In a politically turbulent year President Michel was re-elected in May, while the main opposition contender, Ramkalawan, lost considerable popular support in his fourth electoral challenge for the presidency. Michel was credited with having quite successfully stabilised the economy after the near-collapse in 2008 and with having introduced credible reform measures. A parliamentary boycott by the frustrated opposition precipitated the dissolution of the national assembly by a governmental two-thirds majority and the holding of early new parliamentary elections. In the wake of a further opposition boycott, these were overwhelmingly won by the long-ruling dominant Parti Lepep. Throughout the year, the political confrontation became far more antagonistic than it had been for a long time. Economic performance was again quite satisfactory, with another record year for the tourism industry and continued praise from international organisations. Somali pirate activities remained a serious threat and attracted international attention to Seychelles as an important hub for concerted anti-piracy efforts.

Domestic Politics

Regular **presidential elections**, scheduled for 19–21 May, were expected to be the first key test for **President James Michel** and his long-ruling **Parti Lepep** (PL, People's

Party) since the dramatic financial crisis in late 2008, the subsequent introduction of harsh socioeconomic reform measures and a remarkable recovery of the economy. On 13 March, the main opposition **Seychelles National Party (SNP)** endorsed its leader **Wavel Ramkalawan** for the fourth time as presidential candidate, but amid signs of growing internal dissensions. A little-known MP, Nicolas Prea, was chosen as compromise vice-presidential candidate over two secretary-generals. Deputy secretary-general David Pierre resigned on 3 May in the midst of the campaign, opting out from politics for a while. The 25th PL congress on 16 April nominated Michel and Vice President Danny Faure as its candidates, thus dashing all rumours about a possible early handover to a younger generation. The small **New Democratic Party (NDP)** also put up its leader Ralph Volcère as candidate, while lawyer Philippe Boullé again ran as an independent as he had done since 1993.

The electoral campaign turned out to be a lacklustre affair, with the SNP hit by a number of prominent defectors criticising their former party, while the PL attracted crowds at rallies. The official **election results** showed a high turnout of 85%. The PL tandem obtained clear majorities in 23 of the 25 electoral districts and got 55.5% of the votes, although this was only a slight 2% increase over 2006. Ramkalawan ended up with 41.4%, a drop by 5% to his lowest result since 1998. Boullé (1.7%) and Volcère (1.5%) had no chance. In view of this clear defeat, Ramkalawan hinted at possibly relinquishing the SNP presidency, but later changed his mind and was re-elected on 20 November by an overwhelming vote at a congress, which also brought many new faces into the SNP leadership. Four foreign observer groups (from the Commonwealth, IOC, OIF and SADC) judged the elections to have been "free and fair", but all the opposition candidates rejected the results as flawed and accused the PL of vote-buying and unlawful use of state resources. Ramkalawan announced a **boycott** of **parliamentary sessions** by the SNP, except for discussions on urgent electoral reforms. This boycott was, however, only patchily observed due to the MPs fear of losing their mandates after a prolonged absence.

Michel's new **cabinet** was approved by parliament in the absence of SNP MPs. As a sign of continuity, no personnel changes were made in the line-up, other than the retirement of Land Use Minister Jaqueline Dugasse, who had been in government since 1993. In his National Day speech on 18 June, Michel focussed strongly on aspirations for a 'New Seychelles', which called for a radical transformation, and above all a structural and institutional transformation. He further stated that the country was in need of a moral, spiritual, cultural and social revolution in order to regain traditional values and to inculcate them into the children.

In mid-June, an SNP motion to immediately set up an Electoral Reform Commission was rejected, but at the same time the government started preparations for amendments to the constitution and the elections act with reference to an earlier 2009 constitutional review report. On 12 July, a 6th **constitutional amendment bill** for the creation of a new Electoral Commission was passed in parliament with a two-thirds majority, which was only obtained because a dissident SNP MP, Jane Carpin, voted with the PL. Immediately afterwards the **National Assembly** was **dissolved** by the same majority, thus opening the way for new parliamentary elections within 90 days (rather than the regular scheduled date in April 2012). The PL clearly wanted to capitalise on Michel's victory and the apparent weakness of the opposition camp. However, in response to an SNP petition, the Constitutional Court declared the dissolution unlawful due to a procedural error, since no prior agenda warning had been given to all MPs. This was quickly corrected by a new dissolution vote on 12 July, with Carpin again voting with the PL, but in the absence of all other SNP MPs. Ramkalawan had unsuccessfully tried to sack Carpin as an MP (since she had not been directly elected in a constituency) and thus invalidate the parliamentary majority, but this move was rejected by the Speaker of the House. The Constitutional Court later confirmed that the dissolution had been lawful and that Carpin had still been a rightful SNP MP. A new five-member **Electoral Commission** was duly appointed on 29 July by Michel from nominations made by the Constitutional Appointments Authority, with the former single Electoral Commissioner Hendrick Gappy chosen as chairman. The opposition had always objected that having a single Electoral Commissioner did not allow truly independent supervision of elections.

The country was now faced with a sharp political confrontation and an unexpected election campaign for **parliamentary elections**, set for the end of September (on the outer islands) and 1 October as the main polling day. On 22 August, the existing opposition forces (SNP, NDP and Boullé) announced an election boycott and called for a postponement. A newly-registered Seychelles Freedom Party, led by businessman Christopher Gill, also supported the boycott. However, several SNP defectors, unhappy with the parliamentary boycott since May, registered a new party, the Popular Democratic Movement (PDM), led by David Pierre and Jane Carpin, and attempted at very short notice to challenge the PL. Both the PDM and the PL nominated candidates for all 25 constituencies (including, in the case of the PL, 18 newcomers who had been groomed for some time). A new local NGO observer group, in addition to external observers, monitored the conduct of the election and a largely subdued campaign. Not surprisingly, the PL swept all constituencies with high scores, including former SNP strongholds. The PDM's best result was 20% for Pierre. The 74% turnout, markedly lower than usual, and 32% of spoiled votes were clearly the effect of the SNP's call for a boycott. The PL got 88.6% of the valid votes, and the PDM 10.9%.

Initially, out of the additional nine possible **proportionally-elected seats**, six were allocated by the Electoral Commission to the PL and none to the PDM, based on an interpretation of the constitution that the qualification threshold for these seats was 10% of the votes cast (not of the valid votes). A PDM appeal against this decision was quickly rejected by the Constitutional Court, but the Court of Appeal on 9 December reversed the judgement and allocated one seat to the PDM and two to the PL, which the latter, however, declined to take up. Pierre thus became leader of the opposition in parliament and chairman of the finance committee, tasked to oversee the government's budget. This development was also welcomed by the PL leadership, who were keen to avoid the impression that the elections had brought a *de facto* return to a one-party regime.

The **controversies** between **government** and **opposition** had long centred mainly around demands for a non-politicised public service, independent judiciary and electoral body, and liberalisation of the media. Michel had already broken with many traditions of the former single-party era, but had still to contend with some old socialist elements within the PL and was viewed with suspicion by the SNP. In January, a new seven-member Seychelles Media Commission, widely deemed to be relatively toothless, was appointed amid SNP criticism of the nomination process. A heated parliamentary debate in March about a new law for the Seychelles Broadcasting Corporation (SBC) led to an opposition walkout, with the SNP rejecting the bill as not leading to the genuine independence of the SBC. Demands for electoral reform subsequently formed the core of the political confrontation during the year. After the dilemma of the one-sided elections, it seemed to dawn on all sides that a move towards reaching a new consensus needed to be made. In late November, the Electoral Commission invited reform proposals from the general public and initiated the establishment of a **Forum for Electoral Reform**, with representatives of all five registered political parties and members of civil society, to deliberate on a roadmap for generally agreed electoral reforms. At the end of a confrontational political year, this offered an opportunity for renewed closer cooperation in this tiny community of barely 90,000 people. Major popular events during the year were the first 'International Carnival of Victoria' in March, mainly a tourist attraction, and the 8th Indian Ocean Island Games in August.

Foreign Affairs

The unrelenting threat of **Somali piracy activities** in large parts of the Indian Ocean continued to be a focal point of the country's foreign policy concerns. Seychelles' geographic location made it a strategic hub for many international anti-piracy operations, whose participants used Victoria as a convenient port of call and resource base between long patrol engagements at sea. The wide concern about the dangers of Somali piracy led to far more international focus on Seychelles than was commensurate with its size. It was repeatedly praised for its role in prosecuting apprehended pirates when no other country in the sub-region, apart from Kenya, was able and willing to undertake this important task – one that had become a heavy burden for such a small country. Early in the year about 50 pirates were held in custody, about 10% of the overall prison population. Total piracy-related costs to the economy were estimated by one source at about 2% of GDP. The UAE again gave five patrol boats to Seychelles' coast guard to strengthen its capacity in the anti-piracy struggle. In February, the government signed a landmark agreement with Somaliland, Puntland and the transitional Mogadishu authorities to the effect that convicted pirates could be repatriated to their home regions, but its concrete implementation remained uncertain. In February, another 20 pirates were jailed for 20 years by the Supreme Court.

Michel further underscored his recent concern to adopt a **more active foreign policy** than hitherto. He undertook official visits to India (January), Australia (August) and China (October) and to the UAE in November, where he opened a new embassy in Abu Dhabi. In October, he also attended the Commonwealth summit in Australia. In November, Seychelles re-joined the IORARC, which it had left in 2003 as a cost-saving measure, and it also remained an active member of SADC. In October, it assumed the annually rotating presidency of the IOC. Cordial relations with Tanzania were underscored by President Kikwete's presence as guest-of-honour during the National Day celebrations in June.

Socioeconomic Developments

The government continued successfully to adhere strictly to its reform course, introduced in late 2008 in a desperate bid to prevent a near-collapse of the unsustainably indebted and heavily welfare-orientated economy. This change of policy orientation had since then remarkably stabilised the overall **macroeconomic situation**, and 2011 turned out to be another good year with a generally satisfactory performance. The improved HDI ranking, up by five positions to 52nd, by far the highest of any African country, also reflected this. The PL's election results could be taken as an indicator that the population by and large was appreciative of the improved situation. The **GDP growth rate** was estimated to be 5%, only slightly lower than the 6.2% in 2010. Consumer prices were relatively stable, with an average **inflation** rate of 2.6%, but a clearly escalating trend towards the end of the year (5.5% in December). The Seychelles Rupee (SR) also remained remarkably stable with just a modest depreciation against major currencies in the course of the year. This was a further reflection of confidence in the government's reform agenda and in the rebuilding of a comfortable foreign reserve position ($ 290 m, equivalent to a targeted three months' import cover, compared with just two weeks' in 2008 at the height of the crisis).

The structural deficit of the tiny import-dependent island's **balance of trade** hardly changed, however, with imports ($ 873 m) amounting to almost double the value of exports ($ 495 m), about half accounted for by tuna fish and most of the rest by oil re-exports. FDI, almost all in major tourism projects, was estimated at around $ 200 m, somewhat lower than in 2010, but still substantial. The (provisional) **current-account deficit** was lowered from 24% (2010) to 20.9%, with good prospects for further improvement in coming years, mainly due to growing service industry receipts. The key **tourism sector** had another excellent year and had a major impact on the stabilisation of the economy. Visitor numbers increased by 11.4% to a new record of 194,000, and tourism earnings rose by 8.8% to a new high of $ 298 m.

The government continued with a policy of **strict fiscal discipline** in pursuance of its goal to gradually redress the huge debt that had been accumulated during the period of the welfare-oriented socialist policies under Michel's predecessor, René. For the fourth consecutive year, a **budget surplus** (1.5% of GDP) was achieved. The total public debt by the year's end was down to 76% of GDP (compared with 128% in 2008), with the target for 2018 set at 50%. External debt remained stable at around 50% of GDP, a strong decline from 90% in 2008. In appreciation of these efforts, Seychelles' **credit rating** was upgraded by Fitch to B, with a stable outlook.

IMF missions in March, June and October conducted further reviews of the government's performance under the $ 31 m three-year Extended Fund Facility arranged in December 2009. The programme was found to be fully on track, with all quantitative performance criteria having been met. The IMF was satisfied that all agreed structural reforms were well underway, with an enhanced focus for 2012 on tax reforms and further **privatisations** of parastatal enterprises. In April, a first tranche of shares of the Seychelles Savings Bank was offered to the public. The loss-making Public Utilities Company was to be turned into a commercially viable enterprise, and steep rises in electricity tariffs came into effect in November. Air Seychelles' continuous operational and financial problems, largely the result of increased competition from Emirates, required hefty subsidies from the government; in November a restructuring and downsizing exercise became inevitable and plans were made for a partial sale of the airline to Etihad.

In November, the government reiterated its commitment to comply with OECD **taxation rules** in reaction to a G-20 report in which Seychelles was listed among a number of suspected tax havens that should be 'shunned' by the international community.

Michel occasionally warned against an undercurrent of **xenophobic sentiments**, partly caused by fears of alleged competition from foreigners for local jobs and partly a reaction to a significant increase in high-value land purchases, mainly by Arabs. A special stabilisation fund, established in June, was intended to protect consumers against rising prices. Despite its consistent pursuance of economic reforms, the government was also mindful of attenuating any possible social hardships. In line with its ecological concerns about the dangers of climate change for small island states, repeatedly declared in international forums, the government announced in June that about half of the country's territory would soon be declared protected areas.

Rolf Hofmeier

Somalia

Somalia remained a region of insecurity and crisis, particularly in the south-central area, but the Transitional Federal Government (TFG) and AU Mission in Somalia (AMISOM) forces, aided later in the year by military contingents from Kenya and Ethiopia active in the border regions, succeeded in pushing back the Islamist al-Shabaab movement, which left Mogadishu in August after military setbacks. Nevertheless, al-Shabaab still continued to intensify terror and hit-and-run attacks. The TFG remained very weak and non-functional and did not offer a substantive alternative political model for south-central Somalia or the rest of the country, but it extended its reach and initiated activities to prepare for the post-transition period. The end of the transitional period was extended by one year to 20 August 2012. Southern Somalia was hit by a major drought, resulting in an emergency situation for hundreds of thousands of people. A major international aid effort averted mass deaths. Somaliland and Puntland were more peaceful and less affected by the drought, but clashed with each other on their border. Al-Shabaab's retreat and gradual decline did not spell the end of the movement but opened up new possibilities for the country. The emerging momentum was evident in a growing number of high-profile diplomatic visits and more political and economic activities, notably in the urban areas. Migrant and refugee flows remained quite dramatic. Overall stability was not attained, but some hopes for political and economic improvement were apparent.

Domestic Politics

Somalia, still divided into three main separate political entities – Somaliland, Puntland and the anarchic south-central region – remained the scene of intense political and socio-economic insecurity, with civil conflict and terrorist violence prevalent in the south-central area.

The **Transitional Federal Government (TFG)**, in place after a deal made in Kenya between clan-based Somali political groups in 2004, remained in power in Mogadishu and was able only modestly to extend its reach, in the wake of military offensives aided by the AMISOM forces and Kenyan and Ethiopian military pressure on its adversary, the violent, radical Islamist movement '**Harakat al-Shabaab al-Mujahiddin**'. Universally known as al-Shabaab, this al-Qaida-linked group, which advocated a theocracy on a puritanical and extremist Islamist basis, continued to wreak havoc on the Somali social fabric. The TFG, tasked with preparing a country-wide representative government and a post-transition political future, did not function well and effectively remained confined to Mogadishu and some selected rural areas, secured with allied local authorities and militias. Throughout the year, however, it slowly extended its sphere of influence.

Al-Shabaab's hold on the country was not secure, as they were dependent on local authorities, clan elders and business groups, and often maintained a tenuous grip on power by threats and acts of intimidation. They were able to retain young fighters by paying a $ 150-a-month 'salary', with an additional $ 10 per day of fighting. But their forces lost significant ground in the course of the year and they frequently had to move their troops (ca. 9,000–10,000 in total) around, and keep up their violent Islamist rhetoric and intimidation tactics in order to maintain control over the towns and territory they held, threatened by the TFG and its allied forces. Al-Shabaab's forced recruitment of youngsters, closing of schools, abductions, use of torture, and imposition of draconian punishments on people "infringing on Islam" (as their spokesmen put it) generated more resentment. In addition, it failed to deliver food relief shipments in areas under its control and banned foreign aid agencies. The movement as a whole did not disintegrate, however, and stuck to its ideology (as evident from its websites). It rejected any semblance of democratic politics (such as elections), and refused to engage with other political players in Somalia, let alone with outside forces (except financiers and 'jihadist' foreigners who joined its ranks). It was therefore not possible either to move towards a negotiated end to the violence and forcible Islamisation in south-central Somalia, or to start a process of political compromise with this movement, despite the wishful thinking of several analysts.

In the course of the year, hundreds of people, many of them civilians, women and children, again fell victim to often indiscriminate **bomb and grenade attacks** by al-Shabaab, who frequently used the civilian population as human shields. Among such attacks were the following. On 21 February, there was a suicide car bomb attack on a police camp in Hamar Jabab district, resulting in 11 dead and 40 wounded. On 30 May, a US Somali,

Farah Mohamed Beledi from Minneapolis, carried out a suicide bombing at a TFG checkpoint in Mogadishu. On 9 June, al-Shabaab claimed responsibility for killing TFG Interior Minister Abdishakur Sheik Hassan in a suicide attack on his residence. On 22 June, al-Shabaab targeted an AMISOM contingent in Mogadishu, but they killed four civilians and wounded 13 others. The worst incident took place on 4 October, when a car bomb exploded in front of the ministry of education in Mogadishu, causing the death of over 70 people and injuries to many more.

The military dynamics in south-central Somalia altered significantly when, in mid-October, the **Kenyan army** entered south-west Somalia with a military force of some 2,000 soldiers, intent on clearing al-Shabaab out of border areas from where they had repeatedly threatened Kenya. The invasion was well prepared, but was only prompted by kidnappings of tourists on Kenya's coast and of aid workers in the Dadaab refugee camp, as well as recruitment and the spread of propaganda by al-Shabaab sympathisers among young Kenyan Muslims. On 27 February, al-Shabaab had threatened to attack Kenya "for training Somali government forces and allowing Ethiopian troops to operate from its towns". Kenya decided not to wait and to put pressure on al-Shabaab. It also feared the escalation of the Somali refugee problem in Kenya because of the growing instability, famine and income loss resulting from threats to coastal tourism. The Kenyan attack was not coordinated with Ethiopia or the TFG, and indeed TFG President Sheikh Sharif Sheikh Ahmed initially condemned it, although he soon turned around. The **Ethiopians** later stepped up their own military activities in the Beledweyn area, eventually conquering the town and some smaller places with the help of local Somali allies.

These two invasions followed a relatively **successful offensive** in early August by **AMISOM** and **TFG forces in Mogadishu** (aided by units from Western private security companies, such as Bancroft). This had been preceded by AMISOM getting a stronger grip on the notorious Bakaraha (arms) market in the capital, choking it and denying al-Shabaab the opportunity to derive an income from it. On 7 June, the Comoran Fazul Abdullah Mohammed, a top al-Shabaab military leader and al-Qaida pointman, and one of the most wanted men in Somalia, was killed by TFG troops at a checkpoint near Mogadishu, together with a Kenyan Islamist militant, Musa Hussein. On 13 November, a compound near Afgoye where al-Shabaab leaders were allegedly gathered was hit by missiles, but without a successful outcome. On 24 June, an air strike by an unidentified military aircraft hit a convoy carrying al-Qaida-linked militants near Kismaayo. The presence of some US warships and counter-terror units thus kept up the pressure on al-Shabaab and its leadership.

The mounting military pressure and their declining popularity made **al-Shabaab** decide on 6 August to **"strategically withdraw" from Mogadishu** (except from a few northern suburbs) and turn to a more intensive terror campaign, with hit-and-run attacks and targeted killings of TFG personnel and any individuals or institutions perceived to be TGF supporters. It also continued 'suicide attacks' on Kenyan, AMISOM and Ethiopian forces, and exported terror to Kenyan towns. In the ongoing fighting, there were numbers of victims of cross-fire between TFG, AMISOM and Ethiopian forces and al-Shabaab units.

All parties involved in the conflicts **abused human rights**. Independent **media and journalists** were also frequently endangered and some were killed. A HRW report on war crimes in Somalia, produced in August, tried to divide the blame for the armed violence evenly, but from its own data it was clear that al-Shabaab was the main perpetrator, and added to its actions was a stifling Islamist ideology that denied basic rights to Somalis. On 16 October, the TFG army chief, Abdulkadir Sheikh Ali Dini, called on al-Shabaab rank-and-file to lay down their arms and join the TFG.

Al-Shabaab came under **further pressure** towards the end of the year, faced with internal disagreements, and dispersed and retreated from various central areas, such as Hiraan Region. Some units moved towards Puntland. The movement was not 'defeated', however, but tried to adapt, and kept up its radical Islamist rhetoric and propaganda via a new Twitter account opened in December, among other methods. They also made attempts to extend contacts in Yemen and East African countries, and were reputed to have hosted several militants from the violent Nigerian Islamist group 'Boko Haram'.

The **TFG**, while expanding its reach and territory during the year and slightly gaining in popularity, was **not politically successful**. It remained divided and inefficient, and its army was not a united force but a conglomerate of clan-based or 'big-man' factions, with varying records. It was reputed to be corrupt and unreliable, and did not pay its soldiers on time. TFG President Sheikh Sharif remained in power but, as a relatively weak compromise figure, he was incapable of shaping a stronger and more credible leadership. Government institutions were not built up, political alliances were shaky and unproductive, decisive preparations for the post-transition period were not made, and outreach into the rural areas to provide an alternative authority structure to al-Shabaab was inadequate. The TGF's (financial) accountability, including to the donor community, was also very weak. In the wake of its failure, new regional units claiming autonomous government status gained ground in the south. They included Jubaland (or Azania) and Ximan-Xeeb, in addition to Galmudug, already established in 2010.

On 28 June, a new **TGF prime minister** was appointed: **Abdiweli Mohamed Ali**, a reputed US-educated economist (from the Majerteen/Darod clan), replaced Mohamed Abdullahi Mohamed 'Farmajo' (of the Marehan/Darod clan), a relatively popular politician who after not even one year in office fell victim to TFG infighting and had a dispute with TFG President Sheikh Sharif over various policy issues. The new prime minister claimed that the implementation of a roadmap to transform the transitional government into a permanent one was on course: a **National Security Stabilisation Plan** was crafted in early September. But he asked the donor community to double its financial aid to the TFG. On 4–6 September, the various stakeholders at a 'High Level Conference' in Mogadishu agreed to extend the transition period by one year and draw up a political roadmap towards a post-transition period after 20 August 2012. On 26–28 November, a

consultative meeting of civil society in Mogadishu, facilitated by the UN Political Office for Somalia headed by Tanzanian diplomat Augustine Mahiga, expressed support for the roadmap. The meeting involved 60 religious leaders, clan elders, and representatives of the business community, the diaspora, and youth and women's groups. Representatives of the TFG institutions, the Puntland and Galmudug administrations and the more Sufi-oriented 'Ahlu as-Sunnah wal Jama'a' movement were also present. This meeting made a new start on instigating a nation-wide political process going and engaging as many players as possible (except al-Shabaab, who refused).

The **conflict** between **Somaliland and Puntland** over the disputed Sanag, Sool and Ayn border regions was not resolved. In late February, fighting again erupted in the Buhoodle area. Leaders from the local D'ulbahante clan (from the Darod clan-family) in these areas declared a new mini-state called Khatumo, independent of Somaliland and declaring allegiance to the TFG.

The coasts along Puntland and south-central Somalia remained infested by **pirates**, led by well-organised **criminal networks**. While some commentators pleaded for the pirates to be regarded as 'insurgents' with social grievances, etc., the common motive of the pirates was criminal profit-seeking with armed violence, which had emerged in a lawless environment with weak or absent judicial systems and executive state power. They had no nationalist, all-Somali ideals. The **recruits** of the piracy networks, as in past years, were jobless Somalis, adrift as a result of the civil war and Islamist terror, or sometimes former fishermen. The business remained in the hands of strong organisational networks based in various Gulf States, Kenya and Somalia itself. Piracy endangered the lives of ships' personnel and ocean trading routes and raised the costs of sea traffic substantially because of increased insurance premiums. Both hostages and pirates were killed in several confrontations. On 21 February, four American hostages aboard a captured vessel were killed by pirates. More and more shipowners decided to take their own private security measures.

The **international naval protection force** became more effective and successful than in previous years. According to figures released by the International Maritime Organization, whose activities included the legal and practical fight against piracy, the number of ships and seafarers held captive by Somali pirates fell from 33 and 733, respectively, in February to 13 and 265 in early December. The number of reported attacks also declined from a high of 45 in January to 14 in November. Finally, the proportion of successful attacks was cut from 20% (of all attacks) in January to just 7% in November. However, according to a report by the US Center for American Progress, the costs of piracy incurred since 2007 reached the sum of $ 22 bn, quite apart from the harm done to crews and hostages.

There were indications that **al-Shabaab elements** were moving into a closer **alliance** with some **pirate groups** in southern Puntland. For instance, after taking over the pirate base at Harardheere by force, the 'taxation' income from the pirates was yielding an estimated $ 1.5 m per year. In such deals, al-Shabaab provided protection for the pirate bases and interest groups. Piracy might thus be given a new lease of life by its emerging alliance with al-Shabaab groups. Somaliland, however, effectively prevented piracy from taking root on its coasts.

In international forums, there was more discussion on measures to limit illegal fishing and possible toxic waste dumping by foreign vessels in Somali coastal waters, which was said to have encouraged local people to take up piracy.

Somaliland and **Puntland** were much more peaceful than south-central Somalia, but were not entirely free from violence, in addition to the enduring tension in their border areas. On 19 June, two soldiers were killed in a bomb attack on a Somaliland police station in Las Anod. On 27 November, the Somaliland commander of the Central Investigative Unit of Sool region, Mohamud Mohamed Hirsi, was gunned down in Las Anod. In Puntland, the government was not able to eliminate Muhammad Seyyid 'Atam', an Islamist rebel (from the Warsangeli clan) in the Galgala Mountains south of Bosasso.

In August, **Somaliland** decided to adopt a full multi-party system, after there had previously been only three parties. A registration process for all aspiring parties was started, to be concluded sometime in 2012.

The **Puntland** authorities became more actively involved in combating piracy, adopting measures such as land raids on pirate hideouts in cooperation with Saracen International (a private security company). Coast guard training continued with the assistance of UAE funding and Japanese Coast Guard trainers. As a result, pirate activity shifted southwards to the Galmudug region coast line, making its headquarters in El Danaan, Harardheere and Hobyo.

Foreign Affairs

Somalia continued to demand an inordinate amount of **foreign policy attention** on the part of the **global community**, notably with regard to the persistent political instability, the piracy issue and the humanitarian disaster, including from famine. Al-Shabaab's persistent acts of terror and sabotage and TFG inefficiency and divisiveness remained key issues of concern. Substantial and costly naval forces were maintained against piracy, anti-terror activities continued, and (mainly Western) donor countries continued to support the TFG and urged it to get its act together. The al-Shabaab radicals continued to be seen by the USA and the EU as a major international security risk, responsible for global terror attacks and threats.

In March, the **AMISOM forces** were augmented by the deployment of 1,000 additional Burundian troops and then numbered about 9,300 men, still below the 12,000 target. The majority of the troops and the commander continued to come from Uganda. In December, a first advance group of 250 men from Djibouti joined AMISOM, but no further reinforcements were contributed by other AU member states. On 24 February, a meeting of

AMISOM, IGAD, the AU and the UN representative for Somalia adopted a Joint Regional Strategy designed to help the TFG manage the transitional period.

Kenya's invasion in October, with an armed force of about 2,000 men (Operation 'linda nchi' = 'protect the country'), quickly secured the area along the border, but later got bogged down by the onset of rains in the south. The Kenyans stopped short of attacking Kismaayo, al-Shabaab's chief port and its economic and arms life line. The city came under threat but no attempt was made by the Kenyan army to capture it, as no post-victory scenario had been developed and there was fear that there would be Somali civilian casualties and that too much local resistance would be provoked.

The **humanitarian disaster** in the wake of the **drought** prompted the international community to mount a major operation and provide substantial funds for emergency assistance, with the US being the largest donor (giving in excess of $ 380 m). On 25 August, the AU held its first ever 'pledging conference', raising $ 350 m. Other countries that reacted to the famine crisis included **Turkey**, which provided relief aid and announced that, after the withdrawal of al-Shabaab, it would reopen its embassy in Mogadishu. Turkish Prime Minister Erdogan, who visited Mogadishu on 19 August, was the first high-ranking foreign politician for a very long time to go to Somalia. Ugandan President Museveni was also there on 11–12 June to underscore his country's role as a major contributor to AMISOM, and UN Secretary-General Ban Ki-moon paid a surprise visit to the capital on 9 December.

In February, the **UK**'s Minister for International Development Andrew Mitchell paid a week-long visit to **Somaliland**. Towards the end of the year, the UK government, seeing new momentum in Somalia, started preparations for a major international conference on Somalia's future, to be held in February 2012.

On 28 July, the **EU** extended its security sector support funding to the TFG for another year, to focus on developing command and control structures and educating Somali trainers who could take over the local security and police training programme. The mandate of the EU anti-piracy NAVFOR Atalanta forces, active off Somalia's shores, was extended to 12 December 2012.

On 18 July, the **UN Monitoring Group on Somalia and Eritrea** issued its longest-ever report to the UNSC, addressing issues around the UN arms embargo against Somalia, the development of the armed combat and the flow of contraband supplies, and assessed the chances of stabilising Somalia. Eritrea was accused of continuing to provide al-Shabaab with arms and support, but the evidence for this – in contrast to previous years – was thin.

The **TFG** had no possibility of pursuing a distinct foreign policy but remained committed diplomatically to presenting the vision of one federal Somalia. Its main concern was to keep a tolerable relationship with donor countries so as to sustain its life-line. TFG President Sheikh Sharif undertook several foreign visits to solicit support, including to Ethiopia, Kenya, Djibouti and Qatar.

Puntland and Somaliland had very limited room for foreign policy manoeuvring because of their status as non-recognised political entities. They maintained good political and economic relations with Djibouti, Ethiopia and Kenya, including security cooperation with those countries. **Somaliland** was *de facto* independent – with it own budget, army, government institutions, tax system and political process – and again asked for international **recognition** in various international forums on the basis of its self-generated, independent state recovery, its democratic credentials, and its emerging economy. However, it still did not receive formal diplomatic recognition from the international community, which was clinging to the fiction that it would ultimately have to be part of a united Somalia. Ethiopia did not support the independence option either, afraid that it might spark similar demands in its own Somali-inhabited Ogaden Region.

Socioeconomic Developments

Reliable macroeconomic and social data on the three Somalias were not available, and figures from various sources were inconsistent. Despite the absence of an efficient central state and economic policies, south-central Somalia saw **GDP growth** estimated at 2.6%. GDP was approximately $ 2.4 bn, with a GDP per capita of around $ 600. The mainstay of the economy was still agriculture and livestock (accounting for some 60% of GDP), and the rest came from services (33%) and 'industry' (mostly processing of agricultural and fishery products). The import-export figures were unknown, but imports were about 25% higher than exports. Almost 50% of export earnings were realised through the sale of livestock. According to the Somali National Bank (reopened in 2009), the national debt reached $ 4.7 bn. Claims of overall GDP growth in south-central Somalia were not reflected in an improvement in general socioeconomic and political conditions.

The **TFG's sources of income** were limited. It collected tax revenue from the airport and Mogadishu port as well as from overseas remittances, but it was mainly donor money that kept its operations alive, for lack of any alternative. The TFG's **2011 national budget** was worth $ 98.5 m; 30% of this was expected to come from tax collection and the rest from donor countries. Defence spending was estimated to account for 40%–50% of the total (including salaries for army personnel), 15% went to education, and most of the rest was spent on salaries for government members, parliamentarians, staff and office workers. There was no open information on budget allocation and spending.

Deposits of mineral resources in Somalia were allegedly abundant, including uranium, tin, copper, zinc, gold, coal, zircon, oil and kynite, but little if any exploitation was started. For example, there was no progress towards bringing into production the proven 5.6 bn m^3 of natural gas reserves. Oil exploration was proceeding in Puntland, with promising finds reported.

Somaliland's budget was estimated at $ 90 m, almost 70% higher than in 2010 due to the expected higher tax revenue, notably from business owners. About 40% of the budget went to the army, security and police. **Puntland's budget** amounted to an estimated $ 75 m. Its economic recovery went ahead, with an emerging private sector. Piracy was an unacknowledged source of income for various elite figures and had an impact on real estate prices and certain local business investments. Ill-gotten gains and more money and real estate investments contributed to some local growth and a rise in consumption.

Infrastructure maintenance in Somalia was generally bad, especially roads, but there were **construction booms** (houses, hotels, small businesses) in selected parts of the country, such as Hargeisa, Berbera, Bosasso, Galkaiyo, and several towns with pirate bases. There was a large number of airfields (59), but only seven with paved runways. Bosasso international airport in Puntland was expanded and now had a 3.4-km runway.

The main seaports were Mogadishu (the largest, and controlled by the TFG), Bosasso (in Puntland), Berbera (in Somaliland) and Kismaayo (controlled by al-Shabaab). Berbera gained importance in its role as port for imports to Ethiopia.

The predominant issue for the economy and society of southern Somalia was the **devastating drought**. Lack of rain led to the lowest annual crop production in 17 years, accompanied by high animal mortality and declining livestock prices. Food prices went up by almost 200% in many areas of the south. The drought affected the whole region, but hit especially hard in the south-central areas (Lower Shebelle, Bay and Bakool), which were riven by conflict and al-Shabaab terror. The movement hesitated about what to do, then went into denial, and ultimately refused to cooperate with **international relief** organisations. Its blocking of the inflow of food aid led to further loss of local support. Despite the fact that some 2.4 m Somalis were affected by the drought, which resulted in malnourishment and famine, predictions about imminent mass mortality were exaggerated by the UN's Food Security and Nutrition Analysis Unit, which initially spoke of 4 m people in deep crisis in Somalia, with 750,000 expected to die. In December, it reported that only 10,000 people had died of hunger. The massive emergency aid effort set up by Western donors and WFP averted a more serious crisis. While not all needs could be met, by late October some 2.4 m people had received food aid, and 1.2 m had access to clean water. More than 1.7 m people received livelihood support. These staggering figures (relative to a total population of about 10 m) showed the extent of the crisis and the dysfunctionality of Somali society. The USA was again the largest provider of humanitarian supplies to WFP. Somali diaspora agencies also played a positive role, with small-scale projects reaching many areas, including within al-Shabaab-held territory.

Population growth was estimated at about 1.6%–2% and, despite out-migration, violence and famine, the population rose to a total of about 10 m people (for the three Somalias), with a fertility rate per woman of 6.2 children. Life expectancy fell to an estimated 51 years, and a staggering 45% of the population were aged under 14, while only 2.5% were over 65. The urban population (including peri-urban IDP camps) rose to more than 40% of the total.

Remittances from overseas Somali communities remained the single largest source of income for the country and were estimated at about $ 1.2 bn. Somalia continued its *laissez-faire* system of unfettered business ventures, with no environmental or social regulations, and a weak legal business environment, but showed great dynamics and inventiveness. Nevertheless, a really productive economy failed to take off. Parasitic, rent-seeking economic activities based on import-export levies and 'services' and unregulated resource use, alongside the export of livestock, animal products, incense and charcoal, showed no signs of major value-generating growth via craft production, industrial enterprise or mineral exploitation and sale.

The **education system** remained largely in private hands, but primary schools were operated and expanded substantially, although most were Islamic schools, weak in terms of general curriculum. The majority of Somali children were still not receiving any education, and the general educational standard of the population was very low. Some 15% of the TFG's budget was spent on education. The universities that existed in the three Somalias were not state universities, but largely privately funded. Mogadishu University, for example, was financed by Saudi money and led by Somali academics affiliated to the 'Al Islah' movement (akin to the Muslim Brotherhood).

Corruption, buttressed by the clan favouritism system operating in the absence of a strong state, remained deeply entrenched in Somali society and undermined political institution building, equitable growth, justice and durable environmental management. Somalia was ranked 182nd (and last) in the 2011 TI Corruption Index, meaning it was labelled the most 'corrupt country' on earth. Although not free of corruption, Somaliland was an exception to this score.

More than 1.3 m people still lived in **IDP camps**, such as those in the Afgoye corridor, with close to an additional 250,000 having fled in 2011 to camps in Ethiopia (Dolo Addo, 97,000) and Kenya (Dadaab, 153,000) in the wake of the famine. Many of these famine refugees also told tales of exposure to al-Shabaab abuse. As in previous years, the out-migration of Ethiopian and Somali refugees and migrants to Yemeni shores continued unabated, especially via Bosasso port.

Bleak prospects thus continued for south-central Somalia – an area of persistent insecurity, political instability, lack of respect for human rights, and criminality in the form of power abuse and religion-based terror. But the decline of al-Shabaab, the continuous donor pressure on the TFG to perform better, the emerging building boom in Mogadishu and other towns and the growing positive engagement of Somali diaspora organisations in relief and development work, brought **sparks of hope** for some gradual improvement.

Jon Abbink

South Sudan

On 9 July the **Republic of South Sudan**, a country of about nine million people, became an **independent state** amidst much rejoicing. The ceremony took place at the mausoleum of John Garang, 'Dr John' as he was widely known, the founder and leader of the **Sudan Peoples' Liberation Army/Movement (SPLA/M)** from its establishment in 1983 until his death in a helicopter crash in 2005, shortly after the signing of the Comprehensive Peace Agreement (CPA). The ceremony was attended by a number of African heads of state, including President al-Bashir of Sudan, as well as numerous other dignitaries from around the world, and was presided over by Garang's successor, **Salva Kiir Mayardit**. Kiir's message was that South Sudan had taken its place in the international community after years of suffering. The Turco-Egyptian invasion in the 19th century had carved out southern Sudan – hitherto a heterogeneous area of Africa – which had then experienced and tried to resist widespread slave-raiding. Then, in the 20th century, there had been resistance to the coming of the British-led Anglo-Egyptian condominium. Finally, the coming of Sudan's independence in 1956 had led to the South's need to resist further forceful domination by Muslim Arab governments in Khartoum. Now at last South Sudan was free, but despite oil and other mineral wealth, it lacked all the features of a modern economy and started out as one of the poorest and most vulnerable countries in the world.

Domestic Politics

Salva Kiir's rule of the newly independent state was to be under a **new constitution**, which appeared to be very democratic with an elected bi-cameral parliament, similar in makeup to Sudan's own. There was an upper house consisting of a Council of States – representing the ten federal states – and a parliamentary assembly with 332 members, up from the previous figure of 170. However, there were critics of the new constitution, since it handed greater powers than before to the executive president. In August, **President Kiir** announced the members of his new government, but there were few major changes and it remained dominated by the leading figures of the SPLM. Concern regarding this concentration of power was expressed in the press, which had grown since the CPA and had become increasingly outspoken, though its circulation was limited. There were also signs that the government was prepared to crack down on the press, including if necessary detaining journalists, while the radio and television output was safely under SPLM control.

A number of **opposition parties** had competed in the April 2010 elections, but almost all lacked any significant support base and tended to reflect the personal ambitions of would-be politicians. The main possible exception was a party led by Lam Akol, which called itself the SPLM-Democratic Change (SPLM-DC). However Lam Akol was a controversial figure, having changed sides on a number of occasions, and was widely seen as being backed by Sudan in an effort to weaken the SPLM government politically. At the same time, there were repeated rumours that Lam Akol might be recalled to the government, in which a former ally of his, Riek Machar, was the vice-president, or that he might be offered a job simply in an effort to control him.

It was clear from the outset that there were many **governance challenges**. State structures in Southern Sudan had never been strong and years of civil war had made them non-existent in many rural areas. The SPLA had made some attempts to administer areas under its control, but they were geographically scattered and of limited effect, and so the ten states' governments were also very weak. At all levels of government there was a shortage of trained manpower and internal control of departments was therefore weak, which led to repeated charges of corruption, against which Kiir sought to be seen to act by establishing a new commission. Public services, including health and education, were poor (half the population was under 18), non-existent in some rural areas, or provided by international NGOs, which had proliferated following the signing of the CPA.

Security was also very weak. The largest allocation in the national budget was for the maintenance of the SPLA. In practice, however, this amounted largely to paying young men to stay in their camps, and only limited efforts were made to reduce the size of the new national army. Some of the SPLA were transferred into the police, but training was quite brief and there were few experienced officers. In addition, efforts to disarm the civilian population in a country awash with weapons after decades of conflict had only limited success. On occasion, attempts by the SPLA to collect weapons led to local resentment and even resistance.

Probably the most foreboding development in the early months of the new state was the rise in what was generally described as **ethnic violence**. It occurred in seven of the ten states, and was generally at its most intense in the states of Jonglei, Upper Nile and Unity, towards the border with Sudan. The clashes had some traditional features, such as cattle raiding, which had been a feature of pastoral societies for centuries. However, in recent times this has involved the use of modern weaponry rather than spears and arrows, and the result had been an escalation in the number of fatalities. The UN estimated that there were over 2,000 deaths during the year and other sources suggested even higher figures, while many more fled in search of shelter. The biggest conflict was that between the Lou Nuer and the Murle in Jonglei state; large-scale raids broke out first in April, resulting in the abduction and killing of many local people, as well as the theft of cattle, with the Murle claiming to have lost over 300,000 head to the Lou Nuer. The government tried to broker peace talks, but negotiations broke down when the Murle failed to return abducted children. By the end of the year, some Lou Nuer were calling for the Murle to be entirely driven out by force. Another notable source of conflict was **SPLA mutinies**. That led by George Athor, a senior SPLA figure, was particularly threatening, though in December he was killed when on his way to talks with the government in Nairobi. The government linked these security problems to its **charges** that the Khartoum government was arming and inciting ethnic groups in order to **destabilise the new state**; and the Sudanese government in turn accused South Sudan of fomenting conflicts in Sudan. In some areas, **land disputes** were also a contributory factor, either as people returned from displacement in the north or from refugee camps in East Africa and reclaimed their land, or as a result of urbanisation. The prime example was in the capital city itself: Juba was in Bari territory, but many of the SPLM working in the government were Dinka, and the richer ones sought to build impressive villas. Rising social tensions contributed to a rapid rise in crime, and to a government proposal that a new purpose-built capital be set up at Ramciel in a more central area of the country.

When the CPA was signed, it was envisaged that the UN would play a role in containing ethnic violence and a force of 10,000 troops called the **UN Mission in Sudan (UNMIS)** was established. However, with the independence of South Sudan the mission ended and Sudan made it clear it did not want the mission to continue there. But UNMIS now became the UN Mission in South Sudan (UNMISS), made up of 7,000 troops and 900 police, and as the security situation worsened UNMISS became more concerned. The situation was difficult, with local conflicts breaking out, scattered across a large country with little infrastructure, and the UNMISS mandate was also quite restricted.

Foreign Affairs

In foreign policy, **relations with Sudan** had top priority, especially since the two countries remained interlocked, particularly with regard to oil; several other issues between the two countries also remained unresolved, such as the border demarcation, particularly the disputed status of the Abyei region (see in Sudan article), financial matters, citizenship, and the fate of Southerners residing in Sudan. But the problem was above all one of mutual suspicion with regard to the two countries' domestic conflicts and a lack of trust when they entered into negotiations of any kind. Nevertheless, Kiir's first international visit, shortly after independence, was to Khartoum, amidst hopes that the two presidents might be able to move matters on, though little appeared to have been achieved.

Kiir made another important trip in September, when he visited Washington and met President Obama. The **US** had been a strong supporter of South Sudan and had a substantial presence in terms of both officials and NGOs. It was concerned about issues of governance, and especially the high levels of corruption in top layers of the government. The US ambassador had compiled a dossier on this, which he handed to Kiir personally. The president's response was welcoming but action proved slow since the flow of oil revenues through the state – whether or not corruption was involved – was the lifeblood of the new political system. The US also warned the government against actively supporting the Sudan Peoples' Liberation Army – North (SPLA-N) in the fighting in Sudan.

China was also concerned to develop links with the new state, which was an important source of its oil. As a sign of its commitment, it made a $ 32 m grant in October for new development projects, and also offered to mediate with Sudan, as well as inviting Kiir to visit Beijing. Many **European countries** also wished to offer support, especially when there were fears that, without it, the new state might collapse. Two members of the EU Troika that did so much to achieve the CPA, Britain and Norway, were particularly active.

Many in South Sudan wanted to see the new country orientate itself towards its **African neighbours**. Uganda and Kenya in particular had long maintained close contact, and a number of SPLA leaders had acquired properties in one or both of those countries. **Uganda** had supported the SPLA very openly in the civil war, while **Kenya** had hosted and helped the peace talks that resulted in the CPA. In addition to political links, there were growing economic ties, including much speculation that South Sudan would seek to build a new pipeline for its oil exports, running down to a new Indian Ocean port complex which the Chinese offered to build near Lamu, Kenya. There was also talk of a link being made with a new refinery in Western Uganda, where oilfields were being developed near Lake Albert. **Ethiopia** was also important, especially since the AU-sponsored talks with the Sudan government to resolve outstanding issues were being held there. All three countries were very aware of the security threats if South Sudan should become a failed state. Western Ethiopia could be affected through cross-border ethnic ties; Kenya was concerned about stability in the Rift Valley area, which had been troubled in the past; while Uganda was fearful that the Lord's Resistance Army might once again become a greater threat in its northern border area.

The **Middle East** was less directly involved, but **Egypt** was concerned to press its case on the Nile Waters. Juba had yet to make its position clear and probably felt that the issue could wait, while giving it a measure of leverage with the downstream states. The Gulf states were interested in possible economic opportunities, including further involvement in the oil sector, as well as some possibilities for investment in agriculture. To balance this interest, and perhaps to annoy Sudan, Kiir's government also opened relations with Israel.

South Sudan was also keen to join an array of **international organisations**, which it hoped would provide material help. It quickly joined the UN and other bodies it thought particularly important, such as the World Bank, the IMF, and regional organisations including the AU and IGAD. A decision on a formal application to join the EAC was deferred to 2012 due to its late submission.

Socioeconomic Developments

At independence South Sudan had a **GDP** estimated at $ 13 bn, with oil accounting for 71% of that figure. **GDP per capita** in 2010 had been estimated at $ 1,546, with Gross National Income considerably lower at close to $ 1,000. The government introduced a **new currency** (South Sudanese pound) in July, without consultation with Sudan and with substantial amounts of Sudanese pounds still circulating in the region. The two currencies started at parity, but South Sudan's level against the dollar was pitched quite high, which exacerbated inflation and corruption. **Inflation** reached 61% by September, partly as a result of Sudan's intermittent enforcement of a cross-border trade blockade. The intention was to put pressure on the South with regard to oil negotiations and this forced the South to import more from Kenya and Uganda, which charged higher prices. In October, Thabo Mbeki, former South African president, in his capacity as AU mediator, tried to ease the situation by negotiating an agreement with Khartoum to re-open the border, though the situation on trade remained tense and the oil issue was unresolved. With inflation rising and the value of the new currency falling, it was announced in November that a committee would be established to review the economic situation.

The government would clearly have liked to attract new foreign investment, but there were serious obstacles that made international donors and investors remain wary. In addition to **corruption**, the **bureaucracy** at national and state government levels was difficult to navigate and there was generally a lack of transparency and accountability with regard to finance.

Government revenues were 98% based on **oil**, with production at 350,000 b/d. With independence came a new national oil company, Nilepet. International help for the company under Oil Minister Stephen Dheiu was forthcoming, but its inexperience in dealing with the international companies that develop the fields, such as those from Asia, was still apparent. The ministry planned for new exploration, especially in the southern part of Jonglei state, where the French Total and the Kuwait Foreign Petroleum Company had rights. However, with revenues buoyant and the government unable to absorb more income effectively, there was no great pressure to expand output. In addition, the security situation was such as to deter some foreign companies. The lack of resolution of the pipeline issue with Sudan was also discouraging some and, though the government talked of a new East African pipeline, there were many sceptics.

Negotiations with Sudan over the **rent for the pipeline** were inconclusive. Oil Minister Dheiu claimed that Sudan had been offered a choice. The South would pay $ 2.6 bn over five years, and not pay a further $ 2.6 bn, which it claimed Sudan owed in arrears. Sudan was reported to have demanded $ 10.5 bn, while the AU mediating team suggested a compromise of $ 7.4 bn. The other suggestion offered by the South was a transit fee of $ 0.75 p/b, while Khartoum raised its figure from $ 22.50 to $ 32 p/b. The situation worsened towards the end of the year. As a result of the failure to reach an agreement, together with disputes about payments already due, Sudan announced in late November that it would simply take two shipments of oil and sell them on its own account. The response from Juba was to regard this as theft, and to threaten to cut off supplies entirely, though that had not happened by the end of the year.

In spite of being a substantial oil producer, South Sudan had **no refinery** of its own, though plans were underway. In 2009, there had been a proposal to build a refinery to produce 70,000 b/d in Kiir's home town of Akon, but funding for it had not so far been forthcoming. Meanwhile, the country had to import oil products and, until independence, 90% of its fuel needs were being met from Sudan, which had a Chinese-built refinery just north of Khartoum. After July, the intermittent blockade by Sudan forced the government to import oil products from Kenya and Uganda at higher prices.

As well as oil, there were hopes that other minerals could be developed. South Sudan was believed to have considerable **mineral potential**, but much remained unexplored and, with insecurity rising, exploration might not be carried out for some while. Potential sites included Eastern Equatoria, where there are gold deposits, and the remote area of Hofrat an-Nahas in the north-west, where it has been known for many years that there are substantial reserves of copper. The latter, however, borders on South Darfur and the border had yet to be fully demarcated. In preparation for developments on this front, the government was drafting a new mining law.

In spite of South Sudan's oil wealth, the standard of living of the vast majority of the population was extremely poor. With practically no industry or infrastructure, around 80% of the populace struggled to make a living from **subsistence agriculture**. Many observers saw the longer-term future as lying less in oil than in agricultural development. The country had an abundance of rich agricultural land and plenty of water with good rainfall. It already grew a wide range of crops and had between 10 m and 20 m head of cattle. However, the country was still food-dependent and was estimated to need to grow a further 600,000 tonnes per year to become self-sufficient. The evidence of the suffering of many in South Sudan was clear from the scale of **food support** reported by the WFP, which had been feeding over 2 m people in 2011 and expected the figure to rise to 2.7 m in 2012. In addition to problems of insecurity and conflict, which had damaged crops and sometimes prevented relief supplies from getting through, rains had been erratic and in some cases had damaged the crops. Furthermore, crops in the market were affected by the general inflation, and 51% of the population were estimated to be living below the **national poverty line**.

But while there was **potential for agriculture**, skilled agriculturalists and infrastructure were lacking. It was reported that 9% of the land area had already been leased to foreign companies from a number of countries in an effort to boost agricultural production but, unless handled with sensitivity, this might cause new problems. Property rights were unclear in many areas where much land was traditionally communal and rapid development might lead to local displacement and perhaps increased insecurity. There were also fears that local communities might be turned into poor, landless labourers, which would result in social problems. However, by the end of the year only one commercial project had actually started, located in Unity state and funded by an Egyptian venture capital company. Under present conditions, it was clear that, for the immediate future at least, agricultural expansion would have to be based on small-scale farming rather than on large commercial operations. **Infrastructure** would have to be significantly improved for the strategy to be successful. At independence, the only tarmac roads were in the capital, Juba; the all-weather roads between other towns had been badly damaged by war and many were still in need of repair. The government had an ambitious programme of road and bridge construction, but could make little headway without international support. Improved power generation was also necessary, though there were prospects for hydroelectricity. Some years before, three sites had been identified, but none had so far gone beyond the stage of feasibility studies.

Since the signing of the CPA, South Sudan had also received $ 4 bn worth of **aid**, especially for infrastructure and services. In addition, there had been an influx of **private businessmen**, especially from East Africa. The numerous entrepreneurs were accompanied by long columns of trucks winding their way from the Ugandan border town of Nimule with all manner of goods. However, much of this went no further than Juba, which had become a boom town, with new construction work taking place throughout the city. Apart from that funded through government, much of the work was related to new embassies and offices for international organisations and NGOs. The boom attracted not only foreign businessmen, especially from Kenya and Uganda, but also labour, for the availability of trained Southern Sudanese following the war was limited, while the education system still had a long way to go before the situation would improve. However, the **boom** also had its down-side for the 350,000 residents of the capital. In addition to high inflation, there was a severe shortage of housing, and crime rates rose sharply, as did prostitution, with the danger of a spread of HIV.

The result of all this economic activity was a growth rate of 6% in 2011, and hopes for a slightly higher figure in 2012. However, much was dependent on an agreement with Sudan regarding the export of the South's oil, and improving the expenditure of government revenues that were at the heart of the non-subsistence economy.

As well as becoming the world's newest state, South Sudan was clearly one of its poorest and most vulnerable countries. There was great uncertainty over its ability to improve its position in the years ahead, rather than fragmenting into further poverty and conflict.

Peter Woodward

Sudan

At the start of the year, it was clear that 2011 would be the most momentous year since 1955, at the end of which Sudan had opted for independence from Egypt, officially granted on 1 January 1956. By the end of 2010, it seemed clear that the southern Sudanese would exercise the right to self determination granted to them in the 2005 Comprehensive Peace Agreement (CPA) and choose secession, thus becoming an independent state. The decisive referendum took place in January and the outcome was an even more overwhelming vote for independence – almost 99% of votes cast – than had been expected. From then on, 2011 would be about four key matters: the implementation of the decision, with independence for the new Republic of South Sudan taking place on 9 July; the development of relations between South Sudan and Sudan, many issues still remaining unresolved; the formation of an independent state in the South; and the impact of secession on the now truncated Sudan. The Darfur conflict was still unresolved. The government broadly managed to control the fluid political situation largely because of the continued disarray of the political opposition. The economy experienced a sharp slump, largely due to the loss of 75% of oil production to the South.

Domestic Politics

The January **referendum** on the South's independence passed off comparatively smoothly. Some 3.9 m people registered to vote in the South itself, which included many of the 55,000 who had moved from the north in the run-up to the referendum. A further 116,000 who were still in the north registered to vote, in addition to thousands who voted overseas, including in Britain and the USA. The CPA required that 60% of the electorate should vote in order for the referendum to be valid and the turnout was eventually a high 83%, with even 53% of voters going to the polls in the north. In all there were 22,000 Sudanese and international observers, including representatives of the UN, the EU and the Carter Center. The smoothness of the whole operation owed much to the lack of any significant movement against secession: with the South of one mind, it was a display of unity unprecedented in any free vote ever held in Sudan and in itself provided a ray of optimism that was, however, soon being called into question.

President Omar Hassan al-Bashir had made a visit to the South shortly before the referendum and had made it clear that his government would accept the outcome. Once it was over, he claimed that the choice of secession made **Sudan's identity** far clearer. From then on, it would be a **fully Arab and Islamic state**, under the Sharia, Islamic law.

With the question of the South's future settled, and the result being immediately accepted by both the national government and the international community, the next major political development came as more of a surprise. The start of the 'Arab Spring' in Tunisia in January, followed shortly afterwards by a similar development in Egypt, soon caused unrest in Sudan. Many in the urban centres of the north in particular had **growing grievances**, in spite of the rapid oil-fuelled economic growth since 2000. The benefits of growth had largely flowed to the ruling National Congress Party (NCP) and its supporters, who had a commanding position in the economy. This was resented by those who were excluded, who included those in or from regions of the country that felt marginalised, such as the west, including Darfur, and young people, who made up a large part of the population but experienced high levels of unemployment. In addition, the government had cut subsidies on sugar and petroleum products, raising the already significant rate of inflation; while doing little to address complaints of the high levels of corruption.

The government responded in a number of ways as **demonstrations** broke out from the end of January and continued intermittently for some months. The powerful security services had long developed counter-measures, including the prevention of large numbers of demonstrators gathering in one place, so there was no Khartoum equivalent of Tahrir Square in Cairo. And where there were demonstrations they responded rapidly, attacking the demonstrators and causing a small number of fatalities, as well as detaining some. At the same time, the government tried to identify itself with the Arab Spring, a position it was to maintain repeatedly throughout the year. Its claim was that the coup that had brought al-Bashir to power in 1989 had introduced a moderate Islamic regime, in tune with the powerful forces in Tunisia and Egypt that were having growing success in early 2011. In another effort to win support, al-Bashir announced in March that he would not seek re-election in 2015.

The government's position was strengthened by the **disarray of the major opposition parties**. The leading parties of the pre-1989 democratic periods, the Umma Party and the Democratic Unionist Party (DUP), which had boycotted the 2010 elections, still retained some influence nationally but failed to take united action. There was much speculation that one or the other would join the government, though that failed to materialise until the end of the year, when Mohamed Osman Mirghani, the leader of the Khatmiyya sufi sect, finally decided to take the DUP into government, but the parties remained riddled with factionalism as well as being suspicious of one another. Meanwhile, the leader of the Popular Congress Party (PCP), Hasan al-Turabi, who had been the ideological mentor of the government until his split with al-Bashir in 1999, was arrested and detained until May. In addition, the South's decision to secede weakened the Sudan Peoples' Liberation Movement – North (SPLM-N), despite hopes in some quarters that it might become a significant party in the north.

While the **government** was broadly able to **contain and manage the situation at the centre** (in spite of presiding over the loss of a third of the country's territory, including most of its oil reserves), in the outlying rural areas the position was less clear. **Darfur** remained a continuing **area of conflict**, especially as the rebels were encouraged to fight by the success of the Sudan Peoples' Liberation Army (SPLA) in leading the South to independence. Actual levels of fighting fluctuated, while there was also much political manoeuvring, with seemingly endless rounds of talks between the government and the rebel factions, many of which took place in Doha since Qatar had a growing connection to Sudan. The major rebel groups were the Justice and Equality Movement (JEM) led by Ibrahim Khalil with ethnic support particularly from the Zaghawa, and the Sudan Liberation Army (SLA) factions led by Abdel Wahid and Minni Minnawi with backing from the Fur, the largest ethnic group in Darfur. In March, the government stepped up its armed attacks, especially with the bombing of villages around Jebel Marra, the home of the Fur, and there seemed little that the AU/UN Hybrid Operation in Darfur (**UNAMID**) could do. At the same time, the government sought to re-organise its administration in Darfur in an effort to weaken the rebel groups. They had been seeking a new recognition for Darfur as a whole and many were critical of the existing division of the former region into three states. Fresh opposition was thus expressed to the government's decision, announced in March, to increase the number of states from three to five, while the proposed referendum on the region's structure never took place. In July, the government announced that it had signed a deal in Doha, but only with a new and little known faction, the Liberation and Justice Movement led by former Darfur governor, Tigani Sessi. He later received a senior appointment in Darfur, but with little support for him in the region the security situation remained poor. Conditions for IDPs and the rest of the civilian population remained difficult, with international agencies restricted in their operations by the government.

Meanwhile, **conflict** grew in **three border areas** that had not been resolved under the CPA of 2005. The area that was most problematic after 2005 had been **Abyei**. In addition to its significance as an oil-producing region, Abyei had experienced ethnic tension, mainly over land use, between the Ngok Dinka, who are Southerners, and the northern Misseriyya – semi-nomads who move south in the dry season. During the years of civil war, many Misseriyya had been armed by the government to attack their southern neighbours, while many Dinka in turn supported the SPLA. It had been intended under the CPA that a referendum would be held in Abyei simultaneously with the South's referendum, to discover whether its people wished to stay in the North or become part of the South. However, such was the violence that this referendum could not be held, and instead the government went ahead with an election for the governor of Abyei in May. Victory was claimed for the NCP candidate, Ahmed Haroun, but many disbelieved the result, claiming that Abdel Aziz al-Hilu of the Sudan People's Liberation Movement (SPLM) was the real winner. In May, the government decided to send its forces to occupy the whole of Abyei, inflicting a significant defeat on SPLA forces in the process. Alarmed by the rising level of conflict in June, the UN agreed to deploy a 4,000–strong UN Interim Security Force for Abiyei (**UNISFA**), mostly supplied by Ethiopia, along both sides of the border.

Immediately north of Abyei lies the rest of **Southern Kordofan** state, which with **Southern Blue Nile** had also been a scene of **conflict**. Both these states were to have undergone processes of consultation, but not referenda, to decide their futures. Like Abyei, both included populations that supported the SPLM, but following the South's decision to secede, the government in Khartoum was determined not to lose more territory and, as a result, fighting flared up in both areas that was to continue for the rest of the year. These new areas of conflict, together with Abyei, were spoken of increasingly by the northern opposition parties as the 'New South'. Towards the end of the year, the **SPLM-N** announced that it was forming a new **Sudan Revolutionary Front** to seek to unite the various rebel movements in a collective effort to overthrow the government in Khartoum.

Meanwhile, **in the South** itself, many **challenges** appeared in the six months between the referendum and the planned independence day on 9 July. The civil wars between north and south that had dragged on for decades, becoming Africa's longest war, had in reality always been complex affairs subsuming a number of more localised conflicts. To the outside world, the SPLA in particular had looked like a centralised command under the somewhat autocratic leadership of John Garang, until his death shortly after the signing of the CPA, but in reality it always involved a large element of localism in which local commanders were major figures. In the weeks after the referendum, it was clear that some of these local commanders were beginning to manoeuvre, and in some cases to challenge the autonomous government in the South. A particularly troubled area was **Jonglei**

province, where General George Athor, formerly a senior SPLA figure, turned renegade and attacked local loyal SPLA forces, as well as being reported to have plans to attack Juba. Fatalities in February alone were reported to be some 300. Critics noted that Athor had been frustrated in his failure to win the governorship of Jonglei in the 2010 elections. In the following month, General Abdel Baghi Ayii, from Northern Bahr al-Ghazal, also defected. He gave a press conference in which he claimed that the SPLM leadership in Juba was corrupt and that there was discrimination against southern Muslims in a region that had turned increasingly to Christian churches during the wars. The Southern government in turn claimed that these disturbances in its northern states were being encouraged by the Khartoum government as it sought to pressurise the South in the context of the complex on-going negotiations. There were also growing **ethnic tensions**. The majority of the SPLA had been from the region's largest tribe, the Dinka, but within the Dinka there were clan rivalries and tensions. There were also tensions with other ethnic groups in a number of areas. Ethnic tensions were not new, but longstanding actions such as cattle-raiding were no longer carried out only with traditional weapons, such as spears, for the region was awash with modern weapons like the AK47. Some disarmament programmes were undertaken, but there was often reluctance to hand over weapons for fear of the vulnerability that might result. The return of southerners from the North after the signing of the CPA had also opened up new land disputes in some areas, including around Juba itself. Many barely educated young men were unemployed and added to the intermittent outbreaks of violence. Indeed this was a factor in the slow rate of demobilisation of the SPLA forces: there was fear of further unrest if the troops were demobilised, even though the cost of continuing to pay them took up a major part of the national budget. It had been hoped at the time of the signing of the CPA that the UN Mission in Sudan (**UNMIS**) would make an important contribution to bringing security to the South but, with 10,000 troops in an area as vast as South Sudan, it had only a limited impact.

Within the **government of South Sudan** itself there were also a number of difficulties. Vice-President Riek Machar was appointed to the chair of the Southern Sudan 2011 Taskforce to prepare the way for independence. Opposition figures and media critics said, however, that the Taskforce was too dominated by the SPLM and sought a greater role for themselves and their supporters. In March, nine opposition parties decided to pull out of the committee to prepare a new constitution, complaining that the process was dominated by the SPLM. The government responded by trying to develop south-south talks, in some cases with success, but one prominent resister was Lam Akol, a former SPLM politician and former minister of foreign affairs in the national government, who led his own breakaway party under the banner of the SPLM-Democratic Change (SPLM-DC). The government was also developing its own policies, with ministries instructed to prepare a strategy for the coming four years, including a Southern Sudan Development Plan. New bills were introduced in parliament, including some related to land and mineral extraction. However, there were still complaints about corruption, the large numbers on the public payroll – especially the cost of the SPLA, the shortage of well-trained personnel and the lack of infrastructure.

North-South relations were also evolving in the run-up to independence for the South. It had been intended by the CPA that areas of dispute would be resolved by the time of the referendum, but in practice issues remained unresolved. It was agreed that the various talks would continue after independence, though there were still a number of problems.

Oil was a **major problem**. Three-quarters of Sudan's oil was produced in the South, but the pipeline for it to be exported run through the north to the terminal near Port Sudan on the Red Sea. Under the CPA, it had been agreed that, during the transitional period, the revenue from the South's oil would be split 50–50 between the governments in Juba and Khartoum. However, Juba made it clear that, after independence, it would not continue with that division of revenue and that pipeline fees should instead be negotiated between the two governments. When this proved difficult, both sides decided to talk tough, and in May the Juba government accused Khartoum of a blockade of goods and refined oil from the North. In return, al-Bashir warned the South that, if it did not pay for use of the pipeline, it would be closed. In reality, both sides were indulging in brinkmanship, since oil revenues made up 98% of Juba government revenue, while the South's oil had been providing some 40% of Khartoum's revenue. Nevertheless, the issue was still unresolved when the South became independent in July.

Another issue was the **future border** between the two states. The CPA had stipulated that it should be the border that existed at the time of Sudan's independence in 1956. That sounded straightforward, but in a number of areas the exact border was in fact imprecise and needed to be negotiated both because the future position of some local communities was uncertain and because there were mineral issues involved. Negotiations had proved very acrimonious following the CPA and had still not been fully concluded by the time of the South's independence. Border negotiations were made more difficult by the continuing conflicts on both sides of the border and the mutual accusations of both governments that the other was using them to create instability.

Other **unresolved issues** included Sudan's **debt** after separation, and **citizenship**. The country had a large debt of $ 38 bn and the South was understandably reluctant to take on a significant part of the burden since the debt included the financing of arms used by the government in the civil war. The question of citizenship related particularly to the up to 2 m southerners who chose to stay in the North following the referendum, some of whom were already losing their jobs and suffering other forms of discrimination, which indicated that they would no longer be welcome there. The question of **water** was also carried over. This was potentially of enormous significance since there had long been something of a struggle between Egypt and Sudan on the one hand and Ethiopia and other upstream Nile riparian states on the other, and the arrival of a new state on the scene, in a strategic position on the White Nile, was clearly important. One other issue, the **currency** situation of the South, was settled – not by agreement but by Juba's unilateral issuing of its own currency at the time of the declaration of independence.

Following the South's **secession**, the major issue in Sudan was the **impact** this would have **on politics**. The opposition parties were certainly keen to try to take advantage of the situation, blaming the NCP for the failure "to make unity attractive" in accordance with the terms of the CPA, and thereby losing one third of the country's territory together with about 75% of its oil fields. At the same time, there were also hopes that the dreams of an Arab Spring in Khartoum could be kindled again after the flickers earlier in the year. In addition, the drop in oil revenues was bringing in a new austerity programme at a time of sharply rising inflation – a combination that resulted in **food riots** in October in a number of cities, which were swiftly broken up by the police. On 1 October, the various **opposition groups** came together in London and announced that they would be forming a **new alliance**, which appeared to be the reincarnation of the National Democratic Alliance of the 1990s. A leading element in the alliance was the SPLM-N, now led by Yasir Arman, a longstanding supporter of the former SPLA leader John Garang's vision of the 'New Sudan', in which the regions would work together to reverse the dominance of the traditional power of the centre. It was thus understandable that the alliance was supported by some of the Darfur leaders, especially from the JEM and the SLA, together with SPLM-N supporters from the other conflict areas of Blue Nile and South Kordofan, and from some of the factions of the traditional parties including the Umma, DUP and Communist parties. Attention also focussed on Hasan al-Turabi and his PCP, since he had continued his criticism after his release from prison.

The **government's response** was to **crack down** on the alliance, while trying to woo less hostile parties into the new administration it was in the process of forming. Militarily, it continued to use force against what it saw as the rebel movements in Darfur, South Kordofan and Blue Nile, where the army re-took Kurmuk, a town briefly held by the SPLM-N, on the border with Ethiopia. In December, there was a carefully targeted strike in Darfur that killed the JEM leader, Ibrahim Khalil. The SPLM-N was also made a proscribed organisation and its leader, Yasir Arman, was sought on charges of treason. At the same time, al-Bashir announced in August the start of Sudan's 'Second Republic', which would have a new permanent constitution based on Sharia (Islamic law) and stated that a new government would be formed. In order to give at least the appearance of a new era, the NCP tried hard to woo the veteran leaders of the DUP and the Umma, Mohammed Osman Mirghani and former democratic prime minister, Sadiq al-Mahdi. Al-Mahdi had declined to be linked to the opposition alliance, but remained critical of the government. Al-Mirghani was more amenable and eventually in December decided to take the DUP into the new government, which was finally announced. However, it was still clear that power remained overwhelmingly in the hands of the NCP. In the same month it was announced that one son of each of these traditional leaders was to be made a presidential adviser, a move that was seen as a small gain by the NCP.

Foreign Affairs

With the result of the referendum in the South a foregone conclusion, foreign relations focussed on that, even before the formal secession in July. High on the agenda were relations with the **USA**, the country that had probably done more than any other to conclude the 2005 CPA that had eventually resulted in the split. US sympathy had long tended towards the South, especially in agencies such as USAID. Thus, in the first half of the year, there was a rapid build-up of US government officials and American-funded NGOs in the South, especially the new capital, Juba, which was growing rapidly. The US took a keen interest in the quality of government that was emerging and particularly the spread of corruption with the emergence of new resources and opportunities.

At the same time, the US was careful not to be out of touch with the government in Khartoum. While it had long had its criticisms of the government, it also worried about the dangers of further fragmentation of the country as a result of the fighting in Darfur, South Kordofan and Blue Nile, as well as the failure to resolve the situation in Abyei. In addition, it wished to continue intelligence sharing, particularly with the threat of Islamic terrorism continuing, and even worsening in Somalia, which could prove a threat to the wider region of the 'Greater Horn', as it was sometimes called in Washington. The US also finished building a very large new embassy in Khartoum.

On the government side, there were hopes that its compliance with the referendum and the South's independence would lead to the lifting of **US sanctions**, which were effectively preventing the chances of major Western companies coming into the country. In July, al-Bashir appealed to the US to lift the sanctions in the light of his government's commitment to respect the outcome of the South's referendum. However, under domestic pressure in the US over the continuing conflicts in Sudan and the government's harsh responses, President Obama announced in November that the conditions for lifting sanctions were not yet right.

US sanctions had been one of the factors encouraging Sudan to look towards Asia, especially **China**. China had developed much of Sudan's oil sector, which has been exporting since 1999 and by 2011 was supplying 5% of China's imports. China, of course, sought not to interfere in the politics of states in which it was investing, but the deterioration of security and relations between the two Sudans began to increase the potential for a return to war, which could threaten oil exports. In June, al-Bashir visited Beijing, where the situation was discussed, while in August, shortly after the South's independence, China's Foreign Minister Yang Jiechi offered to act as a mediator. China also continued to express its concern over the conflict in Darfur, not least because it was involved in oil exploration in the region.

The two other Asian states most involved in Sudan's oil development were **India** and **Malaysia**. At the same time as having concern for their investments, they tried to stay out of Sudanese politics. Unlike China, both were concerned not to create a high profile there at a time when they were also trying to look for Western support for their own inward investment plans.

Relations with **neighbouring states** were also important. Probably the biggest breakthrough was the agreement with **Chad** that the two countries would stop supporting their respective rebel groups in eastern Chad and Darfur. Hitherto the two countries had been in opposition, with the Chadian rebels coming close to capturing N'djamena, while Darfur rebels had been supported in a less successful attack on Khartoum. An important factor in the agreement between the two governments was the slow fall of Khadafi's regime in Libya during the year. **Libya** had a long history of involvement in both countries, often using its influence to divide them while also helping their rebel movements. In consequence, Sudan was particularly active during the year in supporting the rebels in Libya. The government hoped that it would win some new support in Europe, where al-Bashir remained indicted by the ICC over Darfur, which was increasingly restricting his overseas travels. Sudan was also assisting **Qatar** in the supply of arms to the Libyan rebels as part of Qatar's support for the 'Arab Spring'.

Sudan's other Arab neighbours were becoming concerned about the situation in Sudan. **Egypt** in particular had long been vigorously opposed to the division of the country, fearing that it would have an impact on the division of the Nile Waters. As a reminder of the importance of this, in April it called for the re-starting of work on the Jonglei canal in South Sudan, which had been intended to improve the flow of water in the Sudd (swamp) area but had been abandoned under early attacks by the SPLA in 1983. The government in the South, however, was determined that it would postpone any decision on the future of the canal project. Egypt's preference for Sudan's unity was shared by **Saudi Arabia**, which feared for future stability. Sudan's relations with Qatar and Iran, however, proved warmer.

In the Horn, relations with **Ethiopia** and **Eritrea** needed careful balancing in view of their continuing animosity and regional ambitions. Eritrea has been important for the maintenance of comparative peace in the eastern part of Sudan; it had backed the Eastern Sudan Peace Agreement of 2006 and continued to have influence with the local communities there. For Sudan, it was a vital region, since Port Sudan on the Red Sea was the country's only port and thus essential for its trade. At the same time, Ethiopia was also vital, since it bordered on both Sudan and South Sudan, and Prime Minister Meles Zenawi sought to maintain good relations with both. He was very concerned about the instability in Sudan and thus contributed Ethiopian troops to the UN security forces in the Abyei border area. He was equally concerned about the deterioration of relations between Sudan and South Sudan as the year went on. Ethiopia backed the AU High-Level Implementation Panel for Sudan based in Addis Ababa in the latter part of the year, and engaged in trying to mediate between the two countries on the issues still outstanding from the CPA. Seeking agreement on oil revenues was particularly important for Ethiopia, since it imported the large majority of its oil from Sudan and failure to reach an agreement threatened the flow of oil from the wells in the South.

For Sudan, relations with the new **Republic of South Sudan** became the number one issue after the latter's independence in July, and oil was the most immediate issue. The position of al-Bashir's government was that, since the South was not prepared to sign a new revenue-sharing deal of the kind that had been in place during the transitional period – a 50–50 split of revenues from oil from the South – Juba should pay pipeline fees to send the oil to Port Sudan for export. Sudan set its sights as high as $ 32 per barrel, while the South was looking for something around the common international figure of $ 1 per barrel. This proved an unbridgeable gap, with both sides trading accusations and some even talking of Sudan's army being sent into the South to annex oil wells near the border. In addition, there were other outstanding issues that had still not been resolved by the end of the year. These included the border, 20% of which was still not demarcated, the liability of the two countries with regard to Sudan's external debt of $ 38 bn, and citizenship. There had also been clashes over currency issues, with both states eventually issuing new currencies. The tensions caused by these disagreements fed into security issues and each government blamed the other for stirring conflict, Sudan accusing the South of sending arms to the SPLA-N in South Kordofan and Blue Nile, and of having links with Darfur's rebels.

At the same time as Sudan was acquiring a new African neighbour in South Sudan, the latter's independence meant that **Uganda** and **Kenya** stopped being its immediate southern neighbours and thus became of somewhat less direct importance. Khartoum had long seen them as generally sympathetic to the South, although their importance to the wider region still made them significant and Sudan endeavoured to maintain working relations. A formal application to join the **EAC** was rejected by an EAC summit in November, due to the non-existence of common borders as long as South Sudan had not yet become an EAC member.

Socioeconomic Developments

Even before the South's independence, the Sudanese government was preparing people for the future **austerity** that would result from the loss of oil revenues, and in July it introduced a three-year austerity programme. Instead of receiving half the revenue from oil in the South, which contributed some 40% of its budget, it would have to rely on its own production of 120,000 b/d, together with whatever was agreed in pipeline fees. At the same time, it was hoping to compensate by improving recovery rates in existing wells on its own territory, as well as encouraging exploration in new areas. There were particular hopes for offshore development being carried out through the Red Sea Operating Company, led by the Chinese, as well as in areas of South Kordofan. The hope was that total output could soon rise to 195,000 b/d.

The separation of the two countries in mid-year had made the calculation of national macroeconomic indicators extremely difficult and provisional. Thus Sudan's **GDP** was tentatively estimated to have **contracted** by about 2.4% in 2011, while the average **inflation** rate for the year attained a new high at 20%. The sharp reduction in government revenues was reflected in the **fall** of the **Sudanese pound**. Its official rate was throughout held at SDG 2.7 to the dollar, but by September the parallel black-market rate had fallen to almost SDG 5 and continued to slide. In response to the declining situation, the Central Bank governor, Mohamed al-Zubeir, appealed for funds from the Gulf states hoping for $ 4 bn. Qatar in particular continued to be a strong investor in Sudan. The government also sought debt relief from the international community.

There were hopes that other areas of the economy might be developed. In the northern region, there was something of a **gold rush**, with hundreds of people taking part following stories of strikes. While there were new finds, the amounts involved scarcely made up for the loss of oil revenues. It has long been thought that Sudan had major agricultural potential, and a number of mainly Arab countries had taken up lands with the intention of boosting production of cotton, sesame, gum Arabic and sorghum. However, the implementation rate was slow with only 20% of land involved being utilised, and rumours that investment was often used for other purposes such as money laundering. Livestock rearing for export was another hope for the economy, but arid conditions were limiting significant expansion. Investment in the transport system, especially the decaying rail network, might also stimulate growth. With inflation reaching 20% by September, it was not surprising that there were **food riots** in a number of towns, which the police broke up, though the situation remained volatile for the remainder of the year.

Following the separation of South Sudan, the outlook by the end of 2011 was one of great uncertainty. Would Sudan now be able to stabilise itself with the long troubled South gone, or would the political effect of separation, coupled with the sharp reduction in government revenues from oil, now mean a deeply uncertain future for what remained of the country?

Peter Woodward

Tanzania

As a result of the October 2010 elections, President Kikwete and his dominant Revolutionary Party ('Chama cha Mapinduzi', CCM) were faced by a substantially strengthened political opposition and by vocal criticism by civil society organisations, but nevertheless remained fully in control. Much attention focussed on discussions about a review of the constitution, but these centred on procedural aspects and did not yet go as far as dealing with the substance of a new constitution. The parliament became much more assertive in attempts to control and criticise the government. Internal power struggles between various CCM factions were evident as the party tried to regain some of its lost public credibility. Zanzibar issues were much less in the limelight than in previous years. Macroeconomic performance remained relatively satisfactory and continued to be commended by international institutions, but the population saw little concrete progress and was increasingly dissatisfied with the services provided by state institutions. There was, however, no sign of a popular uprising.

Domestic Politics

Throughout the year, the **constitution review process** was at the centre of heated political debates and became a trial of strength between the government on the one hand and opposition parties, civil society organisations and wide sections of the public on the other. President Jakaya Kikwete announced this review in his new-year address in response to growing demands from various parts of the society after the 2010 elections. While this initiative was broadly welcomed, criticism was quickly levelled against the government's attempt to take firm control of the process. On 11 March, the government published a draft **Constitution Review Bill**, which it wanted to rush through parliament under a certificate of urgency in order to have it implemented by June. The bill proposed the establishment of a Constitutional Review Commission, tasked to establish and assess public opinion. The bill furthermore elaborated on the announcement of the formation of a Constituent Assembly, which was to be set up to make provisions for the new constitution, and finally proposed a referendum on the new constitution.

Major **concerns of opposition parties** and civil society included the inordinate powers vested to the president throughout the entire process and the perceived attempt to tightly control the proceedings and to restrict public debate and participation by fast-tracking the bill. Fears were also expressed that the government was attempting merely to amend the current constitution rather than allowing the formulation of a genuinely new one. Any restrictions on the debate were heavily criticised. It was claimed that so-called "contentious issues", such as the Union between Zanzibar and the Mainland and some fundamental constitutional principles, were to be excluded from public debate. The criticism was also raised that the draft bill had only been presented in English, although a Kiswahili version was seen as essential for a fully-comprehensive debate.

The Parliamentary Committee on Constitution, Justice and Good Governance conducted **public hearings** on the proposed bill in order to solicit opinions from the general public. Hearings in Dodoma, Dar es Salaam and Zanzibar on 7 and 8 April were chaotic and had to be extended until 10 April. In Dodoma, thousands of people reportedly arrived but were denied entry to the consultation for lack of space. When the confrontation became violent, police used tear gas to disperse the crowds. Similarly in Dar es Salaam, angry crowds demanded entry and the hearings had to be temporarily suspended. In Zanzibar, even representatives of the Zanzibar government rejected the bill, complaining that Zanzibar had been side-lined in the drafting process. Freeman Mbowe, chairman of the main opposition party CHADEMA (Party for Democracy and Development), declared that the fate of 44 m Tanzanians should not be decided by a few people in Dar es Salaam, Dodoma and Zanzibar, and called for countrywide demonstrations to force the government to halt the fast-tracking of the bill. Extensive coverage in the media and criticism from opposition parties, NGOs and academia made the government finally give in and **abandon its fast-tracking approach**. Parliamentary hearings scheduled for 18 April were called off, as were protest demonstrations by CHADEMA. A Kiswahili version of the bill was gazetted in late April. In late June, Prime Minister Mizengo Pinda declared that the government planned to launch the new constitution on 26 April 2014, the 50th anniversary of the Union between Zanzibar and the Mainland.

Civil society played an important role in the process. A variety of organisations (including the Tanganyika Law Society, Legal and Human Rights Centre, Tanzania Retired Judges Association, Policy Forum, University of Dar es Salaam Staff Association, Tanzania Media Women Association, Tanzania Women Lawyers Association, Tanzania Gender Networking Programme, HakiArdhi, and others) took active part in the discussion of the bill and the constitution. They published leaflets and booklets for public information, organised workshops in various parts of the country to discuss the issue, analysed the proposed bill and the current constitution and came up with their own recommendations. They cooperated closely with other NGOs, as well as with academicians, and formed the network 'Jukwaa la Katiba' (Constitutional Forum), representing more than 100 NGOs country-wide.

In late October, Minister of Justice and Constitutional Affairs Celina Kombani presented a **revised bill** to be tabled in parliament for its second and third reading. CHADEMA, NGOs, 'Jukwaa la Katiba' and faith-based organisations immediately rejected the bill, claiming that it did not incorporate many of their recommendations. When it was introduced in parliament on 14 November, CHADEMA's shadow minister for constitution and legal affairs, Tundu Lissu, read a statement on the opposition's views and left the house, accompanied by most opposition MPs. They declared that they would boycott the debate and stage demonstrations instead, but these were immediately banned by the police. Parliament nevertheless passed the bill (after introducing some changes) on 18 November on the strength of the undisputed majority of the ruling CCM. On 27 and 28 November Kikwete quite surprisingly met a **CHADEMA delegation**, which presented him with their recommendations on the issue. The meeting took place in a friendly atmosphere and both sides agreed that the bill needed to be amended. Kikwete emphasised that the government would continue to collect views on the bill and to review the process, but Kikwete nevertheless gave his assent to the disputed bill the following day. Although CHADEMA's public reactions were harsh, analysts argued that a typical Tanzanian compromise seemed to have been reached between the government and the major opposition party, which allowed the passing of the bill but also provided for the incorporation of CHADEMA's views in a later amendment.

CHADEMA's new role as the **first significant opposition party** in Tanzania's history, a result of its impressive performance in the October 2010 elections, led to tensions with state organs throughout the year. Invigorated by its electoral success and by opinion polls that indicated that the party's secretary general and 2010 presidential candidate, Wilbroad Slaa, would emerge as the clear winner in presidential elections, CHADEMA tried to extend its political leverage against the dominance of the ruling CCM, and also against the claims of the previously strongest opposition party, the Civic United Front (CUF). CHADEMA followed a mixed approach of confrontation with CCM and the state on the one hand, and constructive contributions to the public debate on the other. However, it also repeatedly embarked on a populist approach, mobilising support in public rallies where party officials built on widespread dissatisfaction with the government. Its leaders demanded an investigation into the 2010 elections, which they claimed were flawed, and refused to recognise Kikwete as the legitimate president. Hinting at the effects of mass actions in Egypt and Libya, they threatened to use public support to cause the government serious problems.

On 5 January, **five people died** and numerous others were injured in Arusha during clashes between **CHADEMA supporters** and **police**. CHADEMA had called for demonstrations to protest against the election of the chairperson of the Arusha City Council (serving as City Mayor) in December 2010. After initially granting permission, police banned demonstrations but allowed a rally to be held. CHADEMA nevertheless staged its demonstration, which provoked an overreaction by the riot police, who responded to stone-throwing demonstrators with tear gas and live ammunition. More than 40 CHADEMA members, among them the national party leaders, were arrested and charged with unlawful assembly, but were released on bail. Government leaders, including Kikwete, Minister of Home Affairs Nahodha and Foreign Minister Membe, spoke of "unfortunate" incidents and criticised at least indirectly the harsh response of the police. Although the escalation was mainly due to the overreaction of the security forces, CHADEMA was also blamed for going ahead with the demonstration despite the ban. Further demonstrations brought thousands of people to the streets in Arusha, Mwanza and other towns, and were conducted peacefully, but not without incident. In Kahama, secretary general Slaa was one of three senior party leaders who were detained for addressing a party rally without permission. On 5 June, CHADEMA chairman Mbowe was arrested in Dar es Salaam, after an arrest warrant was issued against him and six other CHADEMA leaders who had failed to appear before the Arusha court in May. The same day, CHADEMA MP Zitto Kabwe was arrested in Singida for having allegedly extended a political rally beyond the permitted time. Godbless Lema, MP for Arusha, and 19 other people were arrested on 31 October for unauthorised assembly. CHADEMA announced a seven-day vigil and set up a tented protest, calling for his release. On 8 November, Slaa and other party leaders were arrested after they had extended to early morning a permitted public assembly staged to demand Lema's release. Again, police used tear gas and live ammunition to disperse the crowd. The following day, the party leaders were charged with unlawful assembly and released on bail. Lema was released two weeks later.

Parliament also became an arena for the display of CHADEMA's increased self-confidence, and debates became more heated and emotional. While some observers saw these developments as an indication of a lively democratic atmosphere in the National Assembly, others were concerned that parliamentary rules were being violated and that the quality of debate was falling, focussing more on party interests, polemics and personal accusations than on solving the country's problems. Some **CCM parliamentarians**, however, refrained from pure partisan politics and fulfilled their responsibility to **control the government**. This became most obvious when MPs denounced corruption, especially during the budget sessions in June. The budgets of several ministries came under intense fire. The ministry of energy and minerals' budget was initially rejected and only passed three weeks later after the minister had explained in detail how his ministry intended to tackle the severe energy problems. The budgets of two other ministries were also only passed after amendments and the prime minister's intervention.

CHADEMA's Zitto Kabwe opened a new and popular debate by **questioning additional daily allowances** of TSh 150.000 for **MPs**. The system of allowances had always attracted much criticism from donors, as well as from within Tanzania. Kabwe argued that it was the duty of parliamentarians to participate in meetings and to discuss public affairs and that they were paid their regular salaries in order to do so. He asked the parliament's secretary to stop paying allowances to him, and said he would otherwise donate them to development projects in his home constituency. Kabwe's popular initiative was supported by some opposition MPs, but also earned criticism, even from MPs of his own party, who accused him of being motivated by personal ambition.

Relations within the opposition camp were somewhat cold. CHADEMA, as the largest opposition faction in parliament, broke with an unwritten tradition and formed a shadow cabinet without including members of the other opposition parties, particularly the CUF, which CHADEMA accused of no longer belonging to the opposition after forming a Government of National Unity (GNU) in Zanzibar. The CUF and the other smaller opposition parties appealed in vain for the formation of a joint bloc of all five opposition parties. Towards the end of the year, two smaller **opposition parties were shaken by internal conflicts**. In mid-December, NCCR-Mageuzi (National Convention for Construction and Reform – Change) expelled one of its only four elected MPs, accusing him of undermining the party. In late December, an influential CUF member was threatened with expulsion, together with 13 others, for violating the party constitution.

The arrival of a serious political alternative to the **CCM** posed new challenges for the long dominant party. CHADEMA's strong showing, its persistent campaigning and the continuing popularity of its 2010 presidential candidate, as well as widespread dissatisfaction with the CCM government and perceptions that the CCM had mainly become the home of corrupt politicians, put the ruling party under stress. Internal factionalism and power struggles in the run-up to crucial party elections in 2012 increased the need to act. During the CCM's 34th anniversary celebrations in February, Kikwete, in his role as party chairman, announced that the CCM would undergo a **purge**, introducing reforms and freeing itself of corrupt members. In early April, a **major reshuffle of the top leadership** was undertaken during meetings of the top party organs – the National Executive Committee (NEC) and Central Committee (CC). Several members of the CC, the most important decision-making organ, and the complete seven-member party secretariat stepped down on 9 April. Two days later, new members were chosen. The most significant changes included the replacement of secretary general Yusuf Makamba by the experienced public servant Wilson Mukama, and that of ideology and publicity secretary John

Chiligati by former youth wing leader Nape Nnauye, who became mainly responsible for the purge process, popularised under its Kiswahili name 'kujivua gamba' (skin-shedding). Welcomed as a **first step to clean up the party** was the removal of two formerly influential but highly controversial politicians from the CC, Rostam Aziz and Andrew Chenge, who, together with former prime minister Edward Lowassa, were alleged to have been involved in major corruption scandals in previous years and were seen by many as symbolic of major corruption in the CCM. They remained members of the NEC, however, where Lowassa in particular was still able to mobilise support. The composition of the CCM's new top team indicated that Kikwete was able both to fill the main party organs with supporters of his reform policies, and to satisfy the interests of influential competing factions associated with Lowassa, Chenge, Aziz, Makamba and others. On 13 July, **Aziz resigned** unexpectedly as MP for Igunga constituency and as NEC member, explaining that he was tired of "gutter politics" and intended to focus more on his private business. He also wanted to allow the CCM to concentrate on more important issues.

Observers argued that changes in the CCM's leadership were no more than a first step, which would have to be followed by a revitalisation of the party structure down to grassroots level if the party wanted to regain public confidence. In addition to changes in personnel, **structural reforms were introduced**, such as the establishment of an advisory board of elders, a professionalised secretariat and changes to the mechanisms for the election of NEC members.

By-elections in Igunga on 2 October were heavily contested between the CCM and CHADEMA due to the **highly symbolic** nature of the vote. CHADEMA was keen to take the seat from CCM as a demonstration that it was already on its way to take over power from the ruling party. To the CCM, it was important to bring to a halt what could otherwise be seen as CHADEMA's continuous triumphal progress. Both parties deployed leading personnel during the campaign to ensure victory. The CCM's campaign was headed by former president Benjamin Mkapa and even supported by the ousted Aziz. CHADEMA's top brass appeared in the constituency, including chairman Mbowe and other prominent members. The campaigns were dominated by mud-slinging and aggressive behaviour. The **CCM secured the seat by a small margin** (55.5%) and the CHADEMA candidate finished second with 44.3%. Despite its victory, the CCM suffered a significant fall in support compared with the 73% of votes that Aziz had won only a year before, and CHADEMA had gained, finishing second in a constituency where the CUF had been number two in October 2010. CHADEMA refused to accept the result and claimed that electoral standards had been violated. The media presence and coverage was high, but voters seemed to have been alienated by the ferocity of the campaign, as turnout was only 31.4%.

CCM top-level meetings on 20–27 November raised expectations, mainly in the press, that the party would speed up its cleansing process and expel party cadres widely associated with corruption, namely Lowassa, Chenge and Aziz. Nnauye, who had involved himself in a months-long battle against Lowassa and friends, declared, however, that the popular demands to remove a few individuals from the party would reduce the comprehensive purge to a mere symbolic action. Lowassa and Chenge remained influential NEC members and Lowassa in particular seemed even to strengthen his position. Some observers assumed that Nnauye and other reformers had underestimated the Lowassa faction's power basis. To avoid an open conflict between the competing factions, the purge seemed to have been quietly abandoned.

Zanzibar had come **out of the limelight** somewhat. The GNU, formed after the 2010 elections between the equally strong CCM and CUF, apparently worked smoothly, without any obvious disruptions. The question remained of whether the new arrangement would simply allow the former opposition party, the CUF, to participate in the exploitation of state resources or whether it would also lead to positive developments for the Zanzibari people. The new arrangement at least contributed to reducing tensions among the Zanzibari population. It was reported that party affiliation stopped playing a segregating role in daily activities as it had before the parties' compromise. On the other hand, because it united formerly divergent forces, the GNU contributed to the growth of a **pronounced Zanzibari nationalism**, at least in the context of the debate on the new constitution. Prospects of offshore oil discoveries in Zanzibar waters also led to an emphasis on Zanzibar's nationalist ambitions.

Corruption, irrespective of the government's commitment to curbing it, remained an issue throughout the year, although no major developments were revealed. In May, the Prevention and Combating of Corruption Bureau published its National Governance and Corruption Survey, but the long-awaited report contained hardly any new or surprising information. It named institutions most prone to corruption, such as the police, the judiciary, the education sector and water and electricity supply agencies. This perception was largely shared by **TI's East Africa Bribery Index** in late October. The Index ranked Tanzania the third most corrupt of the five EAC member states, taking the place of Kenya, which now ranked fourth. The BAE scandal about the supply of an air traffic control system in 1999 rumbled on. In early 2010, the British Serious Fraud Office had ordered the arms manufacturer BAE Systems to pay almost £ 30 m to Tanzania. The Tanzanian and UK governments had agreed in late 2010 to invest most of the money in the education sector. BAE, however, insisted on having a say and suggested that a British NGO should supervise the use of the money. This was strongly rejected by the Tanzanian government. The relevant UK House of Commons committee advised BAE to transfer the money to Tanzania as soon as possible.

Celebrations for the **50th anniversary of Tanzania Mainland's political independence** started in July, with numerous small events. The celebrations were themed "We dared, we succeeded, and we are still forging ahead". The main celebrations on

Independence Day, 9 December, were attended by many international representatives, including five African heads of state. The absence of the presidents of the other four EAC member states (which did, however, send representatives) was speculated to have been an expression of dismay at Tanzania's absence at the signing of an agreement **for the establishment of the EAC Political Federation two weeks earlier**. During the festivities, the government highlighted achievements of 50 years of independence, comparing the country's current situation with conditions in 1961, and focussing on education, infrastructure and the economy. These positive views were largely shared by the media, which also questioned, however, the limited extent of these successes as well as the degree of the country's independence, with it being still one of the poorest nations in the world and highly dependent on foreign aid. Some members of opposition parties complained that the costs of the celebrations, reportedly TSh 64 bn, were too high and that the money could have better been invested in the country's development.

Much public attention was given to a **healer** from a village near **Loliondo** in northern Tanzania. The retired Lutheran pastor, Ambilikile Masapila, nicknamed 'Babu' (Grandfather), claimed that the Almighty had revealed to him the recipe for a miracle cure that could treat several diseases, including HIV/AIDS, cancer, diabetes and asthma. About 4 m people, including cabinet ministers and other prominent politicians, reportedly went to his remote village to drink from '**kikombe cha babu**' (Grandfather's cup), causing traffic jams for up to 50 km. People even came from abroad by plane and helicopter, and the authorities had to introduce special regulations to control the traffic. Prime Minister Pinda ordered the district authorities to improve the infrastructure and to establish sanitation facilities and large health centres, as well as cemeteries for the many sick people who died while queuing. The government analysed the brew, consisting mainly of the boiled roots of a certain tree, and found that it did not have any negative effect on the human body, but stated that it was too early to say whether it had any curative properties. However, there were press reports about patients whose conditions had worsened or who had even died, since they had stopped taking their prescribed medication after drinking from 'Grandfather's cup'. Following Babu's success, numerous other self-declared healers claimed that they had also been given secret recipes by God. After several months' excitement, the hype about "Babu's cup" subsided significantly.

Plans to close the remaining two **refugee camps** by the end of the year were postponed to 2012. The government's programme to relocate to other regions refugees who had been naturalised in 2010 proved difficult, because most of these early Burundian refugees (from 1972) had established themselves over decades and refused relocation. Strong competition for jobs and increased immigration from China, South Asia and African countries prompted intensified efforts by the state authorities to **control and reduce illegal immigration** but also led to **increasing xenophobia and economic nationalism**.

Foreign Affairs

Numerous high-profile visitors reflected Tanzania's excellent international relations. In May, **India**'s Prime Minister Manmohan Singh signed bilateral agreements, including a $ 190 m credit for water supply projects in Dar es Salaam and $ 10 m for capacity-building projects in the social and education sectors. Another agreement was signed to construct a heart surgery hospital in Dar es Salaam with Indian aid. Singh offered support for Tanzania's 'Kilimo Kwanza' (agriculture first) programme and envisaged the intensification of trade relations, focussing on small and medium-sized industries, healthcare and human resource development. **US** Secretary of State **Hillary Clinton** paid a short visit on 11–12 June on her way back from a Libya Contact Group meeting in the UAE. Tanzania was one of only four countries to take part in the first set of the new US 'Partnership for Growth' initiative. Clinton spoke with Kikwete *inter alia* about security threats posed by Somali pirates along the East African coast. She visited some US-funded development projects and the memorial site for victims of the US embassy bombings of 1998, only one day after Somali officials stated that soldiers had killed Fazul Abdullah Mohammed, the suspected mastermind behind the bombings. Clinton also co-hosted a high-level forum on the fight against global hunger and malnutrition, together with **Irish** Deputy Prime Minister Eamon Gilmore, who, on a four-day visit, met Prime Minister Pinda and senior members of government, representatives from Irish NGOs and members of the business community.

Somalia's interim president, Sheikh Sharif Sheikh Ahmed, accompanied by several ministers, arrived on 9 August for a two-day visit. Kikwete pledged to donate 300 tonnes of maize as food aid to combat famine and promised further support for Somalia in fighting its manifold problems, including eradicating the al-Shabaab militias and piracy activities. Both phenomena were increasingly perceived as a threat to Tanzania. The authorities reported increased acts of piracy and illegal Somali immigration and alerted the public to the possibility of al-Shabaab terror attacks. Kikwete backed Kenya's military operation against al-Shabaab.

On 6 November, the UK's **Prince Charles** and his wife Camilla arrived for a four-day official visit on Kikwete's invitation as part of the 50th anniversary celebrations of Tanzania Mainland's independence. Although they were warmly received in Dar es Salaam, Zanzibar and Arusha, their visit coincided with threats by British Prime Minister David Cameron to withhold **UK** aid from governments that would not reform legislation banning homosexuality. Several Tanzanian government leaders, along with religious leaders and the media, sharply rejected these demands, calling them a neo-colonial attempt to impose Western ideas on poor countries in violation of their own values and declared that the country would rather go without British funding than legalise homosexuality. The UK High Commissioner tried to smooth the waters, explaining that Cameron had been quoted out of context. Britain would neither enforce acceptance of homosexuality nor cut development aid.

The **donor community** remained concerned about Tanzania's problems in effectively fighting corruption, and doubted the government's willingness to enhance the anti-graft crusade. However, this only slightly affected the generally good relations, which were characterised by continuous support for Tanzania's development efforts.

Despite generally cordial relations with all neighbouring countries, Tanzania's cautious attitude towards faster far-reaching **EAC** integration remained a source of contention. After long-disputed land and security questions re-emerged during a November meeting in Bujumbura, Burundi, the Tanzanian delegation refused to sign an agreement for moves towards an EAC Political Federation, but subsequently agreed to a reformulated text.

The government strongly opposed NATO's intervention in **Libya**, alleging that the UK and France had exceeded the mandates of the UN and the Arab League. Tanzania condemned the killing of Khadhafi as a human rights violation and warned of uncontrollable violence. It initially refused to recognise the National Transitional Council as Libya's new government.

Socioeconomic Developments

The overall **macroeconomic performance** continued to be fairly robust and generally in line with the strong growth trend of the past decade. In this period, Tanzania had become one of the best and most consistently performing countries in Africa, albeit still characterised by a very low absolute level of material wealth. The economy had largely been shielded from the adverse effects of the global economic and financial crisis. The **GDP growth rate** for 2011 was estimated to attain around 6.5%, quite similar to the preceding two years. Expectations for an acceleration of growth were mainly quashed by the effects of severe drought in parts of the country and the resulting power shortages. The agricultural sector again only grew by about 3%, barely higher than the population growth rate.

The deliberate growth stimulus through the government's 2009 rescue plan and extensive public investment programmes had clearly had a positive effect, but also greatly increased the fiscal deficit and now necessitated a return to a tighter monetary and fiscal policy. **Inflation** increased alarmingly throughout the year and was a major cause for growing popular discontent. Consumer price inflation climbed steadily from 6.4% in January to 19.8% in December, with an average for the year of 12.7%. The food price index in December had risen by 25% within a year. The **exchange rate** remained relatively stable during the first half of the year, but then depreciated sharply by 14% against the dollar to a new low in October, before recovering to an annual depreciation of 8% by year's end. The **structural trade deficit** narrowed slightly further, with 63% of Tanzania's import bill now covered by its own export revenues, the highest ratio ever achieved. While imports had grown by 21% to $ 8,650 m, exports had leapt by as much as 26% to $ 5,432 m (preliminary figures). Gold accounted for the bulk of exports (about 40%), but manufactured goods exports to regional markets also featured strongly, while the relative share of traditional agricultural exports declined further. The situation permitted the stabilisation of the (preliminary) **current-account deficit** at around 9.7% of GDP, slightly higher than in 2010. Gross **foreign reserves** also remained largely stable at $ 3.7 bn by the year's end, sufficient for a comfortable import coverage of over five months. While the **external debt** had previously been substantially reduced to a low of $ 4.2 bn in 2006 as a result of concerted debt cancellations, it had crept up again since then, reaching $ 9.7 bn at year's end (compared with $ 7.6 bn at end-2010). In the 2011 **HDI**, Tanzania marked some slight improvement and was ranked 152nd (out of 187 countries) in the low human development category. **GDP per capita** was estimated at about $ 525 and in PPP terms at $ 1,328.

IMF missions in March and October/November conducted the second and third reviews under the current **Policy Support Instrument (PSI)** operative since June 2010. They were generally satisfied with the overall macroeconomic performance and with progress in implementing agreed structural reforms, but stressed the need for a return to a tighter fiscal policy and for reducing inflation. In June, the **World Bank** formulated a new country assistance strategy for the 2012–2015 period, largely in line with support for Tanzania's own current **PRSPs** (generally known by their Swahili acronyms as MKUKUTA II for the mainland and MKUZA II for Zanzibar). In addition to these documents, a Five-Year Development Plan for 2011–2016 was launched by Kikwete on 7 June, creating some confusion about an abundance of policy documents, with the National Development Vision 2025 and the CCM election manifesto also still being used as guidelines.

As common declared principles, all documents focused on accelerating **pro-poor growth** in a sustainable manner by ensuring adequate prioritisation and coordination of policies and harnessing public-private-partnership potentials. Highest priority was accorded to agriculture under the '**Kilimo Kwanza**' (agriculture first) initiative, since it was identified as a growth driver supporting the majority of the poor rural population and offering employment opportunities to the youth. In January at the World Economic Forum in Davos, Switzerland, Kikwete outlined highly ambitious plans for a Southern Agricultural Growth Corridor in Tanzania, with expected investments of $ 3.4 bn over a 20–year period. Visions about more such corridors were also discussed. The government welcomed foreign agricultural investors and offered large tracts of land in little publicised deals. Despite looming problems of unresolved changing land rights, public criticism about 'land grabs' remained largely subdued for the time being. In the plans, greater emphasis was also given to infrastructure, with expectations of attracting more private investment, while progress was also to be maintained in education and health.

On 8 June, Finance Minister Mustafa Mkulo presented the 2011/2012 **budget** to parliament in conjunction with a review of the previous financial year's (provisional) outturn. Both revenue and spending figures had again been below the original budget projections, and the overall **fiscal deficit** had been lower than expected at about 6.9% of GDP. Domestic revenue shortfalls of 7.1% indicated an apparent slackening of revenue collection efforts, while received external grants were as much as 18.1% lower than had been expected, adding up to an overall revenue shortfall of 9.8%. This led to substantially reduced capital (development) expenditure (by 28%), while recurrent spending was only 4.3% below target. Only 23% of the total revenue had by then arrived from foreign donors, a noticeable reduction compared with the situation only a few years earlier (with over 40%). The domestic revenue quota of 16.3% of GDP had remained comparatively low, with a target of 17.9% set for 2015/2016. On the expenditure side, 71% was allocated for recurrent expenses, and only 29% for investments.

The **mining sector** (mainly gold) continued to contribute significantly to overall growth and exports, but by and large remained an enclave activity without substantial linkages to the rest of the economy and without much employment generation. Even the IMF was critical of the fact that the gold mining companies were still not contributing enough to the government's revenue and it called for a review of mining taxes. After lengthy debates, agreement was reached in October to raise royalty payments from 3% to 4% in line with the 2010 Mining Act, to become effective in 2012.

On 22 June, Minister for Natural Resources and Tourism Ezekiel Maige sent a letter to the UNESCO World Heritage Centre, clarifying that the government had abandoned plans to build a **highway** through the **Serengeti National Park**. According to the letter, tarmac roads would only be constructed to towns close to the eastern and western borders of the park. The 53–km section running through the Serengeti would remain a gravel road and be used mainly for tourism and administrative purposes. The government was also seriously considering the construction of an alternative road south of Serengeti and Ngorongoro, which had been suggested by critics of the Serengeti Highway. Environmentalists welcomed the decision, but pointed out that even a gravel road would increase traffic through the Serengeti. Only a few days later, Transport Minister Omari Nundu emphasised that the proposed **railway project from Tanga via Arusha to Musoma** would also be built around the southern end of the Serengeti, thus avoiding the park. On 23 December, Nundu announced that a Chinese company had been commissioned to conduct a feasibility study. Construction of the railway line and ports in Tanga, Musoma and Kampala was envisaged to be completed by 2015. Ecologists were worried that the Tanga port was planned to be built in the Marine National Park at Mwambani Bay. The government asked UNESCO to allow changes to the boundaries of **Selous Game Reserve** so that **exploration of uranium deposits** could go ahead without its World Heritage Site status being affected. Preparations for uranium mining in Ruvuma Region and in Bahi and Manyoni Districts in central Tanzania made progress. Opposition to the uranium mining activities came from various national and international NGOs, scientists, the media, members of opposition parties and affected villagers.

Towards the end of the year, the government was faced with considerable **liquidity problems** and was contemplating cutting a number of planned and budgeted development projects. This was mainly the result of considerable disbursement delays on the part of external donors, who contributed substantially to the regular budget through the General Budget Support scheme, while revenue collection was quite normal. Public employees in local government structures were allegedly only being paid after considerable delays.

Tanzania was less severely affected by **drought** than Kenya and the Horn of Africa, but was nevertheless confronted by serious problems. There was temporary fear of famine in about 42 districts, but the situation was by and large contained with the release of 115,000 tonnes from the Strategic Grain Reserve. In May, the government banned all food exports as a measure to constrain food price inflation, but this was lifted in October, after a good harvest and a grain surplus of 1.7 m tonnes.

The lack of rainfall also led to a lowering of water levels and to renewed **power generation** problems, which affected many industries and the urban population. In May, power-rationing measures had to be introduced and remained in force throughout the year. An emergency power plan aimed to install additional thermal plants (with a capacity of about 220 MW), but this would need time to be realised. The power problems negatively affected economic growth, but also contributed to anger and political frustration among the population. With effect from January 2012, electricity tariffs would be raised by 40% to cover some of the extra costs for the emergency installations, although the power company TANESCO had applied for an even higher increase. In August, the Energy and Water Utilities Regulatory Authority decreed the reduction of **fuel prices** by 8%–9% in an attempt to control sharp price escalations, but this seriously backfired when the oil companies stopped the sale of fuel, causing immediate severe shortages and public anger. After two weeks, the Authority had to backtrack and allow price hikes.

There was growing optimism, based on good longer-term prospects for commercial **oil and gas production**, that the perennial energy problems would soon be overcome. Exploration activities both on-shore and off-shore seemed to indicate a promising future, most concretely in the existing Songo Songo gas-producing area along the coast and around Mnazi Bay on Lake Nyasa. It also seemed that long-existing plans to exploit the Mchuchuma **coal reserves** in the south-west for power generation would become a reality in the near future, with the signing of an investment agreement with a Chinese company.

No viable longer-term solution was yet in sight for either the ailing **Tanzania Railways Ltd. (TRL)** or **Air Tanzania**. In July, the last personnel from RITES of India left the TRL operations after the government's decision in 2010 to terminate the Indian shareholding and management involvement in TRL following a clearly disappointing performance. TRL continued to function very unsatisfactorily under local management, while prospects for extensive upgrading remained uncertain. The same was the case with the national airline. A possible recapitalisation, with public money and a (partial) privatisation, was still contemplated, but the airline remained inoperative throughout the year. The private Precision Air had in the meantime become the leading local airline and started to offer shares in October, with 51% reserved for Tanzanians.

On 11 September, more than 200 people died in a **ferry accident in Zanzibar**, and over 600 people were rescued. The heavily overloaded ferry was apparently hit by a strong current on its way from Unguja to Pemba Island. Only a few weeks later, in late December, the nation was shocked by heavy seasonal rains which caused **flooding** in various parts of the country. Dar es Salaam experienced the heaviest rainfalls for 57 years and was seriously affected, and many parts of the city were flooded for several days. At least 40 people died and thousands lost their homes or other property. The government provided an area of land for the resettlement of almost 3,000 of the more than 4,500 flood victims. Earlier in the year, on 16 February, Dar es Salaam had already been the scene of a tragic accident. More than 25 people died when a military arsenal exploded, and about 400 were injured. The government was criticised for keeping ammunition too close to residential areas.

Despite Tanzania's consistently high GDP growth rates, a better overall socioeconomic development continued to be restrained by a combination of major contributing factors, such as poor education, unproductive agriculture, permanent energy and infrastructural weaknesses, ineffective government structures and cumbersome bureaucracy. In the World Bank's Doing Business 2012 Tanzania was ranked 127th (of 183 countries), thus showing no improvement at all.

Kurt Hirschler & Rolf Hofmeier

Uganda

Somewhat unexpectedly, 2011 turned out to be one of the worst years for Uganda since the current president and his guerrilla force gained control a quarter of a century earlier. Though the incumbent and the ruling party won resounding victories in presidential and parliamentary elections, the markedly deteriorating standard of living resulted in social protest and reinvigorated the opposition, which had done poorly in the polls. State reaction to dissent was heavy-handed, causing the government to lose much of its credibility. The economy slackened. Nevertheless, the internal situation had no effect on the generally good relations with neighbouring states, and on Uganda's standing in African affairs – enhanced by some progress of the AU peacekeeping force in Somalia, led and largely manned by Uganda. The Lord's Resistance Army (LRA) received renewed international attention due to disturbances it caused in three neighbouring countries, though not in Uganda, and to direct US involvement.

Domestic Politics

In power since January 1986, **President Yoweri Kaguta Museveni** and his government spared no expense to win the presidential ballot and to secure once more an overwhelming majority of **National Resistance Movement (NRM)** members in parliament. Both

elections took place on the same day, 18 February. Voter turnout, at 8.3 m (59.3%) out of 13.9 m registered voters was far from impressive, close to one-tenth less than in 2006, and 4% of the ballots were invalid. Out of 7.9 m valid votes cast, Museveni (NRM) received 5.4 m (68.4%); his share was larger than in 2006 (59.3%) and similar to 2001 (69.4%). His main challenger, **Kizza Besigye**, leader of the **Forum for Democratic Change (FDC)** and candidate of the Inter-Party Cooperation (IPC), got 2 m votes (26%, compared with 37.4% in 2006 and 27.7% in 2001); apart from the FDC, the IPC also included the Conservative Party (CP), the Justice Forum (JEEMA) and two smaller groups. Norbert Mao (Democratic Party, DP) received 1.86% of the votes, Olara Otunnu (Uganda People's Congress (UPC) 1.58%, Beti Kamya (Uganda Federal Alliance) 0.66%, Abed Bwanika (People's Development Party) 0.65%, Jaberi Bidandi-Ssali (People's Progressive Party) 0.44% and Samuel Lubega (independent) 0.41%. Like Museveni and Besigye, Bwanika had previously taken part in the 2006 contest. Kamya was the sole female candidate. The losers cried foul, though none of them challenged the results in the Supreme Court. UPC's Otunnu did not even cast his vote, claiming that the exercise was a sham anyway; this did not go down well with many members of his own party. For the first time, Museveni obtained more than half of the votes in all regions. He was most popular in the West (80.3%), followed by the East (68.2%), Buganda (62.7%) and the North (56.9%). Besigye did best in Buganda (31.7%) and in Kampala he even took 46.9% of the vote, relegating Museveni, with 46.0%, to second place.

On 18 February, Ugandans also elected 238 constituency representatives and 112 women district representatives to **parliament**. Representatives of youth, of persons with disabilities and of workers – five each – as well as ten **army representatives**, were chosen in separate procedures. The Uganda Peoples' Defence Forces (UPDF) members were elected by a UPDF Council meeting on 9 March at the Land Forces headquarters in Bombo, after the candidates were nominated by the high command and approved by Museveni; 260 valid votes were cast.

The total number of MPs in the **9th Parliament** was 375. In addition, 11 ex-officio members without voting rights (unelected ministers or state ministers) were appointed by the president. Of the 375 seats, the NRM finally held 262 (69.9%), FDC 35 (9.3%), DP 13 (3.5%), UPC 10 (2.7%), and CP and JEEMA one MP each, as before. There were 43 MPs (11.5%) who had stood as independents, and ten MPs were delegated by the UPDF. The actual NRM majority reached well beyond its 262 seats, given the fact that most of the independents were government-leaning and that this was also expected of all military MPs, though (unlike those of the other special interest groups) they had no formal party affiliation. Thus the NRM camp could muster more than three-quarters of the legislators. Nevertheless, some prominent NRM politicians were among the losers, as a number of ministers either had not been nominated or had lost in the elections. Among them were former minister for the interior Ali Kirunda Kivejinja and former lands minister Omara Atubo.

International observers noted that, notwithstanding some instances of violence and intimidation, the campaign and the polling day generally passed off peacefully and that there was "some improvement" over 2006. But they were dissatisfied with the performance of the Electoral Commission and the police. The EU Election Observation Mission (EU EOM) left no doubt that there had not been a "level playing field". It was "difficult to draw a line between government and the ruling party at local level". Particularly striking was the "monetization" of the election: "The distribution of money and gifts by candidates, especially from the ruling party...was widely observed by EU EOM observers." This was also reflected in large off-budget government expenditure ahead of the elections. Elections for local government councils were held on 23 February and 2 and 7 March, accompanied by malpractices in some places.

The **new legislature** had its first sitting on 19 May. For the first time a **woman**, Rebecca Kadaga, a former minister for parliamentary affairs, was elected parliamentary speaker. Of the legislators, 131 (34.9%) were female, an increase of 5% compared with the previous parliament. This was mainly due to the upsurge in the number of districts, since most of them were elected as women district representatives. Each of the special interest groups for youth, persons with disabilities, workers and the army, had two women among their representatives.

The FDC's Nathan Nandala-Mafabi, hailing from Bugisu in the east and the astute former chairman of the Public Accounts Committee, became the **leader of the opposition** in the House. Criticism of the government, however, continued not to be restricted to the official opposition. Soon it became obvious that many of the new NRM legislators were taking a fresh look at rampant corruption and at oil policy. MPs exercised their powers when it came to scrutinising ministerial appointments that the president intended to make. After the elections, 29 cabinet minister positions were to be filled, plus 47 state minister posts. MPs expressed doubts about the capabilities of some ministers of advanced age and rejected some candidates, among them Hajji Nasser Ntege Ssebagala, a former DP politician and ex-mayor of Kampala, whose biography included a jail term in the US for fraud. The **ministerial appointments** were a mixture of change and continuity; among the reappointed ministers, few continued in their previous positions. The most prominent loser was former vice president Gilbert Bukenya, the post going to Edward Kiwanuka Ssekandi, hitherto parliamentary speaker. As prime minister, NRM secretary-general Amama Mbabazi followed Apolo Nsibambi, who had held the office for 12 years. Defence Minister Crispus Kiyonga and Foreign Minister Sam Kutesa retained their posts. There were some notable female newcomers to the cabinet: First Lady Janet Museveni as minister for Karamoja (having previously served as minister of state for the same area), former principal private secretary to the president Amelia Kyambadde as minister of trade and industry, novelist and founder of the Uganda Women Writers' Association (FEMRITE) Mary Karooro Okurut as minister of information and national guidance, Irene Muloni as minister of energy and minerals, and businesswoman Maria Kiwanuka, formerly on the staff of the World Bank, as minister of finance, planning and economic development. Among the state ministers, former army commander Jeje Odongo continued in the ministry for defence, and, after a stint in the US, Betty Bigombe, who in the early 1990s had personally negotiated with LRA head Joseph Kony, was made minister of state for water. The president also appointed senior presidential advisors; in August, state minister for security under 'Obote II', Chris Rwakasisi, released from death row in 2009, and former chief of staff in Amin's army, Isaac Lumago, were added to a long list.

Of Uganda's **six top executive positions**, again five were held by people representing the western and central regions (where the majority of the population lives). President Museveni and First Deputy Prime Minister Eriya Kategaya came from Ankole, Prime Minister Mbabazi hailed from Kigezi, Second Deputy Prime Minister Henry Kajura was from Bunyoro and Vice President Ssekandi came from Buganda like his predecessor. The north was represented by Third Deputy Prime Minister Moses Ali, a former Amin general, originating in West Nile. Though no easterner was among the top six, the region could be seen as represented by parliamentary speaker Kadaga, hailing from Busoga. The religious architecture was mirrored by the fact that the president was a Protestant, the vice president a Catholic and one of the deputy prime ministers a Muslim. Seven of 29 cabinet positions were occupied by people from the east and the north, with a notably stronger representation of these regions being found among the ministers of state.

The president's ultimate power resource, however, the **UPDF**, continued to be largely run by people dubbed the "Bahima generals", men sharing Museveni's ethnic background and having a common history as guerrilla fighters. Museveni's son, Muhoozi Kainerugaba, who headed the elite Special Forces Group was promoted from the rank of lieutenant colonel to full colonel. For the first time, a woman soldier was promoted to the rank of brigadier. The former girlfriend of one-time UPDF commander James Kazini, who had killed him in November 2009, was found to have acted in self-defence and acquitted of murder, but she was sentenced to 14 years in prison for manslaughter.

In view of allegations of election fraud, some **opposition leaders** considered not taking up their parliamentary seats, but they abandoned this idea before long. Calls for public protest did not attract much attention, but this quickly changed when, soon after the elections, economic hardships became the order of the day. The sharp rise in prices of foodstuffs and fuel was partly due to global developments affecting the country, but it was also attributed to extra government spending ahead of the elections. In April, a group called 'Activists for Change' emerged, organising **demonstrations of discontent** mainly in Kampala. If not inspired by Besigye, this was handed to the FDC on a plate. Besigye joined the **'Walk to Work' protests**, which were confronted by the security agencies with a blend of chicanery and brute force. Various social groups took to the streets or stopped work, including lawyers, market traders, taxi drivers and university students. A strike by teachers was ended after some weeks by the government ordering them to return to classes. By the end of April, nine people (including six in Kampala) had lost their lives as a result of the action of the security forces. A widely publicised incident that contributed to a dramatic loss of government credibility took place on 28 April: whilst seated in his car, Besigye was attacked with pepper spray by a police officer who had smashed the car window; he was then thrown on the rear of a pickup truck and taken into custody, his fifth arrest in the course of the demonstrations. He suffered temporary loss of sight, and went to Nairobi for treatment after his release. On 12 May, Museveni's swearing-in for a new term as president was marred by Besigye's return from Kenya at the same time; he was welcomed by large crowds on his way from Entebbe airport to Kampala.

The following months saw more drawbacks for the president. There were renewed protests, including by city traders over an alleged influx of Chinese competitors. Freshly appointed ministers had to answer **corruption** charges, mainly related to procurement irregularities in connection with the 2007 Commonwealth Heads of Government Meeting (CHOGM) in Kampala. Former vice president Bukenya was detained in October in Luzira prison for a week (but acquitted of CHOGM-related charges in December, possibly thanks to the Catholic archbishop's political manoeuvring), and ministers Kutesa, John Nasasira (government chief whip) and Mwesigwa Rukutana (labour state minister) stepped down on 12 October. Kutesa was also accused of having taken bribes from Tullow Oil company, the same charges being levelled against Prime Minister Mbabazi and Internal Affairs Minister Hilary Onek, although they described as forgeries documents produced in parliament in October by independent youth MP Gerald Karuhanga. Shortly after, Bunyoro princess Kabakumba Matsiko, who was minister for the presidency and Kampala Capital City Authority, was alleged to have used equipment belonging to the Hoima state radio transmitter for her own private broadcasting station; she resigned on 14 December. By the end of the year, Museveni had thus lost four members of his new government.

New **legislation** included the Institution of Traditional or Cultural Leaders Act, much criticised by Buganda's neo-traditionalists, which was passed by parliament on 1 February but signed into law by the president only after the elections. It included provisions barring such leaders from partisan politics. In February, the Regulation of Interception of Communications Act became law, which allowed phone tapping and the interception of private communications.

The country's **human rights** record underwent scrutiny for the first time under the UN's Universal Periodic Review procedure. The Human Rights Council in Geneva examined the country's record on 11 October; among the issues addressed were the infringements of the right of assembly and the action taken by the security forces against demonstrators. The final assessment was to be completed in early 2012.

Two of the perpetrators of the al-Shabaab-inspired **bombings** on 11 July 2010 in Kampala, which claimed almost 80 lives, were sentenced, one to 25 and the other to five years in prison; they were expected to serve as prosecution witnesses against 12 other suspects.

The humanitarian situation in the north and in the north-east improved. Almost all formerly displaced **Acholi** had returned from the IDP camps, but they still faced lack of infrastructure, danger from landmines, and the occurrence of land disputes. In **Karamoja** peace prevailed for the most part and the food situation improved as a result of adequate rainfall.

The famous Uganda Museum in Kampala was threatened by a government plan to erect a 60–storey building on the site. Controversial former Gulu District chairman Walter Ochora died on 3 March; in 1985 he had announced on Radio Uganda the overthrow of President Obote on behalf of the Okello junta. The death occurred on 14 October of Prince John Barigye, who had tried unsuccessfully to re-establish the kingdom of Ankole. Professor Dan Nabudere, an outstanding intellectual who played a leading role in the period following the fall of Idi Amin in 1979, passed away on 9 November.

Foreign Affairs

Uganda's capital again provided the setting for high-level regional and international meetings. The conclusion of the 'Kampala Accord' on 9 June by leaders of various Somali factions laid down modalities for the distribution of power between those groups. Worldwide attention was attracted by the adoption on 18 November of a 'Summary for Policymakers' of a special report on disaster risk management by the 34th session of the Intergovernmental Panel on Climate Change. The 4th Ordinary Summit of the International Conference on the Great Lakes Region (ICGLR) took place on 15–16 December, meeting also as a Special Summit on Sexual and Gender Based Violence (SGBV). The ICGLR states committed themselves to end impunity and provide support for victims of SGBV, to fight the armed "negative forces" active in the region and to set up a Regional Intelligence Fusion Centre in Goma, DRC. ICGLR chairmanship passed to Museveni for two years.

South Sudan's independence on 9 July was most welcome to Uganda, given its longstanding support for this cause and the close trade links between the two countries. Ugandan traders nonetheless complained about harassment in Juba and a local border dispute emerged over a small stretch of land in Moyo district. The disagreement with **Kenya** over ownership of Migingo, the small fishermen's island in Lake Victoria, remained unresolved. But on the whole relations with neighbouring states did not suffer from such irritations.

In view of the events in **Libya**, the AU formed in March a high-level ad hoc committee consisting of five African presidents, including Museveni, but this initiative proved to be irrelevant. After the death of Muammar Kadhafi, with whom Museveni had had a decades-old and rather mixed relationship, the Ugandan president saw one of the slain Libyan leader's mistakes to be his failure to invest in military hardware such as surface-to-air missiles.

In **Somalia**, Major General Fred Mugisha, head of the UPDF field artillery division, took over from Nathan Mugisha as commander of the AU Mission in Somalia (AMISOM). As before, Uganda's approximately 5,000–strong contingent provided the bulk of the force; by mid-September AMISOM troop strength stood at 9,595, the mandated strength being

12,000. AMISOM soldiers cleared Mogadishu of the al-Shabaab militia early in August. Almost 1,000 Somali soldiers passed out on 31 August from the UPDF's Military Training School in Kamwenge district after nine months' training by the EU Somalia Training Mission (EUTM) in cooperation with the UPDF. This was the second intake, the first batch of recruits having passed out in December 2010, and the EUTM received the third intake of Somali trainees in November. At Museveni's invitation, isolated Eritrean President Isaias Afewerki, a known opponent of international (and Ethiopian) involvement in Somalia, came for a three-day state visit in August to discuss regional peace and security. Museveni's own surprise visit to Israel in November may also have served to exchange information on Islamist terrorists active in Eastern Africa.

Though the UPDF presence in the region – accompanied by tensions between the Ugandan and DRC armies – continued, the **LRA** remained able to cause havoc in north-eastern DRC and in parts of the CAR and South Sudan. The UNSC took up the issue in July and November and, in a 21 July press statement, encouraged the UN Secretary-General to support the endeavours of the AU; in presidential statement 2011/21 of 14 November it commended the AU's "efforts to establish a Regional Intervention Force" aimed at the elimination of the LRA. The AU Commission dispatched a technical assessment mission in March and its report was examined on 8 June by a ministerial meeting of the affected countries in Addis Ababa. On 27 June, the International Working Group on the LRA, consisting of interested states, met in Washington. On 22 November, the AU Peace and Security Council authorised an AU-led Regional Cooperation Initiative for the Elimination of the LRA for an initial six-month period, foreseeing the establishment of a Joint Coordinating Mechanism comprising the affected countries' defence ministers, a Regional Task Force (RTF) in brigade strength (5,000 troops) and RTF Headquarters. On 23 November, former Mozambican foreign minister Francisco Madeira, director of the Algiers-based African Centre for the Study and Research on Terrorism, was named the AU's Special Envoy on the LRA issue. Meanwhile, another initiative unfolded. Following a massive campaign by human rights NGOs (and, according to critics, probably also motivated by the discovery of oil in the Albertine Graben), US President Obama operationalised the 'Lord's Resistance Army Disarmament and Northern Uganda Recovery Act', in force since May 2010, by sending "a small group of military advisers to assist the forces that are countering the LRA". The (about 100) soldiers, mostly US Army Special Forces, were based in Entebbe. They established forward bases in Obo in the south-eastern corner of the CAR and in Nzara in the west of South Sudan, where the UPDF was already present.

The deployment of US troops was overseen by the US Africa Command (**AFRICOM**) based in Stuttgart, Germany. The UPDF and AFRICOM continued their close cooperation. In April, a two-week joint aerial rescue training exercise took place at the Civil Aviation School in Soroti and, in June, a week-long leadership training workshop in a number of places involved West Point cadets and Annapolis Naval Academy midshipmen. In September, 35 Ugandan officers participated in the 'Natural fire 11' exercise in Zanzibar.

In October, UPDF Land Forces commander Edward Katumba Wamala visited the US Army Africa command in Vicenza, Italy. In December, eight Ugandans were trained to operate small remote-controlled 'Raven' aircraft systems in Alabama; four of the systems had been bought by Uganda in July for $ 3 m. Also in December, AFRICOM and the UPDF held a combined logistics training exercise at Entebbe Air Base.

A Ugandan was elected for the first time to the UN's principal judicial organ, the **International Court of Justice**. High court judge Julia Sebutinde competed with Sierra Leonean Abdul Koroma, who sought re-election to the bench. Candidates needed the approval of the UNSC as well as the General Assembly. Koroma repeatedly received majority support in the UNSC, while Sebutinde received the endorsement of the General Assembly. The impasse ended on 13 December, when Sebutinde received the majority vote in both bodies.

The party leaders of the centre-right International Democrat Union (IDU), meeting in November in London, welcomed the FDC as a new member; Besigye was elected as one of the IDU's vice chairmen.

International attention to the on-and-off debate on **homosexuality** continued. On 26 January, prominent gay activist David Kato was murdered in his home. According to a statement by President Obama, the US "mourns his murder, and we recommit ourselves to David's work". When it was read at Kato's funeral service, it failed to impress some of the congregation, including the pastor, who sharply criticised homosexual behaviour. Kato's killer was apprehended and sentenced to 30 years in prison on 10 November. While international critics blamed the killing on the prevailing anti-gay atmosphere, the court put it down to personal motivations. Public pressure in support of the rights of homosexuals was exerted by British Prime Minister David Cameron, who threatened African countries with cuts in development aid; annoyed comments in Uganda followed. Lesbian activist Kasha Jacqueline Nabagesera was awarded the Martin Ennals Award for Human Rights Defenders in Geneva on 13 October for the work of the 'Freedom and Roam' organisation, which she headed. She also attended the presentation of the Rafto Price for Human Rights in Bergen, Norway, to Frank Mugisha of 'Sexual Minorities Uganda' on 6 November. On 10 November in Washington, Mugisha also received the Robert F. Kennedy Human Rights Award, together with promises of further financial and organisational support.

Socioeconomic Developments

Global as well as home-grown factors contributed to a much **poorer economic performance** than in previous years. The exchange rate of the Uganda shilling (UGX) depreciated markedly whilst private sector credits soared. A low was reached in September; within three years the UGX had decreased in value against the US dollar by 71%, although the currency appreciated again towards the end of the year, giving a depreciation rate for the year of 6.2%. **Inflation** reached a peak of 30.4% in October, the highest rate since 1993.

The headline inflation was about the same as underlying (core) inflation, which excludes food crops, fuel and electricity. The rise in the cost of living, including food and transport, had fuelled the protests that took place from April onwards. The situation was exacerbated by frequent power cuts, known as load-shedding, due to high fuel costs for thermal generators; the expected coming into operation of Bujagali hydropower plant was delayed.

Uganda became the first country to fail an **IMF** Policy Support Instrument (PSI) review, the PSI being an instrument that concentrates on advice and monitoring. On 11 February, the IMF decided not to complete its first review under the new three-year PSI because of the supplementary budget of UGX 602 bn (about $ 260 m) hastily passed by the outgoing parliament on 4 January. In the IMF's view, this put the programme objectives at risk. The supplementary allocation included payment of UGX 20 m (about $ 8,600) to each MP for the "monitoring" of government programmes. In March, an IMF mission came for discussions to prepare the second review of the PSI. The mission noted "expansionary fiscal spending" necessitating the "rebuilding of cushions in fiscal balances and international reserves" and expressed the hope that the agreement reached with the authorities on fiscal policies would "bring the budget back in line with the PSI". On 29 June, the IMF completed the second PSI review, approving waivers "for the non-observance of the... assessment criteria on net domestic assets and net international reserves". In preparation for the third PSI review, an IMF mission in October commended the government "for adhering to a market-oriented approach to economic policy making, including by resisting the temptation to restrict exports of food products". Part of the disinflation effort and tight fiscal policy was the government's intention to review and rein in tax exemptions and incentives in preparation for the budget for the fiscal year 2012–13. The fiscal year 2010–11, ending on 30 June, saw an increased fiscal deficit. "The sharp increase in Government spending," the IMF stated, "was due to: increased security-related exceptional spending; wages and salaries for the lower-paid cadre of civil servants; unanticipated pension obligations; and higher thermal power costs due rising fuel prices; and unexpected elections costs."

The **budget** for 2011–12 was presented to parliament by newly-appointed Finance Minister Maria Kiwanuka on 8 June, under the heading "Promoting Economic Growth, Job Creation and Improving Service Delivery". Looking back to 2010–11, Kiwanuka pointed out that **GDP** had "rebounded" with a 6.3% **growth** compared with 5.5% the year before. The fastest growing sector was again telecommunication services. Imports grew from $ 4.0 bn to $ 4.5 bn, an increase of 13.2%, widening the trade deficit. Imports were largely destined "for production-related activities", including "increased activity in the oil sector". Total expenditure for 2011–12 was projected to be UGX 9,840 bn, representing an increase of 30% over 2010–11. Of the total expenditure, amounting to roughly $ 4 bn on budget day, domestic revenues and other sources were projected to cover 71%, the remaining 29% to be financed by development partners. The rate of external financing the previous year had been projected to be 25%, then described by Kiwanuka's predecessor as being "in line with our objective of gradually increasing the share of the budget financed through domestic sources". Among budget priorities, infrastructure development in roads and energy again took first place, with reference to railways added this time. Named as other priority objectives were the enhancement of agricultural production and productivity, employment creation, human resource development, and finally the improvement of public service delivery. With regard to the latter, Kiwanuka observed that "there is need to reduce wastage, laxity, and limited responsiveness" and she proposed, among other things, "cuts of 30% on the budget for allowances, workshops and seminars". In order to "encourage supply of solar power to consumers in rural areas by commercial solar producers" solar energy supply would be VAT exempt. Apparently responding to public discontent over recent price increases, Kiwanuka acknowledged "that sugar is a key welfare item in many households" and proposed to cut the excise duty on it by half, leading to an expected revenue loss of about UGX 8.5 bn ($ 3.5 m). The excise duty on paraffin was to be repealed. In line with EAC harmonisation efforts, the pre-budget meeting of finance ministers had been held on 7 May in Kampala. They decided, among other things, to scrap the 10% import duty on hoes with the aim of encouraging food production. In order to promote cross-border investment, the EAC Double Taxation Agreement was concluded.

Non-budgeted expenses were incurred for a $ 740 m **arms deal**, which was justified by the need to protect oil resources. The government bought from Russia six sophisticated Sukhoy-30MK2s fighter planes, the first two delivered in July, as well as other military hardware. The strain on foreign currency reserves was publicly criticised by the governor of the central bank, Emmanuel Tumusiime-Mutebile.

Oil policy was widely discussed, even beyond the corruption allegations levelled in October. Parliament insisted on seeing the Production Sharing Agreements that had been concluded by government with the oil companies but which were shrouded in secrecy; MPs were granted only limited access. On 11 October, parliament demanded that confidentiality clauses in future contracts should be banned. It also resolved to set up an ad hoc committee to investigate issues pertaining to the oil sector. On 23 November, the Tax Appeals Tribunal ruled that Heritage Oil, which had sold its assets to Tullow Oil, was responsible for paying capital gains tax, but the case was to continue in arbitration proceedings between Heritage and Tullow in London.

The 2011 TI **Corruption Perceptions Index** ranked Uganda 143rd, quite a deterioration from 127th in 2010. The area close to Mt Elgon in the east again suffered from torrential rains and landslides, resulting in some deaths and thousands of displacements. Floods and heavy rains were experienced countrywide. In May, the government approved the National Policy for Disaster Preparedness and Management, with emphasis on **disaster reduction**. Among the few encouraging marks of the year was the designation of Uganda as the **No. 1 destination to visit** in 2012 – incidentally the year of the Golden Jubilee of independence – by the publishers of the renowned 'Lonely Planet' travel guide.

Volker Weyel

VII. Southern Africa

The sub-region was largely free from the scourges of war and civil strife for another year, despite ongoing tensions and local acts of politically motivated violence, most notably in Angola and Zimbabwe. Protests in Swaziland and Malawi were met with repression by the state, which erupted in Malawi in an unforeseen act of police terror against demonstrators. Political change took place surprisingly peacefully in Zambia, while the SADC mediators' search for solutions in Zimbabwe and Madagascar produced no results. The economic situation in most countries showed signs of further recovery and benefitted from the absence of major natural disasters such as droughts and floods. Food security improved, though living standards for most people remained modest, if not precarious. All 12 countries were among the 15 members of SADC, the other three being the Democratic Republic of the Congo, the Seychelles and Tanzania. In violation of its own normative legal framework, SADC continued to dismantle its tribunal, while the revenue-sharing formula in SACU and EPA negotiations with the EU remained contested issues.

Elections, Democracy and Human Rights

2011 brought another year of relative stability in the sub-region, with only limited local politically motivated violence and an absence of full-fledged civil strife. Compared with the situation at the turn of the century, many people in the sub-region were experiencing an improved standard of living, although living conditions deteriorated for some. But not every country improved its record in terms of democracy and human rights.

The **Bertelsmann Transformation Index**, one of the global indicators that claims to offer a comparative perspective on good governance worldwide, noted little turmoil in this sub-region but was cautious not to rank it too high in general terms. It remained an unexplained anomaly that Swaziland was omitted from the review, despite the inclusion of all the other countries in the sub-region. The Index registered doubts on the Angolan regime's commitment to democracy. With regard to Botswana, it noted that the record of this "African success story" was not flawless, with deficiencies related to the freedom of the press and the executive's occasional arbitrary actions; particularly noteworthy was the problem concerning the treatment of the Basarwa/San people. In Lesotho, continued wrangling between political parties and rising threats to the free media suggested that the country remained at a crossroads. In Madagascar, political chaos and uncertainty prevailed, in stark contrast to earlier years of relative stability and international legitimacy. In Malawi, some of the legislation passed had the potential to undermine democratic governance, while the future of local government elections was thrown into turmoil. Mauritius remained a functioning democracy, and its economy was able to cope with the effects of the global financial crisis. Mozambique's democracy remained challenged by the dominance of Frelimo, the former liberation movement. According to the Bertelsmann Foundation, Namibia's democratic and economic transformation continued to progress, though the overwhelming strength of the governing party had weakened the constitutional possibilities for parliamentary control. Similarly in South Africa, the opposition remained fragmented and the African National Congress (ANC) continued to dominate. In Zambia, the principles of a democratic system of government were observable, although there was a tendency towards a relatively autocratic style of leadership in both government and opposition parties. Zimbabwe remained marred by political disagreement and stalemates between the coalition partners, which made economic and political reforms a distant vision of the future; political parties suffered from heavy infighting.

The **Ibrahim Index 2011**, released by the Mo Ibrahim Foundation, presented a picture of contrasts. Southern African countries achieved top rankings among the 53 African states classified, with five of them in the top ten: Mauritius (1), Botswana (3), South Africa (5), Namibia (6) and Lesotho (8), the last a very surprising rating, as Lesotho was still seeking to come to terms with the failed 2007 coup and the subsequent party wrangles. Zambia's ranking at 16 on the list was less surprising, but Malawi at 17 was more so. It was followed by Mozambique (21) and – another huge surprise – Swaziland (26), whose middle ranking among all African countries is very difficult to explain. Madagascar (33) saw the biggest fall, from rank 13 in 2007, followed by Angola (42) and Zimbabwe (51), the lowest ranked country in the sub-region. Closer analysis of the rankings shows the dubious value of such undertakings, despite their popularity and the relative prominence they receive in the wider debate and their influence on general perceptions.

Elections remained a contested issue in several of the countries and were among the indicators used to assess levels of democracy – or the lack of it. The two longest serving autocratic rulers in the sub-region, the **presidents** of Angola and Zimbabwe, were both handling electoral issues, but, although the aim of each was to stay in power, they adopted different strategies. Angolan President José Eduardo dos Santos, in office for 32 years, chose to extend his term in office by avoiding presidential elections; a change in the constitution allowed the party or coalition elected into government to nominate the president. This was intended to ensure his re-appointment, but it also provoked the first visible protests against him, mainly by young voters, who at great personal risks went onto the streets in anti-government demonstrations. In contrast, Robert Mugabe, Zimbabwe's president for the 31 years since independence, was eager to push for early elections with the aim securing another term. While he claimed that the constitution gave him the power to implement this initiative, SADC-facilitated negotiations prevented such a unilateral move. Initiatives by Mozambique's President Armando Guebuza to find a way to retain power beyond his two-term limit remained a matter of speculation and showed no direct results, while Malawi's President Bingu wa Mutharika spent time and energy fighting the vice president. Madagascar's President Andry Rajoelina, who had held on to office without legitimacy or international recognition since the coup in March 2009, demonstrated his actual control over domestic policy by once again postponing parliamentary and presidential elections for another year. There were no spectacular developments in power relations on the political front in Botswana, Mauritius, Namibia or South Africa, while in Swaziland King Mswati III continued to eliminate any meaningful political opposition to his reign by the increased use of terror.

The biggest surprise with regard to political developments in the sub-region were the results of the parliamentary and presidential elections held on 29 September in **Zambia**, which resulted in a significant change of political power and a new government under President Michael Sata and his Patriotic Front. Former president Rupiah Banda and the ruling Movement for Multi-party Democracy avoided the risk of large-scale politically motivated violence by accepting the election results. Many observers had doubted that this would be the case.

Municipal elections were held in South Africa on 18 May, when the voter turnout, at over 57%, was the highest since the country's transition to democracy, despite calls by social movements for a boycott in protest against the inadequate provision of housing, public utilities (water, electricity) and other municipal services. While the ruling ANC lost votes and the Democratic Alliance (DA), the official opposition party, made considerable gains, the overall patterns of political dominance remained unchanged. Most notably, the DA once again secured a prestigious success when it won a majority in Cape Town and was able to appoint the mayor. Municipal by-elections on 7 December in three towns in Mozambique signalled the emergence of the Mozambique Democratic Movement as a relevant new political party, which contested Frelimo's absolute dominance by securing a majority in Quelimane. The results of the 1 October local elections in Lesotho confirmed the dominance of the ruling Lesotho Congress for Democracy in most constituencies, although it remained fraught with internal factionalism.

The **human rights** situation generally benefitted from the absence of large-scale political violence and a reluctance to apply state terror. But in several countries the tendency to prioritise control and power over the demands of the people remained a visible sign of disrespect for fundamental rights. In **Malawi**, 18 people were killed by police on 20 July during a peaceful demonstration, and many more were wounded and arrested. Protests by lecturers and students resulted in the closure of the campus of Chancellor College for eight months. The domestic situation rapidly deteriorated into a presidential dictatorship based on repression. In **Swaziland**, the king's autocratic rule, which prohibited political parties from campaigning, provoked growing protest. Students organised mass demonstrations against the monarchy, while, on 1 October, the Law Society launched a boycott of all courts in protest against the subversion of the principle of judicial independence and repeated violations of the rule of law. In **Zimbabwe**, the fragile interim government of national unity managed to limit open political violence and violations of human rights, although incidents tended to increase again ahead of the anticipated 2012 elections. The situation remained anything but peaceful and the authorities continued to abuse their power. Lasting peace remained remote. In **Angola**, media freedom and freedom of expression were once again under attack by the state authorities, who introduced even stricter control over the private use of information technology. The physical violation of human rights, including killings, mainly occurred in encounters with the secessionist movement in Cabinda and in conflicts with miners in the diamond rich provinces of Lunda Norte and Lunda Sul.

Media freedom was also a target and a contested issue in several countries with democratic constitutions. Even in the widely praised democracies of Botswana, Namibia and South Africa, government initiatives targeted press freedom and new laws were in the making that would allow closer scrutiny, interference and control.

Socioeconomic Developments

TI's annual **Corruption Perception Index** for the year presented a mixed picture for the sub-region, corresponding to a large extent with the rankings in the democracy and governance indexes summarised above. Of the 182 countries listed, the best performers in Southern Africa were as follows (their position on the list is followed by their score out of 10): Botswana (32/6.1), Mauritius (46/5.1), Namibia (57/4.4) and South Africa (64/4.1). Considering the known extent of large-scale graft in the last two, this listing is more an indication of the worrying level of organised corruption than of the above average performance of these countries. They were followed by Lesotho (77/3.5), Zambia (91/3.2), Swaziland (95/3.1), Madagascar and Malawi (both 100/3.0) and Mozambique (120/2.7), with Zimbabwe (154/2.2) and Angola (168/2.0) towards the end of the list. The fact that corruption and socioeconomic performance are in no way correlated, or rather that resource-based growth was fuelling the self-enrichment strategies of a political and bureaucratic elite, was evident, particularly with regard to Angola, but it was also indicative of trends in the better-ranked countries of Namibia and South Africa.

The **SADC economies** had a total population of over 250 m and a combined GDP of over $ 400 bn. According to an Integrated Paper on Recent Economic Developments in SADC prepared by the Reserve Bank of Zimbabwe for the Committee of Central Bank Governors in SADC in September, the member states had achieved significant progress towards attaining macroeconomic convergence targets. The lack of FDI was identified as the main challenge. SADC economies were more resilient to the global crisis than most other emerging economies, but remained susceptible to external shocks due to a heavy dependency on commodity exports. The authors of the paper stressed the need for initiatives towards commodity beneficiation (which sets out to leverage long-term benefits from a country's substantial mineral endowment) and value added, and recommended strengthening fiscal surveillance, establishing an infrastructural fund to finance much needed projects in the energy, transport, agricultural, mining and manufacturing sectors, and introducing reforms to unlock productive potential and to promote trade and financial sector development.

Altogether, socioeconomic indicators suggested that most countries in the sub-region had recovered from the effects of the global crisis, and they were spared major natural disasters and subsequent needs for large-scale humanitarian interventions, although food and petrol prices remained an issue for most ordinary people trying to make ends meet. Resource-rich countries continued to prosper. Most notably, **Angola**'s booming oil economy resulted in a kind of reverse trend, in that the money accumulated from the revenue income was invested in the economy of the erstwhile European colonial power **Portugal**. The Angolan oil company Sonangol was estimated to own more than 12.4% of the assets of the Portuguese Banco Comercial Portugues, making it the major stakeholder. Other investments of considerable size were made in media, energy and agro-business. On the other hand, while Angolan capital entered the Portuguese economy on a large scale, growing numbers of qualified younger Portuguese migrants sought employment in Angola and Mozambique.

The **provision of electricity** remained an urgent challenge for the sub-region, with demand far exceeding supply, and shortages continued to be a huge obstacle to economic growth. There was a history of power cuts resulting from major delivery bottlenecks from the main producer, South Africa, which embarked on ambitious plans to generate enough energy by a mix of renewable (solar, wind, water) energy and nuclear and coal based power generation in combination with massive tariff hikes to limit household demand and generate investment. Angola's minister of state announced in September that his government planned to invest $ 18 bn by 2016 to improve the country's power generation and supply system. Power shortages in South Africa forced supply cuts to Botswana in November, with an expected further decline in supply. Malawi was estimated to provide less than 10% of its population with access to electricity. Namibia imported around half of its electricity, mainly from South Africa, and supplied about one third of its population. It invested $ 452 m in sub-regional grid integration to improve electricity transmission between Zambia, Namibia and South Africa, connecting the northern and western parts of the Southern African power pool. Zambia partnered with the Egyptian company El Sewedy Electrometer in an energy efficiency programme and with the China Africa Development Fund and Sinhydro to develop the Kafue Gorge Lower hydropower plant. China also assisted in financing the expansion of the Kariba North Bank power plant. Zimbabwe's estimated energy demands were almost double the operational generating capacity and, despite increased supply from the repaired and expanded Hwange power station and the Kariba hydroelectric scheme, Zimbabwe imported power from Mozambique and Zambia.

The sub-region experienced a relatively satisfactory degree of **food security**, after three consecutive years of average to above-average harvests. Food prices stabilised and even fell in surplus-producing areas. There were, however, pockets of food insecurity in areas affected by floods or dry spells during mid-season. Flood-related higher levels of food insecurity were reported in Lesotho and Namibia. The spot price for white maize escalated to record heights in South Africa as a result of higher demand on international markets due to reduced global supplies, particularly from the USA, the world's primary maize exporter. This was bad news for South Africa's maize deficient neighbours dependent on South African imports, as it was mainly poor households (especially in Lesotho and Swaziland), with their limited purchasing power, who were negatively affected. The governments of Lesotho, Malawi, Mozambique, Zambia and Zimbabwe reportedly subsidised agricultural support programmes to boost crop production, while higher fuel prices hampered the logistics and resulted in transport and distribution bottlenecks.

The need to secure and protect access to **water** as a scarce resource for many parts of the sub-region also remained on the agenda. The 5th annual SADC Multi-Stakeholder Water Dialogue was held on 28–29 June in Ezulwini Valley, Swaziland, with a special focus on ensuring water security and climate resilient development. A report by the University of Cape Town had warned of the rapid deterioration of South Africa's water supplies, not least as a result of the consumption by the mining sector. Other countries in the sub-region faced similar constraints with regard to the depletion of water resources as a result of extractive industry operations.

Malaria Day was commemorated by the SADC ministers of health on 11 November in Limpopo, South Africa. A dramatic decline in malaria cases and subsequent deaths was reported in the sub-region for the previous decade, but it was also noted that the eradication of the disease would require further economic growth to finance the necessary public health interventions and empower people to take adequate protective measures. Similarly, **HIV/AIDS** remained a challenge, but the rate of infection was no longer rising in most countries. The dimensions of the epidemic varied considerably, with estimated prevalence ranging from 0.1% in Madagascar to 23.4% in Lesotho, 24.8% in Botswana and 25.9% in Swaziland, according to the Joint UN Programme on HIV/AIDS. High rates also continued to affect Namibia, South Africa and Zimbabwe. The numbers of AIDS-related deaths again declined as antiretroviral therapy coverage and prevention of mother-to-child transmission of HIV increased.

Sub-regional Organisations

Extraordinary summits of the SADC Heads of State and Government took place on 20 May in Windhoek, Namibia, and on 11–12 June in Sandton, South Africa. Items on the Windhoek summit's agenda originally included Zimbabwe, Madagascar, the suspension of the SADC Tribunal as a regional court, and allegations of corruption in the SADC Secretariat. Just days ahead of the summit, there were doubts as to whether it would take place, since South African President Zuma, SADC's facilitator on Zimbabwe, chose instead to remain at home for the local elections in his country. The communiqué released afterwards made no mention at all of Zimbabwe. The Namibian authorities prohibited all demonstrations ahead of the summit, even those that were properly registered.

The local weekly Namibian newspaper 'Windhoek Observer' reported ahead of the Windhoek summit on 20 May that Namibia's President Pohamba, as hosting SADC chairperson, had been alerted by SADC personnel to massive scales of misappropriation of funds tantamount to graft in the **SADC Secretariat** and called for an audit to be ordered. According to an anonymous source, the secretariat was "an institution of money laundering". Pohamba said he had been aware of the accusations since April and the Council of Ministers would look into the matter. A report on graft within the secretariat had been submitted, but no visible action followed.

With regard to the suspended **SADC Tribunal**, which, subsequent to a ruling against the Zimbabwean government, was de facto stripped of all authority to continue its work as stipulated in the SADC protocol, the Windhoek summit communiqué stated that ministers of justice and attorney generals were mandated to initiate amendments to the relevant legal instruments, and to submit a progress report in August and a final report to the summit in August 2012. SADC's Executive Secretary Tomaz Salomao, when asked whether the recommendations would be made public, responded that neither the media nor SADC citizens needed to know what was in the report. The SADC Secretariat had earlier commissioned an independent review. Submitted in April by University of Cambridge academic Lorand Bartels, it had affirmed the jurisdiction of the tribunal and its legal authority. Notwithstanding compelling arguments, the Windhoek summit decided not to reappoint the judges whose term had ended in August 2010, or to replace the judges whose term expired in October. The tribunal was thereby further dismantled and remained defunct. On 13 June, the four judges whose mandate had not been extended in August 2010 submitted a letter to SADC's executive secretary in which they condemned the decisions as illegal, arbitrary and taken in bad faith, asserting that the treatment of the SADC Tribunal showed that SADC put politics above the law and ignored the legal instruments it had created.

The Windhoek summit also considered the report presented on **Madagascar** by the official SADC mediator and former Mozambican president Joaquim Chissano, but took no decision. It mandated a follow-up meeting to be held on 6–7 June in Gaborone, Botswana, by the so-called Organ Troika, comprised of Namibia's President Pohamba as SADC chairperson, Zambian President Banda as chairperson of the Organ on Politics, Defence and Security Cooperation, and the SADC mediator Chissano, for the further promotion and implementation of the roadmap. Eleven political stakeholders from Madagascar attended the meeting. The Sandton summit on 11–12 June subsequently officially endorsed the roadmap presented by Chissano.

On **Zimbabwe**, the Sandton summit noted the report by the SADC facilitator Zuma with regard to the (lack of) progress made on the implementation of the Global Political Agreement (GPA) and urged further action, including initiatives to continue the dialogue with the Western powers to remove sanctions. Much to his anger, President Mugabe was reminded to adhere to the GPA drafted at the meeting of the Organ Troika on Politics, Defence and Security Cooperation held on 31 March in Livingstone, Zambia, as re-endorsed by the Sandton summit. Mugabe reportedly pleaded in vain for close to 45 minutes at the summit for the Livingstone resolutions to be disregarded. Instead, the final communiqué reiterated that the summit "mandated the Organ Troika to continue to assist Zimbabwe in the full implementation of the GPA".

The **SADC Lawyers Association** held its 12th annual general meeting on 4–6 August in Maputo, Mozambique. Its resolutions reaffirmed that free and fair elections were the bedrock of democracy, the promotion of human rights and the rule of law in the subregion. Three issues featured most prominently and were commented on at length: Deep concern was expressed about the breakdown in the administration of justice and the erosion of the judiciary's independence in **Swaziland**. The extended suspension of the **SADC Tribunal** through the extraordinary SADC summit in Windhoek was declared "illegal and *ultra vires* the provisions of the SADC Treaty and the SADC Protocol"; the resolutions demanded the immediate reinstatement of the tribunal to allow it to function while any potential amendments to the SADC instruments that governed its operations were considered. The use of violence by state security forces against peaceful and unarmed demonstrators in **Malawi** was strongly condemned and the restoration of basic freedoms and fundamental human rights demanded.

The **31st SADC Heads of State and Government Summit** was held in Luanda, Angola, on 17–18 August. The chairmanship moved from Namibian President Pohamba to Angolan President dos Santos, with Mozambican President Guebuza as the deputy chairperson and hence designated next in line to chair SADC for 2012/13. South African President Zuma became chairperson of the SADC Organ on Politics, Defence and Security Cooperation, with Tanzanian President Kikwete as deputy. An agreement on the world's largest **trans-frontier conservation area**, the Kavango-Zambezi Transfrontier Conservation Area (KaZa TFCA), was signed at the summit by the presidents of Angola, Botswana, Namibia, Zambia and Zimbabwe. The area is situated within the Kavango and Zambezi River basins and spans over 444,000 km^2 of parks, game reserves, forest reserves, conservancies and communal land. It includes the Victoria Falls and the Okavango delta as two prominent international tourist attractions. The summit avoided commenting on the repressive situation in Malawi and Swaziland and did not pursue matters further with regard to the SADC Tribunal. Being silent on all contentious issues, the summit closed ahead of schedule. The communiqué welcomed the positive macroeconomic trends in the sub-region as reflected in performance indicators, underscored the role of infrastructure in regional integration and urged member states to promote further initiatives towards gender parity. It welcomed the successful completion of the political mediation process in Lesotho and reaffirmed its support for the mediation processes in Madagascar and **Zimbabwe**. ZANU-PF had called for the resignation of SADC mediator Zuma, which the summit ignored. Frustrated by the SADC position, President Mugabe upon his return to Harare rejected the summit's resolution calling for compliance with the GPA, suggesting that the resolution amounted to interference in Zimbabwe's internal affairs. Back in Pretoria, Zuma indicated that SADC had had enough of the political impasse in Harare.

The **7th Southern Africa Civil Society Forum**, an alliance, composed of churches, NGOs and trade unions, was held ahead of the ordinary annual SADC summit on 8–9 August in Johannesburg. Its statement noted with concern the suspension of the SADC Tribunal and the deteriorating political situation in Madagascar, Malawi, Swaziland and Zimbabwe and the lack of progress in SADC mediation processes in Zimbabwe and Madagascar. It also expressed critical views on the lack of progress in climate change negotiations, as well as the fundamental premises of trade liberalisation and regional economic integration, which did not translate into improved standards of living for the people of the sub-region. It was concerned over the continued restrictions on media freedom in many member states and the lack of protection for media practitioners. The absence of a human security policy framework in many of the countries was noted, along with the continued restrictions on mobility between member states and the harassment of migrants. The continued discrimination against women and the abuse of children were among other issues of concern. The Forum further called for an institutionalised interaction between SADC and civil society in regional integration processes.

Gender was discussed at the meeting of SADC ministers responsible for gender and women's affairs held in Windhoek on 2 June, which was attended by representatives from 11 member states. It was noted with concern that only four SADC countries had a female parliamentary representation above 30%. They were South Africa (45%), Mozambique (39.2%), Angola (38.6%) and Tanzania (36%). On 18 November, an extraordinary meeting of the ministers was held as a follow-up in Johannesburg. Meeting ahead of the 17th Conference of the Parties (**COP17**) to the UN Framework Convention on Climate Change in Durban, it adopted the SADC Engendered Position Paper on Climate Change and supported the initiatives taken by the SADC Secretariat through a regional conference held on 24 to 28 October in Johannesburg to develop a SADC Plan of Action 2011–2016.

A **COMESA-EAC-SADC** Tripartite Summit was held in combination with an IGAD Infrastructure Investment Conference on 28–29 September in Nairobi, Kenya, as part of the three Regional Economic Communities' efforts to establish part of the prospective (continental) African Economic Community. It stressed the need for further improvement of the infrastructure to enhance transport routes and logistics as trade facilitation measures along the defined corridors.

The IMF's Africa Regional Technical Assistance Centre South (**AFRITAC South**) – the fourth of its kind on the continent – was officially opened on 17 October in Port Louis, the capital of Mauritius. It became operational on 1 June and served Angola, Botswana, Comoros, Lesotho, Madagascar, Mauritius, Mozambique, Namibia, Seychelles, South Africa, Swaziland, Zambia and Zimbabwe. AFRITAC South, like its sister institutions, provided capacity-building assistance through a team of resident international experts in financial sector supervision, monetary policy and operations, tax and customs administration, public financial management and macroeconomic statistics. From the start, it was declared under-financed, with important training activities on hold pending additional funding.

An IMF study predicted a significant decline in **SACU** revenue collection, which would massively impact on transfers to the smaller economies of Botswana, Lesotho, Namibia and Swaziland. The analysis concluded that Lesotho and Swaziland would be most affected and pointed to the need for fiscal adjustment. More than a century after its establishment, the oldest customs union in existence remained marred by internal squabbles over the revenue sharing formula. Botswana, Lesotho, Namibia and Swaziland – the so-called BLNS states – followed with concern and frustration continued initiatives by the fifth member, South Africa, to renegotiate a mechanism. One of the options discussed was to increase the development component of the pool with income invested into regional infrastructure projects instead of going into state coffers. A South African draft report on the proposed changes was leaked in February and provoked an outcry by the BLNS states. A heads of state meeting was held on 25 March in Pretoria, South Africa, with no firm outcome and the negotiations continued without concrete results.

EPA negotiations stagnated too. SADC countries were grouped in four different EPA configurations, which added to the complexity of the negotiations. SACU countries negotiated together with Angola and Mozambique in the SADC-EPA, while most other states in the sub-region were grouped in the Eastern and Southern Africa regional grouping (ESA-EPA). Several of these countries had initialled but not signed an Interim EPA, while others had signed but not taken steps to ratify their (Interim) EPA. On 30 September, the European Commission adopted a proposed regulation, which put pressure on those countries required to comply with the EPA provisions or risk being removed from the list of preferred beneficiaries. The proposed regulation exerted pressure on these governments to sign and ratify their EPA before 1 January 2014, regardless of contentious issues pending, or else lose the stipulated benefits. This would particularly harm those countries without least developed country status, namely Botswana, Namibia, Swaziland and Zimbabwe. The unilateral imposition of the regulation was considered as an inappropriate ultimatum and attracted harsh criticism. Technical meetings were held from 10 to 16 November in Johannesburg to clarify outstanding issues in the SADC-EU EPA negotiations, including issues related to market access, rules of origin, services and investment, development cooperation and geographical indicators. While progress was reportedly made in certain areas, it was acknowledged that "more work [was] needed on market access, in particular on agricultural products". In addition, "specific issues on rules of origin for fishery products were discussed with Namibia and Mozambique". According to the European Commission, Botswana, Lesotho, Swaziland and Mozambique had "indicated their willingness to move forward with negotiations" on services and investment issues.

Henning Melber

Angola

The first openly anti-government protests in Luanda and provincial capitals were met with bellicose rhetoric and swift intervention by security forces, showing a certain degree of nervousness on the part of the government. The demonstrations also highlighted the unanswered question of who would succeed President dos Santos, whose dominance of the political system was strongly felt, both among members of the ruling party and by the political and popular opposition. Despite growing popular discontent, opposition parties remained fractured and ineffective. Abroad, Angola emphasised South-South partnerships. The country also consolidated its standing with economic and political initiatives, namely in Guinea-Bissau, although it came under pressure for its stance in the Ivoirian crisis. The economy picked up again after a debt crisis in the previous year, although the majority of the population remained mired in poverty, confined to the informal sector and with low levels of education and health.

Domestic Politics

For most of the year, domestic politics were overshadowed by the question of the **presidential succession** to José Eduardo dos Santos, now in his 32nd year as president, and debates about the 2012 legislative elections. In January 2010, the ruling 'Movimento

Popular para a Libertação de Angola' (MPLA) pushed a new constitution through parliament, which considerably expanded the powers of the president and effectively abolished presidential elections, replacing them by the automatic appointment of the head of the list of candidates presented by the majority party or coalition. This move ensured dos Santos an almost guaranteed re-appointment, but it also led to the first public contestations of the MPLA's crushing dominance of the parliament and its total control of the administration.

In February, a call for an **anti-government demonstration in Luanda**'s Independence Square on 7 March was published on the internet. The call, issued anonymously under an alias, made explicit reference to the on-going Arab revolutions and demanded dos Santos' resignation. Initial reactions were muted and marked by scepticism and disbelief, and were limited to urban circles with access to social media. A popular demonstration explicitly criticising the government and the president had been completely unthinkable in the recent history of Angola. A widespread assumption was that it was a hoax orchestrated by the government to "flush out and identify the troublemakers". However, the government's reaction, combining massive threats against any protestors with the organisation of a 'non-partisan' pro-peace rally two days before the planned demonstration, clearly revealed the regime's nervousness. The 20 people who eventually arrived to demonstrate, including four journalists, were all taken into custody by the police and released over the following days. Several demonstrations followed, with increasing numbers of participants. After a demonstration on 3 September, 50 demonstrators were detained; a week later 18 of them were sentenced in what was widely regarded as a sham trial to up to three months in jail for "public disorder, disobedience and violence against the police". They were then released on the orders of the supreme tribunal, after an example had been made of them. The provincial government of Luanda reacted by designating restricted areas on the periphery of the city where demonstrations would be allowed, while pro-government marches, unsurprisingly, continued unhindered in the city centre. The last demonstration, on 3 December, which attracted over 1,000 protestors, saw plainclothes agents beating demonstrators and spraying them with homemade liquid irritants.

Although the demonstrations in Luanda were by far the most visible, **protests in other provinces** also took place against the dire socio-economic conditions and the government's failing policy responses. In Lubango, the capital of Huíla province, war veterans protested in March against delays in payment of their pensions, but were dispersed by anti-riot police. In May and September, local residents of a Benguela neighbourhood protested against forced evictions to make way for the enlargement of a main thoroughfare; many were arrested. In September, a protest of moto-taxi drivers in Kuito, Bié, resulted in the death of two demonstrators, and in December, several thousand demonstrators took to the streets in various localities in the diamond-rich province of Lunda Sul to protest against the "pillaging" of their natural resources.

In the wake of the fall of North African leaders, the question of the **presidential succession** became a central point of discussion. Even within the MPLA there was some discontent with the president's rule and with the increasing control his children exercised over most sectors of the Angolan economy. Dos Santos therefore announced that he would not stand for a further term of office, although it was noted that his prime concern would be to ensure protection for himself and his family from any future prosecution for embezzlement. In September, sources "close to the MPLA leadership" leaked two possible scenarios to the media, which both envisaged Manuel Vicente, the CEO of the state oil company Sonangol, taking over from dos Santos, either before or after the 2012 elections. Vicente, who in February announced he would resign from his post after the end of his mandate in October, was widely seen as a capable manager who would safeguard the interests of dos Santos' family, but he appeared to lack the credentials as an active party militant needed to gain support from the MPLA's 'old guard'. After the MPLA's fourth extraordinary congress in late April, this idea was seemingly abandoned; in November, dos Santos announced that he would be ready to "serve the party in any capacity" – including as President of the Republic – and, on 12 December, Vicente was reappointed as head of the administrative council of Sonangol.

A few political-administrative **reshuffles** kept government members on their toes and dependent on the whim of the president. José de Lima Massano replaced Abraão Gourgel as governor of the National Bank of Angola, while Gourgel became minister of economy. In a popular move, the governor of Luanda, José Maria Ferraz dos Santos, who had been installed only in November 2010, dismissed half of the municipal administrators of Luanda for incompetence. However, on 5 July, he was himself dismissed for corruption, having privately sold high-value public land in central Luanda for private development to two different companies at the same time. Shortly afterwards, Sebastião Bento Bento, secretary-general of the MPLA for the province of Luanda was appointed as the new governor. Interior Minister Sebastião Martins proceeded to carry out a thorough reorganisation of the migration service, 'Serviço de Migração e Estrangeiros', which saw the dismissal of around 75 mid-level functionaries for corrupt practices and resulted, over the year, in a notable improvement in the service's efficiency.

Opposition parties remained largely ineffective and fractured. Although some ventured to voice tentative support for the causes of student demonstrations, all distanced themselves from any call for protests. Buying into the MPLA's discourse, which equated the expression of dissent with an automatic return to civil war, they all said that they, too, were "for peace and development, and against confusion and disobedience". **UNITA** ('União Nacional para a Independência Total de Angola'), the MPLA's wartime opponent and the major opposition party in parliament, was hampered by internal disputes when its leader, Isaias Samakuva, decided – "reluctantly, as the party needs me" – to stand again at the party congress in December, after having completed two full terms of office. This democracy deficit, expressed in disciplinary action against 'dissidents' such as Lukamba Gato and Abel Chivukuvuku, almost resulted in a rift in the party, and was seen by commentators as causing a further loss of credibility for UNITA.

However, in parliament in August, UNITA successfully blocked the MPLA's legislative proposal for a new electoral law package. The main bone of contention was the composition of the **National Electoral Commission** ('Comissão Nacional Eleitoral'; CNE), as the 2010 constitution stipulated the creation of an 'independent' commission. While the MPLA held that this simply meant independent of the administration, opposition parties demanded independence from any party ties. In the end, UNITA prided itself on the revised compromise version that was finally adopted in December, with the help of the 'Partido da Renovação Social'. The legal formula wrested administrative control of the electoral process from the Inter-Ministry Commission for the Electoral Process, and foresaw a CNE of 17 members, nine from the MPLA and seven from opposition parties, under the leadership of an acting judge. The third 'historic' party, the former liberation movement, 'Frente Nacional para a Libertação de Angola', although vocal in the CNE debate, continued to be paralysed by an internal rift that one of the two contesting leaders, Ngola Kabangu, claimed had been fomented by the MPLA.

In contrast, three **new parties** without parliamentary representation were more outspoken. While 'Bloco Democrático', led by economics professor Justino Pinto de Andrade, and the coalition, 'Partidos da Oposição Civil', led by Manuel Fernandes, criticised the government for its handling of the demonstrations, the leader of the 'Partido Popular', the lawyer Davide Mendes, filed a criminal complaint against President dos Santos for allegedly holding a $ 37 m bank account in Panama.

In an unprecedented move, MPLA deputies refused to vote for a new proposed **law on private investment** in the National Assembly in March, as the proposition raised the threshold for tax breaks on investments from $ 250,000 to $ 1 m, which they felt would disadvantage their own business interests to the benefit of a few super-rich. However, these MPs faced a disciplinary process from the party leadership for opposing the decisions of the Political Bureau and the Council of Ministers. In the wake of the 7 March demonstration and concerned about the influence of 'social media', the executive also proposed in May a new **law on information technologies**, which considerably extended the administration's powers to access private e-mail communication and imposed sentences of up to 12 years' imprisonment for sending messages calling "for conflict". Here again, tensions within the MPLA came to the fore when Vice-President Fernando da Piedade Dias dos Santos 'Nandó' rather ostensibly opened a Facebook account only days after the president had made a speech in which he condemned social networks; the bill was still pending at the end of the year. Commentators observed that, even without this legal basis, the government had extensive control over the networks, as both mobile phone operators Unitel and Movicel, which provide all mobile broadband access, are owned by individuals close to the ruling elite. Ahead of the 7 March demonstration, and repeatedly afterwards, internet access was completely shut down. The operators later blamed the failure on a fibre-optic cable defect.

Media freedom also remained rather restricted. The public radio station, 'Rádio Nacional de Angola', covers the whole national territory, but private radio stations were limited to local broadcasting. Most commercial stations were owned by people close to the regime, while UNITA's 'Rádio Despertar' and the Catholic Church's 'Rádio Ecclésia' were reprimanded for "inciting civil disobedience". Both the public television station (TPA) and TV Zimbo, owned by the regime-friendly Media Nova consortium, cancelled their only weekly live debates, which had till then constituted a limited forum of expression. In print media, the situation was hardly better. Private weeklies such as 'Angolense' and 'A Capital', taken over in 2010 by ESCOM – a holding owned by a Portuguese group with close ties to the president's daughter, Isabel dos Santos, dismissed their most critical columnists. In September, 'A Capital' was issued with two pages blank as a sign of protest, having been prevented by its owners from running an interview with Vicente Pinto de Andrade, a respected old MPLA member, who publicly defended the constitutional right to demonstrate. The two remaining independent publications, 'Folha 8' and 'Novo Jornal', faced several lawsuits for libel. On the other hand, the public 'Jornal de Angola', still the only national daily newspaper, continued to glorify the government's achievements; on 9 September, for example, the director, José Ribeiro, wrote an editorial saying that the Portuguese had "lost their minds" for saying that dos Santos should leave power and suggesting in all seriousness that they "more than anyone else, should put forward his name for the Nobel Peace Prize".

The prevailing climate of intrigue and political paranoia also characterised reactions to a wave of **mass fainting** that swept across middle schools throughout the country from March to August. After the first cases in two polytechnic schools in Luanda, where scores of mainly female teenage students experienced dizziness and fainted, the government attributed the phenomenon to "unknown evildoers", who used a toxic gas to spread panic and "disturb the stability and the gains of peace". Rapid Intervention Police were posted in front of schools to search all students, while those affected were rushed to hospital isolation wards, where they were administered saline drips. The media, meanwhile, reported the increasing number of cases and the futile search for the toxic gas and those responsible, which all contributed to the spread of panic. At the same time, many people expressed the sentiment that the government itself was behind the fainting, and that the Ministry of Interior was testing a new "crowd control gas" on innocent children. The mass hysteria finally subsided when a psychology taskforce pulled off the armed police and imposed a media blackout, combined with psychological interventions in affected schools.

Besides the arbitrary detention of demonstrators, the **human rights situation** was especially concerning in the provinces of Cabinda, Lunda Norte and Lunda Sul. In Cabinda, the low-level guerrilla insurgency of the separatist 'Frente para a Libertação da Enclave de Cabinda' (FLEC) continued. On 31 July, three battalions of the Angolan Armed Forces (FAA) captured 23 members of FLEC in Konde Kavunga, northern Cabinda, as a detachment of 56 rebel fighters was moving to a northern base near Miconje. The following day, FAA units entered DRC territory and started fighting FLEC rebels in the Tshela area of the Bas-Congo province. Despite the military crackdown and increased social spending in the oil-rich province, the situation was tense, precluding a lasting solution to the conflict. Activists and suspected FLEC supporters faced harassment at the hands of the security forces. In June, a delegation of eight ambassadors of EU states visited Cabinda. When about 30 youths tried to speak to the delegation about human rights abuses in the province, they were immediately arrested by the police. In the diamond-rich Lunda provinces, severe human rights abuses persisted. Violent clashes between *garimpeiros* (artisanal miners) and private security agents employed by the company Teleservice led to the death of 14 *garimpeiros* in June.

On 12 September, Leila Lopes, Miss Angola 2010, was elected **Miss Universe 2011** in São Paulo, Brazil. Apart from this triumph, which was greeted by Angolans with great pride, the socio-economic conditions remained dire for the majority of the population. On 15 April, President dos Santos made a speech at the opening of the extraordinary session of the MPLA Central Committee, in which he explained that **poverty** was by no means a creation of the government but that it was, on the contrary, almost a fact of nature, which "already existed at the time of the coloniser", and that the government was taking every imaginable measure to alleviate it. This discourse was widely ridiculed as "an insult to the intelligence of Angolans", considering the dismal socio-economic circumstances experienced by the majority of the population. However, commentators observed that the speech clearly revealed both how far removed from the everyday reality of most Angolans dos Santos was, and his disdain for "ordinary people", and that, in that sense, it had probably been his first honest speech ever. Also, while the MPLA repeatedly accused opposition parties of "political profiteering" by supporting the demonstrators, it saw no such profiteering at work when its female wing, 'Organização da Mulher Angolana', saw fit to call for a nationwide welcome rally for Leila Lopes.

Foreign Affairs

Contrary to the domestic turbulence, Angola's foreign affairs were mainly marked by *courant normal*. The main tensions arose early in the year, when President dos Santos went head-on against the AU, and in fact most of the international community, in supporting the outgoing president, Laurent Gbagbo, against his rival, Alassane Ouattara, in the post-electoral conflict in **Côte d'Ivoire**. Dos Santos, remembering Ouattara's support for UNITA during the Angolan civil war, received a close aide of Gbagbo in the presidential palace in February. It was also rumoured that Angolan troops were being deployed in Abidjan in support of Gbagbo, in what some Angolans said was a 'proxy war' against France. Indeed, after a high-profile corruption case the year before, relations with **France** were still strained, as exemplified by the MPLA's accusations that France had instigated the anti-government protests. After South Africa withdrew its support for Gbagbo, Angola found itself increasingly isolated. Only after the intervention of Angola's new minister of foreign affairs, George Chicoty, with the president in March, did Angola officially adopt the AU position, recommending a negotiated solution to the conflict. Prompted by the UN-sanctioned international military intervention in Libya, and fearing similar foreign intervention at home, Angola also repeatedly condemned any foreign intervention on the African continent.

On 17 and 18 August, Luanda hosted the 31st **SADC Summit** of Heads of State and Government, when Angola took over the rotating chair of the regional body. Opening the summit, President dos Santos promised that, under his auspices, the organisation would review its Regional Development Plan, as well as implement a financing strategy and operationalise infrastructural projects. However, Angola's commitment to the regional alliance remained lukewarm, and greater economic integration was postponed to protect the domestic reconstruction efforts from increased South-African competition. On the margins of the summit, 12 Mozambican journalists and civil society activists were denied entry at Luanda International Airport and sent back on the return flight to Johannesburg. They were to have participated in the 7th Southern African Civil Society meeting, which aimed to contribute to the debates at the summit; five other activists, from Zambia and Zimbabwe, were also expelled. On the margins of the summit, Angola signed a defence agreement with **South Africa**, which remained one of Angola's major trading partners.

2011 saw a new rapprochement with the neighbouring **DRC**. In the two previous years, a spate of expulsions of DR Congolese 'illegal immigrants' was repaid by the expulsion of Angolans from the DRC, and a dispute over the maritime border in the oil-rich offshore waters at the mouth of the Congo River had led to the deterioration of previously good bilateral relations. However, with a view to the DRC legislative elections in November, DRC President Joseph Kabila sought to regain the support of Angola, whose superior military power had saved him before. The DRC's earlier decision to postpone the submission of the border dispute to international arbitration until 2014 was also positive for bilateral relations. The incursion of Angolan troops into DRC territory in pursuit of FLEC guerrillas led to a momentary spike in tensions but, on 4 August, Kabila flew to Luanda to meet with President dos Santos, following which the DR Congolese media reported a notably calmer situation in Tshela and the withdrawal of Angolan forces from the area.

Zambia also tried to improve bilateral relations with Angola: on 17 October, former Zambian president, Kenneth Kaunda, arrived in Luanda as the special envoy of the new president, Michael Sata. On behalf of his government, he apologised for Zambia's support of UNITA during the Angolan civil war, an apology that was widely condemned by civil society groups in both countries – and diplomatically ignored by President dos Santos – but which improved Zambian chances of signing an agreement on imports of Angolan fuel.

Angola also continued at the helm of the **CPLP**. In this capacity, its economic involvement in São Tomé – popularly referred to as "Angola's 19th province" – increased, when the Angolan state oil company Sonangol signed an agreement to take over the management of São Tomé's ports and airports. On the back of the military mission to **Guinea-Bissau**, begun in 2010 to support the country's security sector reform, the Angolan government signed various commercial agreements, which paved the way for Angolan banks and mining interests to expand activities in Guinea-Bissau. The Angolan military mission was also rumoured to have been central in protecting Bissau-Guinean Prime Minister Carlos Gomes Júnior from a failed coup attempt in December.

Relations with Brazil and Portugal remained equally cordial and intense, as both countries pursued their major commercial interests in Angola. In July, the former president of **Brazil**, Luís Inácio 'Lula' da Silva, paid a courtesy visit to President dos Santos, and the new Brazilian president, Dilma Rousseff, arrived in Luanda for a state visit in October. However, she avoided any mention of Angola's internal affairs, focusing instead on economic and commercial partnership, as bilateral trade reached a volume of over $ 1.5 bn. **Portugal** increasingly wooed Angola to prop up its own crisis-stricken economy: the first state visit of the new Portuguese prime minister, Passos Coelho, was to Luanda. President dos Santos stated that Angola was aware of the difficulties Portugal was facing and was ready to assist the brother country by playing its 'trump card' – Angola's cash reserves. Shortly afterwards, Angolan entrepreneurs – primarily the president's daughter, Isabel dos Santos – increased their shares in several Portuguese banks, as well as in the Galp oil company, when Portugal came under pressure from the IMF to privatise key state assets. Indicative of Angola's strengthened position was the warning in November that the Angolan authorities would consider the nationalisation of the Angolan branches of Portuguese banks should the bailout of these banks in Portugal lead to more scrutiny and state oversight.

Angola grew to become the **USA**'s second most important trading partner in Sub-Saharan Africa, as well as its third most important strategic partner after South Africa and Nigeria. The planned highlight of the 2011 diplomatic agenda, however, the first state visit of a chancellor from **Germany** to Angola on 13 July, yielded rather mixed results. While Angela Merkel and her entourage tried in vain to conclude several trade agreements, she came under heavy criticism at home for failing to address issues of human rights and democracy in Angola, and for the sale of six German gunboats to Angola, ostensibly to bolster its border control and peacekeeping capacities.

China remained one of the country's most important economic partners: several visits by Chinese ministers to Luanda underscored the role of Angola, which remained China's main supplier of crude oil and among its most important African trading partners. China's role in Angola's infrastructure reconstruction drive remained evident; amongst other things, construction work on a planned new international airport for Luanda was taken up again in the Bom Jesus area, near Bengo province. Most investments, however, bypassed official channels and were handled between the Angolan president's office and the opaque Chinese Investment Fund (CIF), raising renewed concerns regarding corruption, mismanagement, and poor construction standards. In 2011, Angola also became **India**'s main oil supplier and total trade grew by almost 20% compared with the previous year.

Besides these more established partners, trade – mainly in the form of oil exports and commodity and imports – increased with Norway and the Netherlands, as well as **Russia**. Two visits by the presidential special counsellor for African cooperation, Mikhail Margelov, in July and December served to reinforce cooperation agreements in the finance and energy sectors. Also, on 28 March, the minister of education met with his Vietnamese counterpart, as part of the fifth session of the Angola/**Vietnam** bilateral commission, and they discussed the extension of Vietnam's support in the education sector, notably for teacher training.

Socioeconomic Developments

Angola's economy remained overwhelmingly dependent on oil, with production standing at around 1.7 m b/d, making up about 90% of export revenue and about 75% of tax revenues. Thus, after a slump in world oil prices, the government and the IMF had to adjust their initially optimistic **GDP growth** predictions from 7.1% and 6.5%, respectively, to a more realistic 3.7% in October. Nonetheless, this was a slight increase over the previous year's 3.4%, and the **oil sector** itself progressed: in January, the government awarded exploration licences for new, ultra-deepwater, 'pre-salt' blocks to several foreign operators, including Total and ConocoPhillips but, as the tender was never made public, details of the deals remained unknown. In September, state oil company Sonangol and Total started production in the new Pazflor development in block 17 and, in December, the Norwegian Statoil was awarded operating rights in several of the pre-salt blocks.

However, the oil sector was still characterised by pervasive **non-transparency**. In March, TI cited Sonangol as one of the world's eight most corrupt oil companies, and in December, HRW published government accounts that revealed a $ 32 bn hole in the oil revenues. This was quite a substantial discrepancy, if compared with the country's total debt of $ 29.9 bn, declared by the finance minister in June, or its foreign exchange reserves, which stood at around $ 24 bn at the end of the year. Also, in November, after reviewing Angola's progress, the IMF disbursed the fourth, fifth and sixth tranches of the 2009 $ 1.4 bn standby agreement, bringing the total sum to $ 1.21 bn, noting, however, that there were still improvements to be made in transparency. In turn, the Angolan government refused an additional IMF loan of $ 400 m in June, saying it did not need the money; observers said the refusal was probably intended to avoid greater scrutiny of the public finances.

The government's second main source of revenue was the **diamond** industry. The state mining company Endiama reported a 9% growth in production over the previous year to an estimated total value of $ 3.7 bn. The government also introduced a reform of the mining code in June, which was aimed at removing some of the legal obstacles inherent in previous legislation by unifying the relevant laws in one legal statute. Whereas the old law stipulated three different licences for prospecting, exploration and commercialisation, the new law bundled these three phases into one licence, thereby simplifying the process and guaranteeing that the prospecting company would have the right to explore and sell the product. Moreover, the government also introduced a 25%–30% tax on industrial profits, and 3%–5% royalties, adjusted according to the size of the concession, and announced the introduction of licences for artisanal miners, ostensibly to combat illegal mining and clandestine immigration. However, the sector was still characterised by rampant human rights abuses and opaque business links with Angola's ruling elite. Almost all mining operations were joint ventures between Endiama, foreign operators such as Ascorp and Lev Leviev, and Angolan private companies mainly owned by the president's family and powerbrokers such as General França Ndalu, who was also the president of De Beers Angola.

Although still recovering from the war, which had left large tracts of land mined and unusable, **agriculture** was one of the fastest-growing sectors, thanks to public and private stimuli, including by the Development Bank of Angola, and substantial investment in agro-industrial projects. The domestic beverage industry continued to grow, as did the importation of luxury goods such as cars, clothes, spirits and household electronics.

The government introduced a series of measures to diversify the economy, broaden its tax base, and combat inflation and capital flight: on 26 October, the governor of the National Bank of Angola, Jose de Lima Massano, announced new legislation obliging oil companies to use local banks and local currency to make tax payments, payments to overseas suppliers and subcontractors, and other transactions, in order to boost foreign reserves and stabilise the national currency, the kwanza. In the World Bank's Doing Business report, Angola significantly improved in terms of registering property and dealing with construction permits, but nevertheless fell by one rank to 163rd out of 183 surveyed countries.

Housing remained one of Angola's fastest-growing sectors. The government, which had promised the construction of one million **social houses** by 2012, nonetheless found itself pressed to justify its progress. While forced evictions from poorer central neighbourhoods continued in Luanda and several provincial capitals, the promised new homes failed to meet expectations. The new 'model city' of Luanda, the 'Nova Centralidade do Kilamba', located on the south-eastern periphery of the capital, was inaugurated by the president in July with large parts still unfinished. The new neighbourhood, built by the Chinese company Citic, was planned to include nine primary and eight secondary schools, crèches, shops, car parks, and water, electricity and waste water management facilities. The project came under fire when it was revealed that the management of the sales would be handled by a private Sonangol subsidiary, with prices ranging from $ 175,000 to $ 250,000 per apartment, far in excess of the initially announced $ 25,000 to $ 50,000, and hardly affordable for social housing units.

Infrastructure reconstruction continued throughout the country: in May, the president inaugurated the new Kianda bridge, linking the Luanda Marginal with the Ilha do Cabo peninsula, which greatly improved the chaotic traffic flows of the inner city. In January, the Luanda Railway reopened its first passenger service to Malange after an 18-year interruption due to the war. On 30 August, the rail link from Benguela to Huambo was reopened after the partial upgrading of the Benguela Railway, while construction work on the southern Moçâmedes Railway was almost concluded by December, according to Transport Minister Augusto Tomás.

Socio-economic indicators continued to belie Angola's economic growth. Despite a nominal per capita GDP of $ 5,278 per year, youth unemployment was rampant and two-thirds of the population, estimated at between 15 m and 18 m people, lived on under $ 2 a day. The country also remained the world's worst in terms of infant mortality, with 175.9 deaths under the age of one per 1,000 live births, outranking perhaps more obvious candidates such as Afghanistan and Niger. WHO reported that 27.5% of children under five were underweight, while the malaria mortality rate stood at 89 per 100,000 people, slightly better than the Sub-Saharan Africa average of 94. HIV-prevalence amongst adults remained at 2%, low for the region, although this figure was probably the result of insufficient data and under-reporting. In Luanda, as well as in Cunene province, along the main transport corridors from Namibia, prevalence was as high as 25%, according to independent sources. Life expectancy slightly improved to 51.1 years. Access to clean drinking water remained low, at 50% of the population, although the figure was considerably lower for rural populations, at 23%.

After a revision of the **state budget**, estimated at $ 45.57 bn, expenditure on health and education was reduced by over 5% from the previous year, to 2% and 2.6% of GDP, respectively – while military and public security expenditure rose slightly, to 7% of GDP. Two Angolan NGOs, 'Acção para o Desenvolvimento Rural e Ambiente' and 'Observatório Político Social de Angola', published a critical report on the budget in an effort to improve accountability and the transparency of the budgeting process. They pointed out, for example, that, although the budget stipulated higher spending in the provinces, experience showed that most funding went to Luanda, while some extra social spending was allocated to Cabinda province. The **regional imbalance** was nowhere more marked than in a direct comparison between the two neighbouring provinces of Cabinda and Zaire. Both contribute significantly to Angola's oil production but, while the government kept investing in infrastructure in Cabinda to appease secessionist tendencies, the population of Zaire complained about neglect, poverty and roads in a state of disrepair. Equally, while the national literacy rate was given as 70%, the bishop of Moxico warned in November that the illiteracy rate in the remote eastern province had reached 80%, and that, despite all the church's appeals, there was no funding for literacy education. Nationwide, the average time spent in school education for the population over 25 remained at 4.4 years. The health and education sectors continued to be hampered by a lack of skilled staff, although the return of Cuban medical staff and teachers helped redress the situation somewhat.

Despite the adverse circumstances and the still frequent shortages of electricity and water, Luanda saw the advancement of an emergent, still small and fragile **middle class**. New shops opened and people pursued small business ventures, such as the increasingly popular hot-dog and burger stalls, and there were visible signs of housing improvements arising from private initiatives. And although access to higher education was still limited by the low number of student places and high fees, many young urban Angolans managed to enrol in university or training courses offered by private companies, such as banks.

Jon Schubert

Botswana

This was an interesting year on the domestic political landscape. Despite the first split to rock the ruling Botswana Democratic Party (BDP), which led to the formation of the Botswana Movement for Democracy (BMD) in 2010, the BDP remained a major dominant force. In line with the principles that informed its foreign policy, Botswana continued to make its voice heard on the international stage on matters of democracy, good governance and human rights. Its economy, highly vulnerable to external shocks, showed strong signs of recovery from the global financial crisis. The country continued to be plagued by some social ills, particularly HIV/AIDS, which remained a priority concern.

Domestic Politics

The year marked 45 years of continuous rule by the BDP. However, it was less tumultuous than 2010, when the party split for the first time in its history. The **BDP Congress** that took place on 8–11 July in Mahalapye was the first since the formation of the BMD. Instead of holding elections for positions on the party's central committee, the BDP opted for a compromise list to be compiled from which the party's central/executive committee would be appointed. This was in part because elections were regarded as conflict-ridden. Even then, there were some influential members whose preference prior to the Congress was for elections to determine membership of the party's executive committee. One such was Kentse Rammidi, former assistant minister and BDP MP for Kanye North. He resigned his cabinet position to stand as secretary-general of the party, and was appointed to that office through a compromise list at the July 2011 Congress. The BDP suffered a major set-back when Rammidi resigned from the party on 17 August and later joined the Botswana National Front (BNF). Rammidi cited lack of inner party democracy within the BDP as a reason for his departure. He also criticised President Ian Khama's draconian laws on alcohol, the alcohol levy, and his lack of interests in handling civil servants' issues on the grounds that they were unpopular and devoid of public interest. Another senior member of the party, long-time party chairman and senior cabinet minister Ponatshego Kedikilwe, announced he would retire from active politics in 2014.

The **BMD inaugural congress** took place from 29 April to 2 May. Gomolemo Motswaledi was elected as president, defeating the party spokesperson Sydney Pilane. Botsalo Ntuane (leader of the opposition) was elected as vice president. Guma Moyo, a founder member of the BMD, did not stand for an executive committee position and later resigned from the party to become an independent MP. He explained that he wanted to retire from active politics at the next general elections and concentrate on his businesses. The BDP relentlessly tried to persuade Guma to return to its ranks, a move calculated to spite the opposition and gain political mileage amongst Batswana voters, who were openly beginning to question the party's policies.

Opposition parties were in motion: A former BDP MP, Tawana Moremi, joined the BMD. This brought members of the BMD in parliament to six, the same as the BNF, while the Botswana Congress Party (BCP) had five. An agreement within the opposition bloc, however, allowed Botsalo Ntuane of the BMD to remain as leader of the opposition, with an understanding that the position would alternate between the BMD and the BNF as the two had an equal number of parliamentary seats. Since its formation, the BMD had lost three MPs (Patrick Masimolole, Phillip Makgalemele and Guma Moyo), who went back to the BDP. A major political issue was the holding of opposition talks termed the 'Umbrella', which explored possible cooperation between the BCP, BMD, BNF and Botswana Peoples Party. The discussions were complex, and facilitated through the Committee for the Strengthening of Democracy, led by Lebang Mpotokwane and Emang Maphanyane. The talks collapsed on 22 December over disagreements on constituency allocation.

Another controversial issue was the growing tension between Kgosi Kgafela Kgafela, the paramount chief of **Bakgatla**, and the government. The tension forced Minister of Local Government Lebonaamang Mokalake to cancel a meeting with Oodi residents in Kgatleng after the Bakgatla tribe refused to welcome him to their *kgotla*. Kgafela and some members of the tribal leadership faced charges of flogging people and meting out punishment to wrongdoers and social delinquents without due process of law. The tension continued to unfold when Kgafela made an application to the High Court for the

Constitution of Botswana to be set aside, claiming that it was a fraudulent document enacted in 1966 without any input from Batswana. Kgafela's uneasy relationship with the government disrupted the roll-out of government programmes and prevented government ministers from holding meetings in the Kgatleng District. As a result, on 28 October, the government withdrew its recognition of Kgafela as paramount chief of Bakgatla, although he and his tribe maintained that he was the chief of the area. Mokalake was later moved to the ministry of lands and housing.

Issues affecting the **Basarwa/San**, an indigenous minority (also referred to as 'Bushmen'), continued to make headlines. On 28 January, a five-man bench of Court of Appeal judges ruled in favour of Central Kalahari Game Reserve (CKGR) residents who had sought legal redress following the government's refusal to allow them to either sink a borehole in the reserve or use an existing one at Mothomelo (previously used by De Beers in mineral exploration). The court agreed with the argument raised by the Basarwa that lack of access to water in the reserve caused untold suffering and despair, given the harsh climatic conditions in the Kalahari Desert. The judges declared that Basarwa had the right both to re-commission the borehole at Mothomelo in the CKGR and to sink one or more boreholes at any suitable site within the reserve, at their own expense. Furthermore, the court directed that water abstracted from any such borehole be used for domestic purposes only in accordance with Section 6 of the Botswana Water Act. It remained the responsibility of the Basarwa to service, repair and maintain in good working order any borehole from which they drew water as a result of the court action. However, the court also ordered that, before the borehole at Mothomelo was re-commissioned or any new borehole was sunk, the requisite notice had to be given to the Department of Geological Surveys pursuant to Section 4 of the Borehole Act. During the relocation court case of 2006, the court had held that the Basarwa were "lawful occupiers of the CKGR", and so the Court of Appeal ruled that the Basarwa had an inherent right to sink a borehole within the reserve from which to extract water for domestic purposes.

Another issue that shook the BDP government was a national **public sector strike**. On 10 April, civil servants, led by their umbrella union, the Botswana Federation of Public Sector Unions (BOFEPUSU), embarked on a national strike, demanding a 16% salary rise. The government initially refused any salary increase and threatened to dismiss all essential service workers who participated in the strike in an attempt to cushion the impact of the strike on the health sector and other emergency services. The strike brought most public services, schools and some health centres to a near collapse. The striking civil servants blamed Khama's government for being dictatorial and indifferent to their plight. On realizing the mayhem the prolonged strike was causing, the government responded by offering the workers a 3% salary increment across the board. The workers did not accept the offer but suspended the strike, which had lasted for two months instead of the planned ten days. During the strike, the main opposition parties actively supported the workers and gave voice to their plight in parliament, public ('freedom') squares and council meetings.

In line with the BOFEPUSU model, which brought unions together in a common cause, the major opposition parties formed an 'umbrella' coalition, referred to above, with the aim of unseating the ruling BDP. The BOFEPUSU leadership pledged that its members would only support a united opposition in the 2014 general elections.

While still regarded as the least corrupt country in Africa, allegations of **corruption** against public servants in high government positions continued. Two cases were that of the Minister of Finance and Development Planning Kenneth Mathambo, and that of Minister of Defence, Justice and Security Ramadeluka Seretse. Mathambo was charged with corruption in May. It was reported that, while he was managing director of the public Botswana Development Cooperation (BDC), an investment arm of the government, he had failed to disclose his interest in Tuwana Construction Company, which had dealings with the BDC when it built him a house. Unlike Seretse, who resigned his cabinet position in 2010 when charged with corruption, Mathambo resisted public pressure to resign from his ministerial post. This was against principles of good governance whereby ministers facing charges including corruption would resign from their positions to clear their names. Mathambo's acquittal by a senior magistrate at the end of November followed that of Seretse, who was acquitted in October. Seretse, a cousin of the president, was alleged to have failed to disclose his interests to the president when his family's company had business dealings with the Botswana Police Service, a department that fell directly under his ministry. The anti-corruption body was headed by a relative of the president.

Foreign Policy

In line with its foreign policy, which espouses principles of **good governance**, human rights, rule of law and democracy, Botswana strongly criticised the governments of Egypt, Libya and Syria, amongst others, for violently repressing mass protests. However, Botswana was not consistent in this as it refrained from criticising King Mswati of Swaziland, another autocratic leader.

Botswana continued to enjoy cordial relations with the **USA**, which were reinforced by the visit of American First Lady Michelle Obama on 24 June. She reiterated President Barack Obama's recognition of the importance of Africa to the world and had discussions with Khama on conservation issues, HIV/AIDS and youth leadership, key themes she was promoting in Africa as part of a goodwill mission.

A number of **royal visitors** paid a visit during the year. King Carl XVI Gustav of Sweden visited on 22–25 March and commended Botswana for its transformation from being one of the world's poorest countries to a middle-income economy. Another prominent visitor was the UK's Princess Anne, whose visit was intended to reinforce the friendship and good cooperation between the governments of Botswana and the **United Kingdom**. This was her third visit to the country. During her two-day visit on 4–5 July, she had an audience with Khama and visited a number of charitable and community projects.

Princess Anne, a former British Olympian in 1976 and president of the British Olympic Association, also spoke with members of the Botswana National Olympic Committee and several Olympic aspirants.

A diplomatic row with **South Africa** was narrowly avoided after Julius Malema, president of the African National Congress Youth League (ANCYL) called on 31 July for regime change in Botswana, accusing the Botswana government for being an American puppet. Malema and some members of the ANCYL later faced disciplinary hearings and were suspended from the ANC, which avoided any further damage to bilateral relations.

Socioeconomic Developments

Because of the nature of its economy, which is heavily dependent on diamonds and highly vulnerable to external shocks, Botswana was one of the countries seriously affected by the global financial crisis. However, positive signs of **economic recovery** were recorded, as its GDP grew by 7.8% in real terms during the third quarter of 2011. According to the 2012 budget speech, preliminary estimates suggested a deficit of BWP (pula) 2 bn, lower than the BWP 5.1 bn forecast in 2010 for the financial year 2011/2012, largely because of a recovery in world diamond prices and SACU revenues. Foreign reserves stood at BWP 61.7 bn by the end of November against BWP 50.8 bn in December 2010. This positive growth may be reversed if there is a double-dip world recession.

The economy continued to attract **positive ratings**. Standard and Poor's and Moody's maintained a positive credit rating and Moody's changed the country's sovereign ratings from negative to stable. Similarly, the World Bank's 2011 'Doing Business Report' ranked Botswana third in Africa and 52nd out of 183 countries surveyed. However, the report noted a number of challenges that negatively affected business. **Inflation** continued to be a challenge in the Botswana economy, as it still stood above the target set by the Bank of Botswana. It stood at 9.2% in December, up from 7.4% a year before.

Although Botswana was rated a middle-income country, **socio-economic challenges** included poverty, unemployment and inequality. The national unemployment rate stood at 17.8% in the Botswana Core Welfare Indicators (Poverty) Survey of 2009/10 released in December. The same survey put poverty at 20.7%, down from 30.6% in 2002/2003. The population increased to 2,038,228, according to the Population and Housing Census of 2011, an annual increase of 1.9% from 1,680,863 in 2001.

HIV/AIDS remained another challenge, and threatened to reverse the gains the country had achieved since independence. The HIV prevalence rate, at 17.6%, was one of the highest in the region. The government, in collaboration with several partners, has put in place measures to mitigate the effects of HIV/AIDS.

David Sebudubudu & Maitseo Bolaane

Lesotho

The ruling Lesotho Congress for Democracy (LCD) continued to be gripped by the factionalism that had divided it since 2008. While political turmoil reflected the declining ability of the political class to control events, minimal challenge was provided by the numerous opposition parties, which were themselves rent by internal rivalries , and few of which offered any coherent alternative programmes. In contrast, the Patriotic Front for Democracy (PFD), although small and predominantly urban, continued to promote a left-leaning programme that looked for closer political ties with South Africa. However, by the end of the year, even the PFD had a rival in the newly formed African Unity Movement (AUM), which looked for a "special relationship with the Republic of South Africa which (might) lead to the formation of a union or unitary state".

Domestic Politics

Prime Minister Pakalitha Mosisili, who had inherited the leadership of the LCD in 1997, had led the party to successive election victories in 1998, 2002 and 2007. The last two elections had been secured under a reformed mixed member proportional representation (MMP) electoral system, which sought to address opposition parties' protests about their lack of representation as a result of the imbalance in parliamentary seats that emerged under the previous Westminster-style First Past the Post System (FPTP). MMP secured the opposition parties a proportionate presence in an expanded 120-seat parliament, but the functioning of the electoral system became a matter of perpetual dispute. Although it dominated parliament, there were **divisions in the LCD** and challenges to Mosilili's authority. A break-away group of MPs had formed the All Basotho Convention (ABC) in 2006, and this forced the LCD into a marriage of convenience with the National Independence Party for the 2007 elections, which it won with a much reduced majority. The LCD then became openly split between two factions. The first, 'Lija-mollo' (the fire-eaters), was led by Minister of Natural Resources Monyane Moleleki, the second, 'Litima-mollo' (the fire-extinguishers), by Minister of Communications, Science and Technology Mothejoa Metsing, with Mosisili presiding awkwardly over a deeply divided cabinet. Both factions wanted Mosisili to step aside, for this was essentially a battle for the succession far more than it was about competing visions for Lesotho's future. However, Mosisili, who maintained his grip on the machinery of government, proved reluctant to withdraw from the fray without guarantees of his personal security and comfortable retirement.

A signal that Mosisili was looking ahead was given by the passing of the Prime Minister and Deputy Prime Minister (Retirement and Spouses' Benefit) Bill in January. This granted the prime minister and Deputy Prime Minister Lesao Lehohla (who was also minister of home affairs and public safety) 80% of their basic salaries in **retirement**; an annual allowance for the prime minister's wife of M 357,994 with a pension of 70% of this amount; and, for the prime minister and deputy prime minister, free telephone, water, electricity, gardener and housemaid, along with other benefits such as chauffeurs, bodyguards and free medical care. Whilst apparently opening the door for Mosisili's retirement, the Act simultaneously raised the possibility that ministers and MPs would lobby for the granting of similar benefits, a burden that a deeply troubled economy would find difficult to bear.

Although the LCD was internally divided, this was no barrier to the apparent conclusion to the long running dispute about the **electoral system** that had followed the 2007 election. This had revolved around the spirit of MMP being undermined by the LCD and the ABC by their forming alliances with smaller parties which could only gain admission to parliament via the proportional representation contest (held alongside FPTP). This in effect allowed the larger parties to gain more representation in parliament than their proportion of the vote would allow. The resultant bitter disputes had defied attempted resolution and resulted in the formation of an Opposition Parties Forum, which had succeeded in persuading the government to concede to further dialogue under the chairmanship of retired Anglican bishop, Philip Mokuku. These efforts culminated in an announcement on 28 April that the opposition parties, the LCD, the government and the Independent Electoral Commission had consented to a process of reform that would see the Constitution and Electoral Acts being reviewed to incorporate changes agreed within the two-year mediation process.

Subsequently, Parliament passed a Sixth Amendment to the **Constitution Act** 2011 (gazetted in June), whose major provisions were three-fold. First, whereas previously only individuals qualified to vote, or the Attorney General, had had the right to challenge the nomination of a parliamentary candidate or the designation of a senator, the Act now allowed a political party to do so. This tackled an anomaly whereby a challenge to the 2007 election by the Marematlou Freedom Party had been thrown out by the High Court on the technical ground that the party did not have the status required to raise a challenge. The Act also allowed that challenges denied by the High Court could now be taken to the Court of Appeal. Second, although the previous situation had provided for national referenda to be held to change certain clauses of the Constitution, the Act now enabled the king, upon the advice of the prime minister, to order that a referendum be held to ascertain the opinion of electors on any issues deemed to be of national interest. This device was perhaps intended to ensure that the sort of impasse that had paralysed the political system since 2007 could be avoided by direct appeal to the people. Third, a new addition to the Constitution was the establishment of a Human Rights Commission. Meanwhile, a parallel legislative process saw the passing of the National Assembly Electoral Act 2011, which, amongst other matters, allowed for political parties to petition the High Court regarding the allocation of seats under proportional representation. Even so, opposition parties complained that the Act failed to reflect the reforms that had been agreed on.

The major subsequent electoral development was the release of a **State of the Voters' Roll** as at July, prepared by R.W. Johnson, an independent electoral expert, who had previously exposed shortcomings in the Zimbabwean electoral roll. Johnson's report for Lesotho now revealed that the voters' roll had been inflated by some 100,000 'ghost voters' (people who had died but who had miraculously retained the capacity to vote).

Whilst re-inflaming debates about the previous elections, this more immediately set the scene for the forthcoming **local elections**, which had been repeatedly postponed to enable the passing of legislation to revise local government boundaries. The elections were set for 1 October under a new electoral system that allocated one-third of the seats to women by party on a proportional representation basis, requiring that voters be provided with two ballot papers (one for party lists, and one for councillor positions elected by FPTP). When eventually held, the elections were for a reduced number of local councils, down from 129 to 77 (66 community councils and 11 urban councils). Contests were not held in some 27 electoral divisions in which the LCD was the only party to nominate candidates, and the turnout was low (generally between 20% and 45%, but as little as 9% in key areas such as Maseru). The LCD won majorities in single-member contests in 69 out of the 77 councils, the ABC winning similar victories in three, the Basotho National Party in two, and the PFD in one.

It is not clear how the results of the local government elections reflected the standing of the **LCD's two factions**, although the disunity within the party was such that it was unable to agree on an election manifesto. What is clear, however, is that the divisions within the party continued unabated. The LCD was scheduled to hold an elective conference in January 2012, but this never took place, each side blaming the other. By now, it was widely predicted that the party would split in the lead-up to the forthcoming general elections in May 2012, and it was apparent that the established political players would be faced by the new challenge of the AUM. The AUM was seeking to capitalise upon the inspiration provided by the Lesotho People's Charter Movement, which in 2010 collected some 30,000 signatures on a petition for free border movement between the two countries that was presented to both the Lesotho Parliament and the South African High Commission.

In the lead-up to the 2010 FIFA world cup, South Africa had tightened its borders and had subsequently never relaxed its grip. This resulted in huge queues at border posts, especially at Maseru Bridge, used by thousands of commuters. (Many better-off Basotho and expatriates working in Lesotho have chosen to live in the small town of Ladybrand some 12 km inside South Africa.) The AUM, as the **new party**, called for harmonisation of the immigration and labour laws, possibly including adoption of a common identity card; free movement of people and goods across borders, allowing citizens of South Africa and Lesotho to legally live and work in both countries; and amendment of Lesotho's constitution to allow for dual citizenship. However, for all that the AUM was addressing a matter of increasing concern to huge numbers of Lesotho citizens, its electoral prospects were clouded by its apparent theft of the ideological clothes of the PFD and its opening itself to attack by the political class, which feared any hint of a threat to the independence of Lesotho.

Foreign Affairs

Libya is one of just five countries (the others being China, Ireland, South Africa and the USA) with full diplomatic representation in Maseru. Foreign diplomacy did not therefore rank very high on Lesotho's agenda. Amidst the political conflict in **Libya**, Lesotho's diplomatic representatives were evacuated from Tripoli, arriving back in Maseru on 28 February. The Lesotho ministry of foreign affairs informed Kadhafi's representative in Maseru that Lesotho supported the initiatives of the AU, EU and UN to enable a return to peace and normalcy.

Great Britain, the former colonial power, announced that it would no longer provide aid, as the Cameron government sought to slash public spending. In recent years, British aid had been running at about R 70 m per year. Given that significant numbers of doctors and nurses from Lesotho now work in Britain, it would seem that Lesotho is about to become a de facto aid donor to the UK.

Socioeconomic Developments

The **budget** for the 2011/12 financial year, presented to parliament by Finance Minister Timothy Thahane on 14 February, proposed a total expenditure of M 12,919 m (up by 23% from 2010/11), with recurrent expenditure increasing by 19% from M 6,906 m to M 8,201 m. Budgeted capital expenditure was increased by 32%, from M 3,570 m to M 4,709 m. Even allowing for estimated revenue from domestic sources, development partners and international borrowing, this would mean a record budget deficit of M 2,712 m.

Thahane highlighted that, during 2010/11, there had been a 50% reduction in receipts from SACU and an overall 30% decline in domestic revenue. Agriculture had continued to decline from 4.8% of GDP in 2000/01 to just 1.8% in 2009/10; mining had increased from 0.2% of GDP in 2000/01 to 8.1% in 2007/08; manufacturing, the principal sector of employment, had fallen from 20.6% of GDP in 2002/03 to 14% in 2009/10 as a result of Lesotho's loss of preferential treatment as a 'least developed country' under the Multi-Fibre Agreement and consequent increased Asian competition. Construction, whose contribution to GDP had fluctuated with the various stages of the Lesotho Highlands Water Project (LHWP), had declined to 4.5% of GDP in 2009/10. Fortunately, the award of a $ 85 m contract in August to the Sinohydro Corporation of China for the construction of the Metolong Dam, as part of Phase II of the LHWP, promised something of a recovery of the construction sector in the near future.

A surprising development was the appointment in August of Masupha Sole to the joint Lesotho and South African **Lesotho Highlands Water Commission**, which will be responsible for the implementation of Phase II of the LHWP. Sole had only just been released from jail after serving nine years of an 18–year sentence on 13 counts of fraud and bribery in relation to his performance as chief executive of the Lesotho Highlands Development Authority. This caused concern in South Africa, where the minister of water affairs indicated that that country's government would seek legal advice on whether Sole's appointment could be challenged.

Sole's appointment was an indicator of a growing malaise at wider **corruption and institutional decline**. This extended right up to the prime minister's office, where in February five senior officials were suspended under suspicion of having manipulated tender procedures to favour companies with which they allegedly had connections. Other major pointers were the release of a report by the African Police Civilian Oversight Forum, which indicated extensive corruption, theft and misconduct within the Lesotho Mounted Police, and the release to the press of a hard-hitting report by the new vice chancellor of the National University, Professor Sharon Siverts, which highlighted extensive financial maladministration over decades alongside non-performance of their duties by many academic staff.

Siverts' drive for institutional reform encountered resistance by the Lesotho University Teachers' and Researchers' Union (LUTARU), which combined an end to the restructuring exercise with a call for a 15% pay rise (beyond the 10% increase agreed in December 2010). LUTARU embarked on a strike on 7 October, which was transformed within a matter of days into a lock-out, with the **University** closing the campus and requiring students to leave. On 28 November, the University Council announced that the University would re-open on 28 December, with staff being required to sign a declaration that they would agree to return to work. Subsequently, parliament passed a National University of Lesotho (Amendment) Bill, which brought the University into line with national labour legislation and significantly increased the powers of the administration to discipline university employees.

Revised figures released by the ministry of finance indicated that Lesotho's **population** was smaller than had previously been thought. Whereas previous official figures had reported a population of 2.5 m in 2007, new estimates indicated a population of just under 1.9 m in 2009.

Roger Southall

Madagascar

Andry Rajoelina, President of the High Authority for the Transition, was in a vastly different position from a year earlier. On the one hand, he was struggling to find new sources of revenue. On the other, he had successfully solidified his hold on power while resisting the compromise sought by international mediation efforts. Prime Minister General Albert Camille Vital, remained a deeply controversial figure in the eyes of opposition parties and the international community, but was pivotal in keeping the military in line and creating new opportunities to profit from Madagascar's natural resources. The peace negotiations among the four living heads of state – Andry Rajoelina, Marc Ravalomanana, Didier Ratsiraka, and Zafy Albert – had failed and Rajoelina's new challenges were internal. Yet, for the Malagasy people the situation continued to worsen, with poverty figures skyrocketing and humanitarian initiatives disintegrating.

Domestic Politics

Andry Rajoelina seized power on 18 March 2009 as a 33-year-old business tycoon with one year of political experience as mayor of the capital, Antananarivo. The political opposition to the ousted president, Marc Ravalomanana, was resolute but deeply fragmented. He subverted the legislature in favour of a 44-member High Authority of the Transition comprised of political operatives from across the ethnic, geographic and power spectrums and retained power by dividing the spoils of office. The opposition movements of former presidents Didier Ratsiraka and Zafy Albert became almost irrelevant and the supporters of the elected president, Ravalomanana, had rights without authority or power.

Rajoelina's power to act unilaterally was demonstrated in his postponement of **elections**. The Constitution of the Fourth Republic was written by a team led by Rajoelina supporters. It cleverly took into account key areas of constitutional design that the international community had marked as missing from the previous constitution, but the final version obfuscated regional jurisdictions while creating a near-imperial presidency. The timing of elections, though articulated in the new electoral code of 11 March 2010, appeared to have fallen to the president. Rajoelina initially announced there would be legislative elections in March 2010. This was revised to September 2010 and then to March 2011, but by year's end there had been neither parliamentary nor presidential elections and no clear date was set.

Rajoelina's power to act unilaterally was also visible in his dealings with international **conflict mediation**. In February, after multiple failed attempts, the SADC mediation team, led by chief mediator Leonardo Simao and the head of the mediation team, former president of Mozambique Joaquim Chissano, presented a new peace roadmap. It was signed by the Rajoelina government and seven opposition parties on 9 March. The significant shift in the roadmap was that it recognised the ascendancy of Rajoelina while abandoning the four movements approach. Under the agreement, Rajoelina remained president for a transition period but shared cabinet positions under an appointed consensus prime minister. In exchange, the international community would confer international recognition on Rajoelina and support elections. To its supporters, the roadmap was a mechanism for recognising the realities of power, while to its detractors, it was rewarding an increasingly autocratic rogue who came to power through a coup d'état. The signatories did not include any of the three other major movements that had participated in the previous mediation efforts.

The roadmap was rejected by the SADC Troika. The primary sticking point was the **return of Ravalomanana** to Madagascar from self-imposed exile in South Africa. Fearing fresh conflict, the roadmap stated that he would return when the security situation stabilised. The SADC Troika supported Ravalomanana's right to return and a new round of negotiations, led by SADC and supported by a UN technical team. After significant negotiations with Rajoelina, the right of return was added to the roadmap. This won the signature of the Ravalomanana camp as well as the camp of Zafy Albert, the majority of significant political movements that had hitherto lacked international recognition, and civil society leaders who had been party to the talks. The new roadmap was signed on 17 September, but there were immediate disagreements over its interpretation. The roadmap gave Ravalomanana the right to return unconditionally. It also stated that necessary legal instruments, including an amnesty law, would be urgently developed. It did not, however, explicitly state that Ravalomanana would have the right to amnesty under that law. (He had been convicted in absentia for his role in the killing of protestors by his presidential guard in February 2009.) Rajoelina stated that, although Ravalomanana could return, he could still be arrested, while Ravalomanana clearly thought that return meant amnesty. A statement by the SADC Troika declared that the implementation modalities were intended to be elaborated after the signing.

The roadmap did make clear that a new government was mandatory, with key posts shared by opposition leaders and a **new consensus prime minister** appointed. On 2 November, Prime Minister General Albert Camille Vital was removed in favour of Jean Omer Beriziky, the candidate of former president Zafy Albert. Former president Didier Ratsiraka, a long-time political opponent of both Zafy and Ravalomanana, rejected the appointment of Beriziky and the roadmap. On 24 November, Ratsiraka returned to Madagascar after nine years exile in France but, given his advanced age and questionable domestic support, he was not viewed as a potent threat. Zafy and Ravalomanana accepted the new prime minister and their nominees took key ministerial posts in a new government. By the end of the year, it became clear that Beriziky was preparing to **run for president**. In order to do so, he needed to turn to the Leader Fanilo party and the l'Union des Démocrates et Républicains pour le Changement (UDR-C), which were both at odds with Rajoelina. The compromise candidate began to look less innocuous and more of a potential threat.

Civil society remained divided. Large gaps divided leadership and its constituent organisations, as civil society leadership, nominally held under the umbrella of the National Coordination of Civil Society Organisations, was divided over the road map. The **private sector** was more likely to impact on Malagasy politics than civil society. Both Ravalomanana and Rajoleina were ethnically *merina*, from the capital region, and both rose to power as part of the new business elite. As Ravalomanana was increasingly viewed as blending the interests of his private corporation, the Tiko Group, with his political interests, he lost the strong support he once enjoyed in the private sector. Rajoelina benefited from this shift by gaining the support of important private sector operators such as Edgard Razafindravahy, CEO of the Prey Group. In 2009, Razafindravahy became President of the Special Delegation (a mayoral appointment) of Antananarivo. In January, his ascendancy came under threat but in April he announced that he would run for mayor when there were municipal elections. Many saw him as a potential presidential candidate. While individuals were to benefit, the roadmap did little to unite a private sector desperately seeking stability.

Foreign Affairs

Madagascar's closest ties were historically with the former colonial power, France. During the Ravalomanana presidency, relations diversified and resulted in closer relations with the US, South Africa, Germany, China and South Korea. Ravalomanana was both praised and criticised for bringing Madagascar into the more Anglophone SADC. With pressure from South Africa, the overthrow of Ravalomanana led to the suspension of Madagascar from both SADC and the AU. The US took the hardest diplomatic line. Since there was no opportunity for Rajoelina to build on existing ties, he turned to China and an increasingly complex relationship with France. **China** increasingly looked towards Madagascar for oil rights, precious minerals, and rare earth minerals for use in technology.

France played a commercial, diplomatic and political role. There were 25,000 French nationals in Madagascar, more than in any other AU member state, and 700 French businesses. The stakes rose as diplomatic pressure on France to maintain the EU position on Madagascar increased. At the same time, French President Sarkozy was strongly lobbied by French business interests on behalf of Rajoelina. The Elysée continued independent conversations with Ratsiraka and Rajoelina while international mediation was taking place, but not with the other interlocutors. There was confusion over the role of French diplomatic activity and that of important French business interests. The complex relationship often made it difficult to know the source of statements and funds without an official communiqué.

The rupture between France and the **rest of the international community** became increasingly apparent. In February, a UN technical team was deployed in order to determine the measures necessary to conduct a successful election and how long it would take to implement them. It decided that it would take 11 months to complete a census and put the necessary mechanisms in place, but a study by the OIF concluded that it could be done in four months. Critics within SADC, the AU and the UN argued that this short timeframe would restrict the likelihood of a fair election and produce a result biased in favour of Rajoelina. In December, Rajoelina met with Sarkozy in Paris to discuss the electoral timetable. French representatives were effusive in their support for Rajoelina's change of government following the signing of the roadmap. They expressed support for the roadmap and for Ravalomanana's right to return without prior amnesty. The US walked away from the table and maintained that a return to constitutionality meant a return of Ravalomanana. SADC, the UN and the AU continued to walk a fine line, supporting the roadmap without weighing in on the precise interpretation of amnesty. The spirit of their comments, however, was that Ravalomanana should be able to run for the presidency, but that nothing was assured.

For their part, **donors** maintained their moratorium without going as far as full suspension. The World Bank kept to its Operational Policy 7.30 policy on de facto governments and confirmed that no direct talks could be held with the government and no new spending could be initiated. Nonetheless, a clear softening of positions took place with more conversation and significant anticipation that a new Interim Strategy Note would soon be forthcoming, allowing for a re-engagement and new spending. The year ended with deep fragmentation in the international community, which could only be to the advantage of the increasingly unilateral and autocratic Rajoelina administration, as he continued with his plan towards legitimating his rule through the ballot box.

Socioeconomic Developments

Rajoelina surprised even many of his closest advisors by successfully adopting **austerity measures** that balanced the books, while diversifying revenue streams. At the beginning of the year, it was unclear whether he could sustain this approach. International direct support was effectively zero and private enterprise faced ongoing internal political conflict and external shocks from a weaker global economy. Rajoelina set his then ministers of finance (Hery Rajaonarimampianina), trade (Freddie Mahazoasy) and mining (Mamy Ratovomalala) to the task of increasing revenues. These initiatives were complemented by efforts to monitor and tax international telephone calls, release new telecom tenders and shake up the banking sector. In May, Rajoelina made clear his intention to extend his role in the central bank by reining in its governor. At year's end, the governor's replacement by a political appointee appeared imminent. While Rajoelina succeeded in many of these efforts towards austerity, by December he was far short of the funds necessary to meet the $ 350 m owed to foreign banks.

When the World Bank and the EU, who were leading donors, froze direct support to the government in December 2008, they did so fearful of lack of transparency and accountability in spending. At that time, **donor funding** accounted for approximately 70% of government receipts. With the overthrow of Ravalomanana, there was continued quiet spending on selected existing projects, but no new funding. Donor funding dropped and shifted to UN organisations focused on humanitarian relief and local interventions.

Rajoelina was widely criticised by international donors for the halt in GDP growth. Whereas real GDP was 6.2% in 2007 and 7.1% in 2008 according to the World Bank, it was –3.7% in 2009, growing to 0.5% in 2010 and 1.0% in 2011. Exports recorded an 8.5% growth while imports showed a marked recovery from –18.7% in 2010 to a projected 12.3% growth in 2011. Inflation, projected at 10.3%, remained steady. International reserves also remained steady, but at low levels. This was all indicative of **resilience in the private sector**. Madagascar ranked low in the World Bank's 'Doing Business' indicator (137th of 183 countries in 2011), but made progress in key areas such as trade logistics, even compared with the Ravalomanana boom years. The African Competitiveness Report 2011 and analyses by most independent scholars concurred that improvement in other private sector growth indicators was unlikely to be tied to financial or entrepreneurial exigencies in the short to medium term. The quality of governance, political stability, corruption and deteriorating infrastructure were more serious obstacles. Nowhere was this more apparent than in the bourgeoning mining and oil sectors, where a breakdown in oversight had increased opportunities for politicians to engage in rent-seeking behaviours related to the awarding of permits, the management of contracts, through revenue generation, and the taxes on the revenue generated. The withdrawal of donors aggravated this **governance problem**. Key oversight programmes, notably the World Bank's Projet de Gouvernance des Ressources Minérales and Projet de Gouvernance et de Développement Institutionnel, did not fund the oversight mechanisms adequately. While the public sector unravelled, mining increased from less than 1% of GDP in 2008 to an estimated 15% in 2011.

At the beginning of the year, the Madagascar Development Corporation was formed as a joint venture between the Malagasy state and the **China** International Fund Ltd. In January, Minister of Mines Mamy Ratovomalala engaged more closely with a consortium led by China-Sonangol. A significant effort was made to revoke oil search permits from the US-based Madagascar Oil in favour of China-Sonangol. On 21 March, Madagascar Oil declared a force majeure largely because Prime Minister Vital retained his post and made clear he would push against the company. The China-Sonangol effort built on a $ 100 m agreement entered into the previous year between the Malagasy state and the Chinese company Wisco to extract iron ore from the Soalala region. Sino Union Petroleum & Chemical International Ltd had already purchased the rights to three oil blocks, completing the first three drill tests in the last week of August and demonstrating significant reservoirs. In June, it announced a plan to invest $ 500 m over two years into making the oil fields operational. Other companies concerned with political exposure and risk voluntarily sold interests in Madagascar's fast-growing extractive industries sectors to Chinese interests. In December, Varun Industries sold its stake in an onshore oil block to Da Qing Oil Field Company for $ 150 m. This all demonstrated that, while aggregate trade figures for Madagascar had not been volatile, the nature of the trade itself had been.

The slow growth in the economy was not nearly as severe as during the 2002 crisis in Madagascar, when it shrank to –12%, or as serious as in similar times of crisis elsewhere. It is also difficult to disentangle the impact of Rajoelina's policies from the effects of the political crisis, the withdrawal of aid and the global economic slowdown. What is clear is that there was a significant and critical negative impact on the health and welfare of the Malagasy people. Using the Atlas method, **poverty** levels had increased by 9% since 2005, to encompass 77% of households in 2011. According to the World Development Indicators, this is higher than in any other African country. Perhaps an even greater concern was the substantial difference in poverty levels and opportunities between regions and between rural and urban areas. The highest poverty rate, recorded in Androy, was more than three times higher than the lowest poverty rate, recorded in the capital region of Analamanga. The 2011 Multidimensional Poverty Index ranked Madagascar as the 21st poorest country, but the intensity of the poverty was amongst the worst in the world, with high variations in key indicators such as sanitation, clean water access, electricity access, schooling, income and assets. A UNICEF study of household vulnerability in the capital, Antananarivo, showed that existence was becoming increasingly precarious, with one in three households surviving on less than $ 0.50 per day.

The largest systemic impacts were in the education and health sectors. The National Health Sector and Social Protection Development Plan 2007–2011 were designed in partnership with the World Bank. Key areas of structural funding, including water, transport, energy, communication aid, financial sectors, mining, industry, commerce, employment, tourism, environment and non-allocated budgetary support, dropped precipitously. Spending on health and education grew dramatically, largely outside of the state apparatus, through UN agencies. UN agency efforts had the effect of staving off human catastrophe but also created extensive **aid dependency** and undermined the existing infrastructure.

Richard R. Marcus

Malawi

2011 was the worst year in terms of political and economic governance since President Mutharika came to power in 2004. Mass demonstrations and unrest on 20 July resulted in the death of 18 people. Issues of academic freedom also dominated the political scene, which saw the closure of the University of Malawi's major constituent college for eight months over the interrogation of a political science associate professor by the police. Foreign currency problems and fuel supply shortages reached a climax, with a decrease in revenue from tobacco. Relations with major donors were generally strained. Strikes took place in both the public and private sector.

Domestic Politics

Various controversial **amendments and bills** were introduced during the year. First, the amended section 46 of the Penal Code empowered the information minister to prohibit the publication of any material, or its importation, if the minister had reasonable grounds to believe that such publication or its importation was contrary to the public interest. The Malawi Human Rights Consultative Commission (MHRCC) went to court to challenge the amendment as unconstitutional and therefore invalid, as it contradicted the constitutional provision that guaranteed freedom of the press and respect for human rights. The government argued that it would use the section only in extreme cases, such as child pornography or incitement to violence. Second, the president assented into law the Pension Bill, which omitted pertinent issues. Third, on 17 June, parliament passed the Suits by or Against the Government or Public Officers (Civil Procedures) Bill, and the president assented it into law on 14 July, despite the need to refer it back to the Attorney General as requested by various parties, including members of the governing Democratic People's Party (DPP). Henry Phoya, chairperson of the parliamentary Legal Affairs Committee and DPP's director of legal affairs, and three others were expelled from the party in June for leading the debate against the adoption of the bill, which sought to control the granting of ex parte injunctions against the government by the courts. The civil society organisations (CSOs) that had unsuccessfully applied for an injunction barring the president from assenting it into law argued that the law was unconstitutional in that it denied citizens their right to instant relief when they were victims of injustice. Donors also condemned the move, but the government rebuked them, arguing that it could not bow to cooperating partners' interests. In addition, the fees charged for seeking injunctions were increased from K 60 to K 25,000, a move tantamount to blocking people from obtaining temporary relief in emergency situations.

It was reported on 27 January that government planned to revert to pre-democracy local courts, which would hear civil and minor criminal cases, but which opposition leader John Tembo argued could easily be manipulated by the ruling party. New proposals for legislative amendments included draft impeachment procedures, which would provide for the president or vice president to be removed from office within 30 days of any indictment. On 15 November, MPs adopted a proposal made by the Public Appointments and Declaration of Assets Committee to raise their salaries and benefits from K 390,000 to about K 1 m. The Civil Servants Trade Union warned of a pending civil action if Mutharika endorsed the proposal. On 27 November, it was reported that the opposition parties as well as analysts had requested the review of a constitutional provision that limited state funding to political parties that had secured more than 10% of the votes in parliamentary elections. A possible amendment was being discussed to decrease the 10% requirement, which was viewed as too high and a threat to democracy.

The DPP-led government frustrated the efforts of **new parties**. On 3 January, the government failed to recognise the newly formed People's Development Movement, despite the High Court having declared it duly registered, and the police prohibited it from holding public rallies. It took eight months for the National Salvation Front to be registered, while Vice President Joyce Banda's People's Party presented its registration papers to the office of the Registrar of Political Parties on 5 April but the party was not registered until 28 July, after protracted wrangles. The president's **conflicts with the vice president** reached a climax when the latter was perpetually excluded from cabinet meetings. She was stripped of her responsibilities as NGO co-ordinator and the roles of Goodwill Ambassador for Safe Motherhood and head of the malaria programme, which were transferred to the First Lady, Calista Mutharika. She was also left out of a new cabinet of 32 members, which Mutharika appointed on 7 September, while the First Lady assumed the position of second to the president.

The **opposition parties** were marked by internal conflicts. The United Democratic Front (UDF) was riddled with leadership wrangles. One camp rallied behind Friday Jumbe and another behind George Ntafu. In May, talks aimed at uniting the two factions collapsed due to lack of trust. Further factors were introduced when former president Bakili Muluzi's son, Atupele, declared his interest in standing in the 2014 elections. He was summoned to a disciplinary hearing accused of gross breach of party discipline and total disregard of the party's constitution, and was finally suspended from the party on 2 October. Through its acting president Friday Jumbe and Secretary General Kennedy Makwangala, the UDF asked former president Muluzi to repay the party K 125 m ($ 750,0000) received from donors for party activities. The Malawi Congress Party (MCP) president expelled dissidents and, in September, the MCP national executive committee fired its secretary general Chris Daza for alleged indiscipline after he openly declared he would challenge John Tembo for leadership of the party. On 16 May, Dowa West MP Abele Kayembe, who defeated MCP president John Tembo as leader of the opposition in parliament, crossed the floor to join the ruling DPP.

The government was also in **conflict with civil society organisations** over various governance and economic management issues. On 23 February, the president invited civil society leaders to a meeting in Lilongwe, where he reportedly lost his temper during the deliberations. Consequently, CSOs planned for mass demonstrations, which took place on 20 July, to force Mutharika to solve the many governance and economic management ills. The president organised a public lecture on the same day to discuss related issues. Ahead of the public lecture, an alliance including churches, NGOs and opposition parties indicated that they would boycott the lecture, as it was not going to address the problems facing Malawi. On 19 July, it was reported that the police had assured marchers of protection during the following day's demonstrations. On the same day, DPP Youth cadets roamed the streets aboard the party's pick-up vehicles. Armed with *panga* knives, they threatened CSOs and protesters with consequences if they showed contempt for Mutharika and his administration by demonstrating. The Public Affairs Committee and MHRCC cautioned the government against allowing its sympathisers to oppose the planned civil society demonstrations. On the eve of the protests, a High Court injunction was obtained to stop nationwide demonstrations. This was challenged through an injunction obtained early on the morning of 20 July and people proceeded to demonstrate. There was chaos in Lilongwe, Blantyre, Mzuzu and Zomba, with the government reportedly restricting media coverage of the protests through the Malawi Communications Regulatory Authority (MACRA). Human rights activists, journalists and marchers were beaten and arrested, and 18 people died, allegedly the victims of shooting by the police.

After the demonstrations, CSOs presented a 15-page **petition**, which referred to 20 concerns and possible solutions. These included the First Lady's contract (as the Coordinator of Safe Motherhood for which she was paid close to K 1 m in addition to other fringe benefits for doing voluntary work); foreign currency and fuel shortages; the investigation of MPs and ministers implicated in the Malawi Housing Corporation house sale scam; the selling of the presidential jet; the bloated cabinet; the reinstatement of the four fired lecturers involved in the academic freedom saga at Chancellor College; the use of MBC radio and television as a tool for castigating and threatening dissenters; and provision of drugs in hospitals, among other things. A Presidential Contact and Dialogue Committee was established to facilitate **dialogue between government and civil society** groups over the 20 issues. However, the dialogue was slow and agreements were not respected by the president. CSOs threatened to make an official complaint to the UN, and Mutharika threatened that he was ready to declare war on his critics if they were not ready for the national dialogue he had initiated. Opposition parties and various CSOs warned of more protests if CSOs and political leaders were arrested, as Mutharika had ordered during his remarks on the demonstrations on 22 July. Meanwhile, demonstration leaders suffered a series of attacks: on 24 July Zodiak Broadcasting Station's vehicle was set alight, human rights activist Rafik Hajat's office was petrol bombed and, on 10 September, the house of renowned human rights activist and acting MHRCC national coordinator, Rev. Donald Sembereka was torched. On 24 September, a Malawi Polytechnic student was found dead within the campus, allegedly killed in a politically motivated reprisal. Both local and international partners called for an independent enquiry into the death. Politically motivated fires were also started in three markets within ten days in the country's major cities. These incidents forced CSOs to give up the UN-facilitated dialogue between government and civil society. Further efforts to stifle the freedom of NGOs were noted with the issuing of a directive for all NGOs to submit quarterly returns to the central bank and not to the Council for Non Governmental Organisations in Malawi, as they had done before.

Conflicts between government and the **University of Malawi** lecturers, and between lecturers and their employer, the University of Malawi Council, also made headlines. In February, lecturers at Chancellor College abandoned classes and marched peacefully to deliver a petition to the Inspector General (IG) of police for summoning and interrogating an associate professor of political science, who, in a public policy class, gave the examples of Tunisia and Egypt to illustrate the causes of mass protest. This was the beginning of a long struggle, as the college remained closed for eight months, with other colleges joining in, all condemning the planting of spies in classrooms. Chancellor College academicians recalled that, in the 1970s–1990s, the University of Malawi had become a target for politically motivated arrests of people who spoke out on unpopular or controversial issues. Lecturers vowed not to enter the "spy infested" lecture rooms until the IG apologised for his actions, guaranteed academic freedom and assured lecturers that such actions would not occur again.

On 1 April, the **Electoral Commission** (EC) was re-opened after being closed by Mutharika on 3 December 2010. A forensic audit report on EC transactions showed that only K 467,603 remained unaccounted for, contrary to the earlier figure of K 1.4 bn claimed by the Office of the President and cabinet. On 23 May, the EC announced that government had deferred the **local elections** scheduled for 20 April to 2014. Opposition political parties and CSOs questioned this postponement, and argued that the president was violating the constitution by failing to hold local polls since 2005. It was reported on 10 June that the government had drafted a Constitutional Amendment Bill to provide for parallel elections on all levels in 2014. On 1 August, the DPP National Governing Council endorsed the candidature of Peter Mutharika for the **2014 general elections** and officially presented him at a political rally on 3 December, clearing the long-term uncertainty about his silence on the candidacy. In a test of its popularity, the DPP lost a seat in a by-election that took place in Rumphi Central on 6 September.

MACRA announced in July that it wanted to buy the Consolidated ICT Regulatory Management System from the US in order to have access to call records of subscribers of all the country's telephone operators. Operators feared this would enable government to use information for security and other reasons without the knowledge and consent of subscribers. This was challenged in court by the government, which maintained the equipment was meant to prevent telecommunication fraud by monitoring revenue from airtime generated and to reduce under-declaration of the same.

Foreign Affairs

The president was ranked 17th out of 52 African leaders in a 2010 Index on Leadership performance released by the Kenya-based Nations Media Group in early January. The Mo Ibrahim Index on African Governance moved Malawi's ranking from 23rd to 17th out of 53, with improvements in security given as the main reason for the rise. Vice President Joyce Banda was ranked the third most powerful woman in Africa by the first edition of 'Forbes Africa Magazine' in October. On 25 January, Mutharika, in his capacity as chairperson of the AU, left for Ivory Coast and South Sudan and later proceeded to the 16th ordinary session of the AU Summit and the 24th summit of the NEPAD in Addis Ababa.

Bi- and multi-lateral aid continued to flow at the beginning of the year. A $ 350.7 m (K 53.2 bn) compact grant from the United States Millennium Challenge Corporation was earmarked to modernise Malawi's troubled power system, including adding 6 MW to the national grid. The French government turned into a grant $ 10.8 m (about K 2.2 bn) that Malawi had paid to service its debt. Similarly, Japan pledged continued assistance in the areas of agriculture, roads and education, and China and Kuwait promised continued financial support.

Relations deteriorated during the year as donors suspended aid because of poor governance and human rights violations. Notable among them were Germany (which, barely a fortnight after cutting its budgetary support to Malawi by half, cancelled a four-day visit by its deputy minister for economic cooperation and development planned for February), the USA (which suspended the Millennium Challenge Corporation grant), France, Norway, Japan, Ireland, Iceland and Britain. The relationship with Britain soured when Mutharika expelled British High Commissioner Fergus Cochraine-Dyet in April over a leaked memo he sent to London, in which he had described Mutharika as arrogant, combative and ever more autocratic. The UK also ordered Malawi's High Commissioner to leave London and an invitation to the Malawian government to a party at the High Commission to celebrate the UK royal wedding on 29 April was withdrawn. On 21 May, the British government suspended the exclusive courtesy visa service (the VVIP service accorded to high-profile people in any country with diplomatic relations with the UK) to Mutharika and his cabinet. Britain announced the indefinite cancellation of general budgetary support for Malawi and that it would not send a new High Commissioner to Lilongwe.

By June, a month before the financial year ended, the government was on the verge of losing K 15.7 bn of pledged foreign aid, since six countries of the key Common Approach to Budgetary Support had by 20 May not yet made a full commitment to support the 2011/2012 budget. This resulted in the adoption of a zero-deficit budget, which was presented, but trashed by the opposition, in parliament on 3 June. In August, the Hunger Project withdrew from Mutharika the $ 100,000 Africa Prize for Leadership for the Sustainable End of Hunger following the deaths and scores of injuries during the demonstrations on 20 July. On 26 August, it was reported that, according to the London based Economist Intelligence Unit, Mutharika had lost support through continued intolerance of criticism, sour relations with donors and foreign exchange shortages.

In September, Mutharika assured the World Bank's country director for Malawi, Zambia and Zimbabwe, Kundhavi Kadiresan, that he was ready to restore relations with international donors, including Britain and the IMF. On 14 October, Mutharika revoked the expulsion of the former British High Commissioner after the UK had refused to start normal relations until Malawi apologised for the diplomatic row. CSOs and opposition parties had also mounted pressure on Mutharika to restore relations with Britain. Mutharika sent high-level delegations to London, Brussels and Washington to discuss relations with Britain, the EU and the US.

Malawi also had strained relations with **neighbouring countries**. These included Mozambique, over disagreements on the Zambezi Water way, and Zambia, over the deportation of President Michael Sata as an illegal immigrant in 2007 when he was an opposition party president on a mission to meet former president Muluzi. As a consequence, Sata did not attend the COMESA summit hosted by Malawi on 11 October. Mutharika apologised to Zambia and withdrew the deportation orders against Sata. At the **COMESA Summit**, which was attended by five heads of state, four deputy heads of state and ministerial representatives from eight countries, Mutharika was appointed chairman for one year. President Omar Al Bashir of Sudan was in attendance and the ICC called for his arrest. Malawi's non-compliance was condemned and contributed to the strained relations with the international community.

Up to the end of the year, Malawi was seeking to **restore diplomatic relations** with neighbouring countries and donors through Minister of Foreign Affairs Peter Mutharika and other cabinet ministers. By 30 December, donors under the Common Approach to Budget Support had not yet disbursed their budget contribution of K 65 bn (over $ 380 m) representing 21% of the 2011/12 national budget because of economic and governance concerns.

Socioeconomic Developments

The costs of **public utilities and services** emerged as a bone of contention. The Malawi Energy Regulatory Authority (MERA) allowed the sole electricity supplier, Electricity Supply Control Commission (ESCOM) to increase electricity charges by 20.2% as from 1 January. Four months later, ESCOM had developed a policy that transferred the financial responsibility for new connections to customers by asking them to supply all materials including poles, cables and meters. ESCOM had previously subsidised the cost of new connections by charging customers a minimal K 25,000, while the company paid K 80,000. In June, the Consumer Association of Malawi gave ESCOM a seven-day ultimatum to revert to the old fees, as provisions of the Energy Regulation Act did not allow the unilateral revision of fees, tariffs, charges and pricing of energy sales without the approval of the MERA, which did not have commissioners in place. Road traffic fees were increased by over 100% and those seeking personalised registration number plates would pay K 200,000, up from K 60, 000.

Foreign currency issues continued to haunt Malawi, which started the year with a foreign currency reserve of 1.5 months of import cover. Furthermore there was shortage of vital drugs and fuel and a general increase in commodity prices. Production in the tea industry plummeted by 30% on average as a result of climate change, but cotton lint continued to fetch high prices on the global market with a record of $ 1 (about K 150) per kg. In May, tobacco sales were disrupted and caused worries that this would have a huge impact on foreign exchange reserve targets. This resulted in scarcity of foreign exchange throughout the year. Coupled with low productivity in the industrial sector, this prompted government to announce a foreign currency policy shift whereby all the foreign exchange proceeds from tobacco were to go straight to the Reserve Bank of Malawi and not commercial banks, as they had before. This attracted a backlash from the IMF, the Financial Market Dealers association, the Malawi Confederation of Chambers of Commerce and Industry and other economic analysts, who argued that the policy shift was retrogressive.

Imports constituted 42% of GDP and served mainly direct consumption purposes, leading to charges that this squandered the country's foreign exchange reserves. In August, the total value of Malawi's imports in the first half of the year was given as K 179 bn, up from K 142.3 bn in the same period in 2010 – a 26% increase. **Exports** to the USA under the AGOA between 2009 and 2010 had declined by 16% from $ 73.6 m (K 11 bn) to $ 61.9 m (about K 9 bn). Trade with China continued to grow, with the latest figures showing a 400% increase since 2008.

On 24 May, Mutharika announced that the **2011/12 budget** would be a zero deficit financial plan. The government would finance its recurrent expenditure from locally generated resources. Both donors and local CSOs condemned this for the detrimental effect it would have on the local people. On 3 June, a zero-deficit budget was presented in parliament and, in June, parliament passed a K 303,724,222,777 budget despite uncertain donor support.

Poor prices, high leaf rejection rates and frequent market closures affected Malawi's **tobacco industry**. The budget forecast a depressing future for the tobacco-marketing season, projecting a decline in earnings from $ 434.4 m (K 66 bn) to about $ 300 m (K 45.6 bn). It was announced in June, during the official launch of the 23rd annual congress of the Tobacco Association of Malawi, which pooled key players in the country's tobacco industry that the government planned to introduce a policy to manage **tobacco production**. The policy was aimed at controlling the production of tobacco in relation to the global trade requirements after noting that tobacco farmers' profit margins had eroded because of a higher rejection rate attributed to oversupply. By 24 June, only 25% of income was realised on burley tobacco compared with the previous year. Burley tobacco revenue during the year was $ 30 m against $ 140 m in 2010. After the 13 weeks of sale, about $ 49.6 m were realised (about K 7.5 bn) from the sale of 51,086,770 kg. This was 76.17% lower than the $ 208 m (around K 31.6 bn) from 105,283,061 kg sold during the same period in 2010. The average price that the leaf fetched in the season was 92.89 cents per kg (about K 140) against $ 1.90 (about K 285) during a similar period the year before, representing a 51% decline. By 30 September, a month before the year's selling season officially closed, revenue from tobacco peaked at $ 210.6 m (K 35.1 bn). This was about 45% down on the $ 386.3 m (K 64.5 bn) raised in the same period in 2010. By 30 December, according to the final figures from Auction Holdings Limited, the year's tobacco brought in only $ 293 m.

Labour disputes were also a cause of concern. In January, civil servants in the Ministry of Transport went on strike over poor conditions of service, teachers in rural areas abandoned classes demanding payment of arrears of their hardship allowances, junior doctors went on strike over a three-month delay in the payment of salaries, and judiciary staff went on strike for similar reasons. The monthly **cost of living** in Blantyre reportedly averaged K 51,589, while in Lilongwe it rose to an average of K 50,460, and in Mzuzu to an average of K 45,632. In November, the Famine Early Warnings Systems Network (Fews-Net) reported that rising maize prices threatened to put 200,000 people in the southern region at risk of hunger by the end of the year. The official ADMARC price of maize by the end of the year was K 60, a 50% hike on the previous K 40, with vendors selling at even higher prices. The inadequate supply of fuel resulted in fuel prices rising by an average of 26.4%. By the close of the year, it was evident that the state coffers were running dry, as was evidenced by a shortage of stationery, the grounding of vehicles, and government delays in paying salaries and allowances for civil servants.

Tiyesere Mercy Chikapa-Jamali & Lewis Baison Dzimbiri

Mauritius

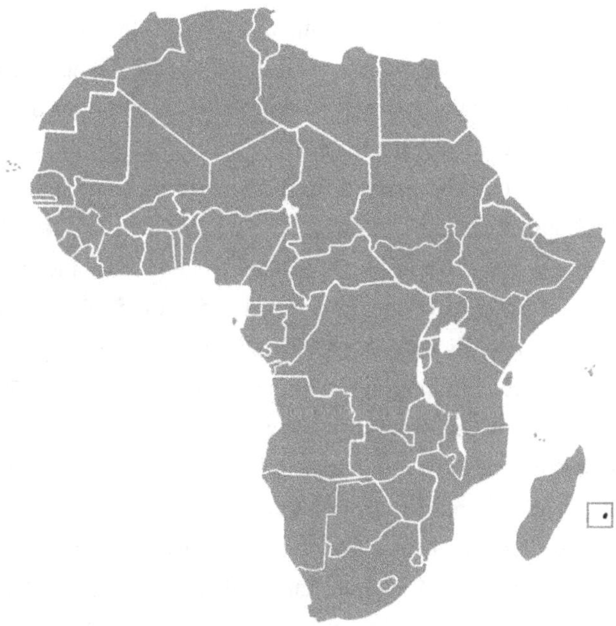

Domestic politics were influenced by allegations of corruption and bribery in the public sector purchase of a geriatric clinic, which was followed by the resignation of the Militant Socialist Movement (MSM) ministers in the Ramgoolam cabinet. The country maintained its remarkable developmental record with one of the highest per capita GDPs in Africa. International analysis lauded the country's stability: the Mo Ibrahim Index on African Governance again ranked Mauritius in first place; the World Bank Index of Doing Business placed Mauritius 23rd, ahead of all other African countries. Mauritius continued to struggle relatively successfully against the negative effects of the global economic environment.

Domestic Policy

Domestic politics remained largely 'triangular'. The Mauritius Labour Party (MLP) was the pivotal member of a **coalition government** under Prime Minister Dr Navin Ramgoolam. The junior partner was the MSM, under the leadership of Pravind Jugnauth, the son of President Sir Anerood Jugnauth, who was assigned the post of minister of finance in the Ramgoolam cabinet. The Mauritius Militant Movement (MMM), led by former prime minister Paul Raymond Bérenger, was the major **opposition** party. Parties such

Xavier-Luc Duval's Parti Socio-Democrate (the third coalition partner in the Ramgoolam government), the National Union, Mauritius Solidarity Front (ex-Hizbullah) headed by the notorious Member of Parliament Cehl Meeah, and other groups, were of minor significance.

On 23 February, the MLP celebrated its 75th anniversary in the presence of delegations from the Indian Congress Party, the South African ANC, the Chinese Communist Party, and Socialist International. Ramgoolam gave the official celebrations the motto "75 years of progressive policy: we construct the future".

Domestic policy was strongly affected by the long-term repercussions of the '**Med-Point' affair**, which had its origins in 2010. The government had decided to acquire a private clinic, partly owned and run by Dr Kishan Malhotra, brother-in-law of Pravind Jugnauth, and to turn it into a government-run 'geriatric clinic', for treating people in an 'aging society'. Although conflict was avoided in 2010 by Pravind Jugnauth's declaration that he had only a negligible holding in the clinic amounting to 0.00135% of the shares, and that he had absented himself from discussions during the cabinet meetings when the matter was on the agenda, the issue arose again when it became evident that government's valuation committees had altered values in the relevant documents. In February, Pravind Jugnauth declared that there had been no open or tacit deal with Ramgoolam with respect to the clinic in order to draw the MSM into Ramgoolam's coalition, but after the arrest of two superior administrators of the government's Valuation and Real Estate Consultancy Services, the widespread lack of transparency became apparent. The Central Procurement Board had rejected the purchase of the clinic because of the costs that would be incurred by additional restoration, but a second valuer, Hooloman Associates, inflated the value from the original 75 m Rupees to 144.7 m Rupees, which affected the purchase. The issue exploded when the Independent Commission against Corruption arrested Health Minister Mrs Maya Hanoomanjee on 22 July. On 26 July, the five remaining MSM ministers resigned from the Ramgoolam cabinet 'in solidarity' but declared that they would stay in the coalition: Minister of Finance Pravind Jugnauth; Minister of Tourism Nando Bodha; Minister for Industry Showkutally Soodhon; Minister for Social Security Leela Devi Doku-Luchoomun; and Minister of Public Service Ashit Gungah – all party heavyweights. Pravind Jugnauth was in serious trouble.

Ramgoolam replaced the resigning ministers with new appointees, either members of the junior party in the coalition (most notably Xavier-Luc Duval, chairman of the Mauritius Social-Democratic Party, as the new minister of finance) or independents, and continued in office, although with a reduced margin of confidence in parliament. In an atmosphere of speculation, any **political re-alignment** between Labour, the MSM and the MMM seemed imaginable, but not really feasible. Pravind Jugnauth had expected Ramgoolam to re-appoint the MSM ministers. The split between the two coalition partners, Labour and the MSM, left room for speculation over the domestic political scenario. One option saw Bérenger's MMM moving towards Labour and Ramgoolam.

On the other hand, Bérenger met Pravind Jugnauth in order to set aside five years of political hostility between MMM and MSM: Bérenger's MMM had tacitly favoured the breakaway group of Ashok Jugnauth, whom Bérenger supported in a bye-election against Pravind Jugnauth. In this climate of domestic political unrest, Bérenger was interviewed by the Central Investigation Department in order to probe what he had meant by his declaration that the institutions of the republic would only act on government orders.

In December, domestic policy discussions took yet another turn, when the French Professor Guy Carcassonne presented his 25-page "Report to the Prime Minister about an Electoral Reform". Carcassonne proposed a proportional **electoral system** which aimed at a fairer democratic representation of all political parties, abolition of the best-loser-system, and a higher representation of women in parliament through a reduction in the number of constituencies from 21 to 11 and the establishment of multi-seat constituencies of four to seven parliamentarians per constituency according to the size of the population, thus increasing the total number of parliamentarians. The reaction of the political elite was generally positive. Similar proposals had already been submitted by the South African judge Geoffrey Sachs in 2000, but, although commissioned by the government and welcomed by the political elite, this 'Sachs reform' was never implemented. The small left-wing party, Rezistans ek Alternativ, demanded the straightforward abolition of the best-loser provision, which allocated parliamentary seats to candidates on the basis of their religious or ethnic affiliation, irrespective of electoral results. This was considered undemocratic and unconstitutional, although it had been followed for 40 years. The Privy Council, the highest court in Mauritius, decided on 20 December that it would not judge on the constitutionality of the best-loser system, giving rise to the reaction of Rezistans ek Alternativ.

On 16 December, President Jugnauth dissolved the **Regional Assembly of Rodrigues**, the satellite island east of Mauritius, which gained interior autonomy in 2001. After its initial constitution in 2001 and a regional election in 2006, the Regional Assembly had reached the end of its five-year term. The forthcoming regional election was to take place on 6 February 2012.

Foreign Policy

Mauritius, in view of its economic interest as a modern economy in a state of transformation, continued to play an active role in Africa and in the Indian Ocean. The African continent was, in the opinion of the Mauritian political and economic leadership, an area of growth and opportunity in which the Mauritian economy as a growing service economy wanted to play a complementary role. Investment banking, management and administration, as well as reform policies in sugar cane cultivation and processing, were areas of foreign economic cooperation with Southern and Eastern Africa.

Traditional close relations with **India** continued. On 24–28 April, Indian President Dame Pratibha Patil paid a state visit. India was looking for a permanent seat on the UNSC and Mauritius supported this ambition, arguing that India had always acted as the voice of those who had no voice in the international order. Economic ties between Mauritius and India were intense as Mauritius functioned as an offshore financial hub for Indian industry. This function, however, drew a lot of attention from Indian tax evasion inspectors. A team from the Indian Central Bureau of Investigation visited Port Louis in May in order to investigate allegations that massive tax evasion and money laundering by Indian companies was organised via offshore financial institutions at the expense of the Indian tax authorities and government.

On 4–7 June, **Singapore**'s President Sellapan Rama Nathan paid a state visit to Mauritius. Ramgoolam declared on this occasion that Singapore was to Asia what Mauritius intended to become for Africa: a service hub for the African market that was growing as a result of globalisation. During this visit, various economic and scientific cooperation agreements were signed between Mauritius and Singapore.

The third pillar in Mauritian external relations was the People's Republic of **China**. Mauritius had supported the 'One-China-only' position since the days of Sir Seewoosagur Ramgoolam and was rewarded by massive Chinese investments in the Shin Fei project and economic zone. Mauritius served China as an entry gateway to Africa, but Mauritius considered the Chinese $ 500 m Fund for Africa to be underutilised by Mauritian entrepreneurs.

With regard to the neighbouring region, Mauritius still suffered from the imbroglio in **Madagascar**. As member of the Indian Ocean Commission (Commission de l'Océan Indien – COI), Prime Minister Ramgoolam proposed in Paris that there should be a Mauritian mediator for Madagascar who would contribute to the settlement of the stalemate there within the framework of the COI, since the SADC settlement initiatives had produced a 'road map' but no actual progress in the easing of the tension. However, this was not followed up.

Mauritian independence in 1968 was conditional on the 'detachment' of the **Chagos archipelago**, a group of islands in the Indian ocean, some 1,000 nautical miles north of Mauritius, and the tacit acceptation by the then prime minister, Sir Seewoosagur Ramgoolam, of the eviction and evacuation of about 2,000 residents of the islands mainly to Mauritius. After this 'ethnic cleansing', the UK and the USA had established a military naval base on Diego Garcia for a period of 50 years with a possible extension for another 20 years to be negotiated in 2014. During 2011, four major political events characterised the intrinsic complexity of the Chagos issue. In January, Navin Ramgoolam was at the AU summit meeting in Addis Ababa, in which Oliver Bancoult, the second-generation leader of the Chagossian people living in exile in Mauritius, participated. The AU endorsed the Mauritian call for the restoration of Mauritian authority over the Chagos Islands. From the British side, the Chagos Islands All Party Parliamentary Group of the House of

Commons affirmed during its 18th session on 26 January that the date set for 2014 would be decisive for settling the sovereignty of the former 'British Indian Ocean Territory' and the re-settlement of its people. Simultaneously, on exactly the same day, a Chagossian subject, Allen Vincatessin, took the oath as the first president of the provisional **Chagos government in exile** in the small town of Crawley, near Gatwick Airport, where about 1,000 Chagos citizens with British passports had chosen to reside. On 25 March, the International Tribunal for the Law of the Sea named three mediators to hear the views of the parties to conflict. At the same time, Oliver Bancoult declared that the Chagossian people had nothing against a marine nature reserve in the Chagos archipelago if the basic rights of the Chagossians were respected and taken into account. With the rising tensions in the Indian Ocean, its rim and adjacent areas (Somalia, Indian Ocean pirates, the Straits of Hormuz, etc.) it was unlikely that the USA would accept the co-existence of resettled Chagossians and the naval base on Diego Garcia. The Chagos issue will therefore continue to be virulent in the years to come.

In December, the Mauritius parliament unanimously approved a Piracy and Maritime Violence Bill, according to which **Somali pirates** apprehended by EU-coast guards or vessels would be put on trial and sentenced in Mauritius.

Socioeconomic Developments

In spite of the global crisis, **macroeconomic variables** remained stable. Real GDP growth was almost constant at 4%. Consumer Price Index Inflation was in the order of 3%. The budget deficit stood at 4.4% of GDP, while the Current Account Deficit rose to 9.2% of GDP according to provisional figures by 'African Economic Outlook 2011'. Public debt was 50% of GDP. The economy registered a rising number of tourists (about 5% more than in the previous year) and an influx of foreign currency. A growing current account deficit due to a constant and robust industrial export performance but a massive influx of investment goods occurred at the same time. In order to avoid Mauritius rupee's tendency to appreciation, the Central Bank bought excess liquidity in foreign currencies from the market on various occasions.

Britain and France remained Mauritius's main European trading partners, but its most important new targets were India, for trade and finance, and China, for trade and future investment. Whilst Mauritius survived the global economic and financial crisis better than anticipated, there was fear of implicit long-term threats to the economic and social model. This was reflected in Pravind Jugnauth's budget speech for 2011 (second reading at the end of November 2010) under the heading "Rebalancing Growth, Consolidating Social Justice". He recalled the euro-zone crisis – an external shock that had a more direct and menacing impact on Mauritius' export sectors than the Great Recession. At the same time, Brazil, Russia, India and China (BRIC) and some other emerging economies were gaining greater prominence as contributors to global output, thus rebalancing the world economy. Consequently, Mauritius aimed at reducing its dependency on Europe and exploring the new global economic structure for opportunities. The government formulated an **Economic Restructuring and Competitiveness Program** (ERCP) that included a far-reaching micro-economic agenda. One of the main thrusts of the budget was rebalancing growth by making a great leap forward in productivity. Instrumental to this, as the finance minister saw it, would be activating economic diplomacy in order to open new markets and facilitate joint ventures and strategic alliances. Embassies located in countries where economic diplomacy would be pursued intensively would be staffed by commercial attachés with relevant expertise. Another objective was to attract a higher share of the more than 60 m outbound tourists from India, China and Russia. Jugnauth repeated in his budget speech that he would continue to develop Mauritius into a "tax free shopping paradise". However, Ashok Subron of the left party Resistanz ek Alternativ argued that this type of growth did not really lay foundations for a new economic model. It was a backward-oriented neo-liberal model, which did not entail a concept of "decent work", redistribution of profits and supportive productive sectors; rather, it remained a prisoner of a cheap labour model and traditional sectors such as a tax-free zone, tourism and financial services, and replaced one form of dependency by another.

The bankruptcy of the call centre "Infinity", a supposed model initiative of the young entrepreneur Jean Suzanne in the prestigious IT-towers at Ebène, was an example of the **fragility of new ventures** in a volatile market. Lack of social security, non-payment of salaries, hunger strikes and protest marches by the workers, showed the dark side of otherwise highly subsidised service companies. Jean Suzanne, who had been appointed counsellor to Prime Minister Ramgoolam, had received subsidies and payments from the Training and Placement Scheme, the Additional Stimulus Package Programme and the National Empowerment Fund for employment creation and service innovation. At the end of March, all these ended in liquidation, mismanagement, fraud, corruption and police intervention.

Klaus-Peter Treydte

Mozambique

Little happened on the domestic political scene, apart from the notable performance of a new political party. Foreign policy played out mainly at the economic interface, with major foreign interests featuring prominently. Mozambique's leap to become a major mineral-energy exporter dominated its economic performance. By the end of the decade, the country is expected to be the largest exporter in Africa of natural gas, electricity and high quality metallurgical (coking) coal. But poverty was not reduced during the year and socio-economic disparities remained a major challenge.

Domestic Politics

Municipal by-elections served as an indicator of **shifting political trends**. The new opposition party, the Mozambique Democratic Movement (MDM), headed by Daviz Simango, mayor of Beira (not to be confused with David Simango, Frelimo mayor of Maputo), was taken seriously by the dominant party, Frelimo. Of the 43 elected mayors, 42 were Frelimo, which in July instructed five to resign. Two in the south where Frelimo was dominant refused. But those in Quelimane (Zambézia province), Pemba (Cabo Delgado) and Cuamba (Niassa) agreed, and by-elections were set for 7 December. It is probable that Frelimo thought that the three unpopular mayors would lose local elections in 2013, and decided to move before the MDM had time to build its organising capacity. Frelimo won two of the cities, but the MDM's Manuel de Araujo won 62% of the vote in Quelimane, making him an important political figure. Renamo did not stand in the municipal by-elections. Its president, Afonso Dhlakama, had moved to Nampula in the north, and little was heard of him – except for regular statements promising anti-government demonstrations that never took place. MDM head Daviz Simango had been expelled from Renamo by Dhlakama in 2008 and other key figures, including de Araujo, had left Renamo to join the MDM. Although Renamo was the second largest party in parliament, it was fading, and it was widely expected that the MDM would replace Renamo as the official opposition after the municipal elections in 2013 and national elections in 2014. Frelimo remained the dominant party, with good organisation and broad support. Nevertheless, patronage remained a key part of party and government, and there were complaints that Frelimo party membership was required for promotion in the civil service, loans from the district development fund, licences, etc. Businesses linked to President Armando Guebuza and Frelimo had an inside track on government contracts, and teachers in several places complained in the press about being forced to make contributions to Frelimo. MDM support initially came largely from disillusioned Renamo members. The test would be MDM's ability to gain support from an increasingly disaffected youth.

There is a two-term limit for the **state president** and Guebuza was half-way through his second term. In a manoeuvre that was never adequately explained, Frelimo had told parliament in 2010 that it wanted a special commission to make changes to the constitution, but refused to say what they were. There was widespread speculation that Guebuza and his allies were looking for a way to keep him in power, either by changing the two-term limit or by strengthening the post of prime minister for him, as had happened in Russia. But gossip from within the party said that the younger generation rejected any attempt to keep Guebuza in power, saying it was time for the post-liberation-war generation to take over. The 10th party congress was to be held in September 2012, and by year's end there was no clear favourite for the position of party president and national presidential candidate.

Frelimo is noted for its strong party unity; few people have ever been expelled from the party, and potential opposition figures have been co-opted, while splits and disagreements have generally not been allowed to spill over. However, there were many fault-lines with the party: between generations, with the young feeling marginalised; between regions and languages, with people from the centre and Nampula province feeling discriminated against by those from the south and the far north; between supporters of former president Chissano and Guebuza backers; and between those who saw the party as mainly for self-advancement and others who saw it as the best way to promote national development.

The **media** remained particularly free and often highly critical of government. Although the front page of the government owned daily 'Noticias' reflected a pro-Frelimo line, articles inside the newspaper, particularly reports from the districts, were frequently highly critical.

Parliament had decided that elections should always take place in the first two weeks of October, but there were sharp divisions between Frelimo and the opposition on a number of other **electoral issues**, including the size and composition of the National Electoral Commission and on means to reduce ballot box stuffing and other fraud within polling stations, which meant that parliament did not meet its September deadline for drafting a new electoral law. The total number of **districts** had been increased to 150 by splitting 13 large districts in half and by defining provincial capitals as districts.

Other domestic events included the publication of a revised highway code, which set a rural speed limit of 120 km/h and banned the use of hand-held mobile telephones while driving. Over 800,000 guns and other items of military equipment had been collected since 1995 under the Mozambique Christian Council's "Transforming Guns into Hoes" programme. Mozambique's best know painter, Malangatana Valente Ngwenya, died on 3 January.

Foreign Affairs

The Mozambican leadership remained sympathetic to Robert Mugabe in Zimbabwe and Muammar Kadhafi in Libya, and former president Joaquim Chissano continued as the unsuccessful SADC negotiator in Madagascar. **SADC** elected Guebuza as its deputy president at its meeting in Luanda, Angola, on 18 August. The next annual summit would therefore be in Maputo, when Mozambique would take over the rotating presidency from Angola. But in practice, international issues were predominantly economic, often related to investment. Mozambique was late submitting its application for membership of the **Export Industries Transparency Initiative** and even then the application was incomplete and was rejected on 23 August.

Tensions continued with **Malawi** over transport. Malawi and coal mining company Rio Tinto wanted to use the Zambezi River for barges to carry cargo to the sea, but the government rejected these proposals on environmental grounds – the extensive dredging required would have too much impact on river flows, and there was a danger of pollution if a barge sank. Despite lack of agreement with Mozambique, Malawi completed the construction of an inland port at Nsanje on the Shire River, which it was not able to use.

The government continued to resist heavy pressure from the international community to renegotiate contracts for so-called **mega-projects**. The first three – the Mozal aluminium smelter, which uses Cahora Bassa electricity, the export of natural gas from Inhambane to Sasol in South Africa, and the Kenmare titanium mine on the coast of Zambézia – benefitted from a wide range of tax and other incentives and contributed little to the Mozambican economy. Contracts agreed after 2007 had fewer incentives, but Mozambique did not gain much from the sharp rises in mineral and energy prices. An IMF staff report in May estimated that mega-projects and mining companies paid Mozambique only 5% of their profits, while they should have paid 30%. The IMF Executive Board, in a statement agreed on 24 May and published on 27 June, called on Mozambique to renegotiate mega-project contracts, and pointed out that other countries, including Peru and Tanzania, had renegotiated contracts. Economist Jeffrey Sachs, in a speech in Maputo on 13 January, also called for renegotiation of contracts. Mozambique Catholic bishops, in a pastoral letter on 20 June, said the mega-projects received "excessive" fiscal benefits and contracts should be renegotiated. But the government remained steadfastly opposed. The sale of the final 15% of Hydroelectrica de Cahora Bassa held by the Portuguese state was still delayed by disagreements over the price.

A **World Bank**-imposed privatisation of the central railways to an Indian company proved disastrous and was finally cancelled. Ricon was a consortium of two Indian companies, Rites and Ircon, and the World Bank gave a $ 104 m loan to upgrade the railway on condition that the Mozambican railways administration be kept at arms length. The project was essential to move coal from Tete to Beira port and should have been completed in 2009; the contact on the incomplete upgrading was finally cancelled.

The issue of **land grabs** came unexpectedly to a head when the major Brazilian daily 'Folha de São Paulo' quoted the president of the Mato Grosso Cotton Producers Association, who claimed that Agriculture Minister José Pacheco had offered 6 m ha of land, without environmental restrictions, free to Brazilian farmers when he visited Brazil on 27 April. This triggered headlines across the world, as well as an angry response from the government. It denied that it would sell land. Brazil could invest, but must create jobs and follow Mozambican regulations. The Council of Ministers had earlier imposed a temporary ban on new land concessions of over 1,000 ha. The local media outcry triggered a strong response from Guebuza; on 22 August he said Mozambicans' conquest of their land must be preserved and that the land law must be scrupulously followed, including with regard to deals between powerful agents. This was clearly aimed at Frelimo party people who had used their positions to obtain land, as well as those who promoted foreign investment.

Meanwhile, existing European investors came into **conflict with local communities** in several parts of the country. The pressure for high profits had pushed foreign companies into seizing land, displacing farmers and threatening their livelihoods and food security. The government accused the Global Solidarity Forest Fund (GSFF), which involves Nordic churches and a major Dutch teachers pension fund, of occupying thousands of hectares of land it had not been allocated, while peasants said they had been pushed off land, and responded by burning forests and chopping down trees. GSFF was forced to replace its entire management in Sweden and Mozambique during the year. Another confrontation was between a Portuguese company, Quifel, a local small soya bean producer backed by the Cooperative League of the USA (Clusa), and the Bill and Melinda Gates Foundation. In 2009, Quifel had told would-be investors it had 30,000 ha for soya in Mozambique, when in practice it apparently had none. In the last concessions before the land freeze, Quifel was given 10,000 ha, but the land included 490 ha occupied by 244 farmers, who had a right to be there as they had occupied the land for more than ten years. Quifel mainly took over a small amount of land already used by the peasant farmers and thus already cleared. By year's end it was still using only a small amount of land, and had never identified the other 20,000 ha it claimed it had been granted. Because land concessions must be put into production within two years, a further confrontation might be expected. But Quifel is well connected; it is controlled by Miguel Pais do Amaral, a Portuguese aristocrat and racing car driver, and Quifel also owns LeYa, which in turn owns two of the most important publishers in Mozambique, Texto Editores and Ndjira, which have published books by local politicians, such as the recent memoires of former president Joaquin Chissano. The land concession freeze was ended in October, and in the final three months of the year five companies were given 330,000 ha – all for trees except for 20,000 ha for sugar and cotton. Meanwhile, SAPPI (originally South African Pulp and Paper Industries), decided not to go ahead with a 150,000 ha eucalyptus plantation in Zambézia province. SAPPI noted that the areas targeted for plantation development had high agricultural potential. They were therefore densely populated, and current land use clearly showed that they were important areas, both at a local and national level, for food production. As a result, any plantation development (own operations and out-grower) would be in direct conflict with agriculture. Trees could only be grown profitably on good farmland which has other potential agricultural uses, and this would lead to conflict with local communities.

China became Mozambique's 10th largest investor, with 7% of FDI in 2010. Chinese companies became increasingly involved in the manufacturing sector, including two cement plants and a cotton gin. China did not have any major involvement in agriculture or mining, although it had been given a heavy sands exploration licence. Illegal shipments of hardwoods continued, organised largely by Chinese businessmen. In July, 561 containers loaded with $ 2 m in valuable timber was stopped at Nacala port; another 1,000 containers of illegal logs were seized elsewhere. There were complaints that government officials were bribed, but government was cracking down. In September, the provincial director of customs in Nampula (which includes Nacala) was sacked. Agriculture Minister Jose Pacheco told parliament on 17 November that more inspectors had been hired, and that 16 Mozambican and foreign companies (including several owned by Chinese citizens) involved in the illegal export of logs and ivory had had their licences cancelled.

Socioeconomic Developments

Tete province has the world's largest known unexploited reserve of high quality **metallurgical (coking) coal**, and exports of thermal and coking coal were predicted to reach 10 m tonnes in 2013 and 100 m tonnes per year by the end of the decade. Coal mining and exports finally started with the first two mines owned by the Brazilian mining giant Vale and Rio Tinto, which bought the Australian mining company Riversdale. More than 30 mining companies were operating in Tete, mostly developing coal mines, but also iron, vanadium, titanium and rare earths. The Indian company, Jindal Steel and Power, expected to produce 6.6 m tonnes of coal per year. A key problem was transport of the coal to port. The newly upgraded railway to Beira can only carry 6 m tonnes per year and even with further upgrading could only handle 12 m t/y. Vale announced its decision to build a new railway to the much better deep-water port of Nacala. This would involve 60 km of new track in Tete, a 137 km new railway across Malawi (for which agreement was announced on 28 December), and a major rebuilding of the existing 650 km railway to Nacala port. The project would take three years and cost $ 3 bn. The northern Mozambique railway line and Malawi railways were operated by a company controlled by Vale, with minority shares owned by a Mozambican consortium headed by Insitec.

Plans were made for three large coalfired **power stations** to be built in Tete. The two big coalmining companies, Vale and Riversdale-Rio Tinto, each planned 2,000 MW plants, and on 3 October, the government authorised Jindal Steel and Power to build a 2,640 MW plant. The main market for the electricity would be South Africa. Meanwhile the Rovuma basin, offshore to the north of Mozambique, was proving to be one of the biggest **gas** fields in Africa. During the year, just one US company, Anadarko, raised its estimate of gas reserves from 10 trillion cubic feet to 30 trillion, and was proposing a plant to produce Liquefied Natural Gas that could process a billion cubic feet of gas a day. The Italian company ENI declared there were 22 trillion cubic feet in its block. Total investments could exceed $ 20 bn. There were no finds of commercial quantities of oil, but there were reports that Niassa province, inland near Lake Malawi, had reserves of high quality coal at least as important as those in Tete, as well as substantial reserves of gas.

A new law was introduced which required that by 2012 petrol must contain 10% ethanol and diesel 3% **biodiesel**. There had been rapid expansion of sugar production, partly for ethanol. But the production of jatropha for biodiesel was proving much more difficult. Originally billed as a miracle crop, which was pest resistant and grew on poor soils, it turned out to be productive only on good soils, where it competed with food crops and had serious pest problems. The most advanced foreign investor, the British company Sun Biofuels, went bankrupt in August, and there was no large-scale production of biodiesel from jatropha. One programme, run by a Portuguese consortium headed by GALP, had the first out-grower scheme, involving 300 small farmers growing jatropha.

The **IMF**, in a report of 24 May published on 27 June, said Mozambique's economic growth had not been as pro-poor as in other countries with comparable high and sustainable growth episodes. It had become less pro-poor over time. It also said that "poverty reduction did not reach the magnitude observed in other high-growth countries", and cited the "sharp contrasts" with China, Vietnam, Brazil "and even Uganda". Expenditure declined for the bottom 30% of the population – the poorest were getting poorer. The report warned that, "as income inequality rises, so does the risk of social conflict – as recent events in the Middle East provide a topical reminder of". Mozambique should put more emphasis on economic diversification, the IMF continued. The stagnation in income poverty reduction and the unrest in September 2010 were clear warning signals that the growth model needed complementation by well-targeted efforts to broaden the country's productive and export base and create employment opportunities. Mozambique needed to "diversify its economy away from capital-intensive, low-valued added products" and should "increase production and productivity in labour-intensive sectors, particularly in agriculture". And, in a total reversal of past World Bank and IMF agriculture policy, an IMF staff report called for "subsidized credit in the form of credit guarantees" and "the provision of public goods such as basic research, infrastructure, and agricultural extension services".

The 2009/10 agriculture census, published on 22 November, showed Mozambique to have the lowest **agricultural productivity** in southern Africa. There were 3.8 m farms in the country, but the average farm was only 1.5 ha. Only 4% of farmers used fertiliser and most of those were tobacco farmers in Tete; only 2% were able to obtain credit, and more than one-third of those were Tete tobacco farmers receiving inputs on credit. Only 3% of farmers used pesticides and only 5% used irrigation. Of all farms, 42% did not produce enough food to feed the farmer's family properly. Major policy shifts were set out in the **Strategic Agriculture Plan** 2011–2020 (PEDSA) approved by the Council of Ministers on 3 May. Donors and foreign investors received hardly a mention; the emphasis was on domestic investment and the development of small and medium commercial farms, making them more productive and competitive. The strategy gave a much more interventionist role to government, explicitly reversing the disastrous farm policies of the World Bank, IMF and donors over the past two decades. There was to be a major expansion of rural extension and agronomic research, both blocked by the World Bank in the past. Priority for state intervention would be input production and supply (including local production and bulk imports of fertilisers), provision of technology packages, animal traction and mechanisation, increased use of water and electricity, and agro-processing. Government would also intervene to ensure seasonal credit for farmers and credit for traders and suppliers, and the provision of insurance, and there would be an expansion of contract farming. The World Bank had also forced the run-down of the **marketing board**, the Mozambique Cereals Institute (Instituto de Cereais de Moçambique – ICM), but the Council of Ministers decided on 28 June that the ICM would return to its traditional role as buyer of last resort, promising to purchase all grain that private traders failed to buy. Agriculture Minister Jose Pacheco declared that one could not risk that farmers increased productivity and output without guaranteeing a market for their surplus.

Another World Bank imposition bit the dust in May, when the state railways company Caminhos de Ferro de Moçambique (CFM) resumed training of permanent way (railway line) maintenance staff. The World Bank had forced privatisation of **railway maintenance** and the dismissal of all the experienced staff who had previously done this work. Other reversals of World Bank policy included the decision not to privatise the state-owned mobile telephone company, mCel, and a decision to open a state-owned grain processing factory in Tete.

A contract was signed in April between the Mozambican government and the Brazilian Development Bank (BNDES) to convert the Nacala military air base into a **commercial airport** with the capacity to handle between 500,000 and 600,000 passengers a year, to promote tourism to northern beaches. The Mozambican government already provided $ 40 m, with the total cost estimated at $ 120 m. Work was to be carried out by the Brazilian company Odebrecht.

After the 1–2 September 2010 riots in Maputo, the government had provided bread subsidies, which in March were announced to be replaced by a subsidised food basket and a subsidised bus pass. By June, however, the government denied that any such thing had been promised, and the ideas were dropped. One reason was action by the Bank of Mozambique to reduce the **exchange rate**. Most food in Maputo is imported from South Africa and in the first half of 2010 the exchange rate had risen from 3.5 to 5 Mozambican Meticais to the South African Rand, causing a major increase in the price of imports, which led to the riots. By the end of 2011, the exchange rate had been pushed back to 3.25 Meticais to the Rand. However, the low exchange rate made it impossible for local producers to compete with imported vegetables.

Minimum wages were raised substantially in April to a minimum for agricultural work of $ 65 per month, a minimum for civil servants of $ 77 and minimum levels in other sectors of $ 90–$ 105 (with one exception – the financial services minimum of $ 173 per month). A study published by the Washington-based Center for Global Development found that there had been a real deterioration of **welfare** in terms of income, food consumption and nutritional status between 2007 and 2008. Meanwhile, a study by KPMG found that Mozambican banks made a profit of $ 143 m in 2009.

The Insitec group became the largest business group, with interests in the second largest bank (BCI), the northern railway and port system, and the company that had the concession for the proposed Mpanda Nkuwa dam (for which the $ 2.4 bn funding was still to be raised). In June, it bought Mozambique's largest building and engineering company, CETA.

In one of the most high-level **corruption** cases, the president of the Constitutional Council (Supreme Court), Luis Mondlane, resigned in disgrace on 17 March after the exposure of his misuse of nearly $ 1 m and his improper dismissal of a court official who had objected. The new president was the highly respected Hemenegildo Gamito. Former transport and communications minister Antonio Munguambe was finally jailed for his part in a $ 3 m corruption case, after his sentence was reduced to four years. On 20 June, Attorney-General Augusto Paulino warned that **organised crime** was directing its profits to real estate. He noted that the Mozambican economy was too small for buildings of the size constructed in the major cities, particularly in the capital. Some of the hotel and private mansions appeared to be funded by drug money.

A revised **budget** was approved by parliament in June. The $ 5 bn budget was financed to 56% by taxes and other state revenue, 42% by aid, and 2% by domestic debt.

Deputy Education Minister Leda Hugo said that the number of higher **education** institutions had increased from 11 in 2000 to 38 in 2010 and the number of students on degree courses increased from 13,200 to 82,000. She also warned about sub-standard higher education institutions and courses. Eduardo Mondlane University (UEM) was to revert to its previous academic curriculum. The previous rector (vice-chancellor), Filipe Couto had decided to shorten four-year undergraduate courses to three years to fit in with the Bologna international standard of three years, and reduce medical training from seven years to six. Couto's deputy, Orlando Quilambo, became rector in May, and in October announced the return to the former curriculum because the Bologna model was not viable for UEM. Maria Celeste Onions, Education Ministry head of human resources, said in October that the pupil/teacher ratio in first level primary education (first to fifth grades) was falling slowly, from one teacher per 71 pupils in 2008 to 67 in 2009 and to 66 in 2010. Of the 147,000 employees of the Ministry of Education, including teaching and non-teaching staff, at least 2,216 had died as a result of HIV/AIDS over the previous three years, and 1,999 were living with the HIV virus, of whom 1,738 were taking antiretroviral drugs (ARVs).

Health Minister Alexandre Manguele reported on 26 April that **malaria** remained the main cause of death, despite a reduction in the number of cases. In 2010, the country registered about 3.3 m cases of malaria, a 21% reduction compared with 2009. Deaths fell 25%. Manguele promised that mass distribution of mosquito nets in the provinces would soon start, prioritising areas that had not benefitted from spraying. Mine clearance was still not complete, and mines from three wars continued to kill. It was reported that land mine explosions had killed seven people and maimed a further 24 in 2010. UNDP estimated it would cost $ 21 m to complete mine clearance.

There was a series of kidnappings of at least 15 members of the Asian-Mozambique community and ransoms of up to $ 2 m were demanded. It was believed that members of the Asian community were involved in the kidnappings. Wild animals killed 86 people, and injured a further 60, according to government spokesperson Deputy Justice Minister Alberto Nkutumula. Over 20 elderly people were killed because they were accused of being witches.

Joseph Hanlon

Namibia

The contest for the up-coming head of state elections emerged as a prominent political feature during the year, which in terms of domestic politics presented no surprises. The results of the 2009 parliamentary elections continued to be contested in a prolonged legal battle. Poverty remained a challenge and the government responded to the high unemployment rate by introducing a new three-year capital investment programme. Despite the lack of visible socioeconomic progress and increased signs of corruption, political stability was maintained. International relations continued to favour new friends over old ties, with the EPA remaining contested and bilateral relations with Germany still tested by memories of the genocide committed more than a century ago.

Domestic Politics

The **disputed elections** for the National Assembly that took place at the end of November 2009 kept the legal system busy. On 14 February, the High Court dismissed for lack of substantial evidence allegations of electoral fraud initiated by nine opposition parties. The ruling Swapo party, however, expressed strong concern over the verdict that the Electoral Commission had failed to maintain a satisfactory state of affairs in organising the elections. On 9 March, the applicants stated their intention to appeal to the Supreme Court against the judgment, but failed to provide evidence to the registrar within the stipulated three months. Judgment in the matter of the appeal was scheduled for 5 October, when the Supreme Court only announced that the merits of the case would be considered at a later stage. At year's end, the legal wrangles had been taking place for over two years without a final settlement.

Meanwhile, it was more or less business as usual as far as politics were concerned, with no initiatives by **opposition parties** significant enough to challenge the dominance of the Swapo party (previously: South West African Peoples Organisation). Given the mediocre level of the challenge represented by the political opposition, often more engaged in internal squabbles than in representing meaningful alternatives, the former liberation movement's de facto one-party rule was not at risk. Hence, policy debates within Swapo and with its affiliated allies such as the National Union of Namibian Workers remained of more interest than any other political discussions.

The **race for the presidency**, with elections due in late 2014 and the new incumbent's term of office to run from March 2015, unfolded with two prominent contestants in the arena. Minister of Trade and Industry Hage Geingob (the former prime minister) and Minister of Justice Pendukeni Iivula-Ithana – the party's deputy president and secretary general respectively – emerged as the most obvious and ambitious candidates. Their early campaigns got under way despite repeated denials and some public speculation about possible factionalism. This prompted Hifikepunye Pohamba, the party president and head of state, to intervene at the party's central committee meeting on 19 November. He appointed a team to investigate allegations of smear campaigns between the two frontrunners, whom he cirticised for divisive politics and creating bad blood in the party. Other potential candidates to succeed him were the party stalwart, Lands Minister Jerry Ekandjo, and Foreign Minister Uutoni Nujoma, son of the first head of state. Pohamba warned against the fomenting of tensions similar to those that had arisen during his nomination as presidential candidate in 2004, which resulted in the break-away of a Swapo faction and the establishment of the new Rally for Democracy and Progress, which became the official opposition.

According to the Mo Ibrahim Foundation's **good governance** index, released in early October, Namibia ranked 6 out of 53 African countries. The Foundation observed, however, that during the previous five years (2006 to 2010) the standard of governance in the country had worsened. The controversy surrounding the repatriation of skulls from Germany in memory of the genocide more than a century earlier (see more details below) culminated in a **spectacular public outburst** by Minister of Youth, National Service, Sport and Culture Kazenambo Kazenambo, who had been the head of the delegation charged with repatriating the skulls. In response to criticism of excessive expenses incurred to fund a large delegation, published in a local newspaper on 11 November, he called a press conference on 16 November, where, enraged over the issue, he lambasted the newspaper that had carried the report, called the journalist a "bloody *boer*" with former links to the South

African army, and threatened that black Namibians' patience with the colonial mentality that surfaced in such criticism was running out. With reference to the continued disproportionately high ownership of land by commercial white farmers, he suggested that the constitution could be set aside if the whites were to "scratch too far". Most of the media and parts of the local community reacted strongly to this apparent lack of diplomacy, but seemed to underestimate the event as an indicator of the growing frustration. The minister's outburst was an over-reaction to the insensitive self-righteousness often displayed by a privileged minority, but it is ignorance of the feelings of the formerly colonised majority that should be seen as a root cause of such displays of emotion. Given the continued scandalous discrepancies between the haves and the have-nots, as well as the minister's humiliating experience during his visit to Germany, when he was refused any meeting at ministerial-level and a state secretary left the only official ceremony after delivering her statement, this outburst should be seen in the context of the lack of progress with regard to national reconciliation.

The year was marked by a public outcry over the fact that hundreds of destitute people of all ages survived by regularly waiting for food that had exceeded its sell-by date to be delivered to the dumping grounds outside Windhoek and other towns. When policy makers pleaded ignorance of this shocking reality, they were accused by the local media of being out of touch. **Poverty** continued to be widespread. According to World Bank statistics, Namibia ranked as the higher-middle-income country with the highest level of poverty in the world. Poverty and unemployment were also considered as root causes of the high suicide rates, especially in the rural northern region, and of a dramatic rate of infant abandonment and infanticide. The director general of the National Planning Commission (NPC) announced on 23 November that the gap between the haves and have-nots was higher in 2009/10 than in 1993/94. The government continued, nonetheless, to dismiss any demands for the introduction of a Basic Income Grant (BIG), promoted for a few years by a local civil society alliance.

In striking contrast, in the course of the year the government purchased a new fleet of Mercedes Benz cars for top ranking officials and a new jet and two state-of-the-art S600L Mercedes Benzes for the president, while a battery of E-Class Mercs remained on the shopping list for ministers and deputy ministers. The leaders of the Swapo Youth League openly criticised the shopping spree in mid-October as **misplaced priorities**. The frustration of ordinary people over the failure of their elected leaders to deliver measures to ease their struggle for survival could emerge as a greater political challenge for Swapo in the years to come than any organised political opposition.

Foreign Affairs

The absence of any coherent foreign policy was ridiculed on 2 December in a weekly editorial by the former editor of the most widely read independent daily newspaper, 'The

Namibian'. In fact, the former president's son, Uutoni Nujoma, who had been foreign minister for two years, did not, contrary to all expectations, use this influential ministerial position to enhance his own profile by formulating a foreign policy concept of his own making. While bilateral relations were promoted through **state visits** by Finland's President Tarja Halonen (22 February) and President John Atta Mills of Ghana (25–28 August), foreign policy continued to reflect increasingly friendly relations with countries such as China, Iran and North Korea without any clearly indicated systematic strategy.

The situation in **Libya** revived the struggle mentality of yesteryear, and the intervention sanctioned by the UNSC was criticised both by members of the government and by leaders of Swapo as an imperialist conspiracy for regime change. In his speech on Namibia's 21st Independence Day on 21 March, President Pohamba condemned the intervention "in the strongest terms", saying: "Our brothers and sisters in Libya are under attack from foreign forces." Former president Nujoma added the same week that this was a "crime against humanity" and a violation of international law. On 11 July, Minister of Justice Pendukeni Ithana confirmed that Namibia would not comply with the ICC arrest warrants for Kadhafi and Sudanese President Omar al-Bashir. Namibia was among the 22 countries that objected in the UN General Assembly on 16 September to accepting the National Transitional Council as the body officially representing Libya. On 23 September, Pohamba declared in his speech at the 66th session of the General Assembly that the intervention in Libya was reminiscent "of the infamous Berlin Conference of 1884/1885, when Africa was carved up by imperial powers".

Zimbabwe's Prime Minister Morgan Tsvangirai visited Windhoek on 28 March to meet Pohamba as head of **SADC** in order to lobby for his party's position on Zimbabwean politics. Despite his office in the government of national unity, the leader of the Movement for Democratic Change was reportedly given the cold shoulder, as in all previous years. In early August, Windhoek hosted leading representatives from another five **former liberation movements** now in political control as governments in Angola, Mozambique, South Africa, Tanzania and Zimbabwe. The final summit on 11 August was preceded by consultative meetings between the youth wing leaders and the secretaries general of the parties. Agreement was reached that such meetings should take place as side events at every SADC summit to strengthen relationships.

An official visit to **Iran** by Foreign Minister Nujoma and Mines and Energy Minister Katali in December underlined the friendly relations between the two countries. It was announced that an Iranian embassy would soon be established and that Iran had decided to invest in an oil refinery in Namibia. This would replace an earlier agreement signed with Nigeria.

During the first nine months of the year, almost 2,000 Namibians applied for **asylum in Canada**, the third highest number of applicants after China and Hungary. Namibians did not require a visa to enter Canada, but in December the Canadian government alerted Air Namibia that Namibians would be scrutinised more closely if they did not have proper travel documents and meet the appropriate entry requirements. According to the local human rights body NamRights, human trafficking was a main reason for Namibians being stranded in Canada, while others were seeking asylum for their links to the Caprivi secessionist movement, which had been prosecuted by the state for high treason.

Bilateral **relations with Germany** remained contested, even though the former colonial power continued to be the biggest single donor country and despite the fact that German Minister for Development Cooperation Dirk Niebel visited the country at the end of August for the second time within 19 months. Early October witnessed the first repatriation of skulls from Germany. They were remains and reminders of the genocide committed by the German colonial army in 1904–1908 and had been taken to Germany for anatomical measurement in line with the Arian obsession with categorising variations between human beings. The visit of a delegation of Herero and Nama descendants to transfer the skulls of their ancestors culminated in a diplomatic wrangle over how to bring about reconciliation with the past. This sensitive issue was exacerbated by **demands for reparation** by the most affected communities, who felt their case had not been adequately recognised. Germany's ambassador to Namibia added fuel to the flames when he suggested, at the signing on 16 November of a new cooperation agreement worth over N$ 660 m, that the Namibian delegation had visited Germany with a hidden agenda and had created a negative impression of bilateral relations between the two countries. Enquiries by opposition parties in the German parliament, as well as a public debate in Namibia and Germany, illustrated the dissonances, also documented in the ministerial outburst reported above.

On 13 September, **EU** Trade Commissioner Karel de Gucht, while on a trip to Southern Africa, met in Windhoek with Pohamba, other ministers and representatives of the trade and business world in an effort to promote the conclusion of an EPA. The meeting ended with no concrete results and the deadlock over unresolved matters continued, while de Gucht made no reference to an ultimatum for the signing of an EPA announced only two weeks later by Brussels.

Socioeconomic Developments

Finance Minister Saara Kuugongelwa-Amadhila tabled the **annual budget** for 2011/12 on 9 March, projecting record expenditure of almost N$ 38 bn, of which N$ 35.8 bn was domestic government expenditure (an increase of 30% on the previous year), with more than N$ 2 bn additional interest costs to service government debt. With estimated revenue of N$ 28 bn, an unprecedented 9.8% GDP deficit was anticipated. This brought the overall debt ratio close to 30% of GDP. The inflated size of new debts took local economists by surprise and resulted in a controversial debate over whether to prioritise fiscal prudence or social investment. The highest allocations were to the ministries of education (N$ 8.3 bn), finance (N$ 3.65 bn), health and social services (N$ 3.3 bn) and defence (N$ 3.1 bn), and totalled over 50% of planned expenditure. The addition of allocations to the ministries of justice, administration, safety and security brought this to 80%, including allocations of N$ 2 bn for the police and N$ 1.2 bn for war veterans. The remaining 20% was allocated to the economic ministries (mines, trade, land, agriculture, fisheries, transport, tourism and planning).

The main budget increase came from the introduction of a Targeted Intervention Programme for Employment and Economic Growth (TIPEEG) with total investments of N$ 14.6 bn over three years for job creation. On the basis of a 2007/8 survey by the ministry of labour, the **unemployment** rate in 2010 was estimated at over 51%. While this figure remained contested, economists agreed that the TIPEEG seemed not to be based on any realistic assessments. Investments through the development budget for the next three years were intended to create over 180,000 jobs in the private sector and public works, but there was little efficient implementation during the rest of the year, due not least to a lack of capacity. On 19 August, Pohamba summoned four ministers to State House to account for the lack of progress. At the end of its yearly mission, which took place from 9 to 22 November, an IMF delegation cautioned that reliance on a TIPEEG would not be enough to combat unemployment.

In contrast to the claim that the budget was pro-poor, no tax adjustments benefited low-income groups, and income **inequality** continued unabated. As observers noted, rising government expenditure over the 20 years since independence had not translated into job creation, reduction of poverty or less income discrepancy. At the end of August, the BIG coalition expressed disappointment over the government's ultimate withdrawal of the planned introduction of a levy on the export of raw materials. The tax reform was shelved after intensive lobbying by the mining industry. The BIG coalition pointed out that the continued zero-rating on the export of **raw materials** gave a free tax ride to those who extracted natural resources.

On 1 December, TI released its latest Corruption Perceptions Index, according to which the country maintained its score of 4.4, and remained in the category of **highly corrupt** although its overall ranking was 57th least corrupt out of 183 economies and second least corrupt in the region – which showed that everything is somewhat relative. A World Bank study presented towards year's end focused on money laundering in Malawi and Namibia. It suggested that government corruption in Namibia was a bigger problem than other forms of organised crime and fraud. Tax evasion was estimated at 9% of GDP and by far the largest source of ill-gotten money. Dubious foreign investments also affected the property market. A considerable cash inflow from Angola was used for the purchase of land and estates, contributing to a boom, fuelled to a large extent by money laundering activities.

Another worrying tendency was the ballooning of **tender exemptions** for public works. A report presented by the Institute for Public Policy Research (IPPR) on 9 September documented that exemptions from normal tender procedures had become the rule, bypassing scrutiny by the tender board, although, with the massive increase of capital investment in public works by the TIPEEG, adherence to the Tender Board Act remained essential to curb large-scale misappropriation of funds through unfair competition and preferential treatment. In mid-December, it was reported that the cabinet had approved another tender exemption for N$ 150 m in emergency spending for the repair of railway lines, allegedly in favour of a company linked to close friends of top officials in the ministry of works and transport. The ministry had previously been accused of being the main culprit when it came to the allocation of large sums for public works without adherence to tender board regulations. On 16 December, the chairperson of the northern branch of the Namibian Chamber of Commerce and Industry (NCCI), in the presence of the finance minister and the director general of the NPC, alleged favouritism and nepotism in awarding tenders under the TIPEEG.

An IPPR report released in December also concluded that mismanagement, lack of transparency and **misappropriation of public funds** were rife in state-owned enterprises, which had mushroomed from 12 to over 60 since independence. Meanwhile, the saga around fraudulent losses of several hundred million Namibian dollars in shady deals through the Development Capital Portfolio of the Government Investment Pension Fund continued. In February, a summary report of the forensic audit was submitted to cabinet and trade union representatives. Details of the massive scale of transactions involving recipients under the banner of Black Economic Empowerment (BEE) were not fully disclosed. In response to public pressure and demands by the trade unions, the cabinet announced on 24 August that it had directed the prosecutor general to lay charges against those officials responsible for the loss and the few politically-well-connected looters who had benefited from the loans.

The finance minister announced at an international **investment** forum at the end of November – during which Ohorongo Cement, a subsidiary of the German company Schwenk, received the international investor award 2011 as the continent's most advanced cement producer – that FDI had increased by 34% during the previous year. This contrasted with the constant net outflow of capital, estimated at between N$ 5 bn and N$ 8 bn. A law reform was initiated to the effect that institutional investors (such as insurance companies, unit trusts and pension funds) should keep a minimum of 35% of their total assets in the country. In early September, the World Economic Forum released its Global Competitiveness Report 2011–12, in which Namibia's ranking dropped from 74th to 83rd out of 142 countries, not least through weak performance in the health and education sectors.

The US-based Wal-Mart Stores Inc. tried to enter the local market through a South African subsidiary. The Namibian Competition Commission and the minister of trade and industry, concerned about the effects of the presence of such a powerful trader on the **retail trade**, tried to prevent this but, on April 28, the retail giant scored a legal victory when the

High Court set aside conditions attached to the approval of Wal-Mart's takeover of South Africa's Massmart group. On 4 November, however, the Supreme Court overturned the ruling and Wal-Mart's objections to the conditions were referred back to the minister.

Mining remained the most important sector in the economy, contributing in 2010 about 15% of GDP and more than 50% of total export revenue. Mines and Energy Minister Isak Katali announced a strategic mineral policy in parliament on 20 April. It transferred control of uranium, copper, gold, zinc and coal to the state-owned Epangelo mining company, including the allocation of exploration and mining licences. The minister admitted that BEE had been exploited in the purchase of exploration licenses, which were secured by local BEE front companies on behalf of foreign-owned companies. Such deals had the sole aim of making "phenomenal amounts" of money for a few to the disadvantage of the state revenue coffers. In July, Katali confirmed rumours that an estimated 12 bn barrels of **oil**, as well as gas, had been identified by exploration companies off the coast. It was announced that systematic drilling would start towards year's end, though a bonanza was not expected to be imminent.

The country remained the world's fourth biggest **uranium** producer. In early December, the wheeling and dealing around the ownership of Swakop Uranium, which controlled the fourth largest known deposit, at Husab, paved the way for further Chinese ownership through a takeover of Kalahari Minerals by China Guangdong Nuclear Power Corp in a £ 632 m ($ 990 m) deal. Kalahari owned 43% in Extract Resources, whose wholly owned subsidiary, Swakop Uranium, received a mining licence to develop Husab as one of the biggest uranium mines in the world. In contrast, the French nuclear fuel and services giant Areva announced on 13 December that it was putting on hold its $ 1 bn investment in the Trekkopje uranium project as a result of worldwide losses of up to $ 2 bn. The originally estimated volume of 45,200 tonnes of uranium was adjusted to 26,000 tonnes, making the investment much less lucrative, since the world market price had dropped from a record high of $ 135 per pound in 2007 to $ 50–$ 55 due to a decline in demand since the Fukushima disaster. Almost bucking this trend, Paladin Energy, owner of the Langer Heinrich uranium mine, announced in late August that new supply agreements had been entered with three US customers with production commitments totalling more than 2.8 m pounds of yellow cake for delivery in 2012–2016. The expansion of Langer Heinrich was expected to increase annual output from 3.7 m pound to 5.2 m pound of yellow cake.

Eastern China Non-Ferrous Metals Investment Holdings, the investment arm of the East China Mineral Exploration and Development Bureau, announced in early December the discovery of 2 bn tonnes of **iron ore** in the Kunene region and plans to open an iron mine and steel plant with an annual production of 5 m tonnes. This promoted speculation about the construction of a third Namibian harbour at Cape Fria, as the government had already allocated funds for a feasibility study in the state budget. NamRights claimed that the Chinese company's local subsidiary had relations with the former head of state, Sam Nujoma, who, according to its investigations, had earlier accepted the role of honorary advisor and senior consultant to the company and received generous donations to his Foundation. Glencore bought 80% of the **zinc** mine at Rosh Pinah, operational since 1969, in a series of transactions during the year. Production during the previous year was reportedly 101,000 tonnes of zinc concentrate and 19,000 tonnes of lead concentrate.

While the Chinese presence in the mining sector expanded further, **trade relations with China** took a dip, according to the NCCI, with a decline in exports from N$ 1.8 bn in 2009 (mainly uranium, copper, lead and other natural resources) to N$ 1.2 bn in 2010. Imports shrank from N$ 2.9 bn in 2009 (mainly cars, telecommunication, furniture, machinery and other manufactured goods) to N$ 1.3 bn in 2010. During a visit to China, Agriculture Minister John Mutorwa signed a bilateral trade agreement on 16 December, which paved the way for the future export of meat and fish, grapes and dates to the Chinese market.

The prolonged negotiations over an **EPA**, which Namibia had refused to sign because of unresolved differences, entered a new chapter with the EU's announcement in October that all preferences in duty- and quota-free market access would end if an EPA were not signed by January 2014. Based on 2009 figures, it was estimated that this would amount to payments of € 58.2 m in duties on Namibian exports to the EU market. Namibia rejected allegations that it was responsible for the delays in finding a solution. On 5 October, Trade Minister Hage Geingob expressed his disappointment and declared that setting such an arbitrary deadline would be no sign of partnership. The continued negotiations towards an adjusted revenue sharing formula among **SACU** member countries, with potentially negative consequences for the public purse in years to come, added to the discouraging indicators with regard to the macroeconomic future and its effects on socioeconomic developments.

Henning Melber

South Africa

While securely established as the ruling power on the eve of its 100th anniversary, the African National Congress (ANC) singled out the press and the judiciary as obstacles to 'transformation', sparking off a civil society coalition against the Protection of State Information Bill. Internal factionalism within the ANC escalated in the build-up to the leadership election in 2012, which had at times a paralysing effect on the functioning of the state. With 2.6% growth, the economy expanded more slowly than anticipated, but picked up in the fourth quarter, largely driven by consumer spending.

Domestic Politics

From 26 to 28 January, South Africa held its breath when **Nelson Mandela** was admitted to Milpark Hospital in Johannesburg, suffering from a respiratory infection. Scenes of alarm and grief spread from Johannesburg to other parts of the country, largely because government communication was badly handled. The nation sighed in relief when Mandela was discharged from hospital after three days and the government began preparing itself for the inevitable day when South Africans would have to face a future without *Madiba*.

The 57.6% voter turnout for the **municipal elections** on 18 May was the highest in local government elections since 1994. Calls for an election boycott under the motto "no land, no vote, no houses, no vote", the campaign slogan used by the Poor People's Alliance, which included movements of homeless or landless people, apparently had little impact, although the number of spoilt ballots was substantial at 235,345. The ANC's share of the vote fell from 66.5% in 2006 to 62.9% while the main opposition party, the Democratic Alliance (DA), increased its share significantly from 14.8% in 2006 to 24.1%. The ANC held control of all the major cities except Cape Town, which went to the DA. On 1 June, Patricia de Lille was inaugurated as the mayor of Cape Town. The ANC lost votes in all provinces except KwaZulu/Natal (KZN), the home base of President Jacob Zuma. The ANC's high rating in KZN was largely at the expense of the Inkatha Freedom Party (IFP), which received only 3.6% of the votes. The Congress of the People (COPE), which had split from the ANC, took only 2.2%. The poor showing of COPE and the IFP may be partially explained as a result of internal wrangling. COPE was already split into factions led by Mbhazima Shilowa and Mosiuoa Lekota, and the IFP now also split: National Chairwoman Zanele Magwaza-Msibi formed her own National Freedom Party (NFP) after veteran leader Mangosuthu Buthelezi refused to step down. The NFP won 2.4% of the vote and became the majority party on two councils in KZN. The elections in KZN were followed by a spate of suspected **political murders**, sparking fears of a turf war between the IFP, NFP and ANC. Within a few months, three NFP leaders, two IFP leaders and one ANC councillor were killed by unknown assailants. A multiparty task force was set up to deal with political violence.

The **Democratic Alliance**'s potential for growth remained limited because of the perception that it represented white interests. As part of a public relations makeover, DA leader Helen Zille predicted that the next leader of the party would be black. The DA support base has widened over the years to include a majority of Coloured voters and substantial numbers of Indians and even Africans. Whites now make up less than 50% of its support base. On 27 October, 31-year-old Lindiwe Mazibuko, who entered parliament only in 2009, was elected leader of the DA's parliamentary caucus, with the strong support of Zille, defeating the incumbent leader Athol Trollip.

Although the ANC had imposed a moratorium on open competition in the **race for the presidential succession**, several rivals emerged in the run-up to the elective conference to be held in Bloemfontein (Mangaung) in December 2012. Apart from Deputy President Kgalema Motlanthe, possible candidates for the ANC leadership were Tokyo Sexwale, currently minister of human settlements and ANC treasurer Matthews Posa. The incumbent, Jacob Zuma, would stand for a second term as leader of the ANC, and thus as State President.

On 24 October, Zuma replaced two ministers: Sicelo Shiceka of Co-operative Governance and Gwen Mahlangu-Nkabinde of Public Works, as part of his much heralded drive against **corruption**. They were succeeded by Richard Baloyi, previously at Public Service and Administration, and Thembelani Nxesithe, former Deputy Minister for Rural Development and Land Reform, respectively. Zuma also suspended National Police

Commissioner Bheki Cele and appointed a board of inquiry into allegations of misconduct. Shiceka, Mahlangu-Nkabinde and Cele had been implicated following investigations by **Public Protector** Thuli Madonsela, a human rights lawyer who had acquired a reputation for vigorous independence. She found Shiceka guilty of misusing public funds for extravagant holiday travel, while Manhlangu-Nkabinde and Cele were found guilty of misconduct in connection with R 1.7 bn leases for new police headquarters. It was estimated that 20%–25% of state procurement expenditure, amounting to roughly R 30 bn a year, was wasted through overpayment or corruption. On 6 May, Sheryl Cwele, wife of Minister of Safety and Security Siyabonga Cwele, was convicted of dealing in cocaine and sentenced to 12 years in jail.

Zwelinzima Vavi, secretary general of the Congress of South African Trade Unions (COSATU), condemned **corruption in government**. In his secretarial report to COSATU's central committee in June, he noted that, in the period after the ANC's Polokwane conference in 2007, "a powerful, corrupt, predatory elite combined with a conservative populist agenda to harness the ANC to advance their interests" had emerged. He also pointed to the "political paralysis" in the state that resulted from the ongoing contestation within the Tripartite Alliance. At the heart of COSATU's dissatisfaction with the Alliance was the question of whether the ANC should lead the Alliance, or whether the Alliance itself should be the strategic centre of power.

On 15 September, Zuma announced a new inquiry into the bribery allegations associated with the notorious 1999 **arms deal**. Judge Willie Seriti of the Supreme Court of Appeal was appointed to chair the commission of inquiry. The 'Sunday Times' reported on 20 November that Zuma spokesman and ANC veteran Mac Maharaj, who was then minister of transport, had been paid 1.2 m French francs by French arms producer Thales, the payments being made into his wife's bank account, using a Swiss bank account owned by Zuma's financial adviser Shabir Shaik as conduit. Shaik was sentenced to 15 years in 2005 for his role in soliciting bribes for Zuma from Thales. He was released on medical parole in 2009. Swedish manufacturer Saab admitted in June that R 24 m had been paid in bribes to secure a contract for Gripen fighter jets, which have since been delivered.

On 7 December, Zuma released the **Donen report**, an investigation by a commission of inquiry into alleged abuses of the UN-sanctioned oil-for-food programme with Iraq. As the Donen Commission had submitted its report in 2006, the timing of the release sparked speculation about Zuma's intentions. Announcing the release, Zuma's spokesman Mac Maharaj said that the report cleared Deputy President Kgalema Motlanthe and Minister of Human Settlements Tokyo Sexwale of involvement in the payment of 'surcharges' or kickbacks, levied on oil allocations by the Saddam Hussein regime in contravention of UN sanctions. The 'Mail&Guardian' pointed out that Motlanthe and Sexwale were in fact neither cleared nor implicated, as the Donen Commission, which had no powers to subpoena witnesses or documents, had not been able to fully investigate the allegations. Motlanthe, then ANC secretary-general, accompanied South African oil trader Sandi Majali, who had good ANC connections, at least three times to Iraq between 2000 and 2003. Majali, who was known to contribute to ANC party finances, was found dead in unexplained circumstances in a Sandton hotel room in December 2010. The Donen report noted that Motlanthe probably knew of the conspiracy to pay kickbacks and "might have become associated in it in some manner". Sexwale never denied that he traded in Iraq under the oil-for-food programme, but stated that his UK-based partner, Michael Hacking, attended to details such as possible kickbacks.

In December, the Supreme Court of Appeal dismissed an appeal by former police commissioner **Jackie Selebi** against his conviction for corruption. The Court upheld the 15-year sentence imposed by the High Court, which had found that Selebi had received R 166,000 in cash from Glenn Agliotti, a convicted drug dealer. In exchange, Selebi had provided Agliotti with confidential police reports. In December, Agliotti was acquitted of the murder of former mining magnate Bret Kebble in September 2005. Proceedings against Selebi were opened after a series of reports in the 'Mail&Guardian'. The paper pointed out that these disclosures would be criminalised once the Protection of State Information Bill was signed into law.

On 6 December, the government took direct control of parts of several provincial administrations in a clampdown on financial mismanagement and inadequate delivery of **public services**. Central government assumed authority over nearly every area of administration in Limpopo province after it asked for a R 1 bn overdraft to pay civil servants' salaries. Under the terms of the takeover, the government assumed direct control not only over Limpopo's finances, but also over the departments of education, transport, health and public works. Minister of Finance Pravin Gordhan announced an investigation into alleged corruption and maladministration. Pretoria also took control of the finances and the police and transport sections of the Free State, as well as the department of health in Gauteng Province. While **Limpopo** in particular was notorious for corrupt and nepotistic practices, the takeover was inevitably also interpreted as a move in the ANC's succession battle. As the 'Mail&Guardian' noted, the drastic intervention was warranted, but the move also deprived one of Zuma's most important opponents of almost all of his power and, crucially, of his patronage network. The moves to stabilise the finances of the Free State and the Gauteng health department were seen as friendly bailouts rather than hostile takeovers. Soon after central government moved in, Limpopo premier Cassel Mathale was re-elected as leader of the provincial ANC with 601 votes against 519 votes for Deputy Arts and Culture Minister Joe Phaahla. Mathale was a key ally of youth leader Julius Malema. The ANC's Limpopo conference marked a triumph for Malema, being the first time that an ANC provincial structure endorsed Malema's views. In the final declaration, the conference called for all productive land to be nationalised, with compensation to be determined through state evaluation.

According to a BBC report on 5 May, the mineworkers' unions alleged that the **Aurora goldmine**, owned by members of the Mandela and Zuma families, was able, because of its powerful political connections, to get away with abuse of workers, non-payment of salaries and refusal to honour commitments. The managing director of Aurora Empowerment Systems was Zondwa Gadaffi Mandela, grandson of Nelson Mandela. The chairman was Khulubuse Zuma, nephew of President Zuma. Another board member, Michael Hulley, was Zuma's personal legal advisor. Aurora took over the goldmines in Orkney and Grootvlei in October 2009, and promised steady jobs, decent housing and education bursaries for the children of the workers. By December 2009, Aurora had already begun to default on the payment of salaries, leaving many of the 5,200 mineworkers dependent on food handouts from the unions. While miners' wages were not being paid, Khulubuse Zuma made a private donation of R 1 m to the ANC. The Grootvlei mine, opened in 2008 at a cost of R 40 m as one of South Africa's most modern mines, had been stripped bare of its headgear and machinery, which had been sold off for scrap. The unions blamed Aurora; Aurora blamed illegal miners.

Julius Malema, 30-year-old leader of the ANC Youth League (ANCYL), made headlines throughout the year. On 16 June (in memory of the Soweto revolt celebrated as public National Youth Day), he came out in favour of a second term for Jacob Zuma, but stated that the League wanted Secretary General Gwede Mantashe replaced by former ANCYL president Fikile Mbalula. Malema's support for Zuma surprised because of his vocal criticism of Zuma's failure to enact pro-poor policies, but later in the year the youth leader made clear that he favoured Motlanthe as Zuma's successor. On 12 September, a court ruled in favour of AfriForum, an Afrikaner rights organisation linked to the trade union Solidarity, which had asked the court to stop Malema from singing a liberation struggle classic that includes a call to "kill the Boers". After Judge Colin Lamont found that the singing of the song under present conditions amounted to hate speech, Malema accused him of racism. Meanwhile, the police had launched an investigation into allegations that Malema had received kickbacks for facilitating state contracts in his home province of Limpopo. On 19 August, the ANC ordered Malema to appear before a disciplinary hearing for "bringing the party into disrepute and sowing internal divisions". He had called Botswana "a puppet of the United States" and had called for "regime change" there. Subsequently, on 10 November, the ANC's disciplinary committee announced a five-year **suspension** for provoking divisions within the party. Malema immediately announced that he would appeal. He had become president of the ANCYL in 2008 and quickly emerged as a key ally of Jacob Zuma in his campaign to oust Thabo Mbeki, but his loyalty faded soon after Zuma assumed the presidency. ANCYL spokesman Floyd Shivambu was suspended for three years, while four other ANCYL leaders received suspended sentences. Under Malema's leadership, the ANCYL has been vocal in campaigning for the nationalisation of the mines and the expropriation of white-owned farmland. He was widely seen as instrumental in the factional battles within the ANC, but analyst Steven Friedman believed that Malema was neither powerful nor popular. According to Friedman, writing in the 'New Age' newspaper, Malema owed his position to the fact that he was useful to one of the factions contesting for power in the ANC, the 'nationalist' or 'populist' group. After his suspension, Malema was elected onto the ANC's provincial executive committee in Limpopo, his home province. Speculation continued that Malema would try to use the 2012 Mangaung conference to stage a comeback.

Archbishop **Desmond Tutu** celebrated his 80th birthday on 7 October with a harsh rebuke to the ANC government for its failure to grant a visa to the Dalai Lama, whom Tutu had invited to South Africa. This was the second time in two years that the Dalai Lama had been refused entry, although he had visited South Africa on three occasions between 1996 and 2004. Tutu criticised the government for pandering to major trade partner China and accused the ANC of conduct worse than that of the apartheid regime. Visibly angry, the archbishop warned that the day might come when people would pray for the ANC's demise. Tutu, widely seen as South Africa's moral compass, celebrated his birthday in St George Cathedral in Cape Town, surrounded by rock stars, politicians and parishioners.

On 22 November, the National Assembly approved the **Protection of State Information Bill**, despite widespread criticism from the media and other advocates of freedom of information. The Bill, commonly referred to as the Secrecy Bill, went through 11 drafts, with over 120 amendments adopted. Despite these substantial amendments, the coalition for press freedom, called the Right2Know Campaign, mounted a sustained campaign for further improvements. With more than 400 affiliates, the Right2Know Campaign had become the most effective public campaign on an issue of government policy since the AIDS activism of the early 2000s. The Bill criminalised the possession and distribution of classified information but was ambiguous as to who had the authority to classify information. The Bill shut off state security agencies from any kind of scrutiny or accountability to the public, with harsh prison sentences for accessing or sharing information related to those agencies. While critics acknowledged that the state might have legitimate reasons to protect sensitive information, it was widely assumed that intelligence agencies were not only used to protect the state, but also served as instruments in internal ANC power wrangles. Outspoken opponents of the bill included two Nobel laureates, Archbishop Desmond Tutu and author Nadine Gordimer. A few dissenters in the ANC parliamentary caucus, notably Professor Ben Turok and Gloria Borman, were threatened with disciplinary action, as MPs were expected to toe the party line. A total of 34 ANC MPs were absent for the vote. The bill was widely criticised as an attempt to silence whistle-blowers and muzzle investigative journalists. Minister of State Security Siyabonga Cwele contended that "foreign spies continue to steal our sensitive information" for their own benefit and at the expense of the people of South Africa. COSATU argued that the Bill could easily be misused to cover up corruption and incompetence in government, and AI called the bill "fatally flawed". The Bill still had to be approved by the National Council of Provinces, South Africa's Upper House, after which opponents could take their case to the Constitutional Court. Both the DA and COSATU announced their intention to do so.

In response to another threat, a government proposal for a **media tribunal**, the print media came up with two initiatives. The existing Press Council reviewed its press code and mounted a campaign to familiarise journalists with its contents; and the South African National Editors Forum and Print Media SA set up the Press Freedom Commission under the chairmanship of judge Pius Langa to look into all forms of regulation as practised worldwide and come up with a proposal. The government was expected to make a revised proposal after the Commission submitted its findings.

The government suffered a number of **setbacks in the courts**, resulting in calls for a radical 'transformation' of the judiciary, and the Constitutional Court in particular. On 8 September, Judge Mogoeng Mogoeng was sworn in as South Africa's new chief justice of the Constitutional Court, in spite of criticism that he had proved to be gender-insensitive in several of his judgments. Zuma had initially attempted to extend the term of the then chief justice Sandile Ngcobo, but this measure was judged unconstitutional. The legislation abolishing the Directorate of Special Operations (known as the Scorpions) as the investigative unit of the National Prosecuting Authority (NPA) and replacing it with the Directorate for Priority Crime Investigations (to be known as the Hawks) was ruled deficient by the Constitutional Court. The Hawks were removed from the NPA and became a unit of the police, whom the Court deemed vulnerable to political interference. Parliament was instructed to strengthen the independent position of the Hawks by September 2012.

The Supreme Court of Appeal ruled on 1 December that Zuma's appointment of Menzi Simelane as **National Director of Public Prosecutions** was inconsistent with the constitution and invalid, as there were unresolved questions about his integrity. The plaintiff DA had argued that Simelane was a Zuma 'acolyte' and that he would be inclined to protect powerful people from prosecution. Zuma appealed to the Constitutional Court but then withdrew his appeal, and on 29 December appointed Simelane's controversial deputy Nomgcobo Jiba. Jiba had briefly acted as head of the Special Investigating Unit (SIU), but she was abruptly replaced after barely a week in the job. She replaced Willem Heath, who had resigned after the publication of a 'City Press' interview in which he alleged that former ANC and South Africa president Thabo Mbeki had initiated rape and corruption charges against Zuma and blocked investigations into corrupt practices. Opposition MP Debbie Schafer (DA) said that Heath had compromised the integrity of the SIU by abandoning his impartiality and siding with Zuma's faction in the ANC. In 2008, Jiba had been suspended from the NPA after accusations that she was part of a conspiracy to have former Gauteng Scorpions head Gerrie Nel arrested before he could bring corruption charges against former police commissioner Jackie Selebi. Zuma appointed Jiba deputy director of the NPA in January, a decision strongly criticised by the DA.

Influential voices in the ANC had been calling for a review of the **powers of the judiciary** and notably the Constitutional Court. Previously, 'transformation of the judiciary' meant speeding up the process of demographic transformation of the Bench, but increasingly the phrase was used as a call to limit the powers of the courts, which were believed to undermine the executive and the legislative. In November, the Cabinet announced plans for the formation of an independent body to assess the judgments of the Constitutional Court in order "to enhance synergy and constructive engagement" between the three branches of government. The most vocal critic of the judiciary was Deputy Minister of Correctional Services Ngoako Ramathlodi, a former chairperson of the Judicial Service Commission. Writing in 'The Times', he lambasted the judiciary as an instrument for the protection of white economic interests. Other prominent ANC politicians had emphasised the legacy of apartheid, stating that courts had been used as an instrument of oppression. Legal experts stressed that the Constitutional Court had a pro-transformation agenda and had generally favoured a progressive interpretation of the constitution.

In his end-of-year speech, Zuma emphasised that the government's expanded **public works programme** had provided opportunities and income for a total of 280,000 people and more than 80,000 job opportunities under the community work programme. The year saw a drop of 5.8% in violent crime. He said that HIV counselling and testing had broken ground in reaching 13 m and 8 m people for HIV and TB screening respectively. In April, a **strike by municipal workers**, who accused the refuse removal company Pikitup of corruption and outsourcing, left the streets of Johannesburg with heaps of uncollected, rat infested litter. Pikitup management resigned and the strike was called off after two weeks. During a service delivery protest in Ficksburg, in the Free State, police shot and killed community leader Andries Tatane. Four police officers were charged with murder.

In October, the Department of Home Affairs lifted a moratorium on the **deportation of Zimbabweans** who had not applied for legal status. The International Organisation for Migration estimated that between 1 m and 1.5 m Zimbabweans were living in South Africa, but only 275,000 had applied to be regularised by the 31 December 2010 deadline, later extended till 31 March. By October, Home Affairs had issued permits to just over half of them, amid reports of massive bribery.

Albertina Sisulu, one of the ANC stalwarts in the liberation struggle, died on 2 June at the age of 92. She was buried next to her husband Walter Sisulu, who had died in 2003. From the 1940s, the Sisulu house in Soweto had welcomed hundreds of activists, including Nelson Mandela. Separated from her husband during his 26-year imprisonment, Albertina became a leader in her own right, instilling the history and values of the ANC in new generations of activists while she worked as a nurse to support her five children. In 1983, she became one of the three national presidents of the United Democratic Front. She was jailed several times and continuously subjected to banning orders that limited her freedom of movement.

On 22 June, **Kader Asmal** died after a heart attack at the age of 76. Asmal, who had served in various cabinets as minister of water affairs and later of education (1999–2004) was known for speaking his mind, even if it deviated from ANC policies. He was an outspoken critic of the Protection of State Information Bill.

In July, one of the most hated figures of the apartheid regime, former minister of defence **Magnus Malan**, died at the age of 81. General Malan was considered the architect of the military repression of anti-apartheid resistance during the decade of widespread popular mobilisation in the 1980s. The wave of repression culminated in the declaration of the state of emergency in 1986 and the bombing of neighbouring countries that provided safe havens for anti-apartheid fighters. In 1995, Malan was charged with conspiracy and 13 counts of murder relating to a massacre carried out by paramilitary forces in 1987 in KZN, but he was acquitted.

Hate crimes against black lesbians were highlighted by the murder of **Noxolo Nogwaza**, who was active in a gay and lesbian rights group. She was raped and stoned to death on 23 April in KwaThema township, which provoked a public outcry by the gay and lesbian community over the brutality to which it remained exposed, despite constitutional rights.

At the stroke of midnight on 31 December, Zuma lit the 'centenary flame' in the Wesleyan church in Waaihoek, Bloemfontein, where the founding fathers of the ANC had met in 1912 to join forces against the dispossession of blacks in the newly established Union of South Africa. A series of **ANC anniversary activities** was planned for the year 2012, culminating in the elective conference in Mangaung in December.

Foreign Affairs

In March, Zuma warned against foreign military intervention in **Libya**, saying that UN members should not go beyond the terms of a 17 March UNSC resolution 1973 to enforce a no-fly zone. As a non-permanent member of the UNSC, South Africa had supported the resolution authorising action to protect civilians from the troops of the Libyan leader Muammar Kadhafi and enforce a no-fly zone. The ANCYL criticised the government for backing what it saw as an attempt by foreign governments to replace Kadhafi's rule with a puppet administration. Zuma was part of a five-man presidential panel tasked by the AU to negotiate in Libya. He later blamed NATO air raids for scuttling the AU mission before it had a chance to succeed.

The president paid a state visit to **France** on 2–3 March, during which a Framework Partnership Document was signed. Zuma urged the French business community to consider infrastructure development, agriculture, mining and beneficiation, manufacturing, the green economy and tourism, which had been identified as key job creation sectors. There were already over 170 French companies operating in South Africa, contributing to a total of bilateral trade of R 32 bn in 2008. However, this dropped to R 23 bn in 2009 due to the global recession. President Nicolas Sarkozy stated that the two countries were going to "harmonise" their positions in the framework of the G20 and announced that France was more than willing to provide South Africa with nuclear energy. Because of an increase in loans to finance large development projects, notably in public infrastructure, the French Development Agency was the second biggest bilateral donor in South Africa.

During the state visit, three agreements worth a total of € 370 m were signed. South Africa and France had strained relations, notably with regard to their Africa policy. In several major conflicts, such as in Côte d' Ivoire and Madagascar, Paris and Pretoria supported opposing sides. France was a firm advocate of military intervention in Libya, while South Africa was involved in AU mediation. In the competition for the chair of the Commission of the AU, France backed the incumbent, Jean Ping from Gabon, while South Africa campaigned for the election of former foreign minister Nkosazana Dlamini-Zuma.

After Swazi King Mswati had prematurely announced that Pretoria would provide a lifeline enabling his government to pay public sector salaries, Finance Minister Pravin Gordhan confirmed on 3 August that South Africa would extend a R 2.4 bn loan to **Swaziland.** Swaziland turned to Pretoria as a last resort after the IMF, the World Bank and the AfDB had declined help because the Swazi government refused to implement austerity measures, including cuts in the public sector. Pro-democracy groups in Swaziland and COSATU reacted angrily, arguing that the loan should have been tied to conditions such as democratic reform and respect for human rights. Swaziland's financial crisis was blamed on a drop in revenue from SACU, financial mismanagement and the extravagant life style of King Mswati and his extended family. South Africa also confirmed that the Swazi currency would remain pegged to the Rand.

South Africa prepared for the launch of a **foreign aid agency**, the South African Development Partnership Agency, which would be partnered by a foreign policy think tank, based at the Foreign Ministry, recently renamed the Department of International Relations and Cooperation (DIRCO). South Africa already provided a modest amount of foreign aid to the IBSA (India-Brazil-South Africa) Fund, which was administered by the UNDP. Now South Africa wanted to bring its foreign aid under its own control.

The **Nordic countries** featured prominently in bilateral relations. During a state visit to Norway in early September, Zuma stated that South Africa would welcome Norwegian investments in energy and partnerships in the green economy. South Africa's trade with Norway had increased significantly over the past five years, tripling from R 963 m in 2006 to more than R 3 bn in 2010. South Africa was a net exporter to Norway. In October, Deputy President Kgalema Motlanthe missed an official state visit to Finland because of mechanical problems in his VIP aircraft, but he made the bilateral meetings with Sweden and a visit to Denmark scheduled for the later stages of this trip.

To promote trade and investment, Zuma paid a state visit to **Burundi** in August. Private investment by South Africans in Burundi had increased significantly over the past years, notably in tourism and agro-business. During a state visit by President Obiang Nguema Mbasogo of **Equatorial Guinea** on 21–22 October, the two countries agreed to work together to increase bilateral trade and investment. Two cooperation agreements were signed during a state visit by President Thomas Yayi Boni of **Benin** on 23–26 November. On 12 November, Zuma and his Congolese counterpart, Joseph Kabila, attended the signing ceremony in Lubumbashi, **DRC**, of an accord to develop a mega-hydroelectric plant on the Congo River. The Grand Inga hydroelectricity complex, which will have a capacity of some 40,000 MW, is aimed at addressing the energy needs of South Africa, the DRC and other countries in the region.

In December, President José Eduardo dos Santos of **Angola** paid his long-awaited state visit to South Africa, the first since 1994. Relations between Angola and South Africa had been somewhat strained as Angola felt that its crucial contribution to the anti-apartheid struggle had not been sufficiently acknowledged. To make up for past negligence, Dos Santos was presented with the Order of the Companions of OR Tambo, the highest honour that can be awarded to non-South Africans. During the struggle years, Angola provided the ANC with hospitality and military bases. Angola's rapidly growing economy was attracting major investment, but most lucrative construction projects went to China, Brazil and Western countries. A number of bilateral accords were signed in areas such as public works, telecommunications, infrastructure and information technology.

Despite international pressure to extend the ban on diamond exports from **Zimbabwe**, South Africa decided to support the export of diamonds from the Marange fields. According to a spokesman of the Kimberley Process, Zimbabwe had complied with the requirements and therefore its diamonds could be traded as 'conflict-free'. Canada and Australia had advocated an extension of the ban on the export of Zimbabwean diamonds because of alleged human rights violations on and around the diamond fields. However, the African Diamond Producers Association accused these countries of having sinister and selfish motives. The Kimberley certification process for conflict-free diamonds was designed to stop devastating conflicts, such as in Angola, Cote d'Ivoire, DRC and Sierra Leone, where the trade in illicit diamonds fuelled civil war. Meanwhile, South African companies expanded their interest in platinum mining in Zimbabwe. In April Anglo-American opened its second platinum mine, a R 4.5 bn investment, in central Zimbabwe.

By the end of 2010, **China** had become South Africa's top export destination. South Africa exported mainly primary products, notably iron ore. As Jakkie Cilliers of the Institute for Security Studies pointed out, the saga of the Dalai Lama and Tutu's birthday party provided a perfect illustration of the fact that South Africa was beholden to China. Trade grew rapidly, and Pretoria was indebted to Bejing for the invitation to join BRIC(S) (Brazil, Russia, India, China, South Africa). Chinese products accounted for 13% of South Africa's total imports. More importantly, South African exports to China grew faster than imports. In 2011, imports were valued at $ 13.5 bn, while exports stood at a record $ 15 bn. Although South Africa was China's biggest market in Africa, it represented only 1% of Chinese trade. A Chinese consortium embarked on plans to open a platinum mine in North West Province in cooperation with Wesizwe Platinum, which would be China's first direct involvement with platinum mining in South Africa.

From 28 November to 9 December, the **COP17** (Convention of Parties) conference of the UN Framework Convention on Climate Change took place in Durban. While the meeting ended inconclusively, it marked the first time that global climate change discussions were held on such prominent scale in Africa. The conference raised South Africa's profile as a host country for world conferences and business tourism.

Socioeconomic Developments

Economic recovery remained hesitant after the 2009 recession, which caused a contraction of the economy by 1.9%. Largely due to the recession in Europe and the USA, **economic growth** lagged behind the predicted 3.5% and remained at 2.6%, although growth accelerated in the fourth quarter. With an ambitious programme for massive spending on infrastructure, the government wanted to move to fixed investment rather than consumer spending as the main driver of growth.

Delivering the **State of the Nation** address on 10 February, Zuma announced the creation of a job fund of R 9 bn over the next three years. The Jobs Fund would co-finance innovative public and private sector employment projects. The government would also set aside R 20 bn in tax relief to promote investment, expansions and upgrades in the manufacturing sector. Support for small and medium enterprises continued as well as support for small scale agriculture. Another important element in the job creation strategy was the beneficiation of minerals to enable South Africa to export finished or semi-finished products rather than raw commodities. A new state-owned company, the African Exploration, Mining and Finance Corporation, was to undertake the mining of minerals of strategic importance. Zuma stated that "the creation of decent work is at the centre of our economic policies". All government departments were to align their programmes with the job creation imperative.

Speaking at the inaugural conference on the **New Growth Path** (NGP), Deputy President Motlanthe called on the social partners to set aside differences in interests and ideology to find solutions to the persistent employment crisis. Despite a return to growth, the economy had not been able to recapture all the approximately one million jobs lost between 2008 and 2010. Minister of Economic Development Ebrahim Patel emphasised that there was no shortage of good ideas, but that the challenge was to work towards purposeful and effective implementation. In the NGP, mining, manufacturing, agriculture and tourism were earmarked as 'job drivers'. The target of the NGP was to create five million jobs over the next decade and reduce unemployment to 15% by 2020. The unemployment rate declined somewhat, from 25.3% in 2010 to 23.9% in the last quarter of 2011.

Inspired by the Chinese model of **state capitalism**, the government was increasingly looking at large infrastructural programmes for state-owned enterprises such as Eskom and Transnet as drivers of sustained growth. Government procurement would be used to encourage the purchase of local products and services. Development finance institutions, such as the Industrial Development Corporation, were also key to the NGP vision of up-scaling the productive sectors of the economy. The NGP gathering ran parallel to consultations in the National Economic Development and Labour Council (NEDLAC) on the NGP. Organised business confirmed that the talks focused on the skills deficit, improving basic education, increasing local procurement, stimulating small business development and galvanising the so-called green economy. Much division remained over the

NGP's macro-economic package, which called for fiscal tightening and monetary loosening. The idea was to use a more flexible monetary policy model to facilitate a weakening of the rand to bolster the competitiveness of South African industry. However, in the light of rising food and fuel prices, there was also strong resistance to calls for a weaker rand.

Organised labour and business remained at loggerheads about proposed **labour legislation**. COSATU and a number of other unions wanted to ban labour brokers because of exploitative practices, while business and government argued in favour of regulation of labour brokers. Business wanted a more flexible labour market, while labour insisted on the gains made in the labour laws. COSATU remained opposed to a proposed wage subsidy to encourage employers to hire more young entrants to the labour market, on the assumption that the scheme would lead to the replacement of existing workers rather than the creation of more jobs. The federation, which had branded labour broking as 'slavery', was also critical of other proposals for more flexibility in the labour market.

In April, the Industrial Development Corporation (IDC) announced that it would invest R 102 bn over the next five years in the NGP priorities: green energy industries, mining and manufacturing would receive the lion's share, while money would also be set aside for tourism and agriculture. To achieve this level of investment, the IDC intended to partner with various stakeholders including business, labour, government and civil society. Tackling **unemployment** was also the main theme of Minister of Finance Pravin Gordhan's budget speech on 23 February. The 2011 budget totalled R 979.3 bn, an increase of 9.1% over the 2010 budget. The lion's share would go to social services, which were allocated R 577.3 bn, an increase of 11.8%. In this category, the bulk of spending was on education (R 189.5 bn), housing (R 121.9 bn), health (R 112.6 bn) and social security (R 146.9 bn). With some 15 m South Africans now qualifying for some kind of social grant, economists warned that the social security system was in danger of becoming unsustainable. The projected budget deficit was 5.3% for 2010–2011, declining to 4.8% in 2012–2013.

Presenting a scheme for **subsidised housing**, Minister of Human Settlements Tokyo Sexwale said in April that there was need for a cut-off point for subsidised housing schemes "where people can begin to do things for themselves". He told Parliament that current increasing dependency and pressure on the state was not sustainable. South Africa had a massive housing backlog because of the legacy of apartheid, migration to the cities and the influx from other African countries. The housing budget was increased by 38% to R 121 bn. About 1.2 m people lived in informal settlements and the priority was to upgrade such settlements in 45 large cities and towns.

Addressing the central committee of COSATU, Zuma announced on 27 June some details of the much-anticipated Green Paper on **land reform**. The review of current land reform legislation was intended to ensure that land reform would result in recipients using their land and that it would not destabilise South Africa's food security. More than 80% of commercial agricultural land remained in the hands of about 50,000 white farmers and agribusiness. Zuma said a three-tier land tenure system was central to the proposals in the green paper: state and public land would be leasehold; other land would be available as freehold property with limitations on the extent of land a person or organisation could own; land held by non-South Africans would be on conditional tenure, which meant it "could revert back to the state should they not meet certain obligations". Zuma also announced the establishment of a value-general's office, which would ensure that the government and citizens were protected from "exploitation by unscrupulous players in the land market". The Green Paper would propose the establishment of a Land Management Commission with powers to investigate land transactions and review title deeds. Zuma also announced new legislation to protect the rights of people working or living on farms. The Extension of Security of Tenure Act has not prevented mass evictions of farm workers. On 23 August, the cabinet approved the Draft Green Paper on Land Reform. Organisations of the – largely white – **commercial farmers** criticised the proposals to cap the amount of land a farmer may own as well as the suggestion that commercial crops should be produced on leased property. Farmers who depended on leasehold would have no security to access loans. Currently, 80% of all food crops were produced by 15% of farmers, but these 15% owned 80% of the land.

An HRW report into the working conditions of **farm workers** in the Western Cape fruit and wine industries revealed shocking instances of human rights abuses. Wages remained very low, while the labour inspectorate failed to monitor working conditions and enforce labour legislation. The majority of workers were not protected from exposure to pesticides, many had no access to safe drinking water or proper toilets, and paid sick leave was routinely refused if the workers could not produce a medical certificate. Only 3% of the 121,000 farm workers in the Western Cape were unionised, as compared with an average of 30% of the general workforce nationwide.

The **strike** season opened in early July with tens of thousands of metalworkers and engineering workers following a strike call by the National Union of Metalworkers (NUMSA). Overall, some 180,000 workers in various industries went on strike. Petrol stations in Gauteng and KZN were running dry before workers in the petroleum sector ended their 18-day strike by accepting a wage increase of 8.5%. NUMSA settled for an increase of 10% and a ban on labour brokers in the metal sector. George Glynos, an economist at Econometrix, criticised COSATU for creating a rigid labour market with annual above-inflation raise demands. While the rate of inflation stood at 4.6% by May, unions demanded pay rises of up to 18%. Several days of strikes in the gold and coal mines ended when the Chamber of Mines and the unions agreed on increases between 7.5% and 10%. The South African Municipal Workers Union, representing some 200,000 workers, demanded an 18% increase.

The National Planning Commission, headed by former finance minister Trevor Manuel, published its Diagnostic Report in May and its draft action plan for the next 20 years in November. The documents, launched with a flurry of digital interaction, presented a candid assessment of successes and failures since 1994. The **National Development Plan**

(NDP) aimed to eradicate poverty and to create 11 m jobs by 2030. About 39% of South Africans currently lived below the poverty line of R 419 per month, but the plan said this figure could be reduced to zero in the next two decades. One proposed instrument was the promotion of labour-intensive industries, making exports more competitive and reinforcing the government's role in economic planning. The plan also proposed several 'experiments' with the labour market. The NDP noted that the number of work days lost to strikes had more than doubled over the past decade and stressed that wage increases needed to be linked to productivity growth. While COSATU and other unions advocated a ban on labour brokers, the plan described the provision of temporary **employment** as an 'essential service'. The NDP advocated a flexibilisation of the labour market, simplifying procedures for dismissal in case of misconduct or underperformance. A ground-breaking agreement was signed in the textile industry to grant a substantial discount (30% and 20% in urban and rural areas respectively) on the wages of newly hired workers, provided 5,000 new jobs were created by employers by 2014.

Despite government plans to reduce dependence on coal, **electricity** company Eskom obtained a $ 805.6 m loan from the US Export-Import Bank to fund the construction of the Kusile power station in Mpumalanga province. Eskom was building two huge new coal plants to address an electricity shortage that brought the economy to a standstill in 2008. South Africa had been criticised by environmentalists for its heavy dependence on coal, which currently provided about 90% of its electricity. The government announced that it wanted to reduce its dependence on coal to about 64% over the next 20 years. On 14 November, Eskom signed a R 1.9 bn loan agreement with the World Bank that would help finance the building of a 100 MW solar power plant near Upington and the 100 MW Sere wind power farm near Vredendal in the Western Cape.

The mini-bus industry, notorious for its violent turf wars, launched on 16 September a **budget airline** targeting smaller cities in remote areas. The South African National Taxi Council (SANTACO) had raised R 100 m for the venture. The SANTACO airline planned to fly initially from Lanseria near Pretoria to Bisho in the Eastern Cape. Since mechanical glitches had repeatedly plagued the **VIP aircraft fleet**, Defence Secretary Mpumi Mpofu resigned under pressure from Minister of Defence Lindiwe Sisulu after the mishap with the deputy president's failure to arrive in Finland on schedule (see above). The head of the air force, Lieutenant General Carlo Gagiano, also tendered his resignation. The Department of Defence had awarded a tender for the acquisition and maintenance of VIP aircraft to Nigerian-owned AdoAir. After AdoAir had made the required changes to the aircraft, the company was informed that the contract would not go ahead. AdoAir took the department to court to force it to honour its commitments.

Presenting his **Medium Term Budget Policy** to Parliament on 25 October, Minister of Finance Gordhan announced a R 5 bn package over the next six years to boost industrial development, assist enterprises and accelerate job creation. The main innovation in government policy was a shift away from consumption to investment in infrastructure as a driver of economic growth, with a focus on electricity, roads, rail, water and telecommunications. Ageing infrastructure, lack of maintenance and insufficient capacity in electricity provision, and the high port costs were seen as bottlenecks limiting growth. As a consequence of this moderate rise in government expenditure, the deficit would rise to 5.5% of GDP in 2011/2012 as compared with an estimate of 5.3% announced in February. Over the three-year medium-term expenditure framework, the infrastructure plan amounted to R 802 bn in energy, transport and logistics, and municipal and housing infrastructure. The government also aspired to draw in private sector investment. Gordhan warned that investment in infrastructure meant that the government's wage bill, which took up 42% of its income, could only grow at a moderate pace. The wage bill had increased from 31% of the budget in 2007 to 42% in 2011. The government spent 10.9% of its total budget on social grants. Expenditure on social security was projected to rise through the inclusion of a contributory retirement pension, in addition to state pensions, and the gradual introduction of National Health Insurance. On 11 August, Health Minister Aaron Motsoaledi unveiled the **National Health Insurance** scheme, to be funded by extra contributions from employers and people earning above a certain threshold.

A few days after Gordhan warned against calls for **nationalisation**, Julius Malema led a march in Johannesburg and Pretoria calling for "economic freedom in our lifetime" and more specifically for the nationalisation of mines and the take-over of white-owned land. According to Malema, some 25,000 people participated in the march to the Chamber of Mines in Johannesburg and the Union Buildings in Pretoria. Police estimates ranged from 5,000 in Johannesburg to 8,000 in Pretoria. An ANC commission, established in September 2010 to study the pro and cons of nationalisation, reported on 28 November, but the ANC asked for further refinements. Nationalisation of mines and other strategic sectors of the economy is one of the key demands of the ANCYL and had the support of many COSATU unions, including the National Union of Mineworkers. However, several ANC ministers stressed that the debate had a negative impact on the economy.

According to the Food Price Monitor released by the National Agricultural Marketing Council, **food prices** increased by more than 10% during the year. The prize of maize, the staple food for the poor, rose considerably because of a relatively poor harvest. Urban consumers paid 30% more for a 5 kg bag of maize meal than in the previous year. The price of bread also increased by 12%. South Africa had not been self-sufficient in wheat for many years and was therefore partially dependent on imports. Heavy rainfall and **floods** that began late in 2010 and continued into the beginning of the year caused widespread damage throughout southern Africa. In South Africa, a national state of disaster was proclaimed in affected areas where thousands of hectares of arable land were destroyed, and torrential rains caused damage to thousands of homes, particularly in KZN.

Ineke van Kessel

Swaziland

2011 was a year in which profound crisis adversely affected every sector of the society. The government struggled to pay its monthly wage bill and severe fiscal cuts were made to public expenditure, including critical welfare programmes. Some social benefits were cancelled altogether. Foreign relations remained limited and negotiations with South Africa for a loan finally failed. The lavish lifestyle of the king and the royal family continued in stark contrast to the increased poverty and destitution of the people, while political resistance grew.

Domestic Politics

Unsurprisingly, given the economic conditions, there was much in the way of **protest**. In March, some 7,000 students, teachers and civil servants staged a peaceful march in the capital, Mbabane, calling on the government to resign. In a rare case of restraint, the protest was not broken up by the police. No such restraint was evident when the Swaziland National Union of Students (SNUS) called a 'day of rage' protest in Mbabane on 12 April, the 38th anniversary of the promulgation by King Sobhuza of an emergency proclamation that centralised political power in the monarchy and outlawed all political parties, and which remained in force. Inspired by events in North Africa, the SNUS called on the Swazi people to rise up in revolt. Curfews and the use of considerable force by the police and military snuffed out the protest. SNUS president, Maxwell Dlamini, and one other student leader were detained and held for several months before being charged with possession of weapons. An attempted general strike in September failed to garner much support after union leaders were rounded up and dropped in a remote location by police and prison officials.

A coroner's inquest into the **death in police detention** in May 2010 of political activist Sipho Jele concluded in March with a finding that Jele had taken his own life by hanging. The finding was widely criticised by political groups, who alleged that he had been severely tortured and killed by the police.

The long-running **trial of Amos Mbedzi**, a South African, continued through another full year. He had been arrested in September 2008 after a bomb explosion destroyed a car in which he was a passenger and killed two colleagues, a Swazi political activist in exile in South Africa, Musa Dlamini, and a South African, Jack Govender, a former member of Umkhonto we Sizwe, the ANC's military wing. Mbedzi claimed he was near the parked car urinating when the explosion occurred. He was originally charged in late 2009 with offences relating to the possession of explosives, but the trial was postponed twice in 2010. After the second postponement, two charges of murder were added. More than a year passed before the new trial resumed in November, when Mbedzi denied all involvement with any plan to use explosives and claimed that Dlamini was a friend who had offered him a ride to Swaziland. To enter Swaziland, the three had left their car and crossed the border fence illegally, where they were picked up by another vehicle. The trial continued into 2012.

On 1 August, the Law Society of Swaziland, which represents attorneys and advocates, launched a **boycott of all courts** as a protest against the subversion of the principle of judicial independence and repeated violations of the rule of law. The triggers were: the dismissal by Chief Justice Michael Ramodibe of his fellow High Court colleague Justice Thomas Masuku, a veteran judge respected for his independence, who on occasions had criticised the monarchy in his judgments; the refusal of the Chief Justice to accept a petition of protest from the Law Society; and the promulgation of Practice Direction 4 of 2011, in which the Chief Justice banned all summonses and applications citing the name of the king or the office of the king, directly or indirectly, thereby rendering the monarch above the law. The Law Society also filed a complaint against the government with the African Commission on Human and Peoples' Rights. Despite the strike, which continued through November, the courts continued to function, giving rise to the conviction and often imprisonment of many unrepresented people.

Political parties continued to be prohibited from participating in electoral politics. Nevertheless, some political groupings went on operating, despite near continual harassment, while some, such as the People's United Democratic Movement (PUDEMO), were banned under Swaziland's anti-terrorism legislation. A coalition of opposition groupings operated from South Africa as the Swazi Solidarity Network, with a close working relationship with South Africa's largest trade union federation, the Congress of South African Trade Unions (COSATU), which provided it with offices and other infrastructural support. A newcomer on the political scene during the year was the Communist Party of Swaziland.

Foreign Affairs

Swaziland is a member of the UN, the AU, the Commonwealth, COMESA and SADC. In 2010–11, King Mswaii chaired COMESA's Council of Ministers but relinquished that role to Malawi in October.

There continues to be only a **limited diplomatic presence** in Mbabane, with most countries being represented by honorary consuls. A major blow to the Swaziland government was the decision by the new Cameron government in the United Kingdom to close its long-standing British High Commission office in Mbabane (established in 1968) and to replace the high commissioner with an honorary consul. This was presented as an economy measure, the same action having been taken earlier with regard to Lesotho. Botswana thus became the only one of the three former High Commission Territories, Bechuanaland, Basutoland and Swaziland, to have full British diplomatic representation.

A second setback was the overthrow of Libya's **Muammar Khadafi**, with whom King Mswati had close ties. Khadafi had made a state visit to Swaziland early in the century and the king had given him a gift of six camels in 2009 to mark the 40th anniversary of his taking power. In addition, one of Mswati's sons had undergone military training in Libya.

The cut in the SACU allocation generated a crisis in the payment of public sector wages. The government first turned to the IMF for a loan in the region of $ 150 m. An **IMF assessment** laid down several pre-conditions for the award of the loan, including a 5% cut in the size of the public sector and cuts in health and education expenditure. It also demanded that the monarchy make a greater contribution to the economy, including taxing the Tibiyo fund, whose asset base was estimated at E 1.3 bn and in 2010 reported profits of E 150.2 m. It also recommended an end to lavish royal events.

Swaziland rejected the conditions and turned to **South Africa**, requesting a R 2.4 bn loan. After direct negotiations between King Mswati and President Zuma, South Africa agreed the loan in June, subject to a number of modest and not very precise political conditions. These included a suggestion that the Swazi authorities broaden a dialogue process to include all stakeholders and citizens of the country in order to determine appropriate reforms, and that the process take place in an open environment that would enjoy credibility amongst the people of Swaziland and the region. Civil society groupings in both Swaziland and South Africa criticised South Africa for the leniency of the terms, but they were too much for the Swazi monarchy. Though Mswati himself never criticised them in public, his older brother, Prince Mahlabu did, describing the offer as "like selling your wife for R 100". By year's end, the Swazi authorities had refused to sign a Memorandum of Understanding with the South African government and the loan, which was supposedly to be paid in three tranches, had not materialised. South Africa's 'Saturday Star' newspaper reported that another stumbling block was the fact that King Mswati had demanded a negotiating fee of R 400 m for himself, although no other media source reported this story.

Socioeconomic Development

Though Swaziland is classified in official IMF/World Bank documentation as a lower middle-income country, about two-thirds of its residents live at or below the **poverty datum line** of E 461 per month per household – equivalent to $ 2 per day – the vast majority as feudal tenants on so-called 'Crown land', held in trust by the king and administered on his behalf by chiefs appointed by, and answerable to, him. The food productivity of this sector has declined steeply in recent decades due to overcrowding, overgrazing, and the HIV/AIDS pandemic, which has depleted the labour supply. Consequently, the majority of rural households have become dependent on monthly food parcels supplied by the government, but these were stopped for lack of funds.

According to the minister of finance, all sectors of the **economy contracted** with the result that Swaziland was in 2011 the worst performing economy of all the SADC member states. FDI in the economy also declined. A number of other factors combined to impact negatively on the economy. These included more closures of textile plants, a phasing out of the sugar export concession with the EU, and the closure of a large paper mill after a fire destroyed over 60% of the trees in the Usuthu Forest, the world's second largest cultivated timber plantation. Each of these resulted in job losses; the paper mill alone accounted for 600 jobs.

To compensate for job losses, the government has increased the number of posts in the police, army and civil service to the point that, by 2010, Swaziland had the largest **public sector** in Africa in relation to population and GDP, and the second largest public-sector wage bill in southern Africa after Lesotho. The public service's share of GDP stood at 18%.

Technically, the government was bankrupt in 2011. The ostensible cause was the severe downturn in the annual receipts from the common customs pool of **SACU**, generated by tariffs levied on imports and exports into and out of the five member countries (Swaziland, Botswana, Lesotho, Namibia and South Africa) and distributed according to an agreed formula. For the past decade, Swaziland had relied on this source for between 60% and 70% of government expenditure. Consequent to the global recession post-2008, SACU's revenues declined severely and the annual payouts fell by 60%, slumping in 2010 to E 1.9 bn from E 6 bn in 2009. In 2011, the payout was in the region of E 2.9 bn.

Nonetheless, King Mswati III and his extensive family of 13 wives and 23 children continued to enjoy their **lavish lifestyle**. The royal household was the one item in the government's budget allocation to enjoy an increase, rising by 23% to total E 210 m, which was used to fund the 13 palaces housing the king's wives and their staff. At the same time as he announced this increase, Minister of Finance Majozi Sithole announced in his budget speech a 10% cut in the salaries of all civil servants. He went on to describe the plight of the Swazi people as one where over 60% of the population lived in poverty. Nearly two-thirds had no bank account. A quarter of all adults were estimated to have HIV and average life expectancy at birth was the lowest in the world. Over half of all young people were unemployed.

In 2010, Forbes magazine named Mswati as the world's 15th richest monarch with a personal fortune of some $ 100 m. He also controls a royal investment corporation, the **Tibiyo Fund**, with assets of several billion Lilangeni, through which the monarchy has acquired shareholdings in virtually every major entity operative in the economy and for which it receives annual dividend payments. The monarchy pays no taxes on its earnings to the Swazi government and neither does any member of the royal family, which comprises not only Mswati's family but also the many surviving offspring (and their families) of the late King Sobhuza who, in a reign of 61 years, produced some 400 children.

The fiscal crisis was portrayed by many commentators as a crisis of revenue generation occasioned by the global downturn and the decline in SACU revenues. This is a superficial explanation. In reality, it is a **political crisis** generated by the fact that the Swazi monarchy – or Swazi Nation as it is referred to locally – operates as a state within a state, an absolutist monarchy accountable to no entity bar itself and awash with funds. The fact is that there would be no economic crisis if the monarchy were integrated into the state and subordinated to the will of a democratically elected legislature, and if it and its investment corporations, such as Tibiyo, paid their share of taxes and dividends to the Swazi government. Instead, the Swazi Nation relates to the government as a parasite, siphoning off ever-increasing amounts to meet its burgeoning running costs and giving nothing back fiscally in return. In July, Mswati took an entourage of 50-plus people to London to attend the wedding of the Duke and Duchess of Cambridge, spending nearly a week at one of London's most expensive hotels – all at the expense of the government, not the monarchy.

The Swazi people paid a heavy price for this extravagance through cuts in **public welfare** services. Payment of the quarterly E 600 state pension was suspended. So, too, was the delivery of monthly food parcels to 40,000 rural households. There were also cuts to the funding of antiretroviral treatment programmes for AIDS sufferers, and bursary programmes for AIDS orphans to enable them to attend school, while the University of Swaziland failed to open for the new academic year in August as the government was unable to fund the annual grants (covering fees, residence and books) payable to Swazi students.

None of the IMF or South African government's fiscal reforms or **austerity measures** with regard to the public sector were implemented. Although it was sometimes late, the Swazi government did still manage to pay its monthly wage bill through the year. How it found the funds was not made clear, but there were reports of loans being arranged with unnamed parties. It was speculated that the government of the Republic of China (Taiwan) may have come to the aid of one of its last two full diplomatic partners in Africa (the other is Malawi), while others named three of the largest **corporations** operating in the Swazi economy. One was the Coca Cola Corporation, which came to Swaziland from South Africa in the 1980s but did not return after 1990. It has since grown into the largest manufacturing employer, contributing about 40% of Swaziland's GDP, as well as being the largest supplier of sucrose to its African operations across the continent. The second was SWAKI (Swazi Kirsh Industries), which has transformed a monopoly granted in the 1970s to a South African businessman, Nathan Kirsh, for milling maize into a wholesaling, retailing and property giant. Now a Swazi citizen, Kirsh is also a global player, who during the year acquired ownership of London's tallest office block. The third was the South African mobile phone operator MTN, which had had a monopoly over cellular communications in Swaziland since 2008. King Mswati is reported to have a personal shareholding in the Swazi operation.

John Daniel & Marisha Ramdeen

Zambia

The presidential and parliamentary elections on 29 September dominated domestic politics. The victory of Michael Sata, elected as the country's new president, and his Patriotic Front (PF), the major opposition party, came as a complete surprise as the re-election of Rupiah Banda and the ruling Movement for Multi-party Democracy (MMD) had been generally expected. The economy continued to recover surprisingly well from the worldwide economic crisis, with a robust growth rate of 6.5%. This contributed to moving the country from the rank of a low- to a lower-middle-income country. Foreign policy activities slowed down because of the elections, but remained largely unchanged under the new president, despite some initial fears about Sata's anti-Chinese stance.

Domestic Politics

On 14 January, violent clashes erupted in Mongu, the capital of Western Province, when the police dispersed an assembly of Lozi-speaking people demanding the independence of their region, known as **Barotseland**. The assembly had been banned because the police judged it to be a threat to national security. The violence left three people dead and 12 hospitalised. Twenty-four people were arrested and charged with treason. A poster campaign by a group calling itself the 'Black Bulls' had urged all 'non-inhabitants' (non-Lozi, mainly the minority Nkoyas and Mbunda ethnic groups) to leave the province by 15 January, or risk being hacked to death. The protests were a reaction to the government's removal in October 2010 of the Barotseland Agreement (1964) from the draft constitution. The agreement united the former British protectorate Barotseland (land of the Lozi) with the rest of Zambia, then Northern Rhodesia. It granted Barotseland a form of regional autonomy within the new Zambian state, although this was never implemented. In fact, the agreement was abrogated by various local government acts during the first republic under the Kaunda government, and in 1969 Barotseland was renamed Western Province. The agreement stated that the Litunga of Barotseland "under the customary law of Barotseland shall be the principal local authority for the government and administration of Barotseland". The interpretation of the agreement and the status of Western Province remained a contentious issue.

The discontent and calls for more autonomy or even **secession**, campaigned for by the Movement for the Restoration of Barotseland, the Barotse Freedom Movement, and the most radical Linyungandambo, was nurtured by the perception that the region was neglected by the central government in Lusaka. Poverty levels there were indeed much higher than in most other parts of the country, at 84% against a national average of 64%, according to the Central Statistical Office. In addition, the province is virtually without industry and has hardly any infrastructure. The government and the traditional leadership of the Lozi, the Litunga and the Barotse Royal Council (BRC) were eager to pacify the tense situation. In February, at a meeting at the State House in Lusaka, a BRC delegation confirmed on behalf of the Litunga that Barotseland was part of Zambia and that agitation for secession was not "in the spirit of the Barotseland Agreement". At the same time, there were fears that the province could become a hotspot for violence during the upcoming elections if the conflict remained unresolved and became a campaign issue. Michael Sata, 74, president of the Patriotic Front (PF), had immediately taken-up the issue and promised the re-adoption of the agreement into the constitution, if his party attained to government.

In February, preparations for the elections and the political parties' infighting about **presidential and parliamentary candidates** started to heat up. The ongoing rift within the ruling MMD re-emerged when Minister of Works and Supply Mike Mulongoti announced that he would contest the party vice presidency at the MMD convention in April. His announcement was accompanied by a strong complaint about the lack of democracy within the MMD. The media reported that the selection of MMD's provincial chairmen was manipulated to favour the president and that rival candidates were intimidated into abstaining from standing. The impression was widespread that the forthcoming convention would be crammed with supporters of President Banda in order to secure a pro-Banda majority in the elections to senior party positions and his re-nomination as the MMD presidential candidate. Mulongoti was dismissed by Banda from his government position for disrespecting the party leadership and the party's national vice president, George Kunda, who was expected to be Banda's preferred choice for the post. The dismissal of Mulongoti signaled that there was no agreement within the party about Banda's nomination as the MMD's presidential candidate. As recently as October 2010, two prominent senior members of the MMD, former finance minister Ng'andu Magande and former defence minister George Mpombo, were expelled from the party after they had criticised Banda's nomination by the National Executive Committee (NEC) and the manipulation of the list of delegates for the convention. Eventually, the MMD convention on 5–7 April safely endorsed Banda's nomination as the unopposed presidential candidate and, in a well-orchestrated election, put mostly pro-Banda men into the leadership of the NEC. Although Banda emerged from the convention as the strong man, not only had the MMD lost a number of prominent members in the internal strife, but some factions within the party were alienated too.

However, the **opposition parties** were not in a much better position. The electoral alliance of the two major opposition parties, formed in 2009 by the PF and the United Party for National Development (UPND), finally came to an end after the tensions it experienced throughout the previous year. On 11 March, after a national committee meeting held earlier, the UPND vice president, Richard Kapita, officially declared his party's withdrawal from the pact. This did not come as a surprise, since the two parties were unable to compromise on a joint presidential candidate or a joint political programme for the alliance. The pact was no more than a simple agreement that the parties would not compete against each other. The split of the alliance greatly raised the morale of the ruling party, since previous election results indicated that the two-party pact presented the only serious threat to MMD's electoral victory. At the same time, the unity of the PF was in danger because Sata had expelled 19 MPs from the party when they defied his directive to boycott participation in the National Constitutional Conference (NCC). Most of them had been elected in Luapula and Northern Provinces where the PF was closely rivalled by the MMD. In June, 23 PF MPs from Luapula, Lusaka and the Copperbelt provinces applied to re-contest their seats on the MMD ticket.

On 18 June, the second Zambian president, **Frederick Chiluba**, 68, died suddenly in Lusaka. Chiluba, who as a trade union leader had led the democratisation movement in 1989 and 1990 and was president from 1991 to 2001, was seen as a Banda supporter. In 2010, in a highly controversial move, Banda had stopped a final attempt by the state authorities to prosecute Chiluba for corruption during his presidency. Banda declared seven days of national mourning for the former president. Some observers expected that Chiluba's sudden death would cost Banda the support of a substantial faction of the MMD, with whom Chiluba still enjoyed some influence.

The **constitutional reform** process finally failed after eight years of discussions and at the cost of more than $ 17 m to the NCC. On 29 March, the second reading of the

Constitution of Zambia Bill 59 failed by ten votes to gain the required two-thirds parliamentary majority. The result was that the vast powers of the president remained unchanged (although the original intention of the reform process to limit the executive role had already been heavily diluted), and that the number of MPs did not increase from 150 to 280 as stipulated in the bill. As before, the first-past-the-post system remained in place for the election of the president, and so the president could comfortably ignore the parliamentary defeat.

On 28 June, Banda dissolved parliament and announced that the tripartite presidential, parliamentary and local government **elections** would take place on 20 September. International observers and domestic opinion polls forecast victory for Banda and his MMD, but the final result, which put Sata and his PF clearly ahead of Banda, surprised not only political observers but even the victorious party and its leadership. Two national polls in July and August showed Banda to be 3%–5% ahead of Sata, reflecting the outcome also expected by international observers. The final results proved them wrong: Sata (PF) won with 42.2% of the votes cast, followed by Banda (MMD) with 35.6% and Hakainde Hichilema (UPND) with 18.3%. In 2008, Banda had won with a small margin of only 35,000 votes. None of the seven other presidential candidates received even 1% of the 2,772,264 votes cast – a 53.7% turnout of the 5.17 m registered voters. The parliamentary elections were won by the PF with 60, MMD 55, and UPND 28 out of the 150 seats; splinter parties such as the Alliance for Democracy and Development and the Forum for Democracy and Development won one seat each, and independent candidates snatched three seats. In two constituencies, no elections were held because of the death of a candidate. The result meant that the president had to work with a hung parliament, since no party had secured an absolute majority. Three by-elections held on 24 November, of which two, Chongwe and Nakonde constituencies, were won by the PF and one, Magoye constituency, by the UPND, did not make a major difference.

National and international election observers judged the election free, but barely fair. Government and opposition parties competed on a completely **uneven playing field**. The ruling party used government resources in an unprecedented way, not only to distribute vast amounts of 'gifts'. In August, the Catholic Church and the Law Association of Zambia (LAZ) issued a strong complaint about "biased reporting" by the state-run Zambia National Broadcasting Corporation, the only radio station that covers the whole country and a government mouthpiece. At the same time, rumours of electoral fraud based on manipulated ballot papers and vote buying were widespread. A glimpse of the misuse of government resources was provided after the elections when the MMD officials had left their offices. The police found numerous abandoned new cars at party buildings and former ministers' homes, which no one claimed to own, 2,000 bicycles at the former finance minister's farm, and millions of Kwacha buried in the garden of another former minister.

A big surprise to observers, as well as to the leadership of the winning party, was that **Banda surrendered power**. The announcement of the results was delayed when the incoming vote counts indicated a clear lead for Sata. Various sources confirmed that Banda seriously discussed with his advisors, the secret service and security men how to rig the result, but they seem to have advised him to accept defeat. The security men were afraid of large-scale rioting in Lusaka and the Copperbelt, since they were aware that the militant PF cadres had been made to believe that anything other than a Sata victory would be the result of election fraud. They had therefore prepared themselves for the worst case scenario and, when the announcement of the result was delayed, violent incidents did indeed begin to occur in the PF strongholds of Lusaka and the Copperbelt. Finally, when it became obvious that the government was prepared to rig the elections, the chair of the Electoral Commission of Zambia (ECZ) threatened to resign, and the US ambassador, who was in close contact with Banda, also insisted that he should accept electoral defeat. The parallel vote tabulation system (PVT) established by the Civil Society Election Coalition (CSEC) and the PF may also have deterred Banda from rigging the result. The PVT was a highly controversial issue between opposition parties and civil society organisations on the one hand and the government on the other, because the latter did not want an independent monitoring system of polling booths that would ensure that the official results announced by the ECZ was consistent with the local result for each polling station. The government argued it would undermine the credibility of the ECZ and be a "recipe for post-election anarchy", especially if it were administered by opposition parties, as the PF planned. The CSEC and opposition parties insisted on the necessity of independent election monitoring, and they pointed out that a similar system had been followed since the 2006 elections, when the ECZ published results at each polling station. Finally, the CSEC's Rapid Response Project, which employed 985 local monitors and had been applied in a number of other African countries, was able to verify official election results with a failure margin of just 0.3%.

The reasons for the **MMD defeat** after 20 years in power were manifold. Banda and the ruling party were unable to capitalise on the booming economy – with more than 5% annual economic growth for about a decade – because little trickle-down was evident to the majority of the population. The MMD election slogan "building tomorrow's Zambia" did not therefore catch the mood of many new voters, who were not interested in macro-economic growth and inflation rates. At the same time, the MMD campaign was poorly organised. The president's national campaign committee operated largely in isolation from the party's officials and members, who were more or less side-lined by the president's national and international advisor team. The factionalism within the MMD contributed to the lack of support from the party, and the defection of a number of prominent party leaders to the PF during the final months before the elections also weakened the MMD. As an insider commented, the MMD organisers mistook the high attendance at carefully selected campaign rallies and voters' "voracious appetite" for party gifts such as t-shirts and *chitenge* cloths for political support. The PF, on the other hand, countered the massive distribution of gifts with the catchphrase "don't *Kubeba*" – which means take the gift, "say nothing", and vote for what you like. At the same time, Sata's central message was clearly directed at the underprivileged majority of the voters: "More jobs, less taxes, more money in your pockets." In the end, Sata's campaign strategy, without state resources and clearly less well financed than during the 2008 campaign, worked in his favour, while Banda's strategy did little to mobilise the electorate. Voter turnout in opposition strongholds in general, and PF strongholds such as Copperbelt and Northern Province in particular, was above the national average, while the turnout in the MMD strongholds of Eastern, Western and Central Provinces was below the national average of about 54%. Sata seemed able to mobilise additional support among the 1.22 m newly registered voters, many of them young, poor and unemployed in urban areas. He won the elections in the Copperbelt, where he attracted over 113,000 more votes than in 2008, and in the mainly Bemba-speaking Northern and Luapula Provinces, with about 54,000 more votes, and Western Province, with 51,000 more votes.

When Sata announced his new cabinet on 29 September, he kept one of his **election promises** by downsizing the government; the new cabinet comprised 19 instead of 23 ministers, and 31 instead of 41 deputy ministers. He appointed as vice president Guy Scott, of Scottish descent and a former minister of agriculture, founding member and former secretary general of PF, who played a pivotal role in the party's and Sata's rise to power. To bolster his cabinet against a hung parliament, Sata also co-opted six MMD parliamentarians as deputy ministers. He ordered a grand corruption investigation into all suspected corrupt dealings by his predecessor's administration in order to live up to another election promise – 'zero tolerance' for **corruption**. He dissolved the board of directors of the Road Development Agency, the Zambia Electricity Supply Corporation (Zesco), the National Pensions Scheme Authority, the Zambia Revenue Authority, the Energy Regulation Board and the Bank of Zambia, citing massive corruption as the reason. Sata also fired all 72 district commissioners on the grounds that these positions had been "politicised" by the former government. In fact, they had originally been created to provide roles for political nominees of the MMD government under former president Chiluba, and the posts were filled by party cadres. Sata announced their replacement by proper civil servants with appropriate professional qualifications. He also sacked the chief of police and, at the end of October, terminated the contracts of 28 senior army officers who had apparently been appointed illegally by his predecessor.

The opposition, and especially the MMD, criticised Sata's sweeping actions as a purge in the disguise of an **anti-corruption policy**. Many local observers also remained sceptical as to whether this was just another twist to the usual actions taken against political opponents under the cover of the fight against corruption. The government under previous presidents had officially fought corruption, but Banda had explained to a World Bank vice president that, since he had a "multiple constituency to satisfy", he had to be "soft" on corruption. Sata's investigation of the Banda administration for misappropriation of funds and procurement crimes was supported by civil society organisations including the local TI and the LAZ. Finally, Sata addressed two other crucial issues raised in his election campaign. As promised, he constituted a commission of inquiry, comprised of respected lawyers and stakeholders, to investigate the protests and riots in **Western Province** earlier in the year and to look into the matter of the Barotseland Agreement. To pacify the situation in Western Province, he also pardoned all those facing prosecution for their involvement in the riots.

Foreign Affairs

President Banda continued with his generally friendly attitude towards authoritarian regimes in the neighbourhood, as well as towards China as a major foreign investor in the country. As the chairman of the SADC Organ on Politics, Defence and Security Cooperation and a member of the **SADC troika**, he was occupied by the security problems of the region. The troika included South Africa's President Jacob Zuma as the incoming chairperson of the Organ and Mozambique's President Armando Emilio Guebuza as the outgoing chairperson. The first time the troika met at the end of March in Livingstone, Zambia, to review the situation in Zimbabwe and Madagascar; among other issues, they also discussed the concept of a uni-visa and the protocol on free movement of people within SADC. For a follow-up, Banda had to attend the troika meeting for two days in May in Windhoek, Namibia, and in early June the troika summit in Gaborone, Botswana, at the SADC-headquarters, to discuss the political situation in Madagascar again; the country was governed by a caretaker government, the High Transitional Authority, which SADC and the international community did not recognise. At the troika summit on 18 August in Angola, Banda handed over the chair of the Organ to Zuma.

The uncertainty about a change in foreign policy after the change of government did not last long. The ministry of foreign affairs was given to Chishimba Kambwili, one of Sata's most trustworthy PF party stalwarts, but inexperienced in foreign affairs and in running a ministry. For a brief period, the relationship with **Malawi** worsened, when Sata declined an invitation from President Bingu Wa Mutharika to attend the COMESA summit in Malawi on 14–15 October. Sata demanded an official apology for his deportation as a 'prohibited immigrant' by the Malawian government in 2007. However, the diplomatic standoff came to an end by the end of the year, after a visit by Malawi's retired president Bakili Muluzi, who was sent by Mutharika as a special envoy.

At the same time, Sata strengthened the relationship with **Angola** by sending elder statesman and former president Kenneth Kaunda as a special envoy to Luanda, where he apologised for Zambia's arms supply to the UNITA rebel movement under the MMD government. Since the end of the Angolan civil war, close cooperation had been established between the two countries. The relationship with **Zimbabwe** remained unclear. Sata had earlier praised President Robert Mugabe's liberation war credentials and his controversial land reform programme and criticised Prime Minister Morgan Tsvangirai as a puppet of

Western governments. Nevertheless, when he was invited in October to attend the Zanu-PF National People's Conference, he only sent a delegation led by PF Secretary-General Wynter Kalimba, although Sata received Mugabe for a private meeting in Livingstone on 3 December.

The biggest challenge to Sata's foreign policy was the relationship with **China**, which was not only one of the biggest foreign investors and aid providers, but had also been held in high esteem as a special partner by former governments, and especially by Banda. Sata was known for his anti-Chinese rhetoric, although this had become muted over recent years and especially during the election campaign: in January, he was talking ambiguously about welcoming Chinese "investors, not infesters". However, Vice President Guy Scott communicated with Chinese officials, and it was rumoured that the Chinese embassy was encouraging Chinese companies to sponsor the PF. This may have contributed to the decline of Sata's anti-Chinese rhetoric. Once in power, Sata confirmed that all foreign investments were safe and no radical change of economic policy should be expected. On 29 October, during a luncheon at State House in honour of the Chinese business people operating in Zambia, he emphasised that his government would support Chinese investors in developing the country. On 21 November, Kenneth Kaunda was used again as a special envoy, when he was sent to China to further improve the relationship. Finally, on 12 December, officials of both countries signed an economic and technical cooperation grant agreement worth K 43 bn and an agreement for an interest-free loan of K 32 bn for the fight against poverty and other projects.

Sata explained at a PF rally at the end of November that, in contrast to his predecessors, he was rarely travelling abroad, because he did not want to "waste" scarce state resources. He only travelled to Kampala, to attend the 4th International Conference on the Great Lakes Region summit on 15–16 December.

Socioeconomic Developments

Due to its increasing per capita income, the World Bank reclassified Zambia from a low- to a **lower-middle-income country**. With an estimated GDP growth of 6.5% (about 1% less than in 2010), the annual growth rate remained at over 5% for the ninth consecutive year, the twelfth year of growth. This was in line with the projection of the national budget, presented by the minister of finance on 8 October 2010, that the growth rate would "exceed" 6% and inflation would fall to 7%. The precise target was missed but, although inflation rose from 7.9% in December 2010 to 8.7% in October, it then declined to 7.2% in December. The economy compared very well with the rest of Africa and the growth figure was above the Sub-Saharan African average of 5.2%. In June, the IMF provided another positive assessment of the country's economic performance – despite a few critical points concerning inaccurate data on net domestic borrowing and shortcomings in the maize marketing system. However, Zambia's ranking in the World Bank's 'Ease of Doing Business' report, which had improved dramatically the previous year, declined again from 76th to 84th.

The good **economic performance** was mainly based on growth in agriculture by 6.8% and industry (mainly manufacturing and construction) by 8.7%. The new government's first budget estimates that production in the mining sector would be far below expectation proved to be wrong; while cobalt production fell to 7,701 tonnes from 8,648 tonnes in 2010, copper output, the major foreign exchange earner, rose to 869,058 tonnes from 852,566 tonnes the previous year. Although the copper price declined by 21% over the year from $ 4,449 to $ 3,432 per tonne, on average it remained clearly higher than in 2010 and contributed to the profitability of the industry and the country's income.

Overall, the **budget performance** was viewed as "satisfactory" by new Minister of Finance Alexander Chikwanda, when he presented the new government's budget for 2012 on 11 November. Due to the economic growth and improved tax collection from valued added tax and from the mining companies, domestic revenue was expected to exceed the original target by 23%; the over performance was twice as high as the previous year. However, the expenditure side was expected to be 18.8% higher than budgeted for the period. To balance the income-expenditure gap, Chikwanda had to increase total borrowing, resulting in a budget deficit of 3.1%, up from the projected 2.9%. The new finance minister gave no explanation for the overspending by the former government.

In line with the economic development, the **external sector** remained strong. The current account surplus was expected to rise by almost 55% to $ 951 m from $ 614.7 m in 2010. This was mainly attributed to higher copper export earnings, which usually account for 80%. Non-traditional exports were expected to increase robustly to a total of $ 1.5 bn compared with $ 1.2 bn in 2010. This also helped the gross international reserves to rise to $ 2.6 bn, which would cover the import bill of about 4.3 months. The Kwacha continued to remain fairly stable and depreciated only marginally by 4.5% against the US dollar.

In line with the pro-poor election manifesto, the **new budget for 2012** reflected some economic and social policy changes without completely reversing established policies. It provided for an overall increase of 30% in public spending. General public sector spending was to be increased by 40%, the health budget rose by 46%, expenditure for agriculture by 38%, and the education budget by about 27%, which would cover 2,000 additional classroom blocks and the recruitment of 5,000 teachers, among other things. The allocation for the transport sector, construction and upgrading of roads and railways was also increased by 41%. As promised during the election campaign, the government doubled the threshold for personal income tax from K 1 m to K 2 m ($ 400) per month. It was estimated that about 80,000 workers would benefit from the tax reform. To compensate for this revenue shortfall, the government increased the royalty rates for precious minerals from 3% to 5%, and for base metals to 6%. The hotly debated 25% windfall tax was not reinstated, since Sata had abandoned his earlier plans. To comply with Sata's long-standing call for the mining sector's contribution to the nation's welfare to rise, government envisaged a new **mining policy**. To improve control over the actual mining output, the government announced that all copper and cobalt exports would have to be verified by the Bank of Zambia prior to export. In addition, the government envisaged an increase in the state's stake in the mining industry by raising its shareholding to 35%. Since the re-privatisation of the mining industry during the 1990s, the state-owned Zambia Consolidated Copper Mines-Investment Holding controlled between 4% and 20% of the assets of the ten big mining companies in the country, except one, which is fully owned by the state. It was not expected that the moderate tax reform or the envisaged stake increase would negatively affect the competitiveness of the copper industry. The World Bank and a number of civil society organisations led by the Civil Society for Poverty Reduction and the Economics Association of Zambia, as well as the doctors' association, praised the government's 'pro-poor' budget and the fact that most allocations exceeded the organisations' expectations.

In one of its first actions, the government put the latest privatisation processes of the Banda government under scrutiny because of suspected **corruption**. In October, Sata ordered the cancellation of the sale of the Finance Bank Zambia (FBZ) to South Africa's FirstRand. The FBZ, purportedly the country's largest privately owned lender, was sold only in September, after having been taken over by the Bank of Zambia in November 2010. The June 2010 sale to LAP Green Networks of a 75% share in the troubled Zambia Telecommunication Company (Zamtel), the state-owned telecommunication company running the sole fixed line service for 400,000 customers, also came under investigation. The controversial agreement with the Libyan investor included the dismissal of Zamtel's 2,341 employees, although a smaller number were to be rehired. Civil society organisations and opposition parties had criticised the sale for lack of transparency, corruption and an inappropriately low sale price. Opposition parties viewed the company as of national strategic interest and considered that it should not be privatised; they had even threatened to re-nationalise the company if they won the next elections.

Sata's populist, pro-labour election promises propelled a wave of **labour strikes** in October. Discontented workers demanded not only substantial wage increases, but also an improvement in working conditions, which were unsatisfactory because the previous government was lax in enforcing labour laws. A HRW report claimed that Chinese mining companies "routinely flout labor laws and regulations designed to protect workers' safety and the right to organize". However, the strikes hit foreign and national businesses, such as three of the four Chinese-owned mines, as well as the state-owned Zesco. On the news of Sata's election, Chambishi Copper Mines, owned by the Chinese Non-Ferrous China Africa, granted its 2,000 workers an 85% pay rise. When the rise was reversed as too costly, the workers went on strike and over 1,000 miners were sacked, but then reinstalled after government's intervention. In general, workers' demands ranged from demands to be paid the minimum wage to calls for 100% wage increases. The government first expressed understanding for the labour unrest but, as the strikes expanded and continued, Labour Minister Fackson Shamenda directed all protesting workers to return to work. The government also promised to raise the minimum wage again, after it had already been increased in January.

Gero Erdmann

Zimbabwe

Dominating the year was the love-hate relationship between the principals in the Government of National Unity (GNU) and mixed signals and disagreements over elections. Though the economy remained somewhat stable, there was persistent controversy over the Zimbabwe African National Union - Patriotic Front (ZANU-PF) indigenisation agenda and the Marange diamonds. Some political tensions persisted and incidents of political violence were reported. There was no major change on the foreign relations scene: the ZANU-PF part of the GNU continued to blame "illegal" sanctions for the country's woes, unrelentingly demanding their removal.

Domestic Politics

The year opened with President Robert Mugabe signalling his intentions to **call for elections**. On 23 January, he insisted that the GNU "was not meant to be a permanent arrangement". Stating that he had the constitutional power to call the elections even if electoral and constitutional reforms were not complete, Mugabe announced he would invoke those powers and call for elections during the year. Senior ZANU-PF politicians repeated the call. In May, Simon Khaya Moyo, the ZANU-PF national chairperson, told the Dutch ambassador that ZANU-PF's position was that the country had to conclude the constitution-making process and go to the polls. He asserted that the inclusive government had failed "because our policies with our colleagues in Government are different". In contrast, ZANU-PF's GNU partners were not so enthusiastic about elections. They insisted that the constitution-making process had to be finalised and outstanding issues in the Global Political Agreement (GPA) sorted out before credible elections could be held.

The **constitution-making process** was mired in similar controversy. ZANU-PF officials wanted the Constitutional Parliamentary Committee (COPAC) to wrap up its work so that elections could be held. The body had insisted that the process could not be finished by year's end, and the projected completion time was March 2012. In October, COPAC announced that the referendum would not be held before February 2012, which meant that elections could not be held before mid-2012. ZANU-PF accused the Tsvangirai-led Movement for Democratic Change (MDC-T) of dragging out the process to postpone elections. On 21 April, negotiators from the three parties in the GNU announced that they had established a framework for holding future elections. It included the need for a new constitution to be in place before the elections, the lifting of sanctions and amendments to the Electoral Act. There was no agreement on security sector reforms as demanded by the MDC factions; nor was there agreement on having election observers in the country six months before elections, or on the demilitarisation of the Zimbabwe Electoral Commission.

There was a change of leadership in the **smaller faction of the MDC** led by Deputy Prime Minister Arthur Mutambara (MDC-M). On 8 January, Professor Welshman Ncube, the party's secretary general and GNU minister of industry and commerce, replaced Mutambara – who did not seek re-election – as party president. Henceforth the party was known as MDC-N. What started as a peaceful transition soon turned into an acrimonious power struggle between Mutambara and Ncube, each of whom had his own faction, and the Mutambara faction challenged the election of Ncube in the high court. On 8 February, Mutambara claimed he was still the MDC president and had fired Ncube. He (Mutambara) would remain president until the high court decided otherwise. The Ncube faction dismissed this and insisted that Ncube should replace Mutambara as deputy prime minister and GNU principal. However, Mutambara remained in post, thanks to Mugabe and Tsvangirai, who turned a deaf ear to requests by the Ncube faction. On 15 December, the high court dismissed Mutambara's challenge. The judge said Mutambara was not the legitimate leader of the party and could no longer 'purport' to be the party president. However, at year's end, Mutambara was still the deputy prime minister.

There was some activity on the **democracy and human rights** front. On 19 February, 45 members of the local chapter of the International Socialist Organisation (ISO) were arrested during an academic meeting where a video on the uprisings in Tunisia and Egypt was shown. Those arrested included Munyaradzi Gwisai, a former MDC legislator and president of the ISO. They were charged with treason and there were claims that the arrested activists were tortured in jail. On 28 February, the UN Special Rapporteur on Torture confirmed that he had written to the Zimbabwean government expressing concern about the torture allegations. On 19 July, the state prosecutor dropped the treason charges against the remaining six activists, who were finally indicted. The charges were downgraded to conspiracy to commit public violence, participating in a gathering with intent to promote public violence, or unlawfully acting together to endanger, promote or expose to hatred, contempt or ridicule the president and government.

Over the year, there were issues regarding **freedom of assembly**, with numerous MDC meetings being barred by the police. On 6 March, police barred most MDC restructuring meetings in Bulawayo, Midlands North, Mashonaland East and Mashonaland West. In Bulawayo, at least 20 police officers in full riot gear besieged the MDC provincial offices and ordered those attending the meeting to disperse, saying the meeting was illegal. On 4 April, police barred an MDC-T Kadoma Central district congress meeting, arguing that they had received orders from the Police General Headquarters in Harare to ban all MDC meetings in the district. Tsvangirai himself was barred from holding several rallies, including on 25 March, when he was prevented from holding a rally in Victoria Falls after police sealed the entrance to the stadium. Analysts took this as a sign of ZANU-PF's jitters over elections scheduled for 2012 and it was also seen as evidence of police partisanship, emphasising the need for security sector reform.

After a decline in 2010, political violence and human rights violations reportedly increased, with the parties blaming each other. Again, the security services and war veterans were fingered in quite a few of the incidents. There was widespread speculation that linked this **resurgence in violence** to the elections anticipated for 2012. On 29 May, Police Inspector Petros Mutedza was murdered outside a pub in the Harare township of Glen View, an MDC stronghold. Police quickly picked up 15 suspects, all members of the MDC-T, and the number soon swelled to 29. Those arrested included Solomon Madzore, the MDC-T Youth Assembly chairperson, who was arrested on 28 October. This again raised questions about the impartiality of the police, who had been accused of being an extension of ZANU-PF. The suspects were to spend the rest of the year in detention and the court was told that the suspects were tortured. On 6 November, there were violent clashes between ZANU-PF and MDC-T supporters in Chitungwiza, after the former stormed an MDC-T rally. On 7 November, Tsvangirai told journalists that the national executives of all three political parties in the GNU would meet on 11 November to discuss the worsening political violence in the country. ZANU-PF Central Committee members and their counterparts from the national executive councils of the MDC-T and MDC-N were expected to attend.

On 10 March, Energy and Power Development Minister Elton Mangoma (MDC-T) was arrested for criminal abuse of office in connection with a fuel deal he had made in December 2010. He was accused of by-passing tender procedures, spent more than a week in remand prison and was released after paying $ 5,000 bail. Some critics dismissed the arrest as a political ploy and as punishment for cutting ZANU-PF heavyweights from fuel deals. Signalling the **tension in the GNU**, Tsvangirai described Mangoma's arrest as a "calculated assault on the people of Zimbabwe". After a sensational high court trial, Mangoma was acquitted on 28 June. There was speculation that the arrest had been part of a broader plan by ZANU-PF to frustrate the GNU. On 18 April, MDC-T Treasurer-General Roy Bennett lost his senate seat after he had missed 21 consecutive sittings while exiled outside Zimbabwe. Bennett, who had been acquitted of treason charges, had left the country following threats that he would be arrested by the Joint Operations Command. All was not well within the GNU. In March, Tsvangirai claimed there were strong indications that Mugabe was no longer in charge of the country. On 27 March, the 'Daily News' quoted Tsvangirai as saying that many of the issues he agreed with Mugabe in their weekly meetings were often later reversed, ostensibly by security chiefs. He claimed that a 'coterie' of senior ZANU-PF officials was seemingly working full-time at undermining his efforts and working relationship with Mugabe. The 'coterie' was made up of senior people in the police, the military and the Central Intelligence Organisation, and included Defence Minister Emmerson Mnangagwa and Jonathan Moyo.

On 10 March, the Supreme Court nullified the election of Lovemore Moyo (MDC-T) as **speaker of the House of Assembly** on appeal. Four ZANU-PF legislators, including former information minister Jonathan Moyo, had challenged the MDC-T chairman's election in August 2008, claiming breaches of House rules on secret balloting. On 29 March, Moyo was re-elected, beating the ZANU-PF national chairman by 105 votes to 93. Earlier, on 21 March, MDC-N had indicated that its legislators would vote for the MDC-T candidate, claiming that ZANU-PF was planning to rig the election by reducing the numbers of MDC-T MPs through arrests. The voting suggested that at least two ZANU-PF MPs had voted for the MDC-T candidate. A witch-hunt followed within ZANU-PF, which saw a ZANU-PF legislator, Deputy Minister for Labour and Social Welfare Tracy Mutinhiri, being expelled from the party on 31 August for being a 'dissident'. She lost her ministerial post in December.

Throughout the year, there were numerous rumours about **Mugabe's purported illness** and failing health, which were mostly fiercely disputed by ZANU-PF. On 16 January, it was reported that Mugabe was in hospital in Malaysia after a prostate operation. On 13 February, presidential spokesman George Charamba announced that Mugabe had gone to Malaysia for eye checks. This was the only official acknowledgement of Mugabe's health problems. Stories of Mugabe's allegedly failing health surfaced again during the SADC summit in Zambia in April. There were further stories of trips to Singapore and Malaysia in October. On 2 October, Mugabe brushed aside reports that he was ill, saying he was in Singapore to rest and see his daughter, who was studying in Hong Kong.

On 15 August, retired **General Solomon Mujuru** died in a fire at his farm. Husband of Vice President Joice Mujuru and widely regarded as the ZANU-PF kingmaker, Mujuru was seen as the power behind one of the factions vying for control of ZANU-PF. There were numerous conspiracy theories about foul play, with some claims that it was an assassination. His death would have a huge impact on the succession issue and power struggles within ZANU-PF. A day after Mujuru's death, his wife, who was then the acting president, implored people to stop making wild statements on the cause of the death. On 20 October, the high court ordered an inquest.

The fallout from the release of diplomatic cables by the whistleblower website, **Wikileaks**, made further headlines. There was continued highlighting of reports of leading ZANU-PF politicians showing disenchantment with the party and Mugabe, mainly focussing on statements by some of his closest lieutenants saying he should retire. Also highlighted were claims that Mugabe had prostate cancer. The same reports also revealed that Tsvangirai had been criticised by his allies, quite a few of whom doubted his leadership credentials. There was speculation that Mugabe and Tsvangirai would act against the 'sell-outs', but no action was taken.

The **12th ZANU-PF Annual Conference** took place on 6–9 December in Bulawayo, with over 6,000 delegates attending. The most important resolutions were the widely anticipated (unopposed) nomination of Mugabe as party leader and an endorsement of the politburo decision that elections should be held in 2012, following which Mugabe would seek re-election. Other resolutions included the reintroduction of the Zimbabwe dollar and the call for NGOs to stay out of politics.

There were intermittent periods of **industrial unrest**, which mainly revolved around salaries of civil servants, dominated by teachers. On 19 January, public sector workers began an open-ended strike after wage talks collapsed, with Finance Minister Tendai Biti insisting there was no cash to meet the workers' demand. Unions affiliated to the umbrella body, the Apex Council, the main public sector union, were demanding a pay hike of 150%; the government had offered them 24%. The salary disputes were not resolved. In June, public sector workers again embarked on an indefinite strike to press the cash-strapped coalition government to more than double their wages. They wanted the lowest paid worker to take home around $ 500 per month. Civil servants were currently earning an average of $ 200 per month. In December, it was reported that a crippling civil service strike was looming in the New Year, again triggered by a groundswell of discontent over public sector remuneration packages. Unions gave the coalition government up to the end of December to have their salary concerns addressed or risk crippling strike action. ZANU-PF politicians and the pro-ZANU-PF media capitalised on the plight of workers to criticise the MDC-T, which was in charge of the labour and finance portfolios in the GNU.

Foreign Affairs

Although relations with most African and Asian countries and organisations remained largely friendly, there was little change in Zimbabwe's relations with the Western world.

On a personal level, the MDC-T arm of the GNU had good relations with ZANU-PF's long-time Western critics. Sanctions, the GPA, Zimbabwe's debt, elections and indigenisation were some of the key issues that dominated foreign relations.

Relations with **SADC** – a guarantor of the GPA – were characterised by support and tensions with the regional body and with various member states. On 2 February, South Africa's President Jacob Zuma accepted Ambassador Phelekezela Mphoko's credentials as Zimbabwe's chief envoy to South Africa. Pro-ZANU-PF analysts saw this as a direct snub of an MDC-T request in 2010 for South Africa and other countries not to recognise ambassadors appointed by Mugabe. On 31 March, Zuma presented a damning report to the SADC troika meeting in Livingstone, Zambia, urging SADC to tighten the screws on ZANU-PF, since the situation in the country could no longer be tolerated and talk of polls was counter-productive. He warned that Zimbabwe could become another Egypt if there were no reforms. Following this report, the troika issued a communiqué calling for reform. The troika summit called for an end to violence and intimidation, the crafting of an electoral roadmap and the appointment of a SADC team to assist in the monitoring and evaluation of the GPA, among other things. This was an uncharacteristic censure of Mugabe and ZANU-PF and was interpreted by many as expressing the regional block's frustration with them.

On 3 April, the state-controlled weekly 'The Sunday Mail' published an **attack on Zuma**, labelling him "disaster prone". This spat resulted in tensions between the two countries, which were added to on 6 April by a piece in the state-controlled daily 'The Herald'. Mugabe's spokesperson distanced him from the attack on Zuma, pointing out that the stinging editorial was not the government view. South Africa's announcement that it would deport undocumented Zimbabweans residing in South Africa illegally (estimated to be more than a million) did nothing to improve relations between the two countries. Nevertheless, the ANC sent a delegation to ZANU-PF's annual conference and, on 8 December, ANC Secretary-General Gwede Mantashe pledged the ANC's support for ZANU-PF in the Zimbabwean national elections, which were then expected to take place in 2012.

SADC 'facilitation' continued throughout the year through a South African team appointed by Zuma. The team was led by Zuma's international advisor, Lindiwe Zulu, who became a target for attacks by the state controlled media because she often expressed critical views that were at odds with ZANU-PF's position. Some of the team's visits included meeting stakeholders beyond the three GNU parties. On 11 August, representatives from several civil society groups in Zimbabwe met with the facilitation team in Harare to present their positions on the electoral roadmap and other crucial issues, ahead of the 31st SADC summit in Luanda, Angola. On 13 December, the team reiterated that the SADC position on Zimbabwe was 'no reforms, no elections'. This was interpreted as meaning that there would be no elections in 2012. On 19 May, the special SADC summit in Windhoek, Namibia, did not have Zimbabwe on the agenda. The 31st ordinary session of SADC in Angola was significant in that Tsvangirai was not invited as prime minister, but attended as an ordinary citizen. NGO activists from Zimbabwe were also barred from the summit, and Zimbabwe was not on the agenda. The Extraordinary Summit of SADC Heads of State and Government was held in Johannesburg, South Africa, on 11–13 June. There was disagreement as to whether the summit adopted the resolution of the Livingstone troika and Zuma's scathing report. While the MDC factions and their allies insisted it did, ZANU-PF-aligned analysts and politicians insisted it did not, but had simply 'noted' it. The communiqué and the statements of the facilitators, however, indicated they did indeed adopt it, which was seen as a blow to Mugabe and ZANU-PF.

On 27 January, Mugabe arrived in Addis Ababa, Ethiopia, to attend the 16th Ordinary Session of the **AU General Assembly**. Despite attempts by activists to drag Zimbabwe onto the AU agenda, there was no condemnation of Mugabe and ZANU-PF. Analysts interpreted this as a result of the AU's preoccupation with urgent issues, among them the unrest in North Africa and Côte d'Ivoire.

At an official level, there was hardly any thaw in **relations with the West**. Mugabe and ZANU-PF officials continued to blame Zimbabwe's woes on "illegal" Western sanctions. This was not helped by the continuation and/or renewal of targeted sanctions by the EU, USA and Australia, among others. In March, Mugabe launched an ambitious campaign to get two million signatures on an "anti-sanctions petition" calling for the unconditional lifting of all measures imposed by the West. On 15 February, the EU announced the extension of sanctions, but removed 35 people from the list of sanctions targets. This left 163 individuals and 31 businesses on the list for 'restrictive measures'. Unsurprisingly, while noting significant progress in addressing Zimbabwe's economic crisis and in the delivery of basic social services, the EU expressed deep concern about political violence. On 9 March, the USA extended by another year its sanctions regime targeting Mugabe and top ZANU-PF officials, citing lack of progress on political reform and continuing human rights abuses. The West was also seen as frustrating Zimbabwe's attempts to sell its diamonds legally. While most developing countries supported the move, Western countries remained opposed. On 12 December, the USA imposed sanctions on two diamond mines located in Zimbabwe's Marange region, the scene of alleged serious human rights abuses in 2008. A mine belonging to state-owned Marange Resources and another owned by Mbada Diamonds were added to a US Treasury Department list targeting entities linked to ZANU-PF. At its meeting in Kinshasa on 1 November, the Kimberley Process Certification Scheme cleared Zimbabwe to resume the supervised export of diamonds from its troubled Marange field. The deal was brokered by the EU. In June, it was reported that the country had exported diamonds worth $ 90 m between January and April, despite the ban on sales.

Good relations with traditional **allies in the east** continued, with China and Iran being particularly close. On 1 February, ministers claimed that Zimbabwe was in line for a windfall of up to $ 10 bn from China, a potentially huge boost to the ailing economy. The

GNU presented a united front on the issue, with even MDC-T ministers insisting that Chinese investment in mining and agriculture could help turn the economy around. On 21 March, Zimbabwe and China signed a raft of agreements worth $ 585 m through the Chinese Development Bank, aimed at reviving the health, mining and agricultural sectors. The signing ceremony was attended by Chinese Vice Premier Wang Qishan, who was in Zimbabwe on an official visit. He pledged support for Zimbabwe's economic recovery and promised to lobby for the lifting of Western sanctions. On 17 November, Mugabe, who was visiting China, held talks with Vice President Xi Jinping in Beijing. Xi Jinping described Mugabe as "a famed leader of the national liberation movement in Africa".

On 6 March, a leaked intelligence report compiled by the International Atomic Energy Agency, the UN nuclear watchdog, suggested **Iran** would be awarded exclusive access to Zimbabwe's **uranium** in return for providing the country with fuel. Zimbabwe's uranium stocks consisted of an estimated 455,000 tonnes at Kanyemba, north of Harare. The report revealed that Iran's foreign and co-operative ministers had visited Zimbabwe to strike the deal, and sent engineers to assess uranium deposits. On 8 March, the USA warned Zimbabwe that it could face international penalties if it helped Iran's nuclear programme in defiance of UN sanctions and a global arms treaty.

Relations with **multilateral financial institutions** were mixed. In March, the AfDB reopened its Zimbabwe office after a ten-year absence, citing an improved political climate, and, on 7 March, announced a $ 51.55 m injection into a fund to aid the economy. The regional lender had left Zimbabwe in 2000 due to a breakdown in its relationship with the government and Zimbabwe's failure to service its external debt. On 10 June, the AfDB and the Zimbabwean government signed a $ 30 m grant agreement in support of the urgent water supply and sanitation rehabilitation project. In June, the IMF said Zimbabwe's economic outlook for 2011 was uncertain, and warned of a "sizeable" fiscal financing gap and uncertainty over the country's business climate. In the statement following the conclusion of Article IV consultations, the IMF executive board applauded the positive economic changes that had occurred since the formation of the GNU, including a 9% increase in real GDP in 2010. The board said, however, that several factors mitigated against similar growth for 2011, noting that the existing policy environment and the controversial indigenisation programme would deter economic expansion. The growth forecast was downgraded from 7% to 5.5%.

Socioeconomic Developments

There were some continued improvements in **key economic indicators**. Reserve Bank of Zimbabwe figures showed that the consumer price index closed the year at about 100%. Economist Intelligence Unit estimates put the nominal GDP at $ 2 bn, up from $ 1.6 bn in 2010. The official budget estimated the 2011 GDP at $ 8.073 bn, indicating a GDP growth of 9.3%. The current account balance, excluding transfers, improved from –$ 1,041.1 m in 2010 to –$ 58.6 m in 2011. In the budget statement, the finance minister put the external debt at $ 6.9 bn, of which $ 4.8 bn were arrears.

In February, it was reported that there were more than 75,000 **ghost workers in the civil service** out of a total of 180,000 public servants employed. Most of these were said to be unqualified ZANU-PF militia members and supporters. The ghost workers were unearthed by a comprehensive payroll and skills audit done by Ernst & Young (India) on behalf of the ministry of public service. The issue was quickly politicised when the Public Service Commission disputed the findings, producing its own figures to prove its argument about the non-existence of ghost workers. ZANU-PF characteristically claimed that the audit had been hijacked by a British employee in the prime minister's office. The scandal lent weight to claims that the civil service had become a haven for ZANU-PF patronage.

On 25 March, Minister of Youth Development, Indigenisation and Empowerment Saviour Kasukuwere gazetted the **Indigenisation and Economic Empowerment Regulations**. The regulations set out key amendments to the implementation of the indigenisation and empowerment programme in mining companies not controlled by indigenous Zimbabweans. The regulations significantly altered the minimum threshold by requiring that the disposal of 51% of the shares in non-indigenous mining companies to designated entities would apply to all companies with a net asset value of more than $ 1 rather than the $ 500,000 threshold stipulated in the 2010 regulations. This drastically widened the scope of the indigenisation programme to encompass all non-indigenous mining companies operating in Zimbabwe. The timeframe for compliance was shortened to six months from the date of publication of the regulations. In addition, the new regulations required that affected non-indigenous companies submit an indigenisation implementation plan by 9 May. Some companies, notably the South African-owned Implants, started facing pressure from empowerment groups, including traditional leaders who were demanding a 10% stake in the company. While ZANU-PF and its allies backed the regulations, industry and the MDC-T expressed concern about their effect on investment. There were reports that the Chamber of Mines had taken legal advice on the legality and practicality of the regulations, indicating that there were possible grounds for appeal.

On 20 April, the government launched the draft **Industrial Development Policy** covering the period 2011–2015, aimed at reviving four key sectors of the economy: agro-processing, the fertiliser industry, pharmaceuticals, and metals and electricals. The policy sought to increase the manufacturing sector's contribution to GDP to 20% from the current 12%, and to increase the contribution of exports from the sector from 26% of GDP to 50% by 2015. On 27 September, the cabinet adopted the policy. On 7 July, the coalition government launched the **Medium Term Plan** (MTP) 2011–2015. The MTP was expected to pave the way for various policies and programmes addressing the macro-economic fundamentals critical for the growth of the economy.

Throughout the year, Zimbabwe's **underperforming parastatals** experienced various problems. Leading in news coverage were the national carrier Air Zimbabwe, integrated steel manufacture Ziscosteel, and the power utility Zimbabwe Electricity Supply Authority (ZESA). There were issues about debt, mismanagement and corruption. In May, the Civil Aviation Authority of Zimbabwe declared Air Zimbabwe's three planes (all Boeing 737s) a public danger, having reached the limit of 34,000 cycles. On 18 May, Air Zimbabwe cancelled all domestic and regional flights, leaving hundreds of travellers stranded. On 4 March, ZESA's CEO announced that the power utility was technically bankrupt. ZESA's debts had mounted to $ 889 m and its liabilities exceeded its assets. ZESA was failing to meet the country's power supply requirements, with national demand of 2,100 MW outstripping internal generation of about 1,200 MW. On 9 March, Industry and Commerce Minister Welshman Ncube described the country's sole integrated steel manufacturing company, Ziscosteel, as "insolvent, valueless and in a state of disrepair". Ncube was responding to questions from the media after the signing of a deal that saw the Indian firm Essar Africa Group take control of the company. The Indian-based company, through Essar Africa Holdings Ltd, had bought a 54% stake in the ailing debt-ridden state-owned steelmaker. The total deal value was $ 750 m, of which $ 340 m was debt.

About 1.7 m people were estimated to have no **food security** during the peak lean season from October through February. About 400,000 of the food insecure people were estimated to be in urban areas, and those in the rural areas outside of the central districts were classified to be moderately food insecure. Food assistance programme plans for the period of January through to March were deemed to be sufficient to cover the assessed needs. According to Reliefweb, food imports would continue to be a significant component of Zimbabwe's food supply in the outlook period. Since many Zimbabweans still relied on markets for their basic needs, global food and fuel price trends were likely to impact the purchasing power for very poor and poor households. Another worrying development was the poor rainfall season experienced in the southern districts of Masvingo and Matabeleland South provinces. It was estimated that the summer harvest would be substantially lower even than the previous year. In the second half of the year, food security remained generally stable at the national level, with staple cereals and basic food stuffs readily available on the market. Own staple cereal production and purchases were the main sources for most households in both urban and rural areas.

In August, it was reported that the **humanitarian situation** in the country still remained fragile, with food security, health, water and sanitation a serious cause for concern. Millions of people were said to be drinking from unprotected water sources and living in unhygienic conditions. Due to the immediate humanitarian needs, aid agencies appealed through the UN Office for the Coordination of Humanitarian Affairs for $ 488 m, an increase of $ 73 m from the original requirements of $ 415 m. Key priorities to be addressed by the revised 2011 Consolidated Appeal Process included improving levels of food security, which had been described as a "pressing issue", nutrition, water and sanitation, and addressing the needs of asylum seekers and other vulnerable groups. About 4.95 m women and children were in need of immediate nutritional facilities.

On 24 November, Finance Minister Tendai Biti presented his **2012 national budget**. He proposed a $ 4 bn budget, with resumed trading in the country's diamond resources expected to contribute an additional $ 600 m. He further projected a growth rate of 9.4% for 2012, with agriculture and mining as the major drivers. The budget revised the tax-free threshold from the $ 225 for 2011 to $ 250, starting on 1 January 2012. One of the major highlights of the budget was the envisaged creation of the three-year rolling finance strategy for the agricultural sector.

Despite some marked improvements, the **education and health** delivery systems continued to experience problems of staffing, equipment and funding. Health and educational personnel remained a substantial part of the brain drain to countries such as Australia, the United Kingdom, and South Africa. Industrial action and threats of industrial action arising out of salary disputes, particularly by doctors, nurses and teachers, were a constant feature throughout the year, further compromising these sectors.

Zimbabwe continued to lose skilled manpower, through **migration**, mainly to Commonwealth countries. According to the World Bank, emigrants from Zimbabwe in 2010 were estimated to number 1,253,100, which amounted to about 10% of the population. The net emigration rate was estimated at 24.83 per 1,000 of the population. Top destination countries were South Africa, the United Kingdom, Mozambique, Australia, Zambia, the United States, Malawi, New Zealand, Canada and Ireland. The situation of Zimbabwean migrants in South Africa remained precarious, with threats of deportation of undocumented migrants looming. Attempts by the government to issue documents to Zimbabweans in South Africa did not remove the threat, as many remained undocumented. In March, thousands of failed Zimbabwean asylum-seekers in the UK faced deportation after asylum judges ruled there was no evidence that those being returned would generally be at risk of harm. The UK Border Agency promptly announced that Britain would resume the forcible return of Zimbabweans whose asylum claims had been rejected. More than 10,000 Zimbabwean failed asylum-seekers were believed to be in Britain, of whom some 3,000 had exhausted all avenues of appeal. The move was strongly resisted by human rights groups, which continued to warn of harassment and persecution of opponents of ZANU-PF.

In November, there was an outbreak of **typhoid** in the densely populated residential areas of Harare, attributed to a lack of clean water and adequate sanitation in the townships. Most of the typhoid infections occurred in the over-crowded township of Dzivaresekwa, where untreated sewage flowed in the streets. Experts warned it might herald the resurgence of cholera, but this did not materialise. According to government figures, the adult

HIV prevalence was 14.3% in 2010. It is not yet known whether the downward trend is a sign of long-term change or merely a temporary respite. The charity Avert warned that, given the large number of homeless and displaced people living in Zimbabwe who were not likely to have been surveyed, the results could not be taken as wholly representative of the situation. In November, there were reports of an acute shortage of drugs for anti-retroviral therapy (ART) in Beitbridge District, where around 20,553 people were in need of life-prolonging drugs. Only 20% of patients with HIV had been placed on ART due to limited resources. The situation was not different in many parts of the country.

Amin Y. Kamete

List of Authors

Jon Abbink, Researcher, African Studies Centre, Leiden, Professor of African Studies at the VU University of Amsterdam, The Netherlands, abbink@ascleiden.nl

Michael Amoah, Associate, LSE IDEAS, London School of Economics, Dr_Michael_Amoah@alumni.lse.ac.uk

Alice Bellagamba, Associate Professor, Cultural and Social Anthropology, Department of Human Sciences for Education "Riccardo Massa", University of Milan-Bicocca, alice.bellagamba@unimib.it

Heinrich Bergstresser, Media Consultant, Freelance Research Associate of the Institute of African Affairs in Hamburg and Freelance Tutor of Deutsche Gesellschaft für Internationale Zusammenarbeit GIZ, Germany, heinrich.bergstresser@web.de

Maitseo Bolaane, PhD, Senior Lecturer, Department of History, University of Botswana, Bolaanem@mopipi.ub.bw

Alicia Campos, Research Fellow, Department of Political Science and International Relations, and Group of African Studies, Universidad Autónoma de Madrid, Spain, alicia.campos@uam.es

Nic Cheeseman, Lecturer in African Politics and Hugh Price Fellow of Jesus College, University of Oxford, UK, niccheeseman@gmail.com

Tiyesere Mercy Chikapa-Jamali, Lecturer at the Department of Political and Administrative Studies, University of Malawi, Tiyeserec@yahoo.com

John F. Clark, Professor, Department of Politics and International Relations, Florida International University, Miami, USA, clarkj@fiu.edu

John Daniel, Academic Director of the School for International Training's programme in Social and Political Transformation in Durban, South Africa, john.daniel@sit.edu

Lewis Dzimbiri, Professor of Public Administration, Chancellor College, University of Malawi, dzimbiri2002@yahoo.co.uk

Gero Erdmann, Senior Researcher, Institute of African Affairs, GIGA German Institute of Global and Area Studies, Hamburg, Germany, erdmann@giga.hamburg.de

Vincent Foucher, associate researcher, Unité Les Afriques dans le Monde, Centre national de la recherche, Bordeaux, v.foucher@sciencespobordeaux.fr

Mark Furness, Senior Researcher, Deutsches Institut für Entwicklungspolitik / German Development Institute (DIE), Bonn, Germany, mark.furness@die-gdi.de

Lansana Gberie, Research Analyst, Security Council Report, New York, USA, lagberie@yahoo.com

Linnéa Gelot, Post-doctoral researcher, School of Global Studies, Gothenburg University, Sweden, linnea.gelot@globalstudies.gu.se; and Researcher, The Nordic Africa Institute, Uppsala, Sweden, linnea.gelot@nai.uu.se

Eric Komlavi Hahonou, Economist & Social anthropologist, Assistant Professor and Postdoc fellow, Department of Society & Globalisation, Roskilde University, Denmark, komlavi@ruc.dk

Joseph Hanlon, visiting senior fellow, Department of International Development, London School of Economics, UK; honorary research fellow, School of Environment and Development, University of Manchester, UK, j.hanlon@open.ac.uk

Kurt Hirschler, Freelance Political Scientist, Hamburg, Germany, kurt_hirschler@web.de

Nicole Hirt, Freelance Research Associate, Institute of African Affairs, GIGA German Institute of Global and Area Studies and Senior Consultant at HACOS – "Horn of Africa Consultancy Service", Hamburg, Germany, nicolehi2001@yahoo.de

Rolf Hofmeier, Former Director, Institute of African Affairs, GIGA German Institute of Global and Area Studies, Hamburg, Germany, hofmeier@giga-hamburg.de

Amin Kamete, Senior Lecturer, University of Glasgow, Scotland, UK, amini.kamete@glasgow.ac.uk

Christoph Kohl, Researcher, Peace Research Institute Frankfurt, Frankfurt am Main, Germany, kohl@hsfk.de

Dirk Kohnert, Retired Deputy Director, Institute of African Affairs, GIGA German Institute of Global and Area Studies, Hamburg, Germany, Dirk-k-iak@gmx.de

Bruno Losch, Economist, Centre de Coopération Internationale en Recherche Agronomique pour le Développement, Montpellier, France, bruno.losch@cirad.fr

Richard R. Marcus, Director and Associate Professor, International Studies Program, California State University, Long Beach, USA, rmarcus@csulb.edu

Mike McGovern, Associate Professor of Anthropology, Yale University, USA, michael .mcgovern@yale.edu

Andreas Mehler, Director, Institute of African Affairs, GIGA German Institute of Global and Area Studies, Hamburg, Germany, mehler@giga-hamburg.de

Henning Melber, Executive Director, Dag Hammarskjöld Foundation, Uppsala, Sweden, henning.melber@dhf.uu.se

Claes Olsson, Political Scientist and Editor at Global Publications Foundation, Uppsala, Sweden, claes.olsson@globalpublications.org

Helena Olsson, M.A. in Political Science and staff member at the Department of Sociology, Uppsala University, Sweden, helena.olsson@soc.uu.se

Krijn Peters, Lecturer in Armed Conflict & Post-war Reconstruction, Department of Political & Cultural Studies, Swansea University, UK, k.peters@swansea.ac.uk

Fanny Pigeaud, Journalist, France, Fanny.pigeaud@gmail.com

Marisha Ramdeen, Researcher with the African Centre for the Constructive Resolution of Disputes (ACCORD) in Durban, South Africa. Marisha@accord.org.za

Jon Schubert, Doctoral Student at the Centre of African Studies, University of Edinburgh, UK, and Analyst Lusophone and Central Africa, Exclusive Analysis, London, j.schubert@ ed.ac.uk

David Sebudubudu, PhD, Associate Professor of Political Studies and Head of the Department of Political and Administrative Studies, University of Botswana, Sebudubu@ mopipi.ub.bw

Gerhard Seibert, Researcher at the African Studies Centre (CEA), ISCTE-IUL, Lisbon, Portugal, mailseibert@yahoo.com

Claudia Simons, Research Fellow, German Institute for International Affairs, Berlin, Germany, Claudia.Simons@swp-berlin.org

Roger Southall, Professor of Sociology, University of the Witwatersrand, Johannesburg, South Africa, Roger.Southall@wits.ac.za

Alexander Stroh, Research Fellow, Institute of African Affairs, GIGA German Institute of Global and Area Studies, Hamburg, Germany, Stroh@giga-hamburg.de

Susan Thomson, Assistant Professor of Peace and Conflict Studies, Colgate University, Hamilton, USA, sthomson@colgate.edu.

Klaus-Peter Treydte, Economist, Dr. rer. pol., Former country representative Friedrich-Ebert-Foundation Madagascar and Mauritius, kp3t@gmx.net

Han van Dijk, Researcher, African Studies Centre, Leiden and Professor of Law and Governance in Africa, chair Law and Governance group, Dept of Social Sciences, Wageningen University and Research Centre, The Netherlands, dijkh@ascleiden.nl

Ineke van Kessel, Researcher, African Studies Centre, Leiden, The Netherlands, Kessel@ascleiden.nl

Martin van Vliet, African Studies Centre in Leiden, The Netherlands, mvanvliet_imd@yahoo.com

Klaas van Walraven, Researcher, African Studies Centre, Leiden, The Netherlands, Walraven@ascleiden.nl

Stef Vandeginste, Lecturer and Post-doctoral fellow, University of Antwerp, Belgium, Stef.vandeginste@ua.ac.be

Aaron Weah, Lecturer in Sociology at the University of Liberia and a Research Associate at the Center for Policy Studies, University of Liberia, abweah.ci@gmail.com

Volker Weyel, Former Editor-in-chief 'Vereinte Nationen' (1977–2004), consultant, Bonn, Germany, weyel@o2online.de

Peter Woodward, Emeritus professor, School of Politics and International Relation, University of Reading, UK, p.r.woodward@reading.ac.uk

Douglas Yates, Professor of Political Science at the American Graduate School in Paris, France, douglas.yates@ags.edu

www.ingramcontent.com/pod-product-compliance
Lightning Source LLC
LaVergne TN
LVHW080113011026
849160LV00013B/1088

* 9 7 8 9 0 0 4 2 3 3 9 8 0 *